BUILDING THE NAVY'S BASES
IN
WORLD WAR II

VOLUME II

NAVY'S FIRST ADVANCE BASE

Madisonville in Massachusetts Bay in the Marquesas Islands, some 800 miles northeast of Borabora, was established by Commodore David Porter to repair the frigate *Essex* after its historic voyage around the Horn in 1813. The *Essex*, which was the first American warship to visit the Pacific, is shown, with her prizes, in this old print, published in London in 1823.

In his book, *A Voyage in the South Seas in the Years 1812, 1813, and 1814*, Commodore Porter wrote that "agreeably to the the request of the chiefs, I laid down the plan of the village about to be built. The line on which the houses were to be placed was already traced by our barrier of water casks. They were to take the form of a crescent, to be built on the outside of the enclosure, and to be connected with each other by a wall twelve feet in length and four feet in height. The houses were to be fifty feet in length, built in the usual fashion of the country, and of a proportioned width and height.

"On the 3d November, upwards of four thousand natives, from the different tribes, assembled at the camp with materials for building, and before night they had completed a dwelling-house for myself, and another for the officers, a sail loft, a cooper's shop, and a place for our sick, a bake-house, a guard-house, and a shed for the sentinel to walk under. The whole were connected by the walls as above described. We removed our barrier of water casks, and took possession of our delightful village, which had been built as if by enchantment."

BUILDING THE NAVY'S BASES

IN
WORLD WAR II

VOLUME II

Foreword

Because the Navy cannot operate without repairs and supplies. bases are as important as are ships and planes and personnel. The 1940 Navy had no properly equipped advance base other than Pearl Harbor. In the succeeding five years, the Bureau of Yards and Docks built or supervised the building of more than 400 advance bases for the Navy in the Atlantic and the Pacific areas, at a cost of $2.135,-427,881. More than ten million dollars, each, was spent at eighteen areas on foreign soil.

Guam	$280,795,700
Leyte-Samar	215,603,201
Manus	131,757,843
Okinawa	113,715,453
Saipan	63,252,622
Trinidad	45,704,394
Argentia	44,912,927
Espiritu Santo	36,369,925
Tinian	35,158,275
Bermuda	34,983,064
Subic Bay	34,916,587
Noumea	24,297,449
Eniwetok	23,085.079
Ulithi	18,580.273
Peleliu	18,489.159
Iwo Jima	15,462,733
Manila	13.349,589
Milne Bay	11,101,000

All except Trinidad, Argentia, Espiritu Santo, Bermuda, Noumea, and Milne Bay had to be captured from the enemy and cleared of debris before construction could begin. Fifteen of these eighteen bases were in the Pacific. As we progressed across that ocean, islands captured in one amphibious operation were converted into bases which became springboards for the next advance.

Advance bases were set up for various purposes. At first, they were mainly air bases, such as those in the South Pacific, at Borabora and Tongatabu, for use in protecting our lines of communication with Australia. Gradually, this changed to the staging bases for the anchoring, fueling, and refitting of armadas of transports and cargo ships, and for replenishing mobile support squadrons which accompanied the combat forces. As we progressed farther and farther across the Pacific, it became necessary to set up main repair bases for the maintenance, repair, and servicing of larger fleet units. Floating drydocks made it possible to repair battle damage and disabilities so that ships could be kept in the battle line without having to return to continental bases, or even to the Hawaiian islands, but even the floating drydocks needed a base.

The first large advance base set up in the Pacific was at Espiritu Santo; the next was a main repair base at Manus in the Admiralty Islands. A base, capable of supporting one-third of the Pacific fleet, was constructed at Guam; another was established at Leyte-Samar; a third was in process of construction at Okinawa when the Japanese surrendered.

Facilities to maintain these bases, including personnel structures, piers, roads, shops, utilities, in large measure duplicated the type of facilities found at any continental navy yard. There was also provided the replenishment storage necessary to restock every type of vessel with fuel, ammunition, and consumable supplies, as well as food. The stocks on hand at Guam by V-J day would have filled a train 120 miles long. For fuel supply alone, 25,000,000 barrels of bulk fuel were shipped to the Pacific in June 1945 for military purposes. At Guam, one million gallons of aviation gasoline were used every day.

As Admiral King pointed out in his final report to the Secretary of the Navy, had it not been for "this chain of advance bases the fleet could not have operated in the western reaches of the Pacific without the necessity for many more ships and planes than it actually had. A base to supply or repair a fleet 5000 miles closer to the enemy multiplies the power which can be maintained constantly against him and greatly lessens the problems of supply and repair. The scope of the advance base program is indicated by the fact that the personnel assigned directly to it aggregated almost one fifth of the entire personnel of the Navy, . . . including almost 200,000 Seabees. . . . In the naval supply depot at Guam there were 93 miles of road. At

Okinawa alone there were more than fifty naval construction battalions building roads, supply areas, airfields and fleet facilities for what would have been one of the gigantic staging areas for the final invasion of Japan.

"As our advance came nearer to the Japanese islands, the rear areas which had been the scene of combat operations in earlier months were utilized for logistic support. In the South Pacific, for example, more than 400 ships were staged for the Okinawa operation. They received varied replenishment services, including routine and emergency overhaul as required. Approximately 100,000 officers and men were staged from this area alone for the Okinawa campaign, including four Army and Marine combat divisions plus certain headquarters and corps troops and various Army and Navy service units. Concurrently with the movement of troops, large quantities of combat equipment and necessary materiel were transferred forward, thus contributing automatically to the roll-up of the South Pacific area. Similarly in the Southwest Pacific area, Army service troops were moved with their equipment from the New Guinea area to the Philippines in order to prepare staging facilities for troops deployed from the European theater. The roll-up was similarly continued and progress made in reducing our installations in Australia and New Guinea."

Bases as a vital factor of sea power have been well defined by Admiral Nimitz.

"Sea power," he declared, "is not a limited term. It includes many weapons and many techniques. Sea power means more than the combatant ships and aircraft, the amphibious forces and the merchant marine. It includes also the port facilities of New York and California; the bases in Guam and in Kansas; the factories which are the capital plant of war; and the farms which are the producers of supplies. All these are elements of sea power. Furthermore, sea power is not limited to materials and equipment. It includes the functioning organization which has directed its use in the war. In the Pacific we have been able to use our naval power effectively because we have been organized along sound lines. The present organization of our Navy Department has permitted decisions to be made effectively. It has allowed great flexibility. In each operation we were able to apply our force at the time and place where it would be most damaging to the enemy."

CONTENTS

PART III — THE ADVANCE BASES

ILLUSTRATIONS

Photographs

Maps

PART III

THE ADVANCE BASES

LTA Steel Hangar, Built by the 80th Seabees, at Carlson Field, Trinidad

CHAPTER 18

BASES IN SOUTH AMERICA AND THE CARIBBEAN AREA INCLUDING BERMUDA

Part I—The Caribbean Area

World War II development of the naval shore establishment throughout the Caribbean and Central American area divides itself broadly into two phases; the defense period and the war period.

Although the defense period is considered as beginning in July 1940, the construction program, as it evolved in the Caribbean area, dates from the fall of 1939, when the expansion of existing bases was begun, in line with recommendations of the Hepburn Board.

With the exception of a radio station at San Juan, Puerto Rico. the naval shore establishment in the Caribbean in 1939 was confined to Guantanamo Bay, Cuba: the Panama Canal Zone: and a small area on the island of St. Thomas in the Virgin Islands. Hepburn Board recommendations called for development of Guantanamo into a fleet operating base with airport facilities to accommodate one carrier group and one patrol squadron. On St. Thomas, a small airfield occupied by the Marine Corps was to be expanded to support a Marine squadron of 18 planes on a permanent basis, and the adjacent waterfront was to be developed to serve a patrol-plane squadron in a tender-based status.

For the Canal Zone, where the Navy maintained a naval air station for patrol planes and a submarine base at Coco Solo, the board recommended an increase in the air facilities sufficient to accommodate seven squadrons of patrol planes, with a supporting industrial establishment capable of complete engine overhaul, and the establishment of a naval station at Balboa, on the Pacific end of the Canal. to support submarines, destroyers, and smaller craft.

For Puerto Rico, the board recommended the development of Isla Grande in San Juan harbor as a secondary air base, to contain facilities for one carrier group. two patrol-plane squadrons, complete engine overhaul, and berthing for one carrier.

Congress approved the base program as recommended by the Hepburn Board in May 1939. and partial financing was provided in the 1940 appropriation bill. The initial construction effort in the Caribbean area began in October with the award of a fixed-fee contract for the air-station development at San Juan, Puerto Rico.

Meanwhile. as 1939 drew to a close, the initial success of Axis aggression in Europe and the increasing submarine sinkings in the Atlantic, resulted in Congress again reviewing naval requirements. Recognizing that security hinged on ability to defend ourselves, Congress, pursuant to the recommendations of the Navy Department, authorized an additional 11-percent expansion in combatant-ship tonnage, with a concomitant increase in naval aircraft to 10,000 planes. The President signed the bill on June 14, 1940. The program for the development of shore facilities was immediately revised upward. and the scope of the Caribbean bases redefined.

Guantanamo, under the new program, was to furnish complete facilities for three patrol squadrons, eight carrier squadrons, and four additional patrol squadrons with tender support. The strategically located air station already under construction at San Juan was to be expanded to accommodate six patrol squadrons and two carrier groups, with additional facilities for the temporary use of two patrol squadrons with tender support. Facilities for ten patrol squadrons were scheduled for the air station at St. Thomas.

Development of the bases recommended by the Hepburn Board began immediately. Two contracts were awarded on June 17 and July 11 for work in

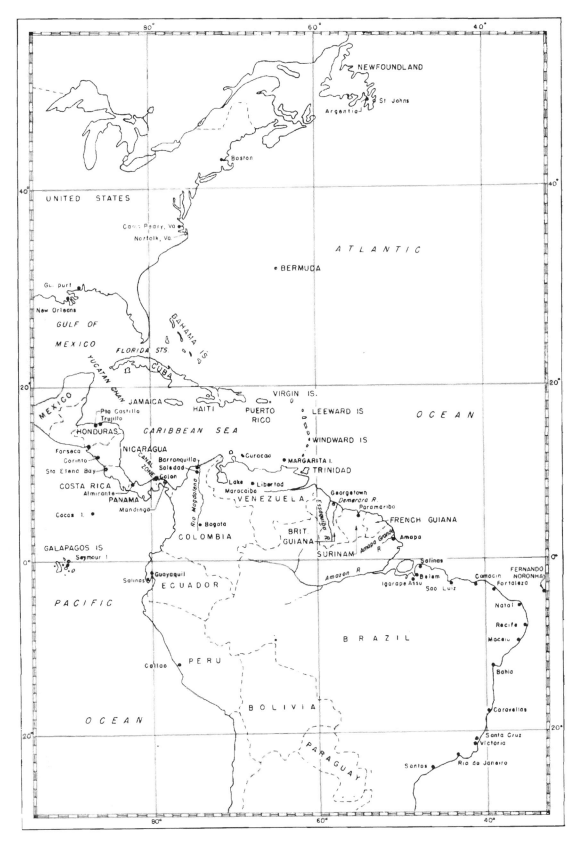

WESTERN ATLANTIC AND CANAL ZONE DEFENSE AREA

the Canal Zone, and a third on July 1, for Guantanamo. Because of St. Thomas's geographic proximity to Puerto Rico, the contract then under way at San Juan was expanded on July 8 to include the work on the neighboring island.

Meanwhile, the German submarine campaign was being prosecuted with telling effect. Britain had been severely affected by the general attrition of operations at sea, particularly in loss of destroyers. The United States needed extra bases to consolidate its defense in the Caribbean. Accordingly, the two governments entered into negotiations which culminated in the "Destroyers for Bases" agreement, signed September 2, 1940. Britain received fifty over-age destroyers. The United States received the right, under terms of a 99-year lease, to construct bases in eight British possessions, all in the Caribbean defense area, except one—Newfoundland (Argentia), which became part of the North Atlantic defense area discussed in Chapter 19. The southern group consisted of Bermuda, Jamaica, the Bahamas, Antigua, St. Lucia, Trinidad, and British Guiana.

On September 11, 1940, the President appointed a board, with Rear Admiral John W. Greenslade as senior member, to survey the naval shore establishment with a view to the requirements of the two-ocean Navy, at that time scheduled for accomplishment by 1946. Beginning its work in the Caribbean, the board, which included Army, Navy, and Marine Corps officers, participated in conferences with British experts to determine the exact location for the new bases. Tentative lease agreements were reached by the end of October 1940, but final agreements, together with decisions on such matters as customs, taxes, and wage rates for local labor, were not settled until March 1941.

The Greenslade Board submitted its recommendations on January 6, 1941. Broadly conceived, these studies divided the strategic concept of our national defense into geographic areas, beginning in the North Atlantic and rotating clockwise through the Middle Atlantic, South Atlantic, Gulf, Caribbean, and Central America, completing the arc in the North Pacific. Insofar as they pertained to the Caribbean and contiguous areas in the Atlantic and the Pacific, they became the basic blue print for all subsequent base development in that area.

Naval defense of the Panama Canal, the focal point of our communications between the two

oceans and South America, is, on the Atlantic side, primarily a matter of controlling the approaches to the Gulf of Mexico through the Florida Straits and the approaches to the Caribbean through the Yucatan Channel and the navigable passes of the greater and lesser Antilles. To accomplish this, the Greenslade Board divided the Caribbean into three areas, focusing major strength at Puerto Rico, Guantanamo, and Trinidad, each major operating base being supplemented by secondary outlying air bases to supply essential air surveillance.

At Puerto Rico, the Greenslade plan called for development of a major operating base as the keystone of the Caribbean defense, with facilities to include a thoroughly protected anchorage, a major air station, and an industrial establishment capable of supporting a large portion of the fleet under war conditions. Puerto Rico was to be the "Pearl Harbor of the Caribbean," furnishing logistic support to outlying secondary air bases developed on Antigua, St. Thomas, and Culebra.

Guantanamo was to be a major supporting base, capable of supplying limited maintenance, training, supply, and rest areas. It would also furnish a link in the supply chain from the Gulf area to other Caribbean bases. Jamaica and the Bahamas, as outlying secondary air bases, were to supply air surveillance in the Guantanamo area.

Bermuda was to be equipped to support carrier and patrol aircraft, cruiser, destroyer, and submarine forces capable of defense against strategical surprise on our middle Atlantic front.

Trinidad was to be organized as a subsidiary operating base, with major air facilities capable of supporting a large portion of United States naval forces. It was also to include training and advance-base operations projected to the south and east. Secondary air bases were to be located at St. Lucia and British Guiana, and emergency advance bases were to be placed along the northeastern coast of Brazil, each to be linked logistically to Trinidad and geared to the defense plan of that area.

Provision for adequate defense of the Canal from the Pacific presented a far more difficult problem. There were no potential sites for air bases, either on American soil or on territory which could be secured by lease or treaty. Only Cocos Island and the Galapagos group, the former controlled by Costa Rica and the latter by Ecuador, presented possibilities.

Early in 1940 the General Board of the Navy and

TENTH NAVAL DISTRICT HEADQUARTERS, SAN JUAN, PUERTO RICO
San Antonio Channel is shown at the upper left

the Army-Navy Joint Board studied the subject and reached the conclusion that preparations must be made for the operation of constant air patrols over a wide area to the west of Panama. They recommended that patrol squadrons of seaplanes, supported partly by tenders and partly by shore installations, be based near Guayaquil on the Ecuadorian coast, in the Gulf of Fonseca in Nicaragua, and in the Galapagos. The Galapagos, it was decided, were to be the key installations, and they were subsequently fortified by both the Army and the Navy, under a program directed by the Army engineers.

By December 7, 1941, basic plans for the defense of the Caribbean and the Panama Canal were rapidly taking shape. The program was further expanded during 1942, with the development of bases at Salinas, Ecuador; Barranquilla, Colombia; Curacao, in the Netherlands West Indies; Puerto Castilla, Honduras; on the Gulf of Fonseca and at Corinto, Nicaragua; on Taboga Island, at the Pacific end of the Canal; and at Almirante, Chorrera, and Mandiga, in Panama. These were all small installations to support seaplanes, lighter-than-air craft, and small surface craft. A chain of air bases was also established along the coast of Brazil.

During the two years that followed, the tempo of construction activity increased steadily, reaching its peak in the early months of 1943. By that time the major features at each base had been completed and were being fully used by the occupying forces. The contractors' forces were withdrawn before the year ended. Station maintenance, as well as minor items of new construction necessary for more efficient operations, was henceforth accomplished by Seabees or by local labor under the direction of the station Public Works Department.

As the progress of the war in Europe became more favorable to the Allied cause and the submarine threat diminished in the Caribbean during 1944, each of the Caribbean bases diminished in importance; consequently, all except the major installations at Trinidad, San Juan, Guantanamo, and the Canal Zone were reduced to a restricted or caretaker status by the fall of 1944.

San Juan, Puerto Rico

Except for a radio station and hydrographic office, the Navy had no installation on the island of Puerto Rico prior to 1939. Construction, which resulted in a major naval shore establishment, was accomplished under a single fixed-fee contract awarded on October 30, 1939.

In its original form, this contract comprised 44 related projects devoted primarily to the construction of the San Juan Naval Air Station on Isla Grande. Subsequent additions increased the scope to include base development on the islands of St. Lucia and Antigua and the naval operating base at Roosevelt Roads.

Isla Grande is a 340-acre site in San Juan Harbor, between San Antonio Channel and San Juan Harbor. Except for an airstrip operated by Pan American Airlines and a small area occupied by the U.S. Public Health Service quarantine station, most of the site was a combination of mangrove swamp and tidal mud flats. Despite the necessity for dredging operations of considerable magnitude to reclaim the low-lying land, the site was selected because of contiguous waters ideal for seaplane operation, unrestricted air approaches, and the nuclear value of the existing airfield.

The layout prepared by the Bureau of Yards and Docks utilized the existing runway as the base of design for the air station. The seaplane operating area used the waterfrontage along the harbor, leaving the area between the two air activities for industrial and personnel structures. Seventy percent of the air station had to be built on a blanket of dredged fill. This site preparation, while an extensive operation, was accomplished simultaneously with, and as a by-product of, the dredging operation necessary to deepen the seaplane runways and

the navigable reaches of both San Antonio and Martin Pena channels.

Facilities initially provided placed the station in the category of a major air base, equipped to serve two squadrons of seaplanes and one carrier group, with an industrial section. The major facilities of the seaplane area comprised two Navy standard steel hangars, an engine-overhaul shop, four seaplane ramps with connecting bulkhead, asphalt-paved parking areas, and a 450-foot concrete tender pier. The center line of the existing airfield was shifted slightly to conform more nearly with prevailing winds, the field was then lengthened, widened, and surfaced with asphalt to make a 5400-by-500-foot runway. This strip and a secondary north-south 2300-by-150-foot runway, together with a utility hangar, became one of the important bases of the Naval Air Transport Service in the Caribbean.

Located in an area frequented by high-velocity winds, most of the buildings were designed as permanent structures, using steel and masonry for industrial buildings and reinforced concrete for personnel units. Flat roofs and a cubical design gave architectural treatment in keeping with local civilian practice. Pile foundations were necessary under all permanent structures, including underground pipe and duct lines, because of unstable soil conditions and a time schedule which demanded immediate use of filled areas.

The Tenth Naval District, including the Bahamas and the Antilles from Cuba to Trinidad, was established November 14, 1939, with San Juan designated as administrative headquarters. Buildings to house the district headquarters were begun in September 1940, on a tract of land bordering San Antonio Channel, directly opposite the air station. The buildings were one-story frame structures, equipped with cable lashings over the roof and anchored to the ground on either end as a safety measure against hurricanes. In addition, the Fernandez Juncos and San Geronimo quarters were erected to house headquarters personnel. Reinforced concrete and prefabricated steel-frame stucco construction was used.

A new quarantine station and hospital were undertaken simultaneously on a tract of land adjoining the district headquarters group. Built of reinforced concrete, these were constructed to replace the 40-year-old buildings of the U. S. Public

Health Service which occupied an area required for seaplane parking.

As the number of naval activities in the San Juan area expanded beyond the original air activity, the fixed dimensions of the Isla Grande site made necessary the purchase of additional land directly south of the air station.

The first of these new activities was a low-cost defense-housing project in suburban San Juan, designated as San Patricio. Added to the contract in October 1940, this facility comprised 200 duplex single-story structures built with prefabricated steel frames, concrete floors, and stucco exteriors.

On February 13, the San Juan contract was further augmented to include construction at St. Lucia and Antigua, and to permit the assembling and fabricating of materials and equipment for temporary shore facilities to house a Marine detachment at each base. This latter item introduced the production-line principle to the construction of bases and was one of the early steps in the development of advance base structures.

As the summer of 1941 approached, gratifying progress was being made toward strengthening the air defenses in the Caribbean. Corresponding facilities necessary to support the Navy's surface craft in that area, however, were seriously deficient, and that at a time when the nation's ship yards were operating on a 24-hour basis, producing vessels for the authorized increase in ships for a two-ocean Navy. There were no drydocks between Charleston and the Canal Zone; nor, except for limited facilities at Guantanamo, were there any bases for repairs, fuel, and supplies.

In order to strengthen this weak link in our defenses, a major program of new construction was added on July 8, 1941, to the San Juan contract. This new program, in addition to the development of a major fleet base at Roosevelt Roads, provided operating and repair facilities in the San Juan area, additions to the air station, a radio station, and an ammunition depot.

Fortunately, the Insular Government had built a graving dock in San Juan Harbor, on a site contiguous with the air station. Functionally complete at the time, this 660-by-83-foot dock was taken over by the Navy in July. The approach channel was deepened and widened, a 600-foot approach pier built, and additional berthing provided by dredging and bulkheading a slip between the approach pier and an adjoining tender pier at the air station. Shops, storehouses, and other supporting industrial facilities were built in the area adjacent to the drydock, and a net depot was also developed.

In September 1941, a public works department was organized to serve all San Juan activities, except the naval air station for which a separate station public works department was established. The San Juan public works department performed station maintenance and operation functions as well as extensive new construction of projects not included in the contract. Except for the public works foreman and quarterman the entire mechanical and labor force comprised local Puerto Ricans, who responded well to a training program in building trades and other skills, under the direction of the public works officer.

Similarly, the combined clerical force of the district public works office and of the San Juan activities public works office, utilized Puerto Ricans under trained supervisors.

The extensive use of Puerto Ricans in mechanical trades and clerical work constituted an interesting innovation in this primarily agricultural land, and the employment of female clerical personnel on so great a scale broke centuries-old sociological precedents.

San Antonio Channel was also deepened to 35 feet adjacent to the north shoreline of the air station, and the waterfront improved with 2000 feet of quay wall and 2000 feet of sheet-pile bulkhead to accommodate carriers and other surface craft.

The San Juan section base, a complete facility equipped with barracks, administration building, warehouses, and waterfront improvements, was constructed under the same program, on a site adjoining the 10th Naval District headquarters.

The air station was improved and increased in all categories to give it complete facilities for the operation and maintenance of five patrol squadrons of seaplanes and one carrier group.

The ammunition depot, built on a 2100-acre site in the hills southwest of the harbor, at Sabana Seca, was planned and developed as a complete and self-contained facility equipped with roads, railroad spur, personnel structures, sewage-disposal unit, magazines, and storage structures.

Concurrently, the radio station, located on a reservation within the city of San Juan, was equipped with a bombproof communications building and a third antenna tower, 250 feet high.

Increased fuel storage, water supply, and hos-

DRYDOCK AREA, SAN JUAN, PUERTO RICO
Administration building (with tower) at right; outfitting and tender piers, upper right

pital facilities were required to keep pace with this growth. Consequently, a fuel depot at Catano and water development at San Patricio were added to the contract in October. The naval hospital was undertaken later, during January 1942, on a site adjacent to the housing project at San Patricio.

The fuel depot comprised seven 27,000-barrel pre-stressed-concrete and three 27,000-barrel steel tanks, built into the hillside for concealment and protection; a timber pier, 350 feet long; a pumping plant, with heating equipment; personnel buildings; and a shop. All buildings were of reinforced concrete.

The San Patricio water development comprised two drilled wells, a filter plant of 500,000 gallons per day capacity, and a 200,000-gallon reservoir.

A 10-inch main, laid under the Martin Pena Channel, served the air station, and a 6-inch main under the San Antonio Channel, served the district headquarters and adjoining activities. The hillside location of the reservoir made possible adequate gravity pressure throughout the entire system.

Two hundred beds were provided at the naval hospital in a compact structure comprising a main central building with eight attached wings and a service building housing garages and heating units. All buildings were single-storied, with reinforced-concrete walls and timber roofs. Buttresses and steel ties held the roofs to the ground as a precaution against wind damage.

Maintaining the flow of materials became a trying and hazardous task subsequent to our entry into the war. The Germans were quick to take advantage of their opportunity and made an incursion into our coastal waters in January 1942. During April and May, enemy submarines sank eight cargo-laden ships en route to Puerto Rico. resulting in costly delays on construction projects.

As 1942 drew to a close. the gradual completion of major construction operations at San Juan permitted a transfer of the major effort to Roosevelt Roads. Early in 1943, all dredging operations were completed, as were the water-filtration plant, the San Patricio housing development, and the ammunition depot at Sabana Seca. The drydock and repair unit were completed in March, and the main plane runway in April. The remaining activities were completed and the contract terminated by August 28, 1943.

New construction as well as station maintenance and operation at Roosevelt Roads was henceforth accomplished by the station public works department, augmented by CBMU 516, which arrived on August 26, 1943. The public works officer was given the additional title of officer in charge of new construction, under which he was vested with authority to hire both persons from the States and Puerto Ricans, giving them a modified civil-service status.

Roosevelt Roads

Roosevelt Roads, on Vieques Passage, at the eastern end of Puerto Rico, was intended to become the major fleet operating base of the Caribbean. As initially planned. it was to be equipped with a protected anchorage, a battleship graving dock, major repair facilities. fuel depot. supply depot. hospital, a major air station for both land- and seaplanes, and numerous other shore-based activities. These were to provide the necessary supporting services for 60 per cent of the Atlantic Fleet. and represented, in broad outline, the requirements indicated by the strategic situation as envisaged in the spring of 1941. It was a tremendous project. requiring five years to complete. at an estimated cost of $108,000,000.

The extreme eastern end of Puerto Rico was the only location on the island capable of accommodating a base of this magnitude. together with sufficient water area for development as a fleet anchorage. The Navy, accordingly, purchased 6680 acres at Ensenada Honda, Puerto Rico, and a substantial portion of the island of Vieques. including all of the western end, 7 miles east of Puerto Rico. Vieques Passage, between the two islands, was to

be developed as an anchorage by constructing two breakwaters. The two sites were similar, with salt flats, mangrove swamps, and steep, weathered hills. some of which were 400 feet high.

In the early summer of 1941, the development of Roosevelt Roads was awarded to the fixed-fee contract then underway at the naval air station at San Juan. The initial award included the dredging necessary to provide channels from the mainland sites into Vieques Passage, the construction of approximately 14 miles of breakwater to provide a sheltered anchorage for the fleet, a battleship graving dock with complete accessories, a bombproof power plant, a large machine shop, and the construction plant and equipment necessary to accomplish a program of this magnitude. The contract was subsequently expanded from time to time, beginning in October 1941 and continuing through 1943, to cover the construction of a fleet supply depot. ammunition storage, personnel facilities, a 200-bed hospital, a section base, a net and mine depot, and a major air station for both landplanes and seaplanes.

No facilities of any kind were existent in May 1941 when work was begun at Ensenada Honda. on a tent camp and access roads.

When the year ended, the number of workmen had increased from 200 to 3000, a temporary construction camp with an expected life of five years had been built, dredging had been started on the approach to the drydock, and a pier had been completed which permitted material and equipment to be unloaded at the site rather than having to be trucked across the island from San Juan. Work was also begun on Vieques Island for the development of a quarry to furnish rock for the proposed breakwater.

The entry of the United States into the war had brought about changes in the plans for Roosevelt Roads. A review of the present and potential enemy naval forces in the Atlantic, the type of warfare conducted by the Axis in the Mediterranean, the necessity for maintaining a large portion of our major naval units in the Pacific, and the shortage of shipping and critical materials led to the decision to reduce the scope of the undertaking.

During February 1942, work was started on the section base, a 120-unit housing project, and an extensive system of roads designed to link the various shore activities then underway. Form work on the drydock was started in April and the first concrete poured in June. In August, certain items

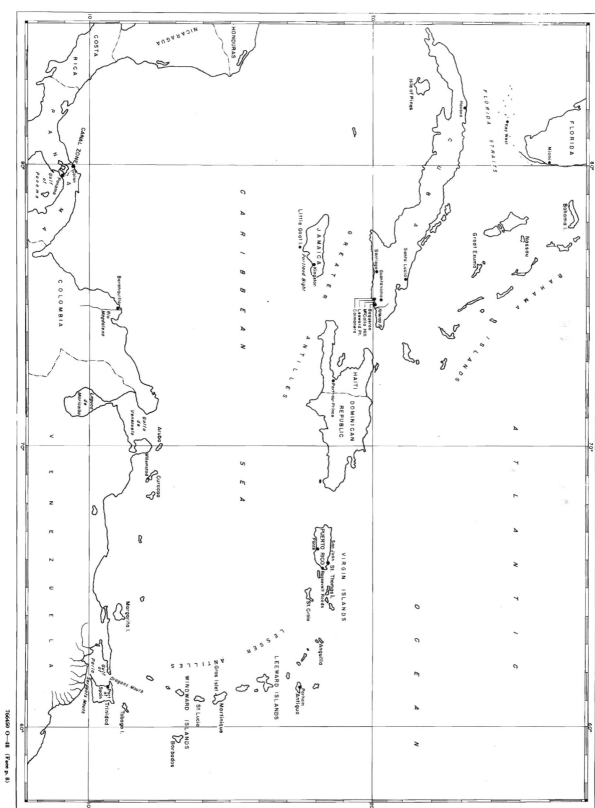

CARIBBEAN AREA

were deferred and others curtailed. Henceforth the priority projects were the drydock with associated industrial facilities, water supply, and the air station for landplanes. Plans for the supply depot, receiving station, hospital, radio station, and seaplane base were abandoned.

Within the industrial area the drydock, a bombproof power plant, a sewage pumping station, and a machine shop were completed. The drydock, 1100 by 155 feet, and built in the dry, was used for the first time in July 1943. The power plant, a bombproof structure with 4-feet-thick concrete walls, was equipped with two 5,000-kw steam-driven generators.

The drydock was dedicated on February 15, 1944, as the Bolles Drydock, in memory of Captain Harry A. Bolles, (CEC) USN, who was killed in Alaska in World War II.

The water-supply system obtained water from the tail race of the Insular Power Plant on the Rio Blanco and delivered it through 11 miles of 27-inch concrete pipe by gravity to a 46,000,000-gallon raw-water reservoir on the base. It was then treated by coagulation, filtration, and chlorination, and delivered to fresh-water reservoirs by pumps, for gravity distribution to the entire base. The treatment plant had a daily capacity of 4,000,000 gallons.

Of permanent construction, the naval air station at Roosevelt Roads was equipped with three concrete runways, 6,000 by 300 feet, concrete taxiways and parking area, a large steel hangar, quarters for personnel, a large concrete storehouse, gasoline storage, and magazines for ready ammunition.

In building the runways, it was necessary to remove unstable clay subsoil and replace it, to a minimum depth of 3 feet, with selected backfill, placed under controlled - moisture conditions. Shoulders were surfaced with a 3-inch layer of rolled coral dredged from the bay. Storage for gasoline was provided in six 50,000-gallon and four 250,000-gallon pre-stressed-concrete tanks. Elsewhere on the base, storage for 118,000 barrels of fuel and diesel oil were built and piped to the completed fuel dock at the section base.

In addition to the quarry, which in itself was a major operation, Vieques Island was developed as a naval ammunition depot. This facility, located on the western third of the island, was equipped with 107 magazines and ammunition storage buildings of the concrete arch type for high explosives. Two 80-foot drilled wells and two large storage

tanks were built for fresh water and fire protection.

The anchorage development was begun in October 1942 when the first rock fill was placed at the Vieques end of the west breakwater. Work continued until the project was deferred in May 1943. When the cease-operations order was issued, 7,000 feet of the breakwater had been completed, and everything was in readiness for major construction involving the quarrying and placing of 20-ton rock.

Field work under the contract was terminated on August 28, 1943. A total of $56,000,000 had been expended on the development, including a considerable amount of temporary construction.

Roosevelt Roads was commissioned as a naval operating base on July 15, 1943; more than a year later, on November 1, 1944, it was redesignated a naval station and placed in a caretaker status under the supervision of a public works officer, assisted by a small detachment of personnel from CBMU 's 507 and 517 and a station labor force of Puerto Ricans.

Culebra Island

Culebra Island, lying midway between Puerto Rico and the island of St. Thomas in the Virgin Islands, was established as a naval reservation in 1917 and at various times during the years between wars was used by the Marine Corps for winter maneuvers. Its two installations, a 2400-foot sod-surfaced airstrip and a camp site, were in a rundown condition when World War II began.

Of value chiefly because of a fine sheltered harbor and potentialities as an emergency landing field, a minor construction effort was expended to rehabilitate the camp for immediate use. The sewerage, fresh- and salt-water systems, cold storage, and messing facilities were renovated and improved under the San Juan contract during the summer of 1942. Further maintenance and repair work was undertaken again during February 1944 by a detachment from CBMU 507 stationed at St. Thomas.

Because of the way the war developed, Culebra remained insignificant throughout the period, and in September 1944 was reduced to caretaker status.

St. Thomas, Virgin Islands

St. Thomas, 50 miles east of Puerto Rico, is 14 miles long, varying in width to a maximum of 4 miles, with an approximate area of 32 square miles. Most of the island rises directly out of the sea in high rocky cliffs, with the major portion of the surrounding water either shallow or made useless

BOURNE FIELD, ST. THOMAS
Industrial area for the Marine aviation facility

by barrier reefs. On the south side of the island, however, there are three excellent bays, so situated that peninsulas and small islands form natural breakwaters. Two of these bays were developed for Navy use; Lindbergh Bay for seaplanes and Gregerie Channel for submarines and deep-draft vessels.

When, in July 1940, the fixed-fee contract operating at San Juan was extended to accomplish the development of St. Thomas, there existed on that island a Marine air base, established in 1935, as well as a radio station and a submarine base, both dating from World War I. The air base, known as Bourne Field, comprised two 1600-foot sod-surfaced runways which were used by the Marines as an outlying training field; the radio station was a minor installation, and the submarine base had long since been abandoned as such.

The initial program called for improvements and additions to existing facilities to accommodate a Marine squadron of 18 planes on a permanent

basis and a waterfront development to serve one patrol-plane squadron in a tender-based status.

The main east-west runway at Bourne Field was extended to a length of 4800 feet, and a 100-foot extension was added to the steel hangar, together with additional quarters, an administration building, additional gasoline storage, a cold-storage building and commissary, extensions to roads and services, and a new 60-bed dispensary and hospital. A concrete ramp, hangar, and utility shop were also built to accommodate seaplane operations in Lindbergh Bay.

Fifty low-cost housing units were added to the contract during October. Financed from National Defense Housing funds, these were built of prefabricated light-steel frames with concrete floors and stucco exteriors, identical with those built at San Juan. Reinforced concrete and structural steel were, in general, used for all other buildings, both

CATCHMENT AREA FOR LAUNDRY AND POWER HOUSE AT THE SUBMARINE BASE, ST. THOMAS

for permanency and as a precaution against hurricanes.

Due to the irregular terrain and the general presence of rock close to the surface, the runway extension was made by dredge-filling a marsh on the eastern end of the field. It was also necessary, because of the shallow soil overburden, to resort to drilling and blasting for practically all excavations necessary for foundations and underground services.

By midsummer 1941 the scope and purpose of St. Thomas had been redefined, in accordance with the Greenslade studies and the requirements of the two-ocean Navy and 15,000-plane program. As a consequence, the contract was again supplemented on July 8, 1941, to provide for further additions to the air station and the development of a completely new facility—a submarine base, on Gregerie Channel and adjacent to the air station.

Under the new construction program, the aviation shore facilities were expanded to meet the operational requirements of two Marine squadrons and the emergency operation of six patrol seaplanes. Additional barracks, services, magazines, recreational facilities, and fresh-water storage were built. Housing for service personnel, when completed, provided for 700 enlisted men in three barracks, one barrack for 40 officers, and 24 housing units for married non-commissioned and commissioned officers.

The waterfront development at the submarine base, built in dredge-deepened waters, comprised three finger piers, each 350 by 30 feet, and twelve 19-pile dolphins. Construction included quarters for 900 enlisted men and 42 officers, an administration building, storage buildings, torpedo overhaul shop, and a bombproof powerhouse in which were installed four 750-kva diesel-driven generators. Two 10,000-barrel steel tanks, with a pump and filter plant, were installed for diesel-oil storage.

Fresh water for both the air station and the submarine base was obtained by collecting rainfall. Five hillside catchment areas, totaling 13 acres, were built by removing the foliage and thin layer of top soil from the underlying rock. The water thus collected was funneled into a number of concrete reservoirs, chlorinated, and pumped directly into the distribution pipe lines.

Under a later program, undertaken in October 1941, a section base and net and boom depot were

McCalla Field Headquarters, Guantanamo Bay

built on the waterfront adjacent to the submarine base. Two additional finger piers, one 500 feet and the other 350 feet long, were constructed, together with the necessary industrial buildings to house these activities. A new radio station, equipped with three 150-foot steel towers and a reinforced-concrete transmitter building, was also constructed to replace the inadequate station built in World War I.

Still further additions and improvements built during 1942 were directed toward bringing into better balance the facilities constructed under the initial development plan. The program was climaxed finally in December by a major increase in liquid-fuel storage and the paving of the east-west runway at Bourne Field. Two 100,000-gallon tanks,

of pre-stressed concrete, for gasoline, and six of a similar type for diesel oil, with a capacity of 135,000 barrels, were built.

On June 11, 1943. CBMU 507. with a complement of 256 enlisted men and 4 officers, arrived at St. Thomas. The civilian contract was terminated 15 days later, the maintenance unit carrying to completion a number of buildings and installations left unfinished by the contractor. Using native labor to augment their own force, they also accomplished an extensive program of miscellaneous construction and improvements to facilitate better operation and make the base more nearly self-sustaining.

Guantanamo, Cuba

At the outset of the emergency, facilities in

existence at Guantanamo Bay comprised a naval station equipped with shops, storehouses, barracks, two small marine railways, a fuel oil and coaling plant, a Marine training station, and an airfield. The station, used by the fleet while on winter maneuvers, reflected the period of strict naval economy between wars, having been relegated to practically inactive status.

The site, acquired by lease from the Cuban government on July 2, 1903, for an annual rental of $2,000, completely encircles the bay and contains approximately 36,000 acres, of which 13,400 acres are land and the remainder water and salt flats. The greater part of the water is navigable, forming an excellent land-locked harbor, with depths ranging up to 60 feet.

Initial development in the bay area consisted of an air station. By 1944, there had been developed a major naval operating base, equipped with ship-repair facilities, fuel depot, supply depot, and other related activities. These new facilities were accomplished under a single fixed-fee contract, awarded July 1, 1940; construction operations began two weeks later.

Included in the initial program were five major projects: a Marine Corps base for 2,000 men, a fuel-oil and gasoline storage depot, two airfields, and improvements to existing radio facilities.

Within the limits of the area under Navy lease, there were two sites suitable for airfields. One of these, McCalla Hill, adjacent to the eastern shoreline of the harbor entrance, was already developed as a field within the tract of land allocated to the Marine Corps. Leeward Point, directly west of McCalla Hill and across the bay entrance, offered the second site.

The area allocated to the Marine Corps was relinquished in order that the existing McCalla Hill airfield might be enlarged and a seaplane base be established there. In exchange, the Marine Corps was provided with a new and self-contained base for a force of 2,000 men, with all necessary utilities, such as barracks, administration buildings, dispensary, mess halls, storage buildings, laundry, roads. The buildings were of semi-permanent character, with concrete foundations, tile ground floors, wooden superstructure, and asbestos shingle or tile roofs.

The airfield on McCalla Hill was equipped with three asphalt runways—one, 300 by 4900 feet, and two cross runways, 200 by 2300 feet built to the limit of the land available. Warm-up platforms, a hangar and utility building, administration and operations building, magazines, quarters, barracks, and mess halls were provided. At the seaplane base, facilities installed included a concrete parking area of approximately 560,000 square feet, two seaplane ramps, each 100 feet wide, and a large, steel hangar.

At Leeward Point airfield, across the bay entrance, two runways, a hangar, storage facilities, distribution systems for water, diesel-oil, and gasoline, a small power plant, a magazine, a barrack and a small-boat landing were built. The main runway, 6000 feet long, and a cross strip, of 3500-foot length, were paved with asphalt 150 feet wide.

Fuel-oil storage, constructed under the original program, included 18 tanks of 25,000 gallons each and 10 tanks of 27,000 barrels each, grouped in tank farms at four separate locations. All were built of steel and located underground. Water lines, access roads, and chemical fire-fighting equipment were installed at each of the four locations. In addition to the pumping equipment and distribution lines which were installed to link these systems together, one ethyl-blending plant was provided for ethylizing raw gasoline.

Housing proved a problem from the very beginning of the construction period, for both continentals and Cubans. For those who lived in the two nearest Cuban cities, Caimanera and Boqueron, it meant a 5-mile boat ride each way or a much longer drive by automobile. To help relieve the situation, 200 low-cost homes, built in a community group on the reservation, remote from the area occupied by the principal naval activities, were added to the contract in October.

That month of October 1940 also saw a second major addition to the contract, which provided facilities needed for a fleet anchorage and operating base. Extensive dredging operations, totalling 16,000,000 cubic yards, were undertaken to deepen certain areas of the bay to permit mooring of deep-draft vessels. Also constructed were 17 destroyer, 10 cruiser, and 3 battleship moorings. These were of steel sheet-piling, cellular in design, filled with dredged material, and capped with concrete.

The October supplement to the contract also included three storehouses, a chapel, additions to an existing machine shop, a net and boom depot, and miscellaneous small projects.

For years, one of the main drawbacks to the development of Guantanamo Bay as a fleet operating base was the lack of fresh water. During the early days. water had to be purchased on yearly contract from the neighboring cities of Caimanera and Boqueron, barged from there to the station, and pumped into storage tanks. This method of supply was costly, unreliable, and even dangerous when considered from the point of view of health. In 1934, Congress authorized the Navy Department to enter into a 20-year contract for water to be supplied to the station by pipe line. The pipe line was placed in operation in July 1939, water being obtained from the Yateras River, 10 miles distant, and pumped to the station through a 10-inch main.

As this system was definitely limited by the size of the pipeline, it became necessary, in view of the development planned for Guantanamo, to increase its capacity. This project, begun in September 1941, furnished an additional 2,000,000 gallons per day. A new pumping plant, installed at the Yateras River, pumped water through 50,000 feet of 14-inch main to two treatment-plants on the station. Midway along the pipe line a 500,000-gallon concrete reservoir was built for reserve water storage and as a fire precaution; three steel tanks, with a combined capacity of 2,000,000 gallons for treated water, were built on the station.

A new section base and an underground hospital were also begun during September 1941. The U-shaped pier, supported on timber piles, with a 260-foot base and two wings, each 350 by 30 feet, was built at the section base. Twelve barracks, each with a capacity of 230 men, a mess hall, and a new machine shop were also provided.

The underground hospital, a bomb-proof structure, comprising four concrete arch-type units built into a hillside, was fitted with 192 beds and complete hospital equipment, including two stand-by power plants for light and forced ventilation.

With the advent of war, the importance and value of Guantanamo as a major link in the chain of Caribbean defenses was reflected in the steady increase in construction activity throughout 1942. The capacity of the fuel depot was greatly expanded, beginning with the addition of a diesel-oil filter-plant in February 1942, two 27,000-barrel pre-stressed concrete tanks in April, and seven 50,000-barrel tanks during May. These underground tanks were interconnected, with pipe-line extension, to a floating oil-dock in the fleet anchorage area.

A degaussing and deperming installation was authorized in March 1942; a 30-ton marine railway and a 3000-ton timber floating drydock, in June; and an anti-aircraft training center, in July. In November extensive ship-repair facilities and an auxiliary outlying airfield were begun.

Included in the ship-repair project were three timber piers, 625 feet, 1120 feet, and 250 feet long, respectively; a timber causeway, 400 feet long; and a 236-foot marginal wharf, the platforms of which were a composite of wood and concrete. Two large buildings, a repair shop and rigging loft, and several small industrial buildings were also included.

The outlying airfield, at Los Canos, 30 miles north of McCalla Hill Field at Guantanamo, was built to serve as an emergency landing field and as a training area for carrier-based aircraft. It was built on 450 acres of land leased from the Guantanamo Sugar Company and equipped with three 4500-foot runways, one of which was paved with a penetration asphalt surface, 150 feet wide. Quonset huts served for personnel housing and administration offices.

Upon completion of the Los Canos project in September 1943, this field, with the facilities provided at the McCalla Hill and Leeward Point fields, composed the naval air station, which supported the operation of three squadrons of patrol seaplanes, one carrier group of 90 planes, and one utility squadron, in addition to the temporary operation of four additional patrol squadrons with tender support and one additional carrier group with the parent ship present.

Upon the termination of the contract on September 30, 1943, the Public Works Department, augmented by 1800 men transferred from the contractors' payrolls, carried on all uncompleted contract projects. These consisted primarily of completing the ship-repair facilities and the installation of machinery in otherwise completed structures at various locations. The peak of operational activity was reached during the summer of 1944, when, because of the Allied advances in the European theater and the almost complete elimination of the submarine menace in the Caribbean area, orders were issued for the curtailment and consolidation of the activities at the base.

Haiti

Using Lend-Lease funds, the Navy constructed a 1000-ton marine railway at Port-au-Prince for use by the Haitian Coast Guard. This facility, built under the Guantanamo contract, was completed in April 1944 and turned over to the Haitian government the following month. Except for the railway, no other construction was done on Haiti.

Part II—The Canal Zone

When anxious eyes were directed toward the defenses of the Panama Canal in the fall of 1939, the naval shore establishment then in existence in the Zone was limited on the Atlantic side to an air station for seaplanes and a submarine base at Coco Solo, a radio station at Gatun, and a small section base at Cristobal. On the Pacific side, at Balboa, were located the administrative headquarters of the 15th Naval District and, directly across the Canal, on the west bank, an ammunition depot. Another radio station, located at Summit, about one third of the distance from Balboa to Coco Solo, and half a dozen fuel tanks at either end of the Canal, and a few minor installations completed the list. For fueling and ship repairs, the Navy was entirely dependent on the industrial plant owned and operated by the Panama Canal. These centered around a battleship graving dock at Balboa and a smaller dock, 390 feet long, at Cristobal on the Atlantic end of the canal.

Using these existing facilities as a nucleus, the Navy began to strengthen and enlarge its installations during the summer of 1940. Guided by the Hepburn Board recommendations, the initial effort was undertaken by two fixed-fee contracts, awarded June 17 and July 11, and devoted primarily to enlarging the air station and submarine base at Coco Solo and constructing housing and a new office building at Balboa for the administrative offices of the 15th Naval District.

The scope of each contract was enlarged considerably during the pre-war period, as defense plans for the Canal were broadened and new installations authorized. When war was declared, several entirely new activities were well underway, with work concentrated in the Coco Solo area and on a new tract of land on the west bank of the Canal, directly across from Balboa.

By the end of 1940, work had begun on a new supply depot at Balboa, and on the Farfan Radio Station on the west bank, together with the enlargement of the two inland radio stations at Gatun and Summit. Two net depots were started in December, one at each end of the Canal, and during the same month a third contract was awarded for 1400 housing units, 1100 at Coco Solo and the remainder on the west bank at Balboa. The following summer two naval hospitals, one at Coco Solo and the other at Balboa, were begun.

That summer of 1941 also saw the start of intensive work on the development of a new naval operating base on the west bank at Balboa. With further expansion impossible along the congested waterfront, this west bank area became the locale for the major war construction effort in the Canal Zone.

The war years of 1942-1944 saw an enormous increase in the tempo of construction activity, the major effort being concentrated in three categories; fuel storage, ship-repair facilities, and the development of several advance bases to support distant air patrols. The Gatun tank farm on the Atlantic side, and the Arraijan farm, on the Pacific, were started in February 1942, and subsequently these huge storage reservoirs, 32 miles apart, were connected by a multiple pipe-line, installed under a fourth fixed-fee contract, awarded August 4, 1942 and completed in 1943.

In April 1942, work was started on a second graving dock adjoining the existing Panama Canal dock at Balboa, a bombproof command center, additional housing in the district headquarters area, and additional frame warehouses at the supply depot. In June, a third graving dock, to adjoin the other two at Balboa, was put under contract, and work was begun on two new marine railways, adjacent to the existing drydock at Cristobal. Meanwhile, the ammunition depots at Coco Solo and Balboa were enlarged, as were the facilities at the Coco Solo submarine base and air station and the Balboa operating base.

Advance bases were established during 1942 and 1943 on Taboga Island at the Pacific entrance to the Canal, on the Galapagos Islands off the coast of Ecuador, at Corinto in Nicaragua, Salinas in Ecuador, Chorrera and Mandinga in Panama,

Puerto Castillo in Honduras, and Barranquilla in Colombia.

The peak of construction activity was reached in the summer of 1943, and three of the four major contracts were terminated during the late fall of that year. After the termination of the fourth contract in April 1944, several smaller lump-sum contracts were awarded for minor additions and improvements and to care for current needs.

Two groups of Seabees, Detachment 1012, which arrived September 9, 1942, and Maintenance Unit 555, which arrived in December 1943 as a replacement for the first group, served in the 15th Naval District. Due to the difficulty of procuring civilian labor for work in outlying areas, both units were used mainly at the advance bases. Some of the men, however, were stationed within the Zone, to operate power houses and perform specialized maintenance work.

Coco Solo

Naval Air Station.—The Coco Solo air station occupies 185 acres of hard land, on the east side of Manzanillo Bay. Existing facilities in 1939 included a small landing-field, three plane hangars, one blimp hangar, barracks, officers' quarters, three seaplane ramps, and a few miscellaneous buildings.

When the development of the station was begun on August 1, 1940, the approved plan contemplated expansion sufficient to serve seven patrol squadrons of seaplanes. The original site, though limited, was considered to be the most advantageous that could be found in the Canal Zone; consequently, maximum expansion was advocated rather than construction of an additional base in another locality.

The greatest single deficiency existing at the station was the lack of sheltered water for full-load take-off immediately adjacent to the base. There was a wide gap of open water between the eastern breakwater and Margarita Point, through which heavy ocean swells entered Manzanillo Bay, frequently making seaplane operations hazardous. In addition, the station lacked sufficient hangars, ramps, parking aprons, housing, storage, and repair facilities.

The initial construction effort, therefore, was concentrated on closing the 3800-foot gap in the Margarita breakwater. Rubble-mound construction, laid on a 15-foot coral mat, was used, the wall itself having a coral-fill core, covered with heavy rock

and armored with pre-cast concrete blocks. It was built entirely from a temporary timber trestle, without the use of floating equipment other than the hydraulic dredge used for placing the foundation and core.

At the air station proper, three large steel hangars, four seaplane ramps, 700,000 square feet of concrete parking area, engine test stands, and a large aircraft assembly and repair shop were added to the operating area fronting on Manzanillo Bay. To make expansion possible, it was necessary to reclaim 30 acres of beach by dredge. A steel sheet-pile sea-wall, 2100 feet long, was driven to enclose two edges of this newly made land.

Other construction accomplished at the station included a barrack and mess hall for 1000 men, a new wing to an existing barracks to care for 400 men, a bombproof command center, an operations building, a large administration building to house the administrative offices of both the air station and the adjoining submarine base, and several large warehouses.

Dredging operations at the air station were also extended to furnish coral fill for the construction of new runways at Army's adjacent France Field. When that field was completed, 1700 feet of concrete taxiway, 66 feet wide, was built to connect the two stations. The Navy, henceforth, used Army facilities for the operation of its landplanes in the Coco Solo area.

Submarine Base. Established in 1917, and later modernized, the submarine base occupied a 130-acre peninsula bounded on the north by Margarita Bay and on the west and south by Manzanillo Bay. Important additions to all existing facilities were accomplished under the wartime construction program begun during the fall of 1940, developments being confined entirely within the limits of the existing boundaries.

A mole pier, 300 feet wide, enclosed with steel sheet-piling, was built as an extension to the original north quay wall, to provide additional berthing space and increase the basin area. This pier, paved with concrete, was equipped with water, oil, and air lines, a railway spur, a large transit shed, several storehouses, and shop buildings. The south quay was likewise extended a distance of 500 feet and equipped with water, oil, and electric services. A net depot, comprising a large storage building and a 16,000-square-foot paved weaving-slab was

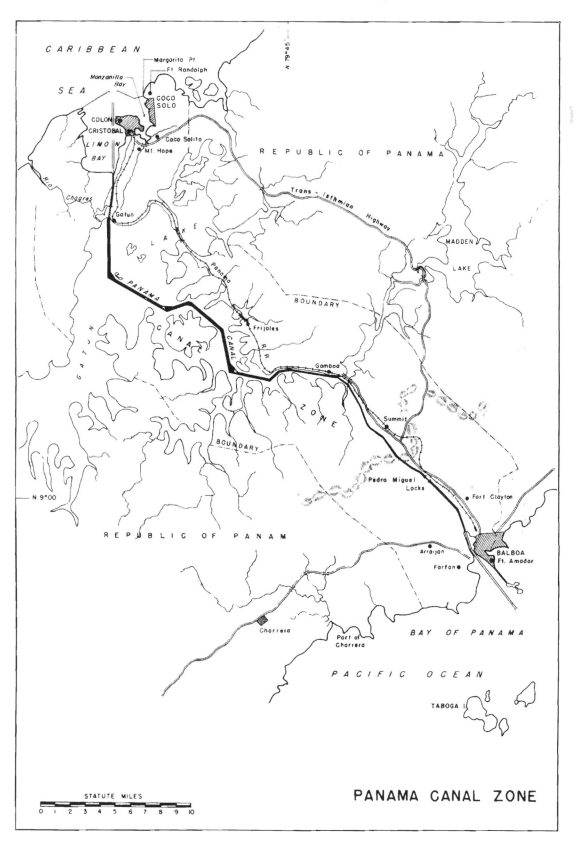

PANAMA CANAL ZONE

built along this quay, and the basin dredged to a depth of 32 feet.

In the industrial area, extensions were made to the torpedo shop, ship fitters' shop, and battery shops. A large storehouse and a three-story structure to house the machine and optical shops were erected.

A low-lying, 20-acre area fronting on Margarita Bay was inclosed with 3200 feet of steel sheet-pile seawall, brought to a usable elevation with coral fill dredged from the bay. This was later developed as the main housing area for the station, construction including seventy four-family two-story houses and two large bachelor-officer dormitories. These units were constructed of concrete, with the first floor placed 6 feet above the ground for ventilation and garage space. A chapel and library, a theater, tennis courts, and a recreation building for enlisted men and officers were also located in the area.

Fuel Storage

In 1940, fuel storage in the Canal Zone presented a serious hazard. There were two tank farms—one at Balboa, on the Pacific side; the other at Mount Hope, on the Atlantic side—neither of which was protected against air attack. Not only were their positions exposed, but each was served by one unprotected pumping station. The Balboa tank farm was on high ground adjoining the harbor entrance channel, and its tanks presented an excellent target for air attack. Had these farms been destroyed it would have been impossible to refuel shipping in the Canal Zone. The solution to the problem was clearly underground bombproof storage tanks, located at points removed from the harbors.

At the same time, it had become increasingly apparent that in event of war, additional fuel-handling facilities would be required. All Navy vessels were fueled at the Panama Canal docks at Balboa and Cristobal, with the exception of diesel-powered craft based at Coco Solo. The Balboa farm had only limited bunkering facilities at the congested Panama Canal docks, had no reserve capacity, had no land for expansion, and could not be developed as a terminal for the proposed Trans-Isthmian pipeline.

In January 1941, the Secretary of the Navy recommended that the commanding general of the Canal Zone call a conference of all interested parties, including the governor of the Canal Zone and the commandant of the 15th Naval District, to develop a project for placing all storage of liquid fuels underground at the earliest practicable date.

Four localities were considered, final decision being left to the Navy. Plans were also considered for a pipe line connecting both coasts in order to replace tanker shipment through the Canal, but the difficulties and cost of construction caused that matter to be dropped until 1942, when the course of the war made it a project of vital urgency.

In June 1941, the Navy Fuel Storage Board submitted its report relative to the quantity, type, and location of liquid fuel storage to be provided in the 15th Naval District. It recommended fuel oil, 1,000,000 barrels; diesel oil, 220,000 barrels; aviation gasoline, 5,900,000 gallons; and suggested distribution of storage on the Pacific and Atlantic sides in proportions of 60 and 40 per cent, respectively. It was further recommended that an additional reserve 3,800,000 gallons of gasoline be stored on the Atlantic side near Coco Solo, in order to be readily available to the naval air station, and that on the Pacific side, 2,100,000 gallons of reserve gasoline storage be combined into a single project under the cognizance of the Army. All storage was to be underground.

The sites selected were a 1700-acre tract, near Cristobal, designated the Gatun farm, and an 820-acre tract near Balboa, known as the Arraijan farm.

The original scope of the Gatun project, which was begun in February 1942, included fifteen 27,000-barrel steel tanks for fuel oil, two 27,000-barrel gasoline tanks, and four pumphouses. When emergency conditions required more extensive underground oil-storage, the Gatun project was enlarged in May and September 1942, and again in January 1943. It eventually included fifteen 27,000-barrel and eleven 50,000-barrel steel tanks and seven 27,000-barrel tanks of pre-stressed concrete.

The Gatun tank farm was connected with the existing 27-tank Mount Hope farm of the Panama Canal and the Cristobal piers by two 20-inch lines for fuel oil and two 12-inch lines for diesel oil. Booster pump stations were constructed in the line to enable a tanker to discharge at the rate of 8,000 barrels per hour for fuel oil and 6,000 barrels per hour for diesel oil.

The development of the tank farm at Arraijan progressed concurrently with the project at Gatun. Planned originally to consist of eighteen 27,000-

barrel and two 13,500-barrel tanks. the Arraijan farm eventually included two 13,500-barrel and twenty-six 27,000-barrel steel tanks, four 27,000-barrel and six 50,000-barrel pre-stressed concrete tanks, and four pump houses. Two 18-inch and one 12-inch pipelines connected the farm with the fueling piers at Balboa. The tanks, pump-houses, all design details, and method of construction were similar to the Gatun project.

To provide reserve storage for aviation gasoline, seven 13,500-barrel steel tanks were installed in the naval magazine area, adjacent to the Coco Solo air station. This project, which likewise was begun in February, eventually expanded to include five additional tanks of 27,000-barrel capacity for ready diesel-oil storage to supply the submarine base. These were connected through an 8-inch pipe to the eight 25,000-gallon tanks at the air station. The diesel tanks were, in similar fashion, connected with the Panama Canal tanks at Mount Hope, the fueling piers at Cristobal, and, eventually, with the tank farm at Gatun, making the entire system mutually flexible.

Japanese seizure of the oil fields in the Netherlands East Indies during the early days of the war made it necessary to rely entirely on the Americas for oil deliveries to the Pacific theater of operations. With a large portion of the United States refineries located along the Gulf of Mexico and the East Coast, and those in South America likewise accessible from the Atlantic and Caribbean, fuel deliveries to the Pacific depended upon the use of tankers and the Panama Canal. A certain and continued supply of liquid fuel was a strategic imperative.

During the summer of 1942, German submarines took a heavy toll of our tanker fleet plying the Atlantic and the Caribbean, which, apart from the loss of oil involved in these sinkings, seriously reduced the number of fast tankers available to transport oil in the quantities needed. These losses were a matter of grave concern in view of the oil demands involved in future operations planned for the Pacific campaign.

Accordingly, the installation of the proposed pipe line across the Isthmus, connecting the Gatun and Arraijan tank farms, became a project of immediate military necessity. Such a pipe line would confine the use of older, smaller, and slower tankers to a shuttle service between the fueling piers at Cristobal, the supply sources along the Gulf of

Mexico, and the huge refineries at the Dutch islands of Aruba and Curacao. It would also serve to eliminate tanker traffic through the Canal and materially speed up the loading and return of the large, fast tankers carrying oil to the Pacific.

The installation of this pipe line was accomplished under a fixed-fee contract, awarded specifically for this purpose, on August 4, 1942. As initially planned, the project called for the installation of one 20-inch and one 10-inch welded-steel pipe lines, each 33 miles long, connecting the Gatun and the Arraijan tank farms. Construction was started in October.

In addition to one Canal-crossing, 4 miles of the run was under the waters of Gatun Lake. The rugged terrain and jungle along the route presented many problems in ditching, grading, and placing of the pipe itself. Even Gatun Lake had to be cleared of submerged obstacles.

In spite of an unduly severe rainy season, the two pipe lines were completed and used for the first time on April 18, 1943. By the end of 1943 the entire system was completed and in full operation.

In April 1944, a year after the first test had been run, work was started to double the capacity of the pipe line. A second 20-inch fuel line and a 12-inch line to carry gasoline were laid directly over the original 20- and 10-inch pipes.

Built at a cost of $20,000,000, the Trans-Isthmian pipe line was built to handle a daily flow of 265,000 barrels of fuel oil, 47,000 barrels of diesel-oil and 60,000 barrels of gasoline.

Housing

As a part of the general expansion program undertaken in the Canal Zone, two housing developments, totaling 1400 units, were built to provide for the families of married enlisted personnel and civilian employees of the 15th Naval District. These units, built under a contract awarded in December 1940, were divided. 1104 being on the Atlantic and 296 on the Pacific end of the Canal.

The larger development, Coco Solito, was constructed on a 33-acre, filled-in site, one mile south of the air station at Coco Solo. Laid out with six east-west streets and three north-south ones, Coco Solito contained 91 twelve-unit, one eight-unit, and one four-unit apartment buildings. The structures were of similar type and design, three stories high, of concrete and frame, with galvanized-iron roofing and the ground floors available for garages and laundries.

The housing area at the Pacific end of the Canal encircled San Juan Hill on three sides, spreading over approximately 100 acres of rolling ground which required considerable clearing and leveling. It included 60 four-unit apartments, 2 officers' houses, 2 bachelor officers' quarters, and 5 B-1-type barracks, together with several community buildings, storehouses, a public-works shop, administration, subsistence, and service buildings.

At Lacona, 296 apartments for civilian personnel were completed in December 1941. This group comprised 24 twelve-unit and one eight-unit apartment houses.

A new 12-inch water main replaced the former 8-inch one supplying Balboa, and a 750,000-gallon water reservoir was built on San Juan Hill to serve naval activities.

Hospitals

To care for the large increases in personnel which accompanied the expansion of the naval establishment, a new 200-bed naval hospital was built on a 40-acre tract of high land, on the north side of the new Trans-Isthmian Highway, about 3 miles from the Coco Solo air station. This facility consisted of a four-story structure, with additional buildings for quarters, laundry, garage, and sewage plant, all of reinforced concrete. It was commissioned in September 1942, and later enlarged by the addition of two temporary wards of frame construction, to provide 500 beds.

A second hospital was built on a 50-acre tract adjoining the operating base on the Pacific side. Construction of this 400-bed facility was begun in the late fall of 1941. It was commissioned August 15, 1942, and put to immediate use, though only partially completed.

All the buildings were of temporary frame construction, one-story high, and well ventilated. They included six standard H-type wards, connected by covered passageways, quarters, an administration building, and laboratories, messhalls, and garages. Location and general layout were chosen so as to be readily adaptable if permanent structures were eventually erected on the site.

Ammunition Storage

The naval magazine area at Coco Solo, originally completed in 1937, was more than doubled both in storage capacity and in area, during the war-

construction period. Under the initial program, begun in November 1940, new additions were confined within the original area of 700 acres. After war was declared, further increase in storage facilities was ordered and the area of the reserve increased to 1500 acres, of which 140 were devoted to the Coco Solo tank farm. Both the earlier work and the later additions required a considerable amount of clearing, excavating, and road building. Altogether, 40 storage structures of various types, ranging from concrete arch-type underground magazines for high explosives to frame storehouses, were built.

The capacity of the existing West Bank Ammunition Depot, commissioned in September 1937, was increased fourfold during the period from 1941 to 1943, a total of 47 ammunition magazines being built, of which 34 were concrete arch-type high-explosive magazines.

These were linked together by a system of access roads, and the newly developed area enclosed by 7 miles of wire fencing. In addition, sentry stations, telephone lines, quarters for assigned personnel, and a temporary mine-anchor storage building were included in the development.

Radio Stations

The two major radio stations, located at Gatun and Summit, were considerably enlarged, and a third, known as the Farfan Radio Station, was installed at Balboa.

At the Gatun station, three existing towers were removed and replaced by three 150-foot steel towers; a new two-story reinforced-concrete, bombproof transmitter and command post was added.

To the station at Summit, which had been completed in 1935, were added housing, an extension to the transmitter building, a new bombproof transmitter and receiving building, and a 300-foot and an 800-foot tower.

Erecting the 800-foot tower presented an unusual construction problem. Approximately 135,000 cubic yards of excavation were necessary to level the surrounding terrain before placing the ground grid-system, which comprised 240 bare copper wires extending radially for a distance of 600 feet. The 20-foot square tower rested on a single, huge insulator and was supported vertically by eight equally spaced guy cables, attached at a height of 515 feet.

The Farfan Radio Station, an entirely new development, located on an 860-acre reservation south of the Balboa operating base, was equipped with complete services. The installation included five steel towers, a two-story bombproof operations building, and housing facilities.

Cristobal

The Panama Canal maintained its ship-repair facilities serving the Atlantic end of the canal at Cristobal. These, comprising the Mount Hope shops and a graving dock, 390 feet by 80 feet, were supplemented by two marine railways of 1000-ton and 3000-ton capacities and a 1000-foot marginal wharf.

As a part of the fuel-storage program, the dock was equipped with fuel, diesel-oil, and gasoline pipe lines to facilitate the transfer of liquid fuel to the Gatun tank farm. Dredging to a depth of 35 feet provided an adequate turning basin in the vicinity of the marine railways and the marginal wharf.

The old section base at Cristobal was supplemented by new buildings to house and feed 450 men assigned to the inshore patrol.

Balboa

An area opposite Balboa, the only practical location for the expansion of waterfront facilities at the Pacific entrance, had been under study for several years as a possible site for a submarine base. In the summer of 1941, the development of a small operating base was begun at a point where a pier had been built four years previously, to afford access to the ammunition depot. An extension was made to this pier and two new finger piers were added.

The two new piers, each 40 by 704 feet, were built of reinforced concrete. Concrete piles were cast at the concrete plant at Fort Randolph, on the Atlantic side, then producing piles for the Margarita breakwater, and shipped through the Canal. Pipe tunnels built into the piers provided space for fuel-oil, water, and power lines. The original ammunition depot pier was lengthened 220 feet and the waterfront area dredged to provide a 45-foot depth alongside the old pier, and a 33-foot depth at the new ones. A fourth pier, 1000 feet long, north of the ammunition pier, was planned and the necessary dredging completed, but the project was cancelled.

Several hundred feet out from the shoreline a head quay, or transverse wharf, 50 by 834 feet, was built to join the inboard ends of the three piers. A

fill of dredged material was to be placed behind the quay, but after filling had progressed behind the first completed section, a serious slide damaged that portion of the quay. The damaged part was not rebuilt, and no more fill was placed.

An industrial area for the new base, adjacent to the piers, was provided with shops for repair and overhaul of torpedoes, batteries, communication equipment, and other items of comparable magnitude. In addition, a three-story general storehouse, 100 by 300 feet, was erected to house top-off stores for Pacific-bound convoys.

South of the industrial area, a net and boom depot was established, equipped with a steel-frame net and boom building and several temporary storehouses. In addition, the depot was provided with a paved area of 12,000 square feet for net weaving and 74,000 square feet for storage.

The 15th Naval District headquarters area, covering 40 acres, was increased to 65, and a new, 3-story, reinforced-concrete office building, a bombproof command center, and additional housing for service personnel were built.

A four-story concrete store house, 80 by 220 feet, adjacent to the Balboa piers, completed in November 1941, formed the nucleus of the Balboa supply depot. After our entry into the war, when the Zone became the last stopping-off place for vessels en route to the Pacific, eight temporary frame structures, each 50 by 300 feet, were erected on an 18-acre plot, half a mile north of the main warehouse. These structures were completed in March 1943, together with a sorting and handling shed and a 75,000-square-foot lumber-storage yard. A much-needed refrigerator storehouse to replenish ships' food-lockers was completed during May 1944.

During World War I, when the construction of the Pacific terminal of the Canal was under discussion, it was decided to build two graving docks at Balboa; one to take any vessel that could pass through the canal locks and the other to care for smaller ships. Construction of both was started, but only the larger, known as Drydock Number 1, was completed. When work on the smaller dock, Drydock Number 2, was stopped, early in 1915, the head wall and south side wall had been completed and the floor of the dock excavated into rock to the required depth. Thereafter, Dock Number 2 was carried in the shore development plans as an essential project to be provided at Balboa.

After the outbreak of World War II, Drydock

Number 2 was approved as a project in January 1942, and construction begun immediately. It was redesigned to accommodate two destroyers or two submarines abreast, and a third dock for small vessels was built alongside, so located as to use the north wall of Dock Number 2 as one of its own.

All three drydocks share the use of the adjoining shops operated by the Panama Canal.

A pumping plant and electrical substation, a wharf along the north wall of Dock Number 3, a pier between Docks 2 and 3, and a cellular sheet-pile extension of the north and south walls of Dock Number 2, to form an approach pier, aiding the lateral control of vessels during docking operations, were also built. Some new machinery was purchased and installed in the Panama Canal shops to improve the repair capacity. By the end of 1943 the total repair facilities available in the Canal Zone were estimated as equal to those at Pearl Harbor on December 7, 1941.

Part III — The Destroyer Bases

The eight bases, popularly known as "Destroyer Bases" because of their acquisition from Britain in exchange for over-age destroyers, operated to advance our sea frontier several hundred miles into the Atlantic on a board arc, with Argentia, Newfoundland, as the north anchor and Trinidad as the south anchor, with Bermuda between. Individually and collectively they were of significant value in that they afforded strategically located sites upon which to base tactical and patrol aircraft for the control of the Caribbean.

Development and fortification of each base took into account the limitations imposed by location and character of terrain. Santa Lucia, in the Windward Islands, Antigua, Jamaica, British Guiana, and the island of Great Exuma in the Bahamas were equipped as secondary air bases and the remaining three, Trinidad, Bermuda, and Argentia, as major air bases. For immediate strategic reasons, Trinidad, Bermuda, and Argentia were given top priority and eventually became important bases for the operation of ships as well as planes. Argentia is discussed in the chapter dealing with bases in the North Atlantic.

A major air base, as visualized by the Greenslade Board, was to be equipped with complete facilities for operation, storage, and supply, engine overhaul, and complete periodic general overhaul of all types of planes. A secondary air base was a smaller installation, having facilities primarily for the operation, routine upkeep, and emergency repair of aircraft.

At the very beginning of their construction history these bases shared a common plan calling for the installation at each of emergency shore facilities to house a Marine detachment. This phase of their development was initiated by the Bureau of Yards and Docks on October 30, 1940, by assigning to the fixed-fee contract then operating at San Juan, the task of purchasing the necessary materials and equipment in advance of operations on the site. This beginning permitted the preliminary work attending a project of this magnitude to progress simultaneously with the negotiations attending the transfer of these Crown lands.

The Greenslade Board submitted its recommendations to the Secretary of the Navy on October 27, 1940, and tentative leases for the lands required were drawn, based on these findings; the necessary topographic and hydrographic surveys were begun. Remoteness of the sites, unknown bidding conditions, and the pressing necessity for speed contributed to the decision to undertake the construction at each location by negotiated cost-plus-fixed-fee contracts.

At first, there were some difficulties as the local governments did not have a clear picture of the agreement between the British and the United States governments concerning the use of the leased areas, and it was necessary for the Bureau to secure temporary leases in order to avoid delaying construction until such matters as customs, taxes, wharfage fees, and wage rates for local labor could be settled. The Navy Department received authority to enter Bermuda, Trinidad, and British Guiana, on January 3, 1941; Antigua and St. Lucia, on January 13; Great Exuma, March 27. The Jamaican government authorized entry into Little

BARRACKS AT TRINIDAD NAVAL BASE

Goat Island on January 16. Final lease agreements for all the bases were consummated March 27, 1941.

Trinidad

The strategically important island of Trinidad, commanding a vulnerable approach to the Panama Canal and the South American trade routes, lies off the coast of Venezuela. It is roughly 35 by 55 miles, with two long, narrow peninsulas extending westward toward the continent to form the Gulf of Paria, completely landlocked except for two easily guarded channels, each 7 miles wide.

The site for the naval shore establishment, on the northwest tip of the island, was acquired under two separate lease agreements, the first of which, dated April 22, 1941, involved 7940 acres, including five small islands in the Gulf of Paria, the property of the Crown. The second acquisition, made during December 1942, involved 3800 privately owned acres. The site consisted principally of steep hills and ridges, interspersed with flat valleys extending from four well-defined bays along the southern shore of the northwest peninsula. This location had the patent advantage of being remote from Port of Spain, the principal Trinidad city and port. From an engineering standpoint the flat areas along the shore, though limited, contained a minimum of swampy lowland, and the bay waters, with a minimum of dredging, were deep enough for accessibility by ships. The four bays—Carenage, Chaguaramus, Teteron, and Scotland—and two valleys—Chaguaramus and Tucker —each became the locale of a separate naval activity. Of the 11,740 acres acquired, only 1200

NAVAL SUPPLY DEPOT, TRINIDAD

acres were developed, at widely separated locations.

The original plans for Trinidad called for the immediate construction of a naval air station with facilities to support the operation of one patrol squadron of seaplanes and the development of a protected fleet anchorage in the Gulf of Paria. The ultimate goal was the development of a subsidiary operating base and a major air station with facilities for two patrol squadrons and the temporary operation of two carrier groups.

On January 24, 1941, a fixed-fee contract was awarded covering the construction of the air station and the first installment of dredging. Construction operations, which began during March, were confined to the Carenage Bay area. Included in the initial phase of the program were a 500-by-50-foot tender pier, seaplane facilities, including a concrete-paved beach and a macadam parking area, two concrete seaplane ramps, a steel hangar and control tower, gasoline storage, and associated

industrial, storage, administration, and personnel buildings. These major features of the station were of a permanent character, built of steel and concrete.

During the early months of the construction period the contractor's efforts were devoted to the many preliminaries attending a project of this magnitude. It was necessary to relocate a settlement of several hundred persons, build access roads, develop a quarry, and perform extensive clearing operations. One of the earliest projects undertaken was, of necessity, an aggressive campaign to combat malaria. Swampy bogs along the shore and the wet lowlands of Tucker Valley were drained, sprayed with oil, and later filled with dredged material. A force of 200 men devoted full time to the malaria program during the life of the contract.

Almost from its inception, the Trinidad contract, by a steady increase of added projects to its scope, reflected the trend of world events. The first increase, made in June 1941, was directed toward

SECTION BASE DISPENSARY, TRINIDAD

developing Trinidad as a fleet base. A net depot, additional dredging, a fueling pier, and a fuel and diesel-oil storage depot were added to the contract. The fuel storage comprised five 27,000-barrel steel tanks and two 27,000-barrel pre-stressed-concrete tanks. The fueling pier was a 450-by-50-foot structure with a composite deck of concrete and laminated wood.

Dredging operations, begun in August 1941, were continued over a two-year period, during which time a total of 13,000,000 yards of material was moved to provide navigable channels to the various piers, water approaches to the seaplane base, a fleet anchorage in Carenage Bay, and the fill necessary to reclaim waterfront area. Of this total, more than 2,000,000 yards were placed in swamps to eliminate mosquito-breeding areas.

Shortly after the declaration of war, the long-range plans made for Trinidad were translated into a vigorous construction program through a series of major additions made to the contract during 1942. The first of these, a section base at Teteron Bay, was incorporated with the air station on February 20. At the same time, contracts were let for five large fleet warehouses and a radio station, a high-power link in the major radio network of the Western Hemisphere. The station was located in Chaguaramus Valley and was of unusual design in that its main antennae were strung across the valley, supported by the mountain ridges on either side.

In March construction of a 150-bed hospital in upper Tucker Valley was begun. May brought new additions to the air station, including a third seaplane ramp, additional parking area, and more personnel buildings, increasing the station's handling capacity to five squadrons of patrol planes. At the same time, two timber floating drydocks,

ADMINISTRATION AND SUBSISTANCE BUILDINGS, TRINIDAD NAVAL BASE
Showing Carenage Bay and, beyond the Five Islands, the Gulf of Paria. Mountains in the background (upper
right) are in Venezuela

one of 3000-ton capacity and one of 1000-ton capacity, were incorporated in the contract. These were built on the site, in two dredged basins especially equipped for the operation.

In June, work was started on two 250,000-gallon concrete gasoline tanks, built underground and connected to the water displacement system installed to handle aviation gasoline at the air station. The total capacity of liquid-fuel storage constructed was in excess of 7,900,000 gallons.

Our entry into the war made our shipping a target for enemy submarines, and Germany was quick to take advantage of this opportunity by incursions into our coastal waters in January 1942. A squadron of ten Army bombers, equipped with radar detection devices, began operating from Langley Field, Va., in April and, as the year wore on, moved south to meet the shift in the U-boat threat, operating successfully from Florida bases and later from Trinidad. By this time the squadron had been augmented by several hundred bombers, both Navy and Army, under the operational control of the Navy. The coastal convoy system was established in May and expanded, during the summer months, to the Gulf and the Caribbean.

Notwithstanding these measures, there were five ships sunk between April and September, with cargo intended for Trinidad, which not only contributed to the cost but added considerable time loss. One of these ships carried the complete materials for a second seaplane hangar intended for the air station; the hangar was never built.

With each succeeding month during the summer of 1942 new projects were added. In August, a supply depot, comprising 20 large wooden warehouses with concrete floors, was begun on reclaimed swamp land in Chaguaramus Valley. During September, work was started on the assembly of nine steel barges and the installation of a degaussing range on Pelican Island.

From the struggle to combat the German submarine menace and the strategic necessity for adequate strength to protect our southern flank in the Atlantic, came the decision to equip Trinidad with facilities for ship repair. Begun as an air station and commissioned as such on October 1, 1941, Trinidad, a year later, became a complete naval operating base, equipped with a section base, net, supply, and fuel depots, a hospital, a degaussing range, a radio station, and ship-repair facilities.

Building a Dike for Ship Repair Facilities in Chaguaramas Bay, Trinidad

The work at the repair base, on Chaguaramus Bay, included extensive dredging and a waterfront development comprising four finger piers and a 1800-foot quay wall. Two of these piers, one 350 feet and the other 600 feet long, were built on timber piles. The other two, 600 feet long, were supported by concrete piles. In addition, the base was completely equipped with shops, an administration building, a power plant built of reinforced concrete and equipped with six 700-kw diesel generators, five 2-story barracks to house 1000 men, officers' quarters, and a laundry.

These additions beyond the original plan brought about major changes in site planning, making it necessary to develop overall plans for highways, electric-power distribution, communications, and water and sewerage systems.

A few roads of good surface quality existed on the reservation, but they had eventually to be replaced as a result of heavy usage or relocated as the station expanded. Of the 57 miles of roads built within the reservation, 30 miles were hard surfaced,

11 miles were given a heavy penetration, and the remainder were coral-surfaced or dirt. Fortunately, road-building materials were readily at hand — native coral sand dredged from Carenage Bay and emulsified asphalt produced locally, combining to yield a durable wearing surface.

Tucker and Chaguaramus valleys, the two principal watersheds, contain water-bearing sand and gravel deposits which were developed as a source of water supply by means of 25 wells, driven at scattered locations. The wells were connected to a system of 20 reservoirs, so located as to maintain gravity pressure in the distribution mains. The water was chlorinated at each well and required no filtering.

All supervising personnel, and the majority of the skilled trades labor used in construction in Trinidad were hired in the States and brought to the station under contract. Upon these men fell the task of leading and teaching the local labor employed. Exclusive of a few outstanding individuals, the majority of the local workmen had

NAVAL HOSPITAL, TRINIDAD

received little or no education, were unaccustomed to United States procedures, and had difficulty in understanding the English of the continentals, who had equal difficulty understanding them. There was a definite caste distinction, not only among the different races but among the different employment classifications. They were temperamental among their own groups, which often resulted in serious fights, particularly between the men of Trinidad proper and those of the smaller islands. They had to be taught, checked, and coached, from the beginning of the operation to the end, which threw an enormous burden on the supervisors, intensified by the large labor turnover and the wide diversification of the project as a whole.

On December 30, 1942, when the 30th Construction Battalion arrived at Trinidad, the contractor was maintaining all completed and partially completed facilities in addition to performing his current construction program. The Seabees immediately took over the maintenance and operation of all completed or usably completed facilities,

permitting the contractor to concentrate his personnel on construction work.

In January 1943, the Public Works Department was organized, officers and men of the 30th Battalion being assigned to the various maintenance and operating divisions. Those Seabees having specialized training were shifted into power house, refrigeration, transportation, and other activities. The remainder, other than administrative personnel, were used on minor construction jobs.

In April, the Bureau of Yards and Docks requested termination of the contract by June 30, 1943, and at the same time directed the station Public Works Department to take over new construction activities in addition to base maintenance. With more than 600 Seabees assigned to maintenance and 900 civilian employees to be replaced, the 30th Battalion was hard pressed to satisfy all demands for personnel. Accordingly, the 83rd Battalion was assigned to Trinidad, the first echelon arriving the latter part of May and the remainder during June. When the contractor terminated his activities on June 30, these two battalions carried

SMALL BOAT LANDING, TRINIDAD

on with the uncompleted portion of the work, which amounted to 25 per cent of the authorized program.

Upon the termination of the contract, the Navy purchased a hydraulic dredge, and dredging operations were continued under a new contract, awarded primarily for the purpose of indoctrinating Seabees in the operation of this type of dredge. After six-months training the Seabee crew assumed complete supervision of this piece of equipment, and the contract was terminated in January 1944. Dredging operations were completed in the Trinidad area in June 1944, at which time the dredge was transferred to the Pacific area for further operations.

The original lease agreement did not include the upper reaches of Tucker Valley and the Maqueripe Bay area fronting the Caribbean on the north side of the peninsula. After our entry into the war, control of this area became essential to the military security of the base. In the supplemental lease consummated in December 1942, whereby these acres were included in the 99-year lease, it was agreed that the United States would build and turn over to the local government a roadway along the northern shore of the peninsula to permit the general public to have access to the beach at Maracas Bay in lieu of facilities formerly available at Maqueripe.

Work on this 7½-mile highway was started late in March 1943 by the contractor, continued by the Seabees upon termination of the contract in June, and completed and turned over to the local government in April 1944. Requiring the removal of

NAS BERMUDA IN THE PROCESS OF CONSTRUCTION
Morgan Island (foreground) and Tucker Island in the process of being made one. Large building (center) is
a seaplane hangar

1,000,000 cubic yards from perilous mountainside heights, the road, as built through virgin jungle, was 24 feet wide, paved with asphalt macadam for a width of 14 feet, and nowhere exceeded a 10-percent grade, despite its climb from sea-level at Port of Spain to a 1335-foot elevation within a distance of 2 miles.

While the Navy was engaged in developing the operating base on the Gulf of Paria, the Army was engaged in building two major airfields, known as Waller Field and Carlsen Field, which were also used by the Navy as bases for carrier planes and transport service.

When the Navy began lighter-than-air operations in the Caribbean in the fall of 1943, the 80th Seabees were brought in to build a station at Carlsen

Field. To supplement the eight Army-owned buildings taken over by the Navy, the 80th Battalion built a large, steel blimp hangar, a mooring circle, paved runways, a helium-purification plant, and other operational appurtenances.

Upon the arrival of the 80th Battalion, the 11th Construction Regiment was formed to furnish the administrative framework within which the three battalions, augmented by 10,000 natives, functioned during the construction peak in the fall of 1943. The strength of the regiment was further augmented on December 16th by the arrival of CBMU's 559 and 560. From the date of their arrival, men of both units were assigned the maintenance and operational duties performed by the 30th Battalion, thus permitting the release and reassignment of this group, which was effected January 31, 1944.

By May 1944, the construction program at Trinidad was substantially accomplished, and the 80th Battalion, having completed the work at Carlsen Field, left on May 4, followed by the 83rd Battalion during the succeeding month. Immediately thereafter the 11th Regiment was disbanded, leaving the two maintenance units, raised to a strength of 750 men and 13 officers, to carry on public-works activities.

Bermuda

Bermuda, a group of small islands, chiefly coral and limestone, about 600 miles off Cape Hatteras, occupies a strategically important position, commanding sea and air approaches to the Middle Atlantic coastline. Both the Army and the Navy, recognizing its value as a base for air and surface craft, undertook an extensive construction program.

The Bureau of Yards and Docks awarded a fixed-fee contract on February 15, 1941, initially, to accomplish the construction of an air station for seaplanes, and subsequently expanded to include a fuel-oil depot, a supply depot, an operating base, a submarine base, and an anti-aircraft training school.

Adjacent water, ideal for seaplane operation, and proximity to existing ship channels resulted in the choice of Morgan and Tucker Islands, situated in Great Sound, within the hook of the western end of Hamilton Island, together with an adjacent area on Hamilton Island at Kings Point, as sites for the air station and the operating base. Darrell Island, also in Great Sound and about a mile and a half to the east, then in use as an air station by commercial airlines, was developed as an auxiliary seaplane base. Submarine facilities were constructed on Ordnance Island, at the eastern end of the Bermuda group, in St. Georges Harbor, adjacent to the town of St. George. This location, while remote from the operating base, was chosen because of the availability of the site, the existing facilities, and its proximity to the sea lanes serving the islands.

The general topography of the leased areas was gently rolling, varying in elevation from sea level to a maximum of 40 feet.

The base development plan issued by the Chief of Naval Operations to support the 15,000-plane program, indicated Bermuda as a major naval air station, with facilities for the operation of two patrol squadrons of seaplanes on a permanent basis and one additional squadron with tender support.

In addition, facilities were to be provided to support the emergency operation of one carrier group from an airfield to be developed by the Army.

The initial construction effort began March 29, 1941. Dredge-filling the narrow funnel-shaped channel between Morgan and Tucker islands more than doubled their original combined area of 40 acres. The one island thus formed was then connected by causeway to King's Point, on Hamilton Island.

The principal structures built at the air station comprised a tender pier, three seaplane ramps and parking area, a large seaplane hangar, barracks for 1100 men, quarters for 140 officers, a bombproof power plant, and the usual industrial, administration, and storage buildings. At the Hamilton Island site, underground storage was provided for fuel oil, diesel oil, and gasoline, as well as barracks for fuel depot and air station personnel, a 50-bed dispensary, a large magazine area, a radio station, and a 10-acre water-catchment area with storage for 5,000,000 gallons of rain water. All these installations were of a semi-permanent character.

Soon after construction began, it became essential that naval air patrols be placed in operation as quickly as possible. This was accomplished by using the established facilities owned by British Imperial Airways on Darrell Island. By an informal agreement with the British and local governments, permission to use this island on a temporary basis was granted. Here, existing facilities were augmented by barracks, water supply, paved parking areas, landing floats, and other temporary essentials. This work was undertaken in May and the island put to immediate use, continuing so until March 1942, at which time the permanent naval air station was usably complete and in operation.

In June 1941 the contract was supplemented to undertake the development of submarine facilities on Ordnance Island. Under this program, and its subsequent additions, a number of existing buildings were rehabilitated to provide housing and messing facilities for crews while ashore, improvements and additions were made to the existing water and sewer systems, waterfront structures were repaired, and offshore moorings installed. The use of Ordnance Island was obtained under a lease extending to December 1955, under the terms of which the United States could regain all removable improvements placed by or on its behalf at any time before the termination of the lease. The island was returned to its owners in July 1945.

During the late summer of 1942 the Riddle's Bay area, which had formerly been used as a golf course and resort area, was rehabilitated and equipped as a recreational area for naval personnel.

Concurrent with the construction program underway at the several areas leased by the Navy, the Army was developing Kindly Field, on Long Bird Island, at the eastern end of Bermuda. At this airfield the Army, pursuant to Joint Board directives, provided all landplane facilities constructed at Bermuda, including those used specifically by naval aircraft. Here, within the base area, the Army contractor, on a reimbursable basis, built facilities for the temporary support of one carrier air group of 90 planes. These included barracks for 550 men and 125 officers, messing facilities, storage buildings, nose hangars, and radio aids.

Inasmuch as Bermuda had no fresh water from ground sources, it was obtained for the air station and the operating base by use of seven evaporating units with a daily capacity of 50,000 gallons, and a system of rain-water catchment areas, which, including roof areas, totaled 20 acres. The water thus collected was stored in reservoirs and chlorinated before entering the distribution system.

Southlands, located along the south shore line of Hamilton Island, was secured under a short term lease for the development of an anti-aircraft training school. Construction included a night-vision training building, repair shops, magazine loading sheds, magazines, instruction buildings and barracks, gun platforms and control tower, roads, walks, and services. This activity was transferred to Guantanamo Bay in January 1945.

On April 8, 1943, construction under the contract was terminated and a new contract negotiated with the original contractors to complete several major items of dredging still unfinished. This second contract remained active until June 28, 1944.

The 31st Construction Battalion arrived in Bermuda on December 5, 1942, with 27 officers and 1027 men. Completed activities at the operating base, air station, and submarine base were then in full use.

On February 27, 1943, the 49th Battalion, with 27 officers and 1080 men, arrived a month before the contract's termination, to augment the 31st Battalion. Together the battalions completed such unfinished projects as roads, utilities, grading, accessory buildings, and general clean-up. In addition, they undertook the operation, maintenance, and repair of the entire naval establishment under the cognizance of the Public Works Department.

During mid-October 1943, the 31st Battalion, which had served continuously on Bermuda for nearly two years, was returned to the mainland after being replaced by CBMU 540, which was followed by the CBMU 551 on December 11, 1943, to replace the 41st Battalion; the two maintenance units were then merged into one unit and designated CBMU 540.

Activities at Bermuda gradually diminished in importance during the fall of 1944, as the progress of the war in Europe became more and more favorable to the Allies. Consequently, the submarine base on Ordnance Island was reduced to caretaker status by January 1945, and all training activities were moved to Guantanamo. The anti-aircraft training center was decommissioned on April 1, 1945.

Shortly after V-E Day further reductions were effected. Ordnance Island was returned to its owners, and the naval facilities at Kindly Field transferred to the Army for future custody. On July 31, 1945, the air station and operating base were reduced in status to an air facility and a repair unit.

Great Exuma

The naval air station on Great Exuma Island was constructed, under the Guantanamo contract, to support a squadron of seaplanes used for patrol operations along the southeastern coast of the United States and the numerous passages through the Bahamas leading to the Florida straits and the Caribbean. It was a compact development of 324 leased acres on the southeast tip of the island, which occupied a strategic central position in the Bahamas. Construction was begun during December 1941, and the station was commissioned on May 15, 1942.

The principal operating facilities, comprising a 50-foot timber seaplane ramp, a concrete parking area, 400 by 300 feet, and a 180-foot barge pier, were located on a partly natural and partly dredged-in beach adjacent to the seaplane landing and takeoff area. This area of water, 3 miles long, is protected from the open sea by Stocking Island, which forms a natural barrier, one mile offshore, directly opposite the station.

The buildings erected had previously been fabricated and assembled under the San Juan contract for installation at each of the eight "Destroyer Bases." These, when later augmented by 28 quonset huts, totaled 79, including quarters for 80 officers

NAS BERMUDA
The completed facility, showing causeway and seaplane hangar (right) pictured on page 30

and 180 enlisted men, a 10-bed dispensary. an administration building, storehouses, a chapel, a bakery, a power house, and several industrial buildings. Located on high ground adjacent to the beach, they occupied an area of 59 acres. The remainder of the tract was devoted to magazines.

Great Exuma, like all the Bahamas, is of limestone and coral, which require crushing to proper size before being used for either road building or as concrete aggregate. During the early construction period, pieces of rock and stone were picked up from around the island by local labor at a set price per yard, and broken into usable size by women laborers using small hammers. Later, as the program expanded, portable crushers were imported to supplement this primitive labor method.

Dredging operations created a seaplane operating

area with a minimum depth of 6 feet, improved the small-vessel anchorage in Stocking Harbor, and deepened the approach channel to the anchorage. A considerable portion of the 750,000 cubic yards of dredged material was used to reclaim the beach area needed for seaplane operating facilities.

Fresh water for the station, obtained from seven drilled wells, was filtered, chlorinated, and stored in a 100,000-gallon underground reservoir built of concrete.

The summer of 1942 saw the completion of basic construction at the station. Henceforth, all minor items of new construction and station maintenance were done by the Public Works Department, using local labor. No Seabee personnel participated during either the construction or the maintenance period.

The station was commissioned on May 15, 1942, and was used continuously for patrol operations until its disestablishment in June 1945.

Jamaica

The naval air station on Jamaica was built under the Guantanamo contract, to provide base facilities for two squadrons of seaplanes whose mission was to patrol the approaches to the Caribbean via the Windward Passage.

The station was located on Little Goat Island, on the south side of Jamaica, in Portland Bight, about 30 miles from the city of Kingston. Leased in its entirety, the island had approximately 150 acres of firm ground surrounded by 150 acres of salt flats and mangrove swamps. The site afforded an excellent land-locked harbor, ideal for seaplane operations, and a satisfactory channel for shipping.

From the standpoint of type and number of buildings and of general layout, the station was essentially a duplication of the development on Great Exuma, in the Bahamas. It was equipped with two timber piers, a concrete seaplane ramp, a parking area, and a complement of buildings, which had previously been assembled and fabricated under the San Juan contract. These included quarters for 75 men and 25 officers, two administration buildings, a 10-bed dispensary, a power plant, a shop, utility buildings, and a warehouse. Fresh water was brought in by barge from the main island and pumped from the dock to storage tanks for treatment and distribution.

A total of 2,800,000 cubic yards of dredging was necessary to remove shoals from the seaplane runway and to deepen the anchorages and channel approaches to the piers. Gasoline storage, totaling 75,000 gallons, was provided in eleven underground steel tanks.

Upon completion of the contract work during the summer of 1942, subsequent maintenance and minor construction items were accomplished by the station Public Works Department. No Seabee personnel were used in either construction or maintenance.

The air station was commissioned April 4, 1941; it was reduced to caretaker status during September 1944.

St. Lucia

The naval air station on St. Lucia, in the Windward Islands, was constructed under the San Juan contract, on a 221-acre site on Gros Islet Bay at the extreme northwest tip of the island. It was equipped to support the operation of a patrol squadron of seaplanes with tender support, having as its principal features a timber seaplane ramp, a concrete parking area, a tender pier, and a compact complement of supporting buildings. Construction began in February 1941 and was carried forward at a rate permitting occupancy by the using forces during the fall of that year.

The buildings, which had previously been fabricated and assembled by the San Juan contractor, included barracks for 200 men, quarters for 25 officers, a 10-bed dispensary, a power plant, ten 5000-gallon steel tanks for gasoline storage, three magazines, a cold-storage plant, and two industrial buildings. Concrete floors, prefabricated lightweight steel frames, and stucco exteriors were used for all buildings.

Rainfall collected on a 60,000-square-foot concrete catchment area furnished the fresh-water supply for the station. It was stored in two 80,000-gallon steel tanks and chlorinated before use.

The waterfront layout, as prepared by the Bureau, centered about a 40-foot timber seaplane ramp, a concrete parking apron, 300 by 800 feet, and a 40-by-350-foot tender pier with a timber deck supported on steel piles. A 500,000-cubic-yard dredging operation was necessary to deepen the water of the bay for the seaplane runways and the approach channel to the tender pier.

With exception of a few minor additions and improvements made at various times during 1942, the station was completed in December 1941. No Seabee personnel participated in its development other than to make a few minor repairs and alterations during the early summer of 1943. These men were drawn temporarily from battalions stationed at Trinidad.

The air station on St. Lucia was decommissioned on September 1, 1943, and placed in a caretaker status by Coast Guard personnel.

Antigua

Crabbs Peninsula and the adjoining waters of Parham Sound, on the north shore of the island, were selected as the site for the naval air station on Antigua in the Leeward Islands. The facilities built were essentially a duplication of those developed on St. Lucia, with regard to general layout, type and number of buildings, waterfront structures, and magnitude of the construction problems involved. The station served one patrol squadron of seaplanes with tender support.

Construction was undertaken on the site during February 1941 under the San Juan contract and progressed concurrently with the work at St. Lucia. Using forces occupied it during the late fall of the same year.

After the conclusion of the contract work in June 1942, the station's Public Works Department, using local labor, made minor additions to the housing and other facilities when it became necessary to increase the operating force to meet the menace of the heightened German submarine campaign at the end of the year.

On February 1, 1944, the station was reduced in status to an auxiliary air facility and to caretaker status a year later. No Seabee personnel were used either in the construction or in the maintenance of the station.

British Guiana

The United States Naval Air Station, British Guiana, constructed under the Trinidad contract and equipped with the minimum essentials necessary to support the operation of a patrol squadron of seaplanes, was located on a 1400-acre site 40 miles up the Essequibo River, at a point where the river provided a sufficiently long and unobstructed landing area in a vicinity free from malaria. Construction began in April 1941 and was completed during the fall of 1942. With the exception of a few supervisors, local labor was used until the station was commissioned in February 1942.

Shore facilities erected had previously been fabricated and assembled under the San Juan contract. These included barracks for 100 men, quarters for 25 officers, a power plant, ten 5,000-gallon steel tanks for gasoline storage, storehouses, water supply, and other related structures. A timber seaplane ramp, a 400-by-300-foot asphalt-surfaced parking area, and a timber tender pier were built to support seaplane operations. Some dredging and underwater blasting were necessary to provide 18 feet of water at the dock and to clear approaches

to the seaplane ramp. All buildings were temporary, either of wood or prefabricated light-weight steel, the tender pier being of native timber.

When the importance of the station increased, following the incursion of German submarines into the coastal waters of South America, it became necessary to expand the shore facilities. The contract was accordingly supplemented in January 1942, to provide a 12-bed hospital, and again in March, to provide two 108-man barracks, quarters for 40 officers, and a new water-supply system. After several unsuccessful experiments with wells, water was finally taken from the Essequibo River and treated.

The contractor carried out the maintenance of the base until February 1943, when one officer and 30 men from the 30th Construction Battalion, stationed at Trinidad, arrived to operate the new Public Works Department. These men were replaced during January 1944 by 12 men from CBMU 559, who carried on normal maintenance until the station was decommissioned and reduced to caretaker status in September 1944.

When the use of nonrigid airships was extended to augment air patrols covering the coastal waters of South America, it became necessary to provide bases for these lighter-than-air craft.

Facilities were provided in British Guiana, at Atkinson Field, the Army air base on the east bank of the Demerara River, 25 miles upstream from Georgetown. A 2,000-foot runway and parking area, two mooring circles with connecting taxiways, a shop, and an administration building, were built by the Army for the Navy on a reimbursable basis. Construction, started in March 1943, was completed in September of the same year.

The field was first used in June 1943. Lighter-than-air operations were discontinued in this area in December 1944, but the base remained in use as a ferry stop for blimps travelling between South America, Trinidad, and the United States. No Seabee personnel participated in either the construction or the maintenance of this facility.

Part IV — Bases in Central and South America

In the interest of national security and defense, the United States Government made its first commitments for military construction in South America more than a year before our entry into the war. By authority of the President, on November 2, 1940, the Secretary of War entered into a secret contract with the Pan American Airport Corporation, a subsidiary of Pan American Airways, Inc. The purpose of this contract was to create a chain of airports and seaplane bases along the coast of Brazil, from the border of French Guiana to Uruguay.

Air facilities constituted most of the naval construction work undertaken in this area. However, on August 17, 1942, the Chief of Naval Operations issued an order basing ten destroyers, 30 corvettes, and destroyer escorts in the Brazilian area. The order further stated that minor bases for voyage repairs and the replenishment of fuel and supplies were to be established along the Brazilian coast. Until bases could be completed and provide adequate coverage, these minor bases materially aided both air and sea patrols against German submarines which operated successfully off the coast of Brazil.

The Dutch island of Curacao was of twofold importance to the war effort of the United Nations. As one of the largest oil-refining centers in the world, it supplied the oil and high-octane gasoline without which the Allied campaigns in Europe and the Pacific would have been difficult almost to the point of impossibility. Moreover, it provided an essential defense base for the protection of the principal trade routes from northern South Amercia, the Caribbean, and Panama, to all the war theaters.

Although there was little danger of an actual invasion of Curacao, there was very great danger that Germany might attempt, by sabotage or commando raid, to stop the flow of oil. Dutch authorities took preliminary steps against sabotage, but lacked effective military forces. Fully aware of the strategic importance of the island and the lack of adequate military protection, the British sent forces into Curacao to take control of the harbor and oil facilities on May 11, 1940, the day after the German army marched into Holland.

Shortly after the Pearl Harbor attack, the defense of Curacao and the adjacent trade lanes was transferred from the British to the United States Army, whose forces arrived February 11, 1942. On February 24th the initial steps were taken to establish a naval operational command. Navy's first operations were directed toward the protection of the Lake Maracaibo tanker lanes, along which crude oil was supplied to the Curacao refineries. The Navy also provided fast convoys of tankers

with destroyer escorts between Curacao and the Mediterranean and the United Kingdom.

Immediately after the outbreak of war in the Pacific, when other assaults following the Pearl Harbor pattern were expected, the Navy hurriedly began the task of establishing a number of advance bases in Central America to weld an outer defense ring around the Panama Canal.

In January 1942, seaplane bases were begun simultaneously at the Galapagos Islands and Salinas, Ecuador, to be followed during the early spring by the establishment of a base for PT boats on Taboga Island, Panama, and another seaplane base at Fonseca, Nicaragua. Unfavorable weather conditions in the Gulf of Fonseca later caused the abandonment of this location in favor of one at Corinto, also in Nicaragua.

Elsewhere in Central America a fueling base for seaplanes and small surface craft was installed at Puerto Castillo, Honduras, in November 1942. The following May, another refueling unit, this time for naval landplanes, was established at Barranquilla, Colombia, using the existing Soledad Airport, whose modernization had previously been financed by the Navy.

After blimps were assigned to the area, in 1943, facilities were provided in Surinam and three temporary lighter-than-air bases were set up at Mandinga and Chorrera, Panama, and at Barranquilla, to expand further the facilities for aerial reconnaissance.

By November 1944, patrol operations were curtailed in the Caribbean and Central American areas, at which time these advance bases either had been, or were, placed in a caretaker status.

Ecuador

Galapagos Islands. — Galapagos was the focal point for a wide arc of aerial patrols protecting the western approaches of the Panama Canal.[1] From these islands, 800 miles from the Pacific Coast, naval seaplanes flew northeast to Corinto, Nicaragua, and southeast to Salinas, Ecuador. Army landplanes assisted in covering the southern route.

South Seymour (or Battra) Island was selected as a base. The island is low, dry, barren, and

[1] Following a cruise in the Panama area by President Roosevelt in 1940, preparations were made to provide a wide arc of constant air patrols west of the Canal. Aviation equipment for a seaplane base in the Galapagos Islands was procured and stored at Balboa. This base was the pioneer of a long succession of mobile units assembled for shipment to locations outside the United States. The list used served as a guide for procurement of aviation materials for seven air bases, thus creating the term *"Galapagos units."* Depots were established November 1940, at Charleston, S.C.; near San Francisco; and at Balboa, where warehouses were constructed by the Bureau of Yards and Docks to house these huge stockpiles.

volcanic, covered with from two to four feet of rocky soil, from which grows only sparse vegetation. It was necessary to import all materials, water, and provisions, as well as Ecuadorian labor.

The naval seaplane base, at Aeolian Cove, on the

SEAPLANE BASE AT AEOLIAN COVE, GALAPAGOS

western side of the island, contained anchorage space in which refueling ships could be hidden.

Five days after the attack on Pearl Harbor, when the Panama Canal was considered in imminent danger of a similar attack, the Navy rushed a token force of 36 men aboard a British tramp steamer, to the Galapagos Islands to establish a refueling depot for patrol planes; a few days later, seaplanes were being refueled by hand pumps from a motor launch. A timber pier to handle unloading of gas drums and a 70-foot timber seaplane ramp were then planned. In January 1942 the Army surveyed for an 8000-foot air strip and let a contract for its construction.

On January 24, 1942, Ecuador granted permission to proceed with essential construction in Ecuador (Salinas and Galapagos), specific agreements to be signed after Lend-Lease details had been settled.

Our immediate occupation of the Galapagos Islands served to provide a key point for aerial patrols, and to prevent the enemy from securing a nearby foothold, as was accomplished in the Aleutians.

The seaplane base, designed for two squadrons of patrol bombers, could accommodate 125 officers

and 1,050 men. Construction by Army contract, which was combined with the contract for the base at Salinas on the Ecuadorian mainland, was fully under way by April 1942, and completed by mid-1943. The base at Galapagos was put into use while under construction, the first plane landing on the temporary wire-mesh parking area May 14. Quarters and dispensary were established; Navy shared the Army hospital.

Two units of Seabee Detachment 1012 were sent to Galapagos and Salinas, respectively, on September 27, 1942, to complete a varied program of construction work begun by civilian contractors, and to install equipment. They built two tank farms for diesel oil, fuel oil, and aviation gasoline, complete with concrete pump houses and submerged pipe lines, a radio building, and a pontoon pier, repaired the concrete seaplane ramp, and assisted with the Army pier, which was later used to land all supplies. The Seabees also installed a water-supply system, distillation units, and storage tanks for 75,000 gallons of fresh-water and 75,000 gallons of salt water. After attempting unsuccessfully to drill wells, the Army imported water by barge.

The units of CBD 1012 were relieved January 1944, by a section of CBMU 555, who continued overhaul and maintenance work through the period of hostilities.

Salinas.—The naval base at Salinas, selected as the southern terminus of the Pacific patrol arc, had its facilities changed, increased, diminished, and removed, all within a short period of time, its strength varying from 60 to 700 men during two years' expansion.

A specific agreement, including payment for expropriation of private property, was signed for the Salinas base on February 20, 1942.

At first, Salinas was scheduled to be a boat base; but it was changed to a seaplane refueling base before construction was well under way. This was developed into a naval auxiliary air facility, servicing and housing a complete patrol-plane squadron. Aviation activities were removed in May 1944, leaving an emergency refueling unit with crash boat service.

Salinas is on a peninsula on the western tip of Ecuador, fronting on Santa Elena Bay. The seaplane base was constructed adjoining the new Army air base, near a former summer resort town, on the north shore of a level tongue of sand, tipped by a promontory. The sheltered bay is suitable for a seaplane landing area, its semi-circular beach being protected somewhat by a line of rock, but the shallow water is stirred by a 10-foot tide and heavy breakers. Ships had to anchor more than a mile off shore and transfer supplies to small boats.

Construction began in January 1942, largely under Army contract, and the base was usably complete and operating in June 1942. The Army and Navy shared utilities—water, power, telephone. Frame buildings were made from local materials, although some quonset huts arrived later, and the first seaplane ramps and parking area were built of steel mats, later replaced by concrete. To allow for swells, the pontoon pier was arranged so that its pontoons, instead of being fixed, could pivot from a concrete emplacement on shore. Other facilities included a nose hangar, two 90-foot radio masts, an aerology and radio hut, twenty-four 1000-barrel storage tanks, a warehouse, eight barracks, twelve quonset huts, quarters, and a dispensary.

Final construction was carried out by Unit 2 of Seabee Detachment 1012, which served from September 1942 until relieved by a section of CBMU 555, which remained from January 1944 until the evacuation of most of the base that summer.

The CBMU section built a taxi strip, 50 by 800 feet, from native materials and surfaced 14 miles of road between Salinas and Libertad.

In June the base was dismantled and machinery, supplies, and personnel were evacuated, heavy equipment, such as refrigerators and generators, being left in a preservation status. All packing, loading, and stowing of 3,000 tons of returned supplies and equipment was done by the Seabees.

Salinas was redesignated as Naval Air Detachment, Army Air Base, on July 24, 1944. The few men remaining to render emergency service were furnished with communication, medical, and messing facilities by the Army. On February 1, 1946, the United States surrendered its jurisdiction over the naval base at Salinas, giving all permanent installations to Ecuador.

Nicaragua

Fonseca.—Advance Base, Nicaragua, which was to be the northern terminus for patrols flown from the Galapagos, was first set up on the shores of the Gulf of Fonseca at Money Penny Anchorage in the early spring of 1942. The bay, which had been surveyed during the calm season, proved too rough for seaplanes the remainder of the year, and the activity was transferred to Corinto.

The Fonseca base was situated in a shallow, bowl-shaped area adjacent to the beach on the western side of the Gulf of Fonseca. At this point the beach slopes gradually away from the shore, affording no deep-water anchorage. Ships bringing supplies had to anchor more than a mile from shore, and unload their cargo into lighters, which were emptied manually. Transportation was limited to air, water, or horseback, no road or railroad facilities being available. The most expeditious supply line was a 40-mile journey by boat to Port Morazon, where train service was available to Managua, capital of Nicaragua.

Maintained as an emergency landing base until October 1943, the Fonseca activity was then decommissioned, all materials, with the exception of permanent fixtures, being transported to Corinto.

Corinto.—The naval base at Corinto was created to accommodate two squadrons of patrol seaplanes, two squadrons of PT boats, and 1300 men. Situated 1,000 miles north of Balboa, its purpose was to serve as northern terminus of the patrol route covering the Pacific entrance to the Canal, and to supply small naval craft. In expectation of actual combat, it was defended by an Army coast artillery unit.

The seaplane base was built on a tip of land at Corinto, on the west coast of Nicaragua. Nearly all of the land was reclaimed from mud flats, mangrove swamps, and even part of the Bay of Corinto by filling it in with 275,000 cubic yards of beach sand.

The climate is sub-tropical, with a long rainy season, the rest of the year being almost completely rainless.

Excellent harbor and docking facilities were offered at Corinto, which provided deep-water anchorage, a dock, and a railroad siding, as well as commercial warehouses and fuel tanks. Native materials, particularly lumber, were utilized to a great extent in the initial construction, and local labor proved very satisfactory.

The naval auxiliary air facility at Corinto was established September 1942, operated at almost full capacity from September 1943 to May 1944, and was of diminished importance for the remainder of the period of hostilities.

Construction, begun in August 1942 by a civilian contractor, was completed a year later at a cost of

UNITED STATES NAVAL BASE, CORINTO, NICARAGUA

about $1,334,000. Observation planes were first stationed there January 21, 1943.

Maintenance, repair, and fueling facilities for seaplanes were constructed, including a concrete ramp and parking area, a nose hangar, aircraft servicing shops, a parachute tower, a radio station, and an aviation-gasoline tank farm of fourteen 1,000-barrel steel tanks connected by an 8-inch pipeline to four 5,000-gallon underground tanks. A unit for charging, repair, storage, and maintenance of torpedoes was projected, but not completed, as PT boats were never based there. Living, messing, and recreation facilities, and a 22-bed dispensary and surgery were provided; 15 warehouses furnished 16,400 square feet of storage space.

The Seabees completed construction work after expiration of the contract in August 1943, and also installed naval equipment. In December 1942, 85 men of the Ninth Battalion arrived; they were relieved in January 1944 by a section of CBMU 555, which remained throughout the period of hostilities. The Army base on Corinto Island (Isla Cardon) was added to the original contract in August 1943. It was begun by the contractors and completed by the Seabees, who continued to supply it until May 1944.

Full use was never made of the base's facilities. At most, one and a half squadrons of patrol bombers were based there from the fall of 1943 through the spring of 1944. When the squadron base was moved to Galapagos, a few observation planes remained, and two patrol planes made a daily reconnaissance flight to Galapagos. Until the end of hostilities, Corinto continued to supply numerous small fleet units with diesel oil, water, and fresh provisions. Water for ships was brought from a point 30 miles inland by railroad tank cars, as the Navy distillation and evaporation units produced only enough for daily needs.

By the spring of 1944, when the prospect of a Japanese attack on the Panama Canal became less likely, the functions of advance bases in the 15th Naval District decreased. Corinto was gradually reduced by removal of the Army defense force and plane squadrons, and surplus equipment was returned to the naval supply depot at Balboa.

On June 6, 1946, the naval air station was disestablished and all fixed installations were turned over to the Nicaraguan government.

Panama

Taboga Island. A home base for PT-boat squadrons operating under the Panama Sea Frontier was set up as a war emergency project on Taboga Island, which overlooks the Pacific entrance of the Panama Canal, 10 miles from the Balboa piers. The island, owned by the Republic of Panama, has a clean, sandy crescent-shaped beach, backed by a stretch of level land, rising to a series of high mounds.

Its purpose was to act as a main maintenance, overhaul, and operating base for a flotilla of PT-boats, and as an operational training center for PT squadrons enroute to combat zones. Construction began July 6, 1942, on a timber pier, two small marine railways, overhaul shops, power plant, light and power systems, refrigeration building, water storage and supply, and a radio building. Later construction included a storehouse, mess hall, barracks, quarters, and 12 storage tanks for fuel oil and gasoline. A torpedo workshop, munitions storage, and numerous other facilities, services, and developments were subsequently added.

The buildings were of frame construction on concrete foundations, many erected without specifically planned designs, time being at a premium. Later additions included two barracks, a galley, dry-stores building, boatswain's locker, garage, armory, berth float, pile dolphins, and a towing platform. Fresh water was obtained from springs augmented by an auxiliary water-supply system. Anchors were fabricated, and cradles on the marine railways were changed to accommodate 80-foot PT boats.

Usable completion for several buildings was reached three weeks after work started, even in the face of lack of material, hard hand-excavating in lava soil, and slow delivery of all materials by barge from Balboa. The work began in July 1942, was half done by the end of August, when the base was commissioned, and 90 per cent complete by the end of the year. At its peak the major overhaul base on Taboga Island operated with 47 PT boats and 1200 men.

The contractors left in July 1943, after finishing installation of materials delayed in shipment from the United States. Seabees from Detachment 1012 took over construction and repair in September, 1943, assembled two pontoon drydocks and erected magazines, warehouses, and other buildings with the help of local labor. A recreation camp was established on Morro Island, accessible by sand bar at low tide. An Army telephone cable furnished direct communication with the mainland.

The Taboga station was decommissioned in March 1946, and all fixed improvements were turned over to the Republic of Panama.

Almirante. In the summer of 1943 a small refueling base was established at Almirante, Panama, on the Caribbean side, to refuel PT boats.

Naval Supply Depot, Balboa, acted as the assembly point for 35 PT-boat squadrons, furnishing material to complete their allowance lists, and rigging the boats and their equipment for secure stowage aboard ship. They were loaded by two 250-ton floating cranes, made available by the Panama Canal authorities.

Mandinga. A lighter-than-air base was established at Mandinga, on the Caribbean side of Panama, 75 miles west of Coco Solo, to furnish aerial patrol for the eastern approaches of the Panama Canal.

Built by the Army on land leased from the Republic of Panama, the airfield was transferred to the Navy February 24, 1944. Three asphalt strips, 3,000 by 150 feet, used by the Army as an emergency fighter field, were taken over, gasoline was stored in drums, and a few temporary buildings were set in land cleared from the jungle.

A detachment of CBMU 555 arrived January 4, 1944, to add facilities required by the Navy and to maintain the base. Jungle was cleared and a portable mooring mast, helium-storage building, and a small radio station were erected.

Eight months later the blimp and its equipment was transferred to Barranquilla, and the Navy vacated the site, which was returned to the Army.

Chorrera. — At Chorrera, about 40 miles from Balboa, an emergency fighter-plane base, with solid runways, was abandoned by the Army in 1943. This base was occupied for a short time in 1944 by the Navy, who set up two portable stick masts. together with special helium equipment to service blimps. The station was disestablished in November 1945.

Netherlands West Indies

Curacao.—Curacao, an island with an area of 173 square miles, lies 46 miles north of Venezuela. On its southern shores, a remarkable series of landlocked bays form excellent harbors, the largest and deepest being Willemstad.

In the summer of 1942, the United States Army began the construction of Camp Parera for Navy use. By January 1943, the camp was usably complete, and the Navy forces, formerly housed in Willemstad, moved in. Initial development of the camp was completed in October 1943. and Camp Parera was transferred to the Navy. Facilities constructed under Army supervision provided housing for 100 officers and 550 enlisted men, a 25-bed hospital, an administration building, shop buildings, recreational facilities, essential utilities, and roads.

At Hato Field. Army construction for the Navy patrol-bomber command included housing for 620 men. storage buildings. an administration building, and a supplementary radio station. Other Army facilities were used jointly by the Navy.

Meanwhile, the first Seabee group, one officer and fourteen men detached from the 30th Battalion at Trinidad, arrived February 9, 1943, to form the Public Works Department for the operation and maintenance of the naval shore installations. Additional Seabees arrived in June. A detachment of 89 men from CBMU 559 in Trinidad replaced the original Seabee group in January 1944 and, together with the Army, accomplished the maintenance and alterations of existing structures and utilities and made minor additions to the facilities at Hato Field and Camp Parera.

Both bases were disestablished in October 1945.

Aruba.—The Dutch island of Aruba, 42 miles west of Curacao. with extensive oil-refining facilities, occupied a strategic position in the Allied war effort similar to that of Curacao. A small American naval force was stationed there, with jurisdiction over shipping control, convoys. and the assignment of escort vessels, to protect the refining facilities and tankers transporting their products.

Four buildings built by the Army engineers and two quonset huts, set up by Seabees in March and April 1943, were the only naval-owned installations built at Aruba. All other facilities were leased from, and maintained by, commercial concerns.

The base was disestablished in October 1945.

Surinam

At Paramaribo in Surinam (Dutch Guiana) the Army constructed a lighter-than-air station for Navy use. It was begun in February 1943, completed the following August, and used continuously until August 1944, at which time it was decommissioned and transferred to the Army in a caretaker status. Facilities, similar to those at Atkinson Field in British Guiana, were constructed, including runway, parking area, mooring circles, taxiways, shops, and an administration building.

Elsewhere in Surinam, the Army erected a stick mast at its Zandry Field for emergency landings of lighter-than-air craft. Several squadrons of Navy landplanes also used the Army facilities at Zandry Field during 1943 and 1944.

Puerto Castilla, Honduras

The dual purpose of the advance base established at Puerto Castilla, on the Caribbean coast of Honduras, was to service small craft enroute to Cristobal and to refuel seaplanes. The activity was never required to handle a volume of ships and planes equal to its capacity.

The base was located on a man-made island on the leeside of a cape, Punta Caxinas, which half way encloses a natural harbor, Trujillo Bay, protecting it from prevailing winds. The site was granted the United States without limitation or cost, with the understanding that, on termination of the Navy's occupancy. fixed facilities would revert to the Honduran government.

Formerly the largest banana-exporting port in the world, the commercial establishment was equipped beforehand to service ships, with dockside rail sidings and experienced personnel available.

The climate was hot, but not unbearable, and malaria-control measures were very effective. Adequate drinking-water. piped 14 miles from a reservoir on the mainland, was also available, and most of the existing buildings were adaptable to Navy use.

Puerto Castilla was commissioned as a naval base and fuel depot on November 10, 1942. Some work had been done previously to convert a fruit-handling activity into a naval base. The small amount of construction materials required was an advantage, as shipping was then at a decided premium.

Construction of a timber seaplane ramp with parking area, a floating pier for a crash boat, and the remodeling of some buildings were carried out in the spring of 1943 by local laborers, under the supervision of Seabees from CBD 1012. An evaporator and two 1,000-barrel tanks with connections to the pier, two pump houses, with eight 1,000-barrel diesel-oil tanks, a 5,000-gallon wooden tank, and a concrete water tank were installed in the fall. In November, all construction was reported complete, and the Seabees were transferred.

Main facilities of the base were a power plant, a large machine shop, several large concrete buildings usable as barracks or offices, ample fuel and storage space, a dock capable of handling vessels of battleship proportions, 4 miles of railroad track, and rolling stock consisting of a locomotive, flat cars, and a dragline. Dockside rail sidings facilitated ship loadings. Living quarters, in existing stucco-type buildings, were excellent.

The chief function of the base was to fuel and provision ships and to make some minor repairs. Although the base was designated a naval auxiliary air facility May 16, 1944, few planes called there, and this function was disestablished July 15 of the same year. Operation as a naval base for refueling small craft continued for another year. Final disestablishment and removal of salvageable naval equipment took place in February 1946, when all land and fixed equipment were turned over to the government of Honduras, in accordance with the terms of the treaty.

Barranquilla, Colombia

Barranquilla, Colombia, served as a naval base for aerial patrol by both landplanes and lighter-than-air craft operating over the Caribbean shipping lanes leading to the Panama Canal and to the Colombian oil ports.

The airport at Barranquilla, which was shared by Navy and the Pan American Airways, is the property of Aerovias Nationales de Colombia (Avi-

anca). It lies inland from the Caribbean, along the Rio Magdalena, 6 miles south of Barranquilla and just south of the town of Soledad. Prevailing trade winds at this location are so strong as to render light construction undesirable.

A naval refueling unit for a small number of observation and scout bomber planes was established at the Soledad airport, in May 1943, Avianca having granted permission to use the landing field without charge and to erect necessary temporary buildings. By informal agreement, the Navy had previously financed improvements made by Avianca to the field, including asphalting the 4,500-by-400-foot turf runway and building a brick control tower. Avianca's facilities included two hangars and a repair shop. As the submarine menace mounted for ships passing through the Caribbean, construction kept pace with the increased need for aerial patrols.

The original naval base consisted of 15 wooden huts with canvas tops, used as barracks, dispensary, repair shop, ordnance shack, storehouses, and a 5,000-gallon water tank, all built by Avianca under contract. As strong trade winds repeatedly tore off canvas roofs, they were replaced with tile the following spring.

In May 1944, the base was designated a naval auxiliary air facility and enlarged to care for patrol bombers and a blimp. It was thought that existing structures should be replaced by permanent ones, but that plan was abandoned and more temporary buildings were added to those already in use, 13 quonset huts being obtained from the base at Salinas, which was being dismantled.

A small detachment of CBMU 555 managed the construction and installation of special equipment, assisted by local labor, paid for by the Navy through Avianca. New installations included a stick mooring mast and a mobile mast, a helium building with pipelines to the mooring circle, two concrete magazines, 22 quonset huts, 29 frame huts with tile roofs, a mess hall, a dispensary, a refrigerator building, a ship's service, a 5000-gallon water-storage tank, and a fire-protection tank and pump, as well as electrical equipment and all services. Further equipment was transferred in August from the blimp base at Mandinga, Panama.

Up to the time expansion was completed, on October 15, 1944, facilities were fully used. The following month, patrol operations in the Atlantic were curtailed, and both landplane and blimp detachments were withdrawn. The base then continued on a maintenance status until its disestablishment in March 1945.

Brazil

Construction accomplished for the Navy dotted the entire coast of Brazil with air and naval bases which were vital to the anti-submarine campaign in the South Atlantic and provided stepping stones on the air route to Africa.

The northern coast of Brazil, an almost entirely flat coastal plain of low elevation, extends from the Brazilian-French Guianan border to the city of Natal. The eastern coast varies from the semi-arid and low-lying coastal region of Natal to the rugged mountain country from Victoria to Santa Cruz just south of Rio de Janeiro. The southern coast is composed of rugged mountain country as far as Rio Grande do Sul and thence develops into a flat, treeless plain extending to the Uruguayan border.

The coastal area, north of Rio de Janeiro, was the site for the major portion of construction. This region is sparsely populated. except in the vicinity of the ports, which are connected, for the most part, only by sea and airlines. Ship transportation became extremely difficult, as an appreciable amount of Brazilian coastwise shipping had been sunk by enemy action. The extremely poor roads between the ports were used during the construction only for the transportation of important strategic material which was too heavy for air cargo.

Most of the airport construction was accomplished by the United States Army, through a cooperative contract with the Pan American Airport Corporation. With the authorization of additional facilities at the airfields and of the projects necessary for the Fleet Facilities Program, further arrangements were necessary. Change orders to the Pan American contract and Army engineer-management contracts were issued, and the Bureau of Yards and Docks awarded cost-plus-fixed-fee contracts. lump-sum contracts, and service requisitions on local contractors. Bases constructed formed an extensive chain along the coast from Amapa, near the border of French Guiana, to Santa Cruz.

Amapa.—Amapa, on the Amapa Grande River, was selected as the site for a naval air base to support the operation of two blimps and three patrol bombers. When naval construction was started on June 22, 1943, the Army had completed 3,000 feet of a proposed 5,000-foot runway, a grass runway

about 5,000 feet long, and a portion of the accompanying permanent housing development. Construction for the Navy included housing and mess facilities for crews and maintenance personnel and a blimp take-off mat. All construction, both Army and Navy, was performed under the Airport Development Program. The base was fully utilized by lighter-than-air craft, but patrol bombers were based there only when the tactical situation required it.

The Amapa base was decommissioned June 30, 1945.

Belem.—The next base along the Brazilian coast was at Belem. Here, Pan American and Brazilian airlines were operating from two 5,000-foot paved runways at Val de Caens and from a seaplane base in Belem harbor. Housing and fueling installations for the Army were well underway, when naval construction began on September 22, 1942. Two paved parking areas, one hangar, and personnel structures were built to provide for the operation of six patrol bombers. The Navy took over two warehouses and four 5,000-gallon gasoline tanks, all locally owned. A seaplane ramp was also built, the facilities, as completed on March 10, 1944, being adequate for the basing of 18 planes, either sea- or land-based, a connecting taxiway having been constructed from the facilities to the seaplane ramp.

The Belem base was decommissioned in June 1945.

Igarape Assu.—On July 26, 1943, construction was started to provide for the operation of two LTA craft at Igarape Assu. There existed at the base two grass runways, 3,000 feet and 1500 feet in length, respectively, built by the Brazilian Air Force. Personnel structures, storage and maintenance facilities, and a blimp take-off mat were constructed for the Navy under the Airport Development Program. The base was fully utilized by LTA craft. It was decommissioned in April 1945.

Sao Luiz.—Naval facilities at Sao Luiz do Marauhao, constructed under an independent management contract let by the Army Engineers, were designed for the operation of two LTA craft and six patrol bombers. Two paved runways were under construction for the Army and two 3,000-foot grass runways were available when naval construction started on June 29, 1943. Housing, mess facilities, warehouses, fuel and helium storage, and shops were provided in five and a half months. The base was fully utilized by LTA craft and intermittently used by planes. It was disestablished in July 1945.

Camocim.—A seaplane base at Camocim was begun on October 1, 1941, and nearly completed when it was determined that the base would not be used. Construction under the Airport Development Program had included a ramp, a paved parking area, and two 6,000-gallon underground storage tanks.

Fortaleza.—When construction of Navy installations to support the operation of two blimps and six patrol bombers was started at Fortaleza on April 14, 1943, the program provided for a paved runway, 5,000 feet by 200 feet, and housing and fueling facilities for the Army. Naval construction, accomplished by a management contract let by the District Army Engineer, required nine months for completion. In addition to personnel facilities, a helium-storage building, four fuel tanks with a total capacity of 20,000 gallons, a paved parking area, a nose hangar, and a blimp take-off mat were constructed. All facilities were used to capacity after completion.

The Fortaleza base was decommissioned in June 1945.

Fernando do Noronha.—Fernando do Noronha, a rocky, volcanic island, situated 210 miles from the eastern coast of Brazil, was developed as an air base, first for the Army and later for the Navy. Prior to the start of naval construction in April 1943, it became apparent that the Army would use the base to a limited degree only. Two runways had been constructed for the Army, one 6,000 feet by 150 feet and the other, 2950 feet by 130 feet, so the only additional construction necessary for Navy involved a blimp take-off mat and a mooring circle. Patrol bombers and LTA craft were based there only as the tactical situation required. The Army Transport Command occasionally used the base for refueling on flights to Africa. It was decommissioned in June 1945.

Natal.—On March 5, 1941, construction was initiated on a seaplane base at the mouth of the Potengy River, near Natal. The only existing facilities there were the Pan American Airways passenger terminal, a pier, and float-fueling facilities, but the Potengy served as a runway with practically unlimited range. Facilities for the basing of six patrol bombers, installed under the Airport Development Program, included a ramp and parking area, a nose hangar, and four gasoline tanks of 20,000 barrels total capacity. This construction program extended over a period of three years.

A landplane base, 8 miles southwest of Natal, known as Parnamarim Field, with two runways, 6,000 feet and 7,200 feet long, respectively, had been constructed for the Army. Construction of Navy housing, shops, and operating facilities was started on May 25, 1942, under an Army Engineer direct contract. In order to provide for expanded activities, additional construction was undertaken under a CPFF contract. Naval construction required 19 months. The base was fully utilized by various types of tactical planes.

The Natal bases were decommissioned in June 1945.

Recife.—Numerous naval facilities were established at Recife and used to maximum capacity. In May 1942, when naval construction was begun at Ibura Field, Army housing and runway development were well underway. The original plan for basing six patrol bombers was amended to provide for the operation of two patrol-bomber squadrons and one carrier group, together with facilities for refueling and the temporary mooring of one blimp.

In addition to housing and storage facilities, one blimp mooring, six hardstands, parking, fueling, and repair areas, and shops were constructed for the Navy. The original construction and that of LTA facilities were under the Airport Development Program; construction of additional housing was under a CPFF contract. Maintenance forces erected additional shops.

Knox Hospital, with a 150-bed capacity, was built during the summer of 1942. Under the original plan, 13 quonset huts were erected by the Airport Development Program forces; a ward, with two 188-by-23-foot wings, was later constructed under a lump-sum contract. In the summer of 1943, a newly built Brazilian government hospital was modified to provide a naval receiving station.

Construction of the fuel-oil storage depot in the dock area at Recife was started on November 4, 1942. Ten 10,000-barrel fuel-oil tanks were erected, with connections to the docks and to Ibura Field; existing storage tanks and pipe lines on the piers were also used. Construction required ten months.

An ammunition-storage base was also built at Recife, partly under the Airport Development Program, partly by Public Works Department maintenance forces, and partly under CPFF contract. The installation consisted of 13 steel arch magazines, three concrete magazines, two fuse and detonator buildings, and a barrack. The project was

ARATU SEAPLANE BASE, BRAZIL

completed in December 1943, one year after construction was initiated.

In December 1942, construction was started to provide for the operation of a destroyer repair unit and to furnish housing for enlisted personnel attached to the staff of the commander of the Fourth Fleet. The necessary shops, warehouses, and personnel structures were completed in two years under the Airport Development Program.

All naval facilities at Recife had been decommissioned by November 1945, and the ship repair facilities were transferred to the Brazilian government under Lend-Lease arrangements.

Maceio.—Construction of seaplane facilities was started on June 1, 1941, on a point of land extending into Lagoa do Norte, 2 miles northwest of Maceio. When installations to support six patrol bombers were 75-percent complete, changes in operational plans indicated that the base would not be used. The construction of Navy facilities had

required 23 months, but only certain storage and housing structures were used.

The establishment of a naval landplane base at Maceio was started on July 22, 1943. At that time, a 4500-by-150-foot runway, an aircraft fueling system, passenger and radio facilities were available. Naval construction, designed for the operation of two blimps and six patrol bombers, consisted of housing, storage and shop buildings, a blimp takeoff mat, and two mooring circles. LTA facilities were provided under the Airport Development Program; other installations, under the CPFF contract.

Maceio was disestablished in November 1945, and transferred, under Lend-Lease agreement, to the custody and control of the Brazilian government.

Ipitanga.—Construction of a landplane base for the Army at Ipitanga was begun in January 1942. There then existed one 1968-by-131-foot paved runways. Naval construction called for operational facilities for half a patrol squadron and two blimps. Shortly after this was authorized, it became apparent that the base would not be used to any extent by the Army; consequently, Army facilities were transferred to the Navy.

Construction of this base involved housing, storage, and administration buildings, two 5,000-foot paved runways, a parking area, two prefabricated nose hangars, a blimp take-off mat with two mooring circles, and repair shops.

Two years were required for the construction of the base, which was fully utilized after completion. It was disestablished in July 1945.

Bahia. -The Aratu seaplane base was built on a steep promontory about 12 miles north of Bahia. Its facilities included housing, two timber piers, storage buildings, 20 gasoline tanks of 5,000-gallons capacity each, a ramp, a parking area, a nose hangar, and shops. The base, begun on December 13, 1941, was used continuously after April 1943 for the operation of half a squadron of patrol bombers. It was decommissioned in June 1945.

A petroleum storage depot was started at Bahia on November 4, 1942. Existing storage tanks and pipelines were available and were interconnected with the new installations, which consisted of two 80,000-barrel and two 10,000-barrel tanks. Construction was completed in ten months.

A ship-repair base was established at Bahia, in January 1943, for half a destroyer-repair unit. Adequate power was not available, and a power plant was built. As existing facilities were available for docking, storage, and repair shops, the only construction necessary was housing for 56 officers and 756 men. A 3,000-ton floating drydock, built in the United States, was assigned to the base. This base was completed in thirteen months, and fully used.

In November 1945 it was decommissioned and the facilities turned over to the Brazilian government under Lend-Lease agreement.

Caravellas.—A base for both blimps and planes was established at Caravellas. The construction of LTA facilities was started in October 1943, at what was formerly the Air France airport. where turf runways and a corrugated metal hangar already existed. In five months, all necessary construction had been completed for the operation of two blimps and the housing of 10 officers and 40 men.

Construction of the landplane base, designed for the operation of six patrol bombers, was started in January 1944, under a management contract awarded by the Army Engineers. Aviation facilities consisted of a paved 164-by-5,000-foot runway, with taxiways, a parking area, a high-speed fueling system of 15,600-gallon capacity, and a radio localizer station. Construction was slowed by difficulty in obtaining a suitable subgrade for paving and by bad weather. The base was completed in ten months, but was used only for emergency landings of patrol planes. However, Naval Air Transport Service planes landed there daily for topping off and for discharging passengers and freight. The base was disestablished August 1, 1945, when it was transferred, under Lend-Lease agreement, to the custody and control of the Brazilian Air Force.

Victoria.—At Victoria Airport, 7 miles north of the city of Victoria, the Brazilian authorities had completed one 5000-by-168-foot runway, a small hangar, and radio facilities. The installation of LTA facilities for the Navy in April 1944 required only the leveling of a take-off area and the provision of mooring circles. The construction was completed in 45 days by a Brazilian contractor who was working under the Brazilian Minister of Air. All naval forces had left the base by October 1945.

Santa Cruz. -At Santa Cruz, the Navy also ordered construction of LTA facilities, and assisted the Brazilian government in the rapid completion of a 5,000-by-168-foot runway, with taxiways and parking areas, for the operation of six patrol bombers. The runway was extensively used by NATS and occasionally used by patrol bombers, as the tactical situation required. The base was decommissioned in September 1945, when it was transferred, under Lend-Lease arrangements, to the custody and control of the Brazilian Air Force.

Uruguay

The United States offered its assistance to the Uruguayan government in the construction of a seaplane base at Laguna del Sauce and of a commercial and military airport at Carrasco. Our participation commenced on February 10, 1944, and consisted of engineering counsel, equipment-operator instruction, and the loan of construction equipment. All work was accomplished, and paid for, by Uruguay.

CHAPTER 19

BASES IN THE NORTH ATLANTIC

In the tense months before America's entry into World War II, a series of agreements with Great Britain gave the United States a set of bases located strategically with respect to the North Atlantic shipping lanes. In 1940, as a part of the "Destroyers for Bases" agreement, an area at Argentia, Newfoundland, was set aside for the development of an American naval base. In July 1941, American Marines replaced British forces who had been defending Iceland, and contract construction for additional facilities in Iceland was begun that fall.

Meanwhile, arrangements had been concluded whereby, under the Lend-Lease agreements of March 1941, contractors from the United States built four naval and air bases in northern Ireland and Scotland. These bases, all located near the northern entrance to the Irish Sea, were designed primarily to service craft for anti-submarine patrol at the eastern terminus of the North Atlantic sea lane to English ports on the Irish Sea.

Argentia, Newfoundland

From the Destroyers-for-Bases agreement entered into between the United States and Great Britain on September 2, 1940, our government received the right to develop a naval base at Argentia, Newfoundland. It had become apparent that an anti-submarine patrol should be established to keep open Atlantic shipping lanes and guard American coastal waters, and the decision was made to develop a major air station on the route between United States and Europe.

Contractors, who were working at the time on the naval air station at Quonset Point, R. I., were instructed to begin preliminary work and site-preparation at Argentia. Field work was started on December 29, 1940.

When the air station was usably complete, early in 1942, an expansion of facilities at Argentia was proposed to include a complete naval operating base.

Work on this expansion was begun by the contractors and continued by Seabees, who first arrived at Argentia on October 12, 1942. Following their arrival, extensive developments were made by both the contractors and the battalions until the contractors were relieved on May 5, 1943. Subsequently, all work was performed by military personnel.

Because the site of construction was in an isolated area where housing, skilled labor, supplies, and utilities for construction were practically unavailable, it was necessary to construct a complete camp, including housing, utilities, shops, warehouses, and office facilities, before actual construction of the air station could be accomplished.

The original "camp" at Argentia was on board the SS *Richard Peck*, which had formerly sailed between New York and New Haven. Originally tied to an antiquated pier, and later to pile-dolphins with a ramp to shore, the *Peck* provided dining facilities and housing for the nucleus of the American construction forces. Local Newfoundland labor lived and subsisted in fishing schooners anchored in the harbor and found their way back and forth to their temporary quarters in dories.

With the arrival of building materials, barracks and mess halls were constructed, and all the problems of community life were immediately presented, not in slow steps, as would happen in a growing community, but suddenly and drastically.

The living quarters of the camp consisted of three groups of barracks for 1,500 men from the United States and three groups of barracks for 4,000 men of Newfoundland, with large, well-

COMMISSIONING CEREMONY, NAS ARGENTIA
Marines take over, July 15. 1941

equipped mess halls located in the immediate vicinity of each group.

At the start of operations, the peninsula of Argentia was covered with a layer of peat varying from a few feet to 20 feet in depth, necessitating the removal of approximately 8,341,000 cubic yards of peat and general excavation. The excavated peat was hauled to disposal points along the outer shoreline.

Below the peat, a formation of sand and gravel proved to be excellent for use as fill and for stock to be run through the crushing plant to produce sand and coarse aggregate. The crushing plant produced approximately 136,000 tons of sand and 186,000 tons of coarse aggregate for concrete and asphalt work.

The airfield contained three runways, 300 feet wide and 5.000 feet long. Included with the runway work were 100-foot-wide drainage slopes, gravel shoulders, and gutters. The runways were surfaced with plant-mixed, hot asphaltic concrete which was applied in two layers by paving machines. Generally, the base course was compressed to three inches and the topping compressed to one and a half inches. Some 193,500 tons of asphalt were produced in blending and mixing plants, erected on the base. At first, the blending plant and fluxing equipment, including tank trucks, were rented from a commercial oil company, but were subsequently purchased through the Navy Supply Office at Argentia; the mixing plant, capable of producing 50 tons per hour, was purchased outright.

Asphalt was processed to a liquid-heated state in the blending plant and supplied to the asphalt mixing plant, whence it was delivered in open trucks to the point of use. Approximately 810,000 square yards of base course were laid, with approximately 740,000 square yards of asphaltic topping.

Because of the importance of the airfield, excavation and grading for runways was given first priority. When the grading was accomplished. the asphalt base course was laid. Three runways were completed for emergency use in the fall of 1941; the top course was applied in the spring and summer of 1942.

Two dredges removed approximately 520,000

THE NORTH ATLANTIC AREA

ADMINISTRATION BUILDING, ARGENTIA NAVAL OPERATING BASE

cubic yards of material from the seaplane-ramp area and 803,000 cubic yards from the outer harbor. Areas were dredged and swept to depths of 30 feet or more.

To care for cargo ships, a 50-by-300-foot extension was added to the original railway wharf. When it became evident that more than one cargo ship would be unloaded simultaneously, another 250-foot extension was added. A stiff-leg derrick was erected for unloading shovels, tractors, and other heavy equipment. The wharf was later used by the operating forces for naval marine equipment.

A 2,000-foot marginal wharf was constructed to connect with the north end of the temporary wharf. Half of the wharf deck, which was supported by creosoted piles, consisted of vertically

laminated planking with steel shear developers over which finished concrete deck was poured. The remaining 1,000 feet was supported in like manner with 4-inch plank decking. Fender piles, bollards, and mechanical services were also furnished.

Concrete was transported to this and various other job sites by mixer-trucks. These were loaded at a batching plant which included a testing laboratory, a cement warehouse, a loading hopper, a batching bin, and a fresh-water well and supply system with a 2,000-gallon storage tank to supply mixing water.

Mechanical services included a system for discharging gasoline from ships to the tank farm and, also, for loading vessels from the underground tanks. A similar system was developed for fuel oil and diesel oil. In addition, fresh-water lines, salt-water lines, and steam service were available at various points along the wharf.

The railroad track was extended to run along the wharf to facilitate the loading, unloading, and distribution of materials and supplies.

At the waterfront of the seaplane-parking area, a bulkhead was constructed of steel sheet-piling, braced and tied into the shore. From this bulkhead, two seaplane-ramps extended into the bay. The ramps were constructed of concrete, cofferdams being used.

Three boathouses, supported on piles, were included in the marine work.

Although the general building-construction program really commenced with the erection of barracks, mess halls, warehouses, offices, and temporary buildings, the first building projects completed for military operations were a temporary bachelor officers' quarters and a Marine barrack. Of semi-permanent wooden-frame construction, they housed the original contingent of 100 Marines and their officers. A mess hall, 14 two-story barracks for naval personnel, and a three-story three-

wing building which housed approximately 300 officers were then built. The structures were of wood on prefabricated structural steel, with asbestos siding and floors of wood and asphaltic tile. Corridors connected the barracks and the mess hall and bakery.

The industrial area buildings, of prefabricated structural-steel with asbestos-protected metal exteriors, included a seaplane hangar, aircraft utility shop, acetylene charging shop, oxygen storage room, alcohol storage room, aircraft storehouse, winter-clothing storehouse, cold-storage building, paint and oil shop, torpedo workshop, and bomb-sight storage room. An operations building and message center and a general storehouse were also a part of this group but were of reinforced-concrete construction. The administration building was built with asbestos-shingle siding.

In a group of buildings along the shore were a fire station and garage, a station maintenance shop, and laundry and dry-cleaning shops. These were all one-story prefabricated structural steel buildings with steel sash and asbestos-protected metal exterior.

WOODEN YFD IN OPERATION AT ARGENTIA
In the foreground is the pontoon bridge, connecting the drydock with the pier

NAS Argentia, as Viewed from the Control Tower

Drill Hall and Gymnasium, Argentia
Timber connector-rings were utilized extensively in structural members of this timber building

This group also included a bombproof power house; the lower slab of the double roof was 4 feet thick and the burster slab, 6 feet thick. The power plant consisted of three boilers, each with a continuous rated capacity of 50,000 pounds of steam per hour, and three turbines capable of producing 4,000 kva. Around the exterior of the power plant, was a protection screen of concrete, 5 feet thick. Steam was delivered through underground mains for use in heating, cooking, and the operation of

laundry equipment. Electrical energy for light and power was distributed through underground cables, in ducts encased in concrete envelopes. Standby units were deemed unnecessary, but an interconnection with a local power line was made for emergency use. The Army power system also was interconnected for mutual service.

The dispensary was a one-story rambling building with many wings. It included a mortuary, a convalescent wing, operating rooms, laboratory, and all the facilities of a complete hospital. A wing of two stories was added subsequently. This building was of wood-frame construction with wooden sheathing and asbestos-shingle siding.

Inert storehouses, high-explosive magazines, fuse and detonator magazines, a small-arms magazine, a pyrotechnic magazine, and warhead magazines were of wire-mesh reinforced-concrete arch construction and were buried for concealment and protection.

Several large buildings, such as the aircraft storehouse addition, the airfield control tower, and the gymnasium, were of timber construction. Timber connector-rings were utilized extensively in the structural members of these buildings.

Construction roads were developed in order to provide access to the various areas under construction. One of the most important of these areas was the storage area for fuels and lubricants.

A fuel-oil and diesel-oil storage farm was developed, consisting of six welded-steel storage tanks and six prestressed-concrete tanks, with an individual capacity of 1,134,000 gallons, making the total capacity for the storage of fuel and diesel oil, 13,608,000 gallons. One of these tanks was later converted to 80-octane gasoline storage.

In the same vicinity, two welded-steel storage tanks of 13,500-barrel capacity, each, were erected for the storage of 100-octane gasoline.

These tanks, of prestressed, gunite-covered, latex-lined, concrete, designed to conserve steel, were all placed underground.

A second tank farm was developed for the storage of 100-octane gasoline. This consisted of 24 tanks with an individual capacity of 25,000 gallons, two bulk tanks of 100,000 gallons, each, and one of 567,000 gallons, making the capacity of the farm 1,367,000 gallons. The farm was fed through a 10-inch pipe from the marginal wharf and an 8-inch line from two finger-piers, and gasoline was disbursed at the parking areas through an aqua system.

The entire operation was electrically and hydraulically controlled. In addition to furnishing 100-octane gasoline at the parking areas, arrangements were made to dispense gasoline to the Army through a tank-car loading-platform.

At the start of building operations the only light and power available was supplied by a line which furnished 50 kva, and by 85-kva diesel generating plants, owned and operated by the local light and power company. With the growth of the camp and the increase in power-consumption for construction purposes, added electrical energy was required. As the result of negotiations with the local company, a power line was constructed from a hydro-electric plant, 64 miles from the base. This line supplied 1,500 kva and delivered it at 33.000 volts to transformers which converted it to 2,400 volts for use on the base. Due to the excessive bad weather during the winter, conditions warranted the installment of two steam turbines in the SS *Richard Peck* to be used as stand-bys. These were fed by the ship's boilers. These generators augmented the local supply by 750 kva.

As permanent buildings were completed and the camp load increased, it became evident that until the permanent power plant was operative, some source of temporary power would be necessary. One of the permanent turbines was selected and arrangements were made for temporary operation. This turbine generated 1.000 kva, using steam from a boiler already installed in its permanent position.

In the final permanent power plant, current was generated from two 1.500-kva and one 1,000-kva alternators.

A 6-inch main from a series of lakes, about a mile from the base, originally furnished the only fresh water. This supply, while pure, was inadequate and uncertain. An attempt was made to drill wells to augment the supply, but salt water was encountered, and the effort was abandoned. The base was connected with an Army supply which was furnished by a larger lake and watershed through a 12-inch line. The water was chlorinated and pumped into nine underground reservoirs of 500.000-gallon capacity each, giving a total underground storage of 4,500.000 gallons. These reservoirs were connected in a loop, thereby ensuring an adequate supply of fresh water if one or more reservoirs or pipe lines were damaged. A fresh-water pumping station delivered the water from the reservoir to the point of consumption.

In addition to the underground storage, three elevated prefabricated riveted-steel water tanks were erected to float on the line in the event of a pressure drop. These furnished sufficient pressure for normal distribution and supplied emergency pressure to the sprinkler systems located in various buildings.

Sprinkler systems for fire protection were in-

SHOPS AND WAREHOUSES AT NAS ARGENTIA

stalled in the seaplane hangar, general storehouse, aircraft storehouse, paint and oil shop, and aircraft utility shop.

The salt-water system for fire protection consisted of lines to hydrants along all roads and at all buildings. A pumping station fed this system.

On October 12, 1942 the first section of the 17th Construction Battalion arrived at Argentia and was assigned to the maintenance and operation of completed utilities and structures, previously operated by civilian employees of the contractors. Additional members of the battalion arrived on March 17, 1943, and most of them were assigned the duties of manning the shops, plants, and equipment. The balance of the group was placed on new construction projects.

On March 27, 1943, the first section of the 64th Battalion arrived, closely followed, in April, by the second section. The 64th was engaged principally in new construction work. On June 17, the 69th Battalion arrived.

On May 5, 1943, the civilian contractors were relieved of all activity, a large portion of the base construction having been completed.

The work performed by the battalions, which were consolidated to form the 10th Construction Regiment, consisted of operations of every character, including the building of heavy industrial structures, wharves, bulkheads, installation of floating drydocks, earth and peat removal, road and runway construction, and general maintenance work.

One of the projects was a reservoir development, which included the formation of a series of ponds to impound 175,000,000 gallons of water. In addition to building a dam, the Seabees constructed a sluiceway from one pond to another, and installed control works at two ponds.

Other assignments included the completion of 84 quonset huts, reconstruction of the BOQ after its destruction by fire, erection of a temporary BOQ during the reconstruction period, and fabrication of a public works warehouse.

During the month of April 1943, the 64th Battalion started work on eleven projects, including a salt-water pumping station, a second boathouse, the drydock development which had been started by the contractors, several radio buildings, and four barracks.

The largest and most extensive job was that of the drydock development. As the first two sections of a 7,000-ton floating drydock were expected, operations were speeded in order to complete the inshore pier, to install a bulkhead complete with tieback system, and to construct a pontoon bridge to connect the pier and the drydock.

The first two sections of the dock arrived early in May and the remaining two sections during the latter part of May. By June 1, all sections were in position and had been secured to the anchorage. During June, concrete sinkers were installed, the main wooden keel blocks were removed and replaced in concrete, the bilge blocks were altered and reinstalled, and temporary mechanical services and energy units were provided to permit operation of the dock before final completion. On June 26, 1943, the drydock was submerged to receive its first ship.

By July 1, all steel work on the shop buildings for the drydock had been completed. This included the erection of two traveling-cranes, the completion of the concrete curtain-wall and of much of the floor slab, roofing, plumbing, and electrical lines.

By September 1, 1943 completed projects included extension of the gasoline-storage area, extension of the water-supply and fire-protection systems, a radio and radar workship, an oil storehouse, a laundry building, and several additional magazines.

During September and October, the entire drydock area was completed and placed in operation. All roads and walks, as well as all railroad tracks, were finished.

One of the most important projects, though not the largest, undertaken by the Seabees at Argentia was the increase in the length of the airfield runways, including the finishing for drainage and the rolling and oiling of shoulders. The project lasted from June 1943 until the latter part of August, at which time it was virtually complete, the only exception being one runway which required the placement and compaction of 100,000 cubic yards of fill plus the oiling of all extended shoulders. By the end of October, all drainage work was completed and the base course of asphalt was laid.

Substantial completion of all new construction was effected during the month of November. The scope of operations included the completion of all authorized runway extensions, laying of approximately 6,700 tons of asphalt paving, and the installation of utilities to service the expanded facilities.

On November 17, 1943, CBMUs 525 and 526 arrived to take over the station maintenance. The next day the 17th Battalion was detached, except for a small contingent of 45 key enlisted men, who were transferred to the maintenance units to indoctrinate the units in their assigned functions.

On December 6, 1943, the 69th Battalion was relieved. The completion of all projects for which materials were on hand was accomplished during December; and on January 1, 1944, the 64th Battalion and the 10th Regiment completed their duty at Argentia.

On February 9, 1944, the two CBMUs were consolidated and the public works officer was designated as officer in charge.

Argentia presented a peculiar situation in regards to roll-up, as construction work was continued during this period. The explanation lay in the fact that permanent facilities were being completed while temporary or emergency facilities were being dismantled.

After January 1944, many projects, started by the battalions and left unfinished because materials were lacking, were completed by the maintenance unit. These included net-depot facilities, a draft curtain for the seaplane hangar and storehouse, sidewalks, and a fuel-oil recovery system. In addition, many new projects were started, including the replacement of quonset huts by more permanent barracks.

Native civilian employees were trained to carry on the regular maintenance operations so that by September 1, 1944, it was possible to reduce the CBMU personnel from 590 men and 11 officers to 296 men and 8 officers.

Iceland

In May 1940, a month after the Axis invasion of Denmark and Norway, the British landed troops in Iceland to protect that country from possible invasion and also to provide a base for patrols to protect shipping to the British Isles.

Military facilities were not available in Iceland for these troops or for bases, so it was necessary for the British to construct them. An agreement between the British and the Icelandic governments stated that no more than 2,200 Icelanders would be used by the British, because no more than this number could be spared from the fishing industry, the main source of livelihood to Iceland, without impairing the local economy.

In the early part of 1941, the British realized

SHOP AT THE NAVAL OPERATING BASE, ARGENTIA
This view was taken in August 1944

that under such an arrangement their required construction could not be completed as rapidly as desired, and requested that the United States construct fuel-oil storage facilities. These facilities, located on the barren and rocky shores of the Hvalfjordur, were to provide storage for 164,000 tons of fuel oil. Part of the storage was to be used for fuel oil used by the British in Iceland, and part to care for the trans-shipment of fuel oil from American bottoms, as the Neutrality Act prohibited American ships from going to England. The labor required for the construction of these fuel-oil storage facilities was to be paid for by the British: the required material, and later the labor costs also, was furnished through Lend-Lease. The United States agreed to this request in the early summer of 1941. It was decided to construct the required facilities by using the organization already engaged, under a CPFF contract, in construction of Navy installations at Newfoundland, drawing on available men and equipment at the construction projects under way at Quonset Point and Davisville, R. I. Although the construction contract was not signed until September 25, 1941, procurement of material by the contractor at Quon-

set Point was underway before this, and the first shipload arrived at Iceland during the latter part of October.

All American labor for work in Iceland was hired by the contractor, but by this time, August and September 1941, there was beginning to be a shortage of skilled workers available for overseas work, partly because of the expansion of the Defense program in the United States and partly because of a reluctance on the part of civilians to sign a contract for a year's work far from home and under unknown conditions.

Meanwhile, upon the invitation of the government of Iceland, United States forces occupied Iceland. On July 7, 1941, the President of the United States informed Congress of this occupation, giving the bases for the occupation as (1) the threat against Greenland and the northern portion of the North American continent, including the adjacent islands; (2) the threat against all shipping in the North Atlantic; and (3) the threat against the steady flow of munitions to Britain.

The need for naval facilities in Iceland developed rapidly. In addition to the fuel-oil facilities originally contemplated, the Commander-in-Chief,

Atlantic Fleet, on September 12 pointed out the necessity for aerial patrol activities, and on September 25, 1941, the Chief of Naval Operations directed that a base be constructed for the operation of one squadron of patrol planes near Reykjavik. This base was to consist of housing and administration facilities, repair facilities, and seaplane ramps, and was to be designated as a fleet air base.

The first contingent of American civilians to reach Iceland consisted of 133 men, who arrived on October 29, 1941. The original intent had been to use all these men on the construction of the fuel-oil facilities; however, 48 of them were sent immediately to begin the air base, leaving 85 men to unload the supplies from the SS *Chattanooga*, on which they had arrived, and the SS *Alchiba*, which arrived a week later.

While the erection of the camp at the fuel depot was proceeding, the 48 men at the air base were erecting housing facilities for aviation personnel. By the end of December 1941, the number of workmen on the project had increased to 50 Americans and 65 Icelanders. In spite of the many difficulties encountered, the base was placed in operation at this time, and on January 21, 1942, the fleet air base was commissioned.

Work was greatly hampered by the severe wind and snow storms of that winter, including a 130-mile gale in the early part of January 1942, which wrecked a partially completed tank at the fuel depot, scattered material over a wide area. Huts were blown down at both the fuel depot and the air base.

At about this time, negotiations by the Army with the Navy for construction of an Army airfield near Reykjavik were under way. Construction was authorized on November 7, 1941, but no site was selected by the Army until the following February. At the time, the officer in charge of construction was directed to proceed with the construction, the Navy contractor doing the construction. The Navy was to do the work; the Army was to furnish the higher echelons of supervision and troops for unskilled labor.

Concurrently, work was started by the Navy contractor on the physical facilities of a naval operating base on the outskirts of Reykjavik. Arrangements for leasing the required land had been undertaken shortly after the attack on Pearl Harbor, and as soon as huts and other materials arrived, construction was started.

On February 13, 1942, the Chief of Naval Operations directed that the fleet air base be constructed for two squadrons of planes. A 100-bed hospital was incorporated in the plans for the operating base, and construction proceeded as rapidly as could be expected with the limited force available.

During February 1942, the Bureau of Yards and Docks requested the British to enter a formal requisition for the construction of a tank farm at Seydisfjord (an informal request had been made some time earlier), and on February 13, 1942, the British made the formal request that there be constructed at Seydisfjord six 10,000-barrel fuel-oil tanks to replace the tanker which was moored there as a refueling base.

To complicate the supply problem further the USS *Lake Osweya*, with a cargo of supplies, was lost while en route to Iceland in the early part of March 1942.

The pioneering nature of the work, including long hours of Arctic darkness and severe winter weather, tended to slow down progress. By the middle of March, only eight American civilians and 32 Icelanders were employed on the construction of the naval operating base. It was at this time that first consideration was given to the use of contingents of the newly organized Seabees.

As the naval activities expanded, it was necessary to initiate construction of ammunition storage, and work was started on this in March—contractors' men being used as they could be spared from other more urgent jobs. The maximum number employed on this project was 25. On March 28, the Chief of Naval Operations approved the construction of a floating pier in the Hvalfjordur at the fuel depot.

The shortage of workmen continued to be serious, and by early April of 1942, there were only 368 American and 325 Icelanders on the various projects.

On May 8, 1942, there arrived 25 of the contractor's men to begin work at the Army airfield. On May 20, a second contingent of 165 workmen arrived, and on May 25, the first of the contractor's heavy-equipment operators and earth-moving men went to work on the first airstrip, called Patterson Field, which was to be a fighter field. Meanwhile, construction had proceeded so well at the naval operating base, that on May 16, 1942, it was formally commissioned as Camp Knox.

In the latter part of May 1942, the Bureau of

TANK FARM AT REYKJAVIK, ICELAND
General view of the living and work camp

Yards and Docks proposed to the commandant of the operating base that Seabees be used to replace the contractor's men on the various projects, it having become evident that it would be impossible to obtain enough American civilian workmen to accomplish the authorized construction within the time allotted. As a result, arrangements were begun to ship Seabees to Iceland.

On July 2, excavation was started on the east-west runway of the huge central airfield, called Meeks Field. During the middle part of the month, 15 Seabee welders arrived and were immediately put to work at the fuel depot. By the last of the month storage space for 240,000 barrels of fuel-oil was ready and fuel oil was being stored. All 44 of the oil tanks had been erected, and 30 of them were complete with piping and appliances.

The arrival on August 18, 1942, of the 9th Construction Battalion, comprising 704 enlisted men and 17 officers, signaled the beginning of a new and busier phase of construction.

The Seabees rapidly replaced the contractor's forces. On the first of September, all the contractor's employees, except 71 of the key men at the Navy fuel depot and the Army airfield left Iceland on the same ship that had brought the Seabees. The civilian workmen at the fuel depot were relieved by September 20, 1942, and those at the airfield by the middle of October.

October signalized the end of good construction weather and the start of a winter-long struggle to meet the goals set for the completion of the various projects. This was particularly true in the case of the Army airfield, which was scheduled to be completed by April 1, 1943.

On October 28, 1942, the naval ammunition depot was commissioned. In addition to the heavy earth-moving, paving was started on the Army Patterson Field on October 26, in an attempt to get at least one strip in operating condition before winter weather set in. By November 25, a landing strip, 3,500 by 100 feet, had been paved, before heavy rains and snows caused the filled-in material to bog completely.

The difficulties encountered in getting this strip paved were varied. The main difficulty was that the surface materials of the well-compacted runway fill had frozen, and when hot asphalt was spread

PIER TO DEEP WATER AT THE TANK FARM, REYKJAVIK, ICELAND

on this frozen surface, the frost melted, forming mud pools under the impervious asphalt. This condition was overcome by laying a porous-mix base course that allowed the water to escape in the form of steam.

The first large concrete job to be undertaken at the Army airfield was for a 175-by-206-foot steel hangar at Meeks Field. The 44 footings for the columns were poured while snow was on the ground; steel erection was made difficult by the high winds.

On December 4, 1942, the first contingent of the 28th Construction Battalion, consisting of 310 enlisted men and 10 officers, arrived and was immediately sent to the Army airfield where they were put to work with members of the 9th Battalion. On December 22, the remainder of the 28th Battalion, consisting of 674 enlisted men and 16 officers, arrived. These men were immediately distributed among the Army airfield, the fleet air base, and the fuel depot forces.

Logistics, climate, and geography combined to offer almost every conceivable obstacle to construction. The terrain was tundra-covered, broken with boulders and ledge outcroppings. It had been vaguely mapped, was devoid of roads and subject to violent winds. Ingenious engineering improvisations and utter disregard for physical hardships

were necessary to overcome innumerable obstacles.

The major task was placing sufficient asphalt paving. A quota of 1,500 square yards of asphaltic concrete paving per day for 121 days (December 1 to March 31) was essential to meet the requirements.

Early in February 1943, a series of break-downs occurred in both the asphalt plant and the rock crusher. In spite of all these difficulties, the first plane to use the field, landed on March 26, 1943, five days in advance of the originally scheduled completion date.

In April 1943, construction was completed at the ammunition depot. By the first of May 1943, the first 376,000 square yards of asphalt paving at Meeks Field had been completed. The placing of the second 189,000 square yards of asphalt was done in less than three months as compared to the five months required for the placing of the first 189,000 square yards.

The new asphalt plant, which had been ordered in December 1942, arrived and was placed in operation at the Army airfield on May 20, 1943. By this time, the fill at Patterson Field had dried out sufficiently for operations to proceed. The bulk of the grading had been done the previous year and all that was necessary to get ready for paving was to dress up the runways and two taxiways. Three new taxiways, new dispersal areas, and the hangar apron were filled to grade.

By July 1, 1943, all paving was completed at Meeks Field, a total of 1,074,419 square yards of base course and 895,309 square yards of topping having been laid, and efforts were redoubled at Patterson Field. Paving was completed there on August 21, a total of 427,788 square yards of base course and 427,778 square yards of topping having been laid. By the first of August 1943, the fleet air base was essentially complete.

The first of the Seabees to be returned to the United States were 34 enlisted men from the 28th Battalion who left Iceland on July 27, 1943. On August 25, CBMU 514, composed of 5 officers and 267 enlisted men, arrived at Reykjavik. In addition to the maintenance at the naval operating base, Seabee personnel were assigned duties with the port director, took over all master-at-arms duties at the naval operating base, were given key commissary and galley assignments, and were assigned to the recreation division and the disbursing office.

With the arrival of the CBMU, members of the 28th Battalion were relieved of duties at the fleet air base, leaving only the detachment at the fuel depot and CBMU 514 to do the necessary construction and maintenance at the several bases. The 28th Battalion left the area on October 2, 1943.

On November 22, 1943, the transfer of the naval fuel depot to the British was authorized and word was received that the British would take over about the first of the year. By this time, the fuel depot was 100-per cent complete and had been in use for some time.

Early in December, Icelandic civilians, who were to work for the British, began arriving at the fuel depot and were indoctrinated by the Seabees.

On December 20, 1943, the fleet air base was closed with the provision that if turned over to the British it would be returned to United States control upon 60 days notice. In January 1944, the 28th Construction Battalion detachment at the fuel depot was redesignated as CBMU 586, and then was redesignated Construction Battalion 146.

On January 21, 1944, the fuel depot was turned over to the British. Ten days later, the fleet air base was evacuated by United States naval forces, the huts and a limited amount of equipment being turned over to the British. Most of the equipment, such as comfort gear, recreation gear, technical apparatus, galley and bakery equipment, and

the major proportion of the refrigeration apparatus, was packed and crated by CBMU 514 and accompanied the 146th Construction Battalion to its new assignment.

After turning the fuel depot over to the British, the 146th Seabees moved to the naval operating base to await further transportation. On February 2, 1944, a portion of the battalion departed from Iceland for the United Kingdom, and on February 18, the remainder left for the same destination to act as a special petroleum unit in preparation for the invasion of France. During the spring of 1944, only routine maintenance work was done.

On May 16, 1944, the Chief of Naval Operations directed that naval personnel in Iceland be reduced to an overall total of about 200 officers and men, exclusive of the Marine detachment, and the ammunition depot be dismantled except for such huts or buildings as might be desired by the British.

The maintenance unit did the salvage work, surplus materials and equipment in usable condition being shipped to the European theater of operations.

In November, 1945 the British returned the air station, the fuel depot, and the ammunition depot to the United States Navy. Seabees were used as guard forces.

Jan Mayen Island

On September 24, 1943, the officer in charge of CBMU 514, then stationed in Iceland, was directed to confer with the officers of the United States Coast Guard and the representatives of the Royal Norwegian Navy concerning the construction of a radio direction finder station on Jan Mayen Island, situated in the Arctic Ocean, between Greenland and Norway.

The most serious obstacle encountered during construction operations at Jan Mayen was not the rugged mountainous terrain, the cold Arctic weather, the frozen ground, or the volcanic structure of the rock, but the landing of supplies, material, and equipment through the heavy surf in small boats. The problem was solved by prefabricating as many items as possible in Iceland, where shop facilities were available, and limiting their size and weight to permit beaching through the surf in the boats.

During the time that a Coast Guard cutter was surveying the island to determine the exact location of the proposed installation, the buildings, equipment, and accessories were being constructed,

assembled, marked, and crated for shipment. This
entailed a great deal of scurrying around and fer-
reting out of crucial equipment, and improvising
when certain items were not available, for there
was not sufficient time to order and receive the
necessary items from the United States. Army
Engineers cooperated fully, so that by November 4,
when the specially selected construction crew departed for Jan Mayen, they were able to complete
their assignment within a month, and that despite

keep it in operation for some time. This group
returned to Iceland on August 3, with the report
that the work had been completed ahead of time.

Greenland

As a result of an agreement reached on April 9,
1941, between the governments of Denmark and
the United States, American troops occupied
Greenland on June 13, 1941.

The Navy's general tasks in Greenland were to

TANK FARM ON THE SHORES OF HVALFJORDUR, ICELAND
Construction was begun early in 1941 at the request of the British, under Lend-Lease agreements

adverse weather conditions and the long Arctic
night.

The Seabees erected a two-story main building
to house the delicate instruments and equipment;
a 20-by-48-foot hut with prefabricated built-in cup-
boards, bunks, and bulkheads for berthing and
messing of the operating Coast Guard personnel,
and a storage building.

The buildings had to be designed without much
definite information as to the frozen terrain, velocity of the winds (reported as being well over
100 knots part of the time), snow load, and the
camouflage problem (enemy reconnaissance planes
came over at regular intervals). For these reasons,
conventional design methods were discarded and
the buildings were laid out in a manner that would
make them as strong and as rigid as the available
materials would allow and also permit the erection at the site in as short a time as possible. There
was little daylight and no sun at the island during
the period the men were working.

In the spring of 1944, members of another special
detail from CBMU 514 were sent from Iceland on
June 12 to Jan Mayen, with orders to make the
station more livable, as it had been decided to

defend sea communications between Greenland
and North America, to defend shipping in the
coastal waters of Greenland, and, supported by the
Army, to prevent access to the territory and terri-
torial waters of Greenland by any hostile elements
or the nationals or agents of belligerent non-Amer-
ican nations.

All construction work in Greenland was done by
private contractors, working under the direction of
the Army. In the construction of Navy facilities,
the Bureau of Yards and Docks, directed by the
Chief of Naval Operations, made arrangements
with the Army for the construction work. The
Army supplied labor and construction implements,
and the Navy supplied all materials except in cases
where the Army happened to have a surplus.

From July until December 1943, when the contractor's work was completed, one CEC officer from
the Atlantic Division of the Bureau of Yards and
Docks was attached to the construction site in
Greenland.

In July 1943, a CEC officer from the Fire Protection Section of the Construction Department
went to Greenland to investigate the fire-protection
facilities there. It was on his recommendation that

a foam system for the protection of the tank farm was installed.

Naval projects at Greenland included a naval operating facility at Grondal, a naval facility at Narsarssuak, a radio station at Gamatron, and a loran project at Frederiksdal.

The operating facility at Grondal was used as a fueling station and minor repair base. The following installations were constructed: a 105,000-barrel tank farm, a camp for 16 officers and 130 enlisted men, a radio and visual signal station, a crib pier with 580 feet of berthing space, two cruiser-type moorings, a machine shop, a 250-pontoon drydock, 2,000 square feet of ammunition storage, emergency seaplane facilities, general storage facilities, and base maintenance shops.

The facility at Narsarssuak was used as a command center and an operating point for naval patrol planes. It was located on part of the Army air base at Narsarssuak. This facility's installation consisted of a camp for 70 officers and 310 enlisted men, an administration office for the commander of the Greenland Patrol, ammunition storage space, facilities for the operation and maintenance of seven PBY's, a radio station, general storage facilities, base maintenance shops, and one cruiser-type mooring.

The radio station at Gamatron consisted of a radio and direction-finder station with a camp for one officer and 40 enlisted men. Military protection of this installation was maintained by the Army.

The loran project at Frederiksdal, which was operated by the Coast Guard, contained housing facilities for one officer and 20 men.

Lend-Lease Bases in the British Isles

In April 1941, arrangements were made with the British government to construct four naval bases in Northern Ireland and Scotland, at Londonderry and Lough Erne in Ireland and at Rosneath and Loch Ryan in Scotland. Funds for the construction of these bases were to be provided by both the British and the American governments, in accordance with Lend-Lease agreements reached in March 1941.

Londonderry and Rosneath were to provide repair and fueling facilities for destroyers and submarines, ammunition storage, hospitals, and barracks for shore-based personnel; Lough Erne and Loch Ryan were to be used principally as operations centers for seaplane squadrons.

After the entry of the United States into the war the construction of a huge pipe line in the vicinity of Rosneath was begun.

Approximately 1,150 American workers and 4,800 local workers, mostly Irish, were employed in the construction of these bases, which represented the initial effort of the United States Navy to erect portable facilities overseas. Supervision was given by 25 officers of the Civil Engineer Corps.

Base I. Londonderry. With the advent of war, Londonderry immediately became a port of inestimable value as a base for North Atlantic convoy escorts. These escorts consisted principally of destroyers and lesser craft of the United States, Canadian, and British navies. The essential North Atlantic sea lane had its terminus in ports bordering the Irish Sea in western Scotland and England. As the maintenance of this thin supply line through the ever-tightening German blockade was imperative to the continuance of British resistance, the top priority was given the project of establishing at Londonderry the first United States naval base in the United Kingdom.

Londonderry is situated some 4 miles up the River Foyle, on the northern coast of Ireland. Its location also made it the most suitable port for the allocation of supplies to other projects.

Four miles downstream from the city of Londonderry, and on the opposite bank, an area, known as Lisahally, offered deep water and adjoining landspace sufficient for unloading and storing large quantities of supplies.

A week before the contract was signed in Washington on June 12, 1941, the CEC officer-in-charge arrived in Londonderry to prepare the way for the arrival of contractor's forces and construction materials and equipment.

Many activities were to be scattered within a 4-mile radius of administration headquarters, located in the center of Londonderry. An abandoned shipyard, where the Admiralty had been engaged in the construction of a small slipway and services for that work, became the center of industrial facilities for ship repair. At Lisahally a deep-water unloading wharf, storehouses, and a tank farm were established. Tanker and fueling berths were available along an existing Admiralty jetty. Three personnel areas, to accommodate 6000 men, a 500-bed hospital, an ammunition depot, and a radio station were constructed in the surrounding countryside. In planning the project, considerable em-

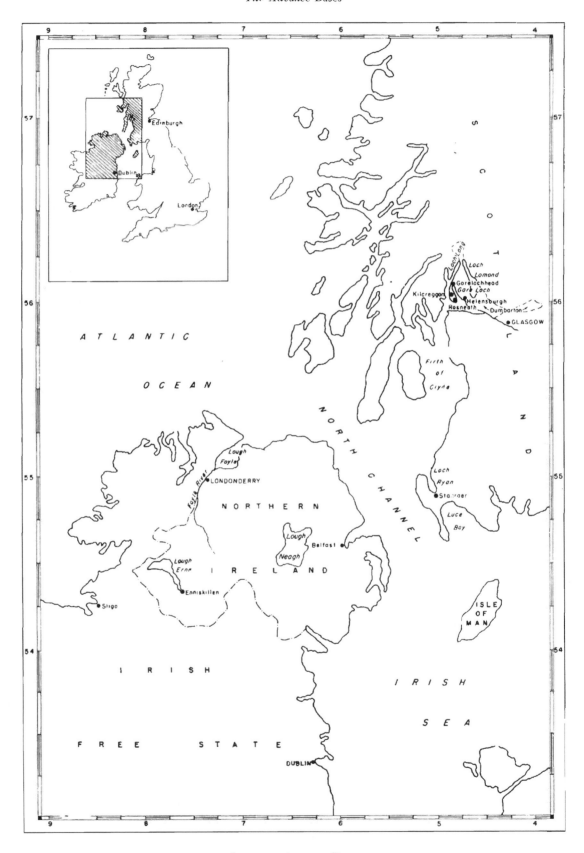

IRISH AND SCOTTISH BASES

phasis was placed on dispersal as a defense against bombing attacks, which, except for one minor incident, never materialized.

Work on the most pressing projects—the first of the personnel areas at Beech Hill, the storage area at Lisahally, and the ship-repair facilities—began in mid-July, when the first ship loaded with tools, equipment, and materials arrived from the States. In September the job expanded to include the second large hut camp at Beech Hill and the administration area. By October, the first pile-driving rigs had been received and assembled, and pile driving was begun for the loading wharf at Lisahally. At the same time, work was in progress on all the major projects except the tank farm, for which materials were a long time in arriving.

With the United States' entry into the war, a new plan of strategy was evolved which materially changed the base-building program in the European theater. Under this program, Londonderry was commissioned as a naval operating base. Notable additions were a 750-foot extension to the 1000-foot loading wharf at Lisahally and enlarged radio installations. The size of the hospital was reduced from 500 to 200 beds.

By the first of the year, work was being pressed to the utmost in spite of the almost incessant rainfall and the much-shortened daylight period characteristic of northern latitudes. Almost 600 Americans and a considerably larger number of Irishmen were employed. In January, most of the magazines in Fincairn Glen were completed, and the first materials for the new warehouses arrived at Lisahally.

With the Navy's efforts in European waters centered on escorting convoys, not only to Britain but also to Murmansk, as American aid to Russia was increased. Londonderry promised to remain essential to the fleet and there was no question of relinquishing its control to the British.

Londonderry was commissioned as a naval operating base on February 5, 1942, the first outpost of the Navy's shore establishment in the European theater. The first American warship had arrived in December 1941. As enlisted personnel arrived, facilities were placed in operation as quickly as they were usably complete. By February 22, many of the ship-repair facilities and shops were being readied for use; by March 3 the first major group of United States naval personnel had arrived and were quartered in the barracks at Springtown.

Much of the original work remained to be done

and base operations were constantly expanding, which allowed no let-up in construction activity. By the middle of April both the hospital at Creevagh and the ammunition depot had been substantially completed. By May 1, work in the industrial area was completed, and a week later the new extension to the loading wharf at Lisahally was ready for use.

As the remaining major projects moved rapidly to completion, the attention of the contractor's force was shifted to maintenance, and many skilled workmen were released for transfer to projects in progress in Scotland. The tank farm, begun in April, had been continually delayed by the difficulty in obtaining materials from the United States. However, this did not materially handicap the activity, as the delay had been anticipated and adequate supplies of oil from British sources had been made available. Operating activities along the waterfront were then at a peak in preparation for the invasion of North Africa.

A 250-man addition to the barracks at the Lisahally storage area, approved in August 1942, was completed on September 5. Londonderry ceased to be the focal point of construction effort, and headquarters of the officer-in-charge were moved to Helensburgh, Scotland, where the Dumbartonshire pipe line was the last major project to be constructed under the CPFF contract. A small local office was left in Londonderry, to supervise the force of 1,000 men handling base maintenance and the remaining construction.

During the course of the civilian contract at Londonderry, a great naval base had been constructed and put into operation. The work, dispersed over an area of 425 acres, included 1,350 separate buildings, of which 55 were structures either 40 by 100 feet or 60 by 90 feet; more than 90,000 square feet of wharfage; construction and paving of more than 12 miles of roadway; 12 miles of water pipe; 8 miles of drainage ditches; 20 miles of electric cable; 27 miles of fencing; electric generators; and 11 radio masts. In addition, a tank farm for storage of fuel and diesel oil had been erected.

Hindered by mud, rain, and the swampy banks of the River Foyle, the contract force, and later the Seabees, often waited in vain for materials and equipment. An innovation was the prefabricated type of building shipped from the United States, including the newly devised quonset huts. Long-span frames were used not only for warehouses

GENERAL HEADQUARTERS, LONDONDERRY

and shops, but also for the theaters and recreation buildings; the huts served as living quarters,
hospitals, and offices.

By January 1943, with the successful completion
of the North African landings and the imminent
transfer of the Rosneath base to the British, most
of the members of the 29th Battalion were available from Rosneath to relieve the 900 contract
employees at Londonderry. The 29th carried on
maintenance and improvement until relieved by
the 97th Battalion, in September 1943. A portion
of the 97th also relieved a 29th detachment at
Rosneath.

Fresh from training, the 97th took over the task
of completing such construction as was left unfinished. They completed the tank farm, assembled a boiler plant which had been shipped in
pieces from the United States, and built pump-
houses, quonset huts, and roads. Often, their work
was impeded by shortage of materials and by worn-
out equipment. On one occasion, using an old pile-
driver that was literally falling apart, they built a

wharf from such materials as they could salvage.
When completed, it supported a 10-ton crane and
a 20-ton derrick.

In nine months the 29th completed several projects which had previously been in progress under
the CPFF contract, including a 300,000-barrel tank
farm, three pumping stations and fuel lines, three
boiler houses, a 150-foot pier with roads and services, 50 quonset huts, a recreation building, and
anti-aircraft gun emplacements.

By mid-April, it was possible to assign the bulk
of the 29th Battalion forces who had been engaged
on the tank farm to the Scottish pipe-line project,
where the Seabees again relieved civilian personnel. With the tank farm in partial operation by
May, all projects originally planned for construction at Londonderry under the contract were complete.

On June 4, 1943, to integrate construction battalion forces with the operative control of the base,
the officer-in-charge of the 29th Battalion was assigned additional duty as public works officer of

GENERAL VIEW OF LIVING QUARTERS AT SPRINGTOWN BASE, LONDONDERRY

the naval operating base, with general responsibility for maintenance of the shore establishment and operation of the transportation department and the tank farm. This precedent of assigning operative control to Seabees was widely followed in subsequent bases in the United Kingdom.

With the arrival of the 97th Construction Battalion in September 1943, it was decided to increase the capacity of the tank farm, in anticipation of the Normandy landings. An unusual Seabee assignment was the mounting of 40-mm. and 20-mm. guns on a large number of landing ships and craft in the spring of 1944.

Later, when the base was relinquished to the British, the Seabees removed all critical material for shipment home. Inasmuch as the radio station was to be the sole remaining activity in the area, Seabees erected 40 nissen huts for personnel, before the 97th was transferred to England between June and November, 1944.

The naval operating base at Londonderry was decommissioned in July 1944. All the men were transferred with the exception of a few storekeepers, a small administrative staff, and two companies of Seabees, who remained to operate the radio station. After they moved to their new location, the base was turned over to the British, September 3, 1944.

During the course of the war, Londonderry was of great importance. Convoy escorts were refueled for their return trip across the Atlantic, and ships which had run the gauntlet of submarine-infested sea lanes, had their damaged hulls and machinery repaired, and such other repairs and improvements as were necessary. Until the creation of Exeter, Londonderry was the main supply depot for our naval activities in the British Isles, and throughout the war, it was the major United States naval radio station in the European theater.

Lough Erne. The original plan for the Lough Erne base was to provide facilities for four seaplane squadrons, with maintenance, repair, and ammunition-storage facilities, which would require quarters for 3,000 men and a 200-bed hospital.

Lough Erne was identical in plan with the project at Loch Ryan, Scotland. However, as the importance of bases in Ireland became greater than those in Scotland, Lough Erne became the larger. Although planned as a United States naval seaplane

CREEVAGH HOSPITAL BASE, LONDONDERRY
Here, quonset huts were sunk into the earth

base, it was not used by the Navy, but, to meet the changing situation, was turned over to the Army as a training camp, the seaplane repair and operating facilities being used by the Royal Air Force.

Lough Erne lies 35 miles southwest of Londonderry and 10 miles from the Atlantic coast of Northern Ireland. Shaped like a crescent, it is about 16 miles from tip to tip and 5 miles wide. Its ample, protected waters and its strategic location on the westernmost British land in the Isles, near the shipping lanes, made it an excellent site for a seaplane base.

The site selected was at Ely Island, 5 miles above Enniskillen, a small village at the end of the lake. On the opposite shore, at Killadeas, less than a mile across the Lough, it was planned to establish the repair base. A suitable site for the hospital was found at Necarne Castle, 8 miles north of Enniskillen and 3 miles from the Lough. The ammunition depot was located 3 miles farther north, at Kiltierney deer park.

Preliminary organization began in June 1941. By August 15, equipment, materials, and the contractor's employees had arrived and were ready to carry out the full construction program, which began with personnel quarters for two seaplane squadrons at Ely Island. Next undertaken were the projects at Killadeas, consisting of repair-base and operating facilities for two squadrons. Road construction was given first priority in all areas, as the soil had turned into thick mud by continuous rainfall. An adequate supply of rock was obtainable locally, so the principal roads were usable for heavy machines before the onset of winter weather.

In September, work at Ely and Killadeas was temporarily spurred by the announcement that the project would provide for eight squadrons instead of four. Further surveys were conducted and more property was requisitioned before this order was countermanded. There had been no interference with the construction in progress, however, and by mid-October, facilities for the original four squad-

LISAHALLY BASE, LONDONDERRY
Fueling wharf, with its pipe lines connected with the tank farm

rons were 60-per cent complete. The construction of additional roads then allowed work to begin on the hospital and the ammunition depot.

In November, when the end of the original work was in sight, further expansion was ordered to accommodate 1,000 men of a Marine battalion, for base defense, and after our entry into the war, the tempo of the job was further increased, until, in February, there were 1,700 men on the payroll, including 130 Americans.

However, Lough Erne was never used as a base for American seaplanes, as our participation in an all-ocean war required their immediate use elsewhere. The United States Army, already in the northern British Isles and beginning to concentrate troops which were to invade North Africa, saw here an excellently equipped and well-situated camp and hospital, and requested possession of the base upon its completion. The Royal Air Force also desired to use the camp. The base had been commissioned by the United States Navy, February 5,

1942, and shortly thereafter Chief of Naval Operations approved its temporary transfer to the Army. Later arrangements were made to allow the Royal Air Force use of the seaplane repair and operating facilities.

As the Army required an increase in dispensary facilities, the 200-bed hospital, then more than 90-percent complete, was expanded during April 1942 to 500 beds. Late in the month, the first Army forces relieved the naval CEC officer, who remained to effect the formal transfer on July 11. As rapidly as possible, construction was terminated and equipment and material not required by the Army were sent to Londonderry. By June 20, the contractor's forces had been released or withdrawn to Londonderry, and the Army was in full possession.

Although not so large as the projects at Londonderry or Rosneath, the facilities acquired by the Army were considerable. About 825 buildings of all types had been constructed, including nine major buildings, 10 miles of new road with three

WAREHOUSES IN THE LISAHALLY STORAGE AREA, LONDONDERRY

bridges, an ammunition dump, seven electric generators, and all the other facilities required for accommodating and feeding a community of more than 5,000 persons. The installations along the waterfront included 32,000 square feet of beaching area for seaplanes, four boat slips, six piers, and limited aircraft-overhaul shops, hangars, and storage buildings.

The changing fortunes of war precluded use of the base by the Navy, but the base proved of great value to the Army in staging the successful African assault. After that invasion, Lough Erne was officially turned over to the British Army and the Royal Air Force. It continued to serve as a base for anti-submarine patrols in the battle of the Atlantic, and as a British assembly and training camp in preparation for the landings in France.

Base II, Rosneath.—On the rugged western coast of Scotland, the Rosneath peninsula, 2 miles wide and 7 miles long, is bounded by Loch Long, Gare Loch, and the Firth of Clyde.

The deep-water channels of the Firth of Clyde and the adjacent lochs are excellent for ship operation. Steamers and small boats connecting the various Clyde ports call at Kilcreggan on the peninsula. Rail facilities, adequate only for small shipments, are located at Garelochhead, 7 miles, and Helensburgh, 14 miles from Rosneath. Rosneath is 40 miles by road from Glasgow, the main railroad, shipping, and industrial center of Scotland.

Hilly wooded land adjacent to waterside flat land afforded protective covering for American-built personnel buildings. The ground at different places was characterized by peat, conglomerate-rock, and blue clay which made drainage a problem. Almost-continuous rain greatly hindered all phases of the work. Historic Rosneath Castle, built in 1860 by the Duchess of Argyl, was used as a transient officers' quarters and mess.

Funds were made available for the construction of a naval base at Rosneath under the provisions of the Lend-Lease Act. Shipments of men and materials started in June 1941. Contract work continued until late in 1942, when completion was undertaken by the Seabees.

The original intention was to provide facilities for the operation and repair of destroyer squadrons and submarines, with accompanying fleet-supply facilities, ammunition and fuel storage installations, plus personnel accommodations for 4,500 men and hospital facilities for 600 men.

Locations near the village of Rosneath were selected for the industrial and storage areas, tank farm, and submarine operations area. The destroyer operating base was to be 2 miles north, along the shore of the loch. Separate sites up the peninsula could be used for the hospital and the ammunition depot.

A detachment of Royal Engineers was already engaged in building a shallow-water unloading jetty for barges along the Gare Loch waterfront when the naval forces arrived in July 1941. The contractors began work with 150 Irish workmen in August. Considerable delay on major projects was caused by lack of a rock crusher which was needed for road construction. The nearest commercial quarry was 25 miles away.

Pile-driving for the pier, and construction of personnel buildings, hospital, roads, reservoirs, and a water-filtering and purification plant were under way when the United States entered the war in December 1941.

The scope of the proposed work was reduced one-third at that time. It was decided to provide the submarine facilities and the repair shops as planned, but to delete destroyer facilities, especially as the critical machine tools were required elsewhere. The British agreed to install whatever tools were required for the modified program. Waterfront work for destroyers, which had not been started, was cancelled, and a substantial reduction was made in the size of supporting activities, the tank farm, hospital, and others.

In April 1942, all projects except the tank farm, materials for which had been delayed, were well under way, and the British were progressively occupying the base. Shortly thereafter, in June, the contractor's crew was shifted to the Dumbartonshire pipe line.

The decision to undertake the North African campaign occasioned the return of Rosneath to the United States Navy as a staging and training base for amphibious forces. It was commissioned a United States naval training base, August 24, 1942, and part of the contractor's force was returned to assume maintenance. Two important activities conducted there in the preparation for the invasion were a fire-fighting school and a practice-landing activity.

In October, contract work at the other bases was nearing an end. Lough Erne and Loch Ryan were finished, and Londonderry was nearly so. Emphasis in American work was swinging to the pipe line.

Rosneath was turned over to the British for occupancy, a detachment of Seabees remaining to assist in the maintenance of the base and of special United States equipment.

Facilities at Rosneath included a large wooden wharf which provided 4,750 lineal feet of deep-water berthing space and 1,500 lineal feet of shallow-water berthing space, including four submarine slips: 64 dolphin berths for LCM boats: a calibration range and degaussing slip; a marine railway for amphibious landing craft; an ammunition dump; 21 storage warehouses; a 200-bed hospital; eleven 10,000-barrel fuel-oil tanks and ten 14,400-gallon gasoline tanks with a distribution system to the waterfront; 153 air-raid shelters; housing and messing facilities for 4,500 officers and men (in 1944 Rosneath subsisted more than 6,300 officers and men); and 10 miles of water-bound macadam roadway. For the wharf and finger piers, 1,400 piles, from 65 to 80 feet long, and 400 piles, 80 to 90 feet long, were used. Many of the piles required splicing.

In this sparsely populated and relatively inaccessible section, adequate labor could be obtained only by preparing living quarters for the laborers. One of the first tasks was to build Camp Clachen, just north of Rosneath village, with facilities for 400 men. At the height of the work of preparing for British occupation in April and May 1942, there were 325 Americans, 1000 Irishmen, and 250 British working on the project.

Huts at Rosneath were divided into groups centering around galley units, each group designed for 500 men, on a basis of 10 men for each sleeping hut. Huts were placed in an irregular fashion among trees, with bomb shelters and miscellaneous service huts evenly distributed.

At the hospital, located a mile from Rosneath, on a hillside field overlooking the Firth of Clyde, 68 hospital huts were arranged in fan shape, with the galley unit at the hub, and connected by covered concrete walks. Portkil Hotel and its near-by cottage were repaired for use as quarters.

On the other side of the peninsula, 3 miles from Rosneath, ordnance was stored in 14 magazines, each 20 by 50 feet. Three houses were renovated for quarters.

Two water reservoirs were repaired and enlarged to provide a supply of 10,000,000 gallons. Because of the peaty nature of the surrounding soil, the water had to be both filtered and sterilized.

One result of plans for reduction of the base was the modification in orders so that certain material could be procured locally whenever possible. These materials included electrical equipment, gasoline-storage tanks, brick, cement, concrete aggregates, and drain pipe.

The 29th Seabees, which arrived in November and December of 1942, took over construction and maintenance work as the last of the contractor's force was withdrawn to the pipeline project.

Work done by the Seabees included completion of a marine railway and erection of four workshops, 20 nissen huts for quarters, eight 10,000-barrel fuel tanks, two pumping stations and fuel lines, a laundry, and roads, as well as the renovating of buildings for a hospital and administration offices.

When a temporary lull in European naval operations occurred after the successful accomplishment of the North African venture, need for the continued use of Rosneath by our Navy, for the moment subsided, and it was agreed to return the base to the British, with some reservation, on February 1, 1943.

Except for piers and quarters required for a United States Navy submarine squadron which continued to operate, the base was placed under British control. All except a maintenance force of 230 Seabees were transferred to Londonderry to relieve contract civilians there. The 29th Battalion was replaced by the 97th in September 1943, when the 29th went to southern England to build bases in preparation for the invasion of Normandy.

Then, on August 20, 1943, Rosneath was recommissioned to act as a receiving station for United States naval activities in the United Kingdom. Between August 1943 and August 1944, thousands of men were received there from the United States and transferred to various ships and stations in the United Kingdom. Rosneath also acted as a training, supply, and maintenance base for large units such as the gunfire support group of the 11th Amphibious Forces, with 1900 men, three units of 1500 each, and another unit with 1250 men.

Up to the time of the Normandy invasion the harbor at Rosneath was continuously occupied by ships and craft which were being repaired and furnished with supplies. After the invasion, hundreds of survivors were accommodated, 3,200 in the month of June. Later, 2,000 to 3,000 men were processed each month for transfer.

With the war's end fast approaching in Europe, the need for the base declined and men and materials were shipped to more active areas. The last major work was the construction of a large Red Cross club for the recreation of personnel at this isolated post.

The base was officially closed on May 5, 1945, and in June the Seabees were withdrawn, with the exception of one officer and a few men who remained for a month or so to instruct the British in the use of American equipment. Thus, for the final time the Rosneath base was returned to the British, and the United States Navy's partnership with the British in Scotland was dissolved after four years of close cooperation.

Dumbartonshire Pipe Line (Rosneath). — The rapid progress which was made by Navy contractors in the construction of the four bases in the United Kingdom made it evident, late in 1941, that skilled American engineers and mechanics soon would be available from these high-priority projects. It was decided that they might well be used to augment the facilities existing in Great Britain for the distribution of petroleum products. Enlisting the assistance of major American oil companies, and in consultation with the British Admiralty and Petroleum Board, the Bureau of Yards and Docks planned a pipe line in Dumbartonshire, Scotland.

This 25-mile pipe line, a part of the Gare Loch installation, was laid between Old Kilpatrick (Bowling) and Loch Long, off the Firth of Clyde. The purpose of the line was to provide a connection between the pipeline network already installed between Edinburgh and Glasgow, and Old Kilpatrick, and to extend this connection to Finnart on Loch Long, where discharging of tankers and fueling of surface craft might proceed in an unrestricted channel which could not be closed by sinkings through bombing attacks.

The pipe line was a double line, consisting of a 12-inch line for fuel oil and an 8-inch line for refined products. The terminus for refined products was in existing space at the British Petroleum Board tank farm at Old Kilpatrick. In addition, there was an 8-inch branch line which ran south the length of the peninsula, some 7 miles, to serve the tank farm at Rosneath.

The system was designed for high-pressure operation (the first in the British Isles) without intermediate pumping stations, and it was to have a capacity of 42,000 barrels per day through the 12-inch line and 30,000 barrels through the 8-inch

ROSNEATH, SCOTLAND
Dock area at the Seabee base; tanks and industrial section in the center background

line. The 25-mile route rose from near sea-level at both ends to an elevation of more than 600 feet at the summit. Pumping plants capable of handling pressures up to 750 pounds per square inch were required for both lines at Finnart, and, as the system provided for two-way flow. they were duplicated for the 8-inch line at Bowling and for the 12-inch at Old Kilpatrick. At the Finnart terminus, on Loch Long, other requisite facilities also were installed: a tanker berth (reinforced-concrete pier with 35-foot depth of water at low tide), 110,000 barrels of fuel-oil storage (with boilers for steam-heating the oil), and storage capacity for 75,000 barrels of lighter oils. The two fuel-oil tanks (55.000 barrels each) had been removed from the old Teapot Dome installation. Because of the acid condition of the soil. a bitumastic felt-wrapped coating was applied at a coating plant brought over from the United States.

Installation began in May. As work on higher-priority projects was "topping out," more materials became available for this project, and it was possible to build the force up to 1,800 men. Just as the actual laying of pipe got under way in August, it was necessary for some of the contract personnel to

undertake maintenance of Rosneath because of its return to the United States Navy.

Though every effort had been made to get as much accomplished as possible during the favorable weather and long summer days, the task was not easy on the main lines. A more difficult terrain for pipeline construction could scarcely be imagined than this route through the southern highlands of Scotland. Sparsity of adequate highways necessitated the building of construction roads, a task which was made especially difficult by rugged country, peat bogs, and subsoil drains. These drains, which were spaced 25 feet apart. presented a dual problem. Not only did they have to be replaced in workable order, but also, when cut by the ditchers, they had to be repaired immediately because they poured water into trenches dug for the line. The incessant rainfall, 5 to 10 inches per month, kept the earth perpetually saturated.

The installation was 70-percent complete by February 1943, but pumps and special equipment had not yet arrived from the United States when the contract was terminated for the civilian forces on March 31, 1943. In April. the Rosneath detachment of the 29th Seabees, aided by five officers and

TANK FARM. ROSNEATH, SCOTLAND
Photograph taken at the Seabee base in August 1944

194 men from the battalion who had completed their work at Londonderry, set out to finish the project. Shipments of material arrived. By July, both lines had been completed and tested, and the installations were turned over to the British Petroleum Board for maintenance and operation. On July 31, 1943, all Seabee personnel were withdrawn.

Loch Ryan. The original plan for a naval seaplane base of Loch Ryan, at Stranraer, was to provide facilities identical with those at Lough Erne, in Ireland. Its location, overlooking the North Channel and the Irish Sea, made it an ideal springboard for seaplanes guarding the western approaches to the British Isles. Because of subsequent expansion in Ireland and reduction in Scotland, Loch Ryan was outstripped in size by Lough Erne, and eventually was the smallest of the four bases.

Loch Ryan, a narrow bay, 8 miles long and 2 miles wide, on the southern tip of Scotland, is almost enclosed by a hook of land. Just south of the Firth of Clyde, the bay lies only 25 miles from Ireland. Between lay a favorite hunting-ground for German submarines, the North Channel, which led from the Atlantic Ocean to the Irish Sea.

Engineering problems were somewhat simplified by the local terrain. At Wig Bay, on the western shore of the Loch, a headland narrowed its neck

to less than a mile, and open fields sloped gently upward from the level shore to provide suitable sites for seaplane installations; wooded areas inland furnished excellent dispersal area. Stranraer, a little village at the base of Loch Ryan, served as principal terminus for construction cargoes.

The Royal Air Force was already operating seaplanes from the Loch and was occupying a considerable stretch of the shore, so that it was necessary to pair the new squadron areas to the north and south of the Royal Air Force location. In the wooded area behind the shore, near station headquarters at Corsewall House, was built the administration area for headquarters personnel, and farther north, part of the ammunition-storage magazines. Seaplane facilities built near Corsewall included five nose hangars, sixty-six 5,000-gallon tanks for aviation gasoline and diesel oil, and 1,800,000 square feet of mesh-surfaced parking area.

The main personnel camps, for 1500 men, the 700-bed hospital, and the remainder of the ammunition depot were scattered 4 miles to the south and west, around Lochnaw Castle, near the middle of the 5-mile-wide peninsula which separates Loch Ryan from the North Channel.

With previous experience in Ireland indicating the desirability of overcoming mud as soon as possible, the bulk of the rough road construction in the Corsewall area was begun in July 1941 and was complete by the end of August. Rented rock-crushing equipment supplemented local purchases of stone for this operation.

In spite of this start, it was not feasible to expand the scope of the construction as rapidly as might have been desired. Other bases, particularly Londonderry, had first priority, and the trickle of materials reaching Loch Ryan was small.

Early efforts were confined to essential projects around Corsewall. In September the contractor's force moved into newly completed huts, and as rapidly as they could be quartered, three companies of Royal Engineers arrived to unload shipments of construction materials and to supplement the scarce local labor. By the time October rains made work difficult, the Corsewall projects were well out

of the mud, and grading had commenced for the operations area south of the Royal Air Force station, as well as at the main hut-camp at Lochnaw.

The United States' entry into the war had an immediate and dual effect on the project. Not only did the rapid completion of essential naval facilities in the British Isles appear imperative, but even higher priorities had to be assigned to the Irish bases. The result was a drastic reduction in the scope of the work at Loch Ryan. Operating facilities for two squadrons, planned south of the Royal Air Force station, were deleted, as well as half of the ammunition depot planned at Lochnaw and one-third of the personnel area there. Work on the remaining projects was continued with redoubled vigor.

The first of the year 1942 saw construction pro-

INDUSTRIAL SECTION AT THE SEABEE BASE, ROSNEATH
Tank farm in the background

gressing as rapidly as receipts of American materials (via Londonderry) and the weather would allow. Camp facilities at Corsewall were now adequate to quarter as large a labor force as could be employed profitably, and there were more than 800 men. including 110 Americans and 450 Royal Engineers, at work. Pressure was exerted to complete remaining projects in the Lochnaw area, the 200-bed hospital and 1000-man camp. in addition to the Corsewall work.

By March, broad strategic considerations had forced the decision to alter the future of the two flying-boat bases. No United States Navy seaplanes were to operate from the British Isles.

As a result of this change in plan the Navy transferred the base to the Royal Air Force to augment their facilities at the Loch. In order that the immediate value of the installations could be fully realized, it was agreed that as rapidly as each facility was completed it would be transferred to the Royal Air Force and put into operation. The Corsewall camp was occupied in May by 600 Royal Air Force personnel, who took over the squadron operating and repair areas along Wig Bay.

This marked the turning point. More than three-quarters of the job was done. Steady progress continued, but the pace slackened as personnel and equipment were directed to the Dumbartonshire pipe line and to the more immediately essential work at Londonderry and Rosneath. During September the last of the contractor's American force was gradually withdrawn to other jobs. On September 24, the formal transfer was completed with the proviso. as at Lough Erne, that. if necessary, it would be returned, intact, to the United States Forces.

Work at Loch Ryan, the smallest of the United Kingdom contract bases, was completed under difficulties heightened by its isolated location and the low priority assigned. In all, 610 buildings were constructed. including seven major structures. and 10 miles of surfaced roads were laid. As at the other bases the utilities and services installed would suffice for a small city, in this case one of 2500 population. In the seaplane-operating areas, almost two million square feet of steel mesh had been laid. and there was fuel-storage capacity for 330,000 gallons of petroleum products.

It was never necessary for Loch Ryan to be returned to the United States Navy for its European operations. However, the increasing part played by seaplanes in waging and winning the vital battle against the submarine menace was aided in considerable measure by the facilities of this base.

CHAPTER 20

THE MEDITERRANEAN AREA

The start of World War II saw the balance of power in North Africa divided between the French on the west and the Italians and British in the east. The Italian invasion of Ethiopia in 1936 marked the opening of a new and bloody era in the history of North Africa which was to continue until May 12, 1943, the day that saw the final capitulation of the last remnants of the Axis forces in that area.

British and Axis armies struggled for two years in a see-saw brand of warfare across the sands and desert wastes of Libya and Egypt to gain control of the transport lines of the Mediterranean and the traffic routes of the Suez Canal. The entry of the United States into the war found the Axis forces capturing Bengasi and opening a drive which pushed the British back to El Alamein, just 27 miles west of Alexandria and the Suez Canal. Here the British stood throughout the summer of 1942, while the United States shipped nearly a billion dollars' worth of supplies, planes, tanks, and armored trucks to its ally.

In October 1942, the Allies launched a full-scale drive that cleared Axis forces from Egypt and pursued them into western Libya. Timed with this drive, on November 7, 1942, a powerful American force landed on the Mediterranean and Atlantic coasts of the French colonies in the west. This was called "the greatest amphibious operation in history," and was launched from an invasion armada of 850 vessels which split to strike the African coast at Casablanca, at Oran, and at Algiers, simultaneously.

The mission of the Navy in this campaign, as in any campaign, was to transport safely the Army and its materials across the open sea, to provide adequate offshore protection for our supply lines afloat and our forces ashore, and, at the same time, to prevent the enemy navy from performing this same function in behalf of its own war effort.

As soon as the initial assault was concluded and land became available, it became necessary to establish bases at which the ships of the Navy could put in for fuel, munitions, and supplies, and could obtain repairs from battle and operative damage, and from which, as the front progressed, additional assaults could be launched or supported.

Included in the invasion forces at Casablanca were members of the second section of the 17th Construction Battalion, later augmented by the second section of the 53rd Construction Battalion and reformed to constitute the 120th Construction Battalion. Early in 1943, in the Oran area, the 54th Battalion was put ashore at the town of Arzeu, which is approximately 30 miles east of the city of Oran, but connected with it by a fine highway. Other members of the 17th Battalion landed at the Moroccan ports of Fedala and Safi. These were the only full battalions which were ordered to the Mediterranean area, as most shore establishments were to be constructed and manned by the Army.

The primary function of these units was to cooperate with the Army in establishing a port of entry and in clearing invasion damage. The initial movements of material and construction personnel were held to a minimum in view of the uncertainty of the enterprise at that time.

As success crowned our efforts and the campaign continued, additional men and materials were sent for the construction of adequate naval facilities. In April 1943, the 70th Construction Battalion left the United States for Arzeu. In the French Moroccan area, the gateway, as it were, to North Africa, a complete naval operating base was set up in and about the city of Casablanca. At the same time at Port Lyautey, which lies approximately 75 miles north, toward the Strait of Gibraltar, a naval air station (with blimp facilities for submarine detection) and an advanced amphibious training base were built. At Agadir, several hundred miles to the south, an additional naval air facility was established. Section bases were established at Fedala and Safi.

Eastward in Algeria, the Oran area was devel-

NAVAL SUPPLY DEPOT AND CAMP, ORAN

oped into a major ship-repair base, with vast hospital facilities and storage areas. Originally a major French naval base, utilizing one of the few harbors offered by the peculiar shoreline of northwestern Africa, Oran was a natural site for an operating base for our fleet units in the western Mediterranean and as a base for supplying those forces which were soon to conduct amphibious operations against Sicily and, finally, Italy and France.

After the enemy had been completely forced out of Africa, in May 1943, various training bases, in preparation for the assaults soon to be launched across the Mediterranean, were established at Bizerte, Tunis, and Ferryville in Tunisia, and at Mers-el-Kabir, Beni-Saf, and Tenes in Algeria.

The small Algerian towns of Cherchel, Bone, Nemours, and Mostaganem, sites used as assembly points for the formation of the mighty Allied invasion armadas, became the scene of practice invasions. Detachments from the 54th, 70th, and 120th Construction Battalions were responsible for whatever naval establishments were required, but these towns required little in the way of installations. A ship's salvage unit, a naval radio station, and a fuel depot were established in Algiers, which

was also the site of the headquarters of Vice Admiral H. K. Hewitt, USN, Commander Naval Forces in Northwest African Waters. It was at Oran and vicinity that most of the construction work was done by the Seabees in Algeria.

Oran

Oran, with a pre-war population of 200,000, the capital and principal seaport of Algeria, lies almost on the Greenwich meridian on the north coast of Algeria. The city proper occupies a shelf about 450 feet above the level of the Mediterranean and commands a well-protected harbor where large ships may anchor. The port had been well developed by the French as one of their major naval stations. The harbor at Mers-el-Kabir, 5 miles west of Oran, is similarly large and well protected; the one at Arzeu, 30 miles east of Oran, is adequate for ships drawing 20 feet. The entire area, serviced by excellent highways, was destined to play a large and vital role in our winning of the Mediterranean.

The principal sources of water in North Africa were wells of many types, each requiring different equipment. In Oran, most of the wells were deep and required deep-well turbine pumps. Although all water from the wells was contaminated and had excessive hardness, nevertheless, it was infinitely superior to that distributed throughout the city lines since the city supply had a saline content which made it unsuitable for drinking. Consequently, the water-supply requirements for the

NAVAL RECEIVING STATION, ORAN

American forces were taken over from the local authorities and operated by the United States military forces under proper medical supervision.

Available areas for Navy housing, storage, and supply were limited. Consequently, it was necessary to take over various buildings in scattered locations throughout the city and in some cases, in order to simplify distribution and control, to erect temporary buildings. In one instance, in order to provide adequate supply-storage space, the Navy was forced to construct a supply depot. The 120th Battalion erected this depot, utilizing 56 standard 40-by-100-foot utility buildings. By combining two for each building, end to end, twenty-eight 200-foot warehouses were obtained. Three 20-by-48-foot quonset huts were erected for general storage and one 40-by-200-foot quonset was erected for the receiving of shipping. Proper electric lighting and heating provisions were made; proportionate outside storage space was graded; and concrete access roads were built.

In addition, storage facilities were taken over in approximately 14 other locations in the city. These, however, were all excellent buildings and required only minor modifications of the structures. It was

necessary, however, to construct refrigerator storehouses in the port area. Two storehouses were erected, each of approximatly 48,000 cubic feet, of cinder-block construction with concrete flooring and tile roof. These were the only permanent-type Navy structures erected in Oran.

The next large building program undertaken was that of a camp for a navy supply depot. This work was performed chiefly by the 70th and 120th Battalions. The camp, south of Oran, consisted of 81 quonset huts, adequately supplied with city power and sewage disposal facilities, and, with the aid of additional tents, at one period housed as many as 1,500 personnel.

A 500-bed hospital (U.S. Navy Base Hospital 9), constructed by the 120th Battalion, 3 miles south

MOBILE HOSPITAL CAMP, ORAN

of Oran, consisted of 110 quonset huts. The hospital was equipped with ample electric power, water-supply, and sewerage systems. Covered concrete walks connected the huts.

Adjacent to the base camp, a receiving station for 1,500 was erected, consisting of 75 quonset huts. The receiving station obtained its own electric energy from advance-base-type electric generators, and shared the water-supply system jointly with the hospital. The electric power in the city of Oran was 50-cycle, 110-volt; and due to the inability of the power companies to expand during the active years of the war, the reliability of the French system was not good. The U. S. Army took over

PONTOON CAUSEWAY ABOUT TO GO OVER THE SIDE OF AN LST, ARZEU

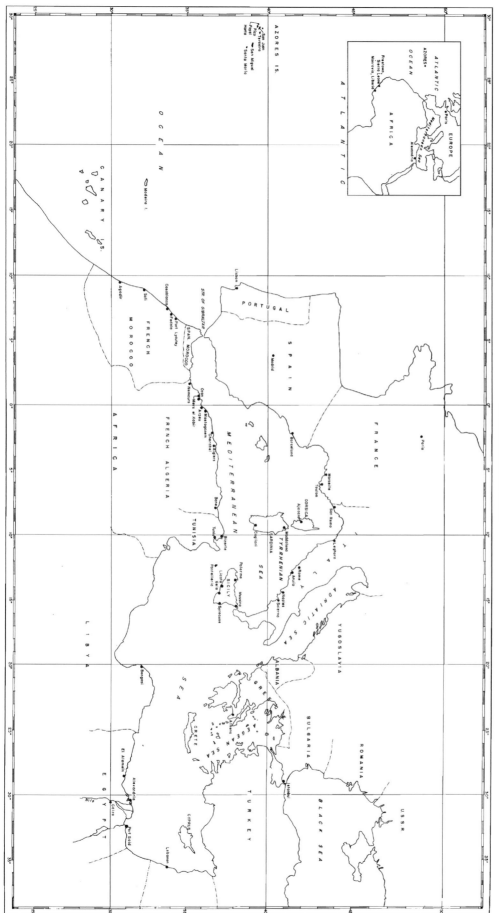

MEDITERRANEAN AREA

control of the powerhouse and dictated which lines were to be cut out when necessary. Under such conditions, it was of real importance that standby electric power be provided at most places and that advance-base-type electric generators be fully utilized at others.

In Oran, the 120th Battalion erected a 124-tent camp for its own use and constructed 17 quonset huts for general usage such as ship's stores, mess halls, etc. At St. Remy, a small town approximately 10 miles southeast of Oran, the 120th built an ammunition depot consisting of 29 magazines.

In Mers-el-Kabir a standard quonset hut was set up for use in sound attack teaching. Other operations there were housed in renovated requisitioned buildings.

In Arzeu, 148 quonset huts were erected for housing personnel. Incorporated within the area were complete galley, dispensary, and allied facilities. Various necessary buildings were acquired by the Navy from the French through the medium of the U. S. Army. These acquisitions were made under the provisions of Lend-Lease agreements.

Upon the completion of the organization of the base at Oran, CBMU 513 was ordered to the base to care for maintenance, repairs, and transportation.

CBMU 513, consisting of one officer and 100 enlisted men, arrived in Oran on August 14, 1943. It worked with the 120th Battalion, until June 3, 1944, when the 120th returned to the United States and the 513th CBMU, whose complement had been increased to 228 enlisted men and five officers on March 9, 1944, took over the entire camp unit. On June 15, 1945, CBMU 513 was relieved by CBMU 626, which was soon relieved, in its turn, by a small detachment of CBMU 567.

On October 14, 1943, Detachment 1017, a stevedore company, composed of five officers and 254 enlisted men, arrived at the naval supply depot in Oran. Its prime function was to ease the stevedoring burdens of the Army at Oran harbor.

After V-E day, our need for Oran disappeared, and the port was gradually returned to the French. On June 26, 1945, the receiving station was decommissioned, and, one month later, so was the naval station. On July 29, 1945, the naval operating base was disestablished as such and reorganized as a naval detachment. The naval magazine was disestablished September 7, 1945. On September 20, 1945, Commander Naval Forces, Northwest African Waters, proposed to the Chief of Naval Operations that the naval supply depot, Base Hospital 9, and

the medical storehouse be decommissioned on September 30, 1945, leaving a naval detachment to assume custody of all surplus, pending final disposition.

By October 22, 1945, all stores, with the exception of medical supplies, had been concentrated in a single group of warehouses. Medical supplies were stored in a fireproof building in town. Pools of excess motor vehicles and heavy construction equipment were being maintained at harborside and transfers were being made to the Army whenever ship space became available. All stores were boxed, inventoried, and ready for sale. Sales to the French Provisional Government had amounted to $428,851.12 as of October 6, 1945. Oran surpluses of both real and personal property amounted to $6,946,209 of which $6,694,209 had been reported to the Office of Foreign Liquidations Committee. Representatives of this group estimated that disposal of all surpluses could be effected within 60 days of receipt of surplus declarations from the Navy, permitting a satisfactory closeout by December 1, 1945.

All properties occupied by the Navy had been obtained by the Real Estate Section of the U. S. Army, and settlements were handled by the Army through reverse Lend-Lease.

Arzeu

The naval station at Arzeu was used in the early days of the war as an assembly point as well as an advance base. The base made a material contribution to the amphibious war in many ways. It was here that the 1005th and 1006th Detachments perfected the pontoon causeways which proved to be such a valuable contribution to the amphibious landings which later took place at Sicily, Salerno, and Anzio. It was here, also, that the methods of launching and beaching these causeways were developed.

The purpose of the pontoon causeways was to bridge approximately 500 feet of water between the LST's and the shore on the shallow beaches of Sicily and Italy. LST's would run aground about 500 feet from shore, but the water would still be 6 feet deep at their ramps, and there was a 300-foot stretch of water to be crossed before it was shallow enough for vehicles to "wade" to the beach, 30 inches of water being about the maximum depth at which our vehicles could operate in safety. Captain John N. Laycock, CEC, USN, deviser of the Navy pontoon, hit upon the idea of using two 175-foot pontoon assemblies and overlapping them. This made their combined length adjustable, strong enough to withstand surf action, and long enough to fill the 300-foot gap.

The causeways proved themselves in a demonstration at Narragansett Bay. Seabees rode on two strings of pontoons which an LST towed toward the beach. When the LST ran aground, the pontoon strings were cut adrift and continued the journey beachward under their own momentum. The forward end of the lead pontoon grounded in 2-foot water; the after end of the trailing pontoon had a line attached to the bow door of the LST. When the causeway was grounded, it was disconnected in the middle, and the trailing end pulled back to the ramp of the LST, in "slide-rule" fashion. When the entire length of water had been bridged, the two 175-foot sections were clamped together again, and the LST could be discharged.

This method was further perfected at Arzeu and Bizerte in that the pontoon strings were carried on the sides of the LST's and dropped in the water just before the ship began its run to the beach. This permitted the LST to proceed to the scene of action at full speed. At Sicily, both methods were tried, but after that invasion, the method of towing the pontoon-strings was abandoned entirely.

CBD 1005 and CBD 1006 arrived at Arzeu early in May 1943. CBD 1005 set up headquarters, and CBD 1006 left a small unit on detached temporary duty at Arzeu, detachment headquarters being located at Bizerte.

On November 18, 1943, the 578th CBMU, composed of two officers and 100 enlisted men, was formed from the 70th Construction Battalion. This unit reported to Arzeu and conducted maintenance and public works functions until it was returned to the United States on January 17, 1945.

In May 1945, all naval installations not previously removed and transported to other American activities were transferred to the French under Lend-Lease.

Bizerte

Through the invasions of Sicily and Italy, Detachment 1006 used Bizerte as its base, spending the time between invasions perfecting the methods of "momentum beaching" of pontoon causeways and repairing battle-damaged pontoons. Detachment 1005 was assigned the job of constructing the 175-foot pontoon sections. During the month of

June 1943, CBD 1005 moved its headquarters from Arzeu to Bizerte.

The base was decommissioned in May 1945. All naval installations, spare parts, and equipment were removed to other American activities except one 10,000-barrel steel tank, with fittings, which was turned over to the French Navy, under Lend-Lease arrangements. All leased and requisitioned property was returned to the owners.

Port Lyautey

Naval activities in French Morocco consisted of a naval air station at Port Lyautey, a naval operating base at Casablanca, an advance base at Agadir, and an air facility at Dakar.

NAS, Port Lyautey was located 2 miles north of the city. Prior to its occupation by United States forces, this station had been a permanent station of the French Naval Air Forces. Construction begun by the French in 1934 included among its installations two surfaced runways, two hangars, and a barracks for 500 men.

Occupancy by U. S. forces began on November 10, 1942, when Army troops invaded Port Lyautey. The 21st Engineer Aviation Regiment was in charge of construction and improvement of facilities from that time until early February 1943, when the Navy assumed control. The 120th Seabees handled construction at the station after that date.

The Port Lyautey airfield was built upon an alluvial deposit of clay, fine sand, and silt, 12 feet above the average low-water elevation of the Sebou River. The maximum monthly high-water level was $4\frac{1}{2}$ feet below the average level of the field, making an elaborate system of underground drainage necessary. Two existing runways were extended to 6,000 feet and a seaplane ramp, pile-supported, was built. A seaplane pier of pontoons was also provided.

Electric power was obtained from two sources, a local utility and a Seabee-constructed central power plant on the station. A group of 50-kw and 75-kw diesel-operated generators was used. A camel barn, used by the French as a stable for the Camel Corps, and centrally located for power-distribution, was reconditioned. Concrete floors and bases for generators were built. Generators were set loose on the foundations with 2-inch cork-block cushions to prevent crawling and to facilitate easy removal for repair or replacement. All generators were synchronized and operated at 220 volts through

AIRFIELD AT PORT LYAUTEY
Included facilities for landplanes and seaplanes, and temporary facilities for blimps

homemade switch panels, constructed by Seabees from material salvaged under War Shipping Administration authority, from Liberty ships at Gibraltar. Three 100-kva transformers were obtained from the Army to complete the station. Sixty-cycle three-phase power was distributed at 5,500 volts to most points on the station. Transformers allowed distribution of 220-volt or 110-volt current. The output of the station varied from 300 to 650 kilowatts, depending upon the needs.

An agreement between the city of Port Lyautey and the Navy provided that the base be furnished the required quantity of water. Dry periods during the summer months made water available for only

12 hours per day, with shut-off periods usually occurring at times when most needed. Moreover, the quality of this water was not satisfactory to the Medical Department, and a project was started to develop sufficient water from wells, dug within the confines of the base.

The French had attempted to develop water on the base, but the first well sunk produced only 45 gallons per minute. Seabee construction of wells in the immediate vicinity of the one dug by the French produced 250 gpm, and later, in 1945, a well was dug in the same general location, producing 750 gpm. A reservoir, in addition to the 55,000-gallon concrete tank installed by the French,

HOSPITAL AREA, PORT LYAUTEY
Personnel barracks and messhall area in upper right

was provided by erection of 100 standard pontoon sections connected together.

Dredging had to be carried on twice a year to insure adequate deep water at the seaplane ramp and pier. The dredging was accomplished with the only dredge available in French Morocco. Approximately 65,000 cubic yards of dredging was accomplished yearly.

A 100-bed dispensary, including housing and diet-kitchen facilities, was completed on the station in April 1945. Units of five standard quonset huts were joined together in an H-shaped structure, with hollow-tile buildings providing connections under cover between quonsets. Hollow-tile buildings also housed the heating, plumbing, and reception services. The dispensary could be converted into a 166-bed hospital without too much crowding.

Warehouse facilities until early 1945 were located in the port area, 2 miles from the base. To provide adequate security against pilferage, new storehouses were built on the base itself. These were constructed of hollow tile or concrete-block sides, timber trusses, and red tile roofs. A large quonset hut was erected in the warehouse area to provide for paint storage. The new warehouse site was connected to the harbor area by rail.

Buildings constructed by the Seabees at Port Lyautey were sufficient to supply the housing and operational needs of an air station with an overall complement of 4,000 men. Some Arab labor was employed from the immediate vicinity. As many as 1,200 Italians were also used at one time on the base. Payment of Arab and Italian personnel was handled by the Army, but all administration and work assignment was under the control of Seabee officers.

Following the end of hostilities in Europe in May 1945, the Army Transport Command was ordered to set up a staging area at Port Lyautey for processing troops returning to the United States by air. Troops were to be flown from Europe by B-17, and processed at Port Lyautey for further transfer by C-47 to the United States.

This was known as the "Green Project," and called for a tremendous increase in facilities at the air station. In less than one month, the Seabees had completed the construction of new buildings for traffic, billeting, finance, personnel, weather communications, navigation, mess halls, and warehouses. The "Green Project" was characterized in Washington as "the most rapid route-capacity build-up in ATC history." Ten standard-size quonset huts were built for administration buildings; six over-size quonsets were constructed for post-exchange, mess hall, galley, Red Cross office, and warehouse; 4,900 lineal feet of 18-inch pipe were laid for sewerage; and 2,800 lineal feet of 4-inch pipe were laid in the construction of a water system. Pontoons were used to construct a 100,000-gallon water-storage reservoir.

PONTOON CRANE IN ACTION AT PORT LYAUTEY
Seabees helped raise the SS *Belgien*, scuttled in the Sebou River

The transfer of Agadir to the Army in July 1945, and the decommissioning of Casablanca in August 1945, left Port Lyautey as the only U. S. Naval activity in French Morocco. CBMU 566, which had relieved the 120th Battalion in the French Morocco area in February 1944, was decommissioned on November 15, 1945, and maintenance of Port Lyautey was then left to general service, with a CEC officer as Public Works Officer.

Agadir

Agadir was established as an advanced aircraft base of Fleet Air Wing Fifteen in early April 1943, its mission being to establish an advance base for submarine patrol in the vicinity of lower French Morocco and the Canary Islands.

United States naval forces maintained operational control of the field.

Development of the Agadir base, performed by both Seabees and the French Public Works Department, involved an expenditure of $600,000 which was processed through reciprocal aid. The first improvement to the field was a 5,200-foot all-weather runway. Operations and billeting facilities were in tents until June 1943, when it became apparent that the Navy would remain in Agadir indefinitely, and permanent structures were built. These included storerooms, administration offices, class rooms, a control tower, and quarters and messing facilities for officers and enlisted men. All construction was of masonry and timber from local sources.

VP73 AND HEDRON 15 PERSONNEL AT QUARTERS, AGADIR, AWAITING DISTINGUISHED FLYING CROSS AWARDS

AIRCRAFT MAINTENANCE GROUP HUTS AT AGADIR
Note plane on ramp

Naval facilities at Agadir were turned over to Army Transport Command in June 1945.

Casablanca

When the Allied Forces invaded North Africa in November 1942, landings were made at Casablanca and a complete naval operating base was set up there. Construction of Casablanca shore facilities included establishment of barracks, galley and mess hall and a warehouse; building of additional barracks in a theatre; remodeling of a hospital; setting up of an ammunition depot; installment of radio facilities; maintenance of buildings taken over for officers' quarters; development of storage facilities; conversion of a fishing ramp into a small marine railway; construction of a large ship-repair shop and assembly point for pontoon barges and cranes; construction of harbor entrance control posts and signal towers; development of water supply; oil line and tank construction; and maintenance of facilities.

This base, which served also as headquarters for the Morocco Sea Coast Frontier Forces, was maintained by Seabee crews until the order for decommissioning on August 1, 1945. Disposition of all equipment, facilities, and materials at Casablanca was simple; it was turned over to the Army, which

assumed full responsibility for all future disposition of material or facilities. Seabee personnel engaged in maintenance of shore facilities at Casablanca were returned to Port Lyautey.

Fedala and Safi

In the early stages of the invasion of North Africa, bases at Fedala and Safi were set up with comparable facilities on one-third the scale of Casablanca. They served as section bases and were operated for only a short period of time.

Sicilian Landings

The general plans of the Allies called for the use of Sicily as a stepping stone to the European mainland. There was only one barrier to be hurdled first; the little island of Pantelleria stood midway between Tunisia and Sicily. General Carl Spaatz, Commander of the Northwest African Air Forces, attacked Pantelleria from the air. Less than a month after Tunisia fell, Pantelleria surrendered.

On July 10, 1943, our forces moved up from the African bases. With an invasion force of some 3200 landing-craft and ships the Allies landed men and equipment on the southern side of Sicily. It was a perilous undertaking, with inclement weather adding to the difficulties. The landings were

CASABLANCA DOCK AREA AND HARBOR ENTRANCE
Seabees rehabilitated the dockside area which had been damaged in the shelling of the *Jean Bart*, berthed at the
Mol du Commerce (left center background)

made between the cities of Licata and Syracuse, but after bitter resistance, our troops fanned out and within ten days held nearly half of the island; within 38 days the conquest of Sicily was complete.

Seabees played a vital role in the initial landings on Sicily as well as in subsequent consolidation and development of the island.

The amphibious invasion of Sicily presented a different problem from that of North Africa where the invaders had a choice of many landing beaches widely scattered between Algiers and Casablanca. Sicily had a few suitable beaches on the northern shore, which, to the enemy, was a logical place for the Allies to make an invasion attempt.

First Allied plans called for an assault on the northern shores of the island, east and west of Palermo. However, reconnaissance pictures showed that this was just what the enemy was expecting,

and that formidable defenses were being built. Accordingly, the landings were made on the southern coast, where the wide shallow-water shelf had given the enemy a false sense of security. The 175-foot pontoon causeways perfected at Arzeu and Bizerte were the prime factor in permitting our forces to make the sally against the southern shores. The causeways were manned by three platoons from the 54th Construction Battalion, one platoon from the 1005th Construction Battalion Detachment, and twelve platoons from the 1006th Construction Battalion Detachment.

The causeway pontoons worked under tremendous difficulties caused by both the flat beach condition and the high winds. When the invasion fleet arrived off the Sicilian coast at 0200 on July 10, 1943, a five-foot surf was running around both Gela and Licata. The Germans were confident that we would not attempt to land, and, indeed, the decision as to whether or not to land hung in the balance for several hours.

Upon orders to go in, LST 389, carrying a causeway and a platoon of Seabees, opened her bow doors and lowered her ramp to let the DUKW's out. The high waves broke the ramp chains so that the bow doors could not be closed. The run to the beach had to be made under these conditions, the tank deck being two feet under water. All the lead LST's experienced similar difficulties, and Seabees left ashore were soaking wet and without food. During 23 days of round-the-clock work, the Seabees unloaded more than 10,000 vehicles over the causeways.

One difficult operation prior to the actual landing was that of charting the channels, shoals, and bars at the landing points. Amphibious DUKW's and some depth-sounding devices were first employed for this work at Gela, Sicily. In a short time after leaving the LST's, the channels were charted and marked. One instance of the value of such a precaution occurred where a sand bar was located 150 yards from shore, at a depth of only 2 feet. However, just past the bar the water deepened to 8 or 10 feet. Had landing boats started to unload on that bar, undoubtedly many lives would have been lost.

After the charting, the DUKW's were efficiently used for handling causeways, transporting supplies from ship-to-shore-to-firing-line, and evacuating wounded.

At Sicily, the Seabees not only performed their assigned tasks of getting motorized equipment and supplies ashore, but also aided in other ways. Following closely behind the first wave of invaders, the Seabees saved the lives of troops aboard a bombed and blazing LST by throwing a pontoon bridge between their vessel and the stricken ship. Over this makeshift causeway, between 150 and 200 Allied soldiers raced to the Seabee craft and safety.

When one of the causeway pontoon bridges had been blown up, the Seabees went to work as a salvage unit, and, in the first day, salvaged approximately 100 small boats which had broached on the beach.

Palermo Operating Base

With the capitulation of Sicily, elements of the 120th Battalion, some of whom were participants in the original assault, were sent into the city of

Palermo, where it was decided to establish the third U. S. Naval Operating Base in the western Mediterranean area, the others being at Casablanca and Oran. The three bases would provide complete naval coverage of the western Mediterranean Sea, with Casablanca and Palmero equidistant from Oran but in opposite directions.

Located on the north shore of the island and commanding a fine harbor which was capable of handling almost any ship afloat, Palermo had long been the major port of Sicily. The waterfront, developed by local enterprise, contained, among other fine facilities, a major ship-repair yard, complete with graving dock and twelve 65,000-barrel underground fuel-oil storage tanks. Moreover, although the city had been severely bombed, there were sufficient buildings of the proper type remaining to preclude excessive new construction on the part of the United States forces. The buildings were badly shattered, however, and it was the task of the Seabees to clear up the debris and do what construction work was necessary.

All utilities had been wiped out, necessitating the rewiring and installation of generators and communication equipment. Several large buildings had to be completely renovated—all had to be rewindowed and plastered. The ingenuity of Seabee personnel was demonstrated in the results obtained, for the base was developed as a remarkably modern and complete establishment. Additional activities were completed as required.

An ammunition depot was set up at Mondello Beach, 5 miles west of Palermo. Later, recreation facilities were constructed there.

With the base fully operative, the function of the Seabees became a purely maintenance proposition, so that in February 1944, the 567th CBMU arrived from the United States and replaced the 120th Battalion's Palermo detachment.

The naval operating base at Palermo remained one of the major United States supply and repair bases throughout the war, rendering aid to Navy and Merchant Marine alike. In August 1945, the 567th CBMU departed for the United States, and on December 15, 1945, after proper settlements had been made, the ship-repair yard was returned to the Sicilian owners. Staff headquarters and operations moved to Naples, and on December 31, 1945, Naval Operating Base, Palermo, was officially decommissioned, the balance of materials being turned over to the Office of Foreign Liquidations

Commission with a naval detachment resident until final disposition could be ascertained.

During the period that CBMU 567 was based at Palermo, detachments were being continually sent out to other localities, for brief intervals, for the purpose of rehabilitating or creating facilities at those places. Working parties were sent to Salerno, Leghorn, and Naples in Italy and to Cagliari in

PONTOONS IN THE SICILIAN INVASION, JULY 10, 1943
Pontoons of Platoon J of the 1006 Seabees, secured alongside LST 388 on the run into Blue Beach, Licata

Sardinia. In Marseilles, France, a group from this CBMU handled the movement of British Embassy property from Toulon to Paris.

Salerno

Salerno is situated on the west coast of Italy, about 25 miles south of Naples, on the Gulf of Salerno. Around this gulf, a fair beach forms a 12-mile arc, with the town of Salerno on the north side. Behind Salerno the hills gradually rise to the Apennines, but on the southern half of the arc the country is gently rolling.

For the landing at Salerno, the 12-mile beach was divided into two parts—the north section to be invaded by the 46th British Division, landed from LST's with the aid of the 1006th Seabee Causeway Detachment; the south section to be invaded by the American forces, also to be landed on causeways run by Seabee pontoon crews.

Before dawn on September 9, 1943, initial landings by assault Rangers and Commandos took place. The first LST (Number 386) headed into the north beach, carrying platoon C of the 1006th Detachment and a portion of the 46th British Division aboard. The convoy was under attack by German 88's during the landing, and LST 386 was struck by a mine, wrecking the causeways. The ship, however, remained afloat, and all cargo was transferred to LCT's. Other causeways ordered to the north beach reached there as planned. Only one was used, however, for the beach was found to be of such nature that it was possible to beach LST's directly and to unload them after the Seabees had placed sandbags under the ramps and spread mats.

One LST was hit eleven times on the run-in; its elevators were disabled, so that only the tank deck could be unloaded before retracting. Another LST was hit eight times on the run-in. Enemy fire was so severe that one LST actually took three runs to make the beach.

The Seabees bivouacked on the north beach for ten days, clearing traffic and building unloading-slips and roadways, under constant fire.

On the south beach operation, units of the 36th American Division landed at the same time as the British landed on the north beach.

The LST for the south beach landing grounded 300 feet offshore, but the causeways ran clear to dry land. Unloading operations were underway across the causeway ten minutes after the LST grounded.

Before Naples harbor was opened, 190 LST's were unloaded by Seabees over causeways on the south beach.

During the first ten days of the landing, ships were unloaded under constant fire and bombing.

Included in the Seabee personnel were one officer and 15 men from Company D of the 70th Battalion, but the largest part of the Seabee share in the operation was borne by the officers and men of the 1006th Pontoon Detachment. This outfit suffered 28-percent casualties, with one officer and seven men killed.

From actual records, it is estimated that about 11,500 vehicles went ashore over the 1006th Detachment's pontoon causeways during the Italian invasion.

When the Salerno area was consolidated and the port of Naples liberated, the 1006th left in

December 1943, for duty in England, and subsequently participated in the invasion of Normandy.

A detachment, consisting of one officer and 40 enlisted men, of the 567th CBMU from Palermo was sent to Salerno on March 3, 1944. There they worked with the 120th unit until May 9, 1944, when the 120th detachment was withdrawn, leaving the 567th to carry on all maintenance work.

1006TH SEABEES IN THE SALERNO INVASION UNLOADING AN LST OVER A PONTOON CAUSEWAY AT SAFTA BEACH

Work at Salerno was completed on October 16, 1944.

Naples

Naples was captured October 1, 1943. Upon evacuation, the Germans performed a fairly complete job of demolition, adding to the destruction caused by Allied shells. Main railway lines throughout the city were systematically destroyed, although streets and roads had been only slightly damaged. All railway bridges were destroyed, and aqueducts were breached in several places. Generating stations and power houses, as much as 50 miles from the city, were damaged or destroyed, and some of the major sewer mains were blown up by placing dynamite charges in the manholes.

Major industrial buildings and manufacturing plants were also wrecked, and delayed-action charges were left behind in many buildings. The port itself was choked with sunken vessels and debris from buildings which had been toppled into the harbor at berthing spaces.

The Navy set up a post office, a salvage unit, and an ammunition dump. Later, a naval radio station

was established. Fleet facilities continued to be furnished at Palermo. At first the Navy had little need of the Seabees in Naples, for harbor clearing was being done by the Army and no Navy installations were required. However, as the port facilities increased, the Navy's role in Naples became more and more prominent. In August 1944, a detachment from the 1005th CBD, which was then at Bizerte, was ordered to Naples, and later augmented by a similar detachment from the 567th CBMU at Palermo. Their function was to provide the Navy buildings with long-awaited and much-needed re-

1006TH SEABEES USING A THREE-SECTION PONTOON CAUSEWAY AT SAFTA BEACH

habilitation. The detail from the 1005th soon returned to its mother organization and departed for the United States in December 1944, but the group from Palermo remained to finish the job, rejoining the main body of the 567th CBMU in January 1945.

Anzio

On November 20, 1943, the 579th CBMU was organized at the Advance Amphibious Training Base, Bizerte. With a complement of seven officers and 316 enlisted men, drawn from the personnel of the 54th Battalion and the 1005th Detachment, the new CBMU was destined to be a pontoon unit in addition to its prime organizational function.

During the early part of January 1944, various officers and men of this group were temporarily assigned to the staff of Commander, Eighth Amphibious Force, and to numerous LST's within that force. On January 22, 1944, members of the 579th operated the causeways in the assault at Anzio-Nettuno.

Anzio is a small coastal Italian city, 30 miles south of Rome; practically adjacent, but slightly east of it, is the town of Nettuno. The beach here contained a sand bar and shallows which extended several hundred feet from the shore. This underwater condition prevented the operation of the causeways in the usual manner, as the LST's grounded so far offshore that the pontoon strings could not reach the beach. Seabee officers and men accordingly improvised a pontoon ferrying system and for two days succeeded in transporting much equipment ashore over the sand bar. To add to the difficulty, the men were subjected to almost constant bombing and strafing attacks; several were killed, many wounded, and much gear was damaged. Stormy weather began the day after the initial attack, and by the next day, all causeways were washed ashore by the surf. One platoon was returned to Bizerte; the others remained until March 1944, salvaging causeways and landing craft. They then returned to Bizerte.

Corsica and Sardinia

The islands of Corsica and Sardinia fell into our hands with the capitulation of Italy, and because of their convenient location were used as sites for PT-boat bases. These small craft were required to wage constant warfare against German E-boats and other enemy vessels operating out of southern French and northern Italian ports. As the range of PT's is limited, many bases were established, the principal one being on Maddelena, a small island north of Sardinia.

A detail of one officer and 27 men from the 1005th Detachment, at Bizerte, reached Maddelena on April 13, 1944. Here they erected pontoon drydocks, finger piers, and quonset huts. The work was completed by July 3, 1944, and the detail returned to Bizerte.

In southern Sardinia, one officer and twelve men of the 567th CBMU spent nearly a month

(June 1944) at the city of Cagliari, establishing a small base for use of PT squadrons and minesweeping details. When this work was completed, the detachment returned to its unit at Palermo.

The 1045th CBD was assigned to the island of Corsica. This unit of 300 men was actually a petroleum specialist detachment, formed for the purpose of establishing fueling facilities. This group arrived at Ajaccio in western Corsica on April 8, 1944. There they erected seventeen 10,000-barrel oil tanks, numerous water tanks, together with the necessary pumping stations, distillation units, and accessories. The installations at Ajaccio were operated until they were of no further value to the war effort, and were then dismantled by the unit.

Southern France

D-Day for the invasion of southern France was set for August 14, 1944. On that day, as the troops under General Devers poured into the Marseilles and Toulon areas, the causeways were operated by men of the 1040th Seabee Detachment. This invasion was made without any serious casualties. Ironically, though, during the dress-rehearsal stages, a causeway struck a mine near Pazzoulia, Italy, seriously injuring several members of the crew.

After the initial assault, one group helped clear the harbor of Toulon, where the French had previously scuttled their fleet. On August 26, four platoons were ordered to Marseilles for salvage work, removing demolished bridges from the canal, setting up causeways, and making other installations.

On D-Day plus eight, CBMU 611 reported at Toulon. Here, they unloaded gear and installed communication equipment, using captured apparatus and property. At both Toulon and Marseilles, the Seabees rehabilitated the property held by the Navy and operated and maintained transportation facilities. From time to time, detachments were sent out to erect or remove other installations as required. Principal among these was the small PT base at Golfe Juan.

Detachment 1040 returned to Bizerte in echelons as their work was completed. Toward the end of 1944, the larger part of CBMU 611 returned to the United States, one officer and sixty men remaining at Marseilles for maintenance work. By October 1945, the Navy had left all areas in southern France, with the exception of Marseilles, where only a liaison officer remained.

Another Seabee unit actively concerned with operations in southern France was the 1045th (Petroleum) Detachment. Four reconnaissance parties from this unit accompanied the invasion forces into southern France on D-Day. Four days later, two construction parties, totalling 42 officers and men, landed, followed in four days by two more parties. These several groups were divided, 2 officers and 29 men going to Toulon and 6 officers and 99 men to Marseilles.

At Toulon, the objective of the 1045th was to repair existing French petroleum storage and fueling facilities which were badly damaged during the battle. They also erected two additional 5,000-barrel gasoline tanks and installed pumps and accessories.

The group at Marseilles had less damage to repair, and although they did renovate a 55,000-barrel fuel-oil tank and clean ten other tanks, the main task was to install 6 miles of 8-inch pipe line. Included in this figure were two submarine pipe lines, extending from the beach to a fueling-barge anchored offshore.

These groups remained in France only until early November; nevertheless, they erected a 2,000-barrel water tank for the Army and set up a small fuel-oil distribution plant.

Azores

In October 1943, the British Prime Minister announced that Portugal had granted bases in the Azores to aid the Allies in their fight against submarines in the Atlantic. British forces immediately moved into the Azores and began construction of an air base on the island of Terceira.

The Azores lie about 800 miles west of Lisbon. The most important of the nine islands is Fayal, whose chief city, Horta, is a Pan American clipper stop and has a harbor suitable for medium and small warships. Terceira, a volcanic island, 20 miles long by 18 miles wide, has two unprotected harbors, Angra and Praia. Praia, used by U. S. supply vessels, is only 3 miles from Lagens Field, established by the British.

Since British facilities were to be used to protect American shipping, both Army Engineers and Seabees were sent to the Azores to aid in construction. The airfield was used by Army Transport Command and Naval Air Transport Service, and the dominant part of the expansion work was accomplished by the Army Engineer Corps.

The first echelon of the 96th Construction Battalion was charged initially with the construction of a quonset-hut camp for naval activities at the Lagens airfield and of minor docking facilities at Praia Harbor. When the Seabees arrived, on January 9, 1944, the British had completed a pierced-plank runway, 6,000 feet by 150 feet, and were engaged in erecting hangars, shops, and camps.

By February 16, the Seabees had erected Santa Ritta Camp for 600 officers and men. The camp consisted of 85 quonset huts for quarters, mess halls, sick bay, dispensaries, shops, offices, and recreation facilities. Concrete floors were laid in all buildings, as a precaution against plague-bearing rats. Frequent rains and strong winds greatly hampered construction, particularly that of the roads, walks, and earthwork incident to the erection of the huts.

On February 21, 1944, the Commander, U. S. Naval Forces, Azores, requested that the necessary dredging and construction be done to convert Praia Bay into a usable harbor. This included construction of a mole pier and widening of an existing pier to form a boat basin for the anchorage of four LCM's and a pontoon barge. A cargo staging area was constructed in the immediate vicinity. The basin was dredged to a 4-foot depth at low water. Facilities were also provided to make minor repairs on damaged ships.

From the time of landing, the Seabees were used in unloading cargo vessels in conjunction with the Army Air Forces. The Army did the stevedore work aboard ship; the Seabees manned pontoon barges and trucks. At one time, in early March 1944, it was necessary to discontinue construction activities for a short time to concentrate on unloading activities.

In late March 1944, the Seabees began construction of 3,800 feet of 8-inch submarine pipe line for tanker unloading. The installation, completed on May 21, served the Army gasoline tank farms on Terceira and Santa Maria.

In addition to the construction of housing and harbor facilities, the Seabees constructed facilities for the Navy, Army, and British forces at Lagens Field. Pierced-plank taxiways were laid, and parking areas were graded and cinder-surfaced. Nine steel arch-rib buildings and two blimp-mooring masts were also erected.

By the first of May 1944, virtually all authorized construction had been completed; the bat-

PRAIA DOCK AREA, AZORES

talion handled minor construction and maintenance until its departure for the United States on July 27. Before the 96th Battalion departed, four officers and 101 enlisted men were transferred to form CBMU 613.

In addition to maintenance activities and stevedoring, the maintenance unit was responsible for some major construction. At Santa Ritta Camp, an enlisted men's galley and mess hall was erected, using eight quonset huts grouped around a central frame structure. A similar structure, utilizing four quonset huts, was erected for use as a recreation building.

At Lagens Field, the Seabees erected three portable nose hangars, 78 by 30 feet, and laid 35,000 square yards of asphalt-surfaced hardstands for Navy planes. Steel towers and quonset huts were erected for the Villa Nova radio teletype receiving site and the Cinco Picos radio teletype sending site.

The maintenance unit remained at Terceira until after V-E Day. Naval facilities received full use, a great amount of operational flying and air sea-rescue work being performed by the PB4Y-1 Squadron, based at Terceira.

Disposition of Property

As the European theaters of operation shifted and ultimately hostilities ceased, what were once vital bases were no longer needed. Fortunately, a goodly portion of the Navy's shore establishments in the Mediterranean area were housed in permanent structures, either seized from the enemy or contracted for from our Allies, under the Lend-Lease terms. The liquidation of these facilities involved merely the estimating of the amount of improvements made or the damage incurred and the billing thereof to the responsible party, upon settlement of the contract or the vacating of the premises.

In many instances, such as was the case in some of our Oran holdings, damages and improvements practically balanced each other; so "quit claims" were signed, and both parties concerned were satisfied. In cases where new construction had been performed by our forces and where such installations were not subsequently removed, a new value for these establishments was declared to the Office of the Foreign Liquidations Committee. These cost declarations (made by officers of the Civil Engineer Corps) were all comprehensive, including road repair or construction, buildings, sewerage,

all utilities, equipment, land improvements, and anything else that entailed the expenditure of United States funds for construction purposes, for or by the Navy.

The larger portion of the personnel of these stations (including Seabee maintenance crews) were removed to other more active theaters or returned to the United States, leaving small detachments as caretakers until such time as final and satisfactory disposition could be made.

Freetown, Sierra Leone

To establish a garrison against a possible German drive toward South Africa, to set up a port through which supplies could be brought from America to the troops in North Africa, and to establish a base for ships in the South Atlantic, the British Government began, early in 1942, to develop its harbor facilities at Freetown, in Sierra Leone, British West Africa. The plan was to set up a base to take care of vessels up to the size of cruisers by installing one large floating drydock, one small floating drydock, hospital facilities, and ammunition storage space. Accordingly, the British laid out the following program: construction of a 1000-foot deep-water quay with a 30-foot depth alongside, extension of a jetty, erection of repair workshops on shore, storage space ashore for naval and refrigerated stores, shore accommodations for personnel, and an oil and fuel depot with an oiling jetty.

In February 1942, the British asked the United States to assist in the Freetown project by sending supplies. In the spring of 1942, the United States let a lump-sum contract for the towing of the timber floating drydock, *Triumph*, from New York to Freetown by two commercial tugs, one American and the other British.

It was thought at that time that no labor problem would be involved, but by June 1942 it was evident that additional skilled labor and supervision were necessary. There was an abundant supply of unskilled native labor, but without skilled supervision, little work could be accomplished.

On June 8, 1942, two CEC officers, one doctor, a dentist, and 40 enlisted men were ordered to Freetown from Quonset, R. I. In July 1942, an additional ten officers and 250 men were sent to Freetown. These men were organized into an advance base unit and quartered in British-constructed barracks.

In December 1942, Construction Battalion Detachments 1001 and 1002, each consisting of 250 officers and men, were sent to Freetown via Guirock, Scotland, arriving early in January 1943. On March 31, 1943, CBD 1001, CBD 1002 and the advance base unit were combined to form the 65th Construction Battalion.

As the tide of battle in North Africa began to turn in the spring of 1943—Axis forces capitulated on May 12—the need for Freetown as an advance base ceased to exist, and United States forces withdrew in June 1943.

Monrovia, Liberia

As the result of an agreement reached on December 31, 1943, between the governments of the United States and Liberia, the United States agreed to aid Liberia in the construction of a commercial port, the work to be done under the supervision of the United States.

On April 27, 1944, the Bureau of Yards and Docks let a cost-plus-a-fixed-fee contract for the construction of a commercial port, port works, and

SOUTH BREAKWATER. MONROVIA

access roads in Liberia, at an estimated cost of $20,000,000. In this contract, the Navy acted as the agent for the Department of State. Officers of the Civil Engineer Corps supervised the construction.

CHAPTER 21

CONSTRUCTION BATTALIONS IN FRANCE AND GERMANY

Plans for the invasion of Normandy began to take shape by the summer of 1943. Decisions of controlling importance were made in August, when the political and military leaders of the United States and Great Britain conferred in Quebec.

The role of the naval forces was to be primarily that of assuring a successful landing on the French coast, providing the shore facilities necessary to permit the uninterrupted delivery of great numbers of troops and vast quantities of material, and the maintenance of an open supply route across the English Channel.

Participation in the invasion by American naval forces was obviously going to require extensive logistic support. A supply depot, large enough to store and issue great quantities of naval supplies of all kinds, would be needed, and a number of shore bases to support the forthcoming amphibious operations would have to be provided.

In the summer of 1943 the task of building the Navy's base facilities in Northern Ireland and Scotland had been virtually accomplished. Only minor construction remained to be done, and thereafter the problems would be those of maintenance and operation. At the same time, a large new program of base construction in southern England loomed ahead.

In view of these circumstances the 29th Construction Battalion, which had been engaged since the previous November in building the Londonderry and Rosneath bases, was moved to Devon and Cornwall, and the Seabee personnel in the United Kingdom was augmented by the 81st and 97th Construction Battalions and the second section of the 10th Special Battalion. The 97th took over the base operation and maintenance work in Northern Ireland and Scotland, from the 29th, the first section at Londonderry and the second at Rosneath. The second section of the 10th Special was also assigned to duty at Rosneath. The 81st Construction Battalion was dispatched to Milford Haven, Wales, to begin construction of new facilities.

On September 24, 1943 the construction battalions in the United Kingdom were organized into the 13th Naval Construction Regiment, so as to provide an overall command and maximum flexibility of personnel and equipment in connection with construction operations in the area. The regiment was designated as part of the organization of the Commander of Landing Craft and Bases in Europe.

By November, all the Seabee units in the United Kingdom, with the exception of the first section of the 97th Battalion, were at work on the new bases in Devon, Cornwall, and Wales. In December, they were joined by the 1006th Construction Battalion Detachment, which had performed pontoon-causeway work with distinction in the Sicilian and Italian invasions.

The largest single base-construction project undertaken by the Seabees in southern England was the supply base near Exeter, in Devon. On what had been the golf course of a country club, south of the city, the 29th Battalion set up its headquarters, and on October 11, 1943, broke ground for the new depot.

Originally, the plan for the station called for the erection of 79 warehouses, to provide about 400,000 square feet of covered-storage space, personnel facilities for 1,000 men, and the necessary administration buildings. After construction was well under way, in December, the plans for the base were changed to provide a much larger capacity than had been originally intended. A total of 578,000 square feet of covered storage was finally attained. Most of the storage buildings were of the quonset-hut type, 40 by 100 feet; a number of buildings of British design were also put up. Standard-size quonset huts were used for personnel quarters and office facilities. About 7 miles of roadway were built to serve the base.

The depot was commissioned on February 4, 1944.

The principal locations chosen for the amphib-

BASES IN SOUTHERN ENGLAND AND IN NORMANDY

ious bases were Falmouth, Fowey, Plymouth, Salcombe, Dartmouth. and Teignmouth. on the Channel coast. and Milford Haven and Penarth in Wales. In addition, installations of smaller magnitude were provided at St. Mawes (across the harbor from Falmouth), Saltash, Calstock, Weymouth, Poole, Southampton, and Instow (on the Bristol Channel).

There were fully developed port facilities already existing at all those places, and many of them had also been used for many years as British seaside resorts. Consequently, much of the problem of housing naval personnel could be met by utilizing existing hotel facilities and large private homes, with appropriate alterations. As practically all the British Channel coast was designated as a restricted area during the months preceding the invasion, and civilian travel into the area prohibited for reasons of military security, the utilization of existing civilian facilities in that way presented no particular hardship to the British people. Additional capacity for housing naval personnel was found in some existing British army camps, which were turned over to the Navy for that purpose.

After the maximum feasible use had been made of such existing facilities, however, it was still necessary to provide new housing at several locations. At some places, new personnel quarters were provided by the erection of quonset huts, or roughly equivalent huts of a British design; at others, by the erection of tents; and at still others, all those forms of housing were used. The capacity for housing naval personnel provided at each of those locations was as shown in Table VI.

To obtain proper dispersal, in view of the constant hazard of enemy bombing, concentration of more than a thousand men at any one point was avoided whenever possible. Thus, at Plymouth, where far more than a thousand men needed to be housed in the general area, several hut camps were erected, each at some distance from the waterfront hotels and well separated from each other. Similar conditions prevailed at Falmouth.

The building of these advanced amphibious bases was put under way at various times beginning in October 1943. By January 1944, the construction of most of them had reached the stage where occupancy could begin.

Similarly, for the hospital and dispensary facilities necessary to serve the large number of men to be assembled for training and participation in the assault, existing hotels or large homes were taken over by the American forces, and suitable alterations were made to fit them to hospital purposes. Where the available buildings were not adequate, they were supplemented by the erection of quonset-hut annexes.

TABLE VI.—*Personnel accommodations provided in England*

| Location | New camps | | | | Alterations | | | | Total | |
| | Huts | | Tents | | British barracks | | Houses and hotels | | | |
	Officers	Enlisted Personnel	Officers	Enlisted Personnel	Officers	Enlisted Personnel	Officers	Enlisted Personnel	Officers	Enlisted Personnel
Falmouth	48	2059	—	1146	—	—	120	528	168	3733
Fowey	104	1500	—	—	—	—	101	930	205	2430
Plymouth	482	4172	—	186	106	296	45	371	633	5025
Salcombe	32	900	—	—	—	—	105	893	137	1793
Dartmouth	138	750	—	462	150	1750	90	344	378	3306
Teignmouth	8	—	—	—	—	—	48	817	56	817
Milford Haven	71	800	—	—	—	102	—	—	71	902
Penarth	28	425	—	—	—	—	47	514	75	939
St. Mawes	8	264	—	—	—	—	62	530	70	794
Saltash	0	150	—	—	—	—	30	150	30	300
Calstock	—	—	—	—	—	—	20	125	20	125
Weymouth	—	—	80	500	120	1113	26	679	226	2292
Poole	—	—	—	402	150	1160	19	100	169	1662
Southampton	24	34	—	250	—	—	53	366	77	650

NAVAL CONSTRUCTION BATTALION DEPOT, HEATHFIELD
Open storage area, left and upper left; large single quonset hut, transportation department's garage; small
huts, offices and personnel quarters; two double huts (right foreground), messhall and recreation huts; tents
used for temporarily housing transient Seabees.

The largest single installation was at Netley, just outside Southampton, where an old British hospital was remodeled to provide a 3000-bed facility. Two major hospitals were provided entirely of quonset huts—one at Manadon Field, on the outskirts of Plymouth, with a capacity of 500 beds; the other, at Milford Haven, with a capacity of 200 beds. In addition, a large home in Falmouth was converted into a 140-bed hospital.

For ship repair and servicing facilities, little new construction was necessary, as the southern coast of England was already well provided with such facilities. Such work as had to be done consisted

principally of installing additional machinery in existing shops, providing a few small marine railways and "hards," and the erection of a limited number of storage sheds.

In March 1944, authority was received for the establishment of a Seabee base of operations, at Heathfield, near Newton Abbot, in Devon. The 81st Battalion worked on the new camp for about a month, as a "fill-in" job, directing its attention principally to the roads and camp utilities. The project was turned over to the 29th Battalion in the latter part of April. When completed, the camp provided for about a thousand men, one-third in quonset huts and the remainder in tents, together with storage and repair facilities for construction and transportation equipment.

Planning for the Normandy Invasion

A logistics problem of unusual difficulty was presented by the plans for the invasion of France. It was clear that even if all the French ports fell into our hands undamaged at an early stage of the operation, the quantity of stores to be landed for the maintenance of the invasion force would exceed the total port capacity. This meant that supplies would have to be landed over the beaches while ports were being improved. It was estimated that the quantity to be put ashore in this manner amounted to about 12,000 tons and about 2500 vehicles per day, for at least the first 90 days, even in the event of bad weather.

The Bay of the Seine, where the invasion was to take place, is characterized by flat sandy beaches, with an average slope of 1 to 150 feet, and an average range of 21 feet between high and low tides. The duration of high water is about 3 hours. A tidal current runs parallel to the coast, at about 3 knots. A series of low sand-bars, also parallel to the beach exists in the tidal area, with the runnels between them attaining a depth of as much as 5 feet.

The plan adopted to meet this difficult problem was bold. It was decided to prefabricate in England the breakwaters and other port facilities that would be needed to create the necessary artificial harbors on the Normandy coast, to tow them across the English Channel with the invading forces, and to install them at the chosen locations at the time of the assault.

This decision was reached at the Quebec conference in August 1943. The details of the plan were developed under the auspices of the Combined Chiefs of Staff during the months that followed.

Assaults were to be made by American forces at two points on the Normandy coast, one on the

INTERIOR OF TEMPORARY WARD, ST. MICHAEL'S HOSPITAL, FALMOUTH

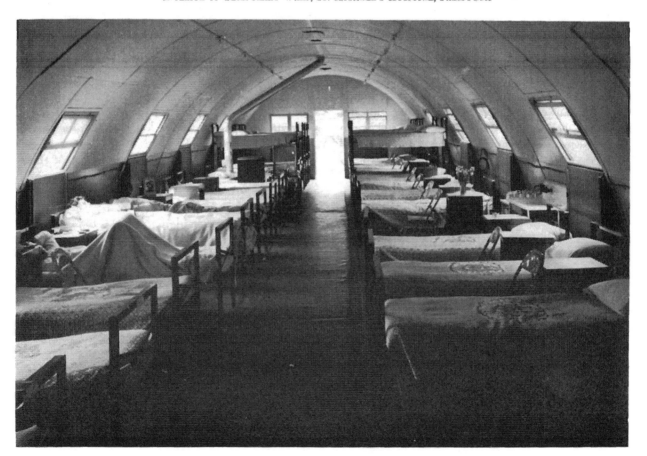

eastern side of the Cherbourg peninsula, northwest of Carentan, at the village of St. Martin de Varreville, and the other some 20 miles farther east, where the coast line runs more nearly east and west, at St. Laurent sur Mer. During the planning of the invasion, these two locations were given the code designations of "Utah" and "Omaha," respectively, and those designations have subsequently come into use as geographic names. Beaches to be assaulted by the British forces were to be east of the American locations, at Arromanches, at Courseulles, and at Ouistreham.

Logistically, Omaha was planned to be the major American location, with Utah fulfilling a supporting and supplementing function. At both beaches there were to be "gooseberries," harbors of refuge for small landing-craft, but for Omaha a great artificial harbor, called a "mulberry," was planned to give a protected anchorage about two square miles in extent, to be provided with moorings for seven Liberty ships, five large coasters, and seven medium coasters. This harbor was to be adequate to handle 5000 tons of stores per day, plus such military vehicles as would be delivered.

For the British beaches, an installation similar to that for Omaha, but somewhat larger, was planned at Arromanches; at their other two beaches, gooseberries only were to be provided.

It was clear from the beginning that the mulberry problem consisted essentially of two parts. First, the protected anchorage could be effected only by means of some sort of breakwater. Second, some way would have to be found to bridge the gap between the ship at anchor and the "dry land" beach, so that supplies and vehicles could go ashore with no delay.

Five methods of constructing the necessary breakwater were studied with great care. They were (1) Lilo floating breakwaters, (2) bubble breakwaters, (3) floating ships, (4) blockships, and (5) concrete caissons. Analysis and tests on models led to the elimination of the first three methods. The choice fell on the blockship and the concrete-caisson methods, and it was decided to employ both—blockships to form the harbors of refuge for small craft, and concrete caissons to form the primary breakwater and provide sheltered anchorage for cargo ships.

Some means had to be provided to take ashore the cargo unloaded from the ships in the harbor formed by the breakwater. From Liberty ships and smaller cargo vessels, vehicles and supplies

could be lightered to the beach by LCT's or other ferry craft. The normal method of unloading LST's, however—beaching and discharging vehicles under their own power, over a bow ramp—appeared to be precluded by the extremely flat beach and the great tidal range. The LST would run aground at the stern, too far out from shore, in water about 4 feet deep at the bow, and a receding tide would leave the ship stranded on an uneven beach for a long time, causing serious de-

UNEVEN OMAHA BEACH
Pontoon causeway is 28 feet wide

lays in maintaining the flow of supplies and probably introducing excessive hogging stresses in the vessel. LCT's could be used as lighters to serve the LST's, but there would not be enough of these smaller landing-craft available to handle the great number of vehicles that would have to pass over the beaches each day.

Five methods of bridging the gap between ship and shore were given consideration: (1) spud pierheads and flexible piers, sponsored by the Director of Transportation of the British War Office, (2) Swiss roll, (3) U. S. Navy lighter pontoons, (4) pontoons as developed by the British Director of Transportation, and (5) Hughes piers. At an early date it was decided to use the spud pierheads and flexible piers to provide the physical connection between ships and shore, and rhino ferries, constructed of the U. S. Navy lighter pontoons, to transport vehicles and supplies from moored vessels to the beach. The Swiss roll, the Director of Transportation's pontoons, and the

Hughes pier were judged impractical to meet the requirements.

The plan called for the installation by D-plus-2 of those "port" facilities that would provide the small-craft harbors of refuge at both Utah and Omaha. Those harbors were to be formed by scuttling a number of merchant ships, bow to stern, roughly parallel to the shore, in about two fathoms of water. in the lee of which small craft, such as barges, LCI's, and LCT's, protected from the force of the sea. could discharge personnel and equipment needed immediately to support the beach assault. Each line of sunken ships was known as a "gooseberry."

Gooseberry One, to be installed at Utah, was to consist of ten ships which, when sunk end to end, would form a breakwater about 4000 feet long and 4500 feet offshore at high tide.

At Omaha, Gooseberry Two was to consist of fourteen merchant ships, an old British warship, the former battleship *Centurion*, heading the western end of the line. The length of the gooseberry at Omaha would be about 6500 feet, and it would lie 4000 feet offshore at high tide.

In all instances the ships, without cargo, manned by Merchant Marine crews, would accompany the invasion forces, and after being sited in their proper locations by tugs would be sunk by setting off explosive charges which would blow out their bottoms.

The artificial harbor for Omaha was to be formed by a breakwater installed just west of the gooseberry. It was to be composed of a series of open concrete-caissons, which would be towed across the Channel, sited in their planned locations, flooded. and sunk. Each caisson was known as a phoenix.

The design of the harbor called for an outer breakwater, 6500 feet long, parallel to the beach. 4500 feet offshore at high tide, at about the 5-fathom line, and a western arm. 1600 feet long. extending to the beach. Between the *Centurion*, heading the gooseberry, and the eastern end of the outer breakwater a 600-foot opening was to be left to serve as a harbor entrance. Another entrance was to be provided by an opening, 200 feet wide, roughly in the center of the outer breakwater. A space, 600 feet wide, separating the outer breakwater from the offshore end of the western breakwater arm, would provide a third entrance to the protected area.

About 2400 feet offshore from the phoenix breakwater, to reduce swells and waves and to provide some measure of protection for large ships

LST Moves in to Secure to a Liebnitz Pier, Omaha Beach

PHOENIXES AT OMAHA BEACH
Note anti-aircraft guns and blimps

which would have to anchor outside the mulberry proper, was to be placed a floating breakwater about 6000 feet long. It was to consist of a series of 24 individually moored steel floats, 200 feet long, called "bombardons." The floats were to be of cruciform cross-section, with the arms of the cross 10 feet long and 5 feet wide. The overall height of the float, like its overall width, would be 25 feet, and it would be so ballasted as to float with a 6-foot freeboard.

The spud pier-heads, sponsored by the Director of Transportation of the British War Office, had been designed and manufactured prior to the inception of the plan to build the mulberries, by a private firm in the United Kindom, and several had been placed in operation in the vicinity of Cairnhead, Scotland, for unloading supplies from ships. They were composed of floating steel barges. 200 feet long, 60 feet wide, and 10 feet deep. Six of these pier-heads were to be provided for installation behind the breakwater at Omaha. They were to be placed far enough out from shore to provide a draft of not less than 9

feet at lowest low-tide; they were to be placed adjacent to each other and so connected by ramps and bridges that they could function together as an articulated structure in the cargo-unloading operation. At several of the pier-heads, LST's could tie up, lower their ramp, and discharge their cargoes of vehicles. Coasters were to unload at the others.

Access to the shore, 3100 feet away at high tide, was to be provided by three multi-span bridges, roughly 500 feet apart. Each bridge would consist of a series of 80-foot steel-truss spans, supported at the ends by moored concrete or steel floats. The western bridge was to be strong enough to pass loads up to 40 tons; the other two were to be capable of handling 25-ton loads. The bridge installation became known as a "whale," and the supporting floats were known as "beetles."

To aid in getting materials ashore in a hurry, particularly military vehicles, from Liberty ships, coasters, and LST's, the rhino ferry was conceived. In view of the limited number of LCT's that could be made available to serve as ferry craft, the

BOMBARDONS MOORED IN POSITION OFF OMAHA BEACH
These floating breakwaters were used for the protection of ships anchored outside the mulberry

Bureau of Yards and Docks was requested to develop a ferry barge composed of pontoons, which could be towed at sea by an LST, and by which an LST could be completely unloaded in two trips. A barge having a capacity of 300 tons, six pontoon strings wide and 30 pontoons long, was made up and tested in August 1943. at the Advance Base Proving Ground at Davisville, R. I. Its performance was observed by a committee composed of representatives of the Staff Commander of the 6th Amphibious Force, the British Admiralty Delegation, the Bureau of Yards and Docks, and the Proving Ground itself. On the basis of tests the tentative design was accepted, with the understanding that further development of the equipment and of the operating technique would be undertaken in the United Kingdom.

It was planned that the rhino, when teamed with an LST, would be made fast, or "married," to the landing ship, stern to bow: vehicles would be able to transfer from the LST to the ferry and leave the ferry at the beach under their own power. When ashore, the ferry would discharge at one of the sunken causeways or, if necessary, discharge its cargo directly onto the beach.

Twenty such rhinos would be needed at Omaha, it was decided. and eleven at Utah.

It was apparent that some means would have to be provided to enable ferry craft coming ashore in the lee of the gooseberries to discharge their cargoes and to retract quickly from the beaches. The invasion plan could not afford the time that would be lost if the craft should be beached and then stranded by a falling tide. Moreover, reconnaissance reports indicated that patches of clay and mud would probably be encountered on portions of the beaches between high and low water and, therefore, that hardways of some sort would be required if vehicles were to move across the tidal area without hazard of miring.

Staff engineers at Allied Supreme Headquarters concluded that Navy lighter pontoons, formed into sunken causeways, presented the only practicable solution using known and tried equipment. It was recommended that the causeways should be installed on the beaches on D-Day or as soon there-

RHINO FERRIES IN ACTION AT OMAHA BEACH
Loaded rhino coming in to the beach; emptied rhino (foreground) being repaired on return trip

after as feasible. Analysis of the expected ferry movements led to the conclusion that causeways would have to handle one-half of the total daily ferry cargo discharged. Taking into account the number of beach exits required, led to the conclusion that four causeways would be needed at the American beaches—two at Omaha and two at Utah —and six at the British beaches.

Made up of the Navy's standard steel pontoons, the causeways were to be two strings, or about 14 feet, wide, and were to extend from the high-water line out to somewhat beyond the line of minimum low-water, a distance of 2450 feet. Flooded and resting on the sand, these causeways would provide a hard roadway to which barges and landing-craft could tie at any stage of the tide, and over which their personnel or vehicles could go ashore in the dry. To facilitate the berthing of these craft, each causeway was to be equipped with eight "blisters," or sunken stages roughly equivalent to pier-heads, staggered on alternate sides, four pontoons wide and twelve long, spaced 250 feet apart.

Organizing for the Invasion

Assembling the Rhinos and Causeways.—To provide for the needs of Omaha and Utah, and a suitable reserve, 36 rhino ferries were assembled by the Seabees at their British bases. Each of these great barges was 42 feet wide and 176 feet long, with deck space enough for 30 to 40 vehicles. At the forward end, a 14-foot-wide ramp, 20 feet long, provided for the discharge of cargo. (The ramp was known as an "Olson ramp," after its designer, Lt. C. E. Olson, CEC, USNR, who was killed in action at Salerno with the 1006th Detachment.) At the stern of the rhino, two vertical timber knee-braces were installed, designed to engage the sides of a lowered LST ramp. Two heavy-duty outboard propulsion-units were provided, so that the barge could be self-propelled.

The provision of the outboard engines was one of the modifications made in the rhino design as a consequence of operating tests made in English waters. The Olson ramp was another, replacing a 60-ton-capacity ramp called for in the original design accepted tentatively at Davisville. Other changes included the addition of plastic-armor shields for the coxswains, the elimination of a hinged fair-lead, and the adoption of a closed cooling-system for the outboard engines.

Assembly of the rhino ferries was begun at Falmouth in late November 1943, by a detachment from the 81st Seabees. While the first unit was being fabricated, a search had been made for other sites along the south coast of England suitable for rhino assembly, and satisfactory sites were found at Plymouth and Dartmouth. The 1006th Detachment arrived from the Mediterranean theater of operations in December and took over the assembly work at Falmouth and the setting up of the new assembly areas at Plymouth and Dartmouth. By the end of January 1944, rhino assembly was under way at all three locations. The 1006th Detachment manned the assembly yards until March, when the 111th Battalion took over the task.

The Plymouth yard continued to build rhinos until early in May, but the yards at Falmouth and Dartmouth turned to the assembly of the causeways as soon as their assigned quotas of rhino ferries had been completed.

For the sunken causeways, 28 pontoon strings, each two pontoons wide and thirty long, were assembled, together with 16 causeway "blisters."

Each causeway string was 176 feet long, a convenient length to tow.

In addition, the Seabees fashioned out of the pontoons, 36 rhino tugs, intended to provide the auxiliary motive power for the rhino ferries: 12 causeway tugs, to assist LCT's in berthing and unberthing at the causeways; 12 warping tugs, designed primarily to pull broached boats off the beach; 2 rhino repair barges, almost as large as the rhino ferries, each fitted with two 5-ton cranes and a toll house; and 2 floating drydocks, of 475-ton capacity, enough to dock an LCT.

The Phoenixes. For installation at Omaha, 51 phoenixes of six different sizes were built by the British in a number of drydocks and in tidal basins excavated especially for the purpose, mostly in the Thames estuary.

The cross-section adopted for the largest caissons, for the outer breakwater, had the shape of an inverted T, 60 feet high. For the first 28 feet of its height, the width was 56 feet 3 inches; for the remainder of its height, 44 feet 1 inch. A set-back, or working platform, on each side, 6 feet 1 inch wide, was formed thereby. When afloat, the phoenix had a draft of 20 feet 3 inches, giving a freeboard of 7 feet 9 inches to the set-back. When sunk in five fathoms of water the freeboard of the breakwater-unit was 30 feet at low tide, and 9 feet at high tide.

Outer walls were 14 inches thick, and the floor thickness was 15 inches, over a portion of which concrete ballast was placed 15 inches thick. A center wall, 9 inches thick, extended throughout the phoenix's length; ten cross walls, of the same

PERSONNEL HUTS AT VICARAGE BASE, PLYMOUTH

NAVAL DISPENSARY, MANADON FIELD, PLYMOUTH

thickness, 16 feet 6 inches apart in the clear, divided the interior of the caisson into 22 cells. In each caisson's outer walls, five sets of 12-inch valves were installed, to serve as sea cocks. Near the bottom of the first, third, fifth, sixth, and eighth cross-walls, 12-inch-square holes were left, so that in the sinking operation the phoenix contained ten separate compartments to be flooded. Large openings, 16 feet high, were left in both the longitudinal and the cross walls, with their sills 34 feet 9 inches above the phoenix's floor.

At each end of the phoenix the space between the end wall and the first cross-wall was decked over with a reinforced-concrete slab, and, forward, an intermediate deck was provided in the space thus formed, and fitted out as quarters for the riding crew. Just aft of the midship point a gun plat-

form was constructed, mounting a 40-mm. Bofors.

The design and construction of the phoenixes was a commitment by the British; the actual design was made by the Director of Ports and Inland Water Transportation of the War Office, with the assistance of several civilian designing engineers. The Ministry of Supply was responsible for the construction of the units, under civilian contracts, and for the inspection of construction.

Preliminary designs were sent to Washington to the Bureau of Yards and Docks in late October 1943, for checking. The analysis in Washington led to the view that the design was inherently weak in view of the conditions likely to be encountered, and an alternate design was proposed, with straight sides and capable of being ballasted with sand for the Phoenix's entire height. When these views were brought to the attention of the British designing engineers, they differed with the conclusions, making the point that the breakwater was to be used for no more than a few summer months.

In the ensuing discussions the Deputy Chief Engineer of the U. S. Army Forces in the European theater participated, and, unsatisfied that the British design would meet all the situation's requirements as to strength and stability, called in a consulting engineer to make a complete examination of the problem. The consulting engineer, Dr. Oscar Faber, reported that in his opinion there were certain defects in the design and made specific recommendations for correcting weaknesses. The recommendations, in general, were directed toward increasing the thicknesses of the interior walls and the amount of reinforcement used. Although the British designing engineers thereupon increased to some extent the amount of reinforcing steel to be placed in the walls, they were firm in their view that the wall thicknesses were adequate.

No further objections were raised by U. S. Forces to constructing the phoenixes as designed.

The Pier-Heads.—Six floating pier-heads for Omaha were manufactured by the British at Cairnhead, Scotland. As has been stated, each pier-head consisted of a steel barge, 200 feet long and 60 feet wide. It was designed to be partially supported by "spuds," or legs, 89 feet long, at the corners, which would extend above the platform. These spuds were built-up steel columns, 48 inches square. Although they were to rest upon the channel floor, they were not intended to support the pier-head's entire weight but, rather, to carry just enough load to anchor and steady it, with buoyance supporting the rest. Accordingly, the pier-head proper was suspended from the tops of the spuds, by an arrangement of sheaves and cables. By means of power-driven winches, it could be raised and lowered as the tide flooded and ebbed so that the amount of load carried by the spuds would remain constant. Raising and lowering operations could be carefully controlled through the use of extensometers, attached to the suspending cables.

The Floating Bridges.—Nearly two miles of "whale" bridge spans were manufactured by the British for the Omaha installation. Each standard span consisted of an 80-foot-long half-through steel truss, designed to be supported on steel or concrete

STORAGE WAREHOUSES AT EXETER SUPPLY BASE

floats. The trusses were lozenge-shaped, with a maximum depth of 8 feet and were fabricated of common structural shapes. with bolted or riveted connections. The width of the bridge was 13 feet 9 inches center to center of trusses, and it carried a steel deck roadway of 10 feet clear width. The only difference between the 4-ton and the 25-ton capacity bridges lay in the weight of the members used to form the trusses. In addition to these standard units, shore-ramp floats of shallow draft were provided to fit the conditions to be encountered at the beach end of the bridges.

Bridge spans and supporting floats were assembled into six-span trains for the tow across the Channel.

Assignment of responsibilities.—The production of the phoenixes, the pier-heads, the "whale"

bridge units, and the bombardons was a commitment of the British, as was the transportation in tow from the points of manufacture to the marshalling areas from which they were to be dispatched to the Normandy coast.

The production of the rhino ferries, the sunken causeways, and all other craft to be built of pontoon gear, the manning of those units while in tow across the English Channel, and their installation and operation at the invasion beaches was the responsibility of the Seabees. In addition, the Seabees were assigned the task of manning the phoenixes, pier-heads, and "whale" bridge trains while in tow across the Channel, their installation at Omaha, and their operation and maintenance after construction had been completed.

Unloading ships in the harbor, operating harbor

RHINO FERRY "MARRIED" TO AN LST

GOOSEBERRY NO. 2 AT OMAHA BEACH

tugs, Dukw's, and providing transportation facilities ashore, from the beaches to the fighting fronts, were responsibilities of the Army.

The magnitude of the role assigned the Navy Construction Battalions in the forthcoming invasion called for an expansion of Seabee personnel and an elaboration of organization. Accordingly, effective April 1, 1944, a new naval construction regiment was formed, the 25th, with its principal function that of participating directly in "Far Shore" activities. It was composed of the 81st, 111th, 108th (a new designation for Section 2 of the 97th), and the 1006th Detachment, all from the 13th Regiment; the 28th, which was a new arrival in the United Kingdom; the 146th, a battalion specializing in P.O.L. work (Petrol-Oil-Lubricants), and the 1048th Detachment, which, newly arrived in England, was made a part of the 111th Battalion. The new regiment was charged with the planning, training for, and execution of, all projects in which Seabees would be involved in far-shore activities; the role of the 13th NCR was

defined as the construction and maintenance of public works in the United Kingdom, and all pontoon construction.

The battalions of the 25th Regiment were given the following assignments for far-shore operations:

28th—Rehabilitation of captured ports.

81st—Manning the rhino ferries despatched to Utah while in tow across the Channel; operation of rhino ferries and beach camp at Utah.

108th—Manning the phoenixes, pier-heads, and "whale" bridge trains while in tow across the Channel; installing, operating, and maintaining them upon arrival at Omaha.

111th—Manning the rhino ferries despatched to Omaha while in tow across the Channel; operation of rhino ferries and beach camp at Omaha.

146th—Installation of P.O.L. facilities at Omaha, Cherbourg, and other captured ports.

1006th—Installation and maintenance of sunken pontoon causeways at Omaha and Utah.

As soon as the first rhino ferry was completed at Falmouth, in December 1943, two operating

UNLOADING ACTIVITIES AT OMAHA BEACH MULBERRY
Photograph on opposite page shows another angle of this scene at a Liebnitz pier

crews were drawn from the 1006th Detachment and trained in handling the big barge. Performance tests carried out by these crews led to the modifications in rhino design noted in an earlier paragraph.

When the 111th Battalion arrived in England in February 1944, it was assigned to rhino-ferry operation, and a large-scale program of crew-training was then set up. Training subjects included seamanship, signalling, aircraft recognition, marrying rhinos to LST's, beaching and retracting, and, in general, in the characteristics of rhino-ferry operation. By April 24, 1944, thirty crews from the 111th had been trained. Crews from the 28th and the 81st Battalions and the 1048th Detachment then reported for duty at Falmouth and were given a similar course of training. Rhino-ferry training was given to 41 crews in all, including 60 officers.

The crews that were to ride the mulberry units across the English Channel were drawn from the 108th Battalion. Phoenix crews were sent to the Thames estuary and rode the units that were built in that area, off Selsey Bill. When the phoenixes arrived, they had to be flooded so that they could be parked while awaiting D-day, and the parking operation served as excellent training for the siting teams. Training in the handling and assembly of whale equipment was carried on at Cairnhead, Scotland.

Invasion

During the last week of May 1944, movement of all equipment to the various marshalling areas began. D-day was not far off. Phoenixes were marshalled at Dungeness and at Selsey Bill; whale units, at Peelbank, on the Isle of Wight; rhinos

SPUD PIERHEAD AND FLEXIBLE PIERS
For detailed view of the piers, see page 113

for Omaha, at Portland: rhinos for Utah, at Dartmouth.

On June 1, information was received that June 5 had been designated as D-day.

On June 4, information was received that D-day had been postponed to June 6.

On June 5, D-minus-1, the rhino ferries and rhino tugs, with their Seabee crews aboard, were taken in tow by LST's and left for the far shore. The invasion was under way. At 0530 the following morning, June 6, D-Day, H-minus-1, the first rhino-LST teams began to arrive at the Omaha assembly point, 12 miles offshore. Upon arrival, they were released from tow and were ordered to marry their LST's according to plan.

The sea was not running according to plan, however, for the waves were 6 feet high, and it had been thought that a 3-foot sea would be the maximum that would permit a successful rhino-LST marriage. The circumstances were extremely severe, but the marriages were successfully made, even though in the first effort most of the rhinos lost the special knee-braces with which they had been provided. The vehicles carried by the LST's moved to the rhino decks, and the ferries started for the beach, 12 miles away, between 0700 and 0800.

Upon arrival at the beach, all the rhinos were ordered to stand out, for beach obstructions had not been cleared. When the order was received

OMAHA BEACH BEFORE THE MULBERRY WAS INSTALLED
Ships unloading on the beach while barrage balloons hover overhead

however, one rhino had already landed between two beach obstacles and was in such a position that it could not be retracted until mines that were astern had been removed. Accordingly, it unloaded on the beach at H-plus-6. All other rhinos retracted from the beach.

They were held off until the afternoon of the next day, June 7. The sea was heavy, and the current, strong; the Seabee crews, on the open deck of a barge having a freeboard of only 18 inches, had absolutely no protection from wind, weather, or enemy action. When finally ordered to the beach the rhinos had to labor for hours to get back into their proper areas.

The rhino tugs were knocked out by mines and collided heavily with submerged abandoned ve-

hicles which began to accumulate as the assault proceeded. Most of the tugs had to be abandoned, and the rhino ferries thereafter were propelled solely by their own outboard engines.

Meantime, rhinos in tow from LST's arrived at 0300 D-day, off Utah, where the sea was at least as heavy as it was at Omaha and where bombing and strafing by German planes added to the severity of operating conditions. Nevertheless, five rhinos succeeded in marrying their LST's and in making the transfer of the vehicle load. The first rhino beached at 1400, and before midnight, four had succeeded in unloading their cargoes including landing 175 vehicles on the beach. Attacks by enemy planes were frequent, and the fire from German 88's was heavy. Rhino tugs had been severely battered during the tow across the Channel, and the rhino ferries either made the trip from their LST's to the beach under their own power or in tow from LCT's or LCI's. At about noon on June 7, the first blockships began to arrive off Omaha and Utah. Surveys for the location had been completed an hour or so earlier, and buoys had been placed to mark the sites at which the ships were to be sunk.

By 2030 that evening, three ships had been sited and sunk in proper position at Omaha. A few minutes after the third ship had been sunk a German 88-mm. battery opened fire on the installation, and the crew was evacuated until the enemy battery had been silenced by naval gunfire. But the installation of the gooseberry had been started. Five more blockships were sited and sunk the following day, June 8, three on June 9, including the *Centurion*, and on June 10, D-plus-4, the Omaha gooseberry was completed by the sinking of the last three ships.

At Utah, the blockships put in their appearance at 1400 on June 7, but at that time the beach area was still under fire from the naval bombardment force and from enemy shore batteries. Although the same severe conditions prevailed throughout the next day, two blockships were successfully sited and sunk. A third ship was sited that day, but, in sinking, it drifted out of position by the stern, because of the difficulties experienced by the tugs in maintaining their positions under the severe enemy shelling. On June 9, efforts to site the fourth ship were prevented for most of the day by fire from the enemy's shore positions; however, at 1700, although still under fire, it was moved into position, and by 2030 its sinking had been completed. The fifth ship was successfully sunk just before midnight. On June 10, two more ships were placed without difficulty, but just as a third was starting for its place in the gooseberry line the site it was to occupy was bracketed by German artillery fire. The ship was brought in, nevertheless, and run aground beside a ship already in place; at high tide, two hours later, it floated off and was towed to its proper position and sunk. The siting and sinking of two more ships on June 11, D-plus-5, completed the gooseberry at Utah. Enemy fire continued to the end, and the installation of the last

AN ARMY DUKW CROSSES ONE OF THE BRITISH-BUILT "WHALE" BRIDGES AT OMAHA BEACH

ship had to be carried on under bombardment. Virtually the entire operation of constructing the Utah blockship-breakwater was carried out in the face of determined enemy opposition.

While the first ships were being sunk to form the gooseberries at Omaha and Utah, the sunken pontoon-causeway equipment began to arrive. On June 7, D-plus-1, the pontoon strings necessary to construct one causeway at each beach, together with the necessary personnel from the 1006th Detachment, arrived.

At Utah the first causeway was laid on the extreme western flank of the beach, according to plan, the next day, and it was in operation on June 8, D-plus-2. Shell fire from the same batteries that were harassing the installation of the Utah gooseberry sought out the causeway group intermittently, but caused no casualties. The second causeway arrived from England on June 14, and the next day was put into place about half a mile farther east.

At Omaha, the actual configuration of the beach was such that the feasibility of the causeway designed on the basis of intelligence reports was thrown into question. Although a section of the first causeway was laid on D-plus-3, a decision was not reached as to the best design to use, thereby permitting the full installation to go ahead, until D-plus-4, June 10. It was finally decided to make the structure four pontoons wide, instead of two as originally planned, to place the "blisters" opposite each other instead of staggering them, and to make the length 1450 feet instead of the 2450 feet originally intended. This would permit LCT's and rhinos to come to the causeway on either side; by making their approach at a 45-degree angle, they could come in at any point along its length. The second causeway at Omaha, installed on June 13, D-plus-7, was also four pontoons wide, and was in full operation June 16.

The causeways were highly successful from the very start. They were immediately put to use by all types of craft up to the size of LCI's. Within the first few hours following the installation of the first causeway at Utah, several thousand troops had gone ashore over it "in the dry."

Phoenixes for the mulberry breakwater were scheduled to arrive at Omaha in the early morning of June 8, D-plus-2. The first tows of the great concrete structures arrived, however, eight hours ahead of schedule, at 2200 on June 7. The survey for the mulberry had been begun earlier that day.

The phoenixes were maneuvered into position in the western breakwater arm the next morning, flooded, and sunk. On June 9 the western arm was extended by one more unit, and a beginning was made on the outer breakwater, by the installation of its first phoenix. By that time the survey work for the mulberry had been completed, and it was possible the next day to install five more units. During the days that followed, phoenixes arrived in tow, were sited, and were sunk with considerable regularity. By June 15 the western half of the outer breakwater was complete, and only two units remained to be installed in the mulberry's western arm.

Moorings for the bombardons had been laid, starting on June 7. Installation of the floating breakwater was begun on June 8 and progressed without serious difficulty until its completion on June 13.

Survey of the site of the floating pier-heads and whale bridges had been attempted on June 7 but had had to be deferred because of the presence of many underwater obstacles and mines in the proposed location. The next day the vicinity was still under enemy sniper fire, and consequently the survey work did not get under way until June 9. Although good progress was then made, mines and underwater obstacles still prevented the start of installation until June 11, when both the western and the center bridges were begun.

The survey had indicated that the depth of water close to shore was greater than had been shown on the charts from which the mulberry operation had been planned. To take advantage of the situation, and to compensate for the loss of one bridge train while in tow across the channel, the length of all bridges was shortened 480 feet. By June 15 the center pier-head and bridge were complete, and the next morning LST's began unloading over them. Observation of unloading operations at the partly completed installation that day showed that LST's could discharge their vehicles in an average time of 64 minutes, or at the rate of 1.16 minutes per vehicle. By June 18 the western pier-head and bridge, with a capacity of 40 tons, was also ready to be put into service. At that point, disaster struck the beaches.

The Great Storm and its Effects

On the morning of June 19 a gale out of the east and northeast caused a stoppage of all construction work. The storm was abnormal both in intensity

OMAHA BEACH AFTER THE GREAT STORM
Ships, boats, and pontoons in a jumbled mass

and direction for the season. Unfortunately, it came at a time when the eastern half of the harbor was still unprotected.

Early in the day it was necessary to evacuate the U.S. Army anti-aircraft gun crews from several phoenixes in the outer breakwater, for heavy seas were breaking over it, sweeping away hand rails and shelters at the base of gun platforms. Before the day came to an end the outer breakwater began to show signs of approaching collapse.

The storm showed no signs of abating the next day. The bombardons had broken loose from their moorings and had been driven ashore by the force of the wind. They piled up against the whale bridges and subjected those structures to forces beyond their capacity to withstand. Gun crews from all the phoenixes had to be evacuated. High seas were still breaking over to the outer break-water units, and they had begun to break up. In a desperate effort to relieve the situation, oil was spread on the water outside the breakwater, but with only temporary benefit.

The fury of the storm continued throughout the third day. Disintegration of the outer breakwater became progressively more extensive, and, consequently, the seas within the harbor became even higher.

On the morning of the fourth day, June 22, the fury of the storm began to abate. Wind velocity fell, and the seas decreased in height. Conditions

SEABEE REPAIR SHIP AT OMAHA BEACH
Quonset hut houses intricate machinery required for repair operations

remained entirely too severe to permit the resumption of port operations, however, until June 23.

When the storm was over, Omaha presented a tragic scene. The entire beach was strewn with a confused tangle of wrecked small craft of all types. Most of the floating bridges and pier-heads had been carried away and damaged beyond repair, as had also the bombardons. The mulberry's outer breakwater had lost 19 of the 27 phoenixes which had been in place when the storm broke, although most of those placed in the western breakwater arm were still intact. All the rhinos had had their mooring lines cut by drifting craft and were broached on the beach. Pounding for three days by heavy wreckage had virtually demolished the engines of all 20 of the great barges, and a great many of the rhinos' pontoons had been smashed.

At Utah there were no phoenixes, whales, or bombardons to be damaged. The blockship-breakwater, which had been installed under such hazardous conditions, had fared as well as its counterpart at Omaha; it was battered but still serviceable. The two causeways had had the sand cut away from beneath them by the force of the sea and had settled two to three feet into the beach. Wrecked small craft littered the beach, creating a scene similar to that at Omaha. Rhino operations had, of course, come to a complete stop while the gale was raging.

The mulberry installation at the British beach at Arromanches also suffered from the storm, but the damage was not so extensive as at Omaha. For one thing, the British beach was more favorably situated, farther inside the Bay of the Seine, and within the lee of the Le Havre peninsula, and considerable protection was afforded by the Calvados Rocks, a rocky shoal area just northeast of the harbor installation. For another, the phoenixes at Arromanches were set in water slightly shallower. Moreover, at Omaha the construction work was about 85 per cent completed when the storm hit, while at Arromanches the work had made far less progress.

When the severe weather at length subsided, there was work to be done on both American beaches. The wreckage had to be cleared away, in order not only to salvage the maximum amount of usable equipment but also to put the beaches again into an operating condition. The Seabees salvaged a number of LCT's, barges, coasters, and small craft.

At Omaha a survey of the mulberry led to the conclusion that it was too far gone to be repaired. As that meant that the gooseberry would be the beach's only protection against the open sea, the blockship installation had to be strengthened. Accordingly, 10 more ships and 21 more phoenixes were brought across the Channel from England and sunk so as to reinforce the gooseberry, by forming a second breakwater immediately inshore from the installation that had been originally laid down.

At Utah the two causeways, which had settled badly, had to be taken up and re-laid somewhat farther west. In the rebuilding, their width was increased to four pontoon strings (28 feet), equal to the causeway width at Omaha; the "blisters" were eliminated; and the length was reduced to 1400 feet.

On June 22, the first day after the storm, the rhinos were back in service at Utah, lightering vehicles and cargo from ship to shore. Because of the great damage done to the barge equipment at Omaha, particularly to the outboard engines, rhino operations there were not fully resumed until July 1.

Marrying rhinos to LST's was discontinued on D-plus-7, for it had been found that the landing ships could be successfully beached. During the first ten days of the invasion, rhinos had accounted for the landing of 5,286 vehicles at Utah and 16,000 at Omaha. Thereafter, they were used to lighter vehicles and cargo from Liberty ships and coasters, the transfer being made by the ships' cargo booms. The causeways continued to carry out the function for which they were intended, the unloading of vehicles from LCT's and personnel from LCI's.

Personnel Camps

It was also the responsibility of the Seabees to construct and operate camps for naval personnel behind the invasion beaches. At Omaha, the de-

tachment having this assignment arrived off the beach at about midnight of D-day. Their schedule of operations called for them to go ashore and begin their camp operations on D-plus-1, but the great number of beach obstructions still in place prevented that plan from being carried out. It was not until the morning of D-plus-3 that the detachment could get on the beach, and it was found, even then, that the area that had been chosen for the camp site, on a cliff overlooking the far eastern end of the beach, was not yet clear of mines. Accordingly, a small bivouac area adjoining the proposed camp site was occupied as temporary measure until the Army could remove the mines from at least a part of the area planned for occupation. For the first few days thereafter, naval personnel who had to be given shelter ashore were accommodated in the temporary camp.

On D-plus-6, work was begun on the beach camp, designed to accommodate 6000 men, that had been planned. Air raids were a nightly occurrence, and foxholes and slit trenches became important items in the facilities provided. By the next day, it was possible for personnel in the bivouac area to begin occupying the pup tents erected in orderly rows along the lines of trenches. Unfortunately, the great number of land mines, still in place, limited the dispersal of the camp facilities; in fact, a number of anti-personnel mines and a few anti-tank mines were encountered even in those areas understood to be "cleared."

Tent erection proceeded steadily during the days that followed, as rhino-ferry crews moved up from the beach and as the number of stragglers and beach survivors mounted. By D-plus-13, all the rhino crews had been billeted ashore.

The population of the camp fluctuated widely; its maximum was reached in the latter part of June, after the great storm, with a total of 3150, which included British as well as American personnel. On one occasion, 12 men from the Norwegian navy were given shelter.

It was found, however, that the camp location left much to be desired; it was too exposed to enemy bombing and strafing. Accordingly, after the great storm had subsided, a start was made on a new camp for Seabee personnel at a more desirable location, and a separate site was selected for a camp for the naval staff. Both new camps were built of pyramidal tents instead of the shelter-halves used for the earlier facility. The 111th Battalion moved into its new quarters late in July;

the other camp was occupied near the end of August.

At Utah, the 81st Battalion erected a tent camp to house 1500 men and 70 officers a short distance behind the beach. This camp included six galleys and a hospital comprising nine tents and one quonset hut. In addition, headquarters facilities for the naval officer in charge were set up, which included two quonset huts, an underground BOQ, and telephone, radio, and visual communication systems for the entire beach.

Cherbourg and Le Havre

After the assault operations were successfully completed, Omaha beach continued to be used as the only available port in northern France until the middle of October when the ports of Cherbourg and then Le Havre were opened to Allied shipping.

At the end of the assault phase, however, most of the Seabees returned to England, leaving the 69th, 28th, and 114th Battalions of the 25th Regiment to close up Omaha beach and open the ports at Cherbourg and Le Havre.

The 69th Battalion remained at Omaha, relieving the 111th, worked the harbor as long as was necessary and then closed it by dismantling all its installations. The other two battalions moved to Cherbourg and went to work rebuilding communications systems, re-conditioning war-damaged houses for occupation by naval personnel, and running a transportation pool.

In August 1944, the 114th Battalion arrived in Cherbourg and made ready to carry out its assigned function of rehabilitating French ports still to be captured from the enemy. In London, the Bureau of Yards and Docks set up a small office to make detailed plans for this rehabilitation. Many of the ports for which rehabilitation work was planned, however, were successfully held by the Germans for a long time, and by the time they were taken had been practically demolished by bombing and gun fire. Moreover, the progress of our troops, moving eastward toward Germany, had been so rapid that the western French ports were no longer of vital importance for logistic-support purposes.

When Le Havre fell on September 20, 1944, the 28th Battalion moved to Le Havre to re-construct the harbor which had been badly damaged by Allied bombings and German demolitions. In No-

vember, the 114th Battalion moved to Le Havre to relieve the 28th.

Like most of the other Channel ports, Le Havre depended upon locked basins for docking facilities because the average rise and fall of the tide is from 25 to 40 feet. The retreating Germans had blown up virtually all the basin gates, in an endeavor to make the harbor of no use to the conquering Allies.

Army engineers set to work repairing the gates to the locked basins, and Seabees began installing floating piers inside the gates. This was accomplished by bringing rhino barges from Omaha Beach, joining two rhinos to make a pier which was made stationary by driving pilings and was connected to shore by a bailey bridge.

Outside the main sea-wall at Le Havre, the Seabees constructed a 60-by-1,000-foot floating pier of pontoons, which was capable of handling six cargo vessels. On the inshore section of the floating pier, they constructed two timber ramps, each connected with the shore by means of a bailey bridge, built by the Army engineers. With their upper ends resting on pontoon units 5 feet high above the deck of the pier, the ramps were made of such length as to give a ten-percent grade. This same grade continued over the bailey bridges at low tide when their outer ends were down, decreasing as the tide rose until, at high tide, the bridges were horizontal. The piers were moored by pile dolphins placed by Army engineers.

The Seabees also built a pierced-plank airfield at Le Havre. The first strip, built by the 28th Battalion, consisted solely of pierced plank laid on the ground. In building the second strip, the 114th Battalion placed the pierced plank on top of a 4-inch fill which was made of debris from battle-damaged Le Havre and of stones obtained in a nearby quarry. The pierced plank used in this construction had to be hauled 150 miles from Omaha beach.

In addition to the work at Cherbourg and Le Havre, the 28th and 114th also sent detachments to other parts of France. In October, the 28th sent a detachment to Calais on temporary duty. In November, the mobile telephone crew of the 28th was assigned to Paris. The 114th Battalion sent one company to Nantes in August and another company to Pontivy in September.

On November 20, 1944, the 25th Regiment was decommissioned, and the 114th Battalion was formed into CBMU's 627, 628, and 629. CBMU 627, consisting of 250 men and five officers, took

FIRST SEABEE CAMP ON THE NORMANDY BEACH

over maintenance duties in Cherbourg, where they remained until June 1945, when they were returnd to Davisville. CBMU 628. with a personnel of 350 men and ten officers handled public works, communications, and transportation in Le Havre, until December 1945 when they also returned to the United States. CBMU 629 moved to Paris to repair Orly airfield. In May 1945, a small detachment was sent to Bad Schwalbach in Germany; they returned to Orly in June. In July 1945, work was discontinued at Orly, and the unit was divided, half of the personnel returning to the United States; the remainder moving across the channel to the United Kingdom.

Seabees at the Rhine Crossing

Three CBMU's—the 627th, the 628th, and the 629th—participated in the crossing of the Rhine. One unit, the 629th, participated in front-line activities. The other two were with the rear echelon. From pontoon assemblies in the ports of Cherbourg and Le Havre, they salvaged pontoons and accessories to fill the bill of materials for 5-by-12-pontoon and 4-by-12-pontoon barges, to a total of 71. They assembled the material in lots for the various destinations of the barges. They also assembled and marked quantities of anti-mine and anti-torpedo netting with flotation gear for various sections of the Rhine. and they expedited shipments to the forward area.

CBMU 629 was split into four detachments of one officer and six men each. Three detachments worked with small boat units in their preparation for the Rhine crossing, and one detachment worked with an Army Engineer unit.

The first detachment became the first Seabee unit to enter Germany, on December 26, 1944. Later. they assembled pontoon barges on the Rhine at Remagen. These barges were to have been used in connection with strengthening the Ludendorf bridge. When that structure collapsed, work on the barges stopped.

The second detachment supervised the construction by the Army Engineers of a pontoon pile-driver barge for use in the construction of a bridge across the Moselle. The rig was completed January 28. 1945. It was later disassembled and transported overland to the Rhine, where it was assembled in preparation for the Rhine crossing. The second detachment also helped load boats for transport to the banks of the Rhine.

The third detachment assembled sea mules along the Meuse River, then built a pontoon pile-driver rig near Maastricht. In March the detachment built sea-mule barges for use as tugs and work barges for bridge construction in the Rhine crossing at Wesel. Operations on the Rhine were carried on day and night; at night, under flood lights; at times, under enemy fire.

The primary function of the fourth detachment was to instruct Army personnel in the assembly and operation of barges on the Meuse River.

Seabees in Germany

The only construction battalion assigned to Germany was the 69th. which had completed demobilization of Omaha Beach. On April 6, 1945, the first echelon, comprising 300 officers and men, left London for Ostend, Belgium, where they docked on April 7. After remaining two weeks at Hengelo, Holland, the Seabees moved on April 24 to Vreden, Germany. After the fall of Bremen on April 27, the first echelon proceeded there, followed soon after by the rest of the battalion.

After setting up camp in the German barracks at Lettow-Vorbeck Kazarene, a few miles outside the city of Bremen, the Seabees immediately set to work re-roofing buildings where artillery had made huge gaps, installing plumbing and lighting, setting up shops and offices where necessary, repairing harbor facilities, and installing and repairing power lines.

Later, detachments were sent to Bremerhaven and Frankfort-am-Main. Bremerhaven was to be set up as the main port of entry into Germany for the occupation army. Quarters for officers and men were made livable: dock installations, power lines, and other facilities were repaired. Frankfurt-am-Main was designated as headquarters for the United States Navy for the occupation of Germany.

In the meantime, employment of German civilian labor was begun in Bremen. These men were trained in the shops, transportation, and the operations of the base so that eventually only a skeleton crew of Seabees remained in Germany in supervisory capacities.

Beginning June 22, 1945, the 69th Battalion was flown in echelons from Germany to England.

CHAPTER 22

PEARL HARBOR AND THE OUTLYING ISLANDS

Development of Pearl Harbor under the National Defense construction program, together with the fortification of other Pacific island possessions, was begun in the fall of 1939.

At that time, the navy yard occupied 498 acres and included one battleship drydock with its supporting industrial establishment, one marine railway, administration offices, two fuel-oil tank farms (above ground), a supply depot, and housing, a total of 190 buildings. The Pearl Harbor naval hospital, occupying 41 acres adjoining the navy yard, was a 1100-bed facility. Ford Island, a 330-acre island within the harbor waters, was the site of the fleet air base. With facilities for seaplanes and a landplane runway 5400 feet long, Ford Island was used jointly by the Army and the Navy. At that time, however, the Army had Hickam Field under construction and was in the process of relinquishing Ford Island entirely to the Navy. The Pearl Harbor submarine base occupied 32 acres of harbor waterfront and was contained in 28 buildings.

Other naval properties on the island of Oahu included a Marine barracks, with a total of 29 buildings on 55 acres of land adjoining the navy yard, an ammunition depot at West Loch and Lualualei, a large radio station at Lualualei, a six-acre reservation at Bishops Point, adjoining Fort Kamehameha at the harbor entrance, a mooring mast for blimps at Ewa, a 152-acre rifle range at Puuloa, a small radio station at Wailupe, and several other small reservations that were used as right-of-way for water supply. An 18-foot macadam highway linked the navy yard with Honolulu, 10 miles distant. Beyond the limits of the Navy-owned property and the land containing Hickam Field, the surrounding countryside was devoted to the cultivation of sugar cane.

Recommendations of the Hepburn Board formed the basis of the first CPFF contract, awarded by the Navy during the war-construction program. As signed on August 5, 1939, the contract covered the construction of a new naval air station at Kaneohe, on the northern shore of Oahu, a major expansion of the existing air base on Ford Island, and the development of air facilities on Midway, Johnston, and Palmyra islands, at an estimated total cost of $15,505,000.

The contractor, designated as Pacific Naval Air Base Contractors, was a combination of three construction companies, each a specialist in its own field.

For some time prior to this beginning, deficiencies other than those concerning aircraft had been manifest at Pearl Harbor. Additional ship-repair facilities were needed; also, fuel storage, housing, electric-power and fresh-water systems, greater anchorage area within the harbor and additional piers and wharves; in fact, improvements and additions of every category were essential to strengthen our main fleet base in the mid-Pacific.

In view of this situation, a second major contract was awarded on December 22, 1939, for the construction of two new graving docks adjacent to the existing battleship dock, then in operation. Dock No. 2 was a 1000-foot battleship dock; Dock No. 3 a smaller structure, 497 feet long, for destroyers and submarines. A lump-sum contract was awarded jointly to two companies for the work at an estimated cost of $7,000,000.

In 1940, two additional contracting firms joined the three known as Pacific Naval Air Base Contractors, and a new CPFF contract, to replace the earlier one, was executed on July 1, 1940, covering construction at an estimated cost of $30,870,000. A year later, in July 1941, three more firms were added to the PNAB contractors. When the contract was terminated, on December 31, 1943, the total construction and procurement costs had exceeded $692,000,000.

On October 12, 1940, a third CPFF contract was awarded jointly to three local contractors, covering a program of miscellaneous construction areas outside the navy yard.

The two-year period between the start of construction in the fall of 1939 and the outbreak of war with Japan was one of intensive and sustained activity. Major extensions were made to industrial facilities in the navy yard, including additional drydocks. power plants, shops, storehouses, piers, wharves, barracks, office buildings. cranes, mechanical equipment. and various utilities. The major undertakings of the approved program for the yard were usably complete by December 7, 1941. Particularly noteworthy was the completion of Dock No. 2, during the week prior to the Japanese attack, to a stage which permitted the emergency docking of the cruiser *Helena*, which was torpedoed during the attack.

Important construction was begun at Kaneohe and at Barbers Point on Oahu. on the islands of Maui, Midway, Guam, Wake, Johnston, Palmyra, and Samoa, and at Cavite in the Philippines. All these facilities, except those at Samoa and Guam, were in use before December 7. 1941. Extensions to submarine facilities were undertaken at Pearl Harbor and Midway. A new supply depot on Kuahua Island, a tremendous underground fuel-storage project. a new hospital, a new radio station, extensions to ammunition storage, and an extensive dredging program were also in progress at Pearl Harbor. Concurrently with these developments. five major housing projects, with a capacity of 20,000, were being built to house civilian and naval personnel. These were accompanied by an extensive program for making personnel. power. and communication structures bombproof.

On October 4, 1941, a fourth fixed-fee contract was awarded for the building of another battleship drydock, Dock No. 4, and a 20,000-kw bombproof power plant. The contractor, already at work on Docks No. 2 and No. 3, began work on these new facilities during November.

To achieve flexible control of the contract, under the emergency conditions following the attack. it was imperative to establish the cost-plus-fixed-fee relationship possible under a CPFF contract. The lump-sum contract was therefore terminated on December 7, 1941, and Docks No. 2 and No. 3, which at that time were 90-percent complete, were finished under a CPFF contract.

In addition to the completion of Docks No. 2 and No. 3, and the construction of Dock No. 4 and the new power plant, the new CPFF contract included construction of a 3000-ton marine railway, several bombproof electrical sub-stations with an interconnecting power-loop system, erection of several 50-ton cranes at each drydock, and salvage operations made necessary by the December 7 attack.

The work under these contracts continued over a period of four and a half years, on sites which extended from Port Hueneme in California to Cavite in the Philippines. a distance of 7000 miles; at one time, 26,000 persons were employed by the contractors.

Extensive dredging operations were required at the outlying islands and at many places in the Hawaiian group. Thirty million cubic yards were dredged; the deepening of Pearl Harbor waters accounted for 13,000,000 cubic yards.

Five quarries were operated on Oahu to obtain the required concrete and paving aggregates. Although the manufacture of cement was considered, no plant was built because of the time element involved. Consequently, cement was shipped from the mainland, largely in bulk, an operation which required the continuous use of two ships.

At Guam, Wake, and Cavite, work was terminated by enemy action. At Midway, Johnston, and Palmyra, the contractors' forces were withdrawn during the summer of 1942 and were replaced by Seabees. The first of these battalions, the 5th, arrived at Pearl Harbor in June 1942, to be followed by the 10th in September and the 16th in October. Each battalion was sent forward immediately to carry on programs left unfinished by the contractors.

Immediately after the December 7 attack, the construction program at Pearl Harbor slackened briefly while a large portion of the contractors' personnel and equipment were engaged in rehabilitation work and emergency defense measures. Following this period, however. the program went forward with renewed vigor and at the same time expanded immensely beyond its pre-war dimensions.

In view of a tightening labor market on the mainland by the spring of 1943, it became necessary to send Seabees to Hawaii to expedite new construction, which had extended far beyond the original navy yard limits.

Initially, these battalions undertook new projects, supplementing the contractors' forces, but eventually they replaced the contractors' personnel and brought about a gradual curtailment of contract activities.

The termination of the earlier contracts by

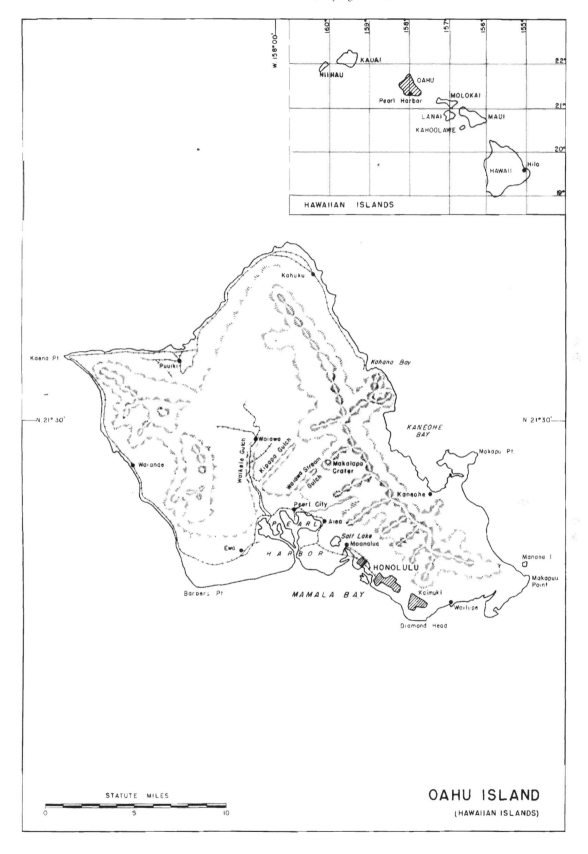

OAHU ISLAND
(HAWAIIAN ISLANDS)

March 31, 1944 and the use of Seabees did not, however, mark the end of contract construction. On August 16, 1943, a new CPFF contract was awarded to one of the eight firms comprising PNAB contractors. In its initial form, it included a 3200-bed expansion of the new naval hospital at Aiea, the conversion of 350 housing units into 700 small apartments, construction of a three-story BOQ in the navy yard, and extension of the water-supply system at the ammunition depot and at the radio station at Lualualei. During 1944 and 1945, this contract was supplemented many times to include extensive new construction in the Navy yard and the Pearl Harbor vicinity, and it was still active when the Japanese surrendered.

Pearl Harbor Navy Yard

Two years before the attack on Pearl Harbor, in December 1939, a lump-sum contract for the construction of two drydocks had been awarded. Built adjacent to the existing battleship dock, which had been in use since 1919, Dock No. 2 was a battleship dock, 1000 feet long and 133 feet wide, with a 46-foot depth over the sill; Dock No. 3, a smaller structure accommodating destroyers and submarines, was 497 feet long and 84 feet wide, with a 22-foot sill depth.

Both docks were built of reinforced concrete supported on steel-pile foundations. Four pumps, located in a pump-house between the two docks, controlled the unwatering. Closures were made by steel caisson-type gates. In building portions of these docks, the tremie method of placing concrete under water was used in preference to the steel cofferdam method used in 1910 for the construction of Dock No. 1.

The tremie concrete-deposition method was evolved from a series of 22 experiments, in which various grades of concrete were deposited under water varying in depth from 51 feet to 67 feet. The method finally adopted utilized nine 17-inch pipes, spaced 10 feet apart, which serviced half of the width of the drydock slab at a time.

In building Dock No. 2, after placing a gravel foundation bed, driving steel piles, placing tremie truss floor units, and pouring tremie concrete floor, side-wall cofferdam form units were erected in six opposite pairs of an average length of 162 feet with 90-foot intermediate closure units. The side walls were poured in the dry. At Dock No. 3, the construction was similar to that for Dock No. 2,

except that, after pouring the tremie floor, a closure cofferdam was built at the entrance to the dock, and steel sheet piling was placed to form the outer form wall for the side and end walls of the dock. After unwatering the entire structure, the wooden inner forms were built, and the concrete was poured in the dry.

On December 7, 1941, Dock No. 2 was usably complete and Dock No. 3 was half finished. After the blocking of Dock No. 1 by the burning of the destroyers *Cassin* and *Downes*, and the sinking of the only floating dock in the harbor, Dock No. 2 was the only drydock available. It was not yet finished, but the caisson gate was in place and emergency use was practicable, a fact of the utmost importance to all subsequent salvage operations. The cruiser *Helena* was docked here on December 10 and remained until the 21st. The dock was unwatered by pumpwell drainage pumps and the contractors' construction pumps. Temporary connections provided the ship with air, fresh water, and salt water. The dock was completed while in use.

A CPFF contract for the construction of Dock No. 4, a power plant, and mooring facilities for aircraft carriers at the navy yard, had been signed on October 4, 1941. After the Japanese attack, the assigned projects were changed in part and augmented. Specifically, the work under the contract consisted of the completion of the two docks then being constructed under the lump-sum contract, and the construction of Dock No. 4, with appurtenances and services for each dock, construction of a marine railway and repairs to an existing one, construction of a bombproof power plant with substations and equipment, and a series of switchstations with an interconnecting power-loop system, together with salvage operations and other emergency work necessitated by the Japanese attack.

Installations for Dock No. 4 included a drydock, 147 feet wide at the floor, 1100 feet long, and 47 feet deep over floor and sill, a floating caisson gate and an extra caisson, a pumping plant, service and track systems, and short quay walls on both sides of the dock entrance. The floor, including finish, was 19 feet thick, with 20-foot thick side walls.

Construction of Dock No. 4 differed from that of Docks No. 2 and No. 3 in two important respects. Although the floors of all three docks were poured by the tremie method, Docks No. 2 and No. 3 were

DRY DOCK NO. 1, PEARL HARBOR NAVY YARD

supported on steel piling, imbedded in the floor slabs, to aid in resisting hydrostatic uplift. Dock No. 4, in contrast, was supported on wood piling, driven to compact the underlying soil. These piles were cut off 6 inches below the slab bottom, to insure against their interfering with the placement of forms. Also, the walls of Dock No. 4 were poured to high-water line by the tremie method, and only the top, or gallery section, was poured in the dry; whereas, in Docks No. 2 and No. 3 the walls were poured entirely in the dry.

The success of construction operations depended upon the skillful integration of many plant set-up items. For example, the 350-foot-span gantry crane, which had been used in the construction of Docks No. 2 and No. 3, was moved without disassembly by extension of its tracks to the new location. The original gantry cantilever extension was removed and a second bridge gantry crane was erected on the same tracks. These two gantries were the primary means of constructing and placing all forms, and carrying concrete buckets to the tremie rigs.

Pile driving, in the dock's inboard portion, was begun on October 12, 1942, as soon as dredging was complete. This was done for a sufficient distance to permit handling of floating equipment without interfering with the dredge. A total of 9,694 piles, averaging 30 feet in length, was driven. The work was completed on December 22.

Piles were cut off by an underwater circular saw, driven by a barge-mounted motor through a vertical shaft. Cutting-off operations were begun on November 4, 1942, and completed on January 14, 1943. Placement of the rock blanket, the foundation for tremie concrete, was begun on November 9, using 3-inch quarry waste. Rock was placed through a 36-inch steel pipe from a 12-yard steel

to a height of 69 feet. It required 24 hours to finish both sides of one section.

By May 20, 1943, all tremie concrete had been placed. Unwatering was begun on June 11, with the caisson in place and the side walls complete, except for pumpwell sections which were enclosed by steel sheet cofferdams. The dock was completely emptied on June 13 and slab surfaces were leveled

BARRACKS AT THE STAGING CENTER, PEARL HARBOR

hopper at the upper end, through the water, to a flat-bottomed section at the lower end, set at the elevation of the top of the rock blanket. A 2-foot layer of rock, topped by a 3-inch layer of sand, furnished a smooth, even bed for setting the forms, which were begun December 7, 1942; the first concrete was poured on December 19.

Tremie concrete for the dock floor was poured through eight 17-inch pipes, supported by pontoons. These pipes led from eight hoppers to the bottom of the floor slab, with an individual drum for each, operated by hoisting engines, which raised and lowered the pipes. This arrangement poured half a bottom form at one pour. For the side walls, two 3-pipe tremie rigs operated simultaneously on opposite sides of the dock. The gantries picked up six-cubic-yard buckets, brought by truck from the concrete plant, carried them out, and dumped them into the pipe hoppers. A form containing 785 cubic yards of concrete was thus poured in three and a half hours. Side-wall forms nearly 50 feet long were poured slowly, in one lift

by chipping and blasting, before the 18-inch floor finish was begun. A 125-man detail from the 62nd Construction Battalion assisted in this operation.

The dock was ready for emergency use by July 19, 1943. By October 1, 1943, the main pumps were ready for operation and the floor and bottom altar were complete, with keel blocks in place and all lines connected. The first docking occurred on October 6, 1943.

The new 3,000-ton, 836-foot marine railway for handling destroyers and submarines, was begun on January 1, 1943, and placed in operation September 15, 1943. It was constructed under water by tremie concrete methods. Dredging entailed the removal of 50,000 cubic yards.

In constructing the marine railway, reinforced-concrete groundway sections, in units approximately 18 by 120 feet, were precast on a casting wharf erected adjacent to the railway site. A 150-ton floating crane lifted sections from the wharf, placed them upon previously driven timber piles, and, after being exactly positioned with jacks, they

SUPPLY DEPARTMENT WAREHOUSE, PEARL HARBOR NAVY YARD

were fixed, by masses of tremie concrete poured around each girder, for the entire length.

As originally planned, the service wharf for the marine railway was to be 60 feet wide and 450 feet long. Upon investigation, it developed that a wider pier would be required to afford sufficient operating range for a 50-ton traveling crane operating on a 28-foot-gauge track, and the dimensions were increased to 70 by 570 feet.

The wharf consisted of a concrete deck, half of which was supported on land and half on piles. In addition to the tracks for the 50-ton crane, it carried narrow-gauge rail tracks. Both tracks connected with Dock No. 3. Heavy reinforced-concrete girders were constructed for the crane rails and bore chiefly on the concrete piles. These girders

rested, at their inboard ends, on concrete columns which bore on stepped spread-footings. The remainder of the wharf rested on concrete piles driven into the hard underlying coral sandstone. Wood form-work was built on the piling, and the concrete was poured in the dry.

The power plant, substations, and associated buildings were of bomb- and splinterproof construction. All bombproof construction was of heavy reinforced concrete.

The bombproof power plant, simple in design, was notable for its massive, windowless construction. It was divided into four nearly equal areas, containing boilers, turbo-generators, and air compressors.

Protected fuel-oil storage was provided in two

SMALL BOMBPROOF POWER SUBSTATION, PEARL HARBOR

pairs of 25,000-gallon underground tanks, shielded by a reinforced-concrete mat.

Two 10,000-kw turbo-generators, with necessary boilers, and with switch-gear and all control devices, were installed.

The new electrical-distribution system, designed to provide 11,500-volt, three-phase, 60-cycle power characteristics, augmented the existing navy yard system. This new system was a modification of the existing service in that it effected a change from radial distribution from the central power house, to a network transmission system in which the navy yard was divided into approximately equal power areas, each supplied from switching stations interconnected to the several independent sources of supply.

Installation of cables, nearly all in underground ducts, was complicated by the necessity for performing the work in the face of constantly multiplying yard activities and power load, by the progress of new construction projects of major importance, and by the demand for temporary power

facilities. Wherever possible, such temporary services were so installed as to permit their later incorporation into the permanent system.

Major additions were made to the industrial shop facilities, principally in areas adjacent to the drydocks.

The administration building was enlarged; water, sewer, and communication facilities were expanded. A bombproof communication center was built, together with concrete personnel shelters and casualty stations. Available berthing space was greatly increased by constructing quay walls and bulkheads. Additional barracks, housing for transient naval personnel, an elaborate system of paved roads, extensive railroad trackage, several laundries, a fuel station, warehouses, and many miscellaneous buildings were also constructed.

In making improvements to the harbor and channels a total of 13,000,000 cubic yards was dredged. The initial dredging program, which was started in May 1940, to provide a turning channel around the periphery of Ford Island, grew to include the

ORDNANCE SHOP, PEARL HARBOR NAVY YARD

deepening of West Loch, Middle Loch, East Loch, and Magazine Loch to provide a mooring area for fleet units within the harbor. The channel to the sea was also deepened.

Salvaging of ships and property and the rescue of personnel began December 7, 1941.

For salvage operations, methods were developed for underwater patching with timber, steel, and concrete, or combinations of these materials; an elaborate system of struts, anchors, tackles and winches was used to right capsized ships.

Salvage work was of two kinds: repairs to damaged vessels still afloat, although seriously flooded, as in the case of the *Pennsylvania, Maryland, Tennessee, Helena, Honolulu. Raleigh, Vestal,* and *Curtiss:* and the raising, flotation, and repair of the sunken or grounded vessels *Shaw, Nevada, California, West Virginia, Oglala, Arizona, Oklahoma.* and *YFD-2.*

Much of the material and equipment necessary for salvage operations had to be shipped from the mainland, and did not arrive until February 1942. Without waiting for its arrival, however, the contractor's forces began work. Divers and available equipment were diverted from work on Docks No. 2 and No. 3 to patch holes in the *Nevada.* Beneath 30 feet of water, holes were patched with concrete or with combinations of timber and steel and were sealed with tremie-placed concrete. The

ship was then pumped out, floated, and placed in drydock, where repairs were made by the Navy.

In salvaging YFD-2, the contractor designed, constructed, and placed a 40-foot-square patch under the bottom shell, so designed that it created a chamber 4 feet deep below the hull, which permitted repairs to the frames and bottom-shell plates. Divers patched more than 200 holes.

From surveys made and data furnished by the Navy, the contractor also designed and constructed steel and timber patches which were applied, under 40 feet of water, to the *West Virginia.*

The contractor's engineers then prepared to raise the *California.* Deck cofferdams, assembled on shore in large units, were placed forward and aft, and the torpedo holes were closed with tremie concrete. When salvage work had reached the pumping-out stage below decks the ship was turned over to the Navy for flotation.

It was decided to occlude water from the main-deck openings by building a fence-type cofferdam around its edge and pumping out the vessel without patching. The ship was successfully floated on March 24, 1942, permanent repair of all underwater damage was made by yard forces, and on June 7, 1942, she was released from the dock.

The *West Virginia* had been moored outboard the *Tennessee* on December 7. She took several torpedoes, and two large bombs damaged the vessel's port side and amidships superstructure. There was also extensive oil-fire damage from internal explosions and the fire which had spread from the *Arizona*, moored a few yards astern. As a result, the *West Virginia* rested on the bottom, with a three-degree list, the port side of the main deck slightly immersed.

Visible damage was extensive, and underwater survey indicated that flotation would be difficult. The initial plan, to drive a sheet-piling cofferdam around the ship which would expose underwater damage and permit temporary repairs, proved impracticable because of the porosity of the coral bottom. Finally, two large cofferdam patches were set, installed in sections 13 feet long by 50 feet deep, with the ends sealed by underwater concreting. The ship was floated on May 17 and drydocked June 9.

On December 7, the *Oglala* had been berthed, port side to, outboard the *Helena*, when an aerial torpedo passed under her and struck the *Helena*. The resultant pressure wave sprung the *Oglala's* port bilge area and permitted slow flooding. As capsizing was likely to foul the *Helena*, the *Oglala* was towed clear, and capsized against the dock, astern of the *Helena*.

It was necessary to salvage the *Oglala* at once as she obstructed a needed berth. The plan was, first, to right her, and then raise her by means of a deck-edge cofferdam. She was righted by attaching ten submarine salvage pontoons to her main weather decks and was placed in Dock No. 2 on July 3, 1942.

In contrast with the foregoing salvage projects, the operations connected with the *Arizona*, *Oklahoma*, and *Utah* were major undertakings. Cables and winches, installed on Ford Island, were used to right the *Oklahoma* and the *Utah*. The *Arizona*, however, was resting on the bottom, her back broken.

The *Oklahoma* had capsized, after rotating through an arc of 150 degrees: masts, cranes, stacks, turrets, and all superstructure were buried in the mud.

The vessel was righted by utilizing submarine-salvage pontoons attached to the mud-buried structures, then reducing the internal water level by air pressure, and, finally, by hauling winches rigged on Ford Island to exert a turning moment through wires running over a leverage strut built on the ship's bottom and attached to the starboard side-blister. She was then raised by means of a fence-type cofferdam, installed around the entire main deck.

As the ship was pumped out, small leaks were plugged by divers. A number of leaks had developed through the hull of the ship, but were concealed by the blister, which had been crushed against the hull when the ship rolled over. Divers had to cut their way through a tangled mass of blister steel to find and plug the leaks in the main hull, a task which required three months. The *Oklahoma* was afloat on November 17, 1943, and was towed into Dock No. 4 on December 28.

The *Utah* (a target ship) had been moored on the west side of Ford Island. She had been struck by three torpedoes on the port side, which caused her to rotate through an arc of 165 degrees, before capsizing.

Naval forces effected considerable salvage of material before any righting operations were undertaken by the contractor. The ship was rolled over, by using approximately the same equipment and methods as those used for the *Oklahoma*. However, after the ship had been raised to within 38 degrees of normal, work was suspended by Navy order.

The *Arizona* had been struck by several bombs and a torpedo. Navy divers found that the forward structure had been completely wrecked. The two forward turrets and the conning tower had dropped 20 feet vertically, indicating collapse of the hull.

It was possible that the after part of the ship might have been floated, after severance from the forward structure, but the value of the salvaged half would not have been sufficient to warrant the work involved and the tying up of drydock facilities. Porosity of the coral bottom prevented use of a sheet-piling cofferdam around the ship.

Work actually done by the contractor had included only exploratory work, method design, and estimates for raising, when, on May 22, 1943, salvage operations were ordered cancelled.

Submarine Base

The Pearl Harbor submarine base was established in 1920 on a 32-acre site adjacent to the industrial section of the navy yard. Under the war program, existing facilities were expanded to the limits of the land available. New work provided additional personnel and industrial facilities and major improvements along the waterfront to supply additional berthing area.

A fourth story, of temporary frame construction,

Dry Dock No. 4, Pearl Harbor Navy Yard

was added to the existing barracks, together with six, 200-man barracks and additions to the officers' quarters.

Within the industrial area, several storehouses, a two-story fire station, a warehouse for submarine spare parts, several shop buildings, and additions to the torpedo-overhaul shop were built. The existing waterfront structures were extended by a 1520-foot quay-wall, quipped with fuel, air, and water lines. A berthing area was developed, with two finger piers and extensive quay-wall area. The battery-charging shop and the electrical-distribution system were enlarged and improved.

During 1944, the 62nd Battalion built a machine shop and a compressor building and developed a related program of minor construction.

Storage Facilities

Before the course of the war required the establishment of bases and staging points in advanced areas, Pearl Harbor was the storage and issue point for most of the stores, fuel, and equipment used in the Pacific. For advanced operations, after the

outbreak of the war, these supplies had to be stock-piled in such quantities as to provide for unforeseen demands, a problem which was solved by the construction of warehouses, storage yards, and fuel tanks.

When the program began, early in 1940, storehouses were added to those already within the navy yard, but, as the demand for space increased, it became necessary to develop new areas outside the yard, a process which continued steadily until the Japanese surrendered. The new areas included Kuahua Island, Iroquois Point, Pearl City Peninsula, Waipio Point, Wiawa Gulch, leased areas in the city of Honolulu, and a wide area which was developed as an advance base supply depot, a Marine Corps storage area, and a supply depot annex.

Kuahua Island.—Kuahua Island was the site of the fleet supply depot. Before large-scale development began, Kuahua was a 47-acre island, connected to the mainland by a narrow causeway. Spoil from dredging operations in Pearl Harbor was used as fill material to extend the island until it formed a peninsula with an area of 116 acres. Reinforced-concrete quays were erected around the periphery of this peninsula to confine the fill and provide additional berthing space.

Existing buildings on Kuahua Island, in the fall of 1941, consisted of eight one- or two-story structures, six of which were ultimately used as storehouses. The other two were converted into shops, one for mine craft and the other for torpedoes.

Six multi-story, reinforced-concrete storehouses were erected for dry provisions and miscellaneous stores, in addition to a five-story cold-storage building. The main portion of this structure was 280 feet long by 120 feet wide. On each floor were two rooms, 120 by 60 feet, each, in which a temperature of four degrees could be maintained. These rooms were flanked by service corridors, each containing two elevators. Other rooms in the building could be maintained at varying temperatures. One-story extensions, 30 feet wide, housed offices and refrigeration machinery. This work was completed by the contractors in the fall of 1943.

To increase berthing space at the depot and to facilitate transshipment of cargo, a 150-by-600-foot pier was built of concrete on concrete piles. It was equipped with railroad tracks and an open transit shed, 75 by 450 feet. Berthing space on each side of the pier brought to twelve the total number of ships which could be docked at the depot at one time.

Merry Point.—Merry Point was also used by the supply department as a storage and shipping area. Prior to the expansion program, quays had been built on two sides of this triangular spit of land and the waterfront developed for ship mooring. There were two buildings; one, near the center of the triangle, was converted to use as a lubricating-oil storehouse, and the other, a one-story frame structure, had recently been constructed as a cold-storage building. The contractors erected five temporary wooden storehouses along the north quay and paved the area at its eastern end for cargo sorting and handling.

Within the navy yard, a five-story reinforced-concrete storehouse was built for general and miscellaneous dry stores. This building, 180 feet wide and 500 feet long, was provided with an 18-inch concrete roof slab, which made it partially bombproof. A bombproof command center was constructed on the ground floor. Six freight and two passenger elevators served the building.

Interposed with the other facilities within the yard, many other warehouses were erected. Most of them were of one-story wood-frame construction, varying in size from a small office building to a temporary shed. Railroad spur tracks and paved roads were provided to facilitate the movement of material.

To relieve congestion in the yard and to disperse supplies, several sites on the island of Oahu were developed for additional storage. A plot of ground, known as the Damon Tract, was one. Here, the contractors erected 25 temporary one-story wood-frame buildings, the largest of which was 240 by 500 feet. One building, 300 feet long, with four 100-foot wings, was used by the Seabees as brigade headquarters. Another, 61 by 160 feet, was used as a dry-cleaning plant, and included equipment for the repair, renovation, and storage of special winter clothing.

Two battalions, the 64th and the 90th, were assigned the completion of the project after the contractor's forces were withdrawn upon termination of the contract. Minor construction was finished by a maintenance unit.

Pearl City.—The base of the Pearl City Peninsula was selected as the site for another storage area. The contractors erected three 130-by-550-foot one-story frame warehouses with concrete floors. A railroad spur was installed with three shorter spurs extending between the buildings. The ground around the structures was paved with asphaltic concrete. A 100-by-500-foot oil-drum shed was also erected. Two smaller open sheds for cable storage and a Marine guard building completed the development.

Pearl City Peninsula was also the site of the spare parts distribution center and other supply depot warehouses, known as the Manana Supply Center. The spare parts distribution center, built by the 117th Battalion, between March and September 1944, contained 18 warehouses which provided 626,000 square feet of covered storage space. Portions of other battalions assisted the 117th in developing 20 buildings for the supply depot.

Waiawa Gulch.—An aviation supply depot was built at Waiawa Gulch, where 50 wood-frame structures were erected by the contractors. Open-storage areas, which stretched along the banks of Waiawa stream for 2 miles, were connected by paved roads. A road also connected the Waiawa development to an auxiliary area, just south of the Manana storage

REINFORCED CONCRETE STOREHOUSE, NAVAL SUPPLY DEPOT, PEARL HARBOR

area, containing 20 warehouses, erected by the Seabees.

A waterfront terminal for the aviation supply depot was built at the southern tip of Pearl City Peninsula, adjacent to the Naval Air Transport station. Two wharves, each 400 feet in length, were built for mooring carriers and supply ships, and six wood-frame sheds were erected for the sorting and temporary storage of cargo.

ABCD Salt Lake.—At the Salt Lake storage area and advance base construction depot, eighteen 80-by-190-foot wood-frame warehouses, together with several smaller utility structures, were erected by the contractors. One of the larger buildings housed a coffee-roasting plant which had been transferred from Mare Island.

Seabees set up fifteen 40-foot-by-100-foot quonset warehouses and graded the entire area, including 20 acres for open storage. They also erected a heavy equipment overhaul depot, consisting of 8 quonset warehouses and 12 wood-frame buildings.

Miscellaneous Storage Construction.—A supply annex, including shipping facilities for the advance base construction depot, was built by Seabees at Iroquois Point. The 98th Battalion started the work in May 1944; it was relieved by the 43rd, which completed the work in the spring of 1945. An area of 342 acres was graded and surfaced with

coral, and 24 quonset warehouses, six 96-by-283-foot, one-story, wood-frame warehouses, and 4 miles of railroad were built. Approximately 2,000 feet of docking space were provided for the receiving and shipment of material.

Within the city of Honolulu, more than 30 buildings and areas were leased by the Navy for the use of the district supply department and for the storage of aviation supplies for the Honolulu naval air station. Five piers and wharves were also leased for use by the supply department and the contractors.

Waipio Point.—A salvage area at Waipio Point was developed for use by the supply department. This activity, which reclaimed usable parts and metal from ships which were damaged beyond repair, was equipped with a 225-foot T-wharf, a 60-by-160-foot warehouse, and a paved working area of concrete and macadam.

Underground fuel storage.—The military risk involved in fuel-oil storage at Pearl Harbor had long been the subject of discussion. In its 1938 report, the local shore station development board had pointed out that experience had proved fueling facilities inadequate for considerable fleet concentrations, even in time of peace. Studies were undertaken to determine the best method of solving the problem. The Bureau of Yards and Docks suggested several methods, including tanks placed underground to the point of concealment only; pre-stressed, circular, reinforced-concrete tanks, concealed by cut-and-cover methods; steel-lined concrete tunnels; and underground steel tanks. It was decided that tunnel-type storage, with vertical-type cylindrical, domed vaults of prestressed, reinforced concrete, with inner steel linings, was the most practical.

designed to use the rock rather than the steel and concrete to resist pressures.

Work was begun late in December 1940.

Construction methods included first the excavation of two concrete-lined tunnels: an upper and a lower access tunnel. The center lines of the tunnels within the tank area were parallel with, and midway between, the center lines of the two rows of tanks. The upper access tunnel entered the ridge

Upper Tank Farm, Pearl Harbor

The underground fuel-storage project, in its completed form, provided for the storage of 5,-400,000 barrels of fuel oil and 600,000 barrels of diesel oil, a total of six million barrels, stored in twenty vaults arranged in two parallel rows. The vaults were cylindrical in shape, 250 feet high and 100 feet in diameter, with dome-shaped tops and bottoms. The interiors were lined with sheet steel and backed with concrete. The tanks were connected by pipelines through a tunnel which was excavated from beneath the vaults to an underground bombproof pumphouse. Oil was received and issued at a concrete fueling pier and transferred from the pumphouse to the pier through underground pipelines.

Construction of the storage vaults involved numerous features for which no precedent was found in design or construction methods. Although many tunnels had been built in lava in the surrounding areas, no construction had been attempted which required the 100-foot rock span necessary in the building of these vaults. The tank structures were

on the north side and was driven at the same grade as the tops of the tanks. The lower access tunnel, which was later used as a portion of the pipeline tunnel, entered the ridge three-fifths of a mile west of the first tank and ran at a grade slightly below the tank bottoms. Cross-tunnels were excavated from the access tunnels to the center of each tank. A belt-conveyor system was installed in the lower tunnel to facilitate removal of excavated material. A crusher and screening plant, erected in the adjacent valley, processed the rock excavated for use as concrete aggregate in the construction of the tanks and tunnels.

On December 16, work was begun on the sinking of pilot shafts, 4 by 5 feet in cross-section, on the vertical center lines of the first four vaults. When these shafts had penetrated to the lower access tunnels, work was begun on the vaults.

The first work done on the tanks themselves was the construction of the upper domes. In order to avoid the necessity of working above a considerable depth of excavation, only enough rock was excavated to allow room for the building operation. A ring tunnel, timbered where necessary, was first driven around the spring line of a dome, and a concrete curb ring was placed with a channel-iron bed in its top. The concrete ring was to serve as a sill for the dome while the main portion of the tank was excavated and the walls formed. To speed the disposal of the excavated material, that portion of the pilot shaft from the dome down to the lower access tunnel was enlarged to 12 by 12 feet. Because of the arch action of the rock formation, it was possible to remove the material in the dome area to make a hemispherical excavation, 10 feet high. and to use the channel iron in the curb as a foundation upon which to erect a structural steel falsework, braced against the undisturbed rock, for the steel dome lining. After the reinforcing steel and lining had been placed and welded, the dome was concreted in one continuous pour of 75 hours. Pumped concrete was piped through the pilot shaft from a mixer at the surface. Next. the dome. 8 feet thick at the spring line and 4 feet thick at the crown. was pre-stressed by forcing grout between the concrete and the surrounding rock.

For the excavation of a vault's main cylinder, the pilot shaft was enlarged to 30 feet in diameter. After the shaft enlargement was completed, excavation was begun at the top of the vault, just below the concrete dome, to bring the tank to its final diameter. This operation consisted of blasting the rock in such a manner as to cause the excavated material to slide down the sides of the pit to the shaft and then into the lower access tunnel. where it was removed from the site on the conveyor belt. When the tank was excavated, the exposed rock surface was coated with pneumatically placed concrete. A wash of mud and water then was applied to prevent bond between the concrete lining and the coated rock.

A steel tower, extending the full height of the tank, was erected in the center of each vault. The tower supported concrete chutes, power cables, and other construction equipment. Piping connections were installed from the lower tunnel to the vault.

For the first, or bottom. section of the lower dome, templates were carefully set along the joint lines for the steel lining. The pre-formed steel-lining sections were welded in place and used as forms for the concrete poured around and under the bottom of the tank. This operation was repeated for the remaining sections of the lower

dome, a ring at a time, until the dome was brought to the spring line.

Construction of the vault side-walls, with a thickness of reinforced concrete varying from 4 feet at the bottom to less than 3 feet at the top, was then begun. The walls were built in 5-foot lifts, using quarter-inch steel lining plates as the inside forms. Delivery of concrete into place behind the lining was made as the lining was installed. In general, lining operations were kept two lifts ahead of concreting. The cycle of operations was repeated until the previously completed upper dome was reached. At this junction of the side walls with the upper dome, an expansion joint was introduced to take up possible settlement and to minimize the possibility of rupture to the lining.

Grouting to pre-stress the concrete was then done. Pre-stressing was necessary because of the practical and economical limitations of providing sufficient reinforcement in the walls to take the hydrostatic pressure of the stored oil. The vaults were designed in such a manner that most of the liquid pressure in the tank was resisted passively by the surrounding natural material rather than by the reinforcement in the walls. Grouting of the annular spaces between the walls of the vault and the material around them was intended to fill any voids, to compress any weak areas in the rock envelope, and to place the inner concrete shell under compressive pre-stress. The reinforcement in the concrete was relied upon for general consolidation of the structure, redistribution of reaction pressures, and to take care of special stress concentrations.

Grout was supplied by a plant on the surface, directly above the tanks. Grout pipes had been inserted in the concrete walls during their construction, and these were used to introduce grout between the rock and the concrete. Grout was fed into the pipes, at one elevation. under a pressure 20 per cent greater than the computed hydrostatic pressure from the oil at the point where the grout was introduced, until the grout was visible in the next series of pipes, 35 feet higher in the tank. The lines were then moved to these pipes and the operation repeated. This cycle was carried out until the entire tank was pre-stressed.

Grouting completed, the tank lining was scrubbed down, with particular emphasis on the joints. The tank was then thoroughly tested by introducing air under pressure beneath the steel lining, applying soapy water to the inner surface, and locating leaks by bubbles. As testing of the bottom section was completed, water was introduced into the vault and testing crews worked their way around the walls in boats. Rise of the inflow was arrested every 5 feet to test horizontal joints. After all disclosed leaks had been stopped. the vault was filled with water as a final check.

Work on the twenty tanks was carried on more or less by an assembly-line method. When a crew finished one portion of the work, it moved on to repeat the same operation on the next tank. In this way, it was not necessary to train a large number of men in all phases of the intricate methods of construction that were developed. The first vault was brought to usable completion on September 28, 1942, and by July 20, 1943, all tanks were ready to receive oil.

In addition to the upper and lower access tunnels and the cross tunnels, there also was a long pipe tunnel leading to the pumphouse. Work on the tank end of this tunnel started as soon as the other tunneling was completed, and as more workmen became available, work was started at the pumphouse end. The tunnel was holed through December 27, 1941. The entire amount of tunnel work on the project, including the access tunnels, was more than 7 miles. Within the tunnels, more than 32 miles of pipe was installed, varying in size from 8 inches to 32 inches.

While construction of the first domes was underway, work on the receiving pumphouse and surge tanks was begun. Both were built in open cut, with heavy reinforced concrete, bombproof walls and roofs. Automatic-closing, oil-tight doors were built to prevent flooding of the pumphouse if breaks occurred in either the tunnel or the surge tanks.

A 54-by-1300-foot fuel-oil pier, built of reinforced concrete, provided berthing space for four ships. The installed equipment made it possible to issue oil from the pier at the rate of 20,000 barrels per hour.

Housing

The tremendous expansion of facilities in the Pearl Harbor area gave rise to a concomitant program of housing construction, which began during the fall of 1940 and continued throughout the war period. This housing was built to accommodate civilian employees of the yard, contractors' employees, and naval personnel on duty in the area or in a transient status.

Altogether, five separate housing areas were built. each planned as an independent community, with schools, fire protection, and recreational facilities.

Area One, occupying 90 acres, contained 500 housing units in 155 buildings. Area Two occupied 61 acres and was identical in every respect. Area Three, built on a 192-acre site, had 1000 units in 238 buildings, and was equipped with a laundry, fire station, two large mess halls, and four recreational buildings. Schools were provided in Area One for the combined housing development. These buildings were all two-story wood and cinderblock structures, built to minimum standards.

Area Four, a 2000-man cantonment, erected to house the bachelor employees of the contractors, was also a complete community.

The fifth area, set apart as officer housing, was built on a 362-acre tract at Makalapa Crater. Designated "Makalapa," this area contained 104 houses of varying size and pattern, five large barracks, the administration headquarters for CinCPac, a radio station, and two large office buildings housing Navy Intelligence. The CinCPac headquarters building was a reinforced-concrete bombproof structure, 60 feet wide, 200 feet long, and two stories high.

Built to house the many thousands of enlisted personnel staging through Pearl Harbor, Aiea receiving barracks was located on a 130-acre tract. Planned to accommodate 10,000 men. the project, begun during the summer of 1942, included two identical camps, each with a capacity of 5000 men. Buildings erected included 117 single-story barracks, two large mess halls, four recreation halls, a dispensary, a dental clinic, a laundry. a bakery, and an administration building. Minimum frame construction was used throughout.

In January 1944, construction was started on a third camp area to house an additional 6000 men in 16 large, two-story frame barracks. This camp was built by the 94th Construction Battalion.

Recreational facilities were developed on a 25-acre site across the highway from the Aiea Barracks, designated Richardson Recreation Center.

Naval Air Stations

Ford Island. Ford Island, in Pearl Harbor, is flat and entirely covered with pavement and buildings.

At the start of the war-program construction, on November 30, 1939, about one-third of the

BARRACKS AND RECREATION FIELD AT KANEOHE NAVAL AIR STATION

island was occupied by the Army, and the waterfront was devoted principally to fleet moorings. Construction was begun by a crew of 40 men, who performed hand excavation to locate buried utilities. By mid-December the construction force had grown to 400 men, engaged in the establishment of material yards and construction plants.

Reconstruction of the Army airfield required removal of the existing pavement and grade correction. Asphaltic concrete was used for the landing mat, which, upon completion in June 1941, was 4,500 feet long and 650 feet wide. A concrete warm-up platform, 1300 feet long and 600 feet wide, landplane hangars, administration building, dispensary, bachelor officers' quarters, underground gasoline storage facilities, the main wharf, seaplane ramps and parking areas, the final assembly shops, and miscellaneous storage buildings were essentially complete by December 7, 1941.

During the attack, one seaplane hangar and the dispensary were damaged, and considerable damage was done to the seaplane parking area. Although repairs were quickly effected, the construction program was disrupted for many days while the landing field and hangar area were being cleared of wreckage.

Revetments, personnel shelters, a bombproof command center, and much splinter-proofing were provided, and one of the old hangars was converted into an emergency barracks. A new 16-inch water main was laid across the channel, and the power cable was repaired.

The advent of war also brought heavy air-traffic to Ford Island, necessitating additional gasoline storage. Forty-eight 25,000-gallon tanks were built underground, and the existing surface tanks were splinter-proofed.

The original seaplane area was augmented by an engine overhaul shop, five concrete ramps, and extensive parking and warm-up areas. Revetments were built, and mooring facilities repaired.

On the northern shore of the island, two T-wharves of reinforced concrete were built on precast concrete piles. The dredging incidental to their construction provided material which was used to enlarge the island to the extent of seven acres. On the southern shore, a bulkhead, a wharf, and several small-boat slips were built, and a T-wharf was rehabilitated. Many buildings of steel and concrete were erected for the various shops, warehouses, training buildings, and administration offices.

A 10-inch gasoline-distribution loop, completed in January 1943, was installed to supply the fueling pits. Most of the initial construction was complete by this time, and until the termination of the contract in December 1943, attention was directed

Facilities built for aircraft operation and maintenance included five steel hangars, five seaplane ramps, concrete parking areas, two warm-up aprons, a maintenance hangar, two seaplane hangars, and two Midway-type hangars. Twenty-foot lean-tos for shops and offices were built adjoining all hangars. As most of the buildings were on filled ground, pile foundations were required. Both corrugated asbestos and asbestos-protected corru-

ASSEMBLY AND REPAIR SHOP, KANEOHE NAVAL AIR STATION

toward the extension and improvement of existing installations.

Kaneohe. — Pursuant to the Hepburn Board recommendations, an adjunct to the Ford Island fleet air base was built at Kaneohe, on a 1830-acre tract on Mokapu Peninsula.

As originally planned, the station was to be a seaplane base with facilities to support five squadrons of seaplanes. Construction commenced in September 1939, under the Pacific Naval Air Base contract, on 42 projects. The major project entailed extensive dredging operations to provide the necessary seaplane runways within the sheltered waters of Kaneohe Bay. Dredging continued for three years, during which time 11,000,000 cubic yards of material were removed.

In the summer of 1940, an airstrip was added to the facilities, with accompanying increases in housing, hangars, parking area, gasoline storage, and industrial buildings. The completed runway, 5,700 by 1,000 feet, was paved with asphaltic concrete.

gated metal were used as walls, partitions, and as roof sheathing on hangars and similar structures.

The gasoline storage and distribution system consisted of 136 underground steel tanks, each holding 25,000 gallons, and was connected with the water-displacement distribution system and five 50,000-gallon and four 25,000-gallon underground, pre-stressed, concrete tanks, equipped with motor-driven, deep-well pumps. The gasoline was pumped from tankers at the fueling pier, through an 8-inch line, to the tanks.

The distribution system included 20 fueling pits on the warm-up apron, each capable of issuing 100 gallons per minute. The 8-inch main around the runway was connected to the concrete tanks and cross-connected to the issue lines, allowing the runway pits to be serviced either directly by pumps from the concrete tanks or from the water-displacement system of the tank farm. Gasoline from the concrete tanks, in addition to being pumped directly to the fueling pits, could be pumped into the storage tanks or directly to the fueling pits at the warm-up apron.

Administration buildings, housing and messing facilities, a hospital, shops, and a storage building were constructed to meet the expanding needs. To care for 9000 men, 23 married officers' quarters, 52 enlisted men's quarters, 15 officers' barracks, and 54 enlisted men's barracks were built. Before the Japanese attack, all barracks were constructed of

runway, 400-by-5000-feet. This field, paved with asphalt, was completed by the 74th Battalion, which replaced the 112th in November 1944. Major construction at Kaneohe was completed during May 1945, and the following month CBMU 596 arrived for maintenance.

Barbers Point.—The naval air station at Barbers Point was originally designed as an auxiliary, or outlying airfield, of Ford Island. Construction

BACHELOR OFFICERS' QUARTERS, KANEOHE NAVAL AIR STATION

reinforced concrete, but after the outbreak of war all personnel facilities were built of wood, to conserve critical materials. When the Seabees arrived, they built 16 additional barracks, two-story woodframe structures which housed 240 men each. Some 30 magazines were built for ready storage of bombs, torpedoes, and small arms.

After the Japanese attack, 50 plane revetments were constructed; vital installations were splinterproofed; and personnel shelters were constructed.

The Seabees arrived on April 1, 1943, to replace the contractor's forces and take over further construction. The 56th Battalion, the first to arrive, began completion of unfinished projects and undertook the construction of a new bombproof powerhouse and an electrical-distribution system which included 14 concrete substations. They also built an assembly and repair building, 160 by 240 feet, a plating shop, a building for testing engines, and an engine-overhaul building. In February 1944, the 112th Seabees started construction of a second

of the field and related facilities was accomplished under the PNAB contract. Original plans were designed to supply accommodations for land-based operations of two aircraft-carrier groups, with provision for station personnel. Included were plane runways, two hangars, necessary shops, storage, and utilities, and quarters for 2,000 men, 250 officers, and 800 civilian workers.

Additional authorizations after the outbreak of war increased the station's capacity to a point at which it could support four carrier groups. Personnel accommodations were increased to a capacity of 4,000 men, 450 officers, and 1,200 civilian workers. Additional magazines and training facilities were added; the size of runways and plane-parking areas was increased.

Barbers Point development had an advantage over earlier projects in that it was authorized in virtually its final form before work had progressed beyond the preliminary stage. Some changes, both in plan and in type of construction, were made;

INDUSTRIAL AREA, BARBERS POINT NAVAL AIR STATION
Assembly and repair shop in center background

but they were made immediately after December 7, when the work was just getting underway.

In the original conception of the air station at this location, the area now designated as the Ewa Marine Corps station was included. However, as the need for operational strips in the Hawaiian area became more urgent, it was decided to develop additional runways in the Ewa location for use during the construction of Barbers Point, which was expected to be a relatively long-time operation. Field work was started on the Ewa project in September 1940, but after the outbreak of the war the plan to relinquish the field was cancelled, and it was developed as a Marine Corps air station.

Work at Barbers Point was begun in November 1941. Some clearing was started, but with the advent of war the men were needed for the early completion of Ewa Field. As crews completed the work at Ewa, they were immediately transferred to the Barbers Point project. The two main runways at Barbers Point, 8,400 feet long and 1,000 feet wide, were originally laid out with four runways, forming an X, or modified radial layout. These runways were to be 500 feet wide with lengths varying from 3,400 feet to 4,800 feet. Later, it was decided to enlarge the runways by increasing the width to 1000 feet and the overall lengths to 8,400 and 8,300 feet, respectively. With this radial arrangement of runways, control of flight operations was facilitated and the necessity for long taxi-ways obviated, with resultant greater operational economy and traffic capacity.

The only adverse condition encountered during construction was that of voids in the sub-grade, some of them 600 cubic yards in extent, which necessitated filling to provide a stable base for the strips. This condition was cared for by a sluicing operation. Beach sand was dumped on the area and washed into the voids by the use of fire hose. After the sluicing, coral was applied over the whole area to the depth required to bring the sub-grade to the proper elevation. The finished surface of the runways was asphaltic concrete.

An asphalt hot-mix plant with a 4,000-pound batch capacity was installed adjacent to the site. It supplied all the asphaltic mix for the 1,650,000 square yards of paving on the runways, warm-up platforms, and taxiways, for the paving on the Ewa runways, and for all the roads, sidewalks, and parking areas in the southwestern portion of Oahu.

Next to the airfield in importance, and even greater in scope, were the buildings for personnel housing, hangars, storage, and schools, many of which were planned as permanent construction.

ADMINISTRATION BUILDING AT PEARL HARBOR NAVAL AIR STATION

After the Pearl Harbor raid, plans were revised to substitute temporary frame buildings, to conserve critical materials and time.

The contractors, however, had stockpiled in the Hawaiian area and on the west coast of the United States some of the materials considered critical, and to conserve the time needed for reordering supplies for the temporary buildings, construction was begun on some buildings, utilizing this material. The administration building, aviation operations building, torpedo and bombsight building. aircraft storehouse. command center, power house, and telephone buildings were built of reinforced concrete. Other buildings were wood frame, temporary structures.

Two steel-frame 370-by-240-foot hangars, with 25-foot wide two-story lean-tos at either side for offices and shops, had exterior walls of asbestos-protected corrugated metal.

The assembly and repair shops were housed in a steel-framed, concrete, block-walled structure. For this building. the only one at the base which required extensive foundation work, 500 concrete piles were driven to depths varying from 40 to 100 feet in order to obtain the necessary bearing values for the foundations.

Housing and messing accommodations for 2,000 enlisted men were provided in nine barracks, a mess hall and galley, and a bakery and cooks' quarters. In August 1942, these facilities were ordered increased to care for 4000 men. The original group of buildings and 70 per cent of the second group were completed before termination of the PNAB contract. The buildings were of wood-frame construction. The barracks were H-shaped, two-story structures. Housing for 400 officers was provided in several two-story, frame buildings.

One-story, wood-frame buildings were erected for a 150-bed hospital. Included in one interconnected building were mess hall, boiler plant, and morgue. Medical stores, the garage, and nurses' quarters were in small separate buildings.

Storage space was provided in 92 buildings. The original plan called for one large warehouse, but later, in conformity with the policy for dispersing stores, eight scattered groups of smaller storehouses were substituted. These buildings were of light, temporary construction, on concrete slabs. In addition, four larger storehouses were built in the main station area.

Aviation-gasoline storage was provided in twenty-four 25,000-gallon, underground, steel tanks, equipped with a water-displacement system. The underground receiving tank, also of steel, had a capacity of 570,000 gallons. Delivery was designed to be by truck or by railroad tank-car. The storage tanks were buried in coral rock. In line with the Navy's policy to disperse important stores, the tanks were built in widely separated groups of four tanks each, with a distance of at least 100 feet between any two tanks. As a further protection against bombs, the pumphouse was built with its floor elevation 24 feet below ground level. Diesel oil and fuel oil were each stored in two 25,000-gallon, underground, steel tanks.

The contractors had completed an estimated 98 per cent of the original contract and its various supplements by the July 15, 1943, when the contract work was terminated. During the 18 months they were employed, they had built, in addition to the installations already described, more than 8 miles of paved and 11 miles of unpaved roads, more than 3 miles of narrow-gauge railroad, and a large sewage-disposal plant. They had also excavated a total of 4,000,000 cubic yards of rock and coral, including the work on the runways, cleared 1500 acres, and installed 54,000 feet of fencing. For various projects, the contractors used 27,000,000 board feet of lumber, 6000 tons of structural steel, 6000 tons of reinforcing steel, and poured a total of 80,000 cubic yards of concrete.

The 16th Seabees, sent to Barbers Point in April 1943, were quartered in the former contractors' camp, midway between the Ewa and the Barbers Point landing fields. They took over maintenance work and the completion of minor construction left undone by the contractor. This included installation of a 1000-line automatic telephone exchange and a 12-mile pipeline connecting the Ewa Junction aviation-gasoline depot with the storage tanks at the Marine Corps air station and the naval air station at Barbers Point. Ewa Junction was interconnected with the fueling pier at Pearl City, and the bulk-storage tank was provided with a transfer pump which allowed transfer of gasoline between any of the four locations.

CBMU 522 relieved the 16th Battalion on March 1, 1944. In November of that year the 14th Battalion sent a detachment to Barbers Point, which, together with personnel that could be spared from the regularly assigned maintenance duties, carried out the last of the major construction work. They erected several wood-frame barracks, a mess-hall, some small buildings to be used as offices, and two hangars.

Honolulu.—During 1942, the Navy enlarged the facilities at the Pan American Airways terminal on the southern tip of Pearl City Peninsula, for use by the Naval Air Transport Service. However, as ship traffic in the adjacent Pearl Harbor waters increased, it became evident that the continued use of these waters by seaplanes would be impractical.

Consequently, the Navy took over the John Rodgers Airport, a commercial facility at Keehi Lagoon on the south shore of Oahu, midway between Pearl Harbor and Honolulu, subsequently designated Naval Air Station, Honolulu.

When the Navy acquired the property, early in 1943, the commercial airlines had four hangars, several small buildings, and two short, intersecting runways. With the exception of the area surrounding these buildings and runways, the land was low and swampy, and only 2 feet above high tide.

Work was started on the project in February 1943, when the contractors brought a dredge into Keehi Lagoon and began the dredging necessary for the seaplane runways. Spoil from this operation was used as fill to bring the land area to a 10-foot elevation. In April it was decided that Army engineers would do the necessary dredging for the runways and Seabees would perform the other work at the station.

The seaplane landing area, as dredged by the Army, consisted of three runways, each 1,000 feet wide by three miles long. The dredged material was handled on the beach by the 5th Seabees, who placed, compacted, and graded the land upon which the landing strips were built.

The 5th Battalion, upon its re-assembly at Pearl Harbor in May 1943, had also taken over the completion of the buildings started by the contractor and begun the erection of aviation-gasoline storage facilities, including twenty 50,000-gallon prestressed concrete tanks, a control tower, several barracks and warehouses, a 10-plane nose hangar, and two seaplane ramps.

In May 1944, the 133rd Seabees were assigned to the air station; during their five months stay they increased the aviation-gasoline storage capacity to 500,000 gallons and completed the two concrete seaplane ramps. They also built eight floating piers for docking seaplanes, five aviation-material storehouses, machine shops, several 250-man frame barracks and two-story, 40-by-100-foot, quonset barracks, an officers' mess, WAVES quarters, and did additional work on the landing field.

The 133rd was augmented by the 13th Battalion in June 1944. This unit assisted on the landing field and road work, in addition to constructing utility systems, a 60-by-205-foot cold-storage building, six line-storage sheds, a concrete-block paint and oil storehouse, and three underground 5,000-gallon oil tanks. The 13th also installed concrete-slab ripraps along the waterfront and moved 35

NOSE HANGARS AT HONOLULU NAVAL AIR STATION

NOSE HANGAR SHOP NAS HONOLULU

houses several miles. The 13th Battalion left in September 1944, and the 133rd followed in November.

From June to September 1944, a portion of the 50th Battalion was engaged in barracks construction. These crews were relieved by the 64th Seabees, to whom was assigned the completion of the air station. The 64th completed the construction that was underway, made additions to the landing-field, and did finish-grading throughout the area. They left in March 1945, when the station was turned over to maintenance crews.

The main runway of the completed field was 7,400 feet long, paved for a 200-foot width, and intersected near its western end by a 6,800-foot runway. Two 6,600-foot parallel runways were also built. These runways, as well as all of the connecting taxiways and parking areas, were paved with

BARRACKS FOR CIVILIAN HOUSING, MARINE CORPS AIR STATION, EWA

asphaltic concrete. Shops, repair facilities, and a large paved parking area were provided, together with housing and living facilities and an administration area.

Marine Corps Air Station

Ewa.—Early in the 1930's, the Navy secured a lease to a 700-acre tract at Ewa, northeast of Barbers Point, and on it erected a dirigible mooring mast and built an oil-surfaced, 150-by-1500-foot emergency landing field.

Field work was started in September 1940 on the grading required for the extension of the existing runway and for a new cross-runway; the strips were in usable condition in the spring of 1941. By June of that year, the paving of the two strips was complete, and Marine personnel moved in, erected their own living facilities, and operated a small number of planes.

In July, work began on two groups of barracks with a total capacity of 3,000 men, a 100-man BOQ, a storehouse, shops, a dispensary, mess facilities, and an operations building.

Two additional runways were laid down, a 300-by-950-foot warm-up platform was added, and one

hangar was provided, an old structure moved from Ford Island.

For some time after the Japanese attack on December 7, which destroyed all the planes stationed at Ewa but left the strips and buildings undamaged, all civilian forces in that portion of the island concentrated on completing the authorized facilities. One runway was brought to usable completion in less than two months; buildings were hastily erected, and splinter-proofing of power transformers and other vital installations was rushed.

In September 1942, Ewa was established as a Marine Corps air station.

Extensive passive-defense facilities were included in the expansion that accompanied the designation of Ewa as a separate base. These measures included 75 reinforced-concrete half-dome revetments, 91 sandbag bunkers, a dressing station, and blast protection for vital installations.

The airfield had four runways, each 300 feet wide, with lengths varying from 2,900 feet to 5,000 feet. Gasoline storage was built underground in four 25,000-gallon and five 50,000-gallon pre-stressed-concrete tanks, which were dispersed in small groups. The work was not completed when the contract was terminated and the Seabees took over on April 1, 1943.

The 16th Battalion, the first Seabee unit in the area, constructed a pipeline connecting the aviation-gasoline storage with the entire southwest portion of the area.

In June of 1943, sixty men of the 10th Battalion were sent to Ewa. By the end of July they had erected 20 quonset huts for their own camp and had completed nine wood-frame barracks, several squadron workshops and storage buildings, an administration building, and a warm-up area, with accompanying taxi-strips.

Maintenance was taken over in October 1943 by CBMU 530, who also engaged in some small construction; any personnel who could be spared from their maintenance duties were loaned to other units whose primary function was construction.

In March 1944 the 10th Battalion was relieved by the 130th, which, during the next eight months completed the administration building, a parachute loft, shops and garages, nose hangars, warehouses, a public-works building, messing facilities, and reinforced-concrete magazines. It also operated a coral pit which supplied material for roads and airstrips.

In November 1944 the 130th was augmented by a portion of the 14th Battalion which undertook

the construction of a recreation building and a dispensary, finished the warehouses, garages, the 3,000-man messhall, and began work on the WAVES barracks. The 123rd Seabees arrived early in January 1945 and were assigned the task of erecting 23 buildings for civilian housing. However, when 20 per cent of this work was completed, on February 28, the remainder of the work was turned over to civilian contractors.

Ammunition Depots

Lualualei.--This depot was originally established by the Navy on February 5, 1931. The 7910-acre site had at one time been a forest preserve, and was transferred to the Navy by the Territory of Hawaii. No additional real property was required for expansion.

Magazine construction under the PNAB contract included fifty-three 25-by-80-foot, eleven 50-by-100-foot, and eight 20-by-25-foot concrete structures buried in the hillside, and 24 frame buildings for storage of projectiles and inert material. Other construction included housing for 600 station personnel, shops, administration buildings, roads, walks, and 15 miles of railroad track.

The 125th Construction Battalion arrived at Lualualei in April 1944 to design and construct additional facilities. Among these were 28 miles of asphalt-paved roads, 10 miles of railroad, sort-

COVERED CONCRETE REVETMENTS, MARINE CORPS AIR STATION, EWA

AIEA NAVAL HOSPITAL
Entrance to the main building

ing sheds, shops, utilities, and housing. This work was completed in 10 months and the 125th left in May 1945. The 52nd Battalion arrived in October 1944 and built 18 miles of roadways, additional railroad facilities, and housing. CBMU 581 arrived in March 1944 and took over all maintenance and minor construction.

West Loch.— For the expansion of the West Loch ammunition depot, 358 additional acres were purchased, which enlarged the tract to 537 acres.

New construction included twelve 25-by-50-foot high-explosive magazines, fifteen 50-by-86-foot, assembled-mine magazines, five 10-by-14-foot and three 20-by-25-foot magazines for fuses and detonators, and 11 magazines for dispersed torpedo storage. In addition, 12 other buildings were constructed to store pyrotechnics, inert material, mine anchors, fixed ammunition, and projectiles. Work on the waterfront included extension of an old wharf and the construction of a new 1000-foot wharf. Also constructed were 9 miles of railroad and personnel structures for 600.

Additional railroad facilities, test buildings, recreational facilities, patrol roads, and sorting sheds were built by the 43rd Seabees. Station maintenance and minor construction were accomplished by CBMU 581.

Waikele Gulch.—The pressing problem presented by the vast amount of explosives stored in the open among the hills and valleys of southern Oahu crystallized in mid-June 1942, when the Commander-in-Chief of the Pacific Fleet directed that "underground ammunition storage of major proportions" be constructed in a location that would "both be readily defended by, and accessible to, Pearl Harbor."

A 350-acre site was selected where steep-banked ravines made possible tunnel construction in such a manner that no two entrances faced each other, and a railroad spur could be built to service the installation.

Most of the tunnel roofs were concreted, and the floors were built of reinforced concrete. Concrete sidewalls were carried to a 7-foot height, mainly as gravity retaining walls. The loading platforms were of concrete.

Facilities included 120 tunnels, each 240 feet long, which required 9 miles of railroad, 10 miles of paved road, 9 miles of patrol road, four bridges, and housing and messing facilities for operating personnel. Work on this project, begun in September 1942, was completed in December 1943.

In April 1944 the 125th Battalion arrived, followed in May by the 95th, to carry out additional construction, upon completion of which the depot was turned over to CBMU 581.

Hospitals

Aiea.—The Aiea Hospital was constructed on the upper slopes of Aiea Heights, whose gentle slope was modified into a series of terraces on levels, 10 to 20 feet apart. The principal ward-and-administration building was built on the upper terrace; quarters and recreation grounds on the lower terraces; and the sewage-treatment plant on the lowest corner of the site. In the original planning the wards were oriented to receive maximum benefits from the sun and tradewinds, and the hospital facilities conveniently arranged to service the wards.

Field work, under the PNAB contract, was started in July 1941. Plans then called for a permanent type of construction, principally reinforced concrete, for the main hospital building, a subsistence building, a bachelor officers' quarters, a powerhouse, and nurses' and corpsmen's quarters.

Although the Japanese attack did not damage any of the hospital facilities, it had an immediate effect on the construction program in that all Japanese, regardless of their place of birth, were not allowed to be employed on any naval project. As most of the carpenters on the hospital job were of Japanese blood, work was almost completely stopped until the order was revoked a month and a half later.

In February 1942, the extent of the project was increased to include an addition of two ward-wings on the main building and the construction of a laundry and a medical storehouse, all of the same construction as those erected under the original authorization. Also built were temporary frame structures to house five wards for 500 patients, an extension of the nurses' quarters, and a BOQ for 100. By October 1942 the hospital was brought to a usable state of completion. However, work continued until the termination of the contract in December 1943.

WARDS AT THE NAVAL HOSPITAL ON MOANALUA RIDGE

NAS PEARL HARBOR

In August of 1943 it had been decided that existing facilities at Aiea could not care for the load of casualties expected as a result of projected operations in the Pacific. Accordingly, a new CPFF contract was awarded for a 3000-bed addition to the hospital, construction of which was begun in September 1943.

The major portion of the expansion consisted of fifteen 148-bed, two-story wards, a 1,000-man messhall, a cold-storage building, and a medical storehouse. In addition, the main building was enlarged by four, two-story, wood-frame wards with a total capacity of 800 patients. The officers' and nurses' quarters were also enlarged by wings to existing buildings.

Construction was completed in April 1944; in July, CBMU 600 was assigned the maintenance of all hospital facilities on the island of Oahu.

Moanalua Ridge.—The hospital on Moanalua Ridge was built as a temporary facility, to assist the main hospital at Aiea to care for casualties from the forward areas. Construction was begun in October 1943 by the 90th Seabees.

The hospital, which covered 115 acres, was of quonset-hut construction exclusively, with the exception of a few wood-frame buildings used for boiler houses, messhalls, galleys, garages, and small miscellaneous storage. The wards, consisting of three quonset huts placed end to end, were 175 feet long by 20 feet wide and had a capacity of 3000 patients in 100 buildings. A group of twelve large quonset huts, used as storehouses, separated the quarters from the wards. A recreational area, containing an open-air theater, was located in the center of the quarters for use by both corpsman and convalescent patients.

McGrew Point. Base Hospital 8, at McGrew Point, was built to augment hospital facilities during the peak of the military operations in the forward areas. Construction of this 1,000-bed facility was begun by the 92nd Battalion during November 1943.

The area was swampy, which necessitated excavation of 50,000 cubic yards of material to drain and reclaim the marsh. For wards, operating rooms, and quarters, 214 standard quonset huts were erected. Galleys, messhalls, and storage space were provided in six large quonsets, and 35 wood-frame structures were erected for shops. Ninety days after the start of construction, the hospital was usably complete, although the Seabees continued work on it for another ninety days.

Bishops Point and Iroquois Point

A section base and net depot was built at Bishops Point, and an annex was constructed directly across the Pearl Harbor entrance channel at Iroquois Point.

Bishops Point, before dredging and filling started, was a gently sloping, sandy beach, rising from the sea to an elevation of about 10 feet at the northern edge of the site. Iroquois Point was level area, a few feet above sea level.

The section base at Bishops Point was initially planned to provide a base and a training establishment for the net-and-boom craft stationed at the harbor entrance. Construction was started on this basis in September 1940; five months later, in February 1941, a net depot at this location was authorized, and the contractor was directed to increase the scope of the project. Still later, in the fall of 1942, work was started on the sub-section base at Iroquois Point.

As practically the entire Bishops Point area required fill, dredging was the first operation. This entailed the moving of 450,000 cubic yards of material.

The 1,000-foot quay was built on precast concrete piles, with a reinforced-concrete deck. After the wall was completed, two concrete piers, 20 by 300 feet, each, were added. Docking space for small boats was provided by a floating timber platform.

To provide drydock facilities for target barges, a 60-ton marine railway was built. Sheet-steel piles were driven to form a cofferdam at its water end, with about 135 feet of piling on each side which later formed the side walls of the railway. For the submarine portion of the railway, precast concrete piles were driven, and capped with reinforced concrete. Tracks at right angles to the railway were installed to facilitate handling and storing of target floats, and racks were built along these tracks to provide target storage. A wood-frame and corrugated-iron building was erected for target-repair shops.

With the exception of an air-raid shelter of reinforced concrete, all other buildings at Bishops Point were of wood-frame construction. They included two 2-story buildings, for barracks and an administration building; one-story frame buildings for the messhall, officers' quarters, storehouse, and shops; two 100-man barracks; and a recreation hall.

At the Iroquois Point annex, the major construction consisted of a 600-foot timber wharf connected to the shore by 140 feet of causeway. The area between the wharf and the channel line was dredged.

Except for the air-raid shelter of reinforced concrete, all buildings were of wood-frame construction. Housing facilities for base personnel were provided in four 30-by-120-foot barracks and a similar structure for officers. A recreation building and a messhall completed the living facilities. Storage was provided in a 60-by-125-foot structure; small buildings were erected for shops, offices, and the dispensary. The contractor completed the project in the spring of 1943.

Haiku Radio Station

The Haiku radio station was constructed at a point where two high, parallel ridges afforded natural supports for an elaborate antenna system.

Construction was begun under the PNAB contract during May 1942. The main projects of station construction included antenna erection, a bomb-proof building for the radio equipment, and housing for operating personnel.

As the first step in the antenna erection, men picked their way to the tops of the nearly vertical mountain ridges, dragging with them thin manila ropes to be used as pilot lines for the heavier cable. Subsequently, a cable way was installed from the valley floor to the anchorage sites on the ridge tops. This was used to haul men as well as materials. These anchorage sites on opposite sides of the valley supported antenna cables which could be raised and lowered for periodic inspections.

Moanalua Ridge

The 127-acre, Marine Corps transient center was built as a tent city to house Marines staging through Pearl Harbor.

Begun in October of 1943 by the 92nd Seabees, the camp was completed in four months. A 10,000-man center, it was broken into two 5,000-man areas, each containing a complete system of utilities.

Housing was provided in 1,250 tents erected over concrete floors, and eight 40-by-100-foot and fifty 20-by-48-foot quonset huts. Wood construction was used for special buildings such as administration offices and post office.

The Seabee encampment on Moanalua Ridge was built by the combined efforts of many construction battalions. Equipped to quarter 25,000 Seabees, the encampment was divided into 20 separate areas,

14TH DISTRICT QUARTERS FOR PERMANENT AND TRANSIENT OFFICERS, MOANALUA

each large enough to house one battalion. Completely self-contained, each area included six two-story wood-frame buildings, one 1,200-man galley, one 1,200-man messhall, eight standard quonset huts for offices and a dispensary, and one large quonset hut for a ship's service store.

More than 4 miles of 24-inch water main serviced these areas, and sewers adequately handled sanitation and drainage requirements. Electricity was supplied to all buildings. There were approximately 19,000 feet of 24-foot roadways, surfaced with 6 inches of crushed rock, throughout the camp area, in addition to 154,000 square feet of similar construction for shops and parking areas. The camp covered 120 acres.

The 73-acre Marine base depot was located adjacent to the Seabee encampment area. The 90th Seabees began the construction in October 1943. Upon completion of the project six months later, in April 1944, they had erected 40 warehouses, 48-by-190-feet each, arranged in four rows separated by paved streets 60-feet wide. They also constructed four larger storehouses and four special buildings for radar storage and shops. About 36 acres were graded to provide open storage.

Waianae Training Center

Naval Anti-Aircraft Training Center, Waianae, covered 42 acres on the west coast of Oahu, about 30 miles from Pearl Harbor.

The installation, authorized in July 1942, was built under the PNAB contract. It included barracks, a messhall, and utilities for 300 enlisted men and 20 officers; a school with 18 classrooms, a trainer building, an armory, and gun mounts. Each of the four barracks accommodated 75 men. Storage was provided in two 25-by-125-foot buildings. All buildings were of temporary construction.

Puuloa Rifle Range

The Puuloa Rifle Range, on the southern coast of Oahu, was already in use as a rifle range in 1940.

Under the PNAB contract, the existing installations were enlarged to increase training facilities. This improvement, begun in September 1940, included the addition of an armory, a frame magazine building, an armory rifle range, a recreation building, a galley and messhall, and 48 additional targets. Later additions were made to provide barracks for 300 men and 20 officers, a 25-by-123-foot dry-storage building, a cold-storage building, and fire-protection service.

Part II — Island of Maui

NAS *Puunene*

The island of Maui, second largest island in the Hawaiian group, is 90 miles southeast of Honolulu and 100 miles northwest of the island of Hawaii. The three principal naval activities were the naval air stations at Puunene and Kahului, and the Kahului section base.

On June 17, 1940, when the PNAB contractors began work it was planned to develop a small base for the use of a naval experimental unit at Puunene, where there existed a landing strip built by the Territory of Hawaii. While Army engineers improved the existing airfield and constructed a cross-runway and taxiways, the contractors built quarters and messing facilities for the 500 men attached to the unit.

Before the work was completed, plans were altered to include facilities for one carrier group. Two 50,000-gallon gasoline tanks were erected and a warm-up platform was laid down. Additional personnel and training facilities were added, including bomb and ammunition magazines. Revetments were constructed and aircraft utility shops erected to service the additional planes. The work was nearly complete in March 1942, when all work was taken over by Army engineers.

In November 1942, the contractors were recalled to construct facilities for a second expansion of plans at Puunene. Four 25,000-gallon tanks and three 50,000-gallon tanks were erected. Work was also begun on seven reinforced-concrete arch-type magazines. A bombsight shop, four storage buildings, and additional improvements to the landing field were other projects completed by the contractors.

On April 1, 1943, the 48th Seabees replaced the contractors and assumed responsibility for the completion of the air station.

Plans were again expanded to permit advanced training and staging for fighter, torpedo-bomber, and dive-bomber pilots. Each airstrip was lengthened 2,000 feet and paved with asphaltic concrete. Upon completion, one strip measured 6,900 feet and the other 6,000 feet.

Base facilities, including an assembly and repair building, bakery, dispensary, torpedo shop, theater, and additional housing and warehouses, were constructed by the Seabees. In addition, they installed complete water and sewerage systems, including a 500,000-gallon circular reinforced-concrete water-storage tank, and a power-distribution system supplied by the local company's existing transmission lines.

The existing 350,000-gallon aviation-gasoline storage system was augmented by five 50,000-gallon and five 25,000-gallon underground reinforced-concrete tanks. On May 15, 1944, the 48th was relieved by the 127th Battalion.

Magazine construction comprised a large portion of the work taken over by the 127th. Seven concrete arch-type magazines, two torpedo warhead magazines, and nine other magazines for fuses and detonators, ready service ammunition, and inert storage were added.

Grading and paving of roads and taxiways, installation of fences, together with additions to existing buildings, constituted the remaining work assigned to the 48th Battalion and completed by the 127th.

Projects assigned directly to the 127th included additional quonset barracks, a large nose-hangar, galley expansions, shop buildings, and warehouse improvements. The fire-protection system was also extended to afford adequate security for the additional facilities.

The 127th Battalion continued to operate on Maui until May 2, 1945, at which time the CBMU 575, which had reported in February 1944, assumed operating duties.

NAS *Kahului*

The site of Kahului Naval Air Station was leased from a commercial sugar company. About one-third of the 1350 acres was cultivated cane land; the remaining portion was pasture containing swamps and fish ponds. The only existing facilities were power and telephone lines, and a narrow-gauge railroad which ran along the highway connecting the villages of Kahului and Sprecklesville. The nearest water supply was in the village of Kahului.

The work of developing a new airfield for

carrier-group operations and training was begun by the PNAB contractors, when they were recalled to Maui in November 1943. They established a complete construction plant, including a camp and utilities, and accomplished the construction of 12 barracks, about 50 per cent of two messhall-galleys, and one bakery, and performed about 25 per cent of the clearing and grading preparatory to runway construction, before April 1943, when they were replaced by the 39th Construction Battalion.

The battalion's first efforts were concentrated on runway excavation and barracks construction. Two strips were prepared, each 500 feet wide by 5,000 and 7,000 feet long, respectively, with work made difficult by the considerable blasting operations required. A warm-up platform, 1500 by 650 feet, was constructed, approximately 190,000 square yards of parking area were laid down, and three nose hangars were erected in the center of the area. Nine ready-rooms, two machine and metal shops, a battery shop, a carburetor shop, and a radio-radar shop were built. Adequate taxiways and parking bunkers were constructed, and the field and taxiways paved with asphaltic concrete. Buildings of the cheapest and most temporary adequate construction were erected for barracks.

Five 25,000-gallon above-ground tanks were erected for aviation-gasoline storage; three were installed underground; and two large bulk-tanks were erected.

Ammunition was stored in 19 magazines, served by paved access roads.

The 39th also constructed a malfunction range, a moving-target machine-gun range, a skeet and trap range, and a machine-gun school. A sewage-disposal plant, sewage lines to the plant, water mains, and an electrical distribution system were installed, together with adequate ditching for drainage. Warehouses, theaters, and supply buildings were erected, built of temporary construction as the need arose. The 39th Battalion was relieved on June 15, 1944 by the 142nd Battalion, which continued operations until the spring of 1945.

CBMU 563 reported for duty in December 1943.

Kahului Section Base

When construction was started at the Kahului section base by Army engineers in 1942, all utilities, power, water, telephone, a railroad, and a paved highway, existed at the site. The harbor had been developed and was being used by a commercial sugar company. Included in the harbor facilities were two 900-foot piers with fuel and water lines, 123,000 square feet of storage sheds, and two un-loading cranes.

Personnel facilities, the only new construction undertaken, included an administration building, a messhall, quarters, and two storehouses. Nine major buildings were started by the Army, continued by the contractors, and completed by the Seabees.

Other Maui Activities

In addition to the two air stations and the section base, several smaller activities existed on Maui. These included the Fourth Marine Division headquarters, when the division was not engaged in combat, as well as several specialized branches of the Navy.

The Fourth Marine Division camp, built on the side of a mountain overlooking Kahului Harbor, was a 30,000-man center with all facilities, completed in four and a half months by the 48th Seabees. It consisted mainly of framing for 16-foot-square tents used as quarters, augmented by quonset huts for galleys, messhalls, ordnance buildings, and shops. The main difficulties encountered during construction were the long haul to an 1800-foot elevation for all materials and the rain, the annual fall of which is 200 inches.

An amphibious tractor camp was erected on Maalaea Bay for the training of Fourth Marine Division amphibious tractor crews. Using tents for quarters and large quonset huts for shops and storage, the 5,000-man camp was completed, with all facilities, in one and a half months. A rifle range with 50 positions and firing lines up to 500 yards was also provided.

The Marine Corps storage depot comprised 40 large quonset huts, on 4-foot concrete walls. A 2,000-foot retaining wall and loading platform was constructed in front of the huts, together with 3,500 feet of railroad siding. This project was started by the 48th Seabees and completed by the 127th. A large open-storage area was utilized to store rolling stock.

With facilities for approximately 800 men, the Naval Amphibious Training and Experimental Base was located in a tent city on Maalaea Bay south of Kamaole. The center was used for the advanced training and staging of underwater demolition teams before sea duty.

Adjacent to the demolition camp, and approxi-

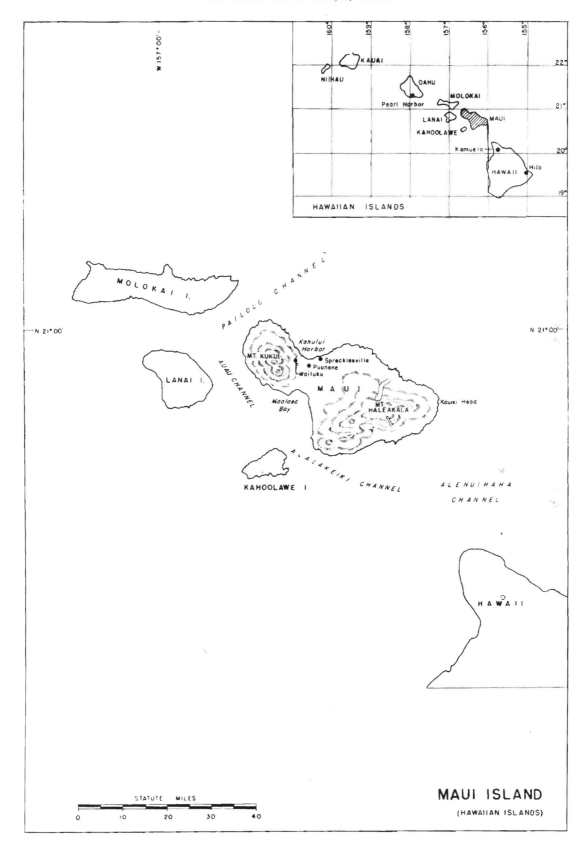

MAUI ISLAND

(HAWAIIAN ISLANDS)

mately the same size, was a training center for
beach parties and small-boat crews. Both shared
the use of a large frame galley and messhall located

between them. A few wooden sheds for food storage were erected by Seabee detachments from the
neighboring Puunene air station.

Part III — Island of Hawaii

NAS *Hilo*

In June 1942. planes to support future operations
were pouring into the Pearl Harbor area from the
United States. Critical construction materials were
at a premium, and it was necessary, as far as possible, to disperse air facilities, both for convenience
of operation and as a precaution against possible
renewal of enemy air attacks. Time was important.
With these factors in mind, the Commander in
Chief of the Pacific Fleet directed a joint board
of Army and Navy officers to submit recommendations for the location of an airfield to support the
operation of two carrier groups. After investigating
the existing facilities of the Army field at Hilo, the
board recommended that it be expanded to meet
the Navy needs.

Existing installations at Hilo included three
runways, 6500, 6000, and 3000 feet long, respectively, storage for 450,000 gallons of gasoline, and
revetments for 24 planes. Quarters and messing
facilities for 70 officers and 1200 men and a gasoline
pipe line from Hilo Harbor were also available.

Construction was undertaken by the 59th Battalion, which arrived during March 1943. Runways were widened from 200 feet to 500 feet, and

additional parking areas built. Supplementary
gasoline storage, comprising ten 50,000-gallon tanks
of prestressed concrete. were constructed underground, and a 500,000-gallon water-storage reservoir was built. In addition. 11 barracks, officers'
quarters, 16 storehouses, and other miscellaneous
structures for shops and administration purposes
were set up. Communication lines, drainage systems, and roads were expanded. Runway surfacing
and road building amounted to 800,000 square feet
of asphalt paving.

Construction was completed in April 1944, when
maintenance was assumed by CBMU 562.

Kamuela

At Kamuela, on the island of Hawaii, Seabees
built a camp, accommodating 20,000 men for the
2nd Marine Division. The 59th Battalion, assisted
by the 18th Battalion, began work in January 1944;
the camp was completed in April.

Facilities included tents for personnel, quonset-
type warehouses, and quonset huts for administration and messing. An airstrip, 75 by 3000 feet, was
built, and a taxiway, 7000 feet long, and a parking
area were later added.

Part IV — The Outlying Islands

Importance of the Islands

When the Hepburn Board made its survey of
the naval shore establishment in the fall of 1938,
the United States had five island possessions west
of Pearl Harbor that were of strategic value as
potential patrol-plane bases. These were the islands
of Midway, Wake, Johnston, Palmyra, and Canton.
The board's recommendations for the development
of each island were the basic criteria upon which
their subsequent fortification was predicated.

From a strategic point of view, an air base at
Midway was considered second in importance only
to Pearl Harbor. At that time, Midway was in
regular use as one of the stops on the air route to
the Orient, and was also the site of a commercial
cable station. The board recommended that Midway be developed as a secondary airbase with
facilities for two permanently based patrol-plane
squadrons. These facilities were to include a pier,
a channel, and a turning basin, with the lagoon

HAWAIIAN AND OUTLYING ISLANDS

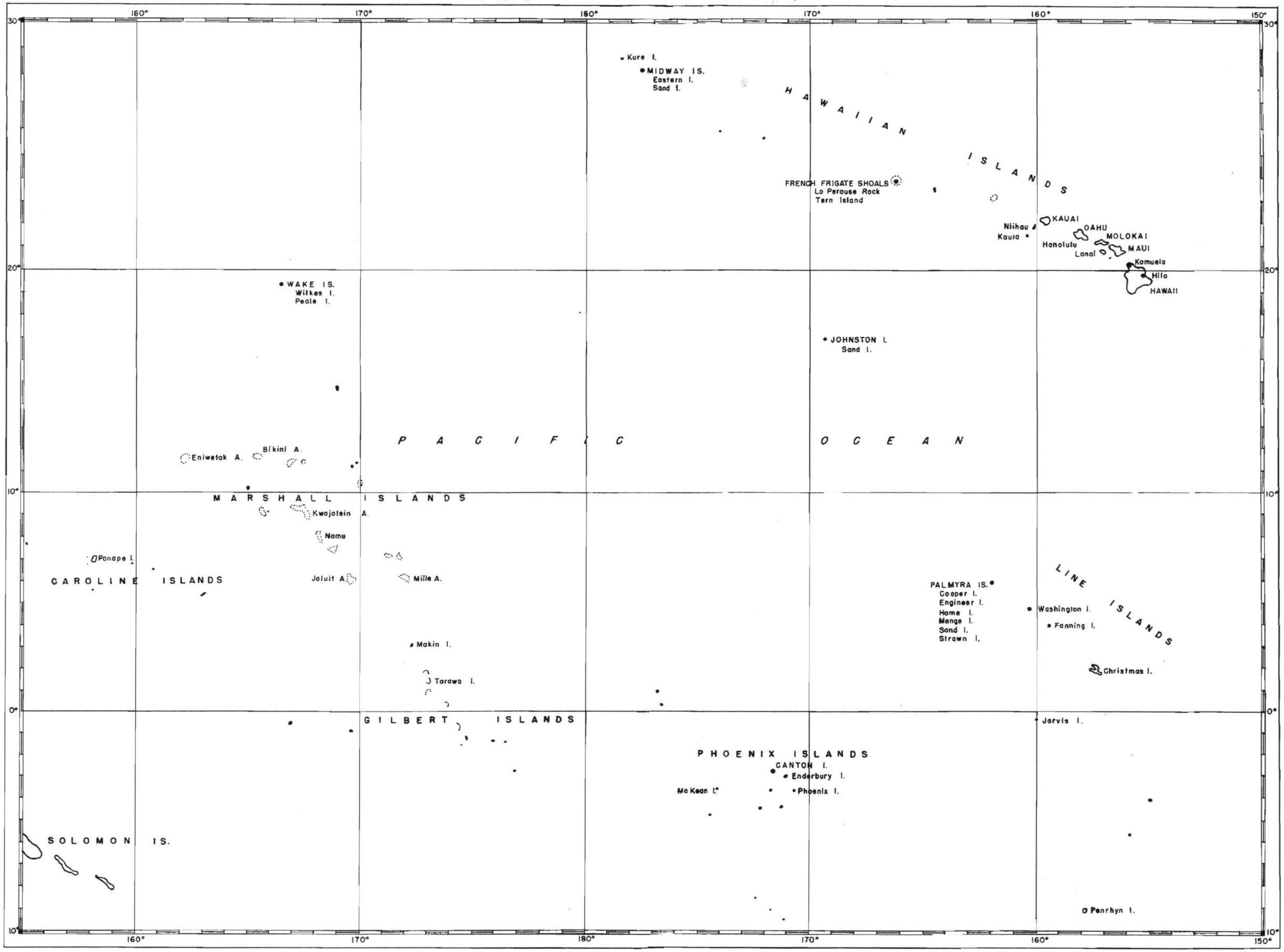
160°
170°
180°
170°
160°
150°
30°
20°
10°
0°
10°
Kure I.
MIDWAY IS.
Eastern I.
Sand I.
HAWAIIAN ISLANDS
FRENCH FRIGATE SHOALS
La Perouse Rock
Tern Island
KAUAI
Niihau
Kaula
OAHU
Honolulu
MOLOKAI
Lanai
MAUI
Kamuela
Hilo
HAWAII
WAKE IS.
Wilkes I.
Peale I.
JOHNSTON I.
Sand I.
PACIFIC OCEAN
Eniwetok A.
Bikini A.
MARSHALL ISLANDS
Kwajalein A.
Namu
Ponape I.
CAROLINE ISLANDS
Jaluit A.
Mille A.
PALMYRA IS.
Cooper I.
Engineer I.
Home I.
Menge I.
Sand I.
Strawn I.
LINE ISLANDS
Washington I.
Fanning I.
Christmas I.
Makin I.
Tarawa I.
GILBERT ISLANDS
Jarvis I.
PHOENIX ISLANDS
CANTON I.
Enderbury I.
McKean I.
Phoenix I.
SOLOMON IS.
Penrhyn I.

dredged to accommodate a large tender or a tanker. Wake Island, considered next in importance to Midway, and also a station on the commercial air route to the Orient, was adapted to, and recommended for, development similar to the one proposed for Midway.

Johnston, Palmyra, and Canton islands were to be developed to permit tender-based patrol-plane operations. This would require the dredging of channels into the lagoons to permit entry of small tenders and the clearing of coral heads within the lagoons to provide sufficient area for full-load take-off.

Construction of these bases, together with the new air station at Kaneohe Bay, was begun in the fall of 1939 under the PNAB contract.

The greatest difficulties attending execution of this work were the wide geographical dispersion, the isolation, and the lack of docking facilities which characterized each of these outposts. Consequently, the sequence of construction operations progressed through three stages: the initial "rowboat stage," in which approach was in small boats and a tent colony was set up, supported for several weeks by a ship lying offshore; next, the erection of rough tent-camp buildings, with portable power plants, distilling plants, and radio, upon completion of which the supporting ship was released; and, finally, the gradual erection of permanent barracks and the completion of the station.

Individually and collectively, these five islands were our first move westward from Hawaii into the Pacific under the new defense measures. They were built before the advent of Seabees and without benefit of the standardized and prefabricated advance-base equipment that came into use during 1942. As coral was the prevalent soil material at each location, it was widely used for the first time as concrete aggregate.

Originally begun as seaplane bases, each of these islands was subsequently equipped with runways for landplanes and with waterfront structures to permit fueling of submarines. Eventually, Midway became a major submarine base and a fueling point for destroyers and cruisers, with two large airfields and extensive seaplane facilities.

The contractors' civilian forces were withdrawn during the spring and summer of 1942 and were replaced by Seabees, who carried the unfinished projects to completion and undertook further expansion of the facilities at each base during 1943

and 1944. In August 1945, Seabees were functioning as maintenance units.

With the exception of Wake, which was captured by the Japanese on December 24, 1941, each of these bases functioned extensively throughout the Pacific campaign. During the early months of the war, Midway, Johnston, and Palmyra supplied aerial reconnaissance on a wide arc westward of the Hawaiian Islands, and with their tactical aircraft formed an outer defense ring around Pearl Harbor. As a submarine base, Midway gave strong support to the fleet as our attack moved westward. Palmyra Island, with its air facilities, was an important stop in the air-transport route to the Southwest Pacific. Johnston Island came into importance after the capture of the Gilbert and Marshall Islands as an air station on the route through the Central Pacific.

Midway

In the initial plans for Midway, it was proposed to develop it as a base for one patrol squadron of seaplanes. Subsequently, it became a major submarine base, a major air station for both land- and seaplanes, and a fueling and repair base for ships.

Midway is a coral atoll situated in almost the exact center of the North Pacific Ocean. Hemmed in by jutting coral reefs enclosing about 28 square miles of shallow lagoon, the two islands of Sand and Eastern, collectively known as Midway, lie 300 miles north and 900 miles west of Honolulu. Sand Island, the larger, measures about a mile and a half long by a mile wide, and was originally capped by a hill rising 42 feet above sea level. Eastern Island, triangular in shape and flat, measured a mile and a quarter long by three quarters of a mile wide.

In 1938, Navy funds to the extent of $1,100,000 were made available to the Army for harbor and channel improvements. The Army was to dredge a channel through the southern reef between Sand and Eastern Islands, scoop out a seaplane basin, and dredge a channel 30 feet deep and 300 feet wide to a proposed submarine basin and an anchorage for small ships. A turning basin was to be provided adjacent to the submarine basin, northeast of Sand Island, and a breakwater was to be built. The Army completed this work in 1940.

The Hepburn report had recommended that a naval air station be built on Midway and facilities for a submarine base be provided. The air station was to be large enough to base one patrol squadron of seaplanes permanently, with emergency provisions for one visiting squadron. All of this work was to be on Sand Island, but subsequent changes provided for an airfield on Eastern Island.

The development of Midway under the Pacific Naval Air Base contracts began on March 27, 1940. A dredge was towed in, and the contractors directed their efforts toward the enlargement of the existing basins and channels. A small-boat channel, 12,000 feet long, 50 feet wide, and 10 feet deep, was dredged between Sand and Eastern islands, and a mooring berth, protected by sheet-piling, was built on the latter. Approximately 3,000,000 cubic yards of material were removed in these dredging operations.

Three asphalt-paved runways were constructed on Eastern Island: each was 300 feet wide and 3250 feet, 4500 feet, and 5300 feet long, respectively. Two hangars were constructed, with parking areas and warm-up mats. Small industrial areas were erected, which included the various necessary shops and storage facilities.

A large seaplane hangar, a parking mat, and one concrete ramp were constructed, and an ordnance shop, radio shop, engine shop, and a storehouse and tool room were built around the seaplane hangar to facilitate major overhaul work.

Fighter, bomber, and patrol ready-rooms were constructed, and housing and messing facilities set up for operational personnel. Quonset huts were extensively used.

Approximately 2800 feet of sheet-piling bulkhead was installed on Sand Island. Dredged material was pumped behind this bulkhead, and upon this fill, a large seaplane parking-mat was constructed. Four, concrete, seaplane ramps were built, together with an additional emergency ramp and approach to the mat, and a large, steel, seaplane hangar was erected on the edge of the mat.

Construction was started on underground gasoline storage in twenty-two 2500-gallon steel tanks.

A naval hospital was built by the contractors, who utilized three of the four existing buildings owned by the commercial cable company. These buildings, located on Sand Island, were later augmented by a large underground structure of concrete.

Barracks for naval and Marine personnel were built, together with all necessary accessories such as messhalls, warehouses, administration buildings, commissaries, and cold-storage buildings. The power plant for Sand Island was housed in a bombproof structure of reinforced-concrete and steel.

Midway was subjected to surface shelling by the Japanese on December 7, 1941, which caused considerable material damage and many wounds to personnel.

As a result of the declaration of war, the construction program was modified to meet the emergency, and all efforts were directed toward defense fortifications and damage repair. Late in December, 800 civilian workers were removed from the island and only the garrison was left to continue repair work. Repeated air attacks after the initial shelling did much to retard the work, although no major damage was experienced until the morning of June 4, 1942, when the Japanese launched a major air attack which caused heavy material damage to many installations. The hospital, a group of fuel-oil tanks, a partly completed torpedo shop at the submarine basin, and other buildings were completely destroyed, and serious damage was done to the administration building, the laundry, and the seaplane hangar.

At the Navy's request, 100 of the contractors' men returned to make repairs and install such replacement equipment as refrigerators, distillers, and power units. When this was accomplished, they returned to Pearl Harbor.

On July 17, 1942, a detachment of the 5th Construction Battalion arrived. This detachment of 225 men and 4 officers directed their first efforts toward preparing living quarters for themselves and the remainder of the battalion, which arrived during August to bring the Battalion's total to 550 men and 12 officers. Work was immediately begun on the construction of an airfield and an underground hospital of reinforced concrete and steel at Sand Island. In September 1942, two full companies of the 10th Battalion arrived, and with these additional men, the work of developing a submarine base on the northern tip of the island was begun.

Construction completed by the Seabees included three strips on the Sand Island airfield, revetments, magazines for high explosives, airfield lighting, and additional quarters and messing facilities.

Early in the spring of 1943, the function of Midway was changed from a defensive to an offensive base, and the construction of a major submarine base was begun. The 50th Battalion, assigned to Midway for this purpose, arrived on

CONTROL TOWER, MARINE CORPS AIR STATION, EWA

April 4, 1943, to relieve the Fifth, which returned to Pearl Harbor. The 50th and the 10th Battalions, acting as a unit, lengthened and paved the Sand Island airfield, two strips to 7,500 feet and one to 8,600 feet; erected four 13,500-barrel underground welded-steel tanks for diesel oil and four 27,000-barrel tanks for fuel oil, complete with piping, and underground pumphouses; constructed six timber finger-piers, complete with electrical, oil, air, and water services; and installed 2,900 feet of cellular steel-sheet piling. They also operated the Navy dredge YD-69.

Late in April 1943, the contractors' men again returned to begin work on an enlarged dredging program. The existing ship channel was widened from 300 feet to 400 feet and deepened to 35 feet. The anchorage area was expanded to a mooring capacity of six cruisers, five destroyers or submarines, and one repair ship.

Three areas were dredged, and 5,000,000 cubic yards of material removed.

CBMU 524 arrived in October 1943 to take over maintenance duties, complete the large underground hospital, and set up a recreation and recuperation center at the submarine base. The 10th Battalion which departed for Pearl Harbor in November 1943, was replaced by CBMU 531. The two maintenance units were then combined and continued to carry on their duties as a unit.

In January 1944, the 50th Battalion began water-front construction near the submarine base. This work included three 471-foot piers, a 769-foot tender pier, and an ARD wharf, all of wood-pile construction. A 1,600-kw power plant at the submarine base was built to augment the bomb-proof structure previously completed on Sand Island. Inter-island electrical and fuel lines were begun and were complete in March.

As a result of severe weather, portions of the shoreline were washed away, necessitating the installation of 1,200 feet of sheet-piling bulkhead on Sand Island and 300 feet on Eastern Island to halt the erosion.

The 123rd Battalion and the 10th Special Battalion reported to Midway in April 1944. These two units continued the waterfront work and enlarged the fuel storage capacity. They also built two additional tender piers at the submarine base, four additional submarine piers, and seven shop buildings.

The 50th completed its work in December 1944, leaving CBMU 534 to continue maintenance operations.

Wake

Conversion of the atoll, collectively known as "Wake Island," into an outlying base was recommended by the Hepburn Board in 1939, and construction work, by a civilian contractor, commenced in January 1941. This work was about 65 per cent complete when it was interrupted by Japanese hostilities and our entry into the war. As originally conceived, the base was to provide an unloading pier, a channel through the reef, a turning basin capable of accommodating a tender or a large tanker, complete facilities for one squadron of patrol planes, and a garrison force of one company of Marines. Later, construction was authorized for a submarine base to support one division operating without a tender.

Lying 2000 miles west of Honolulu and 1700 miles east of Tokyo, Wake forms a rough "V," four and a half miles long and two and a half miles wide at the opening. Wake, the largest of three islets, forms the apex, with two narrow peninsulas jutting from its main body. Separated from the end of the northern peninsula by a narrow channel is Peale Island; Wilkes Island is separated by a similar channel from the end of the southern peninsula. The lagoon, three miles long and a mile and a quarter wide, is almost landlocked as the two channels are narrow and the open end of the "V" is virtually closed by the reef which surrounds the group. Land area comprises 2,600 acres, with a maximum elevation of 24 feet.

Wake was placed under the jurisdiction of the Navy Department in 1934, and in 1935 permission was granted Pan American Airways to establish a way-station airport on Peale Island. This work was completed prior to the start of naval construction.

The first of the contractor's personnel, 80 men, arrived on January 9, 1941, accompanied by large amounts of construction materials and equipment, which included an 80-ton crane on caterpillar treads, two heavy bulldozers, and a large tractor.

The channel between Wilkes and Wake islands was first chosen for development, but surveys indicated that this was an excavating rather than a dredging job, so the preliminary work was done with pneumatic-hammers, bulldozers, and a crane. Sufficient width and depth was obtained by this method to permit entrance into the lagoon of a 1000-ton barge loaded with construction materials.

Work was also started on two of the three airstrips planned, and access roads were built. Simultaneously, erection of a camp and headquarters for civilian workers was begun.

Considerable construction had been accomplished, such as the installation of evaporators and refrigerators and general camp improvements, when the hydraulic dredge "Columbia" was brought in. However, due to its many breakdowns,

only one channel, necessitated by construction requirements, was ever developed.

Tanks were installed for the storage of 150,000 barrels of gasoline, 20,000 barrels of fuel oil, and 6,000 barrels of diesel oil.

Living facilities for the Marines were about 50 per cent complete in December, but very little work had been done on defense installations and fortifications.

On December 8, Japanese planes struck, and during the 16 days before the island's surrender, it was subjected to 14 bombing attacks. Construction work came to an abrupt end, and all resources were turned to defense. During the siege, construction personnel maintained power, water, and communication systems and worked on dugouts. Nearly all construction material was destroyed by bombing and resultant fires.

Heroic but futile delaying action was carried on by the garrison of the island. Fourteen civilians lost their lives, and 1132 were interned by the enemy.

Our forces repossessed Wake in August 1945, after the completion of surrender negotiations. No resistance was encountered.

Johnston Island

Johnston Island, lying 720 miles southwest of Oahu, is a coral atoll roughly 8 miles long and 3 miles wide. The enclosed lagoon contains two islands of which Johnston, with its 40 acres, is the larger; the other is Sand Island.

Before development, Johnston Island was approximately 3000 feet long and 600 feet wide. Sand Island, roughly circular in shape, contained six acres. Both islands were composed of sand and guano overlying the coral and sandstone reef. Vegetation was practically non-existent, and there was no fresh water.

The first use of Johnston Island by the Navy was in 1935, when the personnel of Patrol Wing 2, during the course of patrol-bomber training operations performed some minor construction to develop the atoll for seaplane operation. They erected a few rough buildings and a small boat landing on Sand Island and blasted coral heads within the lagoon to clear a 3600-foot area for use as a runway. A narrow ship-channel was also cut through the reef to afford entrance to the lagoon.

Further development of Johnston Island was undertaken in 1939 with the purpose of providing facilities to support the operation of one squadron of patrol planes with tender support. Civilian forces, under the PNAB contract, began work on November 9, 1939, at Sand Island, for which the initial development was planned.

During January 1940, a barge equipped with a crane and a 6-foot clamshell was brought in and put to work widening and deepening the shallow entrance channel. After the barge had worked its way into the lagoon and had excavated a small turning basin, it was dismantled and moved ashore. A 12-foot clamshell dredge arrived on May 5, and continued the dredging. Within the lagoon, a turning basin, 1000 feet square, was dredged and a narrow channel projected in the direction of Sand Island. Excavated material was used to make a plane parking area, 800 feet long and 300 feet wide, adjacent to the ship channel and connected to Sand Island by a 2000-foot causeway. This parking area was equipped with a 60-foot bulkhead, a concrete seaplane ramp, 50 feet wide, supported on steel piles, and two 25,000-gallon steel tanks for gasoline. The buildings on Sand Island included barracks for 400 men, a messhall, an underground hospital, a radio station, two water tanks with evaporating equipment, an electric power and boiler house, a laundry, and several storehouses. A 100-foot steel tower served as a combination standpipe for the fresh-water system and control tower for plane operation.

Dredging meanwhile was continued in the lagoon to provide safe water for seaplane runways. Three such runways were developed, the major one, 11,000 feet long and 1000 feet wide, with two cross-runways, each 7,000 feet long and 800 feet wide. These were cleared to a depth of 8 feet at low tide.

In September 1941, work was begun enlarging the land mass of Johnston Island to provide an airstrip. The initial plan called for a filled-in area, 200 feet wide and 2500 feet long, to be developed along the south shore of the island, but when this area had been completed, the operation was continued to extend the landing mat to a length of 4000 feet and a width of 500 feet. Material was obtained from the lagoon dredging. With all operations concentrated on Johnston, the contractor vacated the buildings on Sand Island to the naval personnel who moved in to operate the seaplane facilities.

Under the contract, the building program which progressed simultaneously with dredging and runway construction, accomplished the erection of two 400-man barracks, two large mess halls, a 30,000-cubic-foot cold-storage building, a powerhouse, a 50-bed underground hospital, a fresh-water evaporating plant, several shop buildings, three 8-room cottages, 16,000 barrels of fuel storage, and the installation of five 25,000-gallon gasoline tanks. These features were all usably complete by December 7, 1941.

When the news of the attack on Pearl Harbor reached Johnston Island, construction work was temporarily abandoned and all personnel were used for immediate defense preparations. On December 15, 1941, the island was shelled from an enemy submarine firing from beyond the reef. Several buildings were damaged, but none of the personnel was injured.

Landplane facilities on Johnston Island now became a strategic imperative in the defense plans for the Hawaiian Islands. A large hydraulic dredge was brought to the island to speed the work. The dredge remained until January 1943, and completed the main seaplane runway to a length of 5200 feet and a width of 500 feet, and extended the north shore of the island to accommodate an auxiliary runway, 3400 feet long by 200 feet wide, and a large seaplane parking area.

All civilian personnel, with the exception of the dredge crew, were replaced during July 1942 by a force of 500 men drawn from the 5th and 10th Seabees, who took up construction where the contractors left off and carried the current program, except for the dredging, to completion. The 5th Battalion departed during January 1943; but 250 men of the 10th remained until the following December.

Seabee construction included two 13,500-barrel diesel tanks, two 17,000-barrel fuel-oil tanks, and thirteen 25,000-gallon gasoline tanks, with associated pumping, filtering, and issuing equipment; a pier, 460 feet long and 30 feet wide, supported on steel piles; a small-boat pier; a float for seaplanes; a concrete power house; a recreation building; an aviation repair shop; 90 quonset huts for housing; a radio station; and 50 concrete magazines, in addition to the installation of new evaporating equipment which brought the total daily fresh-water production to 30,000 gallons. The 10th was replaced by CBMU 554 in January 1944.

During the summer of 1943, air traffic increased steadily as our war effort gained momentum. Johnston Island was, in addition to being a base for patrol planes and a submarine fueling stop, rapidly becoming an important stop along the westward air-transport route.

As a result, it became necessary to increase the length of the main landplane runway to enable it to accommodate heavy long-range bombers and transports, and a detachment from the 99th Seabees arrived during December 1943 to do this work. By use of a hydraulic dredge, the island was lengthened 800 feet to provide a 6000-foot runway. Ten acres of parking area were also added, adjacent to the seaplane operating area.

By the summer of 1944, when the final dredging program and other improvements were substantially complete, Johnston Island covered an area of 160 acres, as compared with its original 40 acres.

Palmyra

Palmyra Island, 960 miles south of the Hawaiian Islands, is a coral atoll, composed of more than 50 small islets arranged as an elongated horseshoe.

Field work at Palmyra began on January 27, 1940, under the PNAB contracts.

A temporary boat channel, 25 feet wide and 5 feet deep, was developed during the first two weeks. In March 1940, work was begun to enlarge this channel to a width of 80 feet and a depth of 15 feet by use of a dredge towed from Pearl Harbor. Once inside the lagoon, it also dredged access channels to Menge and Cooper islands, the two principal land masses. Following the recommendations of the Hepburn Board, a larger dredge began operations on an 11,000-foot seaplane runway and deepened the existing ship channel.

Later, a revision in plans caused an increase of Palmyra's facilities to support land-based planes. As no single islet provided the necessary length for an airstrip, spoil from the dredging operations was pumped between Menge and Cooper islands and on the lagoon side of Cooper Island. After this coral fill was rolled, no further treatment was necessary, and the ultimate result was a runway, 5000 feet long and 300 feet wide. A smaller runway, 3700 feet by 200 feet, also of compacted coral, was constructed on Menge Island, and a concrete seaplane ramp was added.

In April 1941, a second expansion of plans necessitated additional quarters for a detachment of Marines who were to garrison the island. Four 60-man barracks were built, and extensions were added to a previously completed galley and messhall. Eight tanks with a total capacity of 200,000

gallons were built on Cooper Island, and 43 buildings, largely of frame and corrugated-iron construction on concrete foundations, were erected. These were used for shops, storehouses, and offices.

A second tank-farm was built on Menge Island.

When news of the attack on Pearl Harbor reached Palmyra, civilian labor forces were diverted to the construction of defense installations in preparation for an expected attack, which occurred on December 24, 1941. The only damage was minor; a shell from an enemy surface craft passed through the dredge.

Inter-island transportation, non-existent except by water, became of prime importance in the proposed defense of Palmyra against an enemy landing. Work was immediately begun on the placing of fill between the islets to form a continuous horseshoe-shaped causeway extending from Strawn Island, on the northwest, around to Home Island on the southwest tip of the atoll. Twelve miles of coral highway were constructed on Palmyra.

Due to an increase in air traffic through Palmyra, the detachment from the 5th Construction Battalion, which arrived in the summer of 1942, engaged principally in enlarging fuel and ammunition facilities, and building additional quarters and messhalls, until the arrival of half of the 76th Battalion in April 1943.

Work completed by the Seabees on Cooper Island included a 100-room hotel for transient personnel, two 200,000-gallon tank-farms for aviation gasoline, two 13,500-barrel fuel-oil tanks, two 17,500-barrel diesel tanks, and additional dredging operations for fueling wharves. On Menge Island, they built two aviation-gasoline tank farms, one of 125,000-gallon and the other of 175,000-gallon capacity, a 633-foot sheet-steel bulkhead, a boathouse with five 20-foot slips, and a fuel-oil tank-farm. A small emergency landplane runway, 2400 feet long and 200 feet wide, was built on Sand Island, and a hospital on Engineer Island.

In January 1944 the 76th Battalion was replaced by CBMU 527, which, in turn, was replaced by CBMU 564 in November 1944.

Canton

Canton Island, one of the Phoenix group, was developed as a naval air station to support a squadron of patrol seaplanes and to provide a minor fleet refueling point. In addition to these naval missions, the Army developed three airstrips to support Army Air Force base units and the staging

BACHELOR OFFICERS' QUARTERS, NAS PEARL HARBOR

of itinerant aircraft. Canton also served as a principal stop on the air-transport route to Australia.

Canton, a coral atoll, lies about 800 miles southwest of Palmyra. A hotel and some seaplane installations, previously built by Pan-American Airways, were taken over by the Navy.

When a detachment of the 10th Construction Battalion arrived on March 7, 1943, the Army was operating an air base with all supporting installations. The island was under the command of the Army, and maintained by Army forces. After establishing a tent camp, the Seabees started work on a 17-hut quonset village, complete with a sewerage system, power and light, and a water-distribution system. Extensive blasting operations were also begun in the channel and lagoon.

The seaplane runways were sounded, their depths charted, and tide and current observations made, with the intention of reworking them to suitability for naval patrol-plane operations.

While dredging work was in progress, a construction crew started work on an officers' quarters, an overflow hotel building, which was an expansion of the existing hotel, and several magazines. Other men of the detachment were occupied in maintenance and repair work on the original Army facilities. A seaplane ramp and four prefabricated steel warehouses were also built.

In November, shortage of dynamite made it necessary to halt blasting operations. In April, all projects on Canton were turned over to a detachment of the 99th Battalion. The 10th had by this time succeeded in blasting the lagoon to the required depth and had performed 70 per cent of the required work on an aviation-gasoline system. The 99th continued work at Canton until June 1944, when CBMU 588 relieved it to carry out maintenance and minor construction until inactivated in July 1945.

French Frigate Shoals

French Frigate Shoals, a crescent-shaped reef formed on a circular platform about 18 miles in diameter, 550 miles northwest of Honolulu, was

BARRACKS AT PEARL HARBOR SEPARATION CENTER

developed as a minor naval air facility to support the staging of aircraft and to serve as an emergency fueling stop and as a link in the radio-detection chain centered in the Hawaiian Islands.

The reef forms a barrier against winds and currents around the north and east sides of the platform. The south and west sides are open and are covered by water that averages a hundred feet in depth.

Construction was started during July 1942 by a detachment from the 5th Battalion and was accomplished by March 1943.

The major development centered about Tern Island in the northwest corner of the reef. A ship channel, 200 feet wide, was dredged through the barrier reef, and a seaplane runway, 8000 feet long and 1000 feet wide, was cleared in adjacent waters. Ships entering the lagoon were moored to three wood-pile dolphins.

By use of coral dredged from the channel and seaplane runway, Tern Island was increased in area to permit the construction of a coral-surfaced landing field, 3100 feet long and 250 feet wide. A parking area to accommodate 24 small planes was also provided. Housing in quonset huts was provided for 360 men; four temporary wooden buildings served as storehouses. Fresh water and electric power were provided by stills and generators; 20 steel tanks with a capacity of 100,000 gallons were provided for aviation gasoline.

In addition to the seaplane operating area developed adjacent to Tern Island, an auxiliary water area, 5700 feet long, for landing and take-off was also cleared. This runway was also provided with an adjacent mooring area, 4000 feet square.

CHAPTER 23

BASES IN ALASKA AND THE ALEUTIANS

The growing significance of air power in modern warfare, coupled with concern over Japanese aggression in China, caused the United States, in the late 1930's, to study closely the defensive and strategic position of Alaska. For many years our Alaskan position had been neglected; but a drastic change of policy was proposed by the Hepburn Board in December 1938, when it recommended the construction there of submarine, destroyer, and air bases. The board emphasized in its report that air bases in the Alaskan area would be essential in time of war and that the Aleutians themselves would be of great tactical importance. After surveying the various possibilities offered for development, the board urged the establishment of naval air bases at Sitka, Kodiak, and Dutch Harbor, and submarine bases, as well, at the last two points.

Naval base construction in Alaska, carrying out the recommendations of the Hepburn report, began in September 1939 under a CPFF contract, which called for the construction of naval air facilities at Sitka and Kodiak at an estimated cost of $13,000,000. In July 1940 the scope of the contract was enlarged to include the development of a naval air station and several Army facilities at Dutch Harbor. These bases were to be expanded by the construction of nearby outlying activities. The Sitka and Kodiak areas were each to include six such outlying bases, and Dutch Harbor, five. The estimated cost of these facilities was $160,000,000.

After the bombing of Dutch Harbor and the occupation of Kiska and Attu by the Japanese in June 1942, the contractor's forces were reinforced with Seabees, and by April 1, 1943, all construction in the Alaskan area had been taken over by naval construction battalions. Seabee strength grew from a single battalion to more than 20,000 men and 500 officers by January 1, 1944. At its maximum, there were in the Alaskan area 11 construction battalions, two equipment repair units, three additional battalions engaged wholly in maintenance, five maintenance units, and three camouflage units. It was in Alaska that the first naval construction regiment and the first naval construction brigade were formed, at Dutch Harbor in September 1942 and at Adak in May 1943, respectively.

In connection with our campaign to drive the Japanese from their footholds on Kiska and Attu and to develop facilities of our own in the Aleutians, nine new bases were built by the Seabees in the vicinity of Dutch Harbor and on the islands to westward. The principal new bases were Adak, built before our occupation of Amchitka, and Attu, which was developed after it had been wrested from the Japanese. Other bases were Kiska, after its occupation by our forces; Sand Bay, on Great Sitkin Island; Ogliuga; Amchitka; Shemya; Atka; and Tanaga.

Late in the war period a detachment of Seabees was sent to Point Barrow to investigate petroleum resources there.

Sitka Sector

The naval establishment at Sitka provided an intermediate base between northwestern United States and the island of Kodiak, although its location was, from the strategic point of view, not such that it could serve as a main base. However, the extremely severe weather which prevails throughout the entire area made it imperative that such an intermediate station be available and that facilities be sufficient to accommodate heavy overloads for considerable periods of time.

Sitka, formerly New Archangel, is located on the west coast of Baranof Island, on Sitka Sound, a landlocked harbor, about 100 miles south of Juneau. Temperature is not excessively low, but rainfall is heavy and fogs are prevalent.

Construction of a fleet air base at Sitka was one of the provisions of a CPFF contract, signed on August 29, 1939. Authorization was for thirty projects to cost approximately $3,000,000. The contract was later enlarged to cover 155 projects, and in

NAS SITKA

July 1942 the total cost of work in the Sitka area was estimated at $32,000,000.

Designated as a naval air station on September 12, 1939, Sitka was made a naval section base January 24, 1941, and again redesignated on July 20, 1942, as a naval operating base. The operating base was composed of the naval air station, radio station, naval section base, Marine barracks, and subordinate naval shore activities.

At the air station, seaplane facilities were centered around two 186-by-254-foot permanent hangars, with office and shop space of 14,000 square feet provided in lean-to structures. The aerological and control tower was erected on one of these hangars, and a concrete parking area was placed to form a 170-by-1500-foot landplane runway between the hangars and the seaplane ramps. Three con-

crete-surfaced seaplane ramps were built and arresting gear added to the landplane runway to compensate for its shortness in length.

Service facilities for large craft were confined to two Navy piers of permanent construction and an additional pier leased from private owners, which supplied power, steam, fresh water, and fuel. Small-craft piers, all temporary or semipermanent structures, were built at three locations, and finger floats were constructed to provide fifteen slips for small craft. In addition, a 30-ton marine railway was revised and put into working order to supplement repair facilities located in various small structures.

Most of the storage space was provided at the air station and the section base, with small installations provided at the contractor's establishment. Cold storage consisted of three freezer units with a total capacity of 26,000 cubic feet and five chill units with a total capacity of 18,460 cubic feet. Dry-storage space (32,040 square feet) was provided in three semi-permanent buildings and general-storage space in nine semi-permanent buildings (23,380 square feet). Construction and maintenance storage was in 13 buildings, including a wharf warehouse, a seaplane hangar, temporary sheds, and miscellaneous buildings, with a total space of 138,800 square feet.

Underground fuel-oil storage was in a 27,000-barrel concrete tank; aboveground storage, in a 55,000-barrel steel tank with a 12-foot berm for fire protection. Diesel oil was stored in six 710-barrel steel tanks underground and in two 13,332-barrel and one 595-barrel steel tanks protected by earthen berms. Aviation gasoline was stored underground in sixteen 25,000-gallon permanent tanks. Motor-gasoline storage consisted of four 5000-gallon and six 10,000-gallon underground steel tanks and one 25,000-gallon steel tank above ground. All types of ammunition were stored in 21 magazines of permanent construction. A torpedo overhaul shop was also constructed and two compressors installed.

Administration offices were located in eight buildings, three permanent structures, two semi-permanent, and the others temporary, with a total floor space of 22,105 square feet. Radio facilities included a transmitter building, a receiving station, and two direction-finder buildings.

Hospital facilities consisted of a permanent 15-bed dispensary and two other units of 17 and 16 beds, respectively.

Station maintenance buildings included a laundry, an incinerator, a garage, various shops, paint storage, and a concrete-mixing plant.

Personnel were housed at the air station in three permanent barracks which held a total of 766 men, and in temporary structures for 1444 men at the contractor's camp. Two permanent messhalls at the air station accommodated 400 men and included a bakery and a stewards' dormitory. The contractor's eleven temporary messhalls accommodated 1554 men. Recreational facilities included three permanent buildings with a total area of 22,000 square feet, which contained a gymnasium and a theater with a seating capacity of 800.

Electrical power at Sitka was supplied by four 3000-kw turbo-generator units and a small unit belonging to the contractor. An interconnection with the city of Sitka's power system was also in-

stalled. In July 1944 this connection was used in reverse, when, due to the poor condition of the Sitka generators and the lack of replacement parts, it was feared that some of the sawmills and canneries in the area would have to be shut down.

More than 13 miles of permanent or semi-permanent roadways were built. Sewage disposal was by outfall to the sea. Water was supplied by gravity flow from Cascade Creek and pumped from Indian River. Water storage consisted of two tanks with 200,000- and 300,0000-gallon capacities, respectively.

Fort Ray, the Army garrison at Sitka, was constructed to accommodate 2988 men and 194 officers. Buildings for housing totaled 136; about half of them were semi-permanent, and the remainder, temporary. Eighteen messhalls and 12 recreation buildings were constructed. Storage facilities included 31,440 cubic feet of freezer space, 38,110 cubic feet of chill space, and 66,540 square feet of general storage. Administration offices were housed in 11 buildings with a total floor-area of 10,715 square feet. Utilities were provided by the Navy, with the exception of a small-capacity emergency power equipment. Hospital space, including infirmaries, totaled 127 beds in seven units. Semi-permanent structures made up five of these, and quonset huts the other two. Station maintenance equipment, including a laundry, paint and oil storage, and garage and repair shops, were located in 13 buildings, with a total floor-space of 66,705 square feet. Harbor defenses involved construction of gun emplacements and magazines.

The 22nd Construction Battalion reached Sitka on November 28, 1942, and from then until May 1, 1943, when the contract was closed, there was a gradual conversion of operations from the contractor to the battalion. When the contract was closed, the 155 projects it had included were 65 percent complete, at a total expenditure of 25 million dollars.

The work was carried on by the 22nd Seabees until July 1943, when the battalion moved to Attu Island and the public works department of the station was taken over by CBMU 512. One company of the 45th Battalion was moved from Kodiak to Sitka on September 13, 1943, to complete the Army projects remaining under the original contract. From August 22, 1944, when CBMU 512 left for the United States, public works were carried on by station personnel.

Classified with Sitka in the construction story of

BUILDING AN AIRFIELD IN THE ALEUTIANS
Seabees lay pierced plank on a runway under flood lights

Alaska were the small bases located along the route from Seattle to Kodiak. These stations were built. for the most part, by the Seabees and were established to provide minor services to craft along the extended Alaskan route.

A naval auxiliary air facility, at Annette Island, 174 miles southeast of Sitka, was constructed by the contractors, the Seabees stationed at Sitka, and Army engineers.

Personnel housing, messing, and recreation facilities accommodated 86 enlisted men and 32 officers in quonset huts. Storage facilities included 1500 cubic feet of freezer space, with additional space for dry stores, general stores, and open storage. Fuel and diesel storage were each in one 750-gallon tank; aviation gasoline was stored in a 2000-gallon tank. One small magazine was built.

Aviation facilities constructed included a repair hangar for patrol bombers, a seaplane ramp, and revetment areas for landplanes. Administration offices were housed in two 16-by-40-foot buildings. The radio station, a 6-bed dispensary, and three buildings used as shops and storehouses, were also built.

Facilities supplied by the Army included the operation of two landplane strips as well as storage of necessary aviation gasoline and ammunition. The Army also maintained two 300-foot L-type piers, a 257,000-gallon diesel-oil reservoir, and a 100-bed hospital.

Port Armstrong, 50 miles southeast of Sitka, on Baranof Island, was established as a naval section base on July 24, 1941, and changed to a naval auxiliary air facility on March 17, 1943. Construction was started by the Sitka public works office. was later absorbed by the civilian contractor. and finally completed by Seabees.

The air facility was established at the site of an existing commercial oil-company station. Construction and renovation of existing facilities were authorized under the contract and completed, after its termination, by Seabees.

Completed facilities included housing for 50 officers and men, storage buildings, a small-craft pier, and a radio station.

Storage space included a 40-by-85-foot freezer unit, 11,525 square feet of general storage, and two small magazines.

Service facilities for ships included an existing 140-by-250-foot wharf and two new piers, 50-by-100-feet and 10-by-175-feet, respectively, all of them suitable only for smaller vessels. Administration facilities were housed in a single 228-by-40-foot building and those of the dispensary in an 18-by-27-foot structure.

With the general westward movement of activity, the need for the Port Armstrong section base decreased, and it was decommissioned in July 1943.

Port Althorp, 72 miles northwest of Sitka, on Chichagof Island, was established as a section base on July 9, 1941, but was changed to an auxiliary air facility on March 17, 1943. Construction was started by the Sitka base public works department, was later absorbed by civilian contract, and was finally completed by Seabees. Facilities included limited accommodations for seaplanes and small craft, a radio-transmitting station, and personnel facilities for approximately 110 officers and men.

Storage facilities included two 4250-cubic-foot units for cold storage, a building for dry storage, and one for general stores. Fuel oil was stored in four tanks with a total capacity of 428 barrels; aviation gasoline, in three steel tanks which held 15,000 gallons; and motor gasoline in a 2000-gallon steel tank. Ordnance was stored in six small magazines.

Aviation installations were confined to a beach ramp capable of beaching five planes, and minor facilities for aircraft and engine repair.

Administration offices, communications, a fleet post office, and a 6-bed dispensary unit, completed the facilities. Power was supplied by diesel-electric units.

Yakutat, on a large, flat point of land which forms the southeast shore of Yakutat Bay on the northeast coast of the Gulf of Alaska, was established as a naval air facility on September 5, 1942, and on February 13, 1943, was redesignated a naval auxiliary air facility.

Construction at Yakutat began under the Sitka contract and was completed with the help of Seabees.

Personnel facilities included seven enlisted men's barracks for 84 men, and officers' quarters in three units for 20 men, with messing facilities in separate structures. Storage facilities included 83 cubic feet of cold storage, 345 square feet of dry storage, and 960 square feet of general storage. Fuel oil was stored in a 100-barrel wooden tank.

Yakutat was also an important Army staging field, with two runways and aviation-gasoline storage. Both these facilities were used by the Navy.

Seaplane facilities were set up to accommodate 12 scout observation planes and 4 patrol bombers. The seaplane ramp was of standard concrete construction. The lower portion, or connecting section, of the ramp was a submerged, 50-by-108-foot raft, of log and creosoted timber construction, with concrete counterweights. The completed ramp was 283 feet long and rested on rock-fill, with the outboard end 8 inches below mean low water. The warm-up apron, taxiways, and the parking area involved a total of 27,600 square yards of grading and surfacing. At the ramp, there was erected a nose-hangar of wood-truss construction, with shop space on both sides of the hangar.

Administration facilities included offices in a single 36-by-100-foot temporary two-story structure. The dispensary was housed in a quonset hut, as were also the transmitter and radio receiving stations for the base. A 50-kw and a 30-kw diesel-electric generator supplied power for the various activities. Water was supplied from a nearby lake, with storage in a 100-gallon tank. Sewage treatment was accomplished by a septic tank with drains to the sea.

The Yakutat NAAF operated as planned until June 1944, when the base was placed on a caretaker basis.

The naval section base at Cordova was established on July 24, 1941. Facilities there consisted of several magazines and a single gun emplacement; no other facilities were installed before construction ceased in February 1943. Jurisdiction of the base was turned over to the Coast Guard in October 1942. Construction work was performed under contract by Army engineers.

Ketchikan, on the Tongass Narrows, northwest of Annette Island, was established as a naval section base on July 8, 1941. Construction work was performed under the direction of the Coast Guard, and in October 1942 the base was transferred to them.

Personnel facilities constructed at the base included seven barracks of various sizes, to house 853 men; officers' quarters for 35, in three structures; and a messhall in a single 30-by-120-foot building. Recreational facilities consisted of a 60-by-90-foot combination theater and gymnasium, a lounge, and a reading room. A chapel was also provided.

Storage facilities consisted of 12,850 cubic feet

NAS Kodiak

of cold storage; 5150 cubic feet of chill storage, 9700 square feet of dry storage in four units, and 27,030 square feet of general storage in six units. Most of this storage was in standard quonset huts, supplemented by leased warehouses. Fuel-oil storage was in one 10,000-gallon and one 3000-gallon, permanent tanks. Aviation gasoline was stored in a 19,000-gallon tank rented from a commercial oil company; motor gasoline, in one 3000-gallon and one 1000-gallon tanks.

Station defense required the construction of three magazines of a permanent type and 26 gun emplacements. Aircraft facilities were limited to those for seaplanes and were centered around two semi-permanent hangars with six finger floats for docking.

A 45,150-square-foot permanent pier was constructed with 360 feet of berthing space available which could also accommodate longer ships and offered two fuel-oil lines and two diesel-oil lines. Fresh water was available at three stations on the pier. There were five compressed-air outlets. An 80-ton marine railway was installed in conjunction with a 36-by-120-foot machine shop.

Administration offices were located in seven buildings and occupied space totaling 20,826 square feet, of which 7350 square feet were leased in two buildings. Radio facilities were located in three groups, each consisting of two buildings, and each having its own transmitter and receiving station. The hospital was a semi-permanent structure with a capacity of 26 beds and connected isolation wards for 4 beds. Station maintenance included a laundry, a garage, paint storage, and shops in nine buildings with a total floor-space of 23,000 square feet. Water and power were purchased from the municipal supply; sewage treatment was in septic tanks with drains to a ravine.

Kodiak Sector

A naval base was established on Kodiak Island, in accordance with Hepburn Board recommendations, to guard the approaches to the Gulf of Alaska and to constitute an intermediate point between Dutch Harbor and Sitka.

The group of islands, of which Kodiak is by far the largest, lies off the western shore of the Gulf of Alaska, at the base of the Alaskan Peninsula. The island of Kodiak, with an area of 3588 square miles, has a coastline of about 1500 miles, with numerous deep bays and channels. The terrain is mountainous, with many high peaks and numerous lakes and streams. The heavy rainfall is evenly distributed.

Major obstacles encountered in the construction of the station were stormy weather and bad ground. The climate, in general, is not severe, for the island of Kodiak lies in the path of the Japanese current, which gives it a mild and equable climate. However, during the long, dark, winter months, the weather is often very inclement. Kodiak Island is covered by a blanket of volcanic ash, deposited during the eruption of Mount Katmai in 1912, which varies in depth from 3 inches to 8 feet, and in some places 20-foot drifts were found. This blanket, deposited on muskeg and rock outcrop, provided a difficult and unpredictable base for every foundation and footing installation and presented a continuous, surface-water seepage problem.

Construction of additional facilities on the Kodiak Naval Reservation was authorized by an act of Congress, April 25, 1939. A general order, dated November 8, 1939, withdrew public land and water on "the eastern portion of Kodiak Island" for naval purposes. The first ground was broken on September 23, 1939.

Under the original and subsequent authorizations, naval projects of a total estimated value of $66,320,727 and Army projects of a total estimated value of $28,040,400 were placed under cost-plus-a-fixed-fee contract.

The original plans called for the construction of a naval operating base, to include a naval air station, a submarine base, a net depot, a dispensary, docks, ammunition and fuel storage facilities, provisioning, administration, and personnel facilities. The air station was to include facilities for both landplanes and seaplanes, to consist of ramps, runways, maintenance and repair shops, storehouses, and housing units. The submarine base was to provide repair service for small ships and boats with a floating drydock, shops, and additional housing.

The three paved runways at the air station were of concrete, each 150 feet wide and 6000, 5400, and 5000 feet long, respectively. A 175-foot graded strip on both sides of each runway gave a total clear width of 500 feet. All runways were equipped with a flush-contact lighting system. Hangar space was provided by one permanent 50-by-184-foot hangar and one temporary 112-by-163-foot hangar. A 75-by-5400-foot concrete taxiway extended from the 5000-foot runway to the hangar area.

Seaplane facilities were located on Womens Bay. Three concrete ramps, two of them 50-by-250-feet, and one 50-by-325-feet, were built. Hangar space was provided in two permanent 320-by-250-foot hangars. Aircraft repair facilities were provided in two shops attached to the seaplane hangars and a maintenance shop with a floor area of 200,000 square feet. A 121,500-square-yard parking area, of which 94,800 square yards were paved, was also built.

Docking facilities for large craft consisted of an 800-by-65-foot cargo pier, with four deep-water approaches and a depth of 30 feet at its outboard end; a 450-by-40-foot tender pier, with fresh-water, gasoline, and oil lines, berthing on two sides, and a minimum depth of 26 feet; and a 1400-by-30-foot marginal wharf, with a fresh-water line and a 30-ton stiff-leg derrick. Thirteen piers to accommodate small boats, tugs, patrol, and similar craft were located at various places throughout the base.

Service facilities for ships also included a permanent 175-ton marine railway, 348 feet long. Submarine services were also included. Permanent buildings were erected for shops, battery and torpedo overhaul, torpedo compression, and other work.

Cold-storage facilities, with a capacity of 111,350 cubic feet of freezer space in four buildings, and 37,240 cubic feet of cooler space in three buildings, as well as several portable refrigerators, were constructed. Dry storage was provided in three permanent and four semi-permanent buildings with a total area of 99,455 square feet. General stores required 40 semi-permanent buildings which varied in size from the 110-by-208-foot general warehouse to small transit sheds. The total available area amounted to 203,550 square feet. The 29 construction-and-maintenance warehouses were almost entirely of temporary construction and had a total floor area of 192,450 square feet.

Fuel-storage facilities included four 27,000-barrel underground tanks for refueling ships, with eighteen 600-barrel, steel tanks underground and one 55,000-barrel, steel tank above ground. Diesel oil was stored in two 13,500-barrel, underground steel tanks and four 6666-gallon, splinter-proof, steel, surface tanks. Aviation gasoline was stored in sixty-four 25,000-gallon, steel, underground tanks and three 13,400-gallon tanks. Motor-gasoline storage was also installed at the air station in one 567,000-gallon, underground, steel tank and ten

42,000-gallon, steel, splinter-proof tanks. Lubricating oil was kept in drums and in a 1,000-gallon tank. Ordnance was stored in 39 magazines.

Administration facilities, including offices, radio station, hospital and instruction space, were built. Offices, including those of the air station, submarine base, and the civilian contractor, were established in five buildings with a total area of 65,000 square feet. Radio facilities included a 32-by-82-foot transmitter building, a 16-by-72-foot receiving station, and three small direction-finder buildings.

Medical facilities included a 100-bed hospital for the contractor in a semi-permanent building, a 63-bed dispensary in a permanent building at the air

NAVAL OPERATING BASE AT ADAK
Part of the PT base facilities

station, and an Army ward-type 33-bed hospital in a temporary structure.

Instruction facilities for gunnery were provided in five temporary buildings and eight firing-range shelters at the anti-aircraft training center.

A total of 28 buildings, which included a laundry, a fire station, garages, and various shops, were erected for station maintenance.

Utilities required a 4750-kw steam generator and four 50-kw diesel-electric units. Gravel-surfaced roads, 14 to 18 feet wide, totaling 166 miles, were constructed throughout the base.

Water was obtained from two main sources, from Bushkin Lake and from filter galleries along Sargent Creek and Russian River. Storage tanks at the air station included four 187,500-gallon tanks for naval use and four 175,000-gallon tanks for Army use. In the Bells Flat area a 200,000-gallon tank served the Navy, and a similar one was used by the Army. About 17,000 feet of sewers, up to 48 inches in diameter, were installed.

Housing facilities were constructed for 7,769 enlisted men in 321 buildings, with all buildings of semi-permanent or temporary construction, excepting seven permanent 44-by-181-foot barracks to house 1050 men at the air station. Housing for 401 officers was also provided, with messing and recreational facilities for all personnel.

Construction of Fort Greeley, the Army garrison at Kodiak, was accomplished largely by contractors but was completed by Seabees. Personnel installations included housing, messing, and recreational facilities for 10,829 men and 682 officers. This involved construction of 665 semi-permanent and temporary housing units, 89 messhalls and galley units, two theaters, two libraries, two post-exchanges, and two chapels.

Storage facilities provided 79,910 cubic feet of freezer space, 61,820 cubic feet of chill space, and 88 units for general storage with a total floor area of 229,610 square feet. Fuel-oil storage was in two 10,000-gallon tanks of semi-permanent construction. Aviation gasoline was stored in eight 25,000-gallon underground tanks. Motor gasoline storage was also underground, in fifteen 5000-gallon tanks of permanent construction. Ordnance was stored in 38 semi-permanent magazines.

Aviation facilities for Fort Greeley were at the naval air station and included three semi-permanent hangars, which provided 30,000 square feet of area, and 20 plane revetments. Repair shops were located in six temporary buildings, with a total

floor area of 6560 square feet. An auxiliary strip, constructed by laying steel matting on a sand base, was located at Cape Chiniak, 15 miles to the southeast.

Offices were located in 19 buildings of semi-permanent and temporary construction. Medical installations included a 16-ward, dispersed hospital to accommodate 343 men, and an infirmary of 12 units.

The garrison maintenance force was established in 44 semi-permanent and temporary buildings. These included a laundry, garages, a sawmill, and various shops, with a total floor-space of 224,950 square feet. Power was furnished by nine diesel units, with a total rated output of 1565 kw.

The roadway system comprised 130 miles of gravel-surfaced highways, all 20 feet wide. Sewage disposal was accomplished by outfall to the sea, with pumping necessary in only two small areas. Water was supplied from the naval-base sources and stored in three 200,000-gallon and four 60,000-gallon, semi-permanent, wood tanks.

Harbor defense construction involved gun emplacements and platforms, with necessary magazines and control posts.

In June 1945, the submarine base was decommissioned and the net defense facilities on Woody Island were disestablished.

The contractor's maximum construction strength was 3508 men, reached in December 1942. An average of 880 men remained from October 1, 1939, to April 30, 1943, when all remaining construction, with the exception of dredging, was taken over by the 4th Construction Regiment, composed of the 38th, 41st, 43rd, and 45th Battalions. At that time, it was estimated that 72 percent of the authorized work had been completed.

After the 4th Construction Regiment was disbanded on September 25, 1943, the remaining Army construction was assigned to the 41st and 43rd Battalions for completion and the remaining naval construction was taken over by the station public works department, composed of the 79th Battalion and station personnel.

On September 23, 1944, half of the 26th Battalion arrived to relieve the 79th, which departed on October 4. On August 6, 1943, the 8th Special Battalion reached Kodiak to take over cargo operations; however, half of the unit departed at once for Attu. On February 23, 1944, the unit was again split, to permit sending a detachment to Dutch Harbor. The 12th and 23rd Battalions served at

Kodiak from the fall of 1942 to the spring of 1943.

The base at Kodiak was never developed beyond the original plan. This was due mainly to the fact that many projects originally planned for Kodiak were moved farther west or were reduced as the scene of action shifted. A conservative estimate of materials and equipment from cancelled Kodiak projects which were then moved out along the Aleutian chain has been set at $10,000,000.

Installations at NOB Kodiak were started, and a large portion completed, under the civilian contract. Seabees took over unfinished projects and improved some finished ones. They also installed gun emplacements for harbor defense and performed most of the work involved in the construction of magazines and storehouses.

After their arrival, the Seabees carried on all station maintenance at Kodiak, as well as their construction duties. In addition to this, they were active in salvaging ships gone aground or wrecked during storms in the vicinity. Three of the salvage jobs in which they participated were those concerned with the S S *John Peter Gains*, the Army vessel FB-33, and the Army Transport Service vessel *Elna*. The salvage crews also undertook the job of landing supplies on islands surrounded by very dangerous water.

One of the most important jobs accomplished by the Seabees was the establishment, for the Army, of the outlying coastal defense positions which protected the main base on Kodiak Island. These outlying stations included Chernabura, Sand Point, Woody Island, Cold Bay, King Cove, Chirikof, Chiniak, Entrance Point, Cape Greville, Sanak, and Afognak. A part of the work on these bases was done by the contractors and a small portion by Army engineers, but most of the work was executed by Seabees. The installations consisted mainly of air and sea defenses, with accompanying facilities required for operating personnel.

At Chernabura, the southernmost island in the Shumagin group, 475 miles southwest of Kodiak, a radio and radar beacon was erected as an aid to navigation for surface ships and aircraft.

Chernabura was commissioned in May 1943 and operated in its designed capacity until it was decommissioned June 6, 1945.

Sand Point, on Popof Island, also in the Shumagin group, was first commissioned as a section base in the early part of 1942, but on April 1, 1943, it was changed to a naval auxiliary air facility. A radio range station, commissioned September 22, 1943, was also established, as an aid to air navigation and a weather-observation center. This station was decommissioned on April 28, 1945.

The completed air facility included accommodations for 410 officers and men; storage facilities for general supplies, liquid fuels, and ordnance; seaplane parking areas and repair shops; service facilities for large and small surface craft; and a radio transmitter. All buildings were of temporary construction with the exception of those leased from a local cannery.

On Woody Island, 6 miles northeast of Kodiak, were located a magnetic loop and harbor protection equipment, a net depot, and a radio range station.

In October 1942, a heavy indicator-net for surface and under-water vessels was installed between Woody Island and Kodiak Island. In November 1943, anti-torpedo nets were substituted for the heavier nets. In December 1942, magnetic loop stations were located at the entrance of the channel leading to Kodiak and at St. Paul's Harbor. A naval radio compass station, set up on Woody Island during World War I, was still in operation.

Living facilities for 200 officers and men were provided; all personnel and equipment operation was closely allied with NOB Kodiak.

Cold Bay, near the end of the Alaskan Peninsula, 432 air miles from Kodiak, was commissioned July 14, 1942 as a naval airfield and was changed to a naval auxiliary air facility on April 1, 1943.

The landing strips at Cold Bay comprised two 150-by-5000-foot asphalt-surfaced runways and a gravel-surfaced, satellite field, 150-by-5000 feet. All strips were Army-operated. Aviation gasoline was stored in twenty-eight 25,000-gallon tanks and distributed by tank trucks.

Personnel facilities were constructed to accommodate 500 officers and men, in quonset-type buildings which were also used for offices, communications, and refrigerator and general storage. A net depot, with necessary warehouses and storage area, was constructed at Cold Bay, together with an Army T-type 66-by-810-foot wharf.

At King Cove, considered a part of Cold Bay, repair facilities for small craft were constructed, including a 150-ton marine railway and an adjacent machine shop. Diesel-oil storage was in tanks totaling 65,000-gallon capacity.

The Army garrison at nearby Fort Randall, numbering 298 officers and 4648 men, required the con-

MEMBERS OF THE 86TH BATTALION AT ADAK
Dredging surfacing material from Finger Bay for finish material on roads.

struction of necessary quarters and other living facilities.

NAAF Cold Bay was decommissioned November 7, 1944, and at that time a few necessary services were turned over to the Army.

Seabee personnel involved at Cold Bay consisted of a detachment from the 8th Battalion, which was assigned the initial construction, and one company of the 23rd. which moved to Cold Bay in May 1943 to complete the work. Maintenance was then taken over by a detachment of CBMU 510, which was later relieved by a detachment of the 79th Battalion.

Chirikof Island, southwest of Kodiak Island, maintained a radio range, a radio and radar beacon, and a weather-observation station. Commissioned in December 1942, its installations included six temporary structures to house personnel and radio equipment.

Cape Greville, on Kodiak Island, was commissioned in April 1943, as a radio and radar beacon station and was turned over to the Coast Guard in October 1944.

Construction at the station involved several temporary structures for personnel and radio equipment.

Entrance Point, also on Kodiak Island, was established in the early part of 1942 as an anti-aircraft training center. Buildings were constructed for housing and feeding 100 men and 12 officers and for conducting training exercises. The center was decommissioned in December 1943.

Facilities at Sanak and Caton Island, collectively known as Sanak, 50 miles south of Cold Bay. included a radio range, a radio and radar beacon, and a weather-observation station. It was commissioned in January 1943.

Afognak, on Afognak Island. just north of Kodiak Island, was established in March 1942 as an administration point. The installation included a radio station. The entire area was turned into a recreation center in June 1944, and all personnel stationed at Kodiak were allowed a two- or three-day excursion trip there, based on a rotation program. Excellent hunting and fishing were to be had in the area.

Seward, a section base, on the southern portion of Kenai Peninsula, was placed in commission July 31, 1942. Construction was performed by Army engineers. On April 1, 1943. it became a naval auxiliary air facility.

Personnel facilities consisted of four semi-permanent buildings; general storage was in a single 22-by-50-foot building; and aviation gasoline was stored in a 25,000-gallon steel tank. A seaplane hangar was built and a ramp installed. Two piers were provided; one 25-by-165-feet, the other, 15-by-100-feet. Administration offices were housed in a single building.

The Army operated Seward and maintained Fort Ramone there with a defense garrison. Naval activities at Seward were discontinued July 29, 1943, and facilities turned over to the Coast Guard who supervised shipping operations and maintained a port captain's office.

Dutch Harbor Sector

The purpose of the naval installations at Dutch Harbor was to provide a naval operating base farther west in the Aleutian chain than Kodiak. Air facilities, a submarine base, and numerous minor activities were included.

Dutch Harbor is on Amaknak Island in Unalaska Bay, a bay in the island of Unalaska, the largest and most important island of the eastern Aleutians. Unalaska, 67 miles long and 23 miles wide, is largely mountainous. Unalaska Bay provides one of the best anchorages in the Aleutians, with depths sufficient to accommodate the largest vessels, but the prevalence of bad weather causes

operating conditions there to be even more difficult than at most other Alaskan stations.

Army and Navy construction work at Dutch Harbor began in 1940, as an extension to the cost-plus-a-fixed-fee contract originally awarded for work at Sitka and Kodiak. In July 1942, the estimated total probable cost for this project was $44,000,000, of which $20,500,844 was for Army work, including harbor-defense installations, housing for troops, and the facilities and utilities necessary to serve them.

The construction work was carried on entirely by the contractor until the bombing of Dutch Harbor in June 1942, after which the construction effort was reinforced by Seabees. The 4th Construction Battalion, the first to be ordered to Alaska, arrived at Dutch Harbor on July 5. 1942, improperly clothed and without suitable tools or equipment. On July 14, it was reinforced by the 8th Battalion: on August 26, by the 13th Battalion; and on October 18. by the 21st Battalion.

By the middle of December, all of the contractor's personnel had left Dutch Harbor, with the exception of several members of the supervisory force who remained to assist in the inventory work and the settlement of the contract.

The contractor had completed nine of the original 28 projects, the value of which reached $4,484,428. Work had also been started. but not completed, on an additional 10 projects. This work, as well as all new construction. was taken over by the Seabees.

The air station at NOB Dutch Harbor included a 300-by-4385-foot, gravel-surfaced, emergency runway and concrete parking area, a concrete seaplane ramp and its facilities, for patrol bombers and scout planes. Hangar space was provided in a permanent blast-pen-type hangar, 115 feet by 310 feet. and a semi-permanent kodiak-type hangar. Other buildings included a permanent 72-by-122-foot repair shop and parachute loft. a 30-by-50-foot semi-permanent photographer's laboratory, and an air-operations building. Installed as a part of the air-station equipment was a catapult with a launching platform and arresting gear. Storage facilities included tanks for 1,069,000 gallons of aviation gasoline and complete facilities for storage and handling of small ammunition, bombs, and torpedoes.

The submarine base possessed facilities equivalent to a submarine tender. including hull, machine, electrical, optical, and radio shops. In ad-

BUILDING A ROAD AT ADAK
32nd Seabees working on road to the hospital area

dition, a large torpedo shop and storehouse and three magazines to store types of ammunition other than torpedoes were provided. Diesel oil was stored in seven tanks; three were underground, and the others were of the oil-dock type.

Repair facilities for ships and small craft provided half the equivalent of a destroyer tender. The boat shop was equipped to construct small boats; its slip was capable of taking 50-foot landing barges or boats for repairs or major overhaul. A small marine railway, put into operation during November 1943, was capable of taking craft up to 50 tons. The 250-ton marine railway, operated by a maintenance unit, was capable of handling yard mine-sweepers. The machine shop, carpenter shop, welding shop, blacksmith shop, and electrical shop

were capable of making repairs on small craft and providing maintenance and minor repairs on large ships. The public works machine shop and plumbing shop were also available for heavy ship-repair work.

Facilities for provisioning units of the Fleet included dry-storage capacity of 314,610 cubic feet, in six warehouses, and cold-storage space for 1,037 tons. Fuel oil was stored in 13 tanks with total capacity of 173,000 barrels, of which 135,000 were in underground concrete tanks. Motor gasoline was stored in six tanks with a total capacity of 595,000 gallons.

Docking facilities, provided by various docks and piers, included the 500-by-50-foot Dutch Harbor pier, the 575-by-58-foot Advance Base Depot pier, the 900-by-60-foot Ballyhoo Pier, the 550-by-50-foot fuel pier, the 240-by-60-foot YP pier, the 1845-by-30-foot submarine base pier, and a marine-railway pier, which measured 600 by 40 feet. In addition, several small-boat and finger floats were constructed.

Utilities required four diesel and three steam plants for electric power, and turbine exhaust was used for steam-heating the air-station buildings. Water-supply was obtained through a gravity supply flow from a dam on Unalaska Creek, with 12-inch mains to Amaknak Island, and a gravity supply from a dam on Pyramid Creek, with 16-inch mains to the Amaknak Island distribution system. Water was stored at Dutch Harbor in three storage tanks, which also served the submarine base. Roads and highways in the area totaled 84 miles; all were gravel-surfaced and 20 feet wide.

Administration facilities included 17 office buildings of various types. Radio facilities, which included 20 transmitters and receivers, were located in 15 buildings at various sections of the base.

Housing, messing, and recreation were provided for 174 officers and 1265 men of the base personnel, and for 107 officers and 4179 men of the construction battalions. A dispensary, with units at the air station, submarine base, and outlying points, provided a maximum capacity of 200 beds.

Construction of the Army garrison post at Fort Mears, Dutch Harbor, was completed by Seabees. Personnel requirements included the construction of housing and messing facilities for 9500 enlisted men and 500 officers, with recreational, post exchange, and religious facilities. Storage facilities numbered 68,780 cubic feet of freezer storage, 44,910 cubic feet of chill space, and 331,215 cubic feet of general storage space. The 270-bed hospital was designed and constructed to care for both Army and Navy personnel. A dispensary was also set up, with a capacity of 308 officers and men.

Ammunition was stored in 91 magazines of permanent or semi-permanent concrete or steel construction. Administration facilities were established in 53 semi-permanent or temporary buildings, with a total floor-area of 25,675 square feet.

Diesel-electric generators were installed at three stations. Their total capacity was 1155 kw, made up from a 600-kw, a 300-kw and a 255-kw unit; additional power was obtained through a connection by a submarine line to the air station's power circuit. The water-supply source was Unalaska

Creek. Sewage disposal, as in the case of the naval base, was through 16-inch outfalls to the harbor.

Harbor-defense construction was confined primarily to reinforced-concrete gun platforms and emplacements, with adjacent magazines and command posts. For station maintenance operations and the staff, 27 semi-permanent buildings, with a total floor area of 86,670 square feet, were constructed. These buildings ranged in purpose and use from a laundry to garages and repair shops. Aviation requirements for Fort Mears were served by the naval air station.

The story of Seabee assignments and growth at Dutch Harbor began at the point where the contractors and their personnel were relieved. With four battalions at Dutch Harbor, the need for a military organization beyond the battalion was evident. On September 20, 1942, the Western Alaska Construction Regiment was approved, and on November 25, its headquarters company arrived at Dutch Harbor. On December 19, 1942, its designation was changed to the First Construction Regiment, which included the 4th, 8th, 13th, and 21st Battalions.

During the month of January 1943, the 42nd Battalion arrived from the United States to stage for a month before moving to Adak. The 32nd, which had arrived in December, had been assigned to Adak, but it was considered unwise to unload the 32nd directly into Adak at that time, and consequently it was diverted to Dutch Harbor. From Dutch Harbor, such personnel and equipment as could be accommodated and used were filtered into Adak and Atka. The 51st and 52nd Battalions arrived at Dutch Harbor, but only the 51st remained, the 52nd being gradually moved into the Adak sector. In April, the 5th Special Battalion arrived to take over stevedoring duties previously performed by detachments from various battalions. The 85th Battalion and CBMU's 508 and 510 arrived on May 30, 1943.

The 7th Special Battalion arrived in June 1943 to relieve the 5th Special Battalion, which left for Adak in July. Other departures were the 52nd Battalion for Adak during April and May 1943, and the 4th in June; the 8th and 13th in August for the United States; the 21st for the United States in December 1943; and the 51st for the United States in March 1944. The First Regiment was disbanded on September 1, 1943.

The major portion of construction work at Dutch Harbor and its satellite bases was completed by

HOSPITAL AREA AT ADAK
Main building, surgery and ward (foreground); similar building (left) is the mess hall; other buildings are
x-ray and personnel huts

November 1943, and minor construction was then carried on by maintenance units and detachments from other battalions, in conjunction with Army forces. Also present was a group from the 8th Special Battalion which handled stevedoring until May 1945; on July 15, 1945, the CBMU 635 arrived. It was still on duty there on V-J Day.

Naval facilities, in the meantime. had been reduced and, in some cases, revised. The air station had been reduced to the status of an air facility by June 1945; the submarine base was decommissioned on May 22, 1945. A fueling point for Russian ships had been established to replace the station at Akutan. Other facilities remained largely in their designed status.

An interesting sidelight on Seabee activity was

the raising of the SS *Northwestern* at Dutch Harbor. This ship, which had been used as a barracks for civilian employees, was bombed during the June 1942 raid on Dutch Harbor, by the Japanese, who mistook it for a transport. It was decided that the hulk, which lay on the beach, would yield valuable scrap. Accordingly, the Seabees put her into seaworthy condition and secured her for tow to Seattle, where she yielded 2,700 tons of scrap steel.

Unalga Island, about 16 miles northeast of Dutch Harbor, is flat and low in comparison with adjacent islands. Although it possesses a partly sheltered ship anchorage, in most places the coast is fringed with submerged rocks.

The only installation constructed on Unalga

Island was a radio beacon and range station, manned and operated by the Navy. An attempt was made to construct an airfield in one of the level areas, but the project was soon abandoned. The island and its personnel were under the direct control of NOB Dutch Harbor.

Hog Island, of the Fox group, is in Unalaska Bay, about 2 miles west of Dutch Harbor. Here the Navy installed a radio range station, and the Army set up housing and messing facilities for a garrison of 250 men, with the necessary storehouses and utilities. A 178-by-18-foot wharf was constructed to facilitate the landing of supplies and men. The island was under the control of NOB Dutch Harbor.

Otter Point, on Umnak Island at Umnak Pass, the narrow body of water separating Umnak and Unalaska islands, was selected as the site of a naval air facility.

Construction was carried out entirely by Seabees and the Army. The development of the facility at Otter Point was approved by the Secretary of the Navy on September 18, 1942, and Commanding General Alaska Defense Command assigned the required land on September 25, 1942. The work was done by a detachment of the 8th Construction Battalion.

Housing and messing facilities for 119 officers and 359 men were constructed, as well as recreational and ship's service buildings. Storage facilities consisted of 6975 square feet for general stores and a 150-cubic-foot freezer. Buildings for aircraft included a kodiak-type hangar, 160 by 90 feet, a squadron warehouse, and a terminal for air transport service. Administration offices were housed in five buildings with a total floor space of 3850 square feet. Radio facilities included a transmitting station, a direction-finder station, and a radar station, all with separate power houses and with housing and messing provisions for personnel. The hospital, located in one small building, contained eight beds.

The maintenance force of the station was installed in seven buildings. Electric power was provided by three diesel-electric generators. All other utilities were furnished by the Army at Fort Glenn, which also provided landing strips and revetments, aviation gasoline and fuels of other types, provisions, and repair facilities for aircraft.

An additional activity connected with the Otter Point project was the net-defense station at Cher-nofski Harbor, across Umnak Pass, on Unalaska Island. Housing, storage, and the few necessary operations buildings were constructed to accommodate a staff of 30 officers and men. In April 1945 the facility was disestablished, and the Allied harbor entrance control post was transferred to Army jurisdiction.

At Otter Point, similar developments took place. Naval facilities were reduced to include only a radio-beacon station and a radio station. All other activities were either disestablished or turned over to the Army by June 1945.

In the summer of 1942, the operation of Russian ships between Siberia and our West Coast ports required a base in the Aleutians to be used as a midway fueling, provisioning, and repair station. Akutan, a small island 35 miles east of Dutch Harbor, was selected and negotiations were undertaken to lease the station of a whaling company. By October 1942, an agreement had been reached and work completed to render a 250-foot docking facility usable for Russian ships. A detachment of Seabees, numbering about 40 men from the 13th Battalion on Dutch Harbor, was assigned to perform the necessary construction.

Transformation of the whaling station into a naval fueling station was soon accomplished, as buildings and tanks needed only to be altered in order to meet the Navy's needs. Housing and messing were provided for 80 men and 12 officers. This included 24,160 square feet of storage space for general stores, 288 cubic feet of freezer space, and 930 cubic feet of chill space. Six vats, converted to oil tanks, totaled a 32,000-barrel capacity. Diesel oil and aviation gasoline were stored in smaller tanks and drums. Coal for the Russian coal-burning ships was stored in a 5000-ton, pier storage area. Existing utilities were supplemented, and roads improved. Three mooring buoys were installed for seaplane use, as the harbor furnished a fairly well-protected landing area. The Akutan station was ready to pump oil or to receive an emergency seaplane landing by November 7, 1942.

By June 1945, the need for a fueling point of this type had been practically eliminated. As a result, the Akutan base was reduced to the status of a minor seaplane facility and Coast Guard radio-beacon station.

Adak Sector

Naval installations at Adak were planned to provide support for the fleet through an operating base consisting of an air station, a radio station, a net depot, a PT-boat base, Marine barracks. and other small activities.

Adak, a weather-beaten, uninhabited island in the Andreanof group, 400 miles west of Dutch Harbor. is 30 miles long and has a maximum width of 20 miles. Terrain is rugged and mountainous, with many small lakes and streams. Numerous small bays indent the coast line. The treeless ground is covered with tundra.

Although the climate is not excessively intemperate, the island is subject to frequent storms of rain, snow, and sleet and to high-velocity winds, which result in extremely poor flying conditions. Annual rainfall averages 40 inches, with 100 additional inches of snowfall. The summer months are subject to continuous fogs and rain, with high-velocity winds prevailing during August. The winter months occasionally contain fair days, but are always subject to sudden snow and sleet storms. The two best weather months are September and October.

During the latter part of August 1942, Adak and nearby Atka were occupied by the Army, and it was then considered advisable to start immediately the construction of minimum naval activities to permit the Fleet Air Wing to operate patrol searches from these advanced bases.

Construction work for the various activities which constituted the naval operating base was accomplished by the Seabees. This work included personnel facilities: storage for construction materials, general supplies, fuels, and ordnance; seaplane and landplane landing areas; hangars and repair shops: facilities for small and large craft, including drydocks, a marine railway, and repair shops; a radio station: and construction and maintenance shops.

At the air station, two runways, 5277 by 200 feet and 7145 by 200 feet, respectively, were constructed. Both were surfaced with pierced planking. Hangar space was in five kodiak-type hangars and one smaller building, all of semi-permanent design. One building contained a parachute loft. In conjunction with the runways, 60-foot taxiways which totaled 14,000 feet in length were built, with a parking area of 1,500,000 square feet. Both were surfaced with pierced planking. A semi-permanent, two-story control building and tower was erected. Three temporary buildings furnished 10,150 square feet for photographic laboratories. Repair facilities

for aircraft were provided in four buildings with a total area of 24,700 square feet.

Available to the Navy were the two strips operated by the Army at Sweeper Cove. Hangar space and minor repair shops for naval use were installed there by Seabees.

Seaplane facilities were established at Andrew Lagoon, a fresh-water body near the air station. Three hangars were built, providing 17,000 square feet of space for patrol bombers and 2900 square feet for observation planes. Parking area consisted of 24,000 square feet of pierced-plank surface and a 50-by-70-foot ramp of the same material. Fueling service for all naval planes was by tank trucks from Army supplies. When Andrew Lagoon was frozen, operations were transferred to the salt waters of nearby Clam Lagoon.

Service facilities for ships were located in Sweeper Cove, and those for small craft were divided between the PT base and the section base. Five piers for small craft, ranging in size from 25-by-50-feet to 40-by-300-feet and all of temporary construction, and 108 concrete anchorages, weighing from 2½ to 5 tons, were constructed and placed. Two temporary drydocks were assembled from pontoons and furnished capacities of 100 and 400 tons, respectively. Nine temporary structures, with a total area of 42,125 square feet, were erected to serve as shops. Large-craft facilities included three pile-and-timber piers at the section base. The two operating-base piers measured 75 by 392 feet and 55 by 600 feet; the Navy Pier was 55 by 600 feet.

Fresh-water outlets, a rigging loft, and an optical shop were installed at the section base.

Cold-storage space in five units, totaling 77,000 cubic feet, was provided at the air station, section base, and PT base. Dry-storage space in six warehouses totaled 27,100 square feet, of which 15,800 square feet were in a single building. General-stores space was provided in 41 buildings which gave a total floor space of 234,000 square feet. Construction and maintenance storage was in 17 buildings with a total of 27,325 square feet; medical supplies were in 10 quonset huts, with a total floor area of 5050 square feet. All fuel stores were under Army control, and no extra construction for them was required. Ordnance storage was in 27 buildings, only one of which was permanent. Torpedo overhaul and compressor shops at the PT base were in three quonset huts.

Administration offices for the various other ac-

HEDRON AREA UNDER CONSTRUCTION, ADAK

tivities were housed in 76 buildings, 68 of which were quonsets with a total of 104,800 square feet of floor space. Communication facilities were established in four quonset-type buildings, as were also the various branch post offices. The main fleet post office at the section base was a semi-permanent 70-by-100-foot structure.

Radio facilities were located in two quonset huts, and radar equipment occupied a third. The hospital, with all its attendant features, was also established in quonset huts.

Housing facilities included 1049 tents to house 1234 men and 421 quonsets for 7379 men. Seven buildings and 212 quonsets accommodated 1000 officers. Mess requirements were met with 16 mess-halls and 10 wardrooms.

Recreational facilities included five theaters with an average capacity of 400 men, a 172-by-320-foot recreation center at the air station, and a 40-by-100-foot gymnasium at the section base. Commissary and ship's service stores were established in seven buildings, five of which were quonsets, with a total area of 8050 square feet.

Station maintenance, which included a telephone exchange, garages, a laundry, and various shops, was carried on in 18 buildings, which had a total floor area of 61,745 square feet.

Power throughout the entire base was obtained from twenty 75-kw and eleven 50-kw portable diesel-electric generators, dispersed throughout the base. Water was obtained from wells and was stored in wooden tanks which included one 60,000-gallon, seven 15,000-gallon, and three 6,000-gallon units. Between 30 and 40 miles of roads and walks were constructed and maintained.

To perform the construction during the initial phases of the occupation, small detachments of the 4th and the 8th Battalions were sent to Adak, followed by their equipment as shipping space became available. On December 25, 1942, the first group from the 32nd Battalion arrived from Dutch Harbor; the whole battalion was ashore by the end of January 1943. This battalion began the real construction of the air facilities.

In February the 6th Naval Construction Regiment was formed from forces available at Adak; it was later augmented by the 42nd Battalion, a company of the 23rd, half of the 5th Special Battalion, and the entire 52nd Battalion. Additions during June and July 1943 involved more groups of the 23rd, the remainder of the 5th, and the 12th Battalion. The 66th Battalion and a detachment of the 38th arrived during August, followed, on September 20, 1943, by detachments of the 7th Special Battalion and the 45th.

The 12th Battalion left Adak during September 1943, and the 32nd departed just after the first of the year. By the summer of 1944, most of the work at Adak had been turned over to the 86th Battalion for maintenance, and the only unit then left was CBMU 510, which had arrived on May 22, 1943. When the 86th Battalion departed on November 14, 1944, a detachment from the 138th Battalion was sent from Attu to take over maintenance and necessary minor construction.

All construction at Adak was performed by the Seabees. In addition, considerable work was done on the outlying bases, including Kiska and Attu.

Sand Bay, on the southern end of Great Sitkin Island, about 21 miles northeast of Adak, was established as a naval advance fueling station on May 15, 1943. Facilities for this activity and for a net depot were constructed by the Seabees. This included accommodations for 680 officers and men; provisions for storage of general supplies, net materials, and liquid fuels; small- and large-craft piers.

Housing was provided in 46 quonset huts. Messing facilities were set up in six temporary buildings. Recreational facilities included a theater for 550 men, a recreation hall, and a library.

Storage facilities consisted of 89,200 cubic feet of cold-storage space in two temporary buildings;

18,800 square feet of dry-storage space in two buildings; 64,550 square feet of general-storage space in 11 buildings; and 25,710 square feet of space for construction and maintenance materials in two buildings. Fuel-oil storage required twenty-two 10,000-barrel tanks, three 6000-barrel tanks, and one 15,000-barrel tank, all of which were set in excavations with dike berms. Diesel-oil and aviation-gasoline storage was in sixteen 6000-barrel steel tanks. Ordnance was stored in 19 magazines.

Service facilities for small craft at the net depot were centered around the 40-by-630-foot, semipermanent pier. Four moorings were provided at the fueling station, where a 60-by-800-foot pier was furnished with eight 8-inch and eight 6-inch fuel lines and a fresh-water outlet.

Administration offices were placed in five temporary buildings which had a total floor space of 6090 square feet. The fleet post office occupied two quonset huts. Radio transmitting and receiving stations were placed in separate buildings. The hospital, which consisted of six standard quonset huts, was located at the fueling station. Station maintenance shops were established in nine quonsets which had a total floor area of 8690 square feet. Diesel-electric units supplied power for the entire station.

All work was accomplished by Seabees, with the major portion performed by the 52nd Battalion, which had made the initial landing. Later, small detachments were assigned from NOB Adak to carry on the work. On V-J day, Sand Bay was still functioning as a naval fueling station and net depot.

Ogliuga, one of the Delarof Islands, off the western end of the Adreanof group, 100 miles from Adak, is the lowest and flattest island of the Aleutians. It is 3 miles long and 1½ miles wide, with a rocky, irregular coast.

Construction of the emergency landing field established at Ogliuga for the Army in July 1943, was performed entirely by Seabees. A 100-by-3000-foot runway and four 100-foot-square parking areas were constructed, with a surface of steel matting. The only other construction at Ogliuga was a small building for living quarters.

Amchitka, one of the Rat Islands group in the western Aleutians, lies about 178 miles west of Adak. It extends 34 miles northwest-southeast and averages about three miles in width. The northwest section of the island is rugged but gradually levels out toward the center, and in the southeast portion the terrain is low, rolling tundra and flat tableland dotted with lakes and ponds.

A detachment of the 42nd Seabees arrived at Amchitka on March 16, 1943, at the time it was established as a naval air facility. Construction included personnel accommodations, storage buildings, runways, individual hangars, a small-craft pier, and a radio station.

Personnel facilities to accommodate 1200 men were provided in 69 barracks, most of which were small quonsets; 20 additional ones served as officers' quarters. Messing facilities were set up in two H-shaped structures composed of quonset huts; each structure seated 900 men. A mess hall and galley, combined in a single 20-by-90-foot building, served the PT base. Two structures, each a combination of quonset huts, provided officers' mess facilities. Recreational facilities included two 500-man theaters.

Freezer storage was in ten units with a total capacity of 3468 cubic feet; chill storage, in nine boxes which furnished 328 cubic feet. Dry stores were located in a single large quonset with a concrete floor. General stores occupied six buildings which were combinations of various-sized quonsets and had a total floor-space of 12,585 square feet. Construction-material storage required 2471 square feet in six buildings. All fuel, including diesel oil, was under Army control and no construction was required by the Navy. Ordnance was stored in seven small magazines.

Installations for aircraft included the construction of a 50-by-150-foot seaplane ramp, a 60-by-115-foot parking platform, and nine shop buildings. Landplanes were handled at the Army-operated airstrips.

Service facilities for small craft consisted of a 700-foot barge dock, an 80-foot pontoon dock, and five shops with a total floor-space of 3290 square feet. Ships were serviced at two piers maintained by the Army. At one of these the Navy installed a 6-inch water line for joint use.

Administration offices for all activities were in quonset huts. Post offices were in two quonsets. Ready rooms were provided in five buildings. Radio facilities included two structures each for transmitter, receiver, and direction-finder stations, and a single radar building. Hospital facilities consisted of a main two-story building of three wings, with a separate dispensary and isolation ward.

Station maintenance, including garages and shops, was set up in six quonsets with a total area of 8645 square feet. Power generators were installed in three units, a 200-kw and a 175-kw unit at the naval air facility and a portable unit at the PT base. The four miles of roadway were of temporary construction, with a 20-foot, crushed-rock surface. Sewage disposal was accomplished by three tanks at the air facility and a single septic tank at the PT base, with outfalls to the sea. Water supply was from five lakes, with storage in two 88,500-gallon wooden tanks used jointly with the Army, and 17,600 gallons of storage in three wooden tanks.

All naval construction work under the original plan was completed by December 1943, when the detachment from the 42nd Battalion returned to Adak. Maintenance was carried on by CBMU 509 until September 1944, when the 509th returned to the United States. On V-J day, Amchitka was still operating as a naval air facility, with station personnel accomplishing maintenance work.

Atka Island, 50 miles long and roughly crescent-shaped, is the largest of the Andreanof group. Its coast line is generally irregular, indented with many small bays and inlets with steep, rocky shores. Vegetation consists mainly of tundra.

Atka was established as a naval air facility in November 1942 and re-established as an auxiliary air facility February 13, 1943. On September 1, 1943, the air facility was decommissioned and a weather unit remained as the only naval activity.

Facilities, constructed by the Seabees, included housing and storage buildings and a nose hangar adjacent to the Army landing strip.

The 160 men and 15 officers were housed in tents, and mess facilities were provided in quonset huts. Two small buildings were used for recreation.

Storage installations provided 12,000 cubic feet of cold storage, 2300 square feet of general storage, a 500-barrel steel tank for diesel oil, and two steel igloo-type magazines. All other stores were under Army control.

A single 50-by-80-foot nose hangar for landplanes was built, as all aircraft services and runways were also operated by the Army. Two buildings were erected for administration. The hospital was established in tents. Power was supplied by three 10-kw gasoline-driven generators.

Construction at Atka was accomplished by a detachment from the 21st Seabees. Later, this detachment was relieved by two companies of CBMU 510, which arrived on August 31, 1943. On

86TH SEABEES LINED UP FOR INSPECTION ON MAINTENANCE AVENUE, ADAK, JULY 16, 1944

V-J day the naval weather unit at Atka was still in operation and aircraft facilities were available through the Army.

Tanaga Island, in the western part of the Andreanof group, 51 miles west of Adak, is irregular in shape and very mountainous in the northern part, although the remainder of the island is relatively level, with many small lakes and streams. Tanaga was established as an emergency landing field in July 1943, to be operated as an adjunct to NOB Adak.

On September 24, 1943, a detachment of the 45th Battalion landed to carry out the necessary construction. In January 1944 the airstrip was ready for use and by March, NAAF Tanaga was commissioned as an activity of the Adak sector.

Construction included quarters for 720 officers and men, emergency landplane facilities, and a small-craft pier. Housing was provided in tents; messing and galley facilities for all personnel were set up in a 25-by-110-foot wood-frame, canvas-covered building. Recreation buildings included three smaller structures of the same type.

Storage space totaled 1100 cubic feet of cold storage in four portable boxes, 740 square feet of dry storage, 930 square feet of general storage, and 1200 square feet for construction and maintenance materials. Aviation gasoline was stored in drums, for emergency use only.

A 200-by-5000-foot runway was installed, with a pierced-plank surface and two portable lighting units. Five hardstands with revetments were also constructed. A pier and a mooring area were provided to service patrol craft.

Administration was centered in two office buildings which had a total floor area of 1560 square feet. Radio installations were in tents, but the direction finder was in a small permanent building. Medical facilities consisted of a 12-bed quonset-type dispensary. Station maintenance required three buildings.

Power was supplied by a 75-kw diesel-electric

unit. Water was pumped from a lake to two 3000-gallon tanks. Sewage disposal was by septic tank, with an outflow to a ravine. More than 2 miles of temporary gravel-surfaced roads were constructed.

After the initial construction, maintenance and minor construction were carried on by detachments from NOB Adak. On V-J day the air facility was still in operation.

Attu Sector

Attu Island, of the Near Group, lies at the extreme western end of the Aleutian chain. It is 740 miles from Dutch Harbor and only 700 miles from the Asiatic mainland. The island is 14 miles wide and 38 miles long. Its topography is similar to other islands of the chain, with the rugged coastline, tundra-padded valleys, and the treeless, windswept mountains. The area is subject to violent and unpredictable weather, with wind a constant factor and fog, snow, or sleet possible at any time.

Attu and Kiska had been occupied by the Japanese in June of 1942, after their unsuccessful attack on Dutch Harbor. Approximately 2000 Japanese composed the Attu garrison, and the main installation at Kiska was several times larger and was better developed. By-passing Kiska, American Army units, in two forces, landed on Attu on May 11, 1943, one in Massacre Bay and the other around the western arm of Holtz Bay. Although little resistance was encountered on the beaches, the Japanese made stubborn stands inland, but on May 17 a juncture of our two forces was accomplished. After this union the Japanese were slowly driven back across the island.

The Seabees arrived in Massacre Bay on May 21. A detachment of the 23rd Battalion was the first ashore on May 21, 1943, and by the latter part of June all of the Battalion had arrived and were occupied with construction work. The 22nd Battalion arrived July 15, 1943, the 68th Battalion on July 29, 1943. The 9th Naval Construction Regiment, composed of these units was authorized July 8, 1943. In August, Seabee forces were increased by the arrival of half the 8th Special Battalion and the 66th Battalion. The 66th became part of the 9th Regiment.

Naval construction included accommodations for 7650 men; storage for all materials, fuel, and ordnance; seaplane- and landplane-landing areas; hangars and repair shops; small-craft and sub-

marine piers; a drydock and repair shops; a radio station and maintenance shops.

Housing was constructed to accommodate 3291 men at the Seabee camp, 312 at the ordnance depot, 138 at the submarine base, 40 at the net depot, 264 at the PT base, 583 for the fleet air wing, 913 at the naval air station, 187 at the Marine barracks, and 1428 at miscellaneous activities. This housing involved construction of 239 standard quonset huts, pacific huts, and 238 winterized tents. Quarters for 116 chief petty officers and 410 officers were also provided in quonset and pacific huts located at the various activities. Messing facilities were established in 15 buildings, most of them consisting of several quonset huts. Recreational facilities centered around four theaters, which also served as gymnasiums. Eight libraries and seven ship's service stores were provided in standard quonset huts.

Cold-storage space totaled 53,000 cubic feet in three 8000-cubic-foot units and 42 smaller ones. Dry-storage space was provided in quonset huts. General-stores warehouses consisted of a single 60-by-200-foot building, 23 quonsets, and six other buildings, with a total floor area of 87,640 square feet. Construction and maintenance materials were stored in 11 buildings which totaled 22,700 square feet; medical stores were in three huts, providing 1990 square feet of floor space. Two aviation-gasoline tank farms were erected. One consisted of nine 500-barrel tanks, and the other had twenty 1000-barrel tanks and eight 500-gallon tanks. A reserve store of approximately 5000 drums was also at hand, and 13,500 feet of steel piping was laid. Motor gasoline was stored in a 5500-gallon, elevated, storage tank and 2000 drums. Diesel-oil storage was in a 500-barrel tank, two 600-barrel, elevated tanks, and 500 drums; lubricating oil, obtained from the Army, was also stored in drums.

Ordnance of all types required 38 buildings of various sizes. Aviation bombs were kept in 60-foot, open revetments. Four quonset huts were used for torpedo overhaul.

Seaplane facilities included 15 anchorages in Casco Cove for patrol bombers, a 30-by-400-foot ramp of pierced plank, a 150-by-500-foot parking area, a 10-by-250-foot finger pier, and eight kodiak-type hangars. Two runways, 150 by 5000 feet and 150 by 4200 feet, were constructed of pierced planks, with 12,000 feet of pierced-plank taxiways.

GENERAL VIEW OF THE NAVAL AIR STATION AT ATTU
Plane view of 114th Seabees working on runway

Hardstands were of the same material. Repair and maintenance shops were set up in the hangars.

Small-craft piers were built, together with two 220-foot material piers at the Seabee base and a 70-foot pier at the net depot. Two 1100-foot large-craft piers were constructed at the air station, each provided with fresh-water service and with aviation gasoline service for PT boats. A submarine pier, 1100 feet long, with fueling connections, was built at the submarine base, and seven quonsets were erected to house the various shops.

Administration offices for all activities were located in 51 buildings which had a total floor area of 44,355 square feet. The post office at the Seabee base was located in quonsets, that at the air station was in two pacific huts, and the fleet post office, also at the air station, was in a single 62-by-100-foot semi-permanent building. Radio facilities required construction of transmitter, receiver, direction-finder, and radar buildings.

Hospital facilities included a hospital located at the air station and dispensaries at various activities. Buildings used as wards, surgical centers. and dispensaries totaled 21 quonset and pacific huts.

Station maintenance required seven garages, seven laundries, and various shops, which totaled 38 buildings with a floor area of 49,965 square feet. Power was supplied by eight 75-kw and five 50-kw diesel-driven generators, with 30,000 feet of distribution lines. A total of 16 miles of dirt roadways was constructed.

Water was obtained from local sources, and storage tanks, with a capacity of 10.000 gallons, and 4000 feet of water-lines were installed. Sewage dis-

Hospital Area, Attu

posal was accomplished by outfall to the sea and by septic tanks, 32,000 feet of sewer lines being used.

All naval construction was performed by Seabees.

Kiska Sector

On the last day of 1943 the 23rd Construction Battalion left for the United States; the 22nd followed on March 28, 1944. In the meantime, the 138th Construction Battalion had arrived on February 1, 1944, to take over both maintenance and construction. The 68th and 66th Battalions left for the United States in October and December of 1944. The 138th Seabees remained until April 1945, when they were relieved by the 114th, which was still there on V-J day. The 8th Special Battalion left Attu on April 27, 1945 for the United States.

Attu was established as a naval air station in September 1943 and as a submarine repair facility in February 1944.

Kiska Island, one of the Rat Islands group, is about 45 miles northwest of Amchitka and 165 miles southeast of Attu. It is about 22 miles long, with a maximum width of 6 miles. The island is mountainous in its northern end but slopes southward into a flat tableland. Several lagoons, lakes, ponds, and numerous small streams exist, and tundra and muskeg bogs are characteristic of the lowlands. The shores are generally steep and rocky, with a few sandy beaches. Heavy rains are rare, but precipitation in small amounts is frequent and amounts to between 50 and 70 inches annually.

Kiska was occupied by the Japanese in June 1942. Later, as the American counter-offensive in the Aleutians gained momentum, Kiska was bypassed in our occupation of Attu. With Attu secure, attention was focused on Kiska, and in August 1943 the Army landed to discover that all enemy forces had been withdrawn. On August 21, 1943, a detachment of the 38th Seabees landed at Kiska to construct a naval auxiliary air facility.

Housing for 248 men and 19 officers was in quonsets and tents. Mess hall, galley, and stores were housed in an H-shaped building formed by five quonsets and a 25-by-75-foot building. Recreational facilities included a 130-man theater, a tent library, and a quonset hut used as ship's store and barber shop.

Cold storage included four 600-cubic-foot freezer units and two 150-cubic-foot chill units. General storage space, totalling 10,900 square feet, was provided in five quonset-type buildings. Construction and maintenance materials were stored in a standard quonset hut. Medical stores were in tents. Two small magazines were built. All fuel was stored in drums.

For seaplanes, a 30-by-150-foot nose hangar and a 30-by-150-foot ramp with a steel-mat surface were built. A 3500-square-yard parking area was also surfaced with steel matting. Landplanes used the abandoned Japanese fighter strip, which was under Army control. Service facilities for small craft were limited to a single 20-by-105-foot pier.

Administration offices were located in a T-shaped building made of quonset huts. Radio facilities were also set up in a quonset hut. The dispensary was housed in an L-shaped building composed of two quonsets. Another quonset contained the gunnery instruction classroom.

Station maintenance shops occupied seven buildings with a total floor area of 3145 square feet. Power was provided by two 75-kw diesel-driven generators. Almost 3 miles of roadway were built, and 4500 feet of 6-inch and 8-inch lines, with outfalls to the sea, were installed for sewage disposal. A small stream was dammed to provide water, which was stored in two 15,000-gallon tanks.

All naval construction at Kiska was performed by the original detachment of the 38th Battalion. This group, which returned to Adak on October 31, 1943, was relieved by a detachment of the CBMU 509, which operated the public works department.

Shemya, the easternmost island of the Semichi group, lies 137 miles northwest of Kiska. It is smooth and barren except for patches of scrub growth, and is dotted with small lakes. Shemya was established as a naval auxiliary air facility in June 1943.

Construction by the Seabees included tent and quonset housing and parking area for planes. Enlisted men were housed in quonsets and tents with a total capacity of 193 men, and officers' quarters for 47 included four quonsets and four tents. Messing facilities for all personnel were installed in quonset huts. Recreational facilities were centered around a 25-by-78-foot structure used as a chapel, theater, and gymnasium.

Storage space consisted of 1300 cubic feet of refrigerator space and material-storage space which

SEABEES AT POINT BARROW
Members of the 1058th Detachment setting up the core hole rig for test hole No. 1

totaled 4800 square feet, all of which was in winterized tents.

Aviation facilities included a parking area for two planes and a motor-test shop, also in a winterized tent.

Administration offices were located in three temporary buildings with a total floor area of 2310 square feet. A radio unit was installed in the operations building. Hospital facilities consisted of eight beds.

Station maintenance, including a garage, a laundry, and shops, occupied five buildings with a total area of 2340 square feet. Power was furnished by a single 75-kw diesel-electric generator.

Aviation gasoline, land-plane facilities of all types, radar and radio stations, and other necessities were furnished by the Army. On V-J day the

facility was still operating under the control of the Attu naval base.

Point Barrow Sector

In the spring of 1944, exploration operations were undertaken to determine the petroleum-producing potentialities of Naval Petroleum Reserve Number Four at Point Barrow, Alaska. This reserve, 35,000 square miles in area, had been established by Executive Order on February 27, 1923.

Point Barrow, the northernmost tip of the North American continent, lies at approximately 71 degrees North Latitude and 156 degrees West Longitude.

On March 21, 1944, the Bureau of Yards and Docks, on instructions from the Secretary of the Navy, sent a reconnaissance party of four officers into the reserve for investigations concerning the various problems which would be encountered if a drilling program were to be undertaken. In June 1944, two officers and five enlisted men were flown

which had been selected as the site for the first test well.

The second phase of the mission proved most difficult. This involved the tractor-train operations

A POINT BARROW SUPPLY TRAIN
Seabees use a D-8 to haul supplies to Umiat, February 1945

to Barrow to make surveys on which to base the choice of drilling locations.

In August 1944, Seabee Detachment 1058, a petroleum unit consisting of 181 men and 15 officers, debarked at Barrow with 8000 tons of drilling and arctic equipment. The detachment carried sufficient supplies to maintain operations without reinforcement for a 12-month period. Contact with the unit was maintained by plane and radio. Work was begun immediately on the erection of a camp for shelter and construction of an airstrip for Naval Air Transport Service, which was to serve serve the operation.

The operation during the first year consisted primarily of the surface geological work, the coring operations throughout the reserve, and the drilling of test wells.

The crux of the petroleum exploration problem in the Arctic region was transportation, primarily tractor train and air. Adequate air support was essential. High priority was given to the construction of the airstrip at Barrow and to the planning of a second strip at Umiat, on the Colville River,

over the 330 miles of snow and ice from Barrow to Umiat. The expedition had arrived at Barrow during mid-summer in order to take advantage of the fact that the port would be free of ice. Mapping of the roadless, trackless wilderness between Barrow and Umiat revealed that many streams and swamps had to be crossed. This could be accomplished only when the ground was frozen and the ice thick enough to support the tractors and the sled-loads of heavy equipment. Hence, the movement to Umiat could not begin until January 1945.

The first tractor train carried a cargo of airfield-construction equipment, a dragline, two pans, a grader, and accessory equipment, as well as food and miscellaneous supplies and fuel. The train consisted of four tractors with a bulldozer in front and twenty bobsleds behind. By means of house sleds, called wannigans, travel was able to be continued, day and night, without interruption. The wannigans were used as living quarters, portable machine shops, radio stations, mess shacks, and provision storehouses. A snow jeep preceded the train; difficult crossings were examined by Army scouts on dog sleds; and an air-jeep constantly guarded the train. Radio communications were maintained with the various units of the train, Point Barrow, and Umiat.

After completion of the first trip, the tractors and one wannigan returned to Barrow to begin carrying in the heavier pieces of drilling equipment, and as much fuel as was practicable for the construction of the airfield. By June, three trips had been made between Barrow and Umiat. For the thousand miles covered the average speed was only slightly more than one mile an hour.

During the summer of 1945, the well at Umiat was drilled to a depth of 1,816 feet. At the same time, construction of an airstrip was begun. Extensive reconnaissance surveys were made to determine the route for a proposed pipe line from Umiat to Fairbanks, and preparations were made to shift the scene of operations to a new location following the completion of drilling operations at Umiat.

Geological and geophysical investigations continued to be carried on at Umiat and Simpson, and an additional 17,000 tons of equipment and supplies were unloaded at Barrow.

On January 13, 1945, NATS was directed by the Chief of Naval Operations to provide air support of the expedition both to and within the reserve. By March, the back log of air cargo at Fairbanks had been completely eliminated. A great deal of light-plane service within the reserve was required for support of Umiat and Simpson, of the tractor trains to Umiat, for ice patrol, and the support of the several geological parties. Two commercial planes furnished light-plane support by flying fuel and supplies to a radio aid station at Umiat.

V-J Day, however, and its accompanying demobilization program made necessary a shift from the use of military personnel to employment of civilian contractors.

CBD 1058 was inactivated on March 1, 1946, and three civilian companies were selected to continue the explorations, merged under the title of Arctic Contractors. Future operations were to be carried out under a civilian contract which was to cost $2,125,000. The Seabee camp site and all naval equipment and materials connected with the operation were inventoried, given a computed value of $1,175,000, and turned over to the contractors.

The Director of Naval Petroleum Reserves was given general cognizance of naval petroleum reserves under the Secretary of the Navy, and was to define the scope of the exploratory program.

CHAPTER 24

BASES IN THE SOUTH PACIFIC

By one stroke on December 7, 1941, Japan seized the initiative in the Pacific. Long-made plans for offensive action by our Pacific Fleet in the event of war had to be discarded overnight. The enemy's military forces deployed with almost explosive speed throughout the western Pacific and an early counter-offensive was quite beyond the means of our Army and Navy. Furthermore, overall strategic considerations demanded that we direct our major strength against Germany before turning against Japan; in the Pacific we were forced to accept a defensive role, unsatisfying as well as hazardous.

Within a month after the Pearl Harbor attack our Pacific position was perilous. Our Pacific Fleet had been ruinously weakened; Guam and Wake had fallen to the enemy; the Philippines had been invested and there was no hope of sending them support; the British had lost Hong Kong, and Singapore was under siege; the Japanese had invaded the Dutch East Indies and there was no let-up in the progress of their conquest. To all intents and purposes they would win their war if they could continue their march until Australia and New Zealand were overrun.

Keeping open the line of communications with these two great bastions of the South Pacific was a strategic imperative. The northern route, southwest from Hawaii, was already controlled by Japanese positions in the mandated islands. Only the southern route, via the South Sea Islands, was available for use. If we could hold it, future offensive operations would be possible. We would be able to build up our striking power in the South Pacific and when it was great enough we could attempt to wrest the initiative from the enemy.

But the line was long, 7,800 miles from Panama to Sydney, and only meagerly provided with supporting bases. Our tiny naval station in Samoa was wholly out of scale with the gigantic logistic problems that lay ahead, and would be almost negligible even upon completion of the modest expansion that was under way by civilian contract when the war broke out. A major asset, however, was the fact that the line of communication ran through an island-studded area of the Pacific, still wholly under the control of friendly powers.[1]

A fueling base at Borabora.—On Christmas Day, 1941, Admiral King, already in Washington but not yet formally installed as CominCh, requested the War Plans Division of CNO to "proceed at once to study the matter of a fueling base in the central South Pacific area—the Marquesas, Society, or Cook Islands." Five days later CNO recommended that the base be established in Teavanui Harbor on Borabora, in the Society group, which was under the control of the Free French government. The establishment recommended was one that would provide tank storage for 200,000 barrels of fuel oil and 37,500 barrels of gasoline, a seaplane base, the installations necessary for a defense detachment of 3,500 men, and suitable harbor facilities. Admiral King approved the recommendation the day it was made. On January 8, 1942, a "Joint Basic Army and Navy Plan for the Occupation and Defense of Borabora" was issued, which provided that the expedition depart from the United States on January 25.

Thus was sown the seed that was to grow during the years that lay ahead into the great program of advance-base development in the Pacific.

To organize and equip the Borabora expedition on the fast schedule that was set necessitated the cooperation of many agencies and a great deal of improvising. The plan assigned responsibility to the Navy for shore construction at the new base and for transportation overseas, while to the Army fell responsibility for the defense of the island and subsistence ashore after the expedition had arrived at its destination. Planning for the construction operations, or as much planning as could be

---

[1] Marquesas, Society, Cook, Samoa, Tonga, Fiji, and New Hebrides and the large island of New Caledonia.

done in the time available, including procurement of the necessary equipment and materials, became the duty of the Bureau of Yards and Docks, in cooperation with CNO.

Construction planning, equipment procurement, and construction-force organization all had to proceed concurrently. Advance-base equipment was requisitioned from the stock at Davisville awaiting shipment to bases under construction in Scotland and northern Ireland. Hastily, a group of enlisted men was organized into a Construction Detachment, and assigned to "Bobcat," the code name which had been chosen for the new base. Despite much confusion, inevitable under the circumstances, the departure date of the expedition was January 27, only two days behind schedule. In fact, the convoy would have sailed from Charleston on schedule if one of its ships had not needed some ballasting, an operation which occasioned a two-day delay.

After an uneventful voyage via the Panama Canal the Bobcat expedition arrived at its destination on February 17. Immediately, problems arose which overshadowed those encountered during the planning and mounting of the expedition. The terrain of Borabora was different from what had been shown on the mid-19th-century French map that the planners had had to use. An existing water supply the expedition expected to use turned out to be a myth. Above all, cargo had been badly loaded. Equipment needed immediately had been stowed deep in the ships' holds. Important items of equipment had been omitted from the outfitting lists or left on the wharf in the United States.

Difficulties of unloading, the unforeseen necessity to provide a water supply, and other impeding factors combined to delay until April 2 the start of construction of the tank farm which was Bobcat's primary reason for existence.

In the meanwhile, decision had been made to extend base support to a point farther along the line leading to Australia and two more advance-base expeditions were being prepared.

Bases at Efate and Tongatabu.—From Borabora, the midway point, shipping destined for Australia would have to sail through or close to a number of the South Pacific island groups. First would come the Cook Islands, then the Samoa, Tonga, and Fiji groups, and finally, a thousand miles or so from the Australian coast, the New Hebrides group and New Caledonia, forming the eastern rim of the Coral Sea. Protected and developed, these islands could secure the indispensable shipping route; in the hands of the enemy, our line of communications would be severed and the great continent of the South Pacific would be isolated.

An advance in our supporting positions along the Borabora-Australia route was decided upon. On March 12, 1942 the "Joint Basic Plan for the Occupation and Defense of Tongatabu" was issued, calling for the construction of facilities enabling that island, a British protectorate, to serve as a fueling base and as a staging point on the South Pacific air ferry route; eight days later, on March 20, a "Joint Basic Plan" was issued for the development of Efate, the southernmost New Hebrides island, under joint British-French control, as an advance air base. The fuel depot on Tongatabu would extend our support to South Pacific shipping over another quarter of the distance to the Anzac area. Air operations based on Efate would strengthen the communications line where it seemed to be most directly threatened, for the Japanese were in Rabaul and were marching down the Solomons chain, apparently in preparation for a thrust southward that would cut off both Australia and New Zealand.

Again, as with the Bobcat expedition, Army forces were assigned responsibility for island defense and the construction of the base was made a Navy job. By this time the 1st Construction Battalion had been formed and was in training. For the Efate and Tongatabu assignments, coded ROSES and BLEACHER respectively, the new battalion was formed into two detachments; the one consisting of Companies C and D and half of the headquarters company, designated the 3rd Construction Detachment, was assigned to ROSES, and the other Companies A and B and the remainder of the headquarters company, was designated the 2nd Construction Detachment, and assigned to BLEACHER. The officers were ordered to the Bureau of Yards and Docks to plan for the assembly of the equipment that would be needed for the new bases, while the battalion continued in training and preparing for its departure. On April 10 the 2nd Construction Detachment sailed from Norfolk for Tongatabu, and the Efate detachment sailed from the West Coast two days later.

The 3rd Construction Detachment arrived at Efate on May 4. There they found a detachment

BORABORA
Showing the lagoon and the airstrips on Moto Mutu

of Army engineers, a Marine aviation squadron (without planes), and the 4th Marine Defense Battalion, who had preceded them by about a month. As the purpose in occupying the island was to provide an air base to support New Caledonia and the Fijis, airfield construction was the first and most important task undertaken by the construction detachment. The Marines had already cleared, graded, and surfaced with coral about 2000 feet of a 200-foot-wide landplane runway on the site chosen for the airfield. The completion of the facility to its planned dimensions, 6,000 by 400 feet, immediately became the responsibility of the Navy construction men. Twenty planes for the Marine aviation squadron arrived on May 28; the runway was ready for them.

The 2nd Construction Detachment, the other half of the 1st Construction Battalion, arrived at Tongatabu on May 9. Here the development job was to be two-fold, a fuel-tank farm and an air base.

Although the "Joint Basic Plan" called for the Navy construction forces to "construct aerodrome suitable for heavy bombardment operations," the Army on April 25 had entered into a contract with a civilian construction firm to develop airfield facilities in the South Pacific including landplane facilities on Tongatabu. Moreover, because of omissions in its construction-equipment allowance, improper echeloning, and bad loading, the 2nd Detachment was inadequately equipped to take on the airfield construction along with the other installations planned. Accordingly, it was agreed that the Army should proceed with the work under the contract, and the Navy construction personnel turned their attention to the tank farm and the provision of an emergency seaplane ramp.

Strengthening the Samoan Positions.—The third step in supporting the South Pacific supply line, undertaken concurrently with the establishment of the bases at Efate and Tongatabu, was the strength-

REFRIGERATOR WAREHOUSE, HAVANNAH HARBOR, EFATE

ening of our positions in Samoa. The plan called for the establishment by the Navy of facilities to support land, sea, and air forces on Upolu, an island under New Zealand mandate, and on Wallis, a French possession 300 miles to the west. On both Upolu, coded STRAWHAT, and Wallis, coded STRAWBOARD, combined landplane and seaplane bases were to be built for use of Navy and Marine Corps air units. The existing naval station at Tutuila was already being extended and strengthened by civilian construction forces under the PNAB contract, and it was not intended that the work under way should be altered by the decision to establish the two new advance bases.

Again the Bureau of Yards and Docks was assigned the responsibility for planning the construction of the shore installations, and the 2nd Construction Battalion received the construction assignment. Like the 1st Battalion, the Second was split into two detachments: the 4th Construction Detachment, consisting of the Battalion's Companies A and B, was assigned to Upolu, and the 5th Construction Detachment, comprising Companies C and D, was assigned to Wallis.

The battalion, comprising the two detachments, sailed from Norfolk on April 9, 1942, as part of the convoy destined for the Samoan bases. The convoy arrived at Tutuila on May 2, and the 4th Detachment departed a few days later for Upolu, anchoring in Apia Harbor on that island on May 9. The Wallis detachment, however, was kept at Pago Pago, on Tutuila, for about three weeks while diplomatic negotiations were completed to arrange for their operations on the French island to the west. They arrived at Wallis on May 27.

On Upolu, survey and engineering parties were dispatched immediately to the site of the proposed landplane airfield, 14 miles west of Apia, and in a

SOUTH PACIFIC ISLANDS

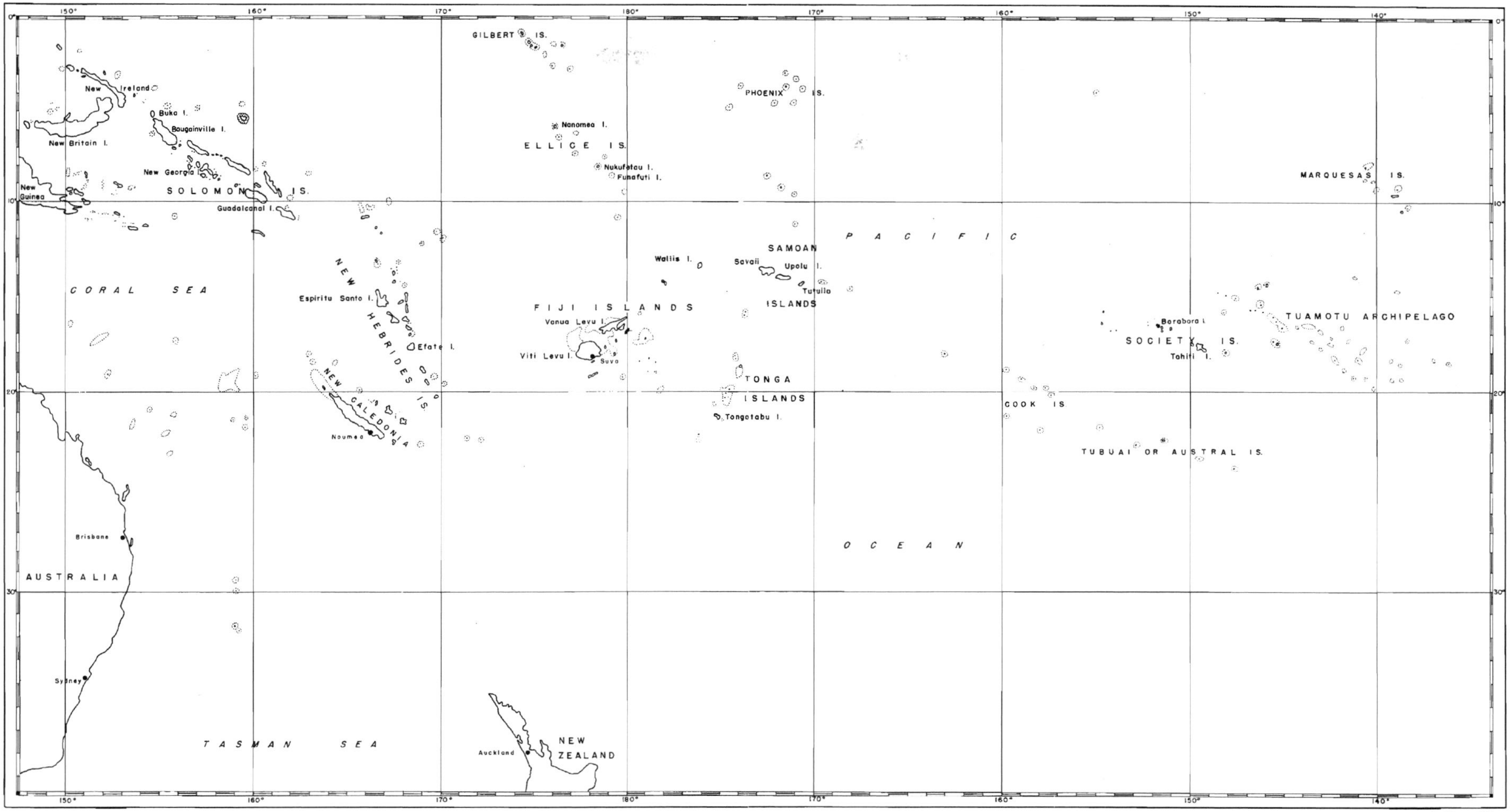
150°
160°
170°
180°
170°
160°
150°
140°
0°
10°
20°
30°
GILBERT IS.
New Ireland
New Britain I.
Buka I.
Bougainville I.
New Georgia I.
New Guinea
SOLOMON IS.
Guadalcanal I.
PHOENIX IS.
Nanomea I.
ELLICE IS.
Nukufetau I.
Funafuti I.
MARQUESAS IS.
SAMOAN ISLANDS
Wallis I.
Savaii
Upolu I.
Tutuila
PACIFIC
CORAL SEA
NEW HEBRIDES IS.
Espiritu Santo I.
Efate I.
FIJI ISLANDS
Vanua Levu I.
Viti Levu I.
Suva
TONGA ISLANDS
Tongatabu I.
NEW CALEDONIA
Noumea
TUAMOTU ARCHIPELAGO
Borabora I.
SOCIETY IS.
Tahiti I.
COOK IS
TUBUAI OR AUSTRAL IS.
Brisbane
AUSTRALIA
OCEAN
Sydney
TASMAN SEA
Auckland
NEW ZEALAND

766450 O—48 (Face p. 194)

short while the necessary grading work was well under way. Small detachments of construction personnel were set to erecting the necessary camp facilities and putting into operation the automotive and refrigeration equipment.

The Wallis detachment, after the delay at Tutuila, got a later start than did their battalion mates on Upolu on the facilities they were to construct. Here too, however, the survey parties began immediately to stake out the airfield, while special detachments erected tentage and temporary messing facilities.

Reinforcing the Fijis. Shortly after the war broke out in Europe in 1939 responsibility for the defense of the Fiji Islands, a British Crown Colony, was accepted by New Zealand. As long as the scene of the war was confined principally to European battlefronts the protection of the islands was a relatively light burden, but when the world conflict was extended to the Pacific the Fijis suddenly became of great strategic importance as a support point on the long South Pacific shipping route. On May 13, 1942 the United States issued a "Joint Army and Navy Plan for the Relief of New Zealand in the Fiji Islands," calling for the replacement of 10,000 New Zealand troops then in the islands with a U. S. Army division.

The joint plan viewed the Fijis as an area to be used as an advance air and naval base and as an air-staging area, and called for an expansion of the existing base facilities on Viti Levu. Of the Navy portion of the plan, the principal new construction item called for was an 80,500-barrel tank farm to be erected near Nandi, on the island's west coast.

The 3rd Construction Battalion had just been commissioned at Camp Allen. Half of it, Companies C and D and a part of the headquarters company, was formed into a detachment and assigned to the Navy construction program in the Fijis. The detachment embarked in June.

Upon their arrival at Viti Levu the detachment was split up again, one company going to Nandi, where the tank farm was to be built, and the other to Suva, the island's principal port.

A Main South Pacific Base at Noumea.—In the meanwhile the other half of the 3rd Battalion had also been given South Pacific assignments. Company A was sent to Borabora to reinforce the 1st Construction Detachment, the Bobcats. Company B was given the task of building another tank farm at Noumea, at the southern end of New Caledonia.

New Caledonia was a French colony. It had committed its loyalties to the Free French organization in September 1940, shortly after France had fallen to the German forces, and for some time prior to the entry of the United States into the war an Australian garrison had been stationed there. The colony marked the end of the island-protected portion of the Australian shipping lane; from New Caledonia westward to Australia there was but the open Coral Sea.

The harbor at Noumea was extensive and well protected, but during the early months of the war it had been considered a bit too far forward for major naval-base development. Until the early summer of 1942, Auckland had been preferred as the site of the principal base facilities for our naval forces in the South Pacific, and a considerable amount of construction had been undertaken there in cooperation with the New Zealand government. The first two Cubs to be sent to the Pacific left the States with Auckland as their destination, but favorable developments in the war situation led to the decision while the shipments were enroute that the advance-base equipment they included should be erected farther north. Accordingly, the Cubs were diverted from their earlier destination; part of Cub 1, including the construction company from the 3rd Battalion, arrived at Noumea on June 26. It had been the Company's mission to erect a tank farm, but shortly after their arrival the project was cancelled.

During the months that followed, emphasis shifted from Auckland to Noumea as the location of Navy's principal fleet base in the South Pacific. On November 8, 1942 South Pacific headquarters was established there. Additional construction battalions were assigned to the area during the latter months of the year, and development proceeded rapidly until Noumea became the most important of the South Pacific installations.

Development of Espiritu Santo.—While the detachment of the 1st Battalion was building the air strip on Efate the Japs were engaged in constructing a field of their own on Guadalcanal. It was a construction race, and the Seabees won. Bombers took off from Efate within a month of the start of construction to harass the Japanese builders. But it was clear that the possession of Guadalcanal would have to be disputed with the enemy and Efate was not quite close enough to provide effective fighter support for our assault forces in the impending action. Another field, farther north, would have to be established.

After a reconnaisance had been made of the islands lying to the north of Efate, extending as far as the Santa Cruz islands, choice for the new airfield site fell upon Espiritu Santo, the northernmost island of the New Hebrides, 400 miles closer to the enemy's position. On July 8 a small group of Seabees from the 1st Battalion detachment on Efate landed on Espiritu Santo and began work on the new field. They were accompanied by an infantry company of the U. S. Army who performed the unskilled work involved in the construction operations. Within twenty days the new field was in operation and offensive action against the Japs in the Solomons was stepped up in intensity. On August 7 the Marines made their landings on Guadalcanal and Tulagi.

The subsequent development of Espiritu Santo as an air base was rapid and extensive. A few days after the Guadalcanal landings, the 7th Battalion arrived on Santo and began building more extensive air facilities. Army Air Forces and Marine Corps personnel on the island increased rapidly until Santo became a major South Pacific base for the support of air activities throughout the year-long campaign for possession of the Solomons.

Borabora

On January 8, 1942, Admiral King, Admiral Stark, and General Marshall signed a joint basic Army and Navy plan for the occupation and defense of Borabora. It called for the establishment by the Navy of a fueling base which would be defended by the Army. The code name and short title for the base was BOBCAT. The importance of establishing and holding such a base to facilitate the use of United Nations shipping routes from the United States and Panama to Australia and New Zealand was obvious. An advance-base expedition to carry out the mission was provided for, including naval construction personnel. According to the plan, the naval personnel were to be withdrawn upon completion of the base. January 25 was designated as the date when the convoy was to leave the East Coast.

Training of the men who formed the construc-

tion force for Borabora was cut to a minimum, and a detachment of 250 men and 8 CEC officers was quickly organized. It included 99 men who had been trained as an administrative headquarters company to function with advance-base construction workers in Iceland, 138 seamen from the boot camp at Newport, R. I., 13 petty officers, mostly gunners' mates, and commissary personnel.

The Army personnel consisted of 4,200 men and 176 officers.

Construction and aviation personnel embarked at Quonset, R. I., their transport stopping at Norfolk to pick up nets and guns. At Charleston, S. C., the convoy assembled for redistribution of personnel and loading operations. It consisted of two cruisers, two destroyers, two transports carrying 2,200 troops each, four cargo vessels, and one tanker. (The Seabees' first job was to correct a 12-degree list on one of the transports, by installing concrete ballast.) On January 27 the convoy sailed from Charleston. They arrived at Borabora February 17, 1942.

Borabora, in the Leeward group of the French-owned Society Islands, is 140 miles northwest of Tahiti, the center of government. The island is small, about 4½ miles long and 4 miles wide. A steep barrier reef, a mile or two offshore, almost completely encircles it; the natural passageway through the reef is curved, adding protection to the harbor.

Vaitape, on Teavanui Bay, is the principal town. When the advance-base expedition arrived the population numbered about 1400, with less than half a dozen permanent white residents.

Negotiations with the French.—Negotiations for the use of Borabora by the United States forces were conducted with Monsieur Charles Passard, Administrator of Borabora, but were subject to ratification by Lt. Col. G. Orselli, Governor of the Society Islands, whose headquarters were at Tahiti. Questions arose regarding arrangements for acquisition of leases, employment of native workers, defense of other islands in the Society group, and other matters. The agreement between the Free French government and the United States for the use, administration, and operation of the proposed naval base on Borabora was signed by Lt. Col. Orselli and Rear Admiral John F. Shafroth at a conference on February 23, 1942 on board USS *Trenton*. Under the agreement the United States

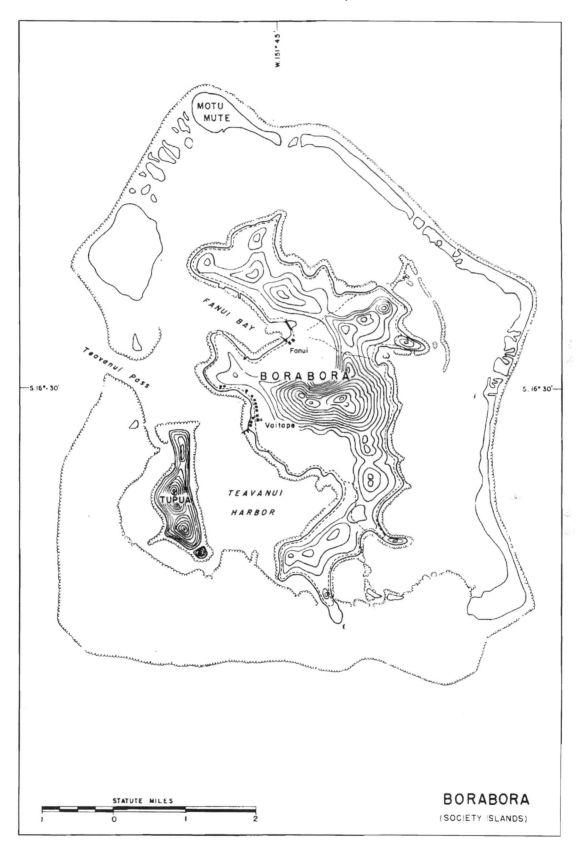

STATUTE MILES

BORABORA

(SOCIETY ISLANDS)

recognized Free French sovereignty. It was agreed that title to the property on which the naval base was established would remain with the Free French government; and all permanent installations, such as buildings and waterfront facilities, were to become the property of the Free French government upon expiration of the agreement.

By October 24, 1942, leases had been consummated for all privately owned property occupied by American installations. The American forces occupied 169 parcels of land, owned by 115 individuals, who received a token payment of $1.00 per annum for each lease. All repairs, alterations, and additions, however, had to be made with the consent of the owner.

Upon arrival of the expedition, unloading commenced at once, but six weeks were required for the operation. Bridge heads to the beach had to be established, as there were only two small coral piers, at Vaitape and at Fanui, available, and these would not support heavy loads.

Moreover, there was only one single-lane road, with a number of small bridges. The heavy Army trucks soon broke down the small bridges and culverts and tore up the roadbed. Road work had to be undertaken at once, but without the proper equipment for there was no road-building machinery available and only one small rock crusher. A large portion of the detachment's continued effort was expended in attempts to improve and maintain in passable condition the roads connecting the installations.

PALLIKULA BAY PONTOON WHARF, ESPIRITU SANTO
USS Tangier unloading supplies

AVIATION SUPPLY ANNEX, ESPIRITU SANTO, UNDER CONSTRUCTION

Unloading cargo from the ships was the detachment's first job, a difficult one owing to improper loading and a lack of landing facilities. No weight-handling equipment was available, and it took three weeks to locate and unload the first crane. Pontoon barges could not be assembled until the tie rods and accessories needed had been uncovered from beneath other cargo. Rain and mud added to the difficulties. Large quantities of construction materials, such as cement, tools, heavy pipe, and special fittings, were scattered along a 2-mile beach.

Eventually, causeways were built out to deep water and a marginal pier, large enough to permit discharging cargo from two hatches, was constructed.

In the course of 18 months, the Bobcats unloaded 60,000 tons of cargo.

Reconnaissance of the island disclosed that much of the information about local conditions used by the base planners, such as character of terrain and availability of water supply, was deficient and erroneous. The water supply the Bobcats expected to find was non-existent, and as the dry season was approaching, rapid steps had to be taken to insure an adequate supply of water. Within two weeks after the landings, construction of a water system

was initiated by building dams on the main streams. At the end of two months four dams had been built and a distribution system, comprising 13 miles of 4-inch pipe, supplied the camps scattered along the perimeter of the island.

Work on the defense batteries was also slow, but by the middle of March, construction on this major project was well under way. Eight 7-inch guns had to be mounted on skids for hauls 1,000 to 2,000 feet up the side of 45-degree slopes. Besides the gun emplacements, eight magazines, four battery command posts, and one harbor-defense command post were built.

By the time the detachment was released from unloading duties, the personnel assigned to the air station had installed temporary facilities sufficient to permit operation of planes. On April 11, the Bobcats took over completion of the project and began work on a concrete seaplane ramp, a compass-calibration rose, permanent gasoline-storage facilities, and the erection of huts for shops and personnel. Ten 5,000-gallon tanks were buried in the mountainside just behind the camp and connected by underground feed lines with the gasoline pits near the ramp. A hangar for VOS aircraft was constructed from a 40-by-100-foot quonset-hut

PONTOON PIER AT THE SEAPLANE BASE, NOUMEA

storage building by raising the entire building 2½ feet above the ground and leaving one side open. There was sufficient depth of water and length of runways within the lagoon to permit the take-off of any type of plane in any direction. The base could accommodate one patrol squadron of 15 planes. PBY's were the heaviest planes that could be handled over the ramp. Concealment of both ramp and aircraft at the naval air station was fairly effective due to the heavy growth of coconut palms.

Thus, construction of the fuel-oil depot, the major facility of Bobcat, was greatly delayed by the many demands upon the extremely limited number of skilled men and the amount of construction equipment available. Rough terrain further complicated the building. Areas had to be blasted out of solid rock, and the soil encountered with the

rock was a clay which was difficult to handle when wet.

The tanks were erected by fashioning a guy derrick from two tubular-steel radio masts. By setting up the derricks at the tank center the sides were hoisted into place and bolted together in a continuous circle, at the rate of 2½ to 3 days per tank. Army personnel, numbering about 725, worked with the detachment seven days a week on three shifts to complete the construction of the first eight tanks by June 9 so that the first tanker to arrive could be promptly emptied. On the day of completion, sea-loading connections were made and pumping to the tanks was begun while some of the bolts were still being tightened. The completed fuel depot consisted of twenty 10,000-barrel storage tanks, two 10,000-barrel diesel-oil storage tanks, and five 1,000-barrel aviation-gasoline storage tanks.

Soon French, American, New Zealand, and Australian ships began to fuel at Borabora on the average of one or two ships per week. Since the docking facilities were poor, the ships had to pull up to one of the two cruiser moorings, anchor, and take on the fuel hose there. Nevertheless, by mid-summer of 1942, Borabora became a filling station for ships going to the Southwest Pacific. The battle-damaged cruiser *Boise* stopped for fuel and water on its way back to the States.

In July 1942, the detachment was reinforced by 100 men from Company A of the 3rd Construction Battalion.

The Army planned to ship fighters to the island, assemble them, and fly them from one island to another on the way to the front. For this reason, in October 1942, construction of an air depot was proposed; the Army was to furnish the necessary equipment and materials and the Navy was to provide the construction personnel. Work was started on December 16, 1942, on a 24-hour day, 7-day-week schedule, on the reef islet of Motu Mute. Construction of an asphalt-paved 6,000-by-

100-foot runway with 100-foot shoulders for bombers and a 3,000-by-150-foot airstrip for fighters was completed in seven weeks, together with installation of radio direction devices and permanent camp facilities for Army flying and operating personnel. By April 5, 1943, all authorized work on the airfield and depot had been completed and Seabee personnel moved back to the fuel-depot construction work. Because of the rapid progress of the war, mail and transport planes made only occasional use of the strip.

The detachment kept an organized crew available for the repair of convoys of the recently commissioned LST's, LCI's, YMS's, and subchasers which passed through Borabora on their way to the Southwest Pacific. The Bobcats repaired refrigerating plants, diesel engines, electrical wirings, and occasionally performed a major overhaul job.

Camouflage activities began early. Protective concealment painting was applied to the tanks, and netting was used to hide their circular outlines. Native labor was employed in planting such trees,

LUGANVILLE FIELD, ESPIRITU SANTO

shrubs, grass, and local vegetables as could be used to the best advantage for camouflage.

Native labor was seldom used for other purposes, partly because the island had just enough manpower to take care of its own needs. Moreover, when it was used, native labor was found to be unskilled and required much supervision. Money was of little value to them.

The only native materials used were coconut logs and coral.

In March 1943 the detachment's commanding officer reported that the original scope of work at the naval fuel depot had been completed and recommended that a CBMU be ordered to Borabora to maintain it. The war had moved ahead so rapidly that the island's other facilities were no longer needed. Two months later, orders were received from headquarters to dismantle and crate half the huts and equipment for shipment. Army personnel moved westward. By June 30, 1943, surplus material and equipment were shipped to Noumea. The tank farm remained intact.

On September 9, 1943 the detachment embarked for New Caledonia to join the 3rd Construction Battalion. Their orders were changed, however, and they went, instead, to Samoa to join the 22nd Marine Regiment for intensive combat training and minor construction work on camps. A detachment of 31 men and 2 officers remained at Borabora to maintain the base until the arrival of the CBMU.

CBMU 519 arrived at Borabora in the fall of 1943 and began construction of a fuel wharf with a network of fuel and water lines to service LCT's. The new facility shortened by one-tenth the time previously required for fueling these craft, and permitted them time to arrive at forward zones several days earlier.

By April 1, 1944 the base had been placed in reduced status, its mission being to provide a fueling and minor repair depot for small diesel-driven craft enroute to the South Pacific. The airfield was also maintained as an emergency landing field.

The base at Borabora was disestablished June 2, 1946.

Efate

The base at Efate was established to serve primarily as an outpost for supporting both New Caledonia, 300 miles to the southwest, and the

Fijis, 600 miles to the east, and subsequently to serve as a minor air and naval base for offensive operations. The U. S. Army had moved into New Caledonia, and the Japanese were moving into Guadalcanal, 700 miles to the north. The U. S. forces went into the New Hebrides to open up airfields from which they could start bombing the Japanese on Guadalcanal and prevent them from completing the airfield which later became Henderson Field.

Efate, the most important island of the New Hebrides group, is 25 miles long from east to west, and 18 miles wide. The northern half of the island is mountainous but the southern part is almost flat. There are two harbors, Havannah, in the northwest, and Vila, in the southeast, both of which afford anchorage for large vessels. The basic formation of the island consists of a lava substratum covered by coral and a shallow top soil of rich humus. The vegetation is tropical and a large part of the island is covered by dense jungle. On the island are several mountain ranges which rise to heights of 2,300 feet. The island is well watered by brooks, streams, and small rivers and, even in the dry season, water satisfactory after chlorination may be obtained from the larger streams. Sufficient distillation equipment had to be provided to supply drinking-water for the U. S. forces.

Politically, the island at the opening of the Pacific war was a condominium of Great Britain and Free France.

Prior to the United States entry into the war, there were a few Australian troops and a seaplane base at Efate. The harbor at Vila contained several small piers in water with a maximum depth of six feet at low tide. There were no facilities at Havannah Harbor.

The charts showed ample space for the construction of a landing field of any size. Seaplane operations could be carried out in Havannah Harbor, but the water was reported as rough in Meli Bay. Vila Harbor would not support patrol-plane operations, but small seaplanes could be used. There was no road between Vila and Havannah and all traffic between them was by water.

Admiral King distributed the joint basic plan for the occupation and defense of Efate on March 20, 1942. Under its terms the Army was to defend Efate and support the defense of ships and positions. The Navy's task was (1) to construct, ad-

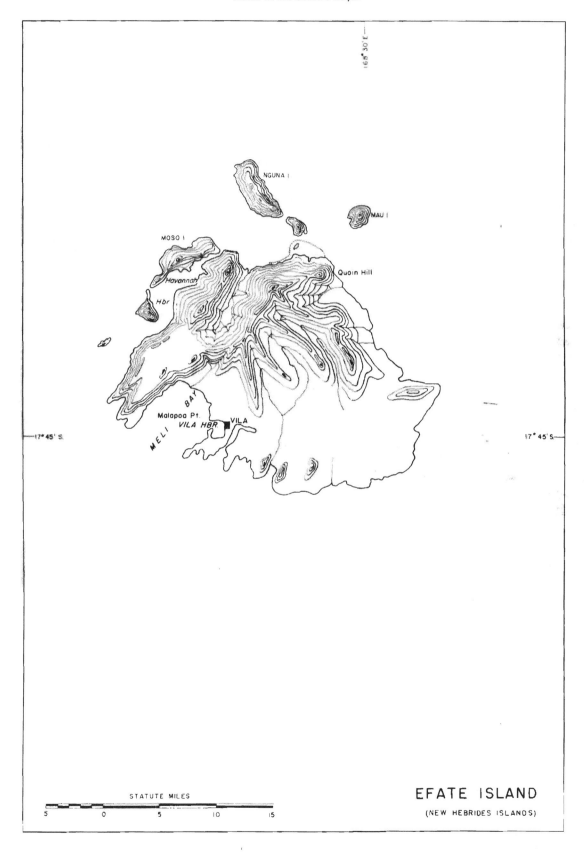

NGUNA I

MAU I

MOSO I

Quoin Hill

Havannah

Hbr

BAY

Malapoa Pt.

MELI

VILA HBR VILA

17° 45' S.

17° 45' S.

STATUTE MILES

5   0   5   10   15

168° 30' E.

EFATE ISLAND

(NEW HEBRIDES ISLANDS)

NAVAL AIR TRANSPORT SERVICE FACILITIES, ESPIRITU SANTO

minister, and operate a naval advance base, seaplane base, and harbor facilities; (2) to support Army forces in the defense of the island; (3) to construct an airfield and at least two outlying dispersal fields; (4) to provide facilities for the operation of VPB-type seaplanes. Navy personnel was to consist of 80 officers and 1184 enlisted men; Army forces were to total 4811.

The plan called for an escorted convoy to be dispatched from the West Coast about April 12, 1942 to transport all Army and Navy personnel and the supplies necessary for sixty days. The defenses, including the airdrome, were to be constructed as rapidly as possible, to be followed by the erection of fuel and housing facilities. Seabees were to be withdrawn, except for a maintenance crew, after the base had been completed.

About March 25, 1942, the Army sent about 500 men to Efate from Noumea, and the 4th Defense

Battalion, 45th Marines, arrived about April 8.

The 3rd Naval Construction Detachment, made up of Companies C and D of the 1st Construction Battalion, 506 officers and men, sailed from the United States on April 12, 1942, and landed at Efate on May 4.

The war at that time was a race between the Japanese and the Americans. Our forces had to get their planes into the air to stop the Japanese construction of an airfield on Guadalcanal, from which they would be able to attack the all-important Allied supply lines across the South Pacific. Therefore, the first and major job at Efate was the construction of an airfield.

When the Seabees arrived they found that the Marines had already cleared and surfaced with coral about 2,000 feet of a 200-foot-wide landplane runway near Vila. The responsibility for construction was immediately assumed by the Seabees who cleared, grubbed, and graded a 6,000-foot runway, 350 feet wide. Finger coral was used as surfacing material.

Available construction equipment was very meager. Even after the Seabees pooled resources with the Army and Marines, the total equipment included one crane, ten trucks, two motor patrol graders, one pull-type grader, seven bulldozers of various sizes. and one scarifier. To keep the equipment from breaking down was a continuous job. Seabees, soldiers, Marines, and natives worked steadily under difficult conditions. and on May 28. the first planes landed on the field.

At the same time, members of the detachment rushed construction of a seaplane base at Havannah Harbor to serve a squadron of PBY's. The Seabees built two ramps of coral, surfaced with wire mesh, and provided buoys for mooring 14 seaplanes. By June 1, the PBY's began operating from the new base, bombing the Japanese posi-

tions on Guadalcanal. In addition to the ramps and moorings, two small piers, two nose hangars, one 40-by-100-foot seaplane workshop, four 5,000-gallon underground gasoline tanks, and housing facilities for 25 officers and 210 men in quonset huts were constructed.

Another project, a 600-bed base hospital. of quonset huts, was also begun. A site at Bellevue plantation, about three miles inland from Vila, was chosen because of its favorable location from the standpoint of drainage, safety, and cover, freedom from malaria causes. and accessibility to other island facilities. Concrete piers were used for support. Mess halls were H-shape, with a serving hut in the center. Vertical panels in several huts were omitted for ventilation. The hospital began to operate on September 15, when wounded Marines were brought in from Guadalcanal.

Two other airfields were soon under construction. Near Quoin Hill, on the northeastern corner

AVIATION OVERHAUL AREA, ESPIRITU SANTO

of the island a site was chosen for a bomber strip in an area of hot springs. The work on the 6,000-by-200-foot runway was begun early in October and was completed by the middle of January 1943. A 3,000-by-180-foot fighter strip was also built at Port Havannah in the early fall of 1942. Fighters were able to land 26 days after construction began, and in another 15 days the field was completed. Two nose hangars were also erected.

In addition to the major facilities constructed, the Seabees built gun emplacements, quonset hut camps for naval personnel, structural-steel storage buildings, pontoon piers, and barges. The main naval camp was located at Malapoa Point, where, by February 1943, fifty quonset huts housed from 400 to 500 men. New roads were built, and some of the original roads, made impassable by heavy traffic, were resurfaced.

At Malapoa Point seven 1,000-barrel bolted-steel tanks for aviation gasoline were completed, as well as two 10,000 gallon diesel storage tanks. At Vila airfield, four 5,000-gallon buried welded-steel tanks for aviation gasoline were provided. Eight similar tanks were built at Havannah Harbor.

In March 1943, the Seabees on Efate were joined by the other half of the 1st Battalion, Companies A and B, which had been working on Tongatabu since the preceding May.

Construction Battalion Maintenance Unit 511, with 3 officers and 196 men, arrived at Efate on July 7, 1943, and was assigned work at Vila and Havannah Harbor. Men of the 1st Battalion, relieved of the maintenance work, were assigned to additional construction at Quoin Hill for the Marines, the improvement of the camp at Quoin Hill, and the extension of the hospital to a 1500-bed capacity.

In January 1944, CBMU 550 left the States bound for Efate, to handle maintenance work in connection with the operation of the three airfields, the roads, and camp facilities.

By the early part of 1944, the principal authorized construction had been completed. The mission of the base was reduced to an emergency landing field and minor fleet operating and communications setup. The base hospital was dismantled and crated for shipment. Other facilities were prepared to be moved forward.

At this time, the medical officer reported that a large number of the men showed signs of operational fatigue and lowered physical stamina caused by long continuous duty in the area. Accordingly, the 1st Construction Battalion was returned to the replacement and recuperation center, Camp Parks, Calif., for reforming and further assignment.

CBMU 511 was moved to Tongatabu, and CBMU 550 remained at Efate.

The base was disestablished and abandoned in February 1946.

Tongatabu

Tongatabu was developed to serve as a fuel base and protected anchorage in the line of communications between the United States and the Anzac area, as an alternate staging point on the South Pacific air ferry route, and as a supporting point for aircraft operating in the Samoan-Fiji area.

Tongatabu, the principal island in the Tonga group, is about 18 miles long by 9 miles wide, and is surrounded by fringing reefs. It is a comparatively level island, its northern shore indented by a large shallow lagoon. Nukualofa Harbor on the north coast, with a depth from six to eighteen fathoms, offers a sheltered anchorage suitable for a large fleet.

Companies A and B, 517 men and 12 officers, of the 1st Construction Battalion, which sailed from Norfolk on April 10, 1942, arrived at Tongatabu on May 9.

The Seabees' first, and major, job at Tongatabu was to provide a fuel depot of twenty-two 10,000-barrel tanks for fuel and diesel oil and twenty-six 500-barrel tanks for aviation gasoline. The basic plan also called for the Navy to construct an airfield suitable for heavy-bombardment operations. However, the Army on April 25 had entered into a contract with a civilian construction firm to develop the Fuaamotu airfield, 7 miles southeast of Nukualofa, the principal city on the island. As the Seabees were inadequately equipped to undertake the airfield construction along with other installations planned, it was agreed that the Army should proceed with the work under contract. However, the Seabees later assisted the contractor in the completion of the field for the Army. Three turf-covered runways, satisfactory in dry weather but requiring strengthening to support heavier aircraft in the wet season, already existed at Fuaamotu. These strips were lengthened and surfaced with coral and marston mat, and other facilities at the field were improved.

In addition, the Seabees constructed a seaplane base, including a coral ramp, three mooring buoys,

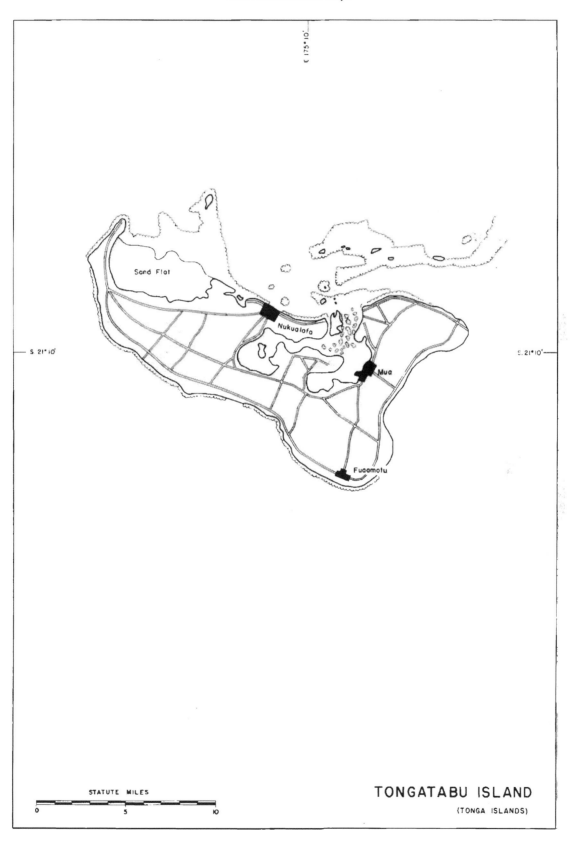

STATUTE MILES

0   5   10

TONGATABU ISLAND

(TONGA ISLANDS)

SHIP REPAIR UNIT SHOP AREA, NOUMEA

a nose hangar, and storage and camp facilities. They also built an Army hospital, comprising 250 buildings, and warehouses, camps, and gun emplacements for both Army and Navy.

Progress on the projects at Tongatabu was delayed by inadequacies in construction equipment, improper loading of the ships, and uncertainties as to the responsible agency for the determination and performance of certain work projects.

One important job performed by the Seabees at Tongatabu was the placing of a concrete bulkhead in the aircraft carrier *Saratoga* when she came in with a large hole in her side. The temporary bulkhead served until the ship reached Pearl Harbor where more permanent repairs were made.

Natives were used extensively for ship unloading, general labor, and carpentry. The Tongans proved to be rather good workmen.

The main part of the construction at Tongatabu was completed in about nine months, and the base was one of the first to be folded up. The facilities installed were never used to capacity except for the warehouses, for the strategic situation changed materially after the island was occupied. If the Battle of the Coral Sea had turned out unfavorably for the Allies, Tongatabu would have been an important supply base for the combat areas. As it was, the mission of the base was reduced to that of a reserve fuel supply base and a service point for the Naval Air Transport Service planes.

In November 1942, orders came to stop building and start tearing down. CBMU 511 was sent to Tongatabu from Efate to accomplish the dismantling.

The Army hospital and the aviation facilities were left for the New Zealand forces, which took over when the Americans moved out. The tank farm was dismantled and moved to Wallis Island. A large number of the huts, magazines, and warehouses were torn down.

On February 23, 1943, the Seabees left for Efate to join the other half of the 1st Construction Battalion.

Samoa

Three of the Samoan group of islands were developed as air and naval bases. Together with bases in the Fijis and New Caledonia the new Samoan bases on Tutuila, Upolu, and Wallis islands provided strong, mutually supporting defense positions.

Tutuila Island, which has been owned by the United States since 1899, is about 17 miles long and 5 miles wide. Pago Pago, the largest village and the seat of the government, is the best harbor in the South Seas. It is formed by the crater of an immense volcano, the south side of which is broken and open to the sea. Good anchorage is found anywhere in the inner harbor in 6 to 25 fathoms. The island is mountainous and heavily wooded.

Upolu Island, mandated to New Zealand, lies 36 miles westnorthwest of Tutuila and is about 40 miles long and 13 miles wide. It is of volcanic

NAVAL HOSPITAL No.3, ESPIRITU SANTO

BOMBPROOF OPERATIONS BUILDING, TAFUNA AIRFIELD, TUTUILA

origin, and mountainous, with rich and fertile valleys. Coral reefs, intersected by channels, form convenient harbors.

The Wallis Islands, a French Protectorate, consist of Uea Island, 7 miles long and 4 miles wide, and several smaller islands surrounded by a barrier reef through which there are three channels. Mata Utu Harbor affords anchorage of 10 to 15 fathoms.

Before the war, the Navy installations in Samoa consisted of a refueling station and a communication center at Pago Pago Harbor. The station was a minor establishment until construction under contract was begun in 1940 as part of the national defense program. At that time the station comprised a 300-foot wharf, a radio station, housing facilities, office space for four desks, shops, and a garage (all poorly equipped), a small power plant, water-supply system, and several miles of narrow, crooked roads.

The PNAB contract, dated July 1, 1940, authorized the construction of fuel-oil, diesel-oil, and gasoline storage facilities at Samoa at an estimated cost of $300,000. By supplementary agreements and

change orders, 98 additional projects at an estimated cost of $10,751,750 were authorized. These projects included expansion of station facilities, an airfield, hangars and facilities, dispensary, war buildings and accessories, net depot, radio station, gun emplacements, shelters, magazines, and facilities for defense forces.

On December 7, 1941, the military governor of Samoa assumed responsibility for all construction operations. Under his direction, the original contract construction plans were altered to meet the wartime emergency. The contractor ceased work on the going projects and started work on the defense of the Pago Pago Harbor vicinity, mainly the construction of bombproof shelters. Moreover, the construction concept for the base was modified. For example, large buildings were considered undesirable, and designs were revised to provide for dispersal.

Marine forces arrived at Tutuila in January 1942, under a brigadier general who was empowered by the President to assume military governorship and command of the defense forces. He

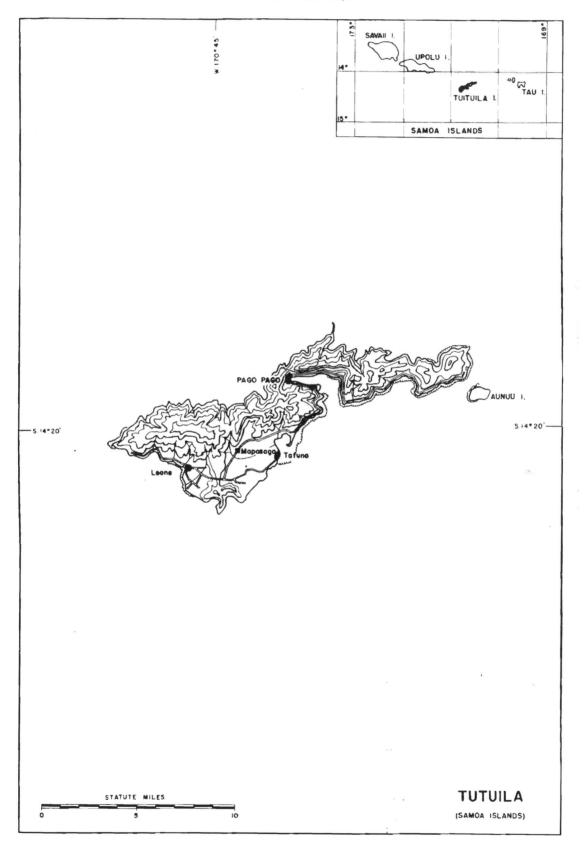

TUTUILA

(SAMOA ISLANDS)

took charge of all construction operations and concentrated attention on the airfield, where a runway was to be completed at the earliest possible moment. Two 10-hour shifts worked daily, and all usable equipment was put on the job. By virtue of concentration, a 2,500-by-250-foot section was ready for operation by April 6, 1942, and the runway was completed in late June.

As the airfield neared completion, work on other facilities was accelerated. Construction of a fuel wharf, an additional power plant, a 100-foot extension of the old naval station wharf, and additions to the net facilities on Goat Island and to storehouses at the naval station were undertaken. In April 1942, facilities for the construction of the 300-bed Naval Mobile Hospital 3 arrived, and the naval personnel attached to the hospital started construction of the unit.

Construction was performed largely by native labor and supervised by imported white superintendents. The maximum feasible number of native laborers was employed and a school was built to train them in welding, carpentry, and other crafts. Work progressed at an unsatisfactory rate, however, due to heavy rainfall, shortcomings of native labor, unavailability of equipment, and frequent breakdowns caused by inexperienced natives, and slow delivery of materials and equipment.

The 7th Construction Battalion reported at Tutuila in July 1942, and prepared to take over from the contractor. The contractor's forces were loaded aboard ship ready to sail for home when the battalion received orders to embark immediately for the New Hebrides. One hundred of the contractor's men volunteered to remain until relieved by another construction battalion. Supplemented by native labor, as before, this group continued to work until the 11th Battalion arrived late in August 1942, and assumed all responsibility for construction. With the exception of two men who remained for work in connection with material procurement and with the native labor pay-roll until September 1943, all contractor personnel then returned to the States.

The major project of the 11th Battalion at Tutuila was the construction of a destroyer repair base. More than 800,000 cubic yards of earth and coral fill were required, for the site of the proposed facility was rugged country and had little level area. Fill was obtained from two rock quarries opened on opposite sides of the island. Quar-

ters for officers and enlisted men, mess hall, water-supply facilities, fourteen 50-by-200-foot frame warehouses, three 20-by-40-foot timber piers, and a 600-foot timber bulkhead were installed. The job, begun in September 1942, was completed the following June.

The Marine airfield, with two coral-surfaced runways—one 6,000 feet by 500 feet; the other 3,000 feet by 500 feet—was completed at Tafuna, together with industrial facilities, warehouses, a 6,000-kw power plant, a 50-bed dispensary, quarters, and mess halls. The Seabees also constructed Leone Airfield, a 6,000-by-400-foot bomber strip, surfaced with volcanic cinders, and necessary supportive facilities.

Mobile Hospital 3 at Mapasaga, which had been started by the hospital personnel assisted by Marines, was completed, with expanded facilities, by the Seabees.

Other work accomplished by the 11th Battalion involved the construction of fuel storage tanks, a pump system and fuel pier, a net depot, the development of the island water supply, power plants and services, and the construction and maintenance of roads.

The 5th Construction Detachment, comprising half of the 2nd Battalion, which had been sent to western Samoa, was assigned to Tutuila in April 1943, and helped to complete the construction projects. In May 1943, CBMU 506 arrived to relieve the 11th Battalion, which was moved to New Caledonia on June 18. CBMU 506 took over all the maintenance work, including the operation of power plants, refrigeration installation, a rock quarry and crusher, and a cinder pit. By January 1944, the entire 2nd CB had been united at Tutuila; it was returned to the States on March 7, 1944.

At Upolu, the Navy's task was to construct and operate an air base and the necessary harbor facilities to support it. The first U. S. forces on the island, the 7th Marine Defense Battalion, arrived on April 1, 1942; the 4th Construction Detachment, comprising Companies A and B of the 2nd Construction Battalion, reached Upolu on May 10.

Pier and sea-wall facilities were found to be of small capacity, and cargo unloading was effected by the use of 3-by-7-pontoon barges, Marine tank lighters, and small native scow-type lighters. Native buildings were used temporarily for warehouses and offices and for a dispensary, supplemented by tentage for wards, messing facilities, and quarters.

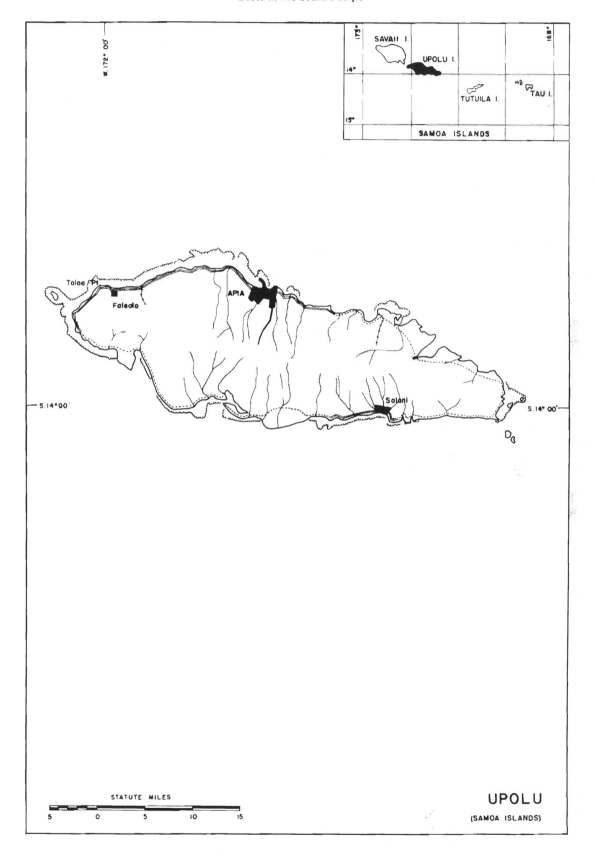

STATUTE MILES

UPOLU

(SAMOA ISLANDS)

SHIP REPAIR BASE, NOUMEA
Warehouses are part of the diesel spare parts sub-depot

The topography of Upolu is not so precipitous as that of Tutuila, and there were many areas suitable for airfields. Construction on a landplane runway, 4,000 feet by 200 feet, was begun immediately at Faleolo, a task which necessitated the removal of a number of native dwellings and many coconut palms. The runway was surfaced with crushed and rolled volcanic ash on a lava rock base, and was able to support planes of the heaviest type. The runway was completed by July 1942.

By March 1943 the Seabees had enlarged the runway to 6,000 feet by 350 feet and had provided a taxiway parallel to the field, parking areas for about 58 VF's or VB's, two nose hangars, and a number of quonset huts for shops and housing.

Meantime, in late May 1942, the Seabees began construction nearby of five 30-foot seaplane ramps of rock fill with concrete surfacing. Six mooring buoys, one nose hangar, and the necessary storage and housing facilities were also installed. The ramps were completed by the end of September.

Twelve quonset huts, two buildings for an operating room and dental office, and seven barracks were constructed for a 108-bed hospital. The Seabees also built a 600-by-20-foot wharf of lava rock surfaced with concrete, several magazines, and numerous quonset huts for quarters.

CBMU 505 arrived at Upolu on May 20, 1943, to relieve the Seabees. It took over the maintenance of all facilities, also operated the sawmill and constructed carpenter, plumbing, and sheet-metal shops. On February 16, 1944, all work was turned over to a detachment of men from CBMU 504 and all personnel of CBMU 505 departed for Tulagi on February 27, 1944.

Wallis Island was occupied by the Free French

forces on May 26, 1942, and on the following day, under an agreement with the French, by U. S. Marines. Companies C and D of the 2nd Construction Battalion assigned to the base-construction tasks at Wallis, arrived at Tutuila on April 28, 1942 and were held there for three weeks, until the necessary diplomatic arrangements were completed for the Wallis occupation.

While at Tutuila, the Seabees completed the assembly of a 3-by-7 pontoon barge and borrowed a 1500-ton steel barge. These two barges were loaded with construction equipment and materials and towed to Wallis by a Pago Pago station tug.

At Gahi village, Wallis, a causeway about 75 feet long, of log framework filled with volcanic rock and covered with coral sand, was built out over the reef to deep water. Material was easily and rapidly unloaded from the barges to the causeway, and from boats and tank lighters to the beach at high tide. Tentage and temporary messing facilities in native-type shelters were set up near the landing point.

Construction on a field for heavy bombers, one of the major activities of the Seabees at Wallis, was greatly delayed by lack of proper construction equipment. The area selected for the runway was a low plateau, covered with relatively light, low bush. The soil was loose, a brown friable clay of volcanic origin. The runway, 6,000 feet by 250 feet, surfaced with crushed rock, was completed by October 1942. Other facilities added included taxiways, plane revetments, two nose hangars, a machine shop, underground magazines, and one 25,000-gallon aviation-gasoline tank.

CRANE HOISTING CONCRETE BEAMS FOR CRIBBING AT THE END OF THE 600-FOOT MARINE PIER, UPOLU

FUEL TANKS AT NOUMEA
Men of the Third Construction Battalion erecting 1000-barrel gasoline storage tanks

A fighter strip, 5,000 feet by 200 feet, with a coral surface, was also built late in 1942. It was originally planned that a catapult and arresting gear be set up at Wallis for use pending the completion of the airfields. Accordingly, construction began on the catapult near the fighter strip on September 20, 1942, and was completed on October 10, but by that time the field was already in operation. Taxiways, 18 plane revetments, and one nose hangar were installed at the fighter strip.

The lagoon provided ample landing and take-off area in all directions for seaplanes. By October, 1942, the Seabees had finished a 150-by-2,400-foot taxiway and a 70-by-200-foot ramp. Later, concealed parking areas for six VPB's or PBY's, camp facilities, and one 25,000-gallon aviation-gasoline tank were constructed.

The Seabees, using local material, also built storehouses for dry and refrigerated storage, a 72-bed hospital, some 70 miles of roadway, and the necessary housing facilities.

In May 1942, CBMU 504 reported to Wallis to assume responsibility for maintenance work, and the Wallis detachment of the 2nd Construction Battalion rejoined the rest of the battalion at Tutuila.

At that time plans were underway for the moving of fifteen 500-barrel tanks from Tongatabu to Wallis. In August 1943, the Tongatabu detachment of the 1st Battalion arrived at Wallis from Tongatabu to erect the tanks. Another detachment, made up of six officers and 201 men of the 3rd Battalion, reached Wallis the same month to assist in the tank-farm construction. The erection was completed by January 1944. The Tongatabu detachment thereupon left for Efate, and the detachment from the 3rd Battalion rejoined the rest of their battalion at Noumea.

The roll-up at Samoa was the first extensive activity of this nature in the South Pacific. By order of the South Pacific Commander on February 19, 1944, dismantling began throughout the Samoan group.

Salvage at Upolu and Wallis was accomplished

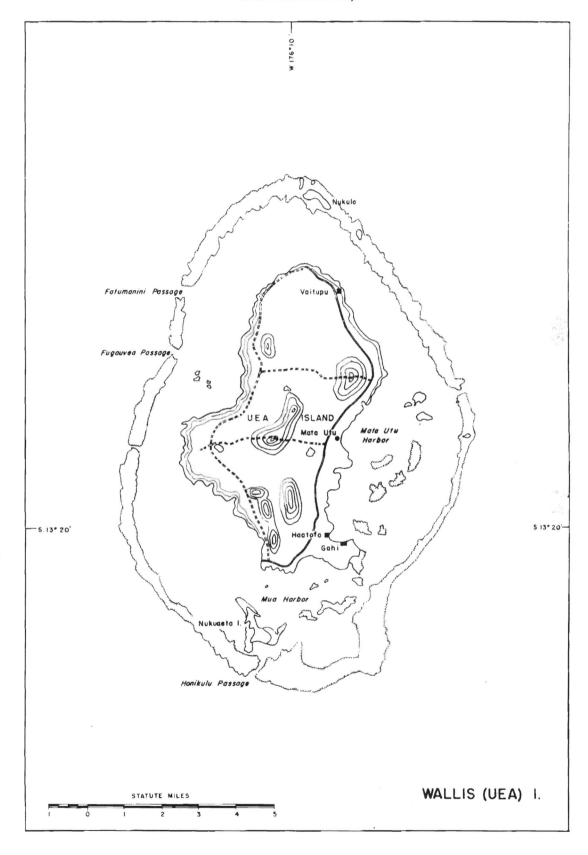

STATUTE MILES

WALLIS (UEA) I.

rapidly by CBMU 504. By July 1944, the salvage operations at Wallis were complete, and the detachment that had been working there joined the rest of the unit at Upolu; the entire unit moved to Tutuila on November 25, 1944. All material was transshipped to Tutuila to await shipment to forward areas.

At Tutuila, CBMU 506 had virtually completed salvage of valuable materials by August 1944. Most of the materials from the Samoan area were sent to Noumea for segregation, improvement of crating where necessary, and determination of future use.

By January 1945, only a token Navy garrison remained in Samoa, and the mission of the base was reduced to emergency seaplane operations, weather reporting, and communications.

Fiji

New Zealand accepted responsibility for the defense of the Fiji Islands, a British Crown Colony, soon after the beginning of the war with Germany and Italy. On May 13, 1942, the United States prepared to take over the defense of Fiji under the joint Army and Navy plan for the relief of New Zealand in the Fiji Islands. At that time, New Zealand had some 10,000 troops stationed on Viti Levu, the largest of the 250 islands which make up the Fiji group. This group was an important link in the line of communications to the south and southwest Pacific areas.

The population, composed mostly of native Fijians and Indians, with a few whites and other races, totals 220,000. Each island is surrounded by a barrier reef, forming a natural breakwater. Fiji has probably the most healthful tropical climate in the world.

Suva, the capital and largest port, is located on Viti Levu. The island, about 90 miles long and 50 miles wide, is of volcanic origin, and, in general, the land rises abruptly from the coast to heights of as much as 4,500 feet. There are several good rivers, the largest of which is the Rewa, which empties into the ocean near the island's southeast corner.

Suva, on the southeast coast, had long been a port-of-call for merchantmen and had many service facilities before the war. Nandi, on the west coast, in a sparsely populated sector, but with a fine large harbor, was chosen as the major location for the United States naval activities. The base was

to provide secure anchorage for a large task force, training airfields, and a staging point for aircraft of all types, fuel storage, and hospital facilities for forward areas.

A number of usable facilities already existed when the U. S. forces assumed responsibility for the defense of Fiji. At Nandi Airfield, there were two runways, both 7,000 feet by 200 feet—one with a clay-gravel surface; the other having 5,000 feet of its runway paved with concrete. There were also hurricane pits, revetments, and storage capacity in two underground tanks for 98,000 gallons of aviation gasoline. Narewa Airfield, with two 5,000-by-200-foot stabilized clay-gravel runways, was made an Army base. There was also a turf-surfaced runway, 3600 feet by 600 feet, at Nausori, 10 miles northeast of Suva.

Suva Harbor was the principal seaplane area, with 1½ miles of water for landing and take-off, eight mooring buoys, extensive repair facilities, and underground storage for aviation gasoline. Lauthala Bay seaplane base, near Suva, was being developed as the principal base for the Royal New Zealand Air Force when the Americans arrived. There was excellent anchorage in the inner harbor at Suva, and three large vessels could be accommodated at a timber wharf. Public and private barges were also available.

Companies C and D of the 3rd Construction Battalion left the United States in June 1942, for Fiji. Upon arrival, Company C was located in the Lautoka area near Nandi, and Company D at Suva. The main project of the detachment, according to the joint plan, was the construction of a tank farm to consist of storage for 50,000 barrels of fuel oil, 20,000 barrels of diesel oil, 10,000 barrels of gasoline, and 500 barrels of lubricating oil. Until the tank-farm material arrived in late October, however, the Seabees were engaged in other construction activities.

After establishing camp, Company C built a jetty, 60 feet long and 300 feet wide, at Lautoka, and a small-boat landing at Vunda Point in Nandi Bay. They also proceeded with the surveying, planning, and drafting work for the tank farm and erected a 10,000-barrel gasoline tank, including camouflage, at Sambeto. For the Saweni Beach seaplane base, 10 miles north of Nandi Airfield, where initial facilities had been provided by the personnel of a naval patrol squadron, the company constructed a seaplane ramp and apron, 50

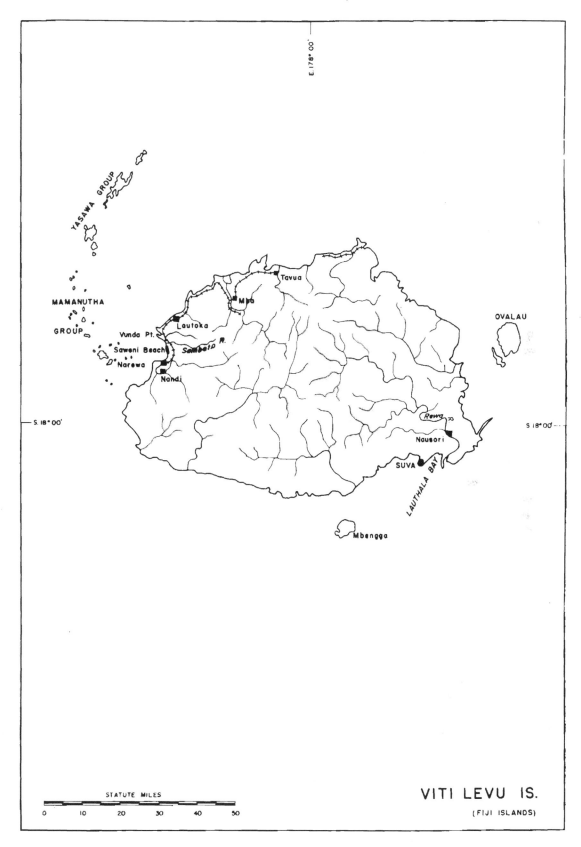

VITI LEVU IS.

(FIJI ISLANDS)

OXYGEN PLANT IN THE INDUSTRIAL AREA, ESPIRITU SANTO
Note 5500-gallon liquid oxygen storage tank (right) and empty oxygen cylinders on platform

feet by 300 feet, a small-boat landing, and camp facilities for 200 men.

Company D, stationed at Suva, carried out extensive work on Lauthala Bay seaplane base, including the construction of a dispensary, guard house, roads, and an underground tunnel for a power house. This company also made repairs on the destroyers *O'Brien* and *Breese*, and engaged in the construction of the 18th General Hospital for the Army.

Upon arrival of the tank-farm material, all efforts were concentrated upon its erection. The personnel at Suva were transferred to the Lautoka area and stationed at the camp already occupied by Company C. The site chosen for the tank farm lay in a small protected depression between two ridges and open to the shore. The nearest wharf was a small pier at Lautoka, accessible to seagoing vessels of light draft. A narrow-gauge railway ran along the beach near the tank farm, connecting the pier with the harbor at Nandi. By April 1943, the tank farm was completed.

The Seabees also provided tents with wood decks for 500 men, galleys, messhalls, a four-building hospital unit, refrigeration and warehouse facilities, and necessary utilities.

At Fleet Air Base No. 2 they erected housing, messing, and galley facilities for 250 officers and 1500 men, and shops for aircraft repair and operations.

The 58th Construction Battalion reported at Fiji on May 3, 1943, with the first echelon of Cub[2] 3. Until the arrival of the 6th (Special) Construction Battalion on May 14 to assume responsibility for all stevedoring activities, the personnel of the 58th and of Cub 3 handled all unloading. All vessels were anchored, and lighters were used between ships and a small pier. To facilitate the unloading, pontoon barges were assembled, two 3-by-7 type with propulsion units and one 4-by-7 tow barge. The harbor at Vunda Point had one T-shaped

[2] Term used to designate an advance base unit consisting of all personnel and material necessary for the establishment of a medium-sized advance fuel or supply base. It had no ship-repair facilities.

pier with a head about 75 feet by 300 feet, a loading capacity of some six tons, and 10 feet of water at low tide.

In addition to their own camp, the men of the 58th erected tent camps with all necessary facilities for Cub 3, the aviation unit, and the 6th (Special) Construction Battalion. A standard steel munitions building and quonset huts were constructed for the Port Director. The problem of safe storage of dynamite was quickly solved by the use of three 150-cubic-foot refrigerators set on top of small mounds about four feet high.

The 58th Construction Battalion left Fiji for Guadalcanal on July 23, 1943.

In May 1943, two other Seabee groups had also arrived at Fiji. CBMU 503 reported on May 6 and prepared to take over all activities previously manned by the 3rd Construction Battalion. Company C of the 3rd had been sent to Funafuti in April, and Company D broke camp and joined the other detachment of the battalion stationed at Noumea in June 1943. The 6th (Special) remained in Fiji until November 6, 1943.

CBMU 503 was engaged in maintenance work on the tank farm and other facilities at Vunda Point. In June and July 1943, a detachment of twelve men from the unit assisted the workmen of a local contractor in Suva to construct NATS facilities, including 16 Army-type medical huts used for housing, galley, and mess halls, and two New Zealand-type 48-by-108-foot warehouses.

By August 1944, when CBMU 503 left Fiji, major activities had been abandoned. The facilities at Saweni Beach seaplane base were discontinued and salvaged. Most of the Army airfields were inoperative. NATS operated from the seaplane base at Lauthala Bay.

Naval installations were turned over to the Army on July 1, 1945.

Noumea

Noumea, at the southern end of the island of New Caledonia, was developed as the main fleet base in the South Pacific, assuming the extensive functions planned originally for Auckland, New Zealand. It served as a staging area for the development of other advance bases, such as Guadalcanal; and on November 8, 1942, became headquarters for the Allied Commander of the South Pacific.

The island of New Caledonia is one of the largest of the Pacific islands. About 250 miles long and 31 miles wide, it has two high parallel ranges of mountains, separated by a central valley, extending through the center of the island. There are numerous rivers, and fresh water is plentiful. The island is almost entirely surrounded by a barrier reef, with a spacious channel, varying in depth from 20 to 50 fathoms, between the shore and the reef.

New Caledonia is a French colony, which has also under its administration several outlying islands—Isle of Pines, the Loyalty Islands, the Wallis archipelago, Futuna and Alofi, and the Huon Islands. The total population numbers about 55,000. Minerals are plentiful, nickel being of special value.

Noumea, with a population of about 11,000, is the chief French city in the Pacific and the seat of government for New Caledonia. It is the only port on the island, its harbor affording shelter to vessels of any size. Between Noumea and Ile Nou, an island in the harbor, there is a channel three miles long and about one mile wide, providing anchorage in any part, with the advantage of complete security and facility of defense.

New Caledonia joined the Free French organization in September 1940. Prior to the entry of the United States into the war, an Australian garrison was stationed on the island. In March 1942, by agreement with the French, U. S. Army forces under General Patch occupied the island, and most of the Australian garrison was withdrawn. On June 10, 1942, a naval officer took over duties as Captain of the Port. With him were 8 other officers and 143 men whose purpose, in addition to forming an administrative unit, was the installation of underwater defenses.

The development of Noumea proceeded slowly at first for effort was being concentrated on the construction of facilities at Auckland, 1,000 miles south. However, in July and August 1942, two Cubs, originally intended for Auckland, were diverted en route, one to Espiritu Santo and the other to Noumea. The Cub unloaded at Noumea formed the nucleus of the subsequent base development. At that time, the only project scheduled for Noumea was a tank farm, providing 30,000 barrels of fuel oil and 20,000 barrels of diesel oil. Company B and one-fourth of the headquarters company of the 3rd Construction Battalion arrived at Noumea on June 26, 1942, to erect the tank farm, but shortly thereafter the project was cancelled.

Plans for building up Noumea as a main air and naval base were soon put into execution, and the detachment of the 3rd Battalion began construction of facilities on Ile Nou. With tents, mess gear, and canteens borrowed from the Army, the Seabees set up camp. No construction equipment or material was available until mid-August, however, so the early projects were accomplished with borrowed equipment. The Army loaned a tug and enough pipe for a 2-inch water line along a shoal from Noumea, and a distribution network on Ile Nou. Later, due to the increase in population, a 4-inch line was run from Noumea, and storage tanks were installed.

The French power cable to the island had been accidentally cut in March, so the Seabees erected a power plant on Ile Nou. A 225-kva generator with a 260-hp diesel engine taken from a Japanese mine at Goro, dismounted and stored in Noumea, was the only power equipment available. The detachment overhauled the machinery, built missing parts, and erected and operated the power plant.

The RAAF had a modest seaplane base at Ile Nou which was taken over by the U. S. Navy to provide fueling and re-arming services for patrol planes and quarters for their personnel. The U. S. Army undertook the construction of a seaplane ramp and apron capable of taking three patrol aircraft. Army personnel completed the excavation and grading, and the paving was laid by the Seabees. By early 1943, the Seabees had constructed 71 pre-fabricated New Zealand-type huts, 180 Dallas huts, seven 40-by-100-foot warehouses, seven quonset hut hangars, and a floating pontoon pier.

In August, the detachment began assembly of pontoon barges, both with and without propulsion units. Most of them were turned over to the Army transportation pool for use in ship unloading.

On December 1, the detachment assumed the operation of a 75-ton crane and its pontoon barge, which they had assembled. It was used to unload PT boats, landing barges, tank lighters. LCT-5's, and P-38's.

Noumea had a large harbor, but servicing facilities were meager. Nickel Dock, 800 feet long with a 24-foot water depth, could take one large vessel. The wharf was equipped with three 7-ton cranes, but it had little storage area. Le Grand Quai, 1400 feet long, with water depth of from 20 to 26 feet,

had some 68,500 square feet of space in transshipment sheds, but had no crane.

Shortage of stevedore personnel impeded the unloading of ships during the summer months. All Navy personnel available were used for unloading, and the construction battalions, as they arrived, handled most of their own unloading. When 600 men of the 20th Construction Battalion arrived in Noumea on October 21, 1942, they concentrated their attention on stevedoring activities. Unloading at Noumea in the first half of December 1942 averaged 5,000 tons per day, but was still not sufficient to keep up with the rate at which cargo was arriving, and a serious congestion of merchant shipping in the harbor resulted.

The 19th Battalion, which reported at Noumea on November 11, 1942, started building an advance base construction depot, the first in the forward area, comprising eleven quonset huts, one steel and two timber warehouses, an electric system, and an area for receiving, sorting, and shipping construction equipment and material. The battalion also operated the depot until the arrival late in the year of the base construction depot detachment, which then assumed responsibility for receiving, inventorying, storing, issuing, and transshipping construction material and equipment, maintaining and operating the detachment camp, and operating the Seabee receiving station.

For the 1st Marine base depot, the 19th Battalion constructed two large piers, one 300 feet and one 200 feet long, and twenty frame warehouses having concrete decks. A vehicular bridge, 20 feet wide, was built at the depot to unload vehicles from barges. The battalion also built warehouses for various naval activities, and operated a rock quarry and crushing plant, a silica pit, and a gravel pit, until transferred to Melbourne in March 1943.

On January 1, 1943, the 24th Construction Battalion, which had arrived in December, undertook the construction of a 600-by-72-foot timber pier at the northern end of the Nickel Dock. The Army Engineers had been working on the pier for several weeks, but due to inadequate equipment, lack of materials, and a shortage of skilled personnel, they had completed only a small portion of the approach. To the newly arrived battalion was assigned the completion of the project. The Seabees developed a pile driver by altering a floating crane. About three-fourths of the bolts

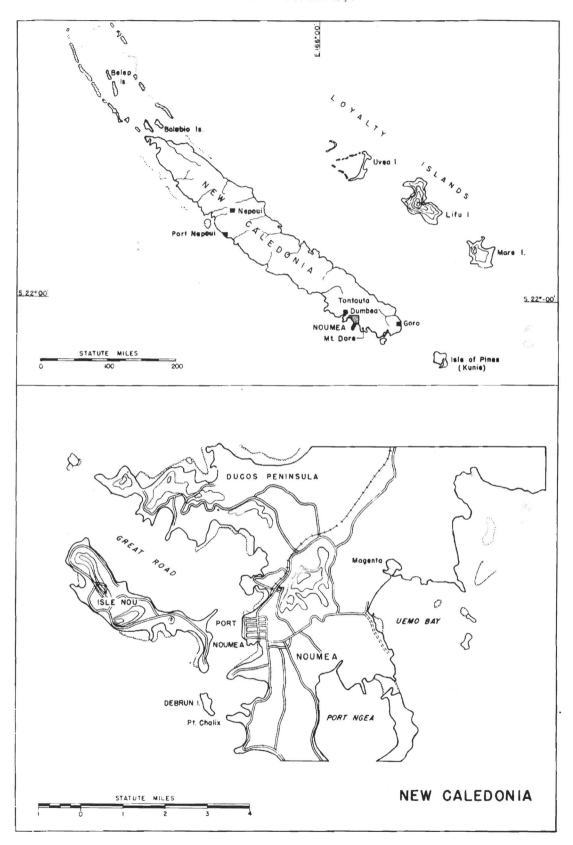

MOBILE HOSPITAL NO. 7, NOUMEA
Beyond Magenta Bay (in the background) is Mont Dore

and drift pins for the pier had to be made by hand. in a small French forge shop. Holes for bolts and drift pins were bored by hand, and most of the piles, of hard native wood, were also cut by hand. In spite of these difficult conditions, the pier was finished and placed in service within the month (January 28). Its completion increased by more than half the berthing capacity of the port.

The detachment of the 3rd Construction Battalion, assisted by a company from the 24th and some fifty men from the 955th Army Engineers, extended the waterfront facilities by means of pontoon assemblies. A Navy landing pier was constructed of two 3-by-12 bridge sections for the wharf and two 2-by-12 bridge sections for the approach. Two 5-by-12 wharf units were installed at Point Chalix for use as a barge landing for the aviation supply depot. Approaches consisted of a landing ramp at each end, hinged to a concrete abutment.

The same personnel handled pontoon erection and assembly until the arrival of PAD 1 on January 18, 1943.

In the fall of 1942, the decision had been made to ship the 15,000 pontoons needed in the Pacific area for 1943 in the form of flat plates and rolled shapes and to assemble them into pontoons at a mobile plant to be located in the South Pacific, because units shipped in knockdown form would conserve much valuable cargo space. On the basis of this decision, a pontoon assembly depot was established at Ile Nou; by March 1943, Seabees had completed the erection of buildings needed to house operations and had installed a narrow-gauge railway in the plant and storage area. The PAD was charged not only with the manufacture of the pontoons, but also with their assembly into barges, wharves, and other units as required.

During the first half of 1943, the construction at Noumea grew rapidly. Facilities at Ile Nou were increased to include an amphibious boat pool, a ship repair unit, NATS facilities, a pontoon assembly depot, an aircraft engine overhaul base, a tank farm for aviation gasoline storage, a section base, and an anti-aircraft school.

In March 1943, the 2nd (Special) Construction Battalion arrived to handle stevedoring.

The construction at the amphibious boat pool was accomplished jointly by Company B of the 3rd Battalion and Company C of the 37th which had arrived at Noumea on January 18, 1943. A marine railway was completely rebuilt, and two others constructed; two New Zealand-type warehouses were erected for LCI storage, and a pontoon pier was increased in size, and relocated.

At the repair base, facilities were provided for the repair and servicing of vessels as large as destroyers, and the base was also equipped to go into the stream and make repairs and alterations to vessels of the transport type. Sixteen 40-by-100-foot steel-arch buildings, 49 quonset huts, five frame storage buildings, and five stone buildings for shops, were erected, together with camp facilities for personnel. A 300-by-70-foot pontoon pier and a 30-by-141-foot small-boat pontoon pier were provided, as well as ARD-2 and AFD-9.

The 3rd Battalion also established facilities for NATS at Ile Nou. This project included the erection of quonset huts for housing and all camp facilities, warehouses, two double nose hangars, and the extension of the existing seaplane ramp. By October 1943, the Seabees had also completed a tank farm for aviation gasoline, consisting of six 1,000-barrel tanks.

Due to the lack of a sufficient pool of spare engines in the South Pacific to permit rotation of engines for overhaul, an aircraft engine overhaul base was set up on Ile Nou, with a capacity of 100

SHIP REPAIR UNIT, ILE NOU, NOUMEA

PONTOON ASSEMBLY AREA, NOUMEA
Third Seabees constructing barges

engines per month. This project was started in February 1943, by Company C of the 37th Battalion, assisted later by the 73rd and the 11th Battalions, which arrived at Noumea in May and June, respectively. Facilities erected included a water-bound macadam apron and a 4500-square-foot concrete ramp, numerous steel warehouses, engine test stands, shop buildings, quonset huts for quarters, and necessary utilities. The work was essentially complete by August 1943. The 78th Battalion, which reported at Noumea in July 1943, assumed responsibility for general maintenance and repair work of the overhaul base.

A section base at Ile Nou, started by the 3rd Battalion and taken over by the 24th in April 1943, had facilities to operate and maintain harbor defense and detection units, to make minor repairs to small craft, and to provide small-boat service for all naval activities around the harbor. There were also two pontoon piers, 120-by-40-foot and 120-by-14-foot, and camp facilities for operating personnel.

Navy medical facilities at Noumea consisted of two 2,000-bed hospitals, MOB 5 and MOB 7. Several construction battalions cooperated in the construction of these facilities, using prefabricated metal huts, native structures, and frame buildings. A convalescent camp was added to MOB 7.

At Noumea, also, a supply depot was established to serve the South Pacific. The construction of some 85 steel warehouses was handled by the 37th and 6th Battalions, while the 78th and 11th established the depot's camp, including barracks, administration building, shops, messing facilities, and all necessary utilities. Steel magazines for an ammunition depot and warehouses for an aviation supply depot were also erected.

The land-plane facilities at Noumea were, in general, under the cognizance of the U. S. Army. On the west shore of Magenta Bay, however, an auxiliary field with a single fighter runway was built for the Navy. In February, the 37th Battalion took over the construction of the airfield, which had been started and brought to some 10-per-cent completion by the 33rd Battalion during its one-month stay in Noumea. Light rod-and-bar mat was laid, covered with coral fill, and tar primer was applied to the surface of the entire runway. To provide additional parking and assembly area, the Seabees hauled material to fill the swampy area at the runway's southwest side. Personnel of the 11th, 6th, and 73rd Construction Battalions assisted in the construction. Two taxiways, four acres of plane assembly, and parking area, shops, dispensary, storage facilities, and housing in tents and Dallas huts were provided.

The 33rd Battalion also started construction of docking facilities at Magenta. This project, completed by the 37th, included the construction of two timber-crib piers extending into the bay about 200 feet.

Two battalions also constructed additional facilities for the Army field at Tontouta, where two runways had been built by the Australians and the Free French. The U. S. Army took over the field in the spring of 1942, resurfaced the runways, lengthened one runway, and provided additional quarters. The 53rd Battalion surfaced 180,000 square feet of airplane-parking area, with nickel ore covered with mesh. The 78th Battalion constructed hardstands, shop areas, and buildings, a nose hangar, service roads, and complete facilities for CASU 3 camp.

On Ducos Peninsula, the 24th Battalion, assisted by the 6th, erected a tank farm for 370,000 barrels of fuel oil and 30,000 barrels of diesel oil. Minor tank facilities were provided at Magenta.

The 53rd Construction Battalion had arrived in Noumea on March 25, 1943, with the First Marine Amphibious Corps. Their major assignment was the construction of three Marine Corps camps, each of 2,000-man capacity. They also drained Lake Gaettege for future Marine camp sites. During its six-months stay at Noumea, the battalion received special Marine training for future combat operations.

During the summer of 1943, Cub 9 was staging in New Caledonia with the 75th and 88th Battalions. The Seabees constructed the staging area, including camp and storage facilities, magazines, a sheet-pile timber bulkhead, and roads at Mont Dore. The 88th also engaged in stevedoring work, unloading the base equipment and supplies and transferring them again to ships at a later date.

CBMU's 536 and 537 arrived at Noumea on January 19, 1944, and shortly thereafter took over all maintenance work theretofore done by the 3rd and 6th Battalions, increased facilities in the former 11th Battalion camp, for their own use, and helped to repair extensive damage caused by a hurricane which occurred on January 18. When the maintenance units arrived, the 6th and 3rd

Battalions, and the base construction depot detachment, were the only Seabees left at Noumea. The 3rd returned to the States in May 1944, and the 6th left Noumea the following September.

In September 1944, the 87th Battalion arrived and had as its major project the completion of an Army staging area at Nepoui in the northern part of the island. The movement of the battalion and its equipment to that location over 150 miles of narrow, winding mountain road presented a formidable problem, and an LST was brought from another island base to take most of the equipment by water, camp equipment being sent by truck convoy. Work began on the staging area on October 12. Some 350 Seabees were used on the project; the Army supplied the materials. The Seabees also built a pier, consisting of one 4-by-12-pontoon floating barge secured to a bulkhead with access to shore by a standard 30-ton ramp.

While at Nepoui for rehabilitation from September 1944 to May 1945, the 82nd Battalion constructed a pier having capacity for berthing two Liberty ships, and reconstructed some 20 miles of highway.

Although little local labor was employed at New Caledonia, native materials were used extensively. The island forests provided a great variety of timber.

Because of the continued, and even increased, use of New Caledonia as a staging and rehabilitation area and the island's position on the line of support to the forward areas in the Pacific, roll-up at Noumea did not get under way until late in 1944. The only activities moved from Noumea were those whose mission could no longer be accomplished in the rear areas, such as the pontoon assembly plant, the aircraft engine overhaul unit, a portion of the advance base construction depot, and a few minor facilities.

In November 1944, the 47th Battalion reported at Noumea and concentrated its attention on dismantling, salvaging, and crating equipment no longer useful there. The advance base construction depot was closed out rapidly. Quonset huts at the receiving station, the ammunition depot, MOB 7, and the section base were dismantled. The Seabees set up a mill and carpenter shop to construct crates, using about one-third salvaged lumber. Frame buildings were razed, and steel warehouses and magazines dismantled. When the 47th left

Noumea in June 1945, roll-up as planned was virtually complete.

CBMU's 536 and 537 were still at Noumea when the Japanese surrendered. The reduction of the naval base left the airfields at Tontouta and Magenta, ship and boat repair facilities, refueling facilities for ships and aircraft, and MOB 5.

Espiritu Santo

When the Japanese moved into the Solomons and began construction of airfields on Guadalcanal, an Allied airbase in an advance area became vital. The choice of Espiritu Santo, 500 miles southeast of Guadalcanal, in the New Hebrides, as a site for a major Army and Navy operating base, brought the U. S. bombers 400 miles closer to the Japanese positions and provided a staging area for the forthcoming Allied invasion of the Solomons. The base provided aircraft facilities capable of supporting heavy bombers, fighters, and two carrier groups; an accumulation of ammunition, provisions, stores, and equipment for offensive operations; repair and salvage facilities for all types of vessels. It became a vital link between Henderson Field on Guadalcanal and the airfields at Noumea and Efate.

Espiritu Santo is the northernmost and largest of the New Hebrides Islands. It has an irregular outline, with numerous small islands near its shores. Heavily wooded and mountainous, particularly in the south and west where the highest peak rises to more than 6000 feet, Santo, as it is locally known, is about 75 miles long and 45 miles wide. Like that of Efate, the government is under joint British and French control.

A small reconnaissance party of three men left Efate on June 28, 1942, to find an airfield site closer than Efate to Henderson Field. Espiritu Santo was chosen, and on July 8, a small group of Seabees of the Efate detachment arrived at Santo with a Marine anti-aircraft battery and a company of colored infantrymen to begin work on Turtle Bay airfield.

The Santo pioneers were given twenty days in which to construct the field. They worked day and night, in the race against time. Equipment for heavy grading was not available and they had to make out with six tractors, two scrapers, one grease truck, one gas wagon, three weapon carriers, and one 50-kw generator. Assisting them were 295 infantrymen, 90 Marines, and 50 natives.

A 6000-foot runway was cleared and surfaced with coral in time to meet the deadline. On July 28, the first fighter squadron came in and was followed the next day by a squadron of B-17's. The planes were fueled from drums and gave the Japs in Guadalcanal their first big bombing on July 30.

Army Air Force and Marine personnel poured into the island shortly thereafter, and after the Marines landed on Guadalcanal on August 7, the new field at Santo gave vital support to that action.

On August 11, 1942, the 7th Battalion arrived and immediately began construction of more extensive air facilities to support the Guadalcanal campaign. In sixty days, they completed a second fighter strip, 4500 feet by 170 feet, with 7500 feet of taxiways and 50 revetments. They then began work on two fields to support bomber operations. A runway, 5000 feet by 150 feet, of steel mat on an 8-inch coral base, was constructed on the shores of Pallikulo Bay (Bomber Field No. 1). Working in cooperation with a company of the 810th Army Engineers, the 7th Battalion also cleared, graded, and surfaced with coral a runway of the same dimensions at Pekoa (Bomber Field No. 2).

When the 15th Battalion reached Espiritu Santo on October 13, 1942, they were assigned the complete overhaul of the grading and drainage of Bomber Field No. 1. They also added taxiways, revetments, and a 1,000-foot extension for air transport operation. In similar fashion, they renovated the grading and drainage of the fighter strip, extended its length 500 feet, and provided it with additional taxiways, revetments, and access roads.

The work at Bomber Field No. 2, which had been begun by the 7th Battalion, was also taken over by the 15th. They completed the construction of a 7,000-foot runway, having a steel-mat surface on coral, and built taxiways, revetments, and miscellaneous structures.

At the same time, both the 7th and the 15th were engaged in providing other necessary facilities for the base as a whole. The 7th erected 60 quonset huts to be used as galleys, wards, operating rooms, dispensaries, and the like for Cub One Hospital, and 40 quonset huts and warehouses for Base Hospital Three. Another hospital of 100-beds, including quarters, wards, mess hall, operating building, and other structures, was established by the 15th for Acorn 2 Hospital. In cooperation with the 822nd and the 350th Army Engineers, the 15th built quarters, wards, laboratories, and messing

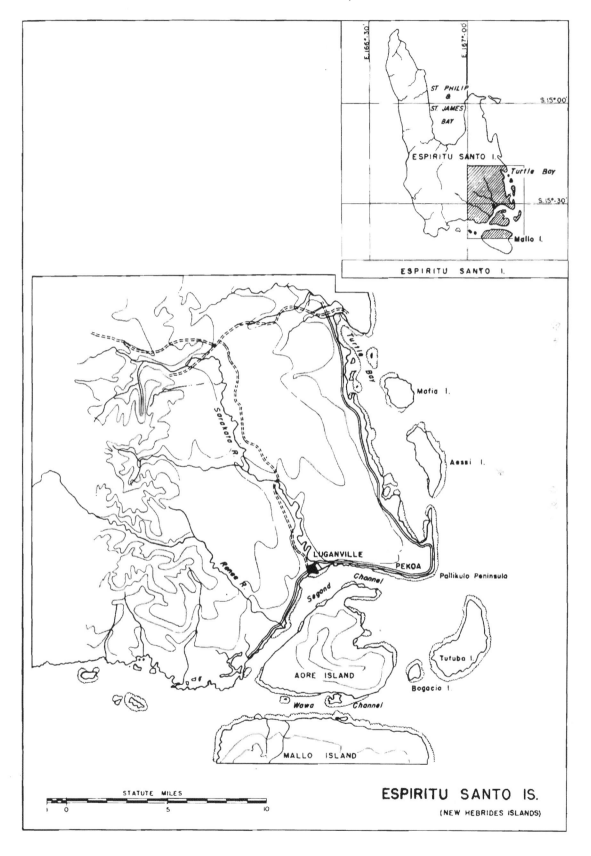

ESPIRITU SANTO IS.

(NEW HEBRIDES ISLANDS)

facilities for the 25th Evacuation Hospital. They also provided surgery and storage buildings and handled electrical and plumbing work. These medical facilities proved to be extremely important for the Guadalcanal campaign in the latter part of 1942.

For a seaplane base, the 7th Battalion constructed a parking area, two pre-fabricated 85-by-100-foot nose hangars, warehouses, quonset huts, and two seaplane ramps in Segond Channel. These Seabees also established a PT-boat base, with extensive facilities.

The 7th built ten camps, varying in capacity from 100 to 1,000 men, with all facilities, roads, and drainage. The 15th provided seven additional camps for various base activities. An outstanding project was the enlisted men's galley and mess hall, equipped to feed 1,000 men in one hour, which the 15th constructed. All decks were of concrete, and complete drainage and plumbing systems were laid out and built with 6-inch quick-coupling pipe and parts of empty oil drums. The Seabees also improvised indirect lighting from discarded tin cans.

The original network of roads—26 miles of new and 8 miles of rebuilt roads—was established by the 7th CB.

The men of these early battalions on Santo were subjected to spasdomic submarine shellings and several air raids.

In the early months of 1943, six additional battalions arrived at Espiritu Santo. The 35th Battalion arrived on January 27th, 1943. After unloading its equipment and setting up camp, the battalion assembled pontoons, constructed a PT-boat base and built roads. In cooperation with the 36th Battalion, which reported on February 10, half of the 35th Battalion constructed Base Hospital No. 3 (500 beds) during the summer of 1943. The other half of the 35th was sent forward to the Russells in March. The rest of the battalion joined them there in late August 1943.

The 40th Battalion reached Santo on February 3, 1943. The principal project of this battalion was the construction of a third bomber field at Luganville. A runway, 6,800 feet by 300 feet, with 27,000 feet of taxiway and 75 hardstands, cut out of dense jungle, was completed in 120 days. Nearly a fourth of the runway was in solid-coral cut ranging from a few feet to 35 feet in depth; 3,000 feet of taxiway and six hardstands were also in solid-

coral cuts averaging 10 feet. Coral for surfacing and necessary fill was obtained from the cuts and from borrow pits. Because of the heavy rainfall in the area, the surface of the coral was treated with an emulsified asphalt binder.

Additional facilities constructed for the operation of the airfield included a tank farm of six 1,000-barrel steel tanks, two truck-loading stations, two repair areas, fifteen 40-by-100-foot arch-rib warehouses, one 100-by-90-foot hangar, eighteen 20-by-48-foot quonset huts for living quarters, six mess halls, and all necessary utilities. Fifteen miles of two-lane road, for access to and operation of the airfield, were cut through dense jungle.

The 40th Battalion moved to New Guinea on November 25, 1943.

Accompanying the first echelon of Lion 1, the 36th Battalion arrived at Espiritu Santo on February 10, 1943. While most of the battalion was engaged in setting up camp facilities and unloading operations, a detachment was sent to Pallikulo Bay to build a pontoon wharf. It consisted of four 6-by-18-pontoon barge sections hinged together and connected to a steel cofferdam by eight 72-foot bridge sections. There was a minimum of 33 feet of water at the end of the pier.

The next major assignment for the 36th Battalion was the construction of an aviation engine overhaul base. This project provided housing for 250 officers and 1,800 enlisted men, as well as facilities for the overhaul of 200 aviation engines per month. The work, begun in February and completed in June, involved the construction of 85 quonset huts for housing, 18 standard 40-by-100-foot arch-rib shop buildings, messing facilities, four quonset huts on concrete decks for offices and instrument shops, and all necessary utilities.

Meanwhile, on March 17, construction was begun on facilities for the overhaul and servicing of torpedoes for the Fleet. This project consisted of the erection of three arch-rib buildings and the installation of torpedo-overhaul equipment, including air compressors and connecting piping, and the construction of all utilities. The work was completed in May.

The 36th Battalion also built an aviation supply annex of twenty arch-rib buildings, and six 1,000-barrel gasoline storage tanks at Bomber Field No. 2, with a connecting pipe line to a tank farm at Bomber Field No. 1. Motor repair facilities and a 300-foot steel-pile bulkhead were built at the PT-boat base, and 75 steel magazines and 16 open bomb-storage areas were constructed for an ammunition depot.

In cooperation with the 35th Battalion, the 36th built 25 quonset huts for quarters and wards, four steel warehouses, and extended the water system, lighting and roads at Base Hospital No. 3.

The 36th Battalion constructed aviation-engine-overhaul facilities at Bomber Field No. 3, additional camp buildings for South Pacific Air headquarters, and further extensions to the road system of the island. On September 12, 1943, the battalion left for the Russells.

The 44th Battalion arrived at Santo on March 18, 1943, and undertook the operation of two coral pits, and the construction of storage tanks, hospital facilities, a boat pool, five piers, utilities for various camps, and an ABSD. The battalion left Espiritu Santo for Manus on April 4, 1944.

The 57th and the 3rd (Special) Battalions reported at Santo late in March 1943. Although the main activity of the 3rd (Special) was stevedoring, camp construction was considered so vital that the entire headquarters company of the battalion worked with the 57th to provide camp facilities. At first, tents were erected, but the torrential rains caused these to wash out almost as soon as they were staked. The tents were therefore floored and raised, and later, screened. Mess and hospital facilities were given equal priority with housing. The 57th soon had quarters and messing facilities for 1,000 officers and men, using floored and screened

Men of the 36th Battalion Erecting Dallas Huts, Espiritu Santo

tents and concrete-floored mess halls. The 3rd (Special) was gradually transferred into quonset hut facilities for 1,000 men.

The 57th Battalion built a seven-acre ammunition dump and ordnance facilities, and rebuilt a portion of the 7,000-foot airstrip at Luganville Bomber Field No. 3.

At Aore Island, the battalion erected quonset huts for housing, 30 magazines for mine storage, and other installations for the mine-assembly, target-repair, and mine-recovery plants. On the same island, they constructed fifty 10,000-barrel bolted tanks for fuel storage, 25,000 feet of 12-inch spiral pipe, and 50 pump units. Other oil facilities provided at Santo included seventeen 1,000-barrel tanks for motor gas storage, two 10,000-barrel tanks for diesel storage, and twenty-three 1,000-barrel tanks for aviation gasoline.

Pontoon assembly was a major activity of the 57th Battalion. Pontoons were assembled into barges with propulsion units, two seaplane drydocks, bridge units, and numerous wharves. They also constructed a cruiser drydock, 840 feet long, 55 feet high, beam inside 140 feet, width outside 180 feet, with 50-foot wing walls.

The 57th built additional facilities for the seaplane base and for Base Hospital No. 3. Hangars were erected at Fighter Strip No. 1 and at Luganville. The battalion also participated in the repair and restoration of a number of warships which had been damaged in battle and put into Santo for repairs.

No local labor was used, but native materials played an important part in construction at Espiritu Santo. Coral quarried from numerous local pits was used for roads. Coral fill for foundations and as aggregate for concrete was useful in the building of quonset huts and warehouses. Palm logs were used for quonset hut footings.

The 57th Battalion left the island on March 15, 1944. CBMU's 535 and 538 arrived late in 1943, on November 23 and December 27, respectively. Three other maintenance units, CBMU's 541 and 542 and Section One of 539, reached Santo in February 1944. These units took over all maintenance work and minor construction. By April 1944, all construction battalions, except the 3rd (Special), which returned to the States in September 1944, had left the island. CBMU 538 moved out in March 1945, and was followed by CBMU's 535 and 541 in July 1945. When the Japs surren-

dered, CBMU 542 and the section of CBMU 539 were still operating at the naval air base at Espiritu Santo.

CBD 1007, which had arrived at Espiritu on August 8, 1943, to operate a truck-repair unit, completely overhauled trucks and construction equipment so that they could be used at one base after another. This was not strictly roll-up activity, but contributed greatly toward the reduction of requirements from the United States.

Major bases, such as Noumea and Espiritu Santo, were not involved in the extensive roll-up activities of the South Pacific area in 1944, as these bases were expected to be utilized in staging the increased forces to be used in the Pacific. The naval base at Espiritu was disestablished June 12, 1946.

Funafuti

Funafuti, an atoll of the British-owned Ellice group of islands, was developed initially in the fall of 1942 to provide an air base and scouting and ferry point for planes en route to the South Pacific area. However, its facilities came into their most important use later in connection with our thrust northwestward into the Gilbert and Marshall islands.

Funafuti Island, the largest of the 30 islets which make up the atoll, is about 7 miles long and from 50 to 150 yards wide, except at the southern end where it forms an elbow about 700 yards wide. The entire island is not large enough to support extensive facilities. However, ships with draft up to 20 feet can enter the lagoon, which is commodious and provides good anchorage. The Seabees brought the first wheels to touch the island.

Two other islands of the Ellice group, Nanomea and Nukufetau, were also used as sites for U. S. air activities. Nanomea, 250 miles northwest of Funafuti, and only 460 miles southeast of Tarawa, is 6 miles long and has no sheltered anchorage. Nukufetau, a group of islets on a reef about 24 miles in perimeter, lies less than 50 miles northwest of Funafuti.

On October 2, 1942, a detachment of the 2nd Construction Battalion, comprising two officers and 120 men from the group on Samoa, went ashore at Funafuti with the 5th Marine Defense Battalion.

The Seabees immediately began the construction on a fairly level site of an airstrip, 5,000 feet long and 250 feet wide. Within thirty days, the field was

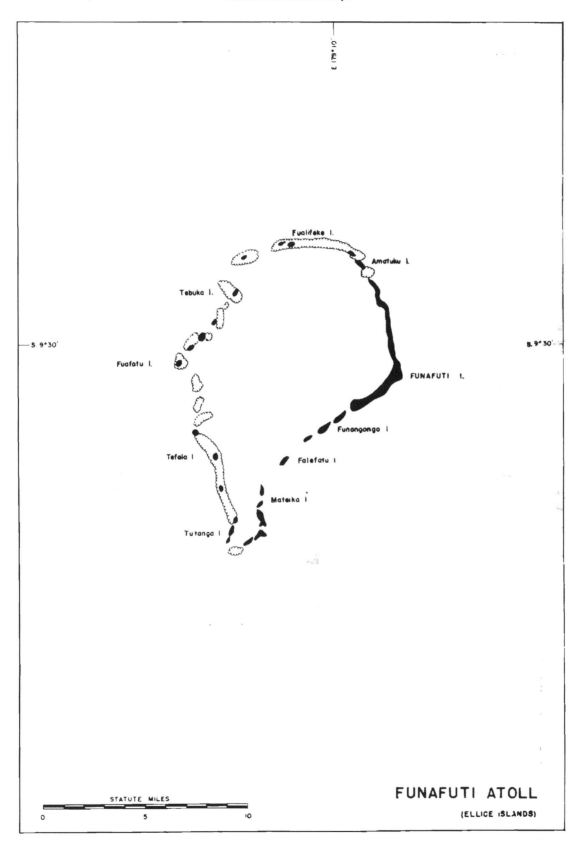

FUNAFUTI ATOLL

(ELLICE ISLANDS)

STATUTE MILES

0   5   10

in use by Navy planes. By early spring, an all-weather runway, 6,600 feet long and 600 feet wide, was completed, together with parking and shop facilities. In April of 1943, B-24's took off from the field in raids against Nauru and Tarawa. The completion of the field marked the completion of the original mission of the Seabee detachment.

The detachment also constructed fifty prefabricated frame buildings for housing, four Marine warehouses, a seaplane ramp, 30 feet wide, a 76-bed hospital, a floating drydock for PT-boat repairs, and a road system.

In April, 1943, a detachment of six officers and 235 men of the 3rd Battalion was ordered to Funafuti for the construction of an aviation-gasoline tank farm, the project comprising ten 1,000-barrel storage tanks, together with connecting piping, a sea line, and moorings. The detachment arrived on May 9, and by May 17 had completed unloading operations and begun construction. The project was completed by June 15.

The detachment then constructed 43 plane revetments, of steel mat and coral fill, and erected a radio repair shop, an airfield operations building, an Army aerological building, and ten frame buildings for base-personnel housing. It moved to Wallis on August 23, 1943.

The 16th Battalion arrived in the Ellice Islands in several echelons in 1943. Two echelons disembarked at Funafuti on August 20 and 24, and were moved to Nukufetau on August 30. Three more landed at Nanomea on September 5 and 7. Two additional echelons were sent to Nukufetau on September 8 and October 7.

All supplies for Nukufetau had to be transshipped at Funafuti, since the entrance channel at the former island could not give passage to a large cargo vessel. Landing craft could get as far as the edge of the reef; from there, men, tractors, and supplies had to be brought ashore at low tide.

The base at Nukufetau was primarily an air operations base, designed to support strikes against Japanese installations in the Gilberts and Marshalls. The 16th Battalion built a fighter strip, 3500 feet by 200 feet, and a bomber strip, 6100 feet by 220 feet. For the latter, nearly 50,000 coconut trees had to be cut down. About 2,000 feet of the runways was built on fill over swamp. The construction as planned was completed in forty days. Two

PT-BOAT DRYDOCK AND REPAIR BASE, ESPIRITU SANTO

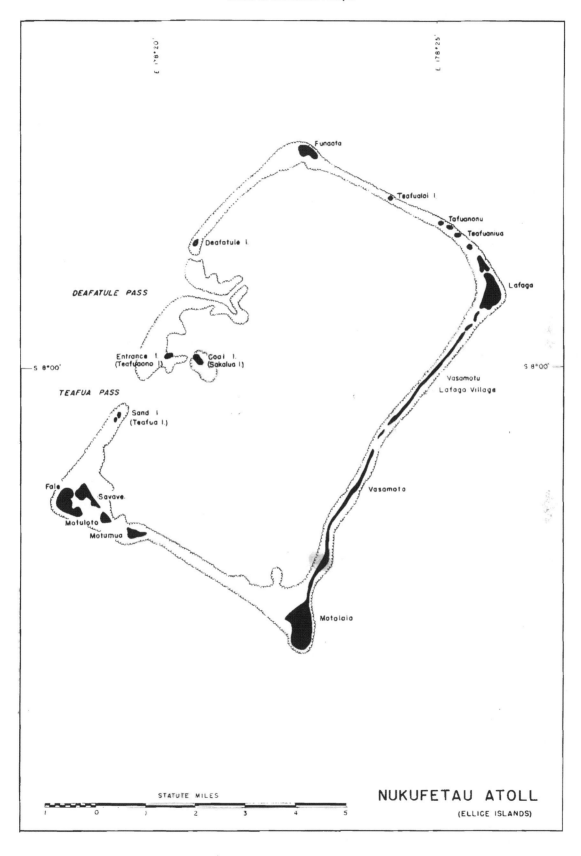

E 178°20'

E 178°25'

Funaota

Teafualoi I.

Tafuanonu

Teafuaniua

Deafatule I.

Lafaga

DEAFATULE PASS

S 8°00'

Entrance I.
(Teafuaono I.)

Coal I.
(Sakalua I.)

Vasamotu
Lafaga Village

S 8°00'

TEAFUA PASS

Sand I.
(Teafua I.)

Vasamoto

Fale

Savave.

Motuloto

Motumua

Motolaia

STATUTE MILES

1   0   1   2   3   4   5

NUKUFETAU ATOLL

(ELLICE ISLANDS)

bombers landed on October 30, and a squadron of VB108's came in on November 7.

A complete aviation-gasoline tank farm, consisting of eleven 1,000-barrel tanks, a filling station, pumps, and off-shore lines for receiving gasoline from tankers, was constructed. Other necessary facilities, such as hangars and hardstands, were provided at the fields. The Seabees often helped to install motors in Liberators.

To link together sections of the atoll, the Seabees built a 1,000-foot causeway, using coconut logs for the foundations.

About fifty natives were used for tasks such as clearing, grubbing, and garbage disposal.

At Nanomea, a detachment of the 16th Seabees went ashore with the Marines in September 1943. Two days after the landing, Japanese fighter pilots hit Nanomea and took advantage of the poor defenses to bomb and strafe at tree-top levels. There were no Seabee casualties.

Work was started on a bomber strip, 7,000 feet by 200 feet, on September 11, and eight days later, planes of a Marine fighter squadron landed on it. The fighter planes continued to use the runway during the remainder of the construction period. The first bombers landed on November 12, although the Japanese had carried out a damaging raid early that morning. The Seabees built the necessary camp and operation facilities for the airfield, including an 8,000-barrel tank farm for aviation gasoline.

The natives proved invaluable in aiding the diving crew in the blasting of obstacles from the lagoon. Capable of diving to great depths, the natives placed the underwater explosives where they would be most effective. Some 80 natives were employed for short intervals.

When the U. S. forces landed at Nanomea, there were no installations, except native churches, council houses, and living quarters. One of the large council houses was utilized for provision storage, and some small huts were used by Marine personnel for offices and living quarters. Seabees and Marines laid out and cleared roads necessary to the placing of defense weapons and detecting devices.

On December 30, 1943, CBMU 517 arrived at Funafuti to relieve the 2nd Battalion, its task being the completion of construction and the maintenance of the installations. The unit also built a NATS pontoon wharf, a log-crib coral-filled LST and LCT wharf for the Marine Corps supply depot,

Marine barracks and warehouses, and handled salvage operations on sunken seaplanes and wrecked landplanes.

CBMU 552 left the U. S. for Nukufetau in January 1944, to assume responsibility for the maintenance of the air strips and all other island facilities, and for stevedoring. On February 2, 1944, CBMU 553 arrived at Nanomea for maintenance duty. They cleared out stumps and other debris along the bomber strip, constructed approximately nine new structures for ATC, made numerous repairs to LST's and LCT's, and maintained roads and equipment.

In May and June 1944, CBMU 517 took over the maintenance of Nanomea and Nukufetau, and CBMU 552 and 553 moved to forward areas.

By May 1944, roll-up activities had begun at the several islands. Before leaving for a new assignment, CBMU 552 began dismantling all buildings and installations not in use and the assembly of all salvagable material at Nukufetau. In June, the majority of the personnel of CBMU 517 were engaged in salvage work. All quonset huts at Funafuti were taken down and crated for shipment. Salvage of the Marine Corps depot was completed by August. One officer and 39 men were assigned to Nanomea for the salvage of structures and the tank farm. One officer and 45 men were assigned to the same duty at Nukufetau.

In September 1944, a detachment of CBMU 506, consisting of three officers and 125 men, arrived at Funafuti and took over the duties of CBMU 517, which was then sent to the Russells. The personnel of CBMU 506 salvaged 72 frame buildings at Funafuti. Six men were sent to Nukufetau to load the salvage materials there. One officer and 20 men were sent to Nanomea to complete salvage operations. The complete detachment returned to Samoa on March 27, 1945.

Auckland

In the opening months of the war, Auckland was chosen as a major fleet anchorage for the U. S. Fleet, and it was planned to develop these facilities to provide for ship repair, training and rehabilitation of combat units, and hospitalization of sick and wounded from forward areas, and to maintain air cover for the allied fleets.

Auckland is on North Island, one of the two principal islands of New Zealand, about 1,200 miles east of Australia. Under the circumstances it

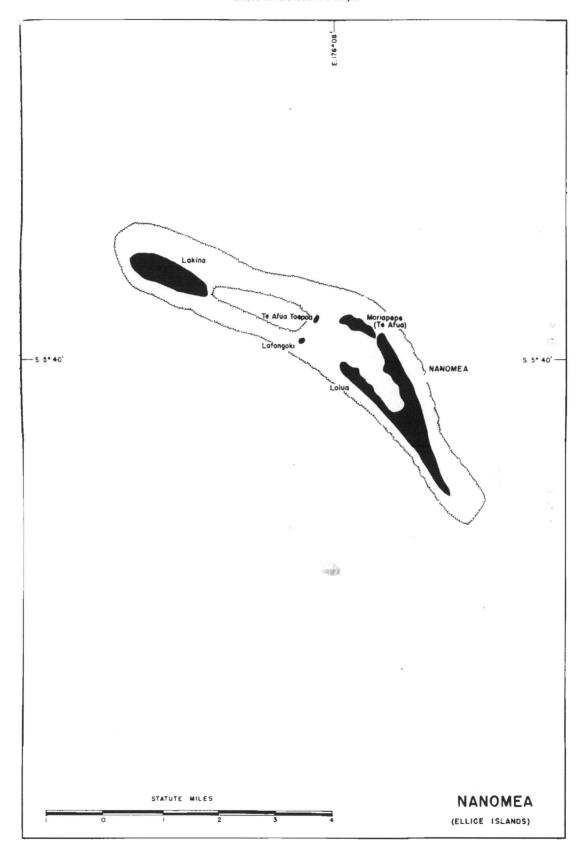

STATUTE MILES

NANOMEA

(ELLICE ISLANDS)

PBY Base, Espiritu Santo
Showing ramps and fill ground

was decided that the construction of the additional facilities needed for the defense of the base and the support of the U. S. naval forces in the area would be carried out with materials furnished by the United States to the New Zealand Naval Board, and that the U. S. Navy would provide experts to supervise the installation and initial operation of the facilities built, but that the actual installation and service operations would be performed by New Zealand personnel. The New Zealand Public Works Department was the construction agency for all government departments.

Consequently, no construction battalions were assigned to New Zealand for construction work. However, the 25th Battalion, which arrived in Auckland on March 11, 1943, attached to the Third Marine Division, and stayed for four months, gave aid to a local contractor in the construction of MOB 6. In April 1943, CBMU 501 and CBMU 502 were assigned to Auckland and took over main-

tenance and minor repair work on all U. S. facilities there.

In April 1942, the Navy ordered an officer to Auckland as port director, charged with responsibility for developing a main naval base, including headquarters for the Commander of Allied Forces in the South Pacific, Vice Admiral Robert A. Ghormley. When the line of U. S.-held bases moved rapidly northward, ComSoPac headquarters in Auckland were closed on November 8, 1942, and were moved to Noumea, New Caledonia. Auckland thereafter had the scope of a minor base.

Housing Facilities.—By May 1942, the increase of U. S. naval activities in the Auckland area had caused a serious problem in connection with the housing of personnel.

On June 3 work was begun on a 500-man camp at Mechanics Bay to provide a receiving barracks for the area. On land donated at no cost by the Harbor Board, the New Zealand Public Works

Department built four 112-man barracks, one C.P.O. dormitory, galley and mess hall, ration storehouse, boiler plant, laundry, recreation building, and officers' quarters. The first barracks were occupied on June 19, and the camp was completed by December.

At Camp Domain, New Zealand workmen constructed facilities for 1,000 men, to be used by headquarters personnel, Marines, and convalescents. This project was also completed by December 1942.

Later, at Victoria Park, a 1200-man camp consisting of 166 eight-man huts, 30 four-man huts, 2 thirty-man quarters for officers, and other necessary facilities was built for Seabee use. However, the camp was occupied by the U. S. Army and Marine Corps personnel.

To house the personnel assigned to ammunition depots at Kauri Point and Motutapu, small camps were constructed. Numerous other hut camps were constructed in the area for the Marine Corps. For example, a 1200-man camp was erected at the Tamaki railway station, location of the Third Base Depot of the Marine Corps.

Hospital Facilities.—To supply medical aid to the U. S. personnel stationed in New Zealand and to the sick and wounded evacuated from forward areas, two mobile hospital units were assigned to Auckland. When MOB 4 arrived, about the middle of 1942, construction was begun on a 1000-bed hospital facility. Prefabricated buildings were erected by hospital personnel; all other construction was carried out by New Zealand workmen. By June 1943, all major construction work on supplemental buildings, such as the recreation hall and quarters, was completed.

For MOB 6, the facilities, begun early in 1943, included 66 BuMed-type buildings for ship's service, corpsmen's barracks, and storehouses. In June 1943, detachments from the 25th Battalion, prior to their departure to a forward area with the Marines, undertook the necessary grading, and built roads, drainage structures, a water system, and a steam-distribution system, erected steel buildings, and remodeled existing quarters. All ward, galley, mess-hall, administration, surgery, and recreation buildings, as well as officer and enlisted quarters, were built by the New Zealand government.

Storage and Ammunition Facilities.—A considerable amount of existing storage space, for fuel as well as for dry materials, was available at Auckland for use by the U. S. forces. In addition, there were built for the Navy 120,000 square feet of covered storage for the Third Base Depot of the Marine Corps at Tamaki Station, a 32,000-square-foot medical storehouse, 550,000 square feet of covered storage at Sylvia Park, and 100,000 square feet of wood-frame storehouses at King's Drive. Additional storage space was leased. The work on these storage facilities was accomplished in late 1942 and 1943.

An extensive tank farm, including storage for 500,000 barrels of fuel oil, was planned for Auckland. However, it was gradually reduced in scope as the line of U. S.-held bases moved forward, until in January 1943, the entire project was cancelled and the materials then on hand were moved to Noumea.

Two ammunition depots were built by New Zealand workmen for the Navy. At Motutapu Island, some 8 miles down the harbor from Auckland, fifty 28-by-80-foot concrete magazines and sixteen brick magazines were constructed, together with 15 miles of road to give access to the site. The project was complete early in 1943.

Harbor Facilities.—One of the main reasons for the choice of Auckland as a naval base was its excellent harbor facilities. However, the drydock facilities for major and intermediate types of ships were so meager that the Calliope Graving Dock at Davenport, owned and operated by the Auckland Harbor Board, was enlarged to take heavy cruisers of the *Indianapolis* class. The only two other graving docks in the area capable of docking heavy cruisers, were the Woolwich and the Cockatoo Island docks at Sydney, Australia. There were also two large floating docks, one at Wellington, N. Z., and one at Newcastle, Australia. Unfortunately, the overhang of the bow and the stern of heavy ships in these docks would have been undesirable for a cruiser in a damaged condition, and the depth over the blocks would have been insufficient.

It was decided therefore, late in 1942, that the Navy should undertake to extend the length of the Calliope Graving Dock by 40 feet. This work was planned by the U. S. Navy, and accomplished by the New Zealand government under reverse lend-lease. The work required about six months for completion and was done without interfering with the use of the dock.

Airfields.—At the opening of the war in the Pacific, all the airfields of the RNZAF were turf-covered. The turf was in excellent condition, but became badly cut up in wet weather under heavy traffic. With the cooperation of the New Zealand Public Works Department and the U. S. Navy, the RNZAF provided some of the fields with concrete or stabilized runways so that they could be used by heavy bombers. At Ardmore Field, the RNZAF began work early in 1943 on two runways—5,100 by 150 feet—to be stabilized and tarsealed. The U. S. Navy took over the project and brought it to 70-percent completion. The field was then turned over to the RNZAF for use as a training field. Construction of strips, taxiways, peripheral roads, and frame structures was accomplished by New Zealand workmen under U. S. Navy supervision.

Maintenance.—CBMUs 501 and 502, the first maintenance units to be commissioned, arrived in New Zealand in April 1943. They performed all major maintenance work on U. S. facilities and made numerous minor repairs. In January 1944, CBMU 501 erected a number of New Zealand pre-fabricated buildings and remodeled existing buildings at the Maungakiekie rest camp for the U. S. Army. This unit also accomplished extensive repairs and remodeling activities at the Tamaki Station Marine Corps camp.

CBMU 502 went to New Georgia in June 1944, and CBMU 501 departed from Auckland for the Russell Islands in October 1944. Auckland soon lay well off the line of flow of support for staging to forward areas. By February 1944, the entire function of the Navy's public works officer was reduced to maintenance. By July, the roll-up was well under way, and even rehabilitation activities were discontinued.

Both mobile hospital units were moved to forward areas in October. Navy's Auckland complement was reduced to 26 officers and 82 men, concentrated at the receiving barracks at Mechanics Bay, thus virtually vacating the naval base at Auckland.

Chapter 25

CAMPAIGN IN THE SOLOMONS

By the early summer of 1942, six months after the bombing of Pearl Harbor, the Japanese had reached the full tide of their conquest of the islands of the Pacific. The Philippines and all of the Dutch East Indies had fallen. The enemy was in control of the north coast of New Guinea and was preparing to push across the mountainous spine of that island to Port Moresby on its southern shore. Although this continued advance to the south by amphibious operations had been checked in May, at the Battle of the Coral Sea, Japanese control of the Solomons was a sharp threat to our own extended position in the South Pacific and to the safety of Australia itself. The necessity of ejecting the enemy from his newly won position in Guadalcanal became increasingly apparent.

The contest for the Solomons opened on August 7, when the 1st Marine Division landed on the beaches of Guadalcanal and Tulagi, initiating a campaign that was to continue for more than a year.

The Struggle for Guadalcanal.—The principal objective of the first phase of the struggle, the contest for Guadalcanal, was to deny to the enemy and to possess for ourselves the airfield that the Japanese had been constructing on the island since early May, the field soon to become known throughout the world as Henderson Field. It was close to completion when our invasion forces struck, and making it operational, and keeping it that way during months of fierce combat, was the principal task assigned to the 6th Construction Battalion, the naval construction force assigned to our first real offensive move in the South Pacific. The 6th Battalion followed the Marines into Guadalcanal on September 1 and thereby became the first Seabees to engage in the combination of fighting and building for which they had been organized and trained.

Japanese resistance was fierce and persistent, and the support we could give our invasion forces was restricted by the shipping demands for the forthcoming invasion of North Africa. For six months, ground, sea, and air forces battled for possession of Guadalcanal. On February 8, 1943, the Japanese evacuated their remaining troops, ending the first phase of the Solomons campaign.

During the six months of struggle for Guadalcanal, however, the enemy had completed the development of an important air base at Munda Point, on the southwest coast of New Georgia, about 175 miles northwest of Henderson Field. From their new base they threatened our position in the southern Solomons, and consequently our next undertaking would have to be their ejection from New Georgia.

Driving the Enemy from New Georgia.—In preparation for the invasion of New Georgia our forces moved into the Russell Islands, 60 miles northwest of Guadalcanal, to build an air base to provide fighter support for the planned operation. The occupation of the Russells, on February 21, 1943, was unopposed. Accompanying the landing forces was a major portion of the 33rd Construction Battalion, which was followed a few weeks later by the 35th Battalion. By early June the Seabees had completed the construction of two air strips and the necessary fuel tanks and other supporting facilities. On June 30 the invasion of New Georgia began.

Naval construction forces participated in the assault of New Georgia at three different points. The 47th Battalion landed at Segi Point at the extreme southeast end of the island, and immediately set to work constructing an air strip. The 20th Battalion, accompanying Marine assault forces, landed at Viru Harbor on the island's southern coast, for the purpose of building a PT-boat base. The third landing was on Rendova, an island separated from New Georgia by a narrow channel, across which the Munda airfield was within artillery range. The assault on Rendova was made by Army forces, accompanied by the

24th Battalion. The Seabees' principal duty became that of building and maintaining roads over which the artillery and its ammunition could be moved.

The New Georgia campaign, the second phase of the campaign for the Solomons, went much faster than did the struggle for Guadalcanal. On August 5, Munda airfield was captured, almost exactly a year after the Marines' first Solomons landing. Speedy rehabilitation of the Munda field by the Seabees and Army engineers permitted our air forces to neutralize effectively the enemy's remaining New Georgia position at Bairoko Harbor and that on Kolombangara Island. Our forces followed up their success promptly and on August 15 landed, unopposed, on Vella Lavella, the northernmost island of the New Georgia group. Participating in the landings was the 58th Battalion, charged with building a small air and naval base to serve as one more step up the Solomons chain. Before the month was out the New Georgia campaign was considered closed; the Japanese retired farther northward to Bougainville, the largest island of the Solomons chain.

The Bougainville Campaign. The third phase of the Solomons campaign revolved around our efforts to drive the enemy from Bougainville. It was his last position in the Solomons, and in our hands would greatly facilitate our attacks on the major Japanese bases at Rabaul and Kavieng.

Invasion of Bougainville was preceded by the assault upon and capture of the Treasury Islands, comprising Mono Island and Stirling Island, 28 miles south of the southern end of Bougainville, and their development as an air and naval base. The assault, on October 27, 1943, was made by New Zealand forces, who were accompanied by a detachment from the 87th Construction Battalion. The landing was strenuously resisted, but, despite severe conditions, by the end of the year the Seabees had successfully completed the fighter field they had set out to build.

On November 1, Bougainville was invaded. Landing with the Third Marine Division at Empress Augusta Bay were detachments from the 25th, 53rd, 71st, and 75th Construction Battalions. Again the principal facilities to be built were airfields, first a fighter strip at Torokina and immediately thereafter a bomber strip and a fighter strip at Piva nearby. Much of the construction plan had to be carried out under fire, but by early December the Torokina strip was complete and work had

begun on the Piva field. By early January 1944, both bomber and fighter strips at Piva were in operation.

Immediately following completion of the Bougainville airfields the next step forward was taken, occupation of Green Island, an atoll 40 miles northwest of the northern tip of the Solomons chain and only 120 miles east of Rabaul. The assault, on February 15, 1944, was made by the Third New Zealand Division, immediately followed ashore by the first echelon of the newly established 22nd Naval Construction Regiment, comprising the 33rd, 37th, 93rd, and half of the 15th Construction Battalions. Japanese opposition to the landing was light. Within twenty days after landing the Seabees had completed the construction of yet another fighter field and by the end of March a new bomber field was completed and in operation.

Occupation of Bougainville was never extended beyond a small area in the vicinity of Torokina, and until V-J Day, Japanese troops in large numbers were present on the island. From our newly won bases, however, the enemy strongholds of Rabaul and Kavieng were attacked incessantly until their effectiveness was reduced to the vanishing point. Enemy troops in the jungles of Bougainville constituted no threat to our offensive strength. Moreover, rapid progress had been made since the landing on Guadalcanal in ejecting the Japanese from positions of advantage in New Guinea and in the Central Pacific. A month before the Bougainville campaign was launched, forces of the Southwest Pacific had captured Finschhafen on the New Guinea coast, and while the struggle for the northern Solomons was under way they had completed their conquest of the entire Huon peninsula. During the last week of November 1943, immediately following our landings at Empress Augusta Bay, Marines of the Central Pacific forces had wrested Tarawa, in the Gilbert Islands, from the enemy, and in early February 1944, just before we went into the Green Islands, a combined force of Marines and Army troops had captured Kwajalein, the dominant position in the Marshalls.

Guadalcanal

Guadalcanal, the second largest island of the Solomons group, a British possession, is about 80 miles long and 25 miles wide, of rugged terrain with mountains rising to 8,000 feet toward the

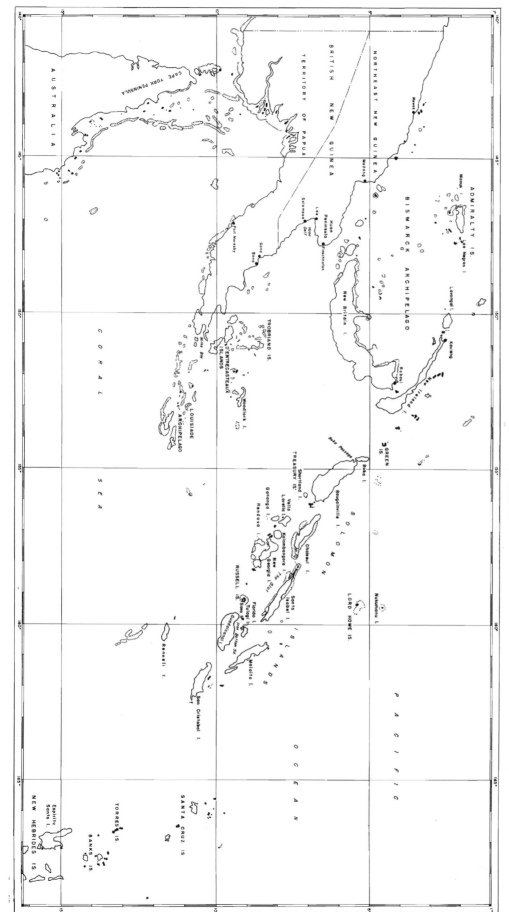

THE SOLOMON ISLANDS

36TH SEABEES ENROUTE TO BOUGAINVILLE
Leaving their base in Espiritu Santo on September 11, 1943, for new work in the Solomons

eastern end. The northeast coast, the most fertile and most thickly populated area, contained many coconut plantations; the population numbered about 14,000 mainly Melanesians. The climate was known to be unhealthful, with an average annual rainfall of about 164 inches.

The Japanese occupied Guadalcanal in May 1942, and immediately began the construction of a field on Lunga Point. It was this field which became the prime objective of our invasion. It was close to completion but not yet in operation when the assault forces of the 1st Marine Division struck the island on August 7. On August 9 the Marines captured it and immediately set about filling bomb craters to make the field usable by fighter planes. It was forthwith named Henderson Field, in honor of Major L. R. Henderson, USMC, a flier lost at the Battle of Midway two months previously. The completion of the field and its maintenance during the forthcoming combat period was the first-pri-

ority task of the 6th Construction Battalion, assigned to the operation.

Thirteen days after the Marines made their landing, the Civil Engineer Corps officer in charge of the 6th, flew to Guadalcanal from Espiritu Santo, where the battalion was being held pending the stabilization of the beachheads. After a quick tour of the area held by the Marines, to size up the situation the Seabees would have to face, he sent word for two companies to come forward immediately.

Henderson Field under fire.—The first contingent of the battalion, selected principally from companies A and D and consisting of 387 men and 5 officers, landed on Guadalcanal on September 1, 1942. They dug in immediately, in a narrow strip of coconut grove adjoining Henderson Field, and the next day a detail took over the construction and maintenance of the airfield. They found a runway 3,800 feet long by 150 feet wide, with 150 clearance zones adjacent to the flight strip. The field had been graded and rolled by the Japanese, but they had made no provision for drainage. Near the center of the strip, there was still about 600 feet not yet completely cleared and graded, but the Marine Engineers had done enough grading to make the runway usable for fighter planes. The soil was generally an unstable muck which had been corrected with a gravel base over a small portion of the field. Use of the uncompleted field by Navy and Marine fighter planes, combined with intermittent rainy weather, had created many bad ruts which had caused a number of plane crashes.

Construction work on the airfield consisted of clearing and grading an additional 1,300 feet of flight strip, building a crown on the existing runway, and surfacing with marston mat. Operations were complicated by the need to keep the field open for use at all times, despite frequent shellings and bombings from the Japanese, who made the field one of their prime targets.

Equipment available at the time for use on the field included two medium-duty bulldozers, six 1½-yard dump trucks, one road grader, one front-end loader, and, later on, a 5-yard carryall scraper and two small scrapers borrowed from the Marines. In addition, the Japanese had left eight small tandem rollers and 15 trucks. The Japanese also had left two 400-kva. diesel power units, hundreds of steel trusses for hangars, a complete radio, large quantities of cement, and other materials. Much of the enemy equipment was of an obsolete design; nevertheless, it was put to use.

The maintenance crew set to work filling and grading the ruts with a mixture of clay, rotten stone, and coral. Another crew began clearing the extension to the runway and building the crown. Hundreds of coconut palms were cut and the stumps blasted with Japanese powder. In locations where the soil was unsuitable for compaction, it was excavated to a depth of 21 inches and replaced with gravel, coral, and clay. Grading for the crown was difficult, for it was necessary to maintain at all times a smooth transition between the uncrowned portion of the runway and the 12-inch crown in order to permit continued plane operation.

The first large-scale laying of marston mat began on September 25, and about that time Flying Fortresses began to use the field. Small sections of mat which previously had been laid over unstable spots were removed, and the base conditions were corrected. Work was also commenced on the matting of taxiway stubs to hardstand areas.

During September, Japanese bombing and shelling threatened vital radio and radar equipment, all of which was surface housed, and it became necessary to get the equipment under ground as soon as possible. The 6th Battalion undertook tunneling operations into Pagoda Hill, just a few feet from Henderson Field. Because of the urgency of the situation, three eight-hour shifts were put to work. Air spades, air drills, and hand shovels were used and Japanese cars, on Japanese rails, were used to remove the spoil. On October 14, all equipment was moved from the Pagoda building on top of the hill into the tunnel, just before a new Japanese shelling took place. In all, four such tunnels were built by the Seabees.

In the early part of October, a Japanese offensive pushed the Marines back to the Lunga River at a point only 150 feet from the west end of the runway. With the Marines entrenched and fighting at one end of the field, the Seabees carried on construction at the other.

In addition to air raids, which at first occurred almost regularly every noon, there was minor sniping from adjacent hills and woods and the more serious annoyance of shelling from a six-inch artillery piece hidden in the hills, which had the range on Henderson Field.

On October 13, the enemy launched an all-out sea, air, and land assault in an attempt to retake the island. About 30 twin-engined Japanese bombers dropped their bombs on the airfield, scoring several direct hits on the bomber-strip. U. S. fighter planes took off immediately in pursuit. As soon as the last plane left the ground, the entire battalion turned out to assist in repairing the damage. Special trucks, loaded with gravel to fill the bomb craters, had been standing by for just such an emergency. Others carried equipment for repairing the marston mat. Peavies were used to pull the pins holding the mat sections together. Entire sections were replaced and fitted into the undamaged mat. As there were not enough shovels to supply all the men, many used their helmets to pick up earth fill and carry it to the bomb craters.

In the afternoon, a second flight of enemy bombers hit the field and repeated the morning's depredations. The men worked all afternoon to get Henderson Field back into service.

That night, star shells marked the beginning of a barrage of 14-inch and smaller shells from an

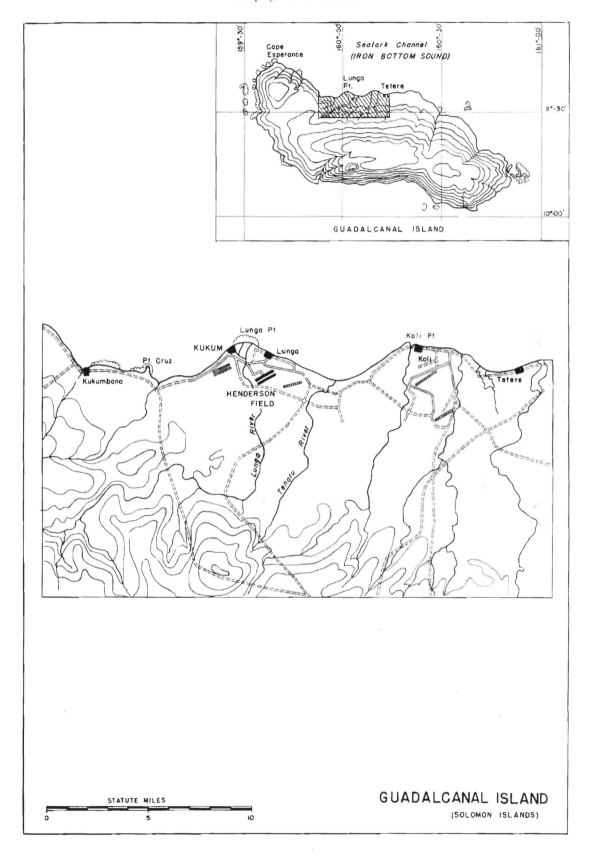

GUADALCANAL ISLAND
(SOLOMON ISLANDS)

STATUTE MILES

enemy fleet consisting of a battleship, cruisers, and destroyer escort. The shelling was followed by bombing from three waves of aircraft. The field received 21 holes in the mat. most of them from the shelling. Of 16 Flying Fortresses which were on the field, one was damaged by the enemy fire and one cut a tire on some torn mat in an attempted take-off and had to be abandoned. The remaining 14 avoided the shell craters and took off successfully, using only 2,600 feet of runway. Repairs to the damaged field began immediately after the Fortresses had taken off. Fortunately, the Japanese cruisers had used armor-piercing shells, and the holes in the field, although deep, were of relatively small diameter.

All the next day, the field was bombed again by enemy craft. The hidden artillery piece also kept sending in shells. Holes were put in the strip as fast as they could be repaired, and then repaired as fast as they were made. Nevertheless, our aircraft were able to use the field throughout the attacks.

Early on the morning of October 15, there was another 50 minutes of heavy shelling by enemy cruisers. and bombers again hit the runway. Within 48 hours the field had been hit 53 times.

On October 16 and 17, the field was again shelled and bombed.

Bombing and shelling continued through the latter part of October and November, but on a reduced scale. In the latter part of November, Henderson Field was turned over to the First Marine Aviation Engineers. At that time, 3,400 feet of mat had been laid and the remaining 1600 feet of the flight strip improved to serve heavy traffic without the necessity for marston mat.

It is the proud record of the Seabees that, despite shellings and bombings. the field was never out of operation for more than four hours and in emergencies was always usable by fighter planes.

To supplement Henderson Field, three secondary flight strips were built close by. Number One Field was a rolled-turf strip, 4,600 feet by 300 feet, constructed in three days, using Japanese equipment entirely. The bush was cut to a height of about 18 inches, hummocks were leveled, old foxholes were filled, and the field was rolled. At one time in October, this fighter strip served all air traffic, including B-17's, when artillery fire made the main field untenable. Number Two Field was a grading job accomplished with a single carryall

and one bulldozer which pulled some Jap trusses rigged into a drag. Number Three was a rolled-turf strip used only for dispersal. These last two strips were on the front line at the time of construction. Marine patrols set up emplacements and stood guard while the construction work was under way.

During the following summer, the 46th and 61st Construction Battalions further extended the main runway with a coral surface, making its total length 6,000 feet and its width 150 feet, with 75-foot shoulders. They also built a second runway. 5400 feet long and 150 feet wide, with 75-foot shoulders. This new runway was placed in operation on October 12, 1943. The field, at that time, had 250 hardstands, 54 with revetments. Taxiways, 80 feet wide, with 75-foot shoulders, were built. Some were surfaced with river gravel and steel mat. and others with coral.

Four more airfields on Guadalcanal. From the beginning, plans for the development of Guadalcanal into a major air base called for the construction of four airfields in addition to Henderson. On Lunga Point, where Henderson Field was located, two fighter fields were projected, one at Kukum and one at Lunga; about 8 miles to the east, on Koli Point, two bomber fields were to be built.

The 6th Battalion began the construction of two fighter runways at Kukum Field. Due to heavy evacuations of personnel, representing nearly half its strength, the battalion was relieved on December 1 by the First Marine Aviation Engineers. At that time, approximately 30 per cent of the subgrading for the runways had been completed. The first strip, coral-surfaced, was placed in operation on January 1, 1943.

An auxiliary strip was constructed by the 46th and 61st Construction Battalions in June-July 1943. It was coral surfaced, 4,000 feet long by 150 feet wide. with 75-foot shoulders. Coral taxiways, 80 feet wide, and 121 hardstands, 15 of them revetted, were also constructed.

On December 5. 1942. the 14th Construction Battalion, which had landed at Koli Point. early in November, in the wake of a small detachment of Marine raiders. began work on an emergency fighter strip at Carney Field, one of the bomber fields built in the Koli Point area. The strip was completed in two weeks, and on December 23, construction was started on the main bomber runway, to be 6,500 feet long and 150 feet wide, with a steel

BUILDING A NEW FIGHTER STRIP ON GUADALCANAL
Seabees laying steel mat on strip No. 1 at Kukum Field

mat surface. On February 3, the construction force was augmented by the 2nd Marine Aviation Engineers, who had arrived at Guadalcanal on January 30.

Heavy rain and day alerts hampered the construction work, but on March 21, an Army night-fighter squadron began using the field; heavy bombardment units began operations on April 1.

Reconstruction work at later dates by the 810th Army Engineers, 873rd Airborne Engineers, and the 26th and 46th Construction Battalions provided the field with three main taxiways, five cross-overs, and 85 hardstands for heavy bombers.

Construction of Lunga Field for fighter planes was started on December 27, 1942, by the 18th Construction Battalion, which had arrived at Guadalcanal two weeks earlier. A request was made to finish construction with all possible speed, but, due to bad weather, the field was not usable until February 9. By this date, the runway, 4,000 feet long and 150 feet wide, of steel mat on a gravel base, and one taxiway were complete. Two squadrons immediately began operating, and by March 7, four squadrons were in operation. An additional taxiway and 110 hardstands for light bombers were later constructed at the field by the 46th and 61st Construction Battalions.

Koli bomber field was constructed during a period when emergency fields for fighters were no longer needed and, therefore, was not put to use until the runway for heavy bombers was completed in October 1943. Work was started on May 22 by the

UNLOADING GAS AND OIL DRUMS ON THE BEACH AT BOUGAINVILLE

61st Construction Battalion. The strip, 7,000 feet by 500 feet, was built of river gravel with a marston mat surface on a silty soil base. Under heavy bomber loads many failures of the mat occurred, traceable to the poor nature of the sub-soil. Emergency repairs were made to permit uninterrupted operation of planes, by filling coral under the mat to provide adequate support. A new site, with a heavy blanket of stabilized soil, was chosen 300 yards northwest of the original strip, and the original strip was reconstructed. The project was under the direction of the 61st Construction Battalion, with additional equipment and men from ten other outfits, both Army and Navy, at various times. The 2nd Marine Aviation Engineers built the south taxiway system, a taxiway connecting with Carney Field, and 101 heavy bomber hardstands were provided.

Tank farms for the Airfield.—Concurrent with construction of the airfields was the erection of tank farms. Late in October 1942, work was begun by the 6th Battalion on three 250-barrel tanks for aviation gas at Henderson Field. Up to that time, fuel drums had been loaded from cargo vessels to landing barges, unloaded at the beach, and thence transported by trucks to fuel dumps near the airfield. Such operations were costly of man power, and at times it was impossible to furnish enough fuel by this method to satisfy operating requirements. The three tanks were located so that it was possible to roll drums from the trucks onto a rack and to empty them into a trough discharging into the tank. Fuel for use on the field was drawn from the tanks into tank trucks. In December, additional storage volume was provided through the erection of one 1,000-barrel and two

10,000-barrel prefabricated steel tanks. The final step in the construction of the tank farm was the laying of a 6-inch welded pipe line connecting a distributing point on the beach to the various tanks.

The 26th Battalion erected two additional 10,000-barrel aviation-gasoline tanks and nine 1,000-barrel aviation-gasoline tanks for Henderson Field and the supplementary fighter strips. At Kukum they built a tank farm providing storage for two million gallons of aviation gasoline, one million gallons of motor gasoline, and 42,000 gallons of diesel oil.

In March 1943, a detachment of 260 men from the 34th Battalion, stationed at Tulagi, was ordered to Guadalcanal to take over the building of a 36,000-barrel tank farm at Koli Point, begun by the 14th and 46th Battalions. The tank farm, with a total capacity of 1,300,000 gallons of aviation gasoline and 500,000 gallons of motor gasoline in thirty-five 1,000-barrel tanks and one 10,000-barrel tank, was completed by May. The tanks were well dispersed and concealed in heavy jungle growth in seven groupings. A submarine line was installed to moorings off Koli Point to permit tankers to discharge their cargoes into the storage tanks.

Waterfront Facilities.—When our forces landed on Guadalcanal, waterfront facilities were virtually non-existent. Unloading from ships to beaches was accomplished by means of light landing-craft, tank lighters, and pontoon barges. Working parties of Marines and the 6th Seabees generally did their own unloading, except during critical periods when the Marines had to man the front lines. Initially, coconut-log ramps, about 35 feet long and wide enough to accommodate a truck, were constructed, extending far enough offshore to float a landing craft at the outer end. Later, three timber piers were built. The first was constructed by repairing an old enemy pier at Kukum, using creosoted telephone poles left by the Japanese. On the day that the pier was completed, enemy artillery got range on the area, forcing its temporary abandonment, and the pier was left unused for quite a while. To substitute for it, two other small piers were constructed at Lunga.

During 1943, harbor facilities were considerably extended. The Seabees assembled pontoon barges to aid in unloading, and built finger piers at various locations around the island. Two T-shaped piers, having 40-foot water depth at their outboard ends, were constructed at Kukum. A pier to accommodate Liberty ships was also built at Point Cruz.

Three (Special) construction battalions arrived during 1943—the 1st in March, the 4th in May, and the 9th in August—to handle stevedoring operations and pontoon assembly. Later, the 2nd (Special) and the 11th (Special) were assigned to Guadalcanal. One Army port battalion and four amphibious truck companies also handled unloading operations.

Road Construction. Initially, road construction on Guadalcanal was delayed by the pressing necessity to complete the airfields and by a shortage of equipment. When the 6th Battalion was relieved of airfield construction, about the middle of November 1942, its attention was turned to road construction. No attempt was made to remove the layer of organic material which formed a sub-base for most of the roads, but a 12- to 18-inch clay blanket was placed over it, traffic-compacted, and surfaced with 6 inches of gravel. Later, the 14th and 26th Battalions, which arrived in the last two months of 1942, added some 96 miles of road to the 24 miles built by the 6th Battalion. At the peak of its development, Guadalcanal had about 135 miles of roads with numerous bridges to permit access between airfields, dock and harbor installations, and camp areas. Furthermore, the 6th Battalion erected four major vehicle bridges, ranging in length from 90 feet to more than 200 feet. For the construction of the Lunga River bridge, which was originally a narrow, coconut-log structure built by the Japanese and not strong enough for trucks, the Seabees fabricated a pile driver from Japanese structural shapes. Work was begun on September 14, 1942, and was more than half completed by October 11. when high water washed out the old bridge and carried it into the new construction, shearing off two piles and tumbling the pile driver into the river. This occurred just before the major Japanese offensive to retake the island on October 13. Because of the immediate need for a river crossing, the Seabees set to work salvaging lumber from the wrecked bridge and used it, in combination with empty fuel drums, to construct a temporary pontoon bridge. During the action of October 13-15, the bridge was used by traffic bearing casualties to the dressing stations at the rear and carrying ammunition to the front. It was kept in use until the new bridge, 225 feet long, with a 20-foot roadway, was completed on October 25.

By December 5, the 6th Battalion had also built

PIVA BOMBER FIELD, BOUGAINVILLE
Men of the 71st Seabees at work, January 23, 1944

the Tenaru River bridge, 209 feet in length, with a 20-foot roadway. By that time the supply of Japanese timber had been used up, and it was necessary to hew many of the timbers from trees cut in the nearby jungle.

It was found that the pile trestle structures were regularly washed out by floods, so later bridges were constructed using high-level pontoon spans supported on pile abutments without intermediate supports. The upper Lunga River bridge, completed by the 61st Battalion in January 1944, and the Malambu River bridge were of this type.

One of the interesting tasks of the Seabees at Guadalcanal was the construction of the "Guadalcanal - Bougainville - Tokyo Railway," 1.22 miles long, in three days by the 26th Battalion. In two more days, the pier terminus of the railway was completed.

Hospitals.—The principal naval medical facilities at Guadalcanal consisted of the 1290-bed hospital for MOB 8, supplemented by a 300-bed hospital for Acorn 1. The work of the Seabees in hospital construction was severely hampered by lack of building materials. To take care of the situation, temporary structures were improvised out of native material to accommodate the overflow of patients until permanent surgical facilities and other requirements could be completed.

Repair and Storage Facilities.—Repair facilities established on Guadalcanal were limited. By November 1943, an aviation repair and overhaul unit had been placed in operation to handle necessary repairs to structural sections of aircraft, manufacture sheet-metal parts, and repair stationary and moveable control surfaces. Boat repair units at Lunga Point and Koli Point were equipped to handle repairs and to overhaul engines for small boats and landing craft.

Quonset huts and 40-foot arch-rib warehouses were constructed by the Seabees for Navy and Army aviation supplies, for a naval supply depot, and for a medical supply depot. In July 1943, a Navy construction-materials depot was set up to supply all construction battalions with much-needed spare parts for repair of their equipment and with expendable materials used in construction. All construction battalions on Guadalcanal at the time furnished personnel to set up this activity, which was in operation within a month.

Malaria Control. The plan to use Guadalcanal for extensive staging operations was greatly handicapped by malaria, which rose to epidemic proportions with the rainy season. Accordingly, 14 officers and 650 men of the 63rd Battalion, which had arrived on June 11, 1943, were assigned to malaria control. With the assistance of native labor, Seabees removed logs, roots, and overhanging trees from the banks of streams and lagoons and submerged snags from the beds. In small streams, this brought about an increase in the rate of flow so that breeding of the anopheles mosquito was checked. In the case of lagoons or the larger, slower-moving streams, clearing their banks permitted easier access for the oiling crews on their periodic missions. In endeavoring to free lagoons on the flat coastal plains from anophelene larvae, it was necessary to surmount the obstacle of sandbars by devising a method to permit egress of infected lagoon water to the sea. Control methods included the clearing of the banks and the installation of culverts, fabricated from discarded oil drums, through the sandbars. The culverts permitted tidal fluctuations alternately to raise and lower the level of the lagoon, flushing it with sea water—an effective breeding preventive. In smaller, sluggish-flowing streams, a rapid cleansing was accomplished by impounding water behind semi-automatic flush dams and releasing it quickly when the water had reached a desired height.

Complete swamp drainage on Guadalcanal was found to be impossible; therefore, the swamps were ditched so that the water could collect in pools, where it could be oiled. More than 50 miles of ditches were dug by hand labor, dragline, and blasting.

Meanwhile, the remaining members of the 63rd Battalion were building dock facilities at Tetere

Beach. Using piling, caps, stringers, and decking obtained from the jungle, they erected a stage, 40 feet square, with a 12-foot driveway extending 60 feet to shore. A ramp on the seaward side facilitated unloading of heavy ordnance and equipment.

General experiences on Guadalcanal. The Seabees on Guadalcanal were subjected to intermittent air raids until the fall of 1943, but the most severe punishment was taken by the 6th Battalion during the first months of airfield construction. Other early battalions were under the constant strain that goes with frequent air raids, but they suffered no personnel losses.

Materials found on Guadalcanal were widely used on construction projects. River gravel, mixed with sand-clay silt as a binder, provided support for airstrip steel-mat surfacing. Decayed coral was later used for runways, taxiways, and hardstands. Gravel and some coral were used for road construction. Good hardwood, mahogany, rosewood, and teakwood furnished piling and timbers for wharves and bridges. Many offices and warehouses were built of native poles, with side and roof materials procured from the coconut tree. The 61st Battalion, from June 1943 to January 1944, set up and operated two sawmills, which produced more than one million board feet of lumber, in addition to numerous piles for camp, bridge, and pier construction. The 46th and 26th Battalions also operated sawmills.

Native labor was used principally in stevedoring operations, handling material at cargo and ration dumps, building native-type structures for warehouses and offices, clearing and oiling streams for malaria control, and, during the early stages of construction, as common labor on airfield construction.

A total of seventeen construction battalions, including five special battalions, were assigned to Guadalcanal. By the end of 1942, the 14th, 18th, and 26th Battalions had reported to Guadalcanal, in addition to the original 6th which was transferred in January 1943. During 1943, the 34th, 46th, 61st, 63rd, 53rd, and 27th Battalions arrived, and the 1st, 4th, and 9th Specials. CBMU 501 took over part of the maintenance duties on Guadalcanal in March 1943, and during the early months of 1944, four maintenance units, CBMU's 532, 533, 518, and 520, assumed responsibility for maintenance and minor construction activities. By that time, all battalions, with the exception of the Specials, had been withdrawn. The 18th, 25th, and 58th Battalions staged through Guadalcanal with Marine divisions, and numerous other Seabee groups were at Guadalcanal for staging activities prior to forward movements to the upper Solomons.

The naval air base on Guadalcanal was disestablished on June 12, 1946.

Tulagi

Concurrent with the building up of the large base on Guadalcanal, Tulagi, across Iron Bottom Sound and part of the Florida Island group, was developed as a small naval base. It provided a well-protected harbor where large ships could anchor, and facilities were established for the reserve storage of fuel and diesel oil, and for the support of seaplanes, landing craft, and motor torpedo boats.

Tulagi, with a circumference of about 3 miles, was the seat of government for the British Protectorate of the Solomons.

In October 1942, a detachment of 59 men of the 6th Battalion was sent from Guadalcanal to Tulagi to build a PT-boat base at Sesapi. The strength of the detachment was later increased to 133 officers and men. First, an emergency outlet channel for Tulagi harbor was dredged and blasted to avoid having PT boats bottled up by enemy warships. Two PT-boat floating drydocks were assembled from pontoons; a 500-man camp was set up; and power and telephone systems to serve the island and harbor area were installed. The detachment also furnished a number of carpenter details to assist with the maintenance and repair of PT boats.

By August 1943, the facilities at the Sesapi base had been augmented to provide more shop facilities and storage areas, to permit major PT-boat overhaul. A repair and service unit was set up able to support 40 PT boats in combat operations. The Seabees also built three small wharves for PT boats. Much of this later work was done by the 27th Battalion.

In addition, PT-boat facilities were constructed on the island of Macambo, with base housing at Calvertville on Florida Island. An existing concrete wharf at Macambo, in need of repair but still serviceable, was used, but it was necessary to build torpedo overhaul and storage facilities.

In July 1943, PT Squadrons 1, 3, and 8 were using the Sesapi and Macambo bases. Two 1,000-barrel tanks for aviation gasoline were erected at Sesapi, and eight 1,000-barrel tanks at Macambo, with loading line to the dock.

Halavo seaplane base.— Before leaving the Tulagi area in January 1943, the 6th Battalion detachment began construction of a seaplane base at Halavo on Florida Island; the completion of this base became the major task of the 34th Battalion when it arrived on Tulagi on February 12, 1943.

A tent camp was erected for 1500 men and 300 officers. In planning for the seaplane facilities, due to the shortage of cement, it was decided to use steel mat on the ramps and apron. A temporary mat ramp, 25 feet wide, had been completed when priorities for work at Halavo were reduced in May to allow concentration on work in the Russells and on Guadalcanal. Priorities were then established as follows: (1) base roads, (2) a 12,000-barrel tank farm, (3) a small apron without mat.

Toward the end of June, a squadron of 15 PBY's was added to the scouting squadron already operating from the base, and another temporary ramp of steel mat was laid for their use. Construction of the tank farm was completed, including a filling line to the beach and a delivery line to the ramp. Thirty wooden buildings for administration and shops were constructed as fast as the output of the local sawmill permitted.

The marston-mat ramps were considered wholly satisfactory in service, and it was estimated that their substitution for concrete saved about two months' construction time.

In late 1943, the scope of the Halavo base was revised upward, the new plan calling for an increase in apron area, structures more permanent than the original canvas-covered ones, and the reconstruction of housing facilities. Two ramps of marston mat, 50 feet wide, and a coral apron, 150 feet by 850 feet, were installed. Dock facilities were constructed, consisting of a small-boat wharf, 16 feet by 72 feet, and a boat refueling wharf, 6 feet by 50 feet. Twelve screened frame wards with canvas roofing were provided for a 200-bed base hospital.

In September, ten quonset huts, 20 feet by 48 feet, were erected for quarters. The aviation-gasoline tank farm was filled to capacity through the newly completed sea-loading line. By December 1943, three PBY squadrons occupied the base, and the scouting squadron had been moved forward.

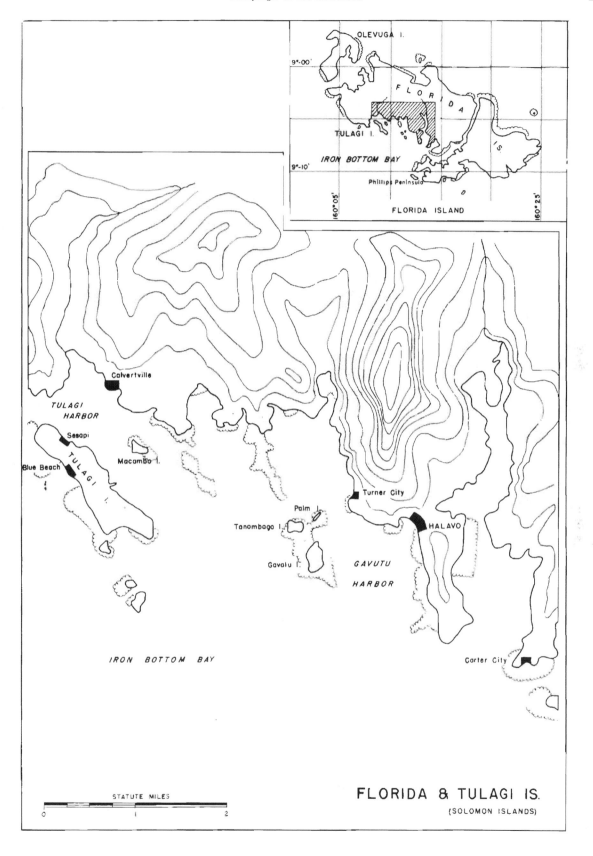

FLORIDA & TULAGI IS.

(SOLOMON ISLANDS)

Work Shops and Marine Railway at the Landing-craft Repair Base. Carter City
Note concrete gutters and ramps and crowned streets

New housing facilities and quonset huts for NATS storage and office facilities were erected.

Tank farms.—One of the major projects at Tulagi was the erection of tank-farm facilities. In addition to smaller farms provided at the different activities in the area, the 34th Battalion erected a large farm, together with two fuel piers, on Phillips Peninsula, on Florida Island, to serve the Fleet. Tanks with a 10,000-barrel capacity were used, 28 for fuel oil, 5 for diesel oil. The task was completed by March 15, 1944.

Landing-craft repair base.—On April 22, 1943, instructions were received calling for the establishment of a base for landing craft in the Tulagi area. The base was to be self-sustaining and mobile, in the sense that disassembly and reshipment of its

facilities to forward areas and resumption of normal operation could be accomplished with a minimum of delay. The base was to be capable of keeping 80 landing craft in repair.

The base called for was established by the 27th Battalion at Carter City on Florida Island, between April and August 1943. Warehouses, tropical-hut housing for officers and men, and other camp facilities were provided. One 350-ton, 6-by-24-pontoon drydock for LCI's was assembled. On August 22, 1943, the operation of the repair base was taken over by CBD 1008.

The 27th Battalion also constructed facilities on Gavutu Harbor for the functioning of two amphibious boat repair and training centers and the training of their crews prior to forward-area assignment.

The base at Turner City, on Florida Island, included camp facilities for 400 men and officers, a pier, 10 feet by 130 feet, a 2-by-12 pontoon finger pier for small craft, and two steel arch-rib warehouses to be used as shops. At the base on Gavutu, steel arch-rib buildings were erected for shops and two 10,000-barrel aviation-gasoline tanks were built concealed in a hillside. An existing concrete wharf, 125 feet by 150 feet, providing 20-foot-draft berthing space, was repaired and equipped with a marine railway. These facilities were essentially completed by August 1943. In December, the 34th Battalion installed a second marine railway on Gavutu and practically doubled the capacity of the boat nest for small landing craft. The boat nests consisted of rows of piling driven in 50-foot squares with heavy steel mooring cables stretched across the top of the piles. Supporting facilities for the Gavutu base, including a 10,000-barrel diesel fuel tank,

were built on the adjoining islands, Tanombago and Palm.

Hospital Facilities.—Illness was even more prevalent on Tulagi than on Guadalcanal. Medical facilities, as established, consisted of a 200-bed hospital at the Halavo seaplane base and the "Blue Beach" Hospital on Tulagi. The first 200-bed unit at Blue Beach, consisting of 35 quonset huts originally part of Cub 2, was completed by the 27th Battalion in May 1943. In August, plans to expand the hospital to a 450-bed unit were formulated, but because of materials shortages, the expansion was not completed until November.

Waterfront facilities.—Waterfront facilities at Tulagi Harbor were improved and extended by the Seabees. The 6th Battalion installed a five-ton stiff-leg derrick, built from Japanese structural steel and powered by a salvaged Japanese automobile engine, on Government Wharf, and the

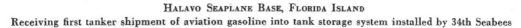

HALAVO SEAPLANE BASE, FLORIDA ISLAND
Receiving first tanker shipment of aviation gasoline into tank storage system installed by 34th Seabees

wharf, built of timber, was enlarged by the 27th Battalion. The 27th also constructed Sturgess Wharf, with a 140-foot face and 40-foot water depth.

The Seabees assembled pontoon barges to aid in unloading operations. In October 1943, Company B of the 9th (Special) Construction Battalion arrived at Tulagi for stevedoring activities. A salvage wharf was built at Tulagi with piling, framing, and decking cut by the 27th Construction Battalion logging and sawmill crews on Florida Island.

General experiences on Tulagi. — Native hard woods, produced by the Seabees' logging and sawmill activities, were extensively used at Tulagi.

Logging was an unusually difficult operation, for the men had to work in mud all day, guarding themselves against crocodiles, poisonous vines, and fungus infection.

The Japanese did not bomb Tulagi until February 1943, after the close of the Guadalcanal campaign. However, from that time until the following June, the Seabees were subjected to occasional air raids. Men of the 27th Battalion were given partial credit for the downing of three Japanese planes.

When CBMU 521 reported at Tulagi in December 1943, all the Seabees had left with the exception of the 34th. That battalion was relieved by CBMU 505 in March 1944.

In early 1945, when the Solomons area was well

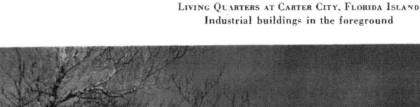

LIVING QUARTERS AT CARTER CITY, FLORIDA ISLAND
Industrial buildings in the foreground

FLORIDA ISLAND CHAPEL

behind the front lines the CBMU's secured several of the activities and crated usable materials for use in forward areas.

Russell Islands

After the Japanese evacuated Guadalcanal, the next phase of the Solomons campaign, the ejection of the enemy from New Georgia, began. On February 21, 1943, Seabees landed in the Russell Islands to construct an air and naval base to lend support.

The Russell Islands, which lie northwest of Guadalcanal, consist of two principal islands, Banika and Pavuvu, and a number of islets.

The topography of Banika Island, where most of the naval development took place, was highly favorable for the projected facilities. Well-drained

shore areas, deep water, protected harbors, and lack of malaria made it a good location for a base to support landing craft, PT boats, and small craft. The gently sloping terrain and well-drained coral subsoil facilitated construction.

Airfield construction.—The major portion of the 33rd Battalion departed from Guadalcanal for the Russell Islands on February 20, 1943, on LCT's and LST's, with whatever equipment could be put aboard. Immediately upon arrival, they started work on the fighter strip. Progress was slow, due to inadequate equipment and lack of personnel, but by April 13 the emergency landing of a P38 was possible. On April 20, 1943, the 35th Battalion, which had followed the 33rd, in early March, was given the task of completing a strip 3100 feet long by 150 feet wide, in twenty days. A detachment of

33RD SEABEES WORKING ON BANIKA AIRFIELD IN THE RUSSELLS
This photograph was taken March 13, 1943

200 men from the 34th Battalion with much of that battalion's heavy equipment was also brought to Banika to help rush the work. The strip was surfaced with coral, which was available in abundance. By early June, in addition to the main runway, a taxiway, two warm-up areas, 60 feet by 450 feet, and 25 revetments for Airstrip No. 1 had been completed.

During June, the 35th Battalion completed the construction of a second 4500-foot strip, with a taxiway and dispersal areas for 60 planes. Work was then started on the lengthening of the first strip to 6,000 feet to make it suitable for medium bombers, and on a bomber taxiway. The hardstands had to be reconstructed to allow them to accommodate heavier aircraft, and more had to be provided.

The two fields were used by the Army Air Force planes in their attacks on enemy positions in New Georgia.

In conjunction with the construction of the airstrips, the Seabees also erected quonset huts and dallas huts for use as quarters, galley, mess halls, offices, operations building, and dispensaries at each field.

Tank farms.—By May 1943, the 33rd Battalion had erected an aviation-gasoline tank farm of eight 1,000-barrel tanks, together with piping and fittings, for Airstrip 1. A second tank farm of six 1,000-barrel tanks, completed in June for Airstrip 2, was connected to the landing dock by a 1,200-foot pipe line.

Enemy bombing on June 25, 1943 caused considerable damage to Tank Farm 1. One tank was set on fire and was completely destroyed; three others were punctured by shrapnel. The piping was also damaged. Repairs were completed in five days. Gasoline service to the airfield was maintained without interruption.

In July, five more tanks were added at Tank Farm 1 and four at Tank Farm 2.

Waterfront facilities.—Development of waterfront facilities at Banika was begun by the 35th Battalion immediately upon its arrival in March 1943. An existing wharf on Renard Sound was

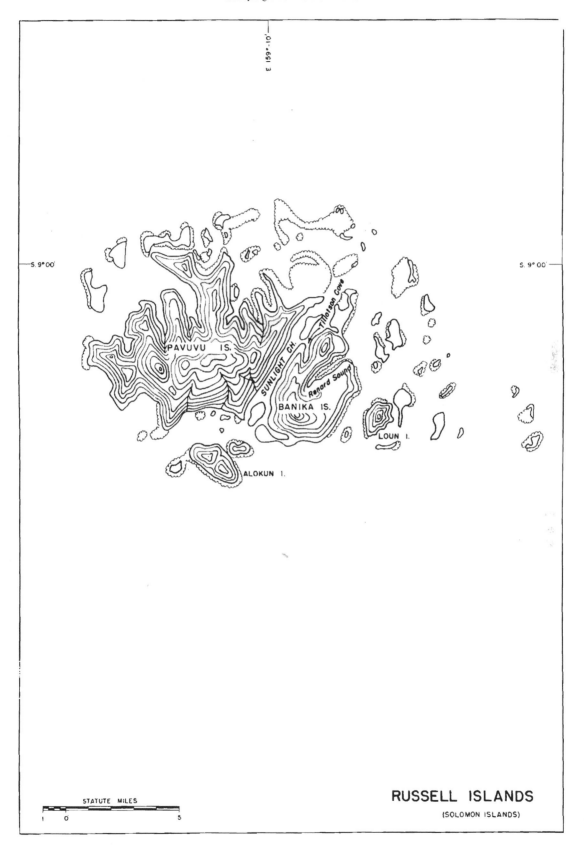

STATUTE MILES

RUSSELL ISLANDS

(SOLOMON ISLANDS)

ADVANCE BASE CONSTRUCTION DEPOT, BANIKA ISLAND
This photograph was taken August 15th, 1944. when the 67-acre depot was approximately seventy-five per cent complete

lengthened to 300 feet, the storage area was enlarged, and dock-access roads were relocated and widened. The 35th also maintained and operated pontoon barges across Renard Sound and to Pavuvu Island, and constructed a barge landing on Pavuvu.

Excellent berthing was developed for LST's and LCT's at Blue Beach and Yellow Beach. Deep water existed close inshore and by building coconut-log bulkheads, backfilled with coral, berthing space having a minimum depth of 3 feet was provided so that the shallow vessels could come to shore and drop their ramps.

In September 1943, the 36th Battalion came to Banika for the purpose of developing transship-

ment facilities. Twin floating pontoon wharves were assembled at Tillotson Cove. Each wharf was 432 feet long and had five bridges connecting it with the shore. The water depth at the outboard edges of the wharves was enough to allow the berthing of the largest ships. Tidal swamps also were cleared at Tillotson Cove for LST and LCT landings. When completed in November 1943, each area was capable of berthing at least six landing craft. Eight standard 40-by-100-foot steel arch-rib buildings were erected for transshipment warehouses. and 50 quonset huts for a transshipment camp.

During the fall of 1943, stevedoring operations were handled by detachments of the 6th and the

9th (Special) Battalions. From early 1944, the 11th and the 12th (Special) Battalions were responsible for those activities.

Road construction.—Considerable time was spent in road construction and maintenance. In March 1943, the 35th Battalion laid out and constructed a two-lane road from Blue Beach around Banika Island, and in the months that followed other coral-surfaced roads were built to connect the various activities on the island.

Hospitals.—The first medical facilities on Banika consisted of several large hospital tents. By May 1943, the 33rd Battalion had supplemented these with two timber-frame hospital wards to accommodate 60 patients, a surgery building, and an underground surgery.

In June 1943, four 35-patient wards were built for a naval dispensary, completely screened, and equipped with emergency battle dressing stations that could be blacked out. An operating room was also constructed. In August, additional construction

was authorized, including a dental laboratory and administration building, two additional wards, and an officers' mess.

Construction was started in December 1943, on a 1300-bed hospital for MOB 10, by the 93rd Battalion, which had arrived in the Russells in November. To meet a completion deadline of March 1, 1944, personnel from the 15th Battalion assisted the 93rd by working on the plumbing and electrical installations, and doctors and hospital corpsmen aided in the erection of the prefabricated-steel building, 20 feet wide and 250 feet long.

Construction facilities.—Late in 1943 several battalions cooperated in constructing the steel arch-rib warehouses for an advance base construction depot annex at Banika. A pontoon assembly depot was also established. In January 1944, the second section of the 20th Battalion arrived to operate the ABCD annex. Operations included the receiving and storage of incoming material; assembly and shipping of outgoing material; uncrating and

ACORN 15 MESSHALL, BOUGAINVILLE, MAY 9, 1944

assembly of jeeps, command cars. water trailers, and fire pumps; erecting, checking, and servicing of cranes, shovels, and bulldozers: and the maintenance of an accurate stock inventory. In June 1944, the first section of the 20th Battalion also arrived. That same month, the 24th Battalion undertook an enlargement of the annex. In January 1945, its operation was taken over by CBMU 501.

In December, the personnel of PAD 2 arrived to operate the pontoon assembly depot which had been constructed by the 93rd Battalion the previous month. CBD 1054 assisted in the operation during the summer of 1944.

One of the most important activities of the 33rd Battalion was the establishment and operation of a sawmill to augment the meager supply of finished lumber available for construction. This mill furnished about 4,000 board feet of lumber daily. However, suitable timber was neither plentiful nor easily accessible. Logging had to be conducted in a jungle difficult to penetrate; trails were cut through by bulldozers, and tractors and bulldozers were used to drag the logs to the mill. In August 1943, demands for lumber became too great for the 33rd alone to supply, and two other battalions also provided logging crews. By October 1943, Banika Island had been practically cleaned out of suitable timber.

The abundant coral supply of the island was used extensively to surface airstrips, roads, and storage areas. In December 1943, the 93rd Battalion set up a ready-mix concrete plant, which greatly increased concrete production while at the same time saving a considerable amount of labor.

The Seabees on Banika were subjected to the constant strain of air attacks until the close of the New Georgia campaign in July 1943. They helped man the 20-mm guns around the island and suffered several casualties. including four men killed.

Most of the construction on Banika was carried out during 1943 by five battalions. In 1944, seven other battalions undertook the construction of additional facilities. The first CBMU arrived in September 1943. During 1944, CBMU's 503, 571, 572, 573. 501. and 580 arrived, and, after the departure of CBMU 503, in January 1945, CBMU 550 took its place.

During the early months of 1945, the maintenance units began dismantling some of the facilities, including MOB 10. All structural parts were marked and packed to facilitate setting up at a new station. Parts found usable were cleaned and repainted. and crated for transshipment. The salvage operation required approximately four months.

New Georgia Group

Our occupation of the New Georgia group in the Solomon Islands took place between June 30 and August 5, 1943. Its purpose was to remove the threat of the Japanese-held airfield at Munda Point and to provide an air and naval base to support further moves into the northern Solomons.

The New Georgia group consists of several large and many small islands. occupying an area about 150 miles long and 40 miles wide. The islands are mountainous, their indented coastlines affording numerous excellent harbors and protected anchorages. New Georgia. the principal island of the group, is about 45 miles long and 20 miles wide at its broadest point. Two other large islands with strategic significance were Rendova, south of New Georgia Island. and Kolombangara to the west of it.

Seabees participated in the assault landings which took place on June 30, 1943, at three different points simultaneously, two on New Georgia—at Segi Point, at the southern end of the island and at Viru Harbor on the southwest coast and one on Rendova.

Segi Point.—In the wake of two small reconnaissance parties, 17 officers and 477 men of the 47th Battalion landed at Segi Point. No enemy resistance was encountered and unloading operations were begun immediately. Before the day was over work was started on clearing an airstrip and preparing revetments.

Nearly continuous rains for the first seventeen days slowed up work on the airstrip and made construction of roads almost impossible. The soil was largely clay, exceptionally difficult to work when wet. Coral was scarce and what little there was had a high content of clay, and consequently drained poorly. Work on the airstrip was carried on night and day until July 18, when enemy air raids seriously retarded night work. By that time, however, the field had been completed to a usable width of 150 feet and length of 3300 feet. By the end of July, two taxi loops with 28 hardstands were complete. Continuous enemy bombing resulted in one casualty, several cases of war neurosis, and damage to several pieces of equipment.

During that first month most of the battalion's

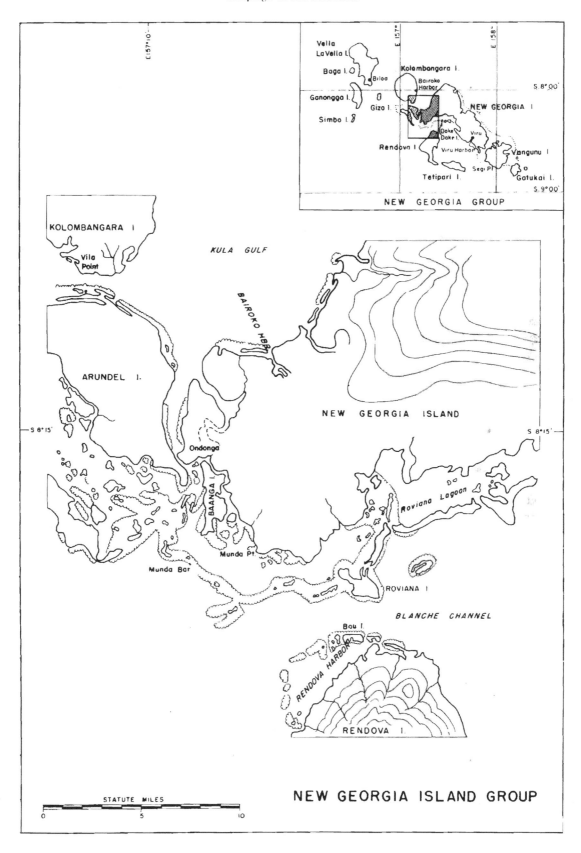

NEW GEORGIA ISLAND GROUP

remaining personnel arrived at Segi Point. They
cleared and graded about two miles of road and
built one permanent and two temporary LCT
wharfs for unloading operations. Permanent camp
facilities were constructed, and a saw mill was set
up and put into operation.

In August, the field was widened to 200 feet and
provided with an all-weather coral-surfaced runway; its shoulders were widened; and warmup
areas were graded and surfaced. Two 42,000-gallon

SEABEES LAYING PIERCED PLANK AT BOUGAINVILLE

aviation gasoline tanks were constructed and put
in use.

The roads, which had been constructed so hurriedly during July, were almost impassable in a
few months, in consequence of the rains and the
heavy traffic. Pit coral proved unsatisfactory for
road construction because of its high clay content,
but satisfactory coral was dredged from the sea by
draglines working from the beach. The coral was
placed two to nine feet thick, to assure roads capable of withstanding rains and heavy traffic.

In September the Segi Point airstrip was extended 150 feet; the parking areas were enlarged; and
52 hardstands were completed. A 30-ton marine
railway was constructed, and two self-propelled
pontoon barges were assembled. The Seabees then
constructed a pontoon pier to accommodate ships
with drafts up to 15 feet, and a 90-foot log ramp for
small landing craft.

By December 1943, about 75 per cent of the

battalion had been moved to Munda. CBMU 580
arrived in November 1943, and assumed responsibility for all maintenance and construction.

Rendova

On June 30, 1943, the same day as the Segi Point
landing, the first echelon of the 24th Battalion
accompanied the 172nd infantry in a landing on
Rendova. The assault was met by Japanese fire,
but bulldozers immediately set to work to cut
roads into the jungle. After enemy snipers had
been driven back into the jungle the transports
were unloaded and then left the harbor.

The Seabees in their road work immediately
encountered extremely difficult ground conditions.
After four or five passages by heavy vehicles over
the marshy terrain, movement became difficult or
impossible. Steel-mesh proved useless after the
passage of eight or ten trucks, and even tractors
bogged down in two to three feet of mud.

The day following the landings the Army and
Marines requested that roads be built so that they
might move their howitzers and anti-aircraft guns
and have access to their ammunition dumps and
bivouac areas. The Seabees then cut down coconut
trees, sawed them into 12-foot lengths, and used
them to build corduroy roads. This was slow work,
however, and even then gave only one-lane passage.
That day, an air attack caused the loss of three
bulldozers and much of the battalion's galley
equipment. Battalion casualties included two officers and 18 enlisted men dead and eight enlisted
men missing. Wounded were evacuated to Guadalcanal.

The Seabees continued to construct and maintain
corduroy roads to assist in the unloading and dispersal on the beaches during the eight days required to secure Rendova. Rainy weather aggra-
vated transportation difficulties. Heavy Japanese
bombing attacks were daily occurrences while skir-
mishing and sniping continued. However, the
corduroy roads permitted the Marines to move
heavy artillery to points from which they could
bring the Japanese stronghold at Munda Point
under fire. By August 1 the entire 24th Battalion
had reached Rendova; on the 15th it moved across
the channel to Munda.

Viru Harbor.—At the third of those June 30th
landings, the one at Viru Harbor, the first echelon
of the 20th Seabees accompanied the landing,
having been assigned the task of building a base
for PT boats. They attempted to enter the harbor

but were driven off by enemy fire. On July 2, they returned and landed after the harbor had been secured by the assault troops. Meanwhile, the second echelon had landed successfully on the west bank of the harbor on July 1. The third echelon landed on July 3.

The Seabees immediately commenced unloading operations. They improved and extended an exist-

Quonset Hut Erected by 73rd Seabees for Field Operations at Munda

ing road and built a new one along the beach to provide for transferral of cargo. A sector of the main defense line was assigned to the detachment, and machine-gun emplacements and rifle pits were constructed and camouflaged. Extensive barbed-wire entanglements were strung in front of the line and fitted with booby traps.

The original plan for the establishment of a PT-boat base was abandoned because the harbor was found to be unsuitable. However, the Seabees remained at Viru Harbor until October, to carry out minor construction projects and maintenance. A marine railway was constructed for the repair of small landing craft, and an existing wharf, 50 feet by 30 feet, was rehabilitated, using earth and coral fill held by coconut-log cribbing.

Munda Point. Immediately after the capture of Munda on August 5, 1943, the 73rd and 24th Battalions began repairing the battle damage to the airfield. The Japanese had surfaced the runway with coral over an area 150 feet by 3,000 feet, but the remainder was overgrown with grass and was soft. By August 13, the strip was ready for use; taxiways and 50 hardstands were ready the next day, when 48 planes arrived for permanent basing

on the field. Four aviation-gasoline issuing points were installed, pontoons, supported by coconut-logs, serving as tanks.

One company of the 47th Battalion, the 828th Aviation Engineers, and the 131st Army Engineers were assigned to Munda to expedite completion of the airfield, which was ready for bomber operations before October 15. By December, the runway had been extended to 8,000 feet, and taxiways had been built along both sides. Quonset huts served for operations buildings, mess halls, and galleys; personnel were housed under canvas.

The construction of a hospital for Acorn 8, and one for Cub 3, was completed in October 1943. Lumber for these structures was produced at the 73rd Battalion's sawmill. The production of the mill was limited, however, by the inadequacy of its power unit, which had difficulty driving the saw through the hard native woods.

In addition to the construction of aviation facilities, the Seabees were responsible for several other projects. In October 1943, the 24th Battalion completed the erection of an aviation-gasoline tank farm of eight 1,000-barrel tanks and one 10,000-barrel tank. Housing was also provided for various naval base activities, as well as numerous steel arch-rib warehouses for the supply depot.

In November 1943, the 73rd Battalion completed the deepening of the channel through Munda Bar to provide a 300-foot channel, 15 feet deep, for passage of LST's and similar craft. Deepening of the channel to 35 feet was completed in April 1944, the 73rd and 47th Battalions cooperating on dredging and blasting. The Seabees also added to the pier facilities on Roviana Lagoon. By November 1943, Companies A and D of the 9th (Special) Construction Battalion had reported to New Georgia for stevedoring operations.

On Ondonga Island, near Munda Point, the 82nd and the 37th Battalions constructed an air and naval base. Ondonga presented many obstacles to construction dense jungle covering a mud bog. Construction of airstrips and roads required excavation down to the natural coral surface, and filling to grade with compacted crushed coral. Here, the Seabees worked against mud and time, under the strain of periodic shelling from Japanese-held Kolombangara Island and intermittent bombing by Japanese planes based on Bougainville.

Nevertheless, they successfully completed a fighter strip, 4500 feet long and 200 feet wide, in 25 days, in time to provide coverage for the forthcoming Bougainville campaign. By February 1944, the two battalions, augmented by additional equipment and equipment operators from the 24th Battalion, completed 20 miles of roads, two fighter strips, several miles of taxiways with accompanying hardstands and revetments. as well as control tower and quonset-hut camps for aviation personnel. A 12,000-barrel tank farm with a submarine filling line and two filling stands was also erected.

During October and November 1943, a detachment of the 20th Battalion improved the island's docking facilities by installation of three LCT landings and one 40-foot-wide boat-pool landing. In February 1944, the 47th Battalion developed the Ondonga base to include offices, headquarters, camp, a net depot, and dispensary.

On Bau Island, beginning in October 1943, a PT-boat base was built by the 20th Battalion. The Seabees first improved docking facilities, built roads and incidental structures. In November, facilities were increased to include three steel arch-rib warehouses, four quonset huts, and water and electrical systems. During March 1944, the 73rd Battalion added an engine warehouse, more roads, and a fuel line.

Two boat pools were established in the New Georgia group, one on Doke Doke Island and one at Liana Beach. For the boat pool at Doke Doke, the 20th Battalion erected during October 1943, camp and administration buildings, roads, three coral-log wharves, a fuel-storage area and fueling pier, and quonset-hut warehouses. The Liana Beach boat pool was completed by the 73rd Battalion in March 1944.

In April and May 1944, CBMU 561 and 568 arrived at Munda for base maintenance and minor construction; by October 1944, all construction battalions had left New Georgia. Before its departure in February 1945, CBMU 561 had dismantled and assembled for forward movement the major installation. CBMU 568 remained at Munda until May 1945.

The naval base in New Georgia was decommissioned in March 1945.

Vella Lavella

The occupation of Vella Lavella by U. S. forces marked the close of the central-Solomons campaign. There a small air and naval base was established, providing one more step up the Solomons chain

toward the strong Japanese positions in the northern islands.

Vella Lavella, measuring approximately 26 miles long by 12 miles wide, lies 14 miles northwest of Kolombangara Island.

Prior to the war there were no roads on Vella Lavella; but an abundance of coral was available for use as concrete aggregate or road surfacing. There were also ample stands of timber.

The 58th Battalion landed on Vella Lavella August 15, 1943, in the wake of the 35th U. S. Infantry, meeting inconsequential opposition. Unloading had begun when Japanese planes staged a heavy air attack, temporarily interrupting operations. The first pieces of equipment off the ships were large bulldozers, which were immediately put to work clearing roadways along the beach and into the jungle to provide access to areas chosen as supply dumps. Unloading under repeated bombing attacks continued all day. Further air attacks that night complicated operations; however, the Seabees kept supplies moving from the beach, and work on roads progressed. The second night brought more bombing and strafing, but marked the end of sustained enemy night activities.

By August 31, four additional echelons of the battalion and one company of the 58th had landed under constant enemy bombing. During the month the Seabees built nine miles of roads, and erected tents for quarters.

The next construction undertaken was a dispensary and sick bay, the latter consisting of four underground shelters, each with a capacity of four beds, and an underground operating room. The dispensary was above ground and consisted of a wooden deck. wooden framing, and a tarpaulin roof.

Surveying and clearing of a 4,000-by-200-foot airstrip was accomplished during August; the auxiliary installations. including signal tower, operations room, aviation-gasoline tanks, and camp for operating personnel, were completed the following month. The first landing on the strip was made September 24, and thereafter the field was in daily use for shuttle service. By the end of November. considerable additions and improvements had been completed, and by December 21 an aviation-gasoline tank farm of six 1,000-barrel tanks, with a sea-loading line, was in operation.

During August 1943, the 58th Battalion provided installations at the naval base, including a radio room, a hospital, and an LST ramp. The radio room and hospital were underground; the sides, built up with sand-filled gasoline drums, were roofed with logs and sand bags, and provided with wooden decks.

During the next few months the channel through the reef was deepened to admit PT boats to the lagoon base. The jetty was improved by widening and the addition of an "L" section at the end. A camp was set up at the naval base, and a marine railway and boat repair locker constructed.

In December the pier at Biloa was further widened by filling in the "L" section with coral. The surface was raised, the water deepened at the outboard end, and pilings and camels installed. From the end of September until late November 1943, the second section of the 6th (Special) Battalion handled stevedoring operations.

The 77th Battalion, which had arrived on September 25, 1943 in the midst of a Japanese bombing attack, had as its major project the construction of three complete hospital units and facilities. During this attack the Seabees manned guns and took over first-aid and evacuation work. In spite of casualties and severe losses of vital equipment, the Seabees immediately set to work clearing jungle, repairing roads and bridges, and constructing gun emplacements and LST landing facilities. During the period from September to December 1943, the 77th Battalion experienced 47 bombings and suffered ten casualties.

The construction of hospital units was rushed to completion in expectation of the Bougainville invasion. Facilities for 1,000 beds, including surgery, laboratories, wards, mess facilities, administration building, underground surgery, and all utilities, were put in operation as scheduled. Proper materials were lacking, but available coral was used in the large amount of concrete necessary for the hospital construction. This substitution resulted in wide deviation from well-known concrete standards, but satisfactory results were obtained.

In September 1943, the 58th Battalion set up a sawmill which produced 5000 to 6000 board feet of lumber daily. The 77th Battalion operated two sawmills to supply lumber for local requirements and the thousands of board feet needed for the Treasury and Bougainville campaigns. From November 1943 to January 1944, a small detachment of the 53rd Battalion set up and operated two portable sawmills to supplement existing production.

In January 1944, the last of the construction battalions left Vella Lavella, and CBMU 502 reported for maintenance duties, beginning salvage operations in May 1944. On June 15, the airstrip was abandoned and all salvageable installations dismantled. The maintenance unit completed all possible salvage operations, including the dismantling of the tank farm, before leaving for Emirau on July 12, 1944.

Treasury Islands

The Treasury Islands, 28 miles south of Bougainville, and about twice that distance northwest of Vella Levella, were chosen as the site of an advance air and naval base to neutralize Japanese strongholds on New Britain, New Ireland, and Bougainville. Emphasis was placed on the establishment of a medium bomber field and a motor torpedo boat base.

The Treasury Islands consist of Treasury, or Mono, Island and Stirling Island. The former, about 6½ miles long and 4 miles wide, is densely wooded. Stirling is a coral island, 3 miles long and a mile and a half wide. Blanche Harbor, between the islands, has a deep channel, half a mile wide through its eastern entrance.

On October 27, 1943, Company A and 25 men of the headquarters company of the 87th Battalion landed with the 8th New Zealand Brigade, in the first echelon making the assault on the islands. Operations were carried out under enemy high-level bombing, mortar and machine gun fire; however, the assault troops soon eliminated enemy resistance. It was during this operation that the bulldozer became famous as a weapon of offense, when the operator, raising the blade to act as a shield, smashed an enemy machine-gun nest.

During November the Seabee detachment, with limited equipment, improved beaches for landing craft, built 21 miles of roads, established gun positions, and built a wharf for PT boats on Stirling Island. The remainder of the battalion arrived on November 28 and immediately began work on permanent camp facilities and on clearing and grading for the air strip.

Within a month, a strip, 5600 feet long and 200 feet wide, had been completed and had received its first fighter squadron. Construction had been carried out on a 24-hour-day basis, hindered by enemy raids and by the unexpected hardness of the coral. The 87th began clearing for taxiways and hardstands, later turning over the construction of these facilities to the 82nd Battalion, which arrived during December. The 88th Battalion, which reported in January 1944, assisted in taxiway construction. Five 1.000-barrel aviation-gasoline tanks were also erected.

In January, two taxiways, complete with hardstands, warm-up and shop areas. were completed. Later, two additional taxiways with complete facilities were constructed. and the strip was extended to 7,000 feet by 300 feet. Tents provided a pilots' camp, and quonset huts were used for operations. For Acorn 12, the Seabees established a hospital of prefabricated steel buildings, a camp, shops, and medical-storage facilities. This hospital, with the 100-bed unit at the naval base, comprised the medical establishment of Treasury.

The 87th Battalion built docking facilities to accommodate large cargo vessels. Four 6-by-18 pontoon. pre-assembled hinge-connected barges, with an over-all dimension of 43 feet by 428 feet, were secured to four 16-by-16-foot timber cribs set on the shore line, by four 16-by-16-foot ramps, consisting of three standard ramp girders covered with heavy planking. On January 30, 1944 the dock was first used by a cargo vessel.

Facilities for a PT-boat base included a fuel station, a wharf, and three pontoon drydocks. A crash boat pier and a small-boat pier were constructed for the naval base.

Miscellaneous activities of the Seabees included preparation of LST landing beaches, erection of magazines and prefabricated steel warehouses for the naval supply depot, and sawmill operation. Road construction in the rugged, heavily wooded terrain was difficult. For malaria control, Soala Lake was cleared of debris, and the shoreline graded and filled with coral. The Seabees built camps for all activities, including naval base headquarters. a Marine bomber squadron. the 42nd Bomber Group, and Acorn 12.

During the first half of 1944, a detachment of the 6th (Special) Battalion took over stevedoring activities.

Major construction was completed by July 1944, and the base turned over to CBMU's 569 and 587. Roll-up began late in 1944, and by January 1945, some facilities had been shipped to Leyte. CBMU 569, the last Seabee group at Treasury, left in June 1945.

Bougainville

Establishment of an advance air and naval base at Empress Augusta Bay on Bougainville Island, largest of the Solomon group, was designed to facilitate attacks against Japanese positions on the island and on New Britain and New Ireland. The major installations planned for Bougainville were airfields and a motor torpedo boat base.

A beachhead was established November 1, 1943, on a large marshy plain along the southwest coast of Empress Augusta Bay, in an area covered with tangled jungle growth through which no roads penetrated. By VJ-day, however, the American zone of occupation was less than one percent of the island area. The lee side of Puruata, one of two small islands off Cape Torokina, proved satisfactory as an LST landing area.

Small detachments of the 71st, 25th, 53rd, and 75th Battalions landed with the Third Marine Division on D-day, under enemy gun and mortar fire, sniping, and bombing and strafing from the air. Immediately after the initial landing the Seabees began unloading operations. Due to shallow water, the LST's were unable to approach nearer than 75 feet of the beach. Portable ramps of sufficient dimensions and strength to accommodate all heavy equipment were constructed to overcome this difficulty. Bulldozers, the first equipment landed. were used at once to make roads, clear dump areas, and move supplies. Unloading of ships continued through the second day under occasional bombing and constant fire from enemy pill boxes, antiaircraft and machine-gun emplacements in the beachhead area. Moreover, the enemy had two airstrips on Bougainville—Kahili. near Buin, on the southeast coast of the island and Kieta, on the northeast coast. about 40 miles northeast of the American beachhead one on Buka Island, and a fourth at Ballale Island in the Shortland group. All fields had been rendered inoperative prior to the invasion, but later were partially repaired by the enemy and used for night raids during the first three and a half months of Allied occupation.

The original plan of the base called for the immediate installation of a small fighter strip at Torokina to provide air cover during construction of a larger bomber-fighter field (Piva Field). The construction of the fighter strip was assigned to the 71st Battalion. Torokina Field, originally planned to accommodate 35 fighter planes or light dive-bombers, handled many times that number

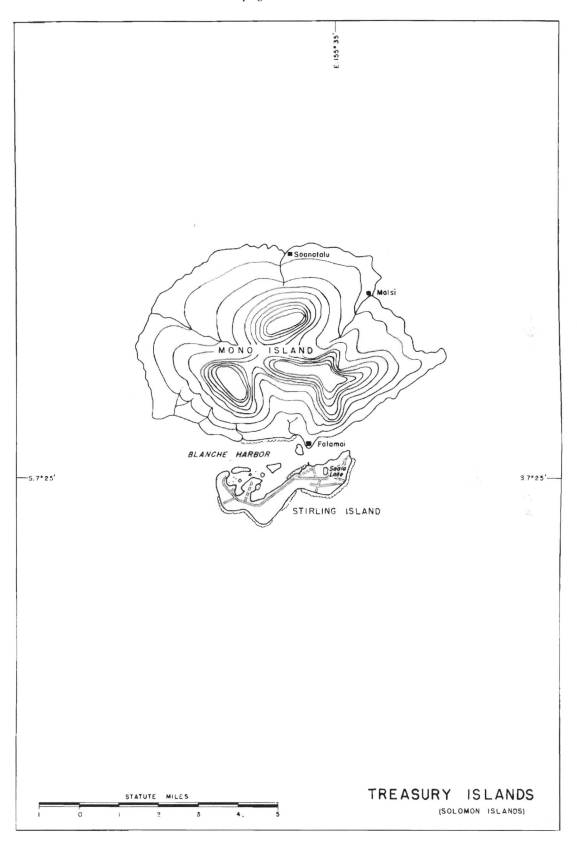

■ Soanotalu

●/ Malsi

MONO ISLAND

—S.7°25′

Falamai

BLANCHE HARBOR

Saala Lake

S.7°25′—

STIRLING ISLAND

E.155°35′

STATUTE MILES

1 0 1 2 3 4. 5

TREASURY ISLANDS

(SOLOMON ISLANDS)

TOROKINA FIGHTER FIELD, NOVEMBER 13, 1943
Snaking logs for use in construction of field facilities. (Compare with pictures of field on pages 272, 273, 276.)

before completion of Piva Field. The original run-way, 200 feet by 5,150 feet, was later enlarged and accompanying facilities were developed.

Surveys for the field and clearing of the area were begun on the third day after landing, subject to continuous enemy action, survey parties often finding themselves targets for snipers. There was little choice as to the location of the first airstrip; however, the area from Torokina Point eastward was considered the most suitable. Considerable difficulty was experienced in clearing jungle growth and removing the slimy muck to reach a suitable subgrade.

Work on the strip was prosecuted as energetic-ally as conditions permitted, the tempo increasing with the arrival of each additional echelon, the last of which arrived November 17. To meet the deadline, night work was necessary; but by No-

vember 24 enough matting was laid to permit an SBD to make an emergency landing. The field was completed December 10, 1943, and the first 18 Corsair fighter planes landed as per schedule.

Simultaneously with the construction of the airstrip and its facilities, camps were erected for aviation personnel, including two galleys and mess halls, storage buildings, a hospital with three wards and an operating room with all utilities. All avia-tion facilities at Torokina were built by the 71st Battalion, with minor assistance from a detachment of the 53rd and from a Marine labor party of 100 men.

On November 29, 1943, the 36th Battalion, which had arrived three days earlier, began construction of the Piva bomber strip. This 8,000-by-300-foot strip, with warm-up aprons at each end, was cleared from dense jungle. The first plane landed on the

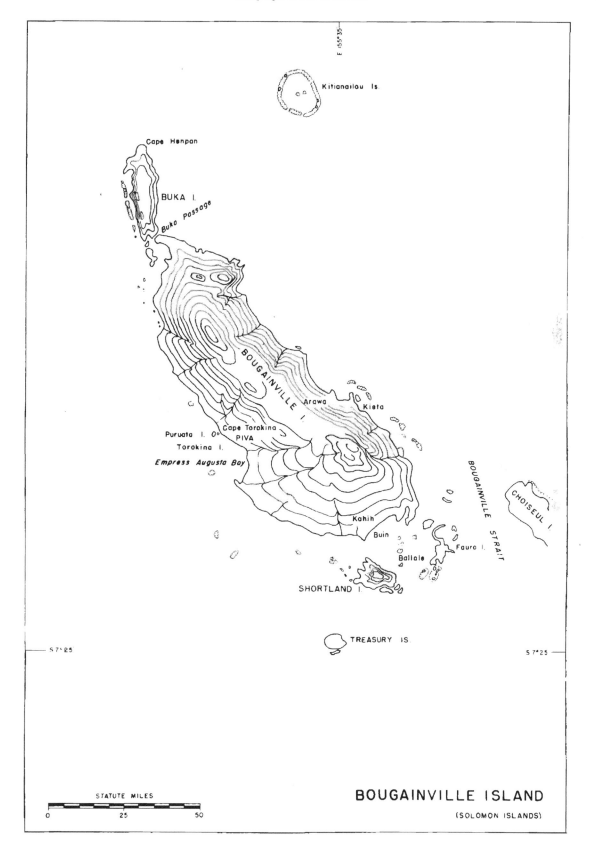

STATUTE MILES

0   25   50

BOUGAINVILLE ISLAND

(SOLOMON ISLANDS)

Torokina Fighter Field, November 15, 1943
71st Seabees Grading Taxiway

strip December 19, and on December 30, the runway was officially put into operation with the landing of ten Army transport planes. A few weeks after the start of operations, it was found necessary to extend the strip an additional 2,000 feet.

Field facilities built by the 71st Battalion included three taxiways with 35 hardstands, a shop area, seven nose hangars, three prefabricated steel huts, and 26 frame buildings. Aviation camps consisted of a 5,000-man camp for Marine Air Group 24 built by the 77th Battalion, and a 2,000-man camp constructed by the 36th.

The 77th Battalion, arriving December 10, 1943, was assigned the task of constructing Piva Field and began this task the second day ashore, work being expedited by working at night whenever possible. The grading of Piva strip was completed December 28, but due to late arrival of steel mat-

ting, final completion was delayed until January 3. The first plane landed on January 9. The project was materially aided by the co-operation of the 53rd Battalion in furnishing and operating equipment. A few weeks later, the 77th was instructed to extend the strip 2,000 feet, and completed the work in eight days.

Another critical deadline was met by the 75th Battalion in the erection of a complete tank-farm system to service the two airfields. Due to shipping difficulties and to the losses of supplies in the establishment of the beachhead, there existed an extreme shortage of pipe fittings, which was overcome by welding joints. Although all work was in marshy jungle, the tank farm, consisting of one 10,000-barrel and eighteen 1,000-barrel tanks, with tanker mooring, submarine pipe line, and 5 miles of overland pipe, was completed in time to support

Torokina Fighter Field, December 2, 1943
West end of the field, taken from the control tower

operations from the fields. Although enemy shelling severed this pipe line eighteen times, repairs were effected each time by the 75th Battalion, frequently under fire, and in no case was delivery of fuel interrupted.

A PT-boat base and boat pool were set up on Puruata Island by the 75th Battalion, assisted by the 71st and the 77th Battalions. Wood-pile and timber construction was used for a PT-boat pier, a crash boat pier, and a PT fueling pier. Complete camp facilities included quarters, mess halls, an emergency hospital, with all utilities, and five prefabricated steel warehouses. Eighteen small-boat moorings, consisting of three pile dolphins, driven and lashed, were provided, and LST landings installed. Stevedoring was handled by the 6th and the 9th Battalions.

The 36th Battalion provided the major medical facilities at Bougainville, supplementing emergency installations at the various camps. The project, completed between February and April 1944, consisted of 70 standard quonset huts and one 40-by-100-foot mess hall, providing accommodation for 500 patients. These installations included an administration building, a general and an underground emergency surgery, as well as quarters for doctors and corpsmen.

Other Seabee activities included operation of sawmills, construction of complete camp installations for air and ground headquarters, and the building of roads. Coconut logs were much used in rough structures, and native mahogany was used in all types of construction.

Much of the construction at Torokina was accomplished under actual battle conditions. In February 1944, it became apparent that the Japanese were preparing an all-out attack on the beachhead in an effort to capture the three airstrips. By this time, the airstrips were in full operation and were contributing much toward the destruction of the enemy. Taking an active part in the defense plan, the Seabees built secondary defense lines and stood by to occupy them in the event of a break-through. On March 8, an unsuccessful Japanese attack was launched with heavy shelling which continued for 20 days, resulting in numerous Seabee casualties.

By July 1944, all major construction had been completed. The 36th Battalion, the last to leave the base, departed in August 1944. CBMU's 586 and 582, which arrived in May, took charge of maintenance. Roll-up of installations was accomplished early in 1945, and in June the maintenance units were ordered to forward areas.

Green Island

Occupation of Green Island, 40 miles northwest of Buka and 120 miles east of Rabaul, provided a new Allied base for offensive sweeps well beyond the previous range of South Pacific air-craft. The base was to provide facilities and fields for the operation of fighter and bomber planes, as well as a motor torpedo boat base.

Green Atoll consists of four, flat, thickly wooded islands which almost encircle a lagoon. Nissan Island, on which the advance base was built, is horseshoe-shaped and by far the largest of the four. The atoll is about 9 miles long and 5 miles wide; the depth of the channels entering the lagoon is 17 feet at mean low tide.

Construction on Nissan Island was begun by the 22nd Construction Regiment, which was established January 15, 1944 and consisted of the 33rd, 37th, and 93rd Battalions and the first section of the 15th Battalion. At the time of commissioning, the 15th and 93rd were staging in the Russells, the 33rd was en route from New Zealand to the Russells, and the 37th was at Ondonga, New Georgia. All battalions were instructed to obtain, so far as possible, all materials and equipment needed, from stocks available in the Russells or on Guadalcanal.

The regiment moved to Green Island in five echelons on D-Day, February 15, 1944, landing against negligible resistance, in the wake of the New Zealand Third Division. Concurrent with unloading operations, artillery was moved into position, road construction begun, and radar installed.

On D-Day-plus-five additional personnel arrived with heavy equipment, and work on the fighter strip commenced.

On D-Day-plus-twenty the strip, measuring 150 feet by 5,000 feet, was opened to full operation. The same day its fighter planes attacked Kavieng in Japanese-held New Ireland. Work was continued on roads, fields, and taxiways, and in late March, the bomber field, 150 feet by 6,000 feet, was completed. Later, it was lengthened to 7,300 feet. Construction of the airfields proved exceedingly difficult. Dense foliage and large trees were encountered, rock blasting was necessary, and all coral used for filling had to be quarried at distant locations, and hauled to the scene of operations. Weather conditions were continually adverse.

Construction of an aviation-gasoline tank farm, completed April 9, 1944, was delayed by changes in plan; however, 14 tanks began operating March 23. The farm included a drum spillway, two tank truck filling racks with separators and strainers, one six-inch sea-loading line, and a PT-boat pier service line with all connections.

The Seabees erected floored and screened tents, galleys and mess halls, dispensary facilities, and all utilities for pilots' camps. Control towers and operations buildings were provided for the two airstrips; 21 buildings were set up for use as shops.

By June, a seaplane ramp, 250 feet by 450 feet, had been built of coral, and three moorings, consisting of four concrete anchors and oil-drum buoys, had been provided.

One company of the 9th (Special) Battalion took over the unloading of cargo ships, from the fifth echelon, thereby releasing the Seabees for construction work only. A fuel pier with a 35-foot outboard end and 11-foot depth was constructed, and the PT-boat base was developed to include a camp, four shops with approach ramps, one prefabricated steel warehouse, and a pontoon-type, T-shaped pier with a 154-foot outboard end.

Medical facilities constructed consisted of floored and screened tents as well as a quonset hut to house the X-ray facilities of Acorn 10 Hospital, and four quonset huts for the naval base hospital. Sick bays and dispensaries were likewise provided at the various camps.

Other activities included the construction of some 25 miles of roads and the operation of a

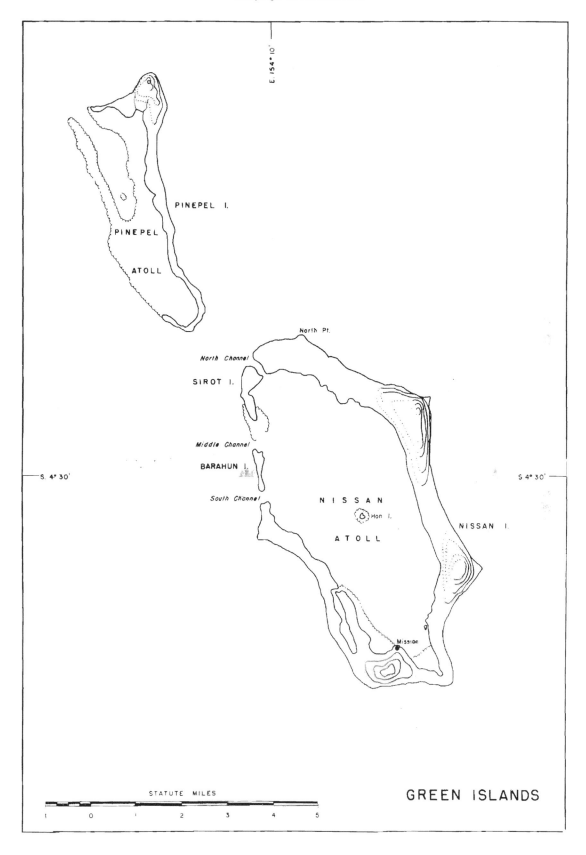

PINEPEL I.

PINEPEL

ATOLL

North Pt.

North Channel

SIROT I.

Middle Channel

BARAHUN I.

South Channel

NISSAN

Hon I.

ATOLL

NISSAN I.

S. 4° 30'

S 4° 30'

E. 154° 10'

Mission

STATUTE MILES

1 0 1 2 3 4 5

GREEN ISLANDS

TOROKINA FIGHTER FIELD, DECEMBER 10, 1943

sawmill, which produced more than a million board feet from native woods. Due to heavy rainfall, patrols were in constant operation to keep roads passable at all times.

Ingenious improvisation met many arising problems. A mess-gear dishwasher and a sterilizer were improvised from salvaged fuel drums. To facilitate feeding men engaged in construction at a distance from the main camp, a portable field kitchen was developed. This kitchen, capable of feeding 200 men per meal, was built over a trailer and could be loaded on an LST. It was complete with

two Army field ranges, refrigerator, sink, and 200-gallon water tank.

By July 1944, all authorized construction on Green Island was complete, and CBMUs 552 and 553 reported to take charge of general maintenance and miscellaneous construction. Late in 1944 the maintenance units began dismantling structures for removal. By January 1945, the majority of the naval facilities had been rolled-up and were awaiting shipment to forward areas. CBMU 552 left Green in March 1945; CBMU 553 remained until August to complete the roll-up.

CHAPTER 26

BASES IN THE SOUTHWEST PACIFIC

When the Japanese scored their initial successes in the Far East, the naval forces of the Allied powers retreated, fighting, through the Netherlands East Indies until they had fallen back to Australia. Refugee units and personnel from our Asiatic fleet began to arrive at northern and western Australian ports within a few weeks of the opening of the war.

The ensuing months showed a picture of considerable confusion. Cargo ships, carrying supplies to destinations which had fallen to the enemy while they were en route, put in at Australian ports and were unloaded. The accumulation of such distress cargo created almost impossible problems of identification, storage, and protection, and much misdirection and loss of valuable material resulted. Gradually, however, storage space was found for Navy material in Brisbane, Sydney, and Melbourne on the east coast and at Fremantle on the west.

The major concern, however, was the development of facilities in Australia which would permit that island continent to serve as a secure base to support naval and military counter-offensives against the enemy. In April 1942, immediately after the command areas in the south Pacific were redefined, a board consisting of Australian and American representatives was convened to determine base-development requirements. It was understood from the beginning that Australia would provide the necessary construction labor and operating personnel and that the United States would be called on to supply only the materials and equipment that could not be obtained locally. Within a few weeks, plans had been formulated which appeared to satisfy the estimated requirements of the combined services and requests were forwarded to the United States for the materials and equipment which would not be available in Australia. Shipments were slow to arrive, however, and in the meanwhile the outcome of the battles of the Coral Sea and Midway had so changed the

military situation that a thorough revision of the plans for base development was in order.

The general effect of the change was to shift major developments northward. The ports of Adelaide and Albany ceased to be important from a military standpoint, and Melbourne declined in importance as a center of activity after naval headquarters for Australia was moved to Brisbane in July 1942.

For the remainder of this first year of the war, work proceeded slowly on naval facilities, handicapped by Australia's severe manpower shortage. Base facilities for submarine maintenance and repair were put under way at Brisbane and Fremantle; PT-boat bases were developed at Cairns and at Darwin; repair and maintenance facilities to service escort vessels were established at Sydney and Cairns; and naval air bases were developed at Brisbane, at Perth, and on Palm Island, just northwest of Townsville. Moreover, a considerable amount of storage and supply space was obtained by lease of existing Australian facilities.

A few advance operating bases, particularly for submarines and PT boats, were also established during this period, at Merauke, on the southern coast of Dutch New Guinea, on Thursday Island in Torres Strait, and in Exmouth Gulf.

By the end of 1942, however, it was apparent that the shortage of manpower and materials in Australia was hampering the base-development program beyond the point of tolerance, and in January 1943 a request was made that naval construction battalions be assigned to expedite the construction work. In response to that request the 55th Battalion arrived in Brisbane on March 24, 1943.

In the meanwhile, it had been necessary to establish advance bases in New Guinea. In the earliest days of the war, Port Moresby on the southern coast of that island assumed considerable importance as a military debarkation point and as a destination of supplies for the forces resisting the

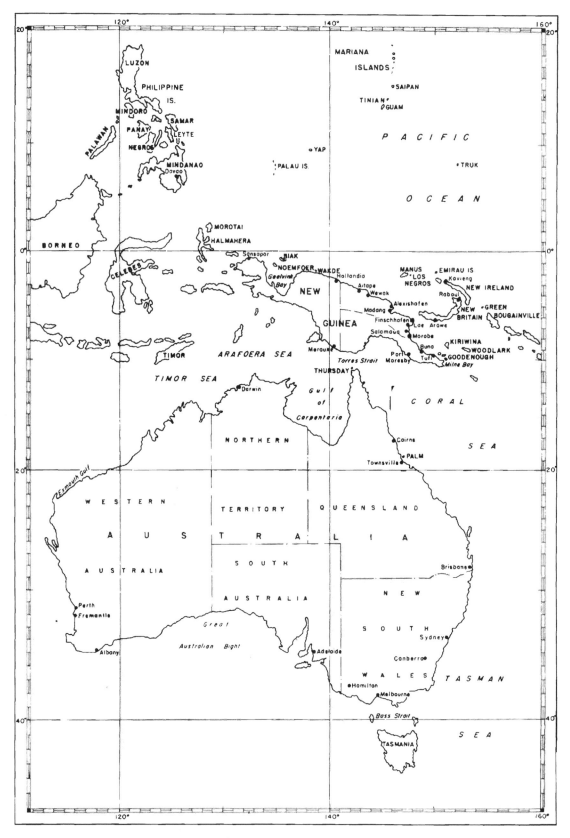

SOUTHWEST PACIFIC AREA

Japanese advance. Existing facilities were augmented by the Australians during 1942 and early 1943, particularly in connection with fuel storage. Milne Bay, at the eastern tip of New Guinea, had been occupied by Allied forces in the early summer of 1942 and a bomber strip had been built to permit air operations against enemy shipping and positions on the north coast.

In September 1942, the Japanese made a strong attempt against Port Moresby, their forces succeeding in pushing across the eastern New Guinea peninsula to within 30 miles of the port. Reinforcement of Allied ground forces and strong air support turned back the advance, however, and the enemy fell back upon his main base at Buna, on the north coast. A campaign by Allied forces to eject the Japanese from that base followed, its success signalized by the capture of Buna itself on December 14. Early in 1943 the northeast coast of New Guinea, from Buna, south, was finally cleared of the enemy.

In late June 1943, after the Buna campaign had come to an end, our forces landed on Woodlark Island and Kiriwina Island, off the eastern end of New Guinea, with the intention of establishing air bases. Parts of the 60th and 20th Battalions participated in the landing on Woodlark; immediately thereafter the 60th set about the construction of the projected air strip. Army engineers undertook the airfield construction on Kiriwina, and in September a detachment of the 20th Battalion was sent from Woodlark to Kiriwina to lend them assistance.

With Port Moresby, Milne Bay, Buna, Woodlark, and Kiriwina firmly in our possession, our next move was directed against the enemy's positions at Salamaua and Lae. Combining an overland drive from Buna and an amphibious assault, our forces succeeded in capturing both enemy bases by the middle of September. Maintaining the momentum of our advance, Finschhafen was taken on October 2, and by February 1944, all of the Huon peninsula was in our hands.

In November 1943, most of the 60th Battalion left Woodlark Island for Finschhafen to assist in the construction of an Army air strip and to build a naval base. During the months immediately succeeding, three more battalions arrived at Finschhafen to aid in establishing the then-forwardmost base in New Guinea.

The next move in our Southwest Pacific offensive was northward, directed toward the enemy's bases at Rabaul and Kavieng. On December 15, 1943, Army troops made landings on the southwest coast of New Britain, near Arawe, and on December 26 the 1st Marine Division went ashore at Cape Gloucester at the island's western tip. The 19th Construction Battalion was attached to the Marines and accompanied them in their landing.

In the meanwhile, our forces had established their positions in Bougainville, in the Solomons, to the east of Rabaul. Encirclement of that major Japanese base was carried forward another step by our invasion and occupation of the Admiralty Islands. On February 29, 1944, advance elements of the 1st Cavalry Division landed on the island of Los Negros on a reconnaissance mission. Finding the area lightly held, the division's mission immediately became one of invasion and occupation. Among the reinforcing elements sent ashore on March 2 were detachments from four of the construction battalions of the 4th Naval Construction Brigade, the 40th, 46th, 78th, and 17th. Development of Los Negros and Manus, the principal islands of the Admiralty group, during the succeeding months, yielded the largest and most important naval and air base in the Southwest Pacific theater. Facilities were established which, together with spacious Seeadler Harbor, made the base at Manus capable of supporting not only the 7th Fleet, attached to the Southwest Pacific command, but also a sizable portion of the Pacific Fleet as well.

Encirclement of Rabaul was completed by the occupation and development of Emirau, of the St. Mathias group, directly north of New Ireland. On March 20, 1944, Marines landed on the island to find it undefended. A few days later, construction battalions of the 18th Regiment, drawn from the Solomons, began to arrive and immediately started the construction of a naval base and two bomber fields for the Army. The once-important enemy base on New Britain was left to share the fate of other by-passed Japanese positions.

The momentum of our offensive was not permitted to run down. Aided by air support from naval carriers, Army forces on April 22 made successful landings on the New Guinea coast at Aitape and Hollandia, 400 miles and more to the west of Finschhafen. On May 9 the 113th Battalion arrived at Hollandia and set to work constructing naval-base facilities on Humboldt Bay to support the 7th Fleet in its future operations, and fleet headquarters facilities in an upland area about 25 miles inland.

The establishment of our position at Hollandia had cut off more than 50,000 Japanese troops to the eastward, and our command of the sea approaches foreclosed their support or reinforcement. Our control of the remaining portions of the New Guinea coast was not far off. In May, our forces assaulted and occupied the island of Biak, the neighboring island of Noemfoor in July, and Sansapor, at the western tip of New Guinea, on July 30. Our control of the New Guinea coast was now complete. By that time, Japanese air strength had almost disappeared in the entire area and our offensive steadily gained momentum. On September 15 our forces invaded and occupied the island of Morotai, north of Halmahera; the reconquest of the Philippines clearly lay ahead.

Australia

Brisbane. Operating bases in the Australian area for patrol and escort craft were needed to anchor the far end of our long supply line to the Southwest Pacific. Accordingly, it was directed early in the war that there be provided in Brisbane, a base to support task forces, submarines, and escort craft.

Brisbane, the capital of Queensland, with a population of 370,460, is located on the Brisbane River, about 14 miles from the east coast. Moreton Bay, at the mouth of the river, affords suitable anchorage for vessels of draft not exceeding 33 feet.

United States naval activities in Brisbane began on April 14, 1942, when the tender USS *Griffin* and her company of submarines tied up at New Farm Wharf, where existing installations consisted principally of wharves and wool-storage sheds. In order to provide the necessary equipment for a naval supply depot, part of these facilities were rented and paid for under reverse Lend-Lease.

Shortly thereafter a submarine supply and repair base was established; necessary facilities were rented or leased from the Australians and renovated by Australian construction men to meet the Navy's needs. Although harbor facilities were limited, the base was eventually expanded until it became the largest United States naval base in continental Australia. Existing buildings and Aus-

tralian materials and labor were used when available; however, some Seventh Fleet units brought with them prefabricated buildings which were set up by their own men or by the Seabees.

Seabees played no part in the establishment of the base until March 24, 1943, at which time the 55th Battalion arrived and established a base for themselves at Eagle Farm, 5 miles northeast of Brisbane, later used as a staging camp for the Seabees in the Southwest Pacific and known as "Camp Seabee." After two weeks in Australia, half of the battalion was sent to New Guinea, while the other half continued work on the camp and also began to build a mine depot. By June 10, other detachments had been sent north to Palm Island and Cairns, leaving only 250 men in Brisbane.

The 84th Battalion landed at Brisbane on June 19, 1943, and moved immediately into Camp Seabee. Here, orders were received sending approximately half the battalion to Milne Bay, New Guinea. The portion of the battalion left in Brisbane assisted the 55th Battalion in constructing the mine depot, additional barracks at Camp Seabee, a Merchant Marine anti-aircraft training station, and Mobile Hospital No. 9. During May and June of 1943 the 60th Battalion staged in Camp Seabee and aided forces there in the construction of projects then under way.

On January 20, 1944 the 544th CBMU arrived to take over all maintenance in the area.

In addition to the projects already mentioned, the Seabees built an advance base construction depot, containing 90,000 square feet of warehouse space and 53 acres of open storage; established a naval magazine at the mine depot by erecting 52 storage huts, 20 by 50 feet. At Hamilton, they renovated existing structures to give a ship-repair unit 5,000 square feet of shop space, and built a wharf, 40 by 130 feet. In addition, many small jobs were done by the Seabees as additions to, or in conjunction with, work performed by the Allied Works Council, including the building of access roads serving the newly constructed warehouses.

The 55th performed logging operations during a period of acute lumber shortage, and also established and operated a river-gravel plant which supplied all the concrete aggregate required at Brisbane by the United States Navy. They also operated a disintegrated-granite pit which provided surfacing material for roads and open-storage areas.

SHIP REPAIR FACILITIES AT LOMBRUM, LOS NEGROS
46th Seabees worked on this project in the Admiralty Islands. Photograph taken August 1, 1944

The Australians had not previously used this disintegrated granite as a surfacing material, but it proved thoroughly satisfactory.

Mobile Hospital 9 arrived at Brisbane with sufficient prefabricated buildings to set up 500 beds; it was later expanded to accommodate 1,000 beds, and subsequently 3,000. All buildings were of prefabricated metal, with the exception of a storehouse, theater-recreation building, laundry, and a sewage pumphouse, and the power plant. All construction was performed by Seabees, with the assistance of station personnel.

No air strips had to be built, for the local airport at Archerfield was made available, and air strips built for the United States Army at Eagle Farm were also used by Navy planes. In addition to 100,000 square feet of existing plane-parking areas, 192,000 square feet and 180,000 square feet were added to Archerfield and Eagle Farm, respectively. Repair shops and a parachute tower were erected, and two hangars, 248 by 105 feet

each, which had been built for the Army, were turned over to the Navy. Leave areas, accommodating 250 men each, were built for naval personnel at Toowoomba, west of Brisbane, and at Coolangatta, on the sea, 65 miles south of Brisbane.

Local labor and materials were used almost exclusively. Australian labor also built a seaplane base on the south bank of the Brisbane River about 3 miles below the city. The existing finger pier was utilized, with barges attached at the outer end to facilitate loading and unloading operations. All station personnel and plane crews were quartered at this site.

The first major installation to be discontinued was the mine assembly depot, which was dismantled and crated in January 1944. The moving of Seventh Fleet headquarters to Hollandia, prior to the Philippines campaign, greatly decreased activities as Brisbane, and many of the facilities were returned to the Australians.

Townsville.—At Townsville, on the northeast

NAVAL RECEIVING STATION, LORENGAU, MANUS, NOVEMBER 1944

coast of Australia. a section base was set up to service convoy and combatant ships operating in the forward areas of the Solomons and New Guinea.

Land was acquired rent-free, from the Townsville Town Council, for the site of a fleet post office. and a frame building, occupied the middle of April, was built entirely by Australian labor for this activity.

A naval magazine, 4 miles from Townsville, was completed August 23, 1943. It consisted of four, prefabricated magazine huts and two wooden-frame buildings for barracks and mess hall. Local labor and some local materials were used. A 120-bed hospital, consisting of a group of quonset huts, was begun October 22, 1943 on the shores of Rose Bay, near Townsville, by Company C of the 55th Battalion and was operative by December 20, 1943.

Meanwhile, on October 25, 1943, another detachment of the 55th Battalion had arrived at Townsville to build a second hospital, on a site 10 miles north of the city. This hospital, also consisting of quonset huts, had a capacity of 100 beds.

The base remained in operation until July 1944, when a detachment of the 84th Battalion began dismantling it and crating material for shipment to a forward area.

Sydney.—The capital of New South Wales, a modern, well-developed city, with a population of 1,250,000, provided a major repair base. an operations and maintenance base for escort craft, and a major port of debarkation.

United States naval facilities at Sydney, consisting of a supply depot, an ammunition depot, and Base Hospital 10, were constructed by civilian contractors, under the auspices of the Australian Allied Works Council, on reverse Lend-Lease. The construction program was not initiated until the summer of 1943.

Storehouses for the supply depot were constructed of standard Australian wood-frame buildings and by rental of existing space. For the ammunition depot, twenty concrete magazines, 25 by 50 feet, and two 30-by-100-foot units were erected.

Base Hospital 10 occupied a small civilian hospital, which was augmented by standard barracks, ward buildings, an operating center, galley and mess hall. The normal capacity of the hospital was 200 beds, with a maximum emergency accommodation of 500 beds.

Commercial port facilities were used. The Australian government had under construction during 1943 and 1944 a graving dock, 1094 feet long and 140 feet wide, with a depth of 40½ feet. Facilities ashore were simultaneously developed equivalent to those of a destroyer tender. During the summer of 1944, a detachment of 90 men from the 84th Battalion was stationed at Sydney to repair the USS *Venus*.

By July 1944, plans had been formulated for the elimination and reduction of our naval facilities at Sydney, with the exception of the ammunition depot, at the earliest practicable date.

Palm Island.—Palm Island, within the Great Barrier Reef, north of Townsville and 20 miles off the coast of Australia, was selected as a naval air station with facilities for the operating and overhauling of patrol bombers.

Palm Island, the largest of several closely grouped small islands, is triangularly shaped and contains 23 square miles. With the exception of a few small areas, the terrain is rugged from the water's edge. The air station overlooked a large stretch of sheltered water, ideal for seaplane operations.

On July 6, 1943, a detachment of 2 officers and 122 men of the 55th Battalion was sent from Brisbane to Palm Island to construct the station. As all the material could not be shipped at one time, a similar detachment, with 1,500 tons of material, was sent from Brisbane to Townsville by rail. Half of this detachment remained in Townsville to unload, store, and reload this material, and the entire

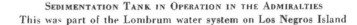

SEDIMENTATION TANK IN OPERATION IN THE ADMIRALTIES
This was part of the Lombrum water system on Los Negros Island

1,500 tons moved to Palm Island by such small craft as became available.

The Seabees on Palm Island set up a camp with all necessary facilities for 1,000 men. Concrete-surfaced seaplane ramps and a seaplane parking area large enough for 12 planes were constructed. Three nose hangars were built, and moorings for 18 planes were provided in the bay. A tank farm with a capacity of 60,000 barrels of aviation gasoline was constructed, using 2000 feet of shore pipeline and 1,200 feet of submarine pipe-line. All buildings were wood frame.

No local labor and little native material were used, but coral aggregate for concrete was obtained from off-shore reefs at low tide.

By September 23, 1943, when personnel for the operation and maintenance of the base began to arrive in large numbers, the major facilities of the base were ready for operation. A month later the base was completed with the exception of the tank farm, construction of which was in progress, and a small portion of two nose hangars. On October 25, the Seabees began moving out, leaving a group of 35 men to complete the nose hangars and other miscellaneous minor jobs, after which the detachment rejoined the battalion at Townsville on November 8.

In addition to the construction of the facilities already listed and the unloading of construction equipment and material, some 3,500 tons of base operational and maintenance equipment and supplies had been unloaded by the Seabees between July 6 and October 22. They had also set up and maintained their own camp.

Housing and operational facilities were fully utilized from October 25, 1943, to May 1, 1944, with an average of four planes per day repaired. On June 1, 1944, a detachment from the 91st Battalion arrived to dismantle the camp, and by September 1, 1944, work was completed, with 5,000 tons of material and equipment loaded on ships for forward areas.

Darwin.—In order to fulfill an agreement with the Australian government, whereby the United States Navy was to supply mines to the Royal Australian Air Forces operating out of Darwin, a mine depot was established there. Facilities were later expanded to service United States submarines and PT boats operating off the northwest coast of Australia.

Darwin, on the northern coast of Australia, oc-cupies a peninsula between Clarence Strait and Frances Bay. With a peacetime population of 3,000, Darwin had no industries, serving only as a port of call for coastwise shipping and as a base for pearling luggers. A civil airfield and a RAAF air-field on the other side of the strait provided air facilities.

The first echelon of Company B, 84th Battalion, arrived at Darwin on August 28, 1943, and imme-diately commenced work on the construction of a 500-foot PT-boat slip, and shortly thereafter erected a quonset warehouse. Existing facilities proved to be inadequate; hotels and private resi-dences were renovated and used as quarters, and existing stores and warehouses were utilized, over-flow space being provided with tents and new con-struction. Commissioning of this section base took place on November 21, 1943.

In January 1944, work was commenced on 12 magazine huts, with a detonator locker in the magazine area on Frances Bay, just south of the RAAF field. Roads were built. This construction, augmented by a warehouse and an assembly shed, was completed by April 6.

During January 1945, the Seabees also built a base camp, consisting of 22 huts, supply tents, and accompanying accommodations. A radio unit with necessary equipment and three quonset huts were set up at Adelaide River, 77 miles from Darwin.

Cairns.—Our base was planned to provide logis-tic support and hospital facilities to serve advance bases and operational forces afloat.

Cairns, on Trinity Bay on the east coast of Australia, is in a sub-tropical region, temperatures often exceeding 100°F. Much of the flat coastal area along the bay is mangrove swamp, requiring considerable fill to make it usable for construction purposes. By dredging, the harbor was kept at a depth of 22 feet.

On October 6, 1943, a detachment of 3 officers and 223 men from the 55th Battalion arrived at Cairns to set up an escort base on the site of small PT repair base, which had been erected by various service units, with no planned construction layout. Practically all installations, however, were ulti-mately incorporated in the base. Although built to accommodate one PT boat, the wharf accommo-dated several more by nesting.

Escort Base One was set up for destroyer re-pair, mine maintenance, patrol-craft repair head-quarters, and supply. The work of grading, filling,

CHAPEL IN THE ADMIRALTIES
Men entering to attend dedication services on Easter morning, April 1, 1945

and erecting buildings was taken over by the Seabees upon their arrival. Construction by the 55th Battalion included a galley and mess hall for 1,000 men, hospital facilities with complete installations for 50 patients, administration and operational facilities, all necessary buildings for radar repair, ships' stores, fleet post office, storage, and base roads.

Ninety days were required for the initial development of Cairns, completion date being January 1, 1944. Major obstacles were poor drainage and unstable material for structures and roads. These were overcome by using disintegrated granite as fill, installing culverts, grading, and ditching.

Development beyond the original plans included construction of a 400-ton floating drydock, a 600-

foot timber wharf, and four 5,000-gallon water tanks. Time required for these developments was thirty days, with the final job completed January 31, 1944. The detachment then returned to Brisbane.

Late in December, it had been decided to provide ammunition-storage facilities, but as participation in this project would prolong too greatly the Seabees' service in a tropical area, another detachment arrived from Brisbane, December 30, 1943. At the dump site, 7 miles inland from the main base, the Seabees set up 18 prefabricated ammunition-storage huts, a frame barrack, and all other necessary camp facilities, which were completed March 19, 1944.

Apart from these projects, the 19th Battalion,

in July 1943, assisted the U. S. 6th Army Engineers in the construction of a large Army operating base, which included a drainage project, power plant, railroad, camp sites, and other facilities.

The naval base was used extensively for repair of all types of small craft and destroyers. During the construction period, as well as upon completion, the base was taxed to capacity.

CBMU 546 started roll-up late in 1944, and by January 7, 1945 all usable material had been sent to forward areas.

Merauke, Dutch New Guinea

Merauke, approximately 2 miles from the mouth of the Merauke River, on the southern coast of Dutch New Guinea, was selected as the site for a base to support PT squadron units, as well as operations of Allied Army, Navy, and Air components.

The area around Merauke consists largely of low land, covered with mangrove swamps interspersed with ridges of more stable sandy clay. The climate is tropical, with an average annual rainfall in excess of 100 inches.

A detachment of 4 officers and 233 enlisted men from the 55th Battalion arrived at Merauke on May 8, 1943, to construct the PT-boat base. As the town jetty had been destroyed by Japanese bombs, material and equipment had to be beached by unloading into leaky scows, which were towed to a makeshift wharf.

Trouble was encountered in selecting a camp site in the swampy terrain. Drinking water was obtained from seepage wells, and then purified. Timber for the construction of a 300-foot pier and a smaller one for PT boats did not arrive until July 15; work was then started immediately, and both were completed by September 3.

The air strip, 150 by 6,000 feet, was commenced on June 28, 1943; eight days later, it accommodated its first plane. This strip was able to handle one squadron of fighter planes and several medium bombers. Twenty miles of roads connected the strip with the town and with gasoline and fuel dumps.

As Merauke at this time was within easy range of enemy air bases, it was subject to numerous strafing and bombing raids. On May 11, three days after arrival, the Seabees experienced their first bombing raid; they sustained no casualties but lost some gear and equipment. Numerous alerts and attempted raids followed, but there were no more bombings until September 9, by which time all assignments had been completed.

Facilities of this base, both harbor and airfield, were used extensively, daily reconnaissance missions and bombing flights being flown from the strip.

Milne Bay

The naval base at Milne Bay was developed to relieve overcrowded ports on the east coast of Australia and to provide facilities nearer the enemy. The major installations consisted of a transshipment and staging area, major overhaul facilities for PT boats, and a destroyer base.

Milne Bay, on the southeastern extremity of New Guinea, is 20 miles in length, with an average width of 7 miles, affording an extensive protected harbor. A dense, swampy, jungle plain extends inland from the narrow coral and mud beaches to the Owen Stanley Mountains. The climate is tropical, with high humidity and heavy rainfall. Population is extremely sparse.

The first Seabees, one company of the 55th Battalion, arrived in Milne Bay on May 23, 1943. Their mission was to construct PT Advance Base Six at Kana Kopa, on the south side of the bay. Personnel of the PT base had arrived in December 1942 and had unloaded supplies and set up a few tents. As the Allied forces moved up the coast of New Guinea, it was found that the major engine-overhaul base at Cairns, Australia, was too far behind the lines to be practicable; accordingly, it was decided to enlarge the base at Kana Kopa.

Despite excessive tropical rains and adverse soil conditions, the Seabees had the base in operation five weeks after work was started, in time for its boats to strike the Japanese at Salamaua and Nassau Bay on June 29 and 30. In four months this small detachment also installed facilities for housing and feeding 800 men, shops and storehouses of quonset huts, three 15,000-gallon water tanks, a tank farm of four 1,000-barrel fuel tanks, a timber pile wharf, and two pontoon drydocks for PT boats.

This base was completed in the scheduled time, despite adverse weather conditions and disease. Severe rains often caused knee-deep mud, and in some places men worked waist-deep in the churned earth. In pouring concrete, it was necessary to keep the slabs under cover, so temporary shelters were erected. An ingenious system for building quonset

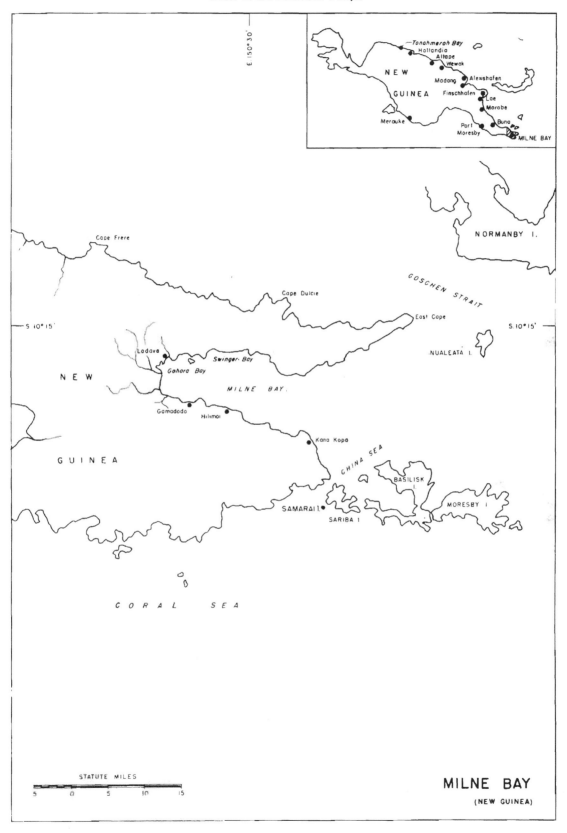

MILNE BAY

(NEW GUINEA)

ADVANCE BASE CONSTRUCTION DEPOT, MILNE BAY, NEW GUINEA
Photograph taken October 10, 1944, showing the general storage yard

huts from the top down was later devised to eliminate the construction of temporary structures for protecting the concrete. Mud sills were set, and on them, blocks were placed at intervals to support a quonset hut, which was then erected. The concrete floors and foundations were then poured under the completed hut.

Milne Bay is in one of the most malaria-ridden areas in the world, and in spite of a rigorous preventive campaign, from 23 to 39 percent of the personnel was incapacitated from this cause alone. This, combined with tropical skin diseases also prevalent, had a pronounced and detrimental effect on the speed with which the project was built.

On July 8, 1943, two companies of the 84th Battalion arrived and immediately began to unload. A temporary camp was set up on the beach, near the native village of Gamadodo. By the middle of August a permanent camp was nearly complete and work had been started on the supply and am-

munition depots, though a major portion of the heavy equipment had not yet arrived.

Construction specified in the original planning was essentially complete by the end of December. After clearing the site, 8½ miles of roads were built, and housing and messing facilities in the staging area for 4,000 men, a dispensary and sick bay for 50 patients, a 40-by-900-foot wharf. 20 quonset and frame warehouses, 54,400 cubic feet of cold-storage space, and 10 ammunition magazines were constructed.

In these developments, more than 400,000 cubic yards of sticky, water-soaked gumbo were moved. A sawmill was set up and supplied all except a small portion of the lumber used. A large portion of the available manpower was engaged in stevedoring until the arrival of a detachment of the 15th Special Battalion in December.

On July 31, 1943, a small detachment of the 84th was sent to the island of Samarai, southeast of

Milne Bay, to construct a small seaplane base. Work was somewhat delayed due to serious material shortages and changes in original plans, but in 42 days the project was substantially complete.

The main features were a 50-foot ramp. leading to a nose hangar and a 40,000-square-foot parking area. Barracks, messing and galley space for 220 men and 50 officers, together with water, power, sanitary, and refrigeration facilities complemented them. Aviation-gasoline storage was provided by the erection of four 1000-barrel steel tanks.

In addition, this same group of men was assigned the task of building a small seaplane operating base in Jenkins Bay, on the north coast of near-by Sariba Island, consisting of a camp for 130 men, a small boat pier, communications building, offices, and general storehouses.

The 91st Battalion, arriving October 21, 1943, relieved a small group of the 84th who were building the base headquarters at Ladava, on the western end of the bay. About one-fourth of the battalion remained at Ladava to improve the camp and construct piers. jetties, roads, electric and communi-

cation systems, warehouses, a hospital unit, and facilities for housing 75 officers and 1,000 men.

Another detachment was detailed to construct a destroyer repair unit at Gohora Bay, half a mile south of Ladava. This project included numerous shops and warehouses. piers, jetties, roads, and housing facilities for 30 officers and 1,000 men. The principal problem confronting this detachment was one of terrain; the site to be used was under water at high tide, necessitating a large amount of fill, which had to be hauled more than 5 miles by truck, over poor roads.

The remainder of the battalion went to Hilimoi, about 5 miles east of Gamadodo, to relieve the detachment of the 84th constructing a 500-bed hospital there. This project was expanded to include a recuperation center for 3,000 men. At the same time a small detail was sent to Swinger Bay, in the northwest corner of Milne Bay, to start an amphibious training center.

A portion of the staff of the 12th Regiment, part of the 3rd Brigade, reached the area on November 29, 1943. and set up headquarters at Ladava. All

FILTERING TANKS AT THE FILTERING STATION, MANUS

units in the Milne Bay area were assigned to this command and worked under its direction.

The 105th Battalion, which reached Milne Bay in January 1944, was given the job of completing the amphibious training center at Swinger Bay. This project comprised housing for 1,500 men in quonset huts, a large frame galley and mess hall, several quonset storehouses, class rooms, and shops, and the development of about 2,000 feet of waterfront. In all, more than 250,000 yards of dirt were moved in grading this project.

Soon after the 105th landed at Swinger Bay a detachment was sent to Hilimoi to assist the 91st in their work on the hospital. Another group of about 150 men was sent to Gamadodo to set up a sawmill, augmenting the one already in operation by the 84th, and to build an additional Libertyship pier.

As work on the amphibious training center neared completion, men thereby released were moved to Gamadodo until eventually only enough were left at Swinger Bay to carry out maintenance and minor construction.

Arriving with the 105th was the 528th CBMU, which took over completion of naval headquarters at Ladava as well as maintenance of naval facilities in that area. Shortly thereafter, Pontoon Assembly Detachment 3 debarked at Gamadodo and commenced operations.

February 1944 saw the arrival of the 115th Battalion, which carried on the construction of the advance base construction depot, begun by the 84th. In March the 118th Battalion landed and assisted the 115th until the depot was complete, their primary function then becoming its operation.

By the middle of 1944, most naval installations were complete. Original plans for Gamadodo were constantly expanded, and before our forces had advanced far enough to render this base unimportant the following developments had been constructed and were in use: a magazine, a staging area with all facilities to care for 10,000 men, a supply depot, a pontoon assembly depot which was assembling pontoon cells as well as barges, and a large advance base construction depot which included a spare-parts warehouse, housed in what was probably the largest building in New Guinea — 120,000 square feet in area.

While work continued on some minor unfinished construction, dismantling was started on facilities which had fulfilled their purpose and were no longer needed by advancing forces. By July 1945, the advance base construction depot had been torn down and crated, and was waiting shipment to a forward area. By October the hospital at Hilimoi had been readied for shipment north. At Gamadodo, as soon as a building was vacated, crews went to work salvaging material which would be needed in the Philippines and Okinawa.

Port Moresby

The naval base at Port Moresby was established to provide major communication facilities and advance headquarters for the Seventh Fleet.

Port Moresby, on the southeastern coast of New Guinea, has a protected waterway, 5 miles long by 3 miles wide, with a sand and clay bottom affording excellent holding ground for anchorage. Temperatures are relatively mild, with rainfall uniform in distribution and not excessive.

A detachment of 70 men from the 55th Battalion arrived at Port Moresby on June 20, 1943. An Army base for forward operations and supply was already in existence there.

The construction project consisted of a radio station, to be used also as a communications center, and Port Director facilities. Constructed at the radio station were 10 quonset huts for living quarters, water supply and storage equipment, 2 transmitter and generator buildings, roadways, and parking areas. The station was placed in operation on July 15, 1943, and 8 additional quonset huts were erected by January 12, 1944.

The Port Director facilities in the original plan were to consist of 17 quonset huts for living quarters and offices, storage facilities, a water-supply system, a generator building, and roads. Work was begun July 28, 1943, and the project was ready for use within a month. As subsequent enlargement became necessary, 19 quonset huts were added and the Port Director facilities became known as naval headquarters.

All construction was accomplished by the original 70 men augmented by 50 men sent from a detachment of the 55th working at Milne Bay. This contingent provided the additional labor required from late September until December 1943, at which time they returned to Brisbane with 20 men of the original detachment. No native materials or labor were used.

A detachment of CBMU 546 arrived on April 3,

1944. to relieve the 55th, which had carried on with routine maintenance after completing the construction program. During October the roll-up of this base was under way, and was completed by November 1. 1944.

Woodlark Island

Woodlark Island, lying northeast of Milne Bay, was occupied by United States forces on June 30, 1943, for the purpose of developing a supporting base to provide air cover for Allied operations along the northeastern coast of New Guinea.

The island has a rolling terrain, covered with dense jungle. Coral barrier-reefs surround it except at Guasopa Bay, the principal harbor, which is accessible through two passages. Limited channel depth restricted the use of the harbor, but LST's could be brought to the beach for operations. Small supply ships anchored just offshore.

The task force which occupied Woodlark Island in a surprise landing on June 30, 1943. included Army and Marine units, the 60th Construction Battalion, and a naval base unit to which about 500 men of the 20th Construction Battalion were attached. Enemy resistance was light. The men of the 20th were assigned the construction of housing, roads, and services. The 60th had as its mission the construction of an airfield and accessory facilities.

On July 2, the first echelon of the 60th Battalion began clearing and grading for the airstrip; 12 days later a coral-surfaced strip, 3,000 by 150 feet. was ready for operations. Work continued on the airfield, and by mid-September the runway was completed to a length of 6,500 feet, with a maximum width of 225 feet. A parallel taxiway, 6,000 feet long, with a minimum width of 60 feet, a dispersal loop, and 110 hardstands were completed by October 12.

Meanwhile, the 20th Battalion concentrated on road and housing construction and the establishment of a water system. The first project after landing had been the cutting of trails into the coconut plantations and the surrounding jungle to allow immediate dispersal of all equipment and supplies. These trails were later developed into suitable roads, and by October a 30-mile network of good hard roads had been completed. Housing was generally in floored and screened tents, although eight prefabricated wooden buildings and

nine quonset huts were provided for the Army Air Force, and a small hospital.

Three 3-by-7-pontoon barges were assembled and turned over to the naval base unit for operation. One 2-by-12-pontoon string was assembled and anchored offshore for use as a PT-boat pier. The Seabees also did considerable repair work on landing craft, picket boats, and PT boats.

Ample water supply was procured locally from several rivers. A sawmill. which was set up, provided 15,000 board feet of lumber per day. A coral pit for road and airstrip surfacing material was also operated.

Spasmodic enemy bombings continued throughout the construction period at Woodlark. causing only minor damage and no casualties to the Seabees.

By November 1, 1943, all Seabees had been detached from Woodlark, with the exception of 309 men of the 60th Battalion who remained for maintenance duties until March 1944.

Kiriwina

Kiriwina Island, the largest of the Trobriand group, lying off the extreme eastern tip of New Guinea, was occupied by United States forces on June 30, 1943, in a virtually unopposed landing, its capture being simultaneous with further landings by U. S. forces on New Georgia and on the New Guinea coast. It was intended to use Kiriwina as an air base to support future moves against the Japanese in New Guinea.

Near the center of this densely wooded island, which is 25 miles long and 6 miles wide at its broadest point, the United States Army Engineers constructed a coral-surfaced airstrip, 6,000 by 150 feet, for fighter and bomber operations. In September 1943, at the request of the 6th Army, 12 officers and 306 men of the 20th Battalion were sent to Kiriwina to assist in the airfield development.

The principal task of the Seabees was the construction of two taxiways, one 7,000 feet long, with 25 fighter hardstands: the other, 5,300 feet long, with 16 bomber hardstands. The first taxiway was completed on October 12, two days ahead of schedule. in time to support a major air raid against Rabaul. About a week later, the second taxiway was completed and the Seabees turned attention to the erection of operations buildings and camp facilities for aviation personnel.

The projects assigned to the battalion were completed by October 28, 1943, when the Seabees returned to Woodlark.

Finschhafen

The advance base at Finschhafen was established to provide supporting facilities for the accommodation of light naval vessels, such as PT boats and amphibious craft, to maintain a staging area for naval units participating in further forward movements, and to serve as a staging and supply point for the Seventh Fleet.

Finschhafen is on the eastern coast of British New Guinea; its harbor affords excellent shelter for moderate-size vessels and anchorages ranging from 5 to 45 fathoms. Climate is sub-tropical, with heavy rainfall.

The base was constructed on a narrow coastal plain backed by mountains. The major part of the area was jungle, with a top soil of deep black mud, underlain by poor-quality coral.

The first naval representatives to arrive at Finschhafen were members of the 60th Battalion, in early November 1943. This battalion, less one company which had remained at Woodlark, aided the Army in completing an airstrip and later developed a naval base.

Landing from LST's in Langemak Bay, near Finschhafen on November 5, the 19 officers and 658 men found the beach a morass as a result of heavy rains the previous night. Trucks and other rolling stock were unable to move more than 100 feet from the ships. The LST's were unloaded, however, and the next morning the work of clearing the beach began. A temporary dump and the camp site selected were about 300 yards from the beach, but in spite of every effort by the Seabees and a company of Army engineers, the road to this site was impassable for four weeks.

As a result, it was impossible for the Seabees to render any assistance to the 808th Army Aviation Engineer Battalion on the airstrip until November 16. The Seabees were assigned the job of rough-grading and mat-laying on the northern half of the field and of producing coral for fine-grading the entire area. In spite of the lack of equipment for road building, this strip was operating by the December 5 deadline.

The 78th Battalion landed at a point south of Finschhafen on December 9, and the 40th Battalion arrived at Finschhafen December 15, on the first Liberty ship to enter this zone. The 46th Battalion landed on the south side of Langemak Bay on January 6 and established a camp site adjoining the area occupied by the 78th Battalion.

Work on base construction was begun December 24. On January 5, 1944, the 808th Army Aviation Engineers departed, leaving the remaining airfield construction and maintenance to the 60th Battalion. The 60th built hardstands for fighters and medium bombers at Dreger Airfield, an aircraft repair area adjacent to the airstrip, four 2,000-barrel aviation-gasoline tanks, complete with piping and pumping units, and a 200-foot pile-and-timber jetty. Assistance was rendered on these projects by the 46th and 78th Battalions.

In the early months of 1944, an operating base for the support of two PT-boat squadrons was built by the 60th Battalion, the facilities including a 30-by-60-foot pier, a torpedo pier, one finger pier, two unloading piers, an 84-foot repair pier, a complete camp, warehouses, torpedo shop, and other work shops. During the late summer of 1944, the 91st Battalion, which had reported in July, improved these facilities with frame buildings and quonset huts for shops, warehouses, quarters, and recreation buildings.

Waterfront facilities were developed early in 1944. The 46th Battalion built four timber piers, each 330 feet long and 30 feet wide, with necessary approaches for Liberty ships.

Progress was slow, for it was impossible to obtain suitable piling, and the material into which the piles were driven was very soft and considerable penetration was needed to attain the required bearing. Two pontoon wharves, with bridge approaches, were erected, and covered storage in prefabricated buildings was provided at the cargo-ship piers. Until the arrival of the 19th Special Battalion in late January, detachments of the several units handled stevedoring.

Base facilities were constructed by the 60th and 78th Battalions. These installations included a 500-man camp of framed and screened tents, quonset huts for administration use, and a 300-bed hospital. Base Hospital 14 consisted of ten 20-by-48-foot quonset huts for dental, surgery, storage, and ward facilities, with nine framed tents for additional wards.

Installations at the supply depot included four

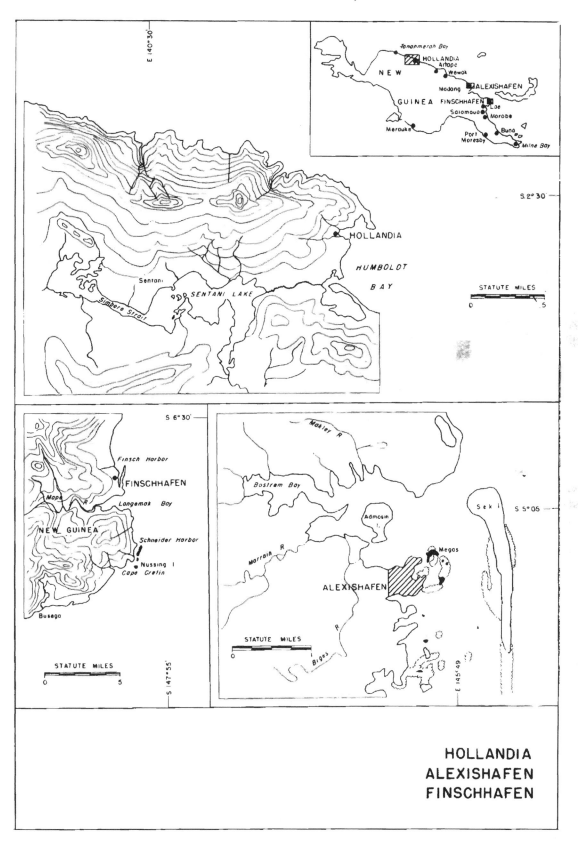

HOLLANDIA
ALEXISHAFEN
FINSCHHAFEN

ADVANCE BASE CONSTRUCTION DEPOT, MANUS ISLAND
This photograph was taken May 24, 1945

6,800-cubic-foot refrigerators, twenty prefabricated warehouses, a 40-by-80-foot timber-and-coral-fill wharf, and ten 20-by-50-foot standard prefabricated steel magazines. The 78th also built a fuel-oil tank farm of five 10,000-barrel tanks, with all necessary piping.

Staging areas were established at Finschhafen for both Army and Navy personnel. The 40th Battalion built an Army staging area for 17,000 men, with camp and storage facilities, 14 LST loading ramps, and 15 miles of two-lane roads with several timber bridges. During the summer of 1944, the 91st Battalion began construction of the naval staging area for 2500 men, with necessary camp and storage installations and roads. This project was about 75-percent complete on November 1, 1944, when orders were received to curtail further work at the base.

From March to June 1944, the 102nd Battalion, while restaging, assisted in minor construction activities. CBMU's 545 and 543 reported in February and April 1944, respectively, in time to aid in the major construction at the base.

Native labor was used, where available, for clearing brush and for logging and milling operations. The 60th Battalion set up a sawmill in November 1943, and the Army furnished the logs. This sawmill was later taken over by the 46th Battalion. Coral for the roads and the airstrip was secured from a nearby coral pit, operated by the Seabees.

Major obstacles to construction were heavy rains and occasional enemy bombings, which caused the Seabees some casualties.

All major projects at the base were curtailed in November 1944, and by January 1945 roll-up by CBMU 543 was well under way. The base was disestablished April 1, 1945, and all facilities were turned over to the Army.

Cape Gloucester

On December 26, 1943, when the 1st Marine Division went ashore at Cape Gloucester, on the northwest tip of New Britain, it was accompanied by the 19th Construction Battalion, whose mission was the building of roads for supplies and access during the assault, and the preparation of beaches and piers for landing craft.

Reconstruction of two enemy airstrips, which were the principal objectives of the attack and from which United States planes could continue raids against Japanese-held Rabaul and Kavieng, was carried out by the 1913th and 841st Army Aviation Engineer Battalions. The strips were captured by the Marines on December 30, and next day, the American flag was raised over all Cape Gloucester.

Road construction, with necessary bridges, continued throughout the Seabees' stay. Pulverized volcanic slag produced a surface so hard that even after continual truck traffic the tread of a large bulldozer did not cut into the surface.

A new method of "drilling" holes for blasting was developed on this work. A 75-mm armor-piercing shell, fired into a rock ledge by a General Sherman tank, left a hole about 10 inches in diameter and 10 feet deep which could be quickly prepared for a dynamite charge.

Waterfront construction consisted of a rock-fill pile-and-crib finger pier, 130 feet long and 50 feet wide, a 160-foot rock-fill approach jetty for a cargo-ship berth, landing-craft unloading pier, and a 350-foot seawall of piles and log-facing, backed with large boulders.

The 19th Battalion, the only Seabee group at Cape Gloucester, was attached to the First Marine Division and left with the division in late April for the Russells. During the first weeks, continuous enemy air raids resulted in 5 men of the battalion killed and 24 wounded.

Manus

A major naval and air base, capable of service, supply, and repair to forces afloat, air forces, and other Allied units in the forward area, was established early in 1944, at Manus, in the Admiralty Islands, about 300 miles north of Lae, New Guinea. and, apart from the St. Matthias group, the northernmost group of islands in the Southwest Pa-

cific area. Manus lay close to the enemy line of communication between Truk and Rabaul, and also near the route between Kavieng and Wewak.

Manus and Los Negros comprise the major islands of the Admiralty group, which includes some 160 small islands and atolls and three first-class harbors. Manus, about 50 miles long and 15 miles wide, is the largest island of the group. The terrain, which rises to a maximum elevation of 3,000 feet near the center of the island, is of volcanic origin, principally basalt, which weathers to a thick, reddish, clayey gumbo.

Seeadler Harbor, one of the largest and best in the Southwest Pacific, lies within the ellipse formed by Manus, the curving shore of adjoining Los Negros, and the reef-bound islands to the north. Its protected waters are capable of accommodating a large fleet of capital ships. Los Negros, roughly crescent in shape, is separated from the much-larger Manus by a narrow passage. The island is low and, for the most part, swampy, with coral just below the topsoil.

The first echelon of the 4th Construction Brigade, consisting of part of the 40th Battalion and small detachments of the 46th, 78th, and 17th Battalions. landed at Hyane Harbor, Los Negros, on March 2, 1944, with the first reinforcements to the original group of 1,000 Army troops, who had landed two days earlier. Only a small beachhead then existed. Enemy resistance, which had been severe, was overcome by March 4.

The Seabees' first job was to rehabilitate Momote airstrip, which had been seized on February 29, by a reconnaissance party of the First Cavalry Division. Although the airstrip was in our hands, the enemy occupied the surrounding areas, and 2 officers and 100 men from the 40th Battalion were placed in the front lines to reinforce the Army unit holding the area. These Seabees remained in this advanced position for two nights, withstanding three enemy attacks. For this action, the 40th was awarded the Presidential Unit Citation.

The captured airfield consisted of a 4,000-foot strip and a number of dispersal areas, none of which was in service, due to poor construction methods and design and to bombing by our forces. The Seabees began work on March 3. the morning after landing. and continued for several days, despite constant sniping and the loss of bulldozers to other activities. The condition of the strip was such that 14,000 cubic yards had to be filled and graded before matting could be laid, as local coral material proved unsuitable as surfacing.

On March 10, RAAF fighters arrived and began operations, although construction continued until June 1, 1944, when the facilities were turned over to the Army for maintenance. Completed installations consisted of an airstrip, 7,800 by 150 feet, with taxiways and hardstands for 90 fighters and 80 heavy bombers, a 17,000-barrel aviation-gasoline tank farm with fuel jetty for small tankers, bomb-storage revetments, roads, operations buildings, and personnel facilities.

Construction of an additional airfield (Mokerang) was the major project of the 104th Battalion, which arrived on April 1, 1944. An Army engineer aviation battalion assisted throughout the operation. The original plan called for a bomber runway, 8,000 by 200 feet; a taxiway, 8,500 by 125 feet, with hardstands and service areas for 50 bombers. This project was completed as scheduled, on April 22, with the use of additional equipment from other battalions. The first landings of 307th Bomber Group planes had taken place on April 21.

The original taxiway was later enlarged and two additional taxiways built. Other installations included a 30,000-barrel tank farm, quonset-hut shops, and personnel facilities. A second bomber strip of equal size, added to the plan, was built by Army engineers aided by Seabee equipment and operators.

By July 1944, the Seabees had constructed numerous other facilities in the Hyane Harbor area, including a 500-bed evacuation hospital for the Army. Waterfront construction consisted of two cargo-ship wharves, a repair pier with fixed crane, and a fuel pier, 800 feet long, to serve major ships.

Facilities at the pontoon assembly depot, operated by PAD 1, which arrived June 19, 1944, involved a pontoon pier, four prefabricated steel buildings for warehouses, shops, and offices, structural-steel factories, and a personnel camp of 40 huts with all utilities for 50 officers and 500 men. The depot could assemble 900 pontoon cells per month.

An aviation-supply depot was established as the central procurement, storage, and issuing agency for all such material and equipment in the Southwest Pacific area. For this activity, the 46th Battalion erected 24 steel warehouses, each 40 by 100 feet, and 83 quonset huts for administration and personnel. Facilities for an aviation repair and overhaul unit were set up, consisting of 25 steel

buildings, 40 by 100 feet, for shops, a personnel camp for 1,000 men, roads, and all utilities. A naval airstrip, 5,000 by 150 feet, with hardstands, a 7,000-barrel aviation-gasoline storage farm, a parking area, warehouses, and a personnel camp were also built. The section base at Hyane Harbor was provided with facilities for small-boat repair, including a wharf, personnel camp, and shops.

In April 1944, two additional locations on Los Negros were selected for development, one at Papitalai Point and one at Lombrum Point.

The projects at Papitalai Point were assigned to the 58th Battalion, which arrived on April 17, 1944. The next day, survey crews were sent ashore to select a camp site. Constant heavy rainfall and the unfavorable terrain, however, made progress difficult. Quarters were finally erected on coconut-log footings at least 2 feet above the ground.

The first major construction assignment was the building of a 30-foot primary road from Lombrum Point to Papitalai Point.

For a drydock storage area and personnel camp, the 58th built seven 40-by-100-foot warehouses, 29 quonset huts, a mess hall, a galley, a water system, and a coconut-log, coral-fill jetty, 40 by 80 feet, the site of which required considerable fill.

Heavy rains, which turned the area into a mass of mud, considerably delayed construction of a PT-boat overhaul base and personnel camp; however, it was found that coral from a nearby deposit furnished a measure of stability. Due to the lack of available access roads, a jetty had to be built entirely by hand labor. Installations upon completion consisted of seven 40-by-100-foot warehouses, three quonset huts, one 30-by-50-foot wood-frame building, and a frame galley and mess hall.

The major project at Papitalai, a tank farm with sufficient storage of fuel and diesel oil to supply a large base and major units of the fleet, was begun on June 23. Lack of suitable coral for surfacing again proved a handicap. Material for tank foundations had to be ferried across the harbor, and roads deteriorated to such an extent that corduroying was the only solution. However, the schedule to complete 25 tanks by August 15 was met despite the difficulties encountered, and work continued until 63 tanks were erected, each having a 10,000-barrel capacity. A two-way pumping system and a drum-filling plant completed the farm, which was split into sections, making it possible to operate from any single unit or series of units.

The 11th Battalion was the first unit to land at

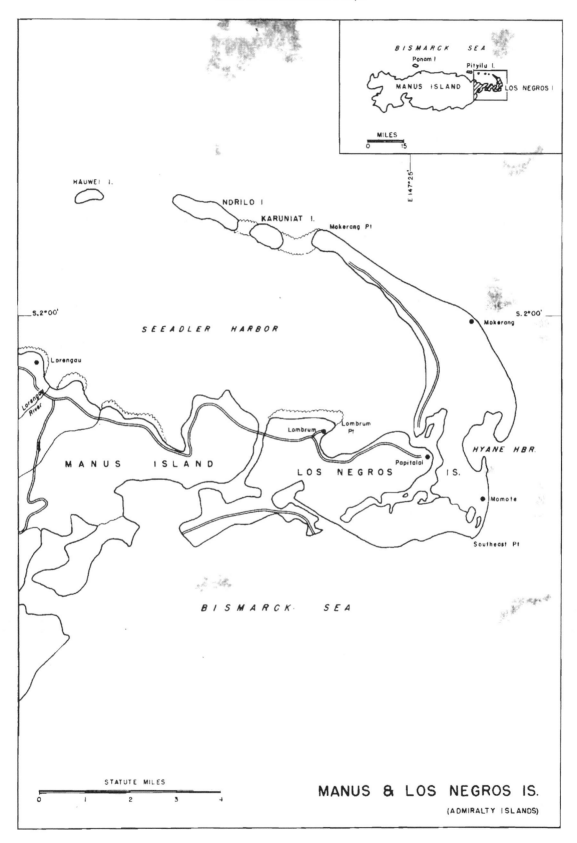

MANUS & LOS NEGROS IS.

(ADMIRALTY ISLANDS)

71ST SEABEES BUILD AN AIRFIELD IN THE ADMIRALTIES
Rough grading on May 28, 1944

71ST SEABEES BUILD AN AIRFIELD IN THE ADMIRALTIES
Coral surfacing on June 1, 1944

71st Seabees Build an Airfield in the Admiralties
Finishing coral surfacing on June 4, 1944

Lombrum Point, on April 17, 1944. A permanent camp was set up and work begun on three main projects—a seaplane repair base, a ship repair base, and a landing-craft repair base.

For the landing-craft repair base, the Seabees erected six warehouses and shops, two quonset huts for administration buildings, and frame quarters and messing facilities. with all camp utilities. A 250-ton pontoon drydock was provided for docking LCT's, LSM's, and smaller landing-craft.

Facilities at the ship-repair base combined docking, repair, and supply services equivalent to those furnished by auxiliary ships. Docking equipment consisted of a 100,000-ton sectional dock capable of handling battleships, a 70,000-ton sectional dock capable of handling most major ships, and an 18,000-ton steel floating dock.

The seaplane base at Lombrum Point was established to furnish operational, service. and repair facilities. Installations included a 50-by-250-foot concrete seaplane ramp. one steel nose hangar with a concrete deck, an 8,000-barrel aviation-gasoline tank farm, a pontoon pier for small boats. four 40-by-100-foot prefabricated shops, quonset-hut shops, and camp facilities.

Development of base facilities on Manus Island was initiated by the 5th Construction Regiment, composed of the 35th, 44th, and 57th Battalions, which landed between April 14 and 20, 1944. There was no enemy resistance, although Army patrols killed three snipers on the beachhead and captured several prisoners in the vicinity during the next ten days. For six weeks, the Seabees maintained perimeter guards at their camps.

The principal installations were made for the supply depot, which was to serve shore-based activities in the Admiralties as well as all forces afloat in the area. The Seabees erected 128 storage buildings. 50 refrigerators, each containing 6,800 cubic feet, built open-storage areas, 5 miles of access roads. an LST landing beach, and two major piers, one 800 feet and the other 500 feet long. Ultimately. the storage floor space was extended to give the equivalent of 180 storage buildings. This was accomplished by lean-to additions. These facilities were located along the Lorengau airstrip,

BLASTING FOR CORAL IN THE ADMIRALTIES
71st Seabees working on the Pityilu airfield

which had been found unsuitable for operational development. The depot was commissioned on July 2.

A major development undertaken by the various units of the Seabees at the Manus naval base was the construction, operation, and maintenance of a water-supply system, capable of producing 4,000,-000 gallons per day.

Two primary systems were developed. The Lorengau system, with its source of supply the Lorengau River, produced a daily average of 2,700,000 gallons. The Lombrum system, utilizing five small streams and impounding reservoirs, produced an average of 600,000 gallons per day.

In addition, 23 unit water systems in outlying areas, using portable purification units, could draw 850,000 gallons per day from shallow wells.

Treatment of both primary supplies incorporated aeration, sedimentation, coagulation, filtra-tion, and chlorination, producing a quality of water that was considered very good for all purposes.

Distribution was accomplished from a gravity-flow system; however, auxiliary pumps were spotted in the lines to boost the pressure in the event of an emergency.

The main reservoir of the Lorengau system had a capacity of 2,142,000 gallons, augmented with five 10,000-barrel steel tanks, one 1,000-barrel steel tank, and various wood-stave tanks at the popula-tion centers.

The Lombrum system was tied in with a main 420,000-gallon reservoir and wood-stave tanks.

All distribution mains were steel pipe, ranging from 6 to 12 inches in diameter. Laterals and aux-iliaries were from half inch to 4 inches in diameter.

The administration area for the entire Admir-alty base was located at the mouth of the Lorengau River. Facilities included 48 quonset huts for officers, a 2,000-man mess hall, 10 quonset huts, signal towers for base communications, all utilities, and a timber pier. On May 4, the 4th Brigade headquarters were moved from Los Negros to Manus.

Original plans contemplated two separate hospitals, but these were consolidated into one 1,000-bed unit, Base Hospital 15. Facilities included 42 quonset huts, a 1,000-man mess hall, 8 wards, 5 operating rooms, storage facilities, administration, dental, and laboratory installations, and all utilities. A receiving station was also established, containing facilities for 5,000 men in 292 quonset huts, with frame galleys and mess halls.

Two additional air bases were constructed on the nearby small islands of Ponam and Pityilu.

At Ponam a fighter base, to provide minor repair and overhaul facilities for carrier-based planes, together with housing facilities for pilots and crews, was established by the 78th Battalion in the summer of 1944. Installations consisted of a coral-surfaced airstrip, 5,000 by 150 feet, a 5,000-foot taxiway with a parking area. 6,000 feet square; 34 quonset huts for repair shops and operations; a 1,500-man camp; and an 8,000-barrel tank farm with sea-loading line for aviation gasoline. Fifty per cent of the work area was swamp land, requiring fill, all of it coral, blasted and dredged from the ocean bed.

The 71st Battalion set up a base for carrier planes on Pityilu, to care for one patrol squadron, to service and repair all types of carrier-based planes, and to provide storage for 350 of these planes, with camp accommodations for 350 officers and 1,400 men. The coral-surfaced runway measured 4,500 by 300 feet, with taxiway and three parking areas. Prefabricated steel huts were erected for administration, operations, and shop use. Other facilities included a 7,000-barrel aviation-gasoline

CORAL EXCAVATION AT PITYILU

PARKING AREA AFTER CORAL SURFACING HAD BEEN APPLIED, PITYILU AIRFIELD

tank farm with sea-loading line, one prefabricated nose hangar, and munition dumps. This work was accomplished in May and June 1944, with assistance from Company C of the 58th Battalion. Later, the field was extended 1,000 feet; parking areas were increased; the camp was enlarged to accommodate 2,500 men; and the dispensary was developed into a 100-bed hospital with all facilities.

The eastern end of Pityilu Island was cleared, graded, and made into a fleet recreation center to accommodate 10,000 men at one time.

Stevedoring for all naval activities was handled by the 20th, 21st, and 22nd Special Battalions.

Although little native labor was employed, native woods and coral were used in abundance.

Arriving September 17 and 18, 1944, the 63rd Battalion was assigned to a wide variety of work. An ammunition depot, consisting of concrete-floored storage buildings, with sorting warehouses, and quonset huts for personnel, was built, together with additional warehouses for the supply depot. Maintenance of all facilities, including roads, boats, and electrical equipment, as well as coral excava-

tion, was also assigned to the battalion. In addition, both a concrete batching plant and a sawmill were set up and operated. These activities, with improvements to docking facilities and extensive power-line installations, were carried out before the 63rd departed for Manila on March 25, 1945.

The 140th Battalion landed at Manus on June 17, 1944, two companies being detailed to Ponam and Pityilu, respectively. On Manus the 140th assisted the 63rd in the establishment of the ammunition depot, later taking over the entire maintenance and development.

On V-J day, the 140th Battalion, the 20th and 22nd Special Battalions, CBMU's 561, 587, and 621, and PAD 1 were still in the Admiralties. All units were engaged in stevedoring and in general maintenance and repair.

Emirau

Continuing the Pacific strategy of by-passing Japanese strong points and occupying intervening islands to aid in cutting the enemy's lines of communication and supply, and to provide landing fields for our shore-based bombers in the coming attacks on Truk, Yap, and Palau, the island of Emirau was occupied on March 20, 1944. In addition to landing fields, the island was to be developed as a naval base, a PT operating base, and a minor repair base.

Emirau, one of the many small islands of the Bismark Archipelago, lies 250 miles north of the once strongly fortified Japanese base of Rabaul, New Britain. The Truk Islands are 600 miles due north, and Yap and the Palau group are 800 miles to the northwest.

The island is approximately 2 miles wide, and 8 miles long in an east-west direction, with an arm in the central section jutting northward for about 2½ miles. The shoreline border of flat land, several hundred feet in width, rises several feet above sea level, and is broken by a parallel cliff formation, which rises abruptly, 75 to 185 feet above the sea at most points, to a comparatively level plateau of about 4,000 acres. The island is covered with light vegetation, second-growth timber, and some heavy forest. Hamburg Bay, a fair harbor, lies on the northwest coast. The climate is tropical, with high humidity and heavy rainfall. About 300 natives inhabit the island.

Emirau was occupied without enemy opposition, March 20, 1944, by two battalions of the 4th Marine Division. Main contingents of the 18th Construction Regiment, comprising the regimental staff, Battalions 27, 61, 63, and the 17th Special Battalion, arrived with the second and third echelons of the division on March 25 and March 30. These contingents were augmented April 14 by the 77th Construction Battalion.

All construction was assigned to the 18th Regiment for distribution among its battalions; the work was inter-related as far as possible, no battalion being assigned projects solely of one type or in one area.

The 27th Battalion took over the construction of the naval base headquarters, PT Base 16, the small-boat pool, Hamburg Bay harbor developments, an LCT floating drydock and slip, and a portion of the roads.

The construction of the main road arteries, aviation housing facilities, ammunition-storage buildings, the runway at North Cape Field, some of the

PARACHUTE LOFT AT PITYILU AIRFIELD

buildings at the PT base, and sawmill operation comprised the work of the 61st Battalion.

The 63rd assisted in the operation of the sawmill and work on the aviation shops, camps, roads, the airfield, harbor facilities, storage warehouses, magazines, and bomb and aviation-gasoline dumps.

To the 77th Battalion fell the task of constructing taxiways and hardstands on Inshore and North Cape airfields, aviation shops, and camps, bomb dumps, and the construction, maintenance, and operation of the aviation-gasoline tank farm.

The Inshore Field runway and approach zones, aviation shops and camps, radio range and radio direction finder stations, and the road and causeway at the eastern end of the island were built by the 88th Battalion.

The two airfields, Inshore and North Cape, were both heavy bomber strips, 7,000 by 150 feet, and coral surfaced, as were the warm-up areas at each end of the fields. Inshore Field had 35 double hardstands capable of parking 210 fighter or light-bomber planes. There were 42 hardstands on North Cape Field, with space for parking 84 heavy bombers. Both fields had all necessary facilities for operations, including a control tower, field operations building, field lighting, and a dispensary. All buildings used for supplies and servicing were of prefabricated steel or wooden frame. Screened and decked tents housed 1,050 officers and 4,200 enlisted aviation personnel.

A tank farm for aviation gasoline was installed with three 10,000-barrel and nineteen 1,000-barrel tanks, two tanker moorings with anti-torpedo nets, two sea-loading lines, and a gravity distribution system to six truck-filling points. In connection with this farm, an adequate reserve of more than 40,000 barrels was maintained in drums. The ammunition and bomb dump provided covered storage, steel magazines, and revetments.

Three hospitals were built on the island. The naval base hospital, with a capacity of 100 beds, and the 24th Army Field Hospital, with beds for 160, were both located in the southwestern tip of the island. Acorn 7 Hospital, located on the extreme northern tip of Cape Ballin, had facilities for 150 patients.

The anchorage in Hamburg Bay accommodated five capital ships; Purple Beach, on the Bay, with three finger piers and one 77-by-120-foot slip was sufficient to handle seven LCT's. On this beach were also eight pier cranes, refrigerators with a capacity

of 42,400 cubic feet, six 40-by-1,000-foot warehouses, and approximately 400,000 square feet of open-storage space, which permitted the handling of 800 tons of cargo a day. An LCT floating dry-dock was also maintained in the Bay. All other beaches on the island were unsuitable for efficient cargo handling; however, five beaches on the western coast were improved to accommodate thirteen LCT's.

Communication facilities consisted of two wooden transmitter buildings with concrete floors, two 16-by-32-foot revetted wood-frame power plants, and two quonset-type receiver stations.

The naval base was established at the southwest tip of the island. Facilities constructed for its operation consisted principally of wooden frame, canvas-covered structures, replaced later by quonset-type buildings, when urgent airfield facilities had been provided.

Quarters and messing for 560 officers and men, engine overhaul and repair shops, a magazine, a total of 350 feet of coral-fill piers, a signal tower, and all the necessary utilities for a PT base, were erected on the island of Eanusau, just off the southwest tip of Emirau. The small-boat pool was also installed there, consisting of a camp for 250 men and 15 officers, 4 quonset-type dry-storage buildings, shops, a sick bay, an armory, a generator plant, ships' service, a personnel pier, and a signal tower. Connecting the various activities and camps were a total of 40 miles of 40-foot coral-surfaced, all-weather highway.

In July 1944, CBMU 502 arrived to relieve the construction battalions of maintenance work. By August, construction was complete, with the exception of minor additions.

The 61st Battalion left in July, and by the middle of December all construction forces, with the exception of the maintenance unit, had left. The 502nd, by that time, was engaged in dismantling quarters and buildings as soon as they were vacated, and crating equipment no longer needed. By the end of May 1945 the roll-up was complete, except for installations which were to remain on the island, and on June 6 the 502nd departed for Manus.

Hollandia, New Guinea

The naval base at Hollandia was established to provide logistic support to services afloat and later to become a supply base for the invasion of the

Philippines. It was to include a base for convoy escorts, a supply depot, a repair base for destroyers and lighter craft, and an ammunition depot. In addition, it was to be advance headquarters of the Seventh Fleet.

Hollandia is located on Humboldt Bay on the north coast of Dutch New Guinea. This area has a tropical climate, with heavy rainfall.

Generally throughout the Hollandia region the terrain is rocky, erosion having caused a jumble of hills and bluffs, some of which exceed 1,000 feet in height. Fresh water is extremely scarce except in the Hollandia valley. A reef, composed of soft coral and silt, lies close along the shore. Humboldt Bay, adequate and well protected, provides the only extensive anchorage between Wewak, about 200 miles to the east, and Geelvink Bay, some 350 miles to the west.

Naval facilities at Hollandia were extensive, including a staging area, fleet postoffice, Seventh Fleet advance headquarters, and a fueling depot. All facilities were located near Humboldt Bay, with the exception of advance headquarters, which was about 12 miles west of the bay, and the fueling depot on Tanahmerah Bay.

Preliminary surveys were made by the officers in charge of the 24th Regiment and the 113th Battalion on D-Day, April 21, 1944. The 113th Battalion arrived on May 9, and was immediately assigned the construction of all base roads, docking facilities, and utility systems, as well as heavy grading and drainage work for dump areas.

Road construction to provide access to the scattered sites of the various base facilities, as usual, took first priority. Accordingly, men and equipment were landed at three different points in order that construction could be pushed. The first day, 4,000 feet were rough graded; within two weeks the roads were open for traffic. In all, 6 miles of road were laid down through particularly difficult country.

The construction of a pier for Liberty ships carried the next highest priority. A temporary camp, to ready and assemble construction material, was immediately set up. Work started on May 25, and 82 feet of the pier was available for use by June 9. From that time until its completion on July 3, 1944, the pier was constantly in use.

At the same time, a water-supply system was under construction. Treated water from small near-by springs, supplementing that truck-hauled from distant streams, was used to supply the camp pending the arrival of pipe. A temporary system to service small landing-craft was constructed in four and a half days, and was put into service on May 27. A supply of 6-inch pipe was received on June 2, and within 24 hours, 960 feet of it had been installed; by June 8 the system had been extended to supply Liberty ships. The permanent system consisted of 58,400 feet of 4-inch, 6-inch, and 8-inch pipe, one 10,000-barrel and twenty 5,000-gallon storage tanks, with a chlorination system that provided 2,500,000 gallons of treated water a day to vessels and to all activities of the base.

Construction of another pier began on September 13, but lack of materials delayed completion until November 23, although 130 feet were ready October 22 and ships were tied up continually from that time on.

Land for sorting and storage areas was obtained by filling and surfacing with concrete a shallow cove between the first pier and the LST watering-point, the edge of the fill being further developed as a landing-craft watering- and loading-point. Similar areas were built at both docking areas, as well as adjacent to the fleet postoffice and harbor administration area.

In addition, the 113th Battalion worked on numerous other projects, large and small, among them the 40-by-494-foot pier for the destroyer repair base. Work there was started on July 31. The pier was completed within a month, during which time a fleet postoffice and harbor administration facilities were also constructed. The communications department of the battalion installed a complete telephone system for the base, including 10 switchboards, 203 miles of telephone line, 76,000 feet of submarine cable, and 351 stations and trunk lines.

The 102nd Battalion arrived at Humboldt Bay, on June 12, 1944, and was assigned the construction of a supply depot, a destroyer repair shop, and a degaussing range, as well as housing facilities at several locations.

The supply-depot warehouses included 16 quonset huts, 40 by 300 feet, with concrete floors. Ten banks of refrigerators, with a capacity totaling 136,000 cubic feet, were built, as well as a complete camp accommodating 200 men. For the destroyer repair shop, it was necessary to fill in approximately 150,000 cubic yards of shore line and set up all

WATERFRONT FACILITIES AT HOLLANDIA

All flat land shown is earth fill from the steep hills which formerly rose precipitously from the water's edge.
Installations shown are (beginning in the foreground) concrete-surfaced sorting platform, landing craft watering,
loading, and unloading ramp, and fleet postoffice and harbor administration area.

facilities, including storage, office, and foundry, quonset huts, and necessary roads.

In addition, the battalion built housing facilities for the various activities of the base, including housing and messing facilities for 100 men at the staging area on Pancake Hill. Other camp areas included housing for 500 men at base headquarters, and housing and messing for the men assigned to the 24th Regiment.

Crews from the 102nd were assigned to the operation of the battalion's pontoon barges and all barges and LCM's which belonged to the 24th Regiment. This equipment was essential to the unloading of ships, especially in the early stages before piers were completed. The 102nd also operated the regimental supply dump, supplying men, cranes, and trucks, and installed 2 miles of overhead and submarine cable incidental to the construction of the degaussing range.

The 119th Seabees reached Humboldt Bay on June 13, 1944, the day after the 102nd landed. On June 19, their ship, with all equipment, was sent to Tanahmerah Bay, 25 miles farther west, where it was unloaded and most of the cargo transported to Lake Sentani, 8 miles in the interior. The battalion was assigned three major projects: a tank farm at Tanahmerah Bay, advance naval headquarters at Lake Sentani, and pontoon assembly at Humboldt Bay.

Although working conditions at Tanahmerah Bay were ideal as far as rain was concerned, the boggy condition of the terrain slowed road construction. Initial plans called for a total of one 10,000-barrel diesel-oil and twenty, later reduced to eleven, 10,000-barrel fuel-oil tanks. The original date of completion was set for September 15, 1944, but due to shortage of materials and the boggy ground, only the diesel-oil tank and seven fuel-oil tanks were ready by that date. By October 7, three additional fuel-oil tanks were in operation. This construction included all necessary piping, manifolds, and pump installations as well as a 12-inch welded fuel line on the Army-built pipeline pier.

Advance naval headquarters at Lake Sentani included quonset huts for administration and for housing and messing 800 men. Completion date was set for August 15, but 34 quonset huts were usable by July 23, and shortly thereafter the Seventh Fleet personnel began moving in. A stevedoring unit of 100 men was furnished by the 119th Battalion during this period.

Important jobs assigned the 122nd Seabees, who arrived June 28, 1944, were the construction of port director's facilities at Wakde and at Aitape. the base water-supply, and, later, G-2 hospital in Hollandia valley. Construction at Wakde and at Aitape was started on July 10 and July 11, respectively. It included administration facilities at Wakde and housing and messing facilities at Aitape. The Wakde project was completed on June 30; the job at Aitape, on July 2.

A radio transmitter was built at Hollandia and a radio receiving station at Leimok Hill. Work was started on the transmitter on July 10 and was completed in 35 days; work at the receiving station required an additional five days. These projects included all buildings for both administration and personnel, and all other equipment necessary for operation of the stations.

A 500-bed hospital, consisting of 78 structures, was begun August 8 and completed September 30. Before this hospital, located in the upper end of Hollandia valley, was begun, it was necessary to make a fill of 85,000 cubic yards and to divert a stream which meandered through the site. A 5-foot dam across the stream and wood storage tanks provided a gravity-flow water system.

Numerous other projects were completed by the

NAVAL SUPPLY DEPOT REFRIGERATOR AREA, HOLLANDIA
102nd Seabees working on the project, September 25, 1944

122nd while at Hollandia, including housing facilities for 350 men at the destroyer repair base and naval base facilities for 1,000 men. A naval base water-supply system, consisting of 3,500 feet of 8-inch water line, was installed in 18 days. A large percentage of all the lumber used on the base was logged and milled by the battalion.

The battalion was constantly handicapped by the urgent need for all facilities. Ships unloaded on piers only half completed, and personnel moved in as soon as even a portion of the administration and personnel areas were usable.

By V-J day only a small part of the base had been rolled-up by CBMU 558, stationed there since the preceding October. Hollandia was strategically important as a base for strikes against the enemy and was a major factor in the invasion of the Philippine, furnishing a large portion of the supplies.

The naval base at Hollandia was disestablished in December 1945. All installations were sold to the Netherlands East Indies Government.

Biak, Owi, Mios Woendi

Biak Island, in the Schouten group, was developed to provide an operating and repair base for seaplanes and PT boats; repair facilities for landing craft, from LST's to the smallest types; and hospitalization for patients evacuated from advance areas. It gave the Allies a base only 900 miles from Davao, P.I., and control of northwestern Dutch New Guinea. However, most of the facilities originally scheduled for Biak were eventually installed on Owi and Mios Woendi in the Padaido Islands. as enemy resistance on Biak was unexpectedly heavy and slowed the time schedule.

The Padaido Islands, which consist of many wooded islands, cover an area 35 by 21½ miles, close to Biak at the entrance to Geelvink Bay in northwest New Guinea. Owi, which is nearest, is less than 5 miles south of Biak. Padaido lagoon, at Mios Woendi. provides an anchorage area of 5 square miles, with 2,100 feet of navigable beach front. The climate is tropical, with an annual rainfall reaching 100 inches.

On June 6, 1944, PT Advance Base 2 arrived at Mios Woendi, accompanied by a detachment of the 113th Battalion, to set up operating and living facilities for two squadrons. The first detachment of the 55th Battalion, with equipment, arrived at Mios Woendi on June 12 and 14, and work was immediately begun on a camp site. On July 5 the detachment from the 113th returned to Hollandia.

Upon the arrival of PT Base 21 on June 26, construction was begun on an operational repair base. Housing, messing, and collateral facilities were provided for 2,000 enlisted personnel and 250 officers. Twelve finger piers were installed to accommodate as many as 50 PT boats, together with a torpedo-change pier, small-boat landing, and a large pontoon pier with crane facilities for changing engines. Five pontoon drydocks were placed in operation for repair work. and two prefabricated warehouses were set up.

Company D of the 55th Battalion accomplished the major portion of the construction program. the finger piers being installed by Company A.

All the shops were in operation six weeks after unloading; on August 7, 1944, the base was usable.

On June 18. half of the 19th Special Battalion arrived with a 100-bed mobile dispensary and immediately started preparation of a camp site and hospital facilities, both of which were more or less temporary. On July 12, materials and equipment for a 200-bed dispensary arrived. The smaller, 100-bed mobile dispensary was absorbed into the larger unit, and became Naval Base Hospital 16. thus providing accommodations for 300 patients.

The 55th Battalion erected 32 quonset huts for use as wards, offices, laboratory, diet kitchen, galley, laundry, and storerooms, as well as 56 tents for living quarters, in connection with the hospital, which was completed August 16.

Mobile Amphibious Repair Base 2, a functional component designed to provide repairs necessary to support the operation of 18 LST's, 18 LCI's, 36 LCT's, 60 LCM's. and 240 LCVP's, arrived at Mios Woendi between July 4 and July 25. For this base, construction performed by the 55th, with additional labor from the repair-base personnel, consisted of a camp of 150 tents, shop facilities of 7 quonset huts, and 5 small miscellaneous wooden structures, all of which were completed by September 15.

The major construction problem at this base was the sorting, assembling, cataloging, and overhauling of machinery and spare parts, which, due to outdoor storage and several transshipments, carried no outside identification. Damaged equipment was repaired and conditioned in the field while the shops were being constructed.

On July 8, 1944, the 60th Battalion (856 officers and enlisted men) arrived at Owi. The Army was already in the process of building two airstrips

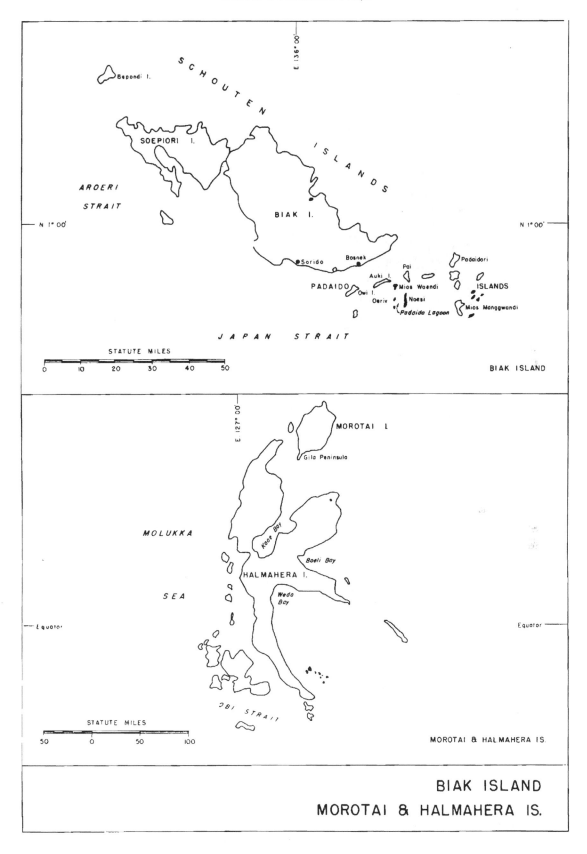

BIAK ISLAND

MOROTAI & HALMAHERA IS.

HOSPITAL WARDS ON OWI ISLAND, NOVEMBER 15, 1944

there, but Army and Navy plans called for the Navy to assist in the construction.

At the time the battalion arrived, one airstrip was completed to 5,000 feet, with approximately 30 hardstands. Plans called for two airstrips, 7,000 by 150 feet each, parallel taxiways, and 219 heavy-bomber hardstands.

All airstrip construction was in coral, and easily performed as the site was level and covered only with scrub growth. Many of the dispersal areas and hardstands, however, were in hard, rough coral and heavy timber, which necessitated much drilling, blasting, and rooting. The construction of all airstrip facilities on Owi was completed on September 25, and the maintenance work was then taken over by the battalion.

Other construction accomplished by the 60th on Owi included camps for Acorn 8, two bomber squadrons, and two air-supply units, the 17th Army Station Hospital, roads, bomb and gasoline storage areas, an aviation-gasoline tank farm, landing facilities for four LST's, and a small-boat pier.

Navy Seaplane Base 2 personnel arrived at Mios Woendi July 16 and were established as an operations and maintenance unit for Fleet Air Wing 17. Facilities installed for their use, by the 55th Battalion, included messing and housing for 850 officers and men, a well-water system of 15,000-gallon capacity, a seaplane ramp and parking area, a nose hangar, an operations tower with three quonset huts for combat-operations structures, a radio station, and shops for various maintenance work, together with roadways and walkways. Use of local materials were, as in all construction in the area, confined to sand and shells for roads and concrete aggregate, and a few logs for foundations and heavy supports.

Construction at Mios Woendi included 8 quonset huts for offices and administration, 136 tents and 18 quonset huts for quarters and messing, 18 quonset huts for storehouses, a 400-by-40-foot wharf, a vehicle-repair shop, and various recreational facilities. Work was completed by August 31.

Other work performed by the 55th consisted of

a tank farm of twenty 1,000-barrel tanks on nearby Noesi Island, the Port Director's office on Biak, and a mine-warfare facilities project and ammunition-storage unit on Oeriv Island, southeast of Mios Woendi. Existing facilities on Mios Woendi were also developed and enlarged to accommodate the increase of shipping handled by the base.

Night air attacks and numerous alerts during the early days, heavy rains, and lack of a proper aggregate for concrete were difficulties met and overcome without halting operations.

With the departure of the 19th Special Battalion on October 14, the 55th, in addition to their other duties, took over stevedoring at the base. In November 1944 the Fifth Air Force headquarters moved from Owi to Leyte, P.I., and the 60th Battalion, after dismantling and shipping their buildings and equipment, embarked for rehabilitation leave in the United States on December 20, 1944.

CBMU 605 arrived at Mios Woendi during the month of November, relieving the 55th, who departed during February 1945. On V-J Day, all facilities were operating as planned.

The naval base in the Padaido group was disestablished January 19, 1946.

Alexishafen-Madang, British New Guinea

The primary purpose of the base at Madang was to provide logistic support, through boat pool and repair facilities, for small craft in the area. The section base constructed at Alexishafen, near Madang, on the northeast coast of British New Guinea, included a section base, boat pool, ship and boat repair facilities, and a fresh-water system.

Alexishafen is located on Bostrem Bay, which provides an ideal anchorage for large ships. The channels are clear, with a depth of 30 fathoms, and the area is protected by Sek Island and a reef. Only a 2-foot tide exists, with a weak current. Rainfall is excessively heavy.

Establishment of this base was requested by the Seventh Amphibious Force in May 1944, and on June 13 a detachment of 200 men of the 91st Battalion arrived. Materials were to be provided by moving part of the facilities from Cape Cretin (Finschhafen) and the remainder from the advance base construction depot at Milne Bay. A camp with all necessary facilities was set up for the 400 men assigned to the base, together with a water-supply system that would provide 500,000 gallons per day of untreated water to ships at the watering-point. The ship and boat repair facilities were floating units, augmented by two pontoon drydocks. The section base, operated by Commander Service Force, Seventh Fleet, was commissioned on August 17, 1944.

Plans for the discontinuance of this base were begun early in November 1944, as the location was then too far behind the area of operations to serve a useful purpose. On November 30, final roll-up was ordered, and a detachment of 80 men from the 91st was sent to Alexishafen on December 25, 1944, for this purpose. The water-supply system was transferred to the Royal Australian Navy when the base was evacuated by the United States Navy and decommissioned on January 28, 1945.

Morotai

The naval installation on Morotai was established to provide an operating base for PT boats and land- and seaplanes, as well as repair facilities for small landing craft, with a supplementary communication system and hospital.

The island of Morotai, which lies about 10 miles east of the northern tip of Halmahera, in the Netherlands East Indies, is 28 miles wide by 48 miles long, with the Gila Peninsula, 6 miles long and a mile wide, at its southern end. This peninsula, with 3 additional square miles, was occupied and developed by American forces. The peninsula terrain is flat, coral sand, covered by fine topsoil, planted with coconut groves. The remainder of Morotai is mountainous and heavily covered with forests, which provided suitable timber. At the northeast corner of the peninsula, about 1,500 feet of shore is ideal for LST landings.

The climate is tropical, and the annual rainfall, which is moderately heavy, is evenly distributed throughout the year.

The 84th Battalion landed from LST's on September 27, 1944, twelve days after D-Day. The original plan called for the construction of an advance base unit and a naval air-facilities camp.

Construction at the advance base involved erection of tents for 1,000-man camp for the 84th Seabees and 24 quonset huts for the base. The Seabees also erected two steel towers for the radio station, two frame buildings, four 6,800-cubic-foot refrigerators, a boat-repair pier, a personnel pier, and a pontoon drydock.

At the air-facilities camp, tents provided living quarters for 1,800 officers and men, and quonset huts were used for the radio station and ships' service. Frame structures with canvas roofs were set up for such facilities as sick bay, galley, storage, shops, and offices. Roads, walkways, and power and water systems to supplement these activities were then installed.

Water was piped from wells drilled by the Army on the north end of the peninsula. Later, when further developed by the Seabees, these wells provided a plentiful supply of fresh water and replaced the stills which had been necessary during the first two months.

The 84th also erected and operated a sawmill which produced 800,000 board feet from native woods.

A 50-bed dispensary, with additional facilities, was constructed of 18 quonset huts and three frame buildings which were used for administration, galley, and storage. The power-distribution system for the whole base included three 75-kw generators, two 50-kw generators, and one 15-kw generator.

The base was complete and usable by November 20, 1944, with the exception of the hospital unit. Naval planes used the Army airstrips.

On nearby Soemsoem Island, a base to service three PT-boat squadrons was established. The camp consisted of tents, except for four quonset huts which were used for storehouses. Here, also, a dispensary was established with a capacity for 1000 men.

The outstanding project for this area was the assembly of a pontoon Liberty-ship pier. The 431-foot wharf section was made up of four 6-by-18-pontoon barges and six 3-by-18-pontoon bridge sections, with necessary hinges, piles, cable, and incidentals, completely fabricated at Milne Bay by PAD 3. All sections and equipment were towed by two Navy tugs from Milne Bay to Morotai, a distance of 1,700 miles. The first ship used this facility on October 8, 1944, just 11 days after the battalion arrived. The pier was used thereafter by the 84th Battalion, which took over all stevedoring of Army and Navy cargo. Enemy action during the construction period was confined to night air attacks.

On February 15, 1945, the 565th CBMU arrived to relieve the 84th, which left Morotai on February 28 for Palawan Island in the Philippines.

The Morotai base was disestablished January 21, 1946. Part of the equipment, materials, and installations were turned over to the Royal Australian Navy, under Lend-Lease agreements. The rest was sold to the Netherlands East Indies Government.

CHAPTER 27

BASES IN THE CENTRAL PACIFIC

In November 1943, our forces were undertaking the final phase of the Solomons campaign, the reduction of Bougainville, and had progressed up the New Guinea coast as far as Finschhafen. Rabaul, the key Japanese position in that part of the Pacific, was under constant bombardment. On November 20 a third thrust against the enemy-held area was opened by our invasion of the Gilbert Islands.

Tarawa, Makin, and Apamama, atoll islands, became the objects of our assaults in this opening move of a major offensive which was to carry us across the Pacific Ocean during the year that lay ahead. The assault on Tarawa was bitterly contested, and casualties to the Second Marine Division ran high. Within four days the islands had been captured, however, and the key position of the Gilberts was in our hands. Immediately thereafter, three construction battalions arrived at the tiny atoll to build airfields for both fighter and bomber planes.

Army units made the landing on Makin, and although the island's defenders put up a belatedly stiff resistance, the position had been taken by November 22.

The landing on Apamama on November 24 met no serious opposition: on November 28 the 95th Battalion arrived to build an airfield.

Control of the Gilberts was only the first objective in the great Central Pacific offensive which had been put in motion. Next came the Marshalls group; at the end of January 1944, our forces moved against Kwajalein and Majuro atolls. After a terrific bombardment by carriers and battleships, on February 1 the Fourth Marine Division, accompanied by the 121st Construction Battalion, landed on Roi and Namur, the northernmost islands of the Kwajalein atoll, while Army forces landed on its southern islands. By February 8 the entire atoll was in our possession. Four more construction battalions followed closely on the heels of the 121st; again, air-base construction became the first task after the assault period was over.

Landings made on Majuro at the same time found that atoll unoccupied by the enemy. A battalion of Seabees, the 100th, went ashore the next day to build a bomber field on one of the islands.

On February 17 our forces, moving still farther westward, landed on Eniwetok, and by February 20 its capture was announced. Engebi, the northernmost island of the Eniwetok atoll, was captured on February 18. Another bomber strip was put under construction within a week by the 110th Battalion, which arrived at Eniwetok on February 21.

Control of these strategic positions in the Marshalls was of vital importance. The by-passed Japanese garrisons at Mille, Wotje, Maleolap, and Jaluit were put in a position of helpless isolation. Moreover, the Japanese line of communication south from Wake Island had been effectively severed.

Great inroads had been made on the Japanese-mandated islands by our successes in the Gilberts and Marshalls. Ahead lay the important Mariana chain of islands. In the summer of 1944 the invasion of Saipan, Tinian, and Guam was put under way, involving some of the most important operations of the Pacific war. An account of the conquest and development of the Marianas is presented in Chapter 28.

Following closely upon the capture of the Marianas, Pacific Ocean areas forces moved to the west and south to attack Japanese positions in the western Carolines. Establishment of our forces in that area would complete the isolation of the enemy-held central and eastern Carolines, including the base at Truk.

Peleliu, in the Palau group of islands, was the point chosen for the first beach assault. On September 15, 1944, units of the First Marine Division went ashore. Within two days the airfield, which had been the prime object of the operation, had been captured, but thereafter enemy resistance stiffened and it was not until the middle of October that the defending forces were completely overcome.

On September 17, Army forces landed on Angaur, 6 miles south of Peleliu. Opposition encountered was much less severe than that at Peleliu, and by September 20 the entire island had been over-run. Prompt steps were taken to develop a heavy-bomber field, to be used in the projected moves against the Philippines.

Control of the western Carolines was completed by the capture of Ulithi atoll on September 23. The Japanese had abandoned the position, and our landings met no opposition. Possession of the atoll gave us an extensive anchorage.

By this time the net was closing on the Philippines; Southwest Pacific forces were in complete control of New Guinea and had extended their strength as far west as Morotai by an operation coincident with the assaults on the Palaus; the Marianas were in our hands and were already being developed as major Central Pacific bases; Rabaul, Truk, and Yap were isolated and neutralized. Recapture of the Philippine archipelago was the task that lay ahead.

Tarawa, in the Gilbert Islands

The Gilbert Islands, which include Tarawa, Apamama, and Makin, are a group of coral atolls lying athwart the equator. Formerly held by the British, they were seized by the Japanese at the outbreak of the war, a move of great strategic significance as they were in close proximity to islands in our possession and immediately south and east of important Japanese bases in the Carolinas and Marshalls. Bases in these islands, therefore, became essential steps in our movement toward Japan.

The assault on Tarawa on November 20, 1943, was bitterly contested. Heavily fortified, and garrisoned by several thousand Japanese troops on Betio, the principal island of the atoll, it had been attacked repeatedly from the air for weeks preceding the assault, and on the previous day had been heavily bombarded by surface craft. Although these attacks silenced the Japanese heavy guns, wrecked everything above ground, and killed approximately half the enemy troops, many dugouts, pillboxes, and bomb-proof shelters were still intact or usable.

The enemy was able to concentrate his forces beside the only beach where a landing was possible, and in spite of air and surface fire support, our casualties were heavy. The assault lasted nearly four days, at the end of which time the island was considered secure, although subjected to air raids and isolated sniper action.

During the remainder of 1943, Army and Navy planes based at Tarawa carried out repeated attacks on enemy holdings in the Marshall Islands and at Nauru, inflicting considerable damage on ships and shore installations.

Tarawa, a triangular-shaped atoll, is composed of a series of islands in a reef, covering 22 miles in length. The enclosed lagoon, about 17 miles long and tapering from 9 miles to less than a mile in width, is open to the west, though partially barred by a section of the submerged reef.

Betio, lying at the southwest corner of the Tarawa atoll, measures roughly $2\frac{1}{4}$ miles in length by less than half a mile in width. The reefs of Tarawa average 500 yards in width, the outer reef being about 2 feet higher than the lagoon reef. The beach is from 30 to 50 yards wide, rising only 5 or 6 feet.

Unforeseen wind and tide conditions uncovered the inner reef to such an extent that it became impassable to assault craft after the landing of the first wave. Ensuing waves were then forced to lie to under heavy fire or disembark their troops at a distance from the beach, in water so deep that wading ashore was extremely difficult. Heavy casualties and the loss of invaluable time resulted.

The first echelons of the construction battalions scheduled for Tarawa, the 74th and 98th, arrived in the lagoon November 24, 1943, D-plus-4, and advance reconnaissance parties went ashore as soon as the islands were declared secure. The 74th immediately began unloading LST's on Betio. The 98th, which was to perform the construction on Buoto Island, was held up on unloading until the final location of the airstrip was decided.

On November 27, a pontoon barge, which had been assembled on the ship, brought the first of the 98th's equipment to the beach. This equipment was used in the construction of a causeway to facilitate the unloading of the small boats and barges, and the work of clearing the fighter and bomber runways was started the next day. By the 29th the entire battalion personnel was ashore ex-

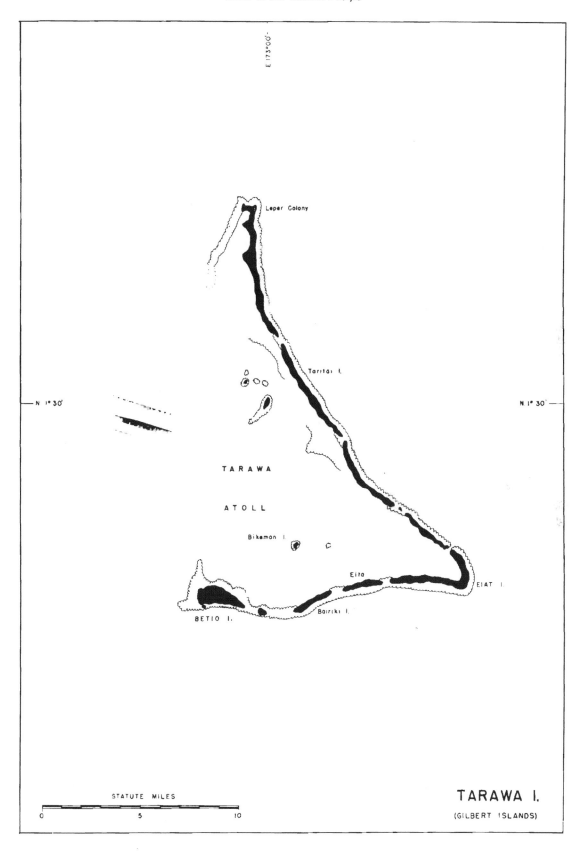

E 173°00'

Leper Colony

Taritai I.

N 1°30'

N 1°30'

TARAWA

ATOLL

Bikeman I.

Eita

EIAT I.

Bairiki I.

BETIO I.

STATUTE MILES

0   5   10

TARAWA I.

(GILBERT ISLANDS)

cept for a crew of 70, left aboard ship for stevedoring purposes.

A temporary camp was established near the beach, and by December 8, the galley was able to serve the first hot meal. The permanent camp was begun on the other side of the island, but work

AIRFIELD AND ADJOINING FACILITIES ON BETIO ISLAND, TARAWA

was retarded through lack of manpower, all available hands being used to expedite completion of the airstrip. On December 4, the second echelon arrived to relieve the manpower shortage, and work on the camp went ahead.

The early completion of an operational strip was the primary objective. By December 18th, or 20 days after work was started, a 4000-foot fighter strip on the eastern end of the bomber strip was usable, and two days later the first planes arrived.

Despite interruptions by enemy air raids, work progressed on the two strips. The taxiways and runways were surfaced with a 10-inch compacted layer of coral, mined from the lagoon below the level of high tide. In order to attain a more durable wearing surface, a coarse grade of coral, approximately one and a half inches in diameter, was worked into the top six inches of the original layer, providing an excellent runway surface. The completed bomber strip was 7,050 feet long with a

surfaced width of 200 feet, and had 27 hardstands. The fighter strip was 4,000 feet by 150 feet and had 18 hardstands. More than 6,000 feet of taxiways were built, leading to an additional 25 hardstands.

Besides the landing fields and their own camp, the 98th built all the necessary housing and living facilities for 1,300 men of the unit which operated the field, a 100-bed quonset-type hospital, ammunition and bomb storage, a control tower, an aviation-gasoline tank farm of 500,000-gallon capacity and ready tank storage of 20,000 gallons. They also moved 30,000 cubic yards of coral fill in the construction of a 2,200-foot causeway at the western end of the landing field.

When the 74th Battalion went ashore at Betio, by far the most heavily defended island in the atoll, organized resistance had ceased, although many snipers were at large, and groups of Japanese were barricaded in underground shelters and in blockhouses.

The greatest obstacle to be overcome was the condition of the island. As a base, it had been wrecked. Chaos, ruins, a litter of corpses and decaying food dumps extended over the entire 285 acres. Flies and mosquitoes, with ideal breeding conditions, existed in countless swarms; all water sources were brackish and polluted, with only salt water available for washing purposes. The menace to health was immediate and alarming, and it was little short of miraculous that no epidemic broke out, although dengue and dysentery appeared. The battalion lost no time in correcting these conditions.

Although no casualties were suffered by Seabee personnel, there was air raid damage to installations, stores, and equipment. Vehicles were burned or destroyed; others were perforated by bomb fragments, which also did considerable damage to tents; and heavy tire damage was caused, not only by the actual explosion of bombs, but by sharp fragments which littered roadways and the strip.

Literally every square foot of the island had to be cleaned, cleared, and graded in order to begin with the installations and improvements. The necessity of unloading supplies on the tidal flat required a disproportionate number of men and created serious maintenance problems due to the exposure of equipment to the corrosive effect of sea-water and to damage from coral entering working parts. Carryalls and tractors were similarly damaged when removing coral from the reef. All

CENTRAL PACIFIC AREA

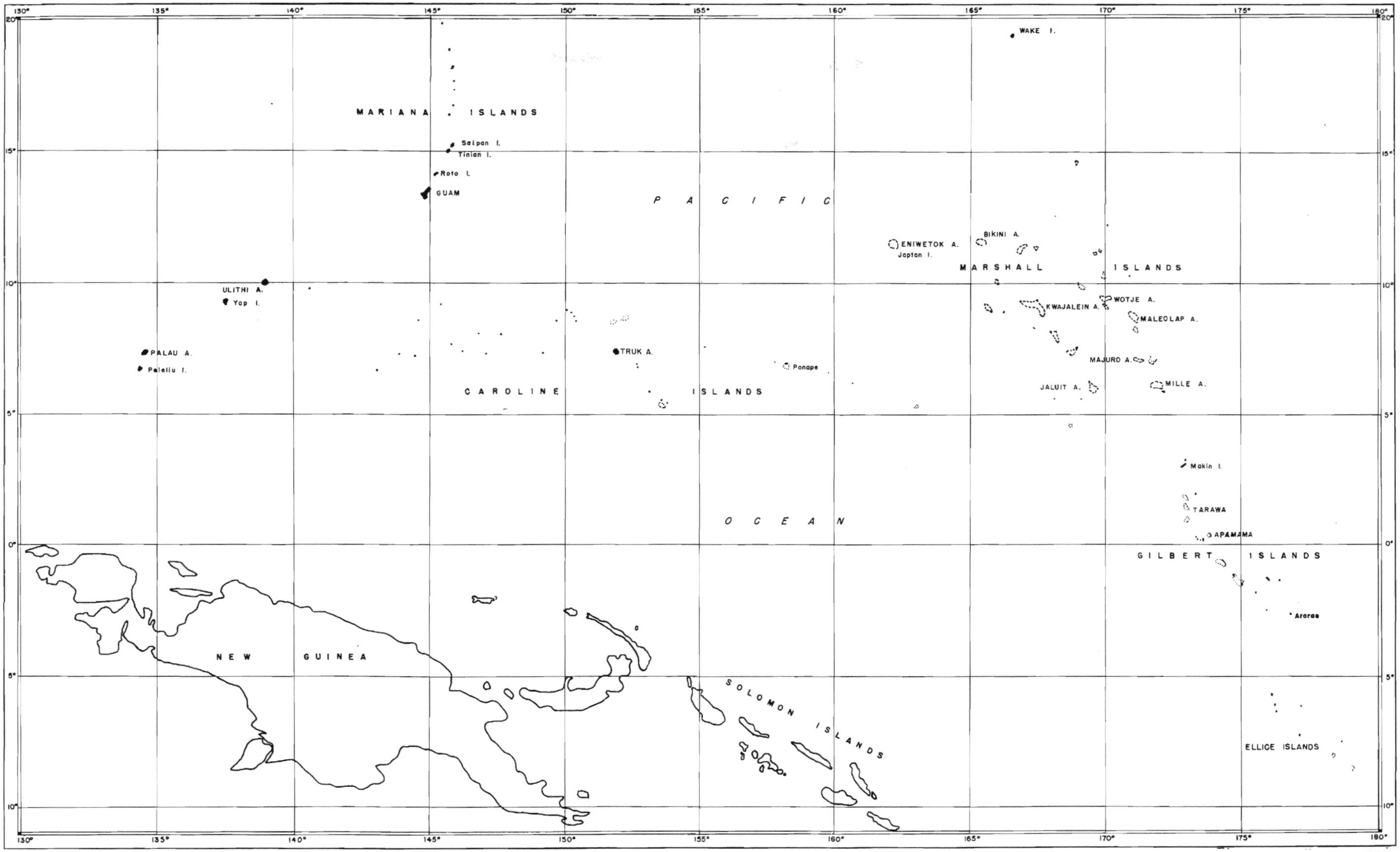
MARIANA ISLANDS
Saipan I.
Tinian I.
Rota I.
GUAM
PACIFIC
WAKE I.
BIKINI A.
ENIWETOK A.
Japtan I.
MARSHALL ISLANDS
ULITHI A.
Yap I.
KWAJALEIN A.
WOTJE A.
MALEOLAP A.
PALAU A.
Peleliu I.
TRUK A.
Ponape
MAJURO A.
JALUIT A.
MILLE A.
CAROLINE ISLANDS
Makin I.
TARAWA
OCEAN
APAMAMA
GILBERT ISLANDS
Arorae
NEW GUINEA
SOLOMON ISLANDS
ELLICE ISLANDS

766450 O—48 (Face p. 316)

grading and excavating work was rendered hazardous by buried mines and unexploded shells. as well as unpleasant by the decomposed bodies frequently uncovered. In the latter connection, Seabees were used extensively as burying details for both enemy and American dead.

Almost as soon as heavy equipment was ashore. the 74th went to work on the enemy airstrip. The existing installations consisted of an air base with all necessary appurtenances. The strip was 4,400 by 150 feet, surfaced with coral concrete of an average thickness of two inches, underlaid with a poorly compacted coral fill. It was relatively undamaged by the bombardment and assault, and temporary repairs made it possible for a squadron of fighters to land fifteen hours after the first Seabees went ashore, and to operate continuously thereafter.

Six days later, six medium bombers landed and commenced patrol operations. The wheel loads of these planes proved so much greater than those of Japanese aircraft that the concrete strip surface began to fail rapidly and was condemned. It was removed and replaced. half the width at a time, continuous flight operations being maintained on the remaining half, and on December 17, 1943, twelve B-24's were staged through the field. Existing hardstands and taxiways were used and were later enlarged and augmented.

When the strip was completed, it was 6,600 by 400 feet, and totally coral-surfaced. The original schedule planned the strip to be operational for B-24's by D-plus-45; the 74th bettered this date by 18 days.

Aside from the air strip, the only Japanese installation of any value was a badly battered, coral-fill quay. It was repaired, but was so unstable that it could be used only for foot traffic and jeeps. As soon as manpower was available, work was started on a 1900-by-32-foot wharf. As there was no timber available for piling, it was necessary to use the rails from an abandoned narrow-gauge Japanese railroad. These piles were braced with Japanese reinforcing rod. Pierced plank was attached with wire to the rails and rods. and sheathed on the inside with light corrugated iron. The resulting structure was then filled with compacted coral.

Additional work of the 74th included housing and messing facilities for aviators and ground crews, and a tank farm of twelve 1,000-barrel tanks with two ready-gas stations. 7.200 feet of buried pipe-line, and 4,500 feet of submarine line for the handling of aviation gasoline. One of the larger Japanese bomb shelters was cleaned and renovated for use by the Medical Corps as an operating room and as shelter for patients during air raids.

The water supply was obtained from evaporators, and 19 wells producing brackish water were drilled to supply them. Evaporators with a total daily capacity of 20,000 gallons were installed and two 15,000-gallon and four 5,000-gallon wood-stave storage tanks erected, together with 7.000 feet of underground pipe-line.

In addition to high-priority jobs, other important construction and maintenance work was subsequently carried out. Surveyors, who had preceded the construction gangs under hazardous conditions, located important sites on Betio and the adjacent islands and made maps of them. Communications, power and light, and refrigeration facilities were built. together with all construction necessary for base operations.

After adequate living quarters were set up, they were improved by additions necessary for morale, such as a post office, theatre, and ship's service. Stevedoring work was aided by native labor, which had been returned to the island and which proved most satisfactory.

Considerable work was done in converting enemy equipment to our own use, as well as salvaging our own worn-out and damaged equipment. A small but effective detail was assigned to diving and salvage. This group recovered equipment and removed obstacles from the ocean floor and on several occasions examined and reported on hull damage to ships. Another group carried out extensive demolition work ashore.

The Seabees worked in close and friendly cooperation with the occupying force of Marines, each making use of the others' equipment and facilities until the departure of the 74th on March 1, 1944.

Apamama, in the Gilberts

Apamama Atoll, in the Gilbert Islands. was occupied and developed as an air base simultaneously with other islands of the group, Tarawa and Makin, and for the same reasons. The atoll. approximately 15 miles long and 6 miles wide, contains a large, well-protected lagoon with an extensive anchorage area. The islands of the atoll have an elevation of about 12 feet, the soil being soft on the sea side but firmer on the lagoon side, consisting of coarse, loosely packed sand.

The initial landing on Apamama was made November 24, 1943. The 95th Battalion followed on November 28, after minor enemy resistance had been overcome, the task being to build an air base.

A 4,000-by-150-foot fighter strip, O'Hare Field, was ready December 10, and the first plane landed on December 13. Extension to 6,000 feet for bomber operations was accomplished by December 21. The 95th Battalion continued the development of the field until March 1944, when CBMU 557 reported to relieve the battalion. At this time, installations at O'Hare Field consisted of a 7,700-by-200-foot coral-surfaced bomber strip, with an additional 1,950-foot sand strip; 21,000 feet of taxiways, with 100 coral-surfaced hardstands, 125 by 150 feet; and quonset huts for ready rooms and repair shops. The final aviation facilities were greater than planned, as the location proved of strategic importance for bombing missions to adjacent Japanese bases in the Gilberts and Marshalls.

The Seabees also constructed 19 miles of coral-surfaced roads, a 12,000-barrel tank farm with a 5,000-foot submarine pipe line, and a causeway to serve as an access pier for unloading and making minor repairs to LST's and smaller craft. Storage space was provided by six prefabricated huts; quonset huts were erected for hospital facilities, offices, and work shops. Personnel were housed in tents.

The total number of natives employed at the peak of construction operations was 426. They proved entirely satisfactory as unskilled workers if sufficient supervision was provided. They were used extensively in the handling of cargo on the beach, and for procuring and placing coconut logs for pier construction. There was an abundance of suitable coral for airstrip and road surfacing, although the source was available only at low tide.

During the construction period, there were four minor air raids, resulting in the loss of one B-24 and slight damage to the taxiways and hardstands. Neither the terrain nor the weather presented any obstacles to construction.

By May 1944, Apamama had definitely become a rear base, its mission of supporting the campaigns in the Marshalls completed. CBMU 557 continued maintenance operations until the fall of 1944, when the base was decommissioned.

Majuro, in the Marshall Islands

The naval base at Majuro Atoll was established to support two Marine dive-bomber squadrons, half of a patrol squadron, and temporary staging for one Army fighter group. In addition, it was to provide Naval Air Transport Service requirements, fleet anchorage without shore-based facilities, medical facilities, and a loran transmitting station. Repair ships, submarine and destroyer tenders, together with tankers and supply ships, were to provide for the needs of the fleet.

Majuro Atoll, in the Marshall group, consists of 56 islands, of which Majuro Island, at its western tip, is largest. The airstrip occupied the major portion of Dalop Island, on the eastern tip, and Uliga and Darrit Islands contained the base facilities, camps, and Port Director's area.

The surfaces of these islands are covered with coral sand which, in some places, had acquired a topsoil through the decay of vegetation. Rainfall is heavy, and the climate tropical.

Within the lagoon, depths run from 25 to 35 fathoms, with variable sand and coral bottom, relatively few coral heads existing other than in the western portion. The channel approach contains ample depth for the largest ships, and sand beaches afford excellent small boat and LST beaching areas.

Army assault forces landed on January 31, 1944, and found the atoll unoccupied. The 100th Construction Battalion followed on February 1, together with the first echelon of a Marine defense battalion.

Darrit Island had once been occupied by the Japanese, who left a 400-foot timber pier, a narrow-gauge track from the pier leading to four frame warehouses, a seaplane ramp, and two steel buildings. At one end of a cleared area a large concrete slab had been poured for a hangar and structural steel was stacked near by, from which a warehouse was constructed. A frame building, located between the pier and the seaplane ramp, became the harbor captain's office. Several food-storage buildings in the vicinity were also utilized. A large frame native workers' barracks became the maintenance shop building. Other barracks were made into quarters for transients and a hospital; a seaplane hangar was converted into a warehouse; and smaller Japanese construction was used for various purposes.

On Dalop Island a coral-surfaced airstrip, 5,800 by 445 feet, was constructed. This was used on D-Day-plus-12 for an emergency landing, and by

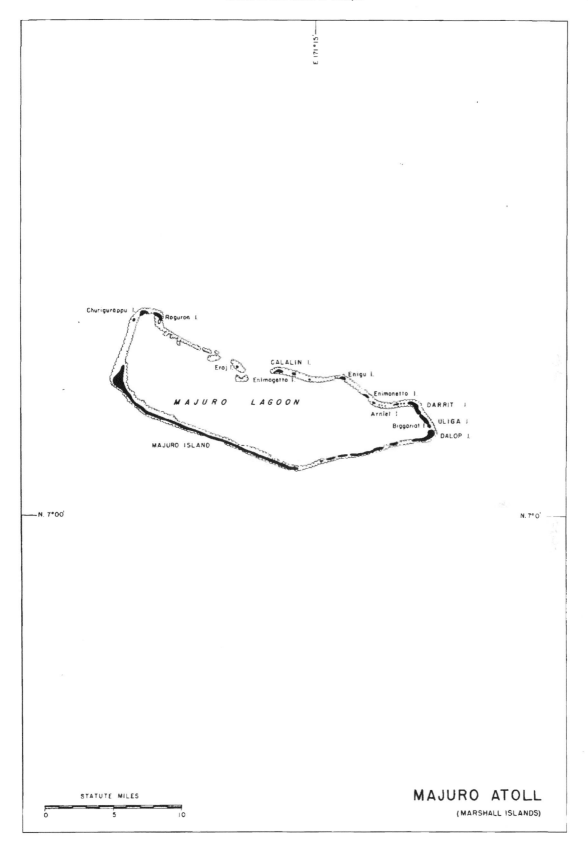

STATUTE MILES

0   5   10

MAJURO ATOLL

(MARSHALL ISLANDS)

April 15, the airfield. taxiways, aprons, housing, shops, and piers, as originally planned, were completed. Additional construction included 10 miles of coral roadways and 11,000 feet of 30-foot coral causeways connecting various islands.

Acorn 8 dispensary. located among former Japanese quarters, was increased by the erection of quonset huts and tents. its final capacity being 150 beds. Fuel-storage facilities were confined to gasoline-storage tanks; aviation gasoline storage was in twelve 1,000-barrel bolted tanks set up on Bigariat Island, connected by 4-inch pipes to the underground ready-gas tanks at the airstrip. Delivery to the tank farm was by tanker, through a sea-loading line.

Water was supplied by distillation, the 21 stills used for this work producing about 50,000 gallons per day. Storage tanks for fresh water included 25 wooden tanks of 160,000-gallon capacity, four 12,000-gallon canvas tanks, and two 8,000-gallon cisterns. The water was distributed to various points by pipe line and tank trucks. A deep-water floating pier, 625 by 28 feet, was constructed, and unloading operations were further facilitated by nine 4-by-12-pontoon and four 3-by-7-pontoon barges.

Storage facilities erected, in addition to Japanese structures, were tents, tarpaulin-covered shelters, and 47 quonsets. Ammunition was stored in several underground magazines, in three quonset huts, and in open-storage revetments.

Shop facilities were located in 17 quonset huts and 6,000 square feet of tarpaulin-covered shelters. The administration buildings included ten quonset huts and 81 tents, as well as the Japanese buildings remodeled for the purpose. On Calalin Island, at the entrance to the approach channel, a signal station and a harbor entrance control post were established.

Bomb-proof shelters were constructed at strategic locations. requiring a total of 350,000 cubic yards of coral fill. Fleet recreation facilities were also provided. all work being done by the 100th Battalion, supplemented in some cases by station personnel. The Seabee unit was housed in two tent camps, two companies living in the area adjoining the airstrip and the balance being based on Uliga, the main housing and administration island.

This construction was the work originally planned. The assignment of additional units to the base and the increased scope of activities necessitated considerable expansion.

Fourth Marine Air Wing headquarters and Marine Air Group 13 were established at Majuro Atoll in the middle of March 1944. These units required the construction of two 750-man camps, shop and storage facilities. At the airstrip, it was necessary to build seven quonset huts. a nose hangar, and several lean-to structures, and to increase hard-stands and apron facilities. A utility air squadron was also assigned to Majuro and required the standard number and types of headquarters buildings. shops, nose hangars, and parking facilities.

When it was decided to locate the carrier replacement plane pool at Majuro, a strip, 175 by 4,000 feet, was cleared and paved on Uliga Island and a two-lane causeway connecting Uliga and Dalop was constructed, furnishing a 30-foot roadway. To accommodate air transport operations, a 150-by-800-foot apron was cleared and paved adjacent to the runway, with four quonset huts to house office and storage facilities. Introduction of the plane-pool activities demanded the doubling of carrier-aircraft service-unit personnel and consequent enlargement of their living and shop facilities. The fleet recreation grounds and facilities were increased, and a submarine base recuperation camp was constructed which involved all installations necessary for a 750-man camp.

All facilities were used to capacity as numerous bomber and fighter squadrons operated from the airfield. The carrier-aircraft service unit serviced the fleet carriers, and the plane pool serviced and furnished replacement planes. The harbor was used as a fleet anchorage and fleet recreation center. The sorting of supplies, mail storage, communications, and personnel replacement taxed the remaining station facilities to the utmost.

Stevedoring duties were taken over from the 100th Battalion in February 1944, when Construction Battalion Detachment 1034 arrived in Majuro. This detachment of six officers and 250 men handled all cargo operations until August 1944, when they moved to Japtan Island in the Eniwetok Atoll.

The 60th Battalion performed all construction and maintenance work until relieved by CBMU 591 on June 18. 1944. The 60th left Majuro on July 5, 1944, for Pearl Harbor, CBMU 591 remaining to take care of construction and maintenance. On V-J Day, all facilities were still operating at capacity, and no roll-up steps had been taken.

Kwajalein Atoll, in the Marshall Islands

To support air offensives against, and maintain surveillance over, the by-passed Japanese bases in

ROI-NAMUR IN THE KWAJALEIN ATOLL

the Marshalls and the Carolines, an advance air base, with minor fleet facilities, was established on Kwajalein Atoll, in the Marshall Islands. Complete facilities were to be provided for the operation of landplanes and seaplanes.

Kwajalein Atoll is 66 miles long and has a maximum width of 18 miles. More than 80 islands and islets lie along the partially submerged reef, which surrounds a lagoon of about 655 square miles.

Land areas large enough to be developed are found at only three points on the atoll. Kwajalein Island and neighboring islands at the southeastern end, Roi Island and nearby islands at the northern end, and Ebadon Island at the western end. The southern islands are covered with a dense growth of coconut trees and smaller vegetation; the islands to the north are wooded.

The Kwajalein area includes Kwajalein Island and the islands on the reef for 12 miles to the north and 10 miles to the northwest. Ebeye Island lies 2½ miles north of Kwajalein, and is separated from the latter by an unbroken reef. It is 1770 yards long and 230 yards wide throughout most of its length. Kwajalein Island, crescent-shaped and open to the lagoon on the northwest, is about 3 miles long and varies in width from 1,000 to 2,500 feet.

In the Roi area, considerable land exists only on Roi and Namur islands. Roi is 1250 yards long and 1170 yards wide. Namur, to the east of Roi and connected with it by a narrow strip of land, is 890 yards long and 800 yards wide.

Kwajalein Atoll was highly developed as a military base by the Japanese. A major air base existed on Roi Island, and on Namur, connected by a causeway to Roi, were barracks, warehouses, a radio station, and a 450-foot L-shaped pier extending into the lagoon. Kwajalein Island contained many buildings, some of which were used as warehouses for a supply center. A 2,000-foot pier extended from the lagoon side of the island. An airstrip, 400 by 5,000 feet, had also been completed. Ebeye Island was the site of a seaplane base with hangars, two ramps, and an L-shaped pier.

On January 30 and 31, 1944, Kwajalein Atoll was subjected to heavy surface bombardment and air attack prior to landings by the Fourth Marine Division on Roi and Namur Islands and by the Seventh Army Division on Kwajalein, on February 1. The 121st Construction Battalion accompanied the first waves of Marines landing on Roi and Namur, as shore parties for combat teams. By February 2, Roi and Namur had been secured despite a strong Japanese counterattack on Namur. Kwajalein Island was under Army control by February 5, and the entire atoll was secured by February 8.

Roi and Namur.—The uprooting of all vegetation and the almost-complete destruction of enemy facilities by the assault caused a tremendous accumulation of debris. Before any progress could be made in setting up camp and storage areas, beach development, or airfield construction, it was necessary for the 121st to remove the debris as quickly as possible.

On February 5, the battalion was ordered to consolidate and begin work on the Roi Island airfield, the 109th Battalion arriving the next day to assist on this project. The 121st, which was attached to the Marine division, had only 20 per cent of its equipment; consequently, the major portion of the heavy construction fell upon the 109th.

Of the three Japanese oil-surfaced airstrips, the runway, measuring 300 by 4,300 feet, was the first to be reconstructed. The existing strip was ripped up and resurfaced. The first fighter squadron arrived on February 13 and operated from the base as construction continued.

By February 12, most of the Marine division had departed and the remainder, with the 121st Battalion, were preparing to leave. On February 13, Japanese bombers launched a heavy attack against Roi, setting fire to a bomb dump. In the resulting destruction, the 109th Battalion suffered 102 casualties and lost 75 per cent of its material and 35 per cent of its equipment. The 121st's losses were 55 casualties, equipment remaining intact. Before the departure of the 121st on February 15, all its remaining equipment was transferred to the 109th to help replace losses from the attack.

The 109th continued the airfield construction. The east-west Japanese runway, lately used as a storage area, was reconstructed by May 1944, with a 2,200-foot taxiway, and a concrete parking area was also provided. The third Japanese runway was then resurfaced for an additional repair and parking area. Including fighters, light bombers, and patrol planes, 100 planes were now based on Roi. The field was commissioned on May 15, and from it daily missions operated against Japanese installations on Wotje, Jaluit, and Truk.

On March 5, 1944, a detachment of 15 officers and 487 men of the 95th Battalion arrived on Namur, their major assignment being the construction of an aviation supply depot, which was commissioned on June 10. Roi was strategically located for use as a center to supply aviation materials to bombing missions against islands of the Marshalls and Marianas. Considerable amounts of supplies from this base also were used in support of the Marianas landings.

The 95th also erected a 4,000-barrel tank farm, with necessary piping; provided hospital facilities at three dispensaries, having a combined capacity of 300 beds; and erected housing accommodations of floored tents, quonset huts, and barracks for all military activities.

As there were no deep-water waterfront facilities in the area, a 4-by-30-pontoon pier was assembled, and a Japanese L-shaped pier, 450 by 33 feet, was used extensively to unload supplies from small craft. Repair installations consisted of overhaul shops for small-boat motors and a 4-by-15-pontoon

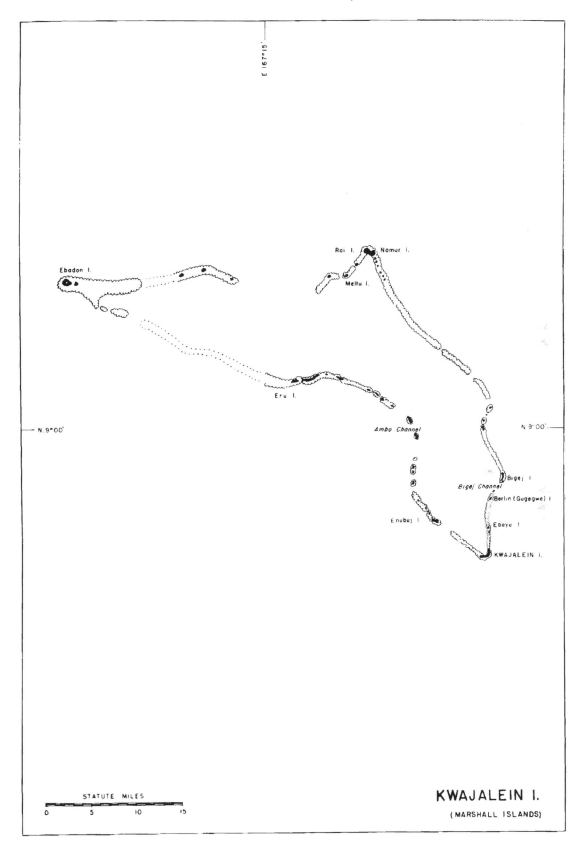

Ebadon I.

Roi I. Namur I.

Mellu I.

Eru I.

N. 9°00'

Ambo Channel

N. 9°00'

Bigej I.

Bigej Channel

Berlin (Gugegwe) I.

 Enubuj I.

Ebeye I.

KWAJALEIN I.

STATUTE MILES

0   5   10   15

KWAJALEIN I.

(MARSHALL ISLANDS)

drydock of 100-ton capacity for aircraft rescue boats, picket boats, and LCM's. Connecting causeways and a perimeter road for each island were also constructed.

Coral found on the islands was not of proper quality for use in surfacing, due to the large percentage of coarse sand, which resisted binding, consequently coral for surfacing purposes was taken from the lagoon. Native woods were used for minor construction, and native labor was employed on clean-up and sanitation details.

CBMU 590 arrived in June 1944 to relieve the construction battalions and continue maintenance.

Kwajalein Island.—The 74th and 107th Battalions reported on Kwajalein Island in March 1944, the 74th setting up headquarters on near-by Berlin, or Gugegwe Island. This island had apparently been used by the Japanese as a supply base and for the repair of small craft. A marine railway with a capacity of 250 tons had been damaged by shelling, but was restored to usefulness for small-boat repair. A concrete pier, almost completed by the Japanese before our occupation, proved small but adequate, when finished for use of the boat pool. Berlin Island then became the site of shops for small-boat repair and overhaul, and of the Seabee camp.

A rock-crushing plant had been set up by the Japanese on Berlin Island and, although damaged, was salvageable for use in connection with the development of crushed coral for airstrip and road surfacing. The Seabees then rebuilt the existing Japanese runway on Kwajalein Island to provide a 6300-foot coral-surfaced strip with two 80-foot taxiways and 102 hardstands for heavy bombers. One hangar with minor aircraft-repair installations was erected, and more than 12 miles of coral roads were built in the area.

Waterfront facilities were developed to provide minor fleet repairs. The Japanese pier was restored, and a 50-by-240-foot boat-slip was added to the outer end, forming an L. The depth alongside was 20 feet, and the pier could safely dock five LST's or a large number of small craft at one time. The Seabees also constructed a log crib, coral-fill quay, 300 feet long, with two 3-by-12-pontoon arms, and established repair facilities for landing craft. A 250-ton pontoon floating drydock was assembled, and a 2,000-ton floating drydock, capable of handling destroyer escorts, was provided for the base.

Half of the 15th Special Battalion was divided between Kwajalein and Roi-Namur for stevedoring.

Personnel were housed in floored and framed tents and in wooden frame barracks. Other base installations included the 200-bed 22nd Station Hospital, 80,000 square feet of covered storage, and a 12,000-barrel aviation-gasoline tank farm.

Between June and September 1944, the two battalions sent detachments to erect a large fuel-oil tank farm on Bigej Island, north of Kwajalein Island. This consisted of four 50,000-barrel tanks and fourteen 10,000-barrel tanks, with all appurtenances.

CBMU 607 arrived in the area in August 1944, to relieve the construction battalions and take over maintenance and minor construction.

Ebeye Island.—On March 7, 1944, four officers and 242 men of the 107th Battalion were sent to Ebeye Island to develop the seaplane base. As the two Japanese seaplane ramps had sustained only minor damage before their capture, construction work necessary for the development of the base, with the exception of paving the parking area and erecting shops and housing, was small.

In April 1944, the atoll commander was instructed to move his headquarters from Kwajalein Island to Ebeye. A detachment of the 74th Battalion was sent there to handle the construction necessary to the development of the headquarters, pending completion of the seaplane base by the 107th.

A Japanese pier, 1600 by 30 feet, with a 50-by-240-foot L extension, was repaired by the Seabees and a 250-foot Japanese H-shaped pier was also used. In addition, the Seabees assembled a pontoon wharf and pontoon barges for transporting damaged carrier aircraft to repair units ashore.

Further installations on Ebeye consisted of housing in floored tents and quonset huts, a 150-bed dispensary, four magazines, 24,000 square feet of covered storage, and a 4,000-barrel aviation-gasoline tank farm.

Although the war moved far forward, no roll-up was contemplated at Kwajalein, as it was necessary to maintain aerial surveillance of the bypassed Japanese bases in the Marshalls and Carolines.

Eniwetok Atoll, in the Marshall Islands

With the capture of Eniwetok Atoll on February 20, 1944, control of the Marshall Islands, which had been in Japanese hands since 1914, passed to the United States. The atoll was to be developed principally as a Navy and Marine air base and a fleet anchorage, with no shore facilities other than a recreational area.

Eniwetok Atoll, consisting of 30 small islands of sand and coral, lies about 326 miles northwest of Kwajalein. The circumference of the atoll is 64 miles and the maximum elevation is 15 feet. There are three entrances to the lagoon.

Eniwetok Island is two miles long and one-quarter of a mile wide. Engebi Island is triangular, each side measuring one mile, and has a good landing beach on the lagoon side. Parry Island is two miles long and very narrow, with a sandy beach on the lagoon side.

The 22nd Marines and elements of the 106th Infantry captured Eniwetok Atoll in a swift amphibious operation that lasted less than five days, landing February 18, 1944, on five small islands in the atoll, just southeast of Engebi Island. Engebi, forming the northern tip of the atoll, was the site of an airstrip, the most important installaion on the atoll. Bombardment of Engebi continued throughout the day and night, and the following morning the assault began. Our forces moved rapidly inland, and the island was in our hands by late afternoon. While mopping-up continued in the northern section of the atoll, other Army and Marine units, on the morning of the 20th, landed on Eniwetok Island, the southeastern anchor of the atoll and the largest island of the group. By late the next morning, enemy forces had been eliminated. On the morning of the 22nd, our forces landed on Parry Island, site of a seaplane base. northeast of Eniwetok, and by evening that island also had been captured. No Seabee units participated in the initial assault.

Echelons of the 110th Battalion arrived at Eniwetok between February 21 and 27, 1944, and immediately began clearing for a bomber strip. On March 11, the first plane landed and on April 5, the first mission by permanently based bomber squadrons was flown from Stickell Field. The completed field, 6,800 feet long and 400 feet wide, had two taxiways, facilities for major engine-overhaul, and housing for aviation personnel in quonset huts.

As activities increased, land area became insufficient to support these activities properly. To overcome this difficulty, quonset huts were erected

atop one-story buildings, a measure which proved very practical.

On Parry Island. the 110th Battalion developed a seaplane base, using the existing Japanese ramp, and provided a coral-surfaced parking area, and shops for minor aircraft and engine overhaul. This base was capable of supporting one squadron of patrol bombers, but activities were limited by the existence of only one ramp and by tides which were unfavorable to beaching activities.

Wrigley Airfield, on Engebi Island. was built to support four squadrons of Marine fighters until sufficient space at Eniwetok became available for their operation. The 126th Battalion arrived at Engebi on March 11, 1944, and took over development of this airfield from the 47th Army Engineers. Aviation facilities, when completed, included a fighter strip, 3950 by 225 feet, taxiways with 150 hardstands, and major engine-overhaul shops.

A tank farm of twelve 1,000-barrel tanks, with piping, a floating pipe-line, 1,200 feet long, and a tanker mooring. was completed for aviation gasoline on Eniwetok Island by May 1944. Completion had been delayed by the explosion of an LCT in March, which reduced the status of completion of the farm from 80 to 30 percent. An aviation-gasoline tank farm. with a capacity of 146,000 gallons and all appurtenances, was also erected on Engebi.

Two coral-fill piers. one 80 and the other 150 feet long, were built on Eniwetok Island, and two beaches were developed for LCT's. Small-boat-repair shops were also built, and a floating dock for small ships was assigned to the base. At Parry Island, a marine railway was installed on an existing Japanese pier, and boat-repair shops were also erected. The Seabees repaired a 30-by-150-foot Japanese pier at Engebi, with timber piling, to accommodate small craft, including LCM's.

Medical facilities were provided by three dispensaries with a total capacity of 200 beds, one each at Eniwetok, Engebi, and Parry islands. Quonset huts and tents were erected for base storage and housing.

By June 1944, the major work projects on Engebi had been completed. and CBMU 594 reported to take charge of maintenance activities. The 126th Battalion, pending its departure in October, was assigned to small projects on several islands in the atoll, including construction of a fleet recreation center on Hawthorne Island. CBMU 608 arrived in

QUONSET-HUT VARIATION AT ENIWETOK
Operations building, showing quonset huts erected atop one-story buildings

August 1944 to relieve the 110th Battalion, which left in September. The air base on Engebi was decommissioned on September 18, 1944, and by May 1945, all activities except a token garrison had been transferred to Eniwetok.

In June 1945, the 67th Battalion reported at Eniwetok, to build a fleet recreation area for 35,000 men and to extend carrier-aircraft service-unit facilities at Parry Island. V-J-Day found the 67th and CBMU 608 still stationed at Eniwetok.

Palau Group, in the Caroline Islands

Guarding the eastern approaches to the southern Philippines, the Palau Islands were developed by the Japanese, in conjunction with Truk, into a powerful naval base. After the virtual neutralization of Truk by repeated Allied air attacks, the Palau Islands replaced it as the principal Japanese advance naval base and assembly point for fuel, ammunition, and supplies moving between Japan

and the southwest Pacific. The islands had also been developed as an air base, and were needed by us as advance airbases to support light, medium and heavy aircraft, in the forthcoming Philippines operations.

The Palau Islands, which lie about 540 miles due east of Davao, are among the westernmost islands of the Carolines. The group is actually a complex atoll, made up of a cluster of volcanic islands, fragmented coral atolls, and islands of limestone composition, the whole surrounded by reefs. Peleliu and Angaur, at the southernmost tip of the group, were the only islands developed by our forces.

Angaur, 2½ miles in length and less than 2 miles wide, rises 15 to 20 feet above sea level. The island is densely wooded, and the soil is generally coral limestone, so hard that it hindered construction. There is only one sheltered water area, a small boat basin on the western side of the island.

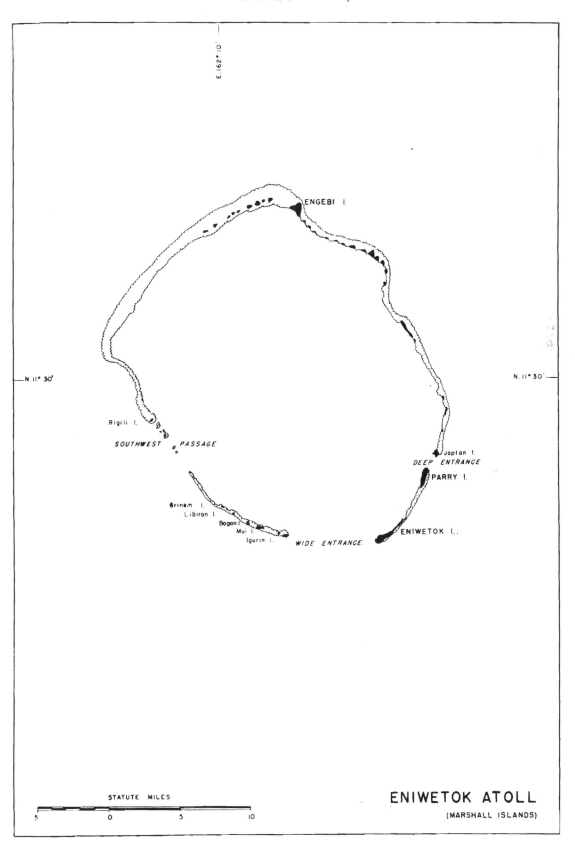

E. 162° 10'

ENGEBI I.

N 11° 30'

N. 11° 30'

Rigili I.

SOUTHWEST   PASSAGE

Joplan I.
DEEP ENTRANCE

PARRY I.

Grinem I.
Libiron I.
Bogon I.
Mui I.
Igurin I.

ENIWETOK I..

WIDE ENTRANCE.

STATUTE MILES

5   0   5   10

ENIWETOK ATOLL

(MARSHALL ISLANDS)

Peleliu is 5½ miles long and 2½ miles wide. The major portion of the land is low and level, but the central and northern portions contain numerous high rock ridges. Swamp areas, extending north and south, divide the island except for a minor strip on which its single east-west road is built. The coastline is mostly rocky but has about 2 miles of scattered sandy beaches.

Although the Palau group offers a spacious and well-protected anchorage for major fleet elements, no major Japanese facilities existed for construction or repair of any except small craft. There were three airfields in the Palau group, the largest of which was located on Peleliu. A new operational strip was on the small island of Ngesebus, just north of Peleliu and connected to it by a bridge in the last stages of construction. A third field was still under construction at Airai, near the southern end of Babelthuap Island.

The Peleliu airfield, a cleared area at the southern portion of the island, contained two runways in an X pattern, one 3,990 feet and the other 3,850 feet long. There were two sizable service aprons, connected with each other, and with turning circles, by hard-surfaced taxiways. Good roads linked the northern coastal areas with this airfield.

Three days of surface bombardment and air bombing preceded the landing on Peleliu. During this time, mine sweepers cleared the waters of Peleliu and adjacent Angaur Island, and underwater demolition teams removed beach obstacles. The landing, on September 15, 1944, was made by units of the First Marine Division. Despite difficult reef conditions, the initial landings were successful, and the troops quickly overran the beach defenses, which were thickly mined but less heavily manned than expected. By the night of the 16th, the Peleliu airfield, which was the prime objective of the entire operation, had been captured. After the rapid conquest of the southern portion of the island, however, progress on Peleliu slowed, as the rough ridge which formed the north-south backbone of the island was a natural fortress of mutually supporting cave positions. Although these were surrounded by September 26, it was not until the middle of October that the assault phase was complete.

The 81st Infantry Division went ashore on Angaur Island, 6 miles south of Peleliu, on September 17. Beach conditions here were more favorable than at Peleliu, and opposition also was less severe. By September 20, the entire island had been overrun, with the exception of a small inland area.

Marines from Peleliu landed on Ngesebus Island, just north of Peleliu, on September 28, by a shore-to-shore movement, and light enemy opposition was overcome by September 29. Later, several small islands in the vicinity were occupied as outposts. From Peleliu and Angaur, the other islands were dominated; enemy forces were neutralized.

Three Seabee groups participated in the initial landing on Peleliu, the 33rd and 73rd Battalions and Construction Battalion Detachment 1054. On D-Day, the two construction battalions assigned men of the shore parties to assist in unloading supplies and ammunition and to aid in burying the dead. Unloading operations were made extremely difficult by the lack of harbors and the nature of the reef.

CBD 1054 operated the 24 pontoon barges with propulsion units. These pontoon barges were used extensively in the Peleliu invasion to transfer cargo between various types of landing craft, by means of cranes, to fuel landing craft, and to serve as floating dumps for high-priority cargo. On D-Day-plus-three, CBD 1054 installed pontoon causeways to the outer reef, and the next day the first LST was beached and unloaded over them. Causeway sections were also used to ferry loads of mobile equipment from LST's.

On D-Day-plus-four, the 33rd Battalion commenced removing land mines, duds, and shell fragments from the airfield, and when the first construction equipment came ashore the next day, it was immediately put to work filling shell holes and making general repairs. The strip was placed in operation 72 hours after the first equipment began work, when three squadrons of fighters arrived to support the remainder of the operation.

No Seabee units participated in the initial assault on Angaur. Army engineers immediately began the construction of a bomber field there.

On September 23, the 33rd Battalion began construction on Peleliu of a bomber strip, 6,000 feet long, with additional equipment borrowed from the First Marine Engineer Battalion and the 73rd Construction Battalion. Land mines were encountered, and during the first six days the field was subjected to mortar fire, but 24-hour air operation began on the seventh day.

Airfield development continued during the early months of 1945. When completed, the bomber strip measured 6,000 by 300 feet, and the fighter run-

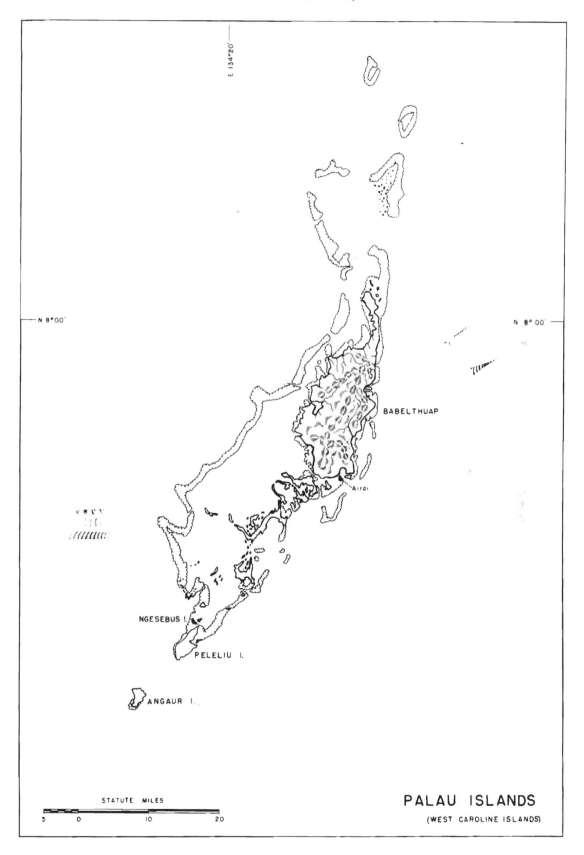

PALAU ISLANDS

(WEST CAROLINE ISLANDS)

way, 4,000 by 250 feet. Taxiways and parking areas were constructed to support the assigned seven squadrons and 100 transient and cargo planes.

The Seabees also erected four quonset-type warehouses for aviation shops, 20 quonset huts for offices and repair facilities, and complete camp installations for aviation personnel.

By January 1945, the 73rd Battalion had completed a tank farm, consisting of one 10,000-barrel tank for motor gasoline, twenty 1,000-barrel tanks for aviation gasoline, and three 1,000-barrel tanks for diesel oil.

Hospitals constructed by the Seabees were the 17th Army Evacuation Hospital and Navy Base Hospital 20. The former had a 440-bed capacity and was completed by the 73rd Battalion in November 1944. The 33rd Battalion then started con-

struction of the naval hospital, and by the end of December, six H-type quonset-hut units, of 100 beds each, had been completed with all facilities. Due to delay in the arrival of materials, the 320-bed annex to Base Hospital 20 was not completed until March 1945. Numerous dispensaries, with a total capacity of 161 beds, were also provided for various naval activities.

By the end of January 1945, minor waterfront facilities were complete. The 33rd had rebuilt a Japanese concrete-block pier, which provided berths for three light craft. The approach channel was dredged to a 10-foot low-water depth and an LCT landing beach prepared.

The 301st Battalion, a harbor reclamation unit, was brought in to dredge access channels to a small boat basin, and to provide sufficient maneuvering

Naval Base Hospital 20, Peleliu

ORANGE BEACH CAUSEWAY AND CHANNEL ENTRANCE, PELELIU
Photograph, taken May 22, 1945, shows Angaur island in the left background

space for small craft at all stages of the tide. A marine railway and shops for small-boat repair were built by the 73rd.

Stevedoring was handled by the first section of the 17th Special Battalion, with the assistance of crews from the 73rd Battalion.

Three major supply centers had been established by early 1945. Construction of the supply depot, begun by Army Engineers, was taken over by the 33rd Battalion in December 1944. Eight quonset-type warehouses, with concrete floors, were built for this activity. For the aviation supply depot, the Seabees constructed five quonset buildings. At the airfield, four 20-by-50-foot steel magazines were erected. The spare parts depot consisted of four quonset buildings, with concrete floors and unloading platforms, and several quonset huts for offices. More than 16 miles of primary roads were built to serve these activities on Peleliu.

Angaur was developed as an Army base, the airfield being constructed by two Army engineer battalions. Installations for the field were an airstrip, 7,000 by 150 feet, adequate taxiways, and hardstands for 120 planes. CBMU 532, which reported at Angaur in October 1944, assisted the Army by the erection of quonset-hut camps for aviation personnel.

The construction program for Angaur was not an extensive one. Detachments of Seabee units stationed on Peleliu were sent to Angaur to handle the erection of a tank farm, to assist the Army in the construction of the 39th Station Hospital, and to develop waterfront facilities.

During late 1944, the 73rd Battalion sent men to Angaur to build the tank farm, comprising twelve 1,000-barrel tanks for aviation gasoline, two 10,000-barrel diesel-oil tanks, and five 1,000-barrel tanks for motor gasoline. The existing phosphate pier was used to carry the pipe line for the tank farm. The project was completed by February 1945. A small boat basin was developed by a detachment of the 301st Battalion, just south of the phosphate loading pier on the western side of the island, and the harbor was dredged to provide a minimum depth of 6 feet at low tide. A natural coral breakwater, forming the western side of the boat haven, was improved on the basin side by the construction of a concrete deck. Pontoon strings

PURPLE BEACH CHAPEL, PELELIU
Stone and timber building, designed and constructed by men of the 73rd Battalion. Chimes (above the entrance) were made of Japanese and American shell cases

were used to form the southern end of the basin. This section was, in effect, a 70-foot pier which could furnish barge berths on the basin side.

The 73rd Battalion built boat shops and a 30-ton marine railway, 130 feet long.

At Blue Beach, one officer and fifteen men of CBD 1054 were assigned to the construction of a pontoon causeway. The installation consisted of two single-pontoon strings, 150 feet long, placed about 150 feet apart at right angles to the beach line. A 2-by-30-pontoon string was then placed at right angles to the offshore end of the first two strings. The enclosed space was filled with coral rock, sand, and gravel, after all sections had been filled with sand and sunk. The pier was ready for use by LCT's on November 1, 1944.

In June 1945, the Army air base was abandoned. CBMU 532 took charge of dismantling and crating salvageable structures; they were secured on July 11, 1945.

Ulithi, in the Western Carolines

The naval base at Ulithi was established to provide a fleet anchorage and an air base to support half of a night fighter squadron, a light inshore patrol squadron, pool for a maximum of 150 carrier replacement aircraft, a utility squadron, and staging facilities for transport aircraft. The basic plan also called for maintaining shore facilities to support the garrison and the fleet.

This atoll, 93 miles northeast of Yap, 370 miles southwest of Guam, and 370 miles northeast of Peleliu, consists of four elements: the main atoll, in the west; the island of Falalop off the northeast point; a small detached reef with several islets, lying east of the main atoll; and Zohhoiiyonu Bank, an incomplete atoll, in the extreme east.

All the islets of the group are of typical atoll structure, with low level land, wooded in spots, and swamp areas, generally covered with thick vegetation. The rainfall is heavy and the climate tropical. Mogmog Island, in the north, is the principal islet; others which were most used by our forces are Falalop, Asor, Potangeras, and Sorlen.

Ulithi Atoll was occupied on September 20, 1944, with no ground opposition by Japanese forces. There were numerous air raids in the early days of the operation, but no damage to Seabees or equipment resulted.

The 18th Special Battalion arrived on October 1, 1944. This unit, consisting of 17 officers and 514 men, was quartered on a barracks barge. The battalion was to stevedore for the fleet rather than to handle straight ship-to-shore stevedoring operations. This type of work was then highly essential at Ulithi, where all supplies, fuel, ammunition, and spare parts were stored afloat. The 18th Special worked at this task until May 25, 1945, when it was detached and ordered to Leyte Gulf. During that period, the battalion handled an average of 20,000 tons of cargo monthly.

On October 10, 1944, a detachment of the 6th Special Battalion arrived at Ulithi to operate as a ship-to-shore stevedoring unit. During its service there, the 6th handled a monthly average of 12,000 tons of cargo. This battalion was detached in June 1945 and returned to Pearl Harbor, where it was inactivated.

The 51st Battalion disembarked on October 8, 1944, with 797 enlisted men and 28 officers, and was assigned the task of widening, lengthening, and improving the Japanese airfield on Falalop

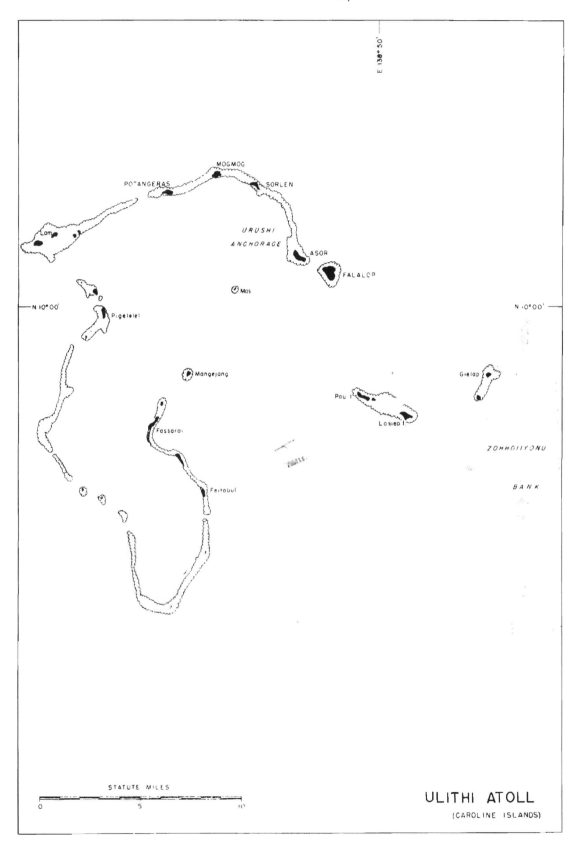

STATUTE MILES

0   5   10

ULITHI ATOLL
(CAROLINE ISLANDS)

Island. A 3,500-by-150-foot runway was completed in 27 days. The east end of the strip extended approximately 20 feet past the natural shoreline of the island, log cribs being used as foundation for this addition to the island. The first plane landed on the strip 15 days after work was begun. Six taxiways were constructed; one, 4,000 by 100 feet; and one, 3,250 by 700 feet; and four, 500 by 100 feet. Also installed were hardstands, lighting, a traffic-control tower, operations buildings, aviation-gasoline ready tanks, and a tank farm: all work was completed by December 1, 1944.

The first section of the 88th Battalion, consisting of Companies C and D and half of the headquarters company, landed at Ulithi on October 10, 1944. Its assignment included construction of the shore facilities necessary to use the atoll as a fleet anchorage; the building of a fleet recreation center; improvement of living conditions on all islands; and the providing of airstrips for light plane operations. Work was also begun immediately on a camp site.

A seaplane ramp was constructed at one end of the main airfield on Falalop Island. This ramp, which extended from extreme low-water mark to the hardstand, was 50 by 95 feet, surfaced with pierced plank, and protected along the outer edges by a concrete slab. Work was begun on November 4, 1944, and completed on December 5, five days ahead of schedule.

A number of pontoon piers of a new and special design were built at Ulithi. These piers, each consisting of three 4-by-12-pontoon sections, filled with sand and gravel, were sunk and anchored in place by guy ropes to deadmen on shore and by iron rods, driven into the coral, with connecting tie pieces running across the tops of the pontoons. Despite extremely heavy weather on several occasions the pontoon piers stood up remarkably well, giving extensive service, with few repairs necessary. Piers of this type were also installed by the 51st Battalion to be used as aviation-gasoline mooring piers near the main airfield.

One of the major construction jobs on Ulithi was that of a fleet recreation area on Mogmog Island. The selected area was cleared, and a swamp area filled with coral, to eliminate mosquitoes and insects. Construction of the recreational facilities began on October 15. Numerous facilities for sports, a band stand, and beverage storage were provided. When completed in January

1945, the center could accommodate 8,000 men and 1,000 officers daily.

A 1,200-seat theatre, including a 25-by-40-foot stage with a quonset hut roof, completed in 20 days was ready for use on December 20, 1944. At the same time, a 500-seat chapel was built. A similar theatre, seating 1600, was constructed on Sorlen Island in 19 days.

The construction of facilities for a standard landing-craft unit on Sorlen Island was another major project. This development involved grading the entire island and covering it with quonset huts for storage, shops, mess halls, offices, and living quarters, and building roads, supply dumps, and necessary facilities to supply water and electricity to all parts of the island. Eleven distillation units, drawing water from the sea, and nine 5,000-gallon storage tanks were set up to provide drinking water.

The Sorlen Island hospital, constructed between November 24, 1944, and January 17, 1945, included quonset huts and supplementary facilities to house and operate a 100-bed unit.

Other construction included the erection of 42 quonset huts for use as a receiving station, and a 1600-man mess hall, complete with galley, warehouses, and refrigeration units. Three strips for light plane operations between islands of the atoll were built between December 12, 1944, and January 27, 1945. Additional facilities included the atoll commander's headquarters, a dispensary, an administration building, a shop, and Marine aviation camp.

All construction was performed by the 88th Battalion between October 10, 1944, and February 7, 1945, at which time the battalion left for Samar.

On November 8, 1944, CBMU 603 arrived, and in addition to general maintenance of the airstrip and taxiways, constructed a sewage-disposal system for the Marines and for the Seabees galleys. Construction of a 3,000-man galley, a refrigeration storage building, a butcher shop, an issue room, a bakery, an officers' mess, and shops for a landing craft unit was another important task. Other construction included enlarging and improving a finger pier and the removal of 10,000 cubic yards of coral to improve beaching facilities for landing craft. With the departure of the other battalions, CBMU 603 took over all duties of construction, maintenance, and stevedoring.

On V-J Day, this base was still operating at capacity, with CBMU 603 still attached.

SORLEN ISLAND, ULITHI

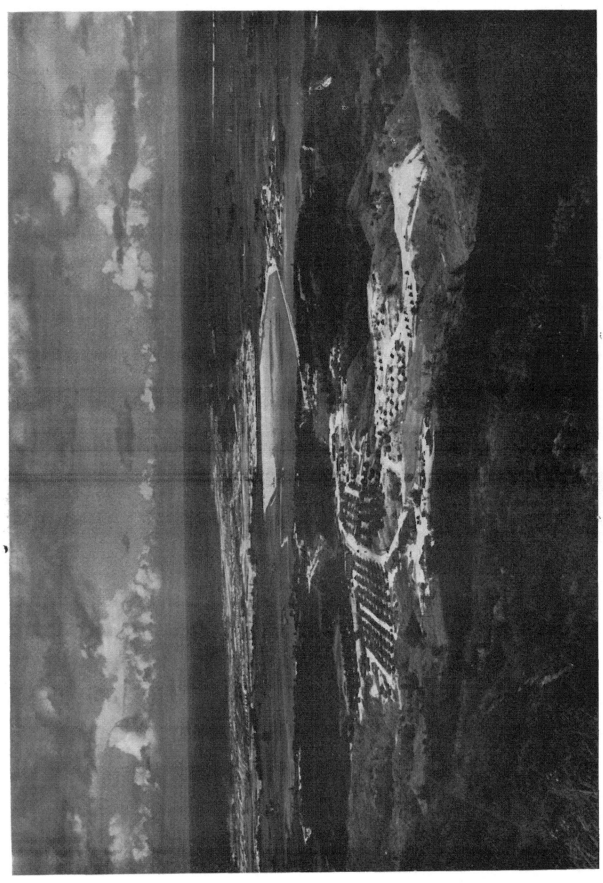

Orote Peninsula, Guam

CHAPTER 28

BASES IN THE MARIANAS AND IWO JIMA

Capture of the controlling positions in the Marshalls and Gilberts early in 1944 gave us command over a strategically vital area of the Pacific Ocean and permitted us to undertake the next major offensive operation, the conquest of the Marianas. These islands formed the southern end of an almost continuous chain, extending southward from Tokyo for 1,350 miles. The Nanpo Shoto, the Bonins, the Volcano Islands, and the Marianas, together, provided the enemy with a series of mutually supporting airfields and bases affording him a protected line of communications from the Japanese homeland to Truk, his major Central Pacific base, and to the eastern Carolines, the Philippines, and conquered territory to the south and west. Wresting the Marianas from him would cut that important line of communication and give us bases from which we could extend our control still farther westward and on which we could base aircraft to bomb the home islands of the empire.

Plans for the Marianas operations called for the development of large-scale facilities on the three largest islands of the group Saipan, Tinian, and Guam. On the two northern islands, long-range bomber fields for the Army's use were to be the dominant features; Guam was to be developed both as a long-range bomber base and as the principal naval base in the Central Pacific west of Pearl Harbor.

The invasion of the Marianas was begun by an assault by the Second and Fourth Marine Divisions on Saipan on the morning of June 15, 1944. Landings were made on the southwest coast of the island, to the north and south of the town of Charan Kanoa. The Fourth Division had the capture of Aslito airfield as its objective; the Second Division's mission was the capture of Mt. Tapotchau, in the center of the island. The 121st Construction Battalion went ashore with the Fourth Division assault forces; the 18th Battalion, with the Second Division.

The landing was vigorously opposed by the Jap-

anese defenders, and it became necessary to commit to the engagement the 27th Army Division which was to have been held as reserve. Despite the severe fighting, Aslito airfield was in our hands by June 19, and the Seabees set about repairing the battle-damaged runway. By June 29, our fighter planes were operating from the Aslito strip, giving the front-line troops land-based air support. By July 9, Saipan was secured.

Originally, it had been intended that the capture of Tinian would follow the Saipan operation after a few days, and that the capture of Guam (by another task force) would take place shortly thereafter. The stiff defense of Saipan, however, upset this schedule. The expeditionary force reserve had to be used; furthermore, the enemy fleet made an unsuccessful attempt to contest our advance into hitherto Japanese waters. Assaults on both Tinian and Guam were delayed, therefore, for about a month, time enough to permit bringing additional reinforcements from Hawaii.

Invasion forces landed on Guam on July 21. Possession of Apra Harbor, together with the development area surrounding it and the airfield on Orote Peninsula, was the initial objective. Landing forces struck north and south of the harbor, the Third Marine Division near Asan and the First Provisional Marine Brigade near Agat. As at Saipan, Seabees participated in the assaults the 25th Battalion and the 2nd Special Battalion on the beaches to the north of the harbor, and the 53rd Battalion, the 13th Special Battalion, and CBMU 515 on the southern beaches. For three weeks, combat and construction proceeded together, until August 10, when Japanese resistance came to an end.

As a development of considerable magnitude had been planned for Guam, calling for the employment of a large number of construction battalions, the 5th Construction Brigade had been formed for the purpose of coordinating and directing all construction on the island. On August 15 the brigade

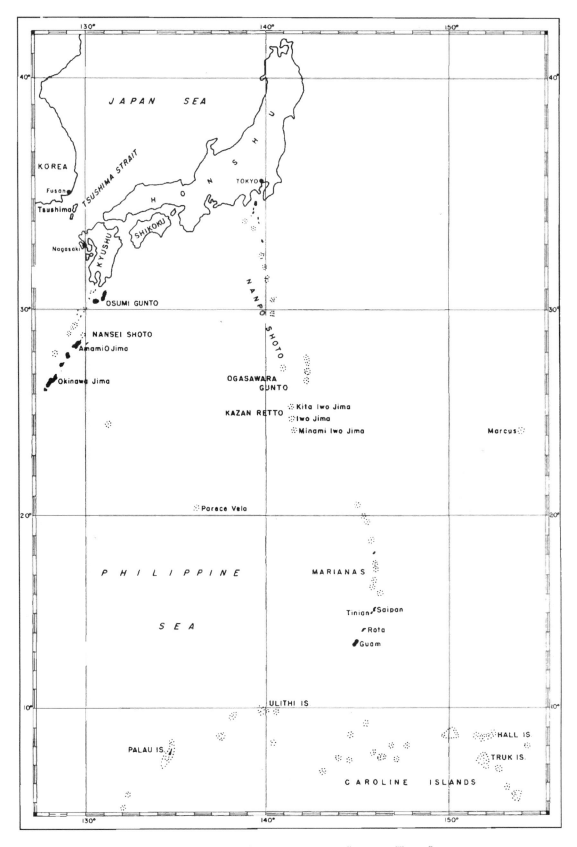

THE MARIANAS, IWO JIMA, OKINAWA, AND THE JAPANESE HOME ISLANDS

SEABEE-BUILT ENLISTED MEN'S QUARTERS OF THE 500TH BOMBARDMENT GROUP, SAIPAN

assumed control of construction, and the development of base facilities for both the Army and the Navy was begun.

Guam became a great Army air base as well as the principal naval base in the western Pacific. In large measure, Army facilities were built by Army engineer troops, and Navy facilities by Seabees, but there was much interchange of construction personnel and resources, made possible by the unified construction command.

Three days after the invasion of Guam, the Fourth Marine Division moved across the narrow strait separating Saipan from Tinian. Again, the Marines were accompanied by the 18th and 121st Construction Battalions. Enemy resistance was relatively weak by this time, and the conquest of the island was quickly completed. Again, all construction was under a unified command, that of the Sixth Construction Brigade, but in this instance, naval construction battalions were made responsible for all construction, even though facilities for the Army Air Forces dominated the base-development plans. During the ensuing months, Tinian became a gigantic air base, primarily for Superfortresses engaged in the long-range bombing campaign against Japan.

By the end of 1944 the long-range strategic bombing of Japan was in full fury. The bases were 1,500 miles away from the target, however, and the B-29's had to make the entire run without fighter-plane escort or the benefit of emergency landing fields. To strengthen the attack, therefore, it became necessary to capture and develop the uninviting island of Iwo Jima, just about half way between Saipan and Tokyo.

On February 19, 1945, the assault took place. Three Marine divisions participated — the Third, Fourth, and Fifth — accompanied by three construction battalions—the 31st, 62nd, and 133rd. Resistance by the defending forces was stubborn and losses ran high, but on March 16 the island was declared secure.

Fighter fields for bomber escorts and bomber fields to serve as intermediate landing points for

Superfortresses were the principal facilities to be constructed. Fifty B-29's, returning from Japan, had made emergency landings at Iwo by the time the island was secured. The Ninth Construction Brigade was formed to control the work of the battalions made responsible for the development of Iwo.

Saipan

As soon as the essential points in the Marshall Islands had been secured, preparations were made for operations in the Marianas. Saipan, the first objective, was the key to the Japanese defenses. It had been in Japanese hands since World War I and its fortifications were formidable. Moreover, the island was surrounded by a reef which made landing extremely difficult. The principal anchorage area, at Tanapag Harbor, was limited in size, and the depth varied from 9 to 25 feet.

The island, second largest of the Marianas, is about 12 miles long and 5 miles wide. Mt. Tapotchau, in the center of the island, is the dominating physical feature. Along the western shore, between Garapan and Agingan Point, there is a low and generally poorly drained coastal plain.

About 70 per cent of the island was under sugar cultivation. The population numbered about 25,000, more than 20,000 being Japanese. Garapan was the largest city and administrative center for the Saipan governmental district.

At dawn on June 15, 1944, the transports, cargo ships, and landing craft of the amphibious forces came into position off the west coast of Saipan. The Second and Fourth Marine Divisions moved in, under heavy fire from enemy mortars and small-calibre guns, to establish two beachheads at the town of Charan Kanoa. Landing with the Marines were men from the 121st and the 18th Construction Battalions, together with small echelons of the 92nd and 67th Battalions.

Aslito airfield was captured on the fourth day of fighting, but not until the strip had been damaged by shell and was covered with shrapnel. It was decided that the northern side of the runway was easiest to repair, and the next day, three companies of the 121st Battalion began work. Holes were filled with coral from stock piles found near the edge of the field. Two Japanese road-rollers were found and put into operation.

By the end of the second day, the entire strip, 150 by 4500 feet, had been repaired, and the first plane, a Navy TBF, landed. The Seabees were then assigned to unloading and storing aviation gasoline in Japanese-built gasoline-storage blockhouses. By D-plus-six, the runway had been widened to 200 feet. An Army aviation engineer battalion then took over the remaining construction, one company of Seabees remaining at the field to assist in laying marston mat. On D-plus-seven, Army planes began patrol operation from the field.

Seabees not assigned to airfield construction were occupied in unloading activities and repair of a Japanese pier.

On June 21, the 121st Battalion was ordered to repair the railroad from Charan Kanoa to Aslito Field, which had been badly damaged by shell fire. Four days later the first train ran from Charan Kanoa to the field. Other railroads were soon repaired and running smoothly, and the Seabees then turned to road repair.

By July 1, American troops had captured the central part of the island around Mt. Tapotchau, gained control of the heights commanding Garapan and Tanapag Harbor on the west coast, and advanced to within 5 miles of the northern tip of the island. Organized Japanese resistance ended on July 9.

On September 13, 1944, the commander of the naval base presented to the island commander a plan for the development of a naval base, to include housing, boat-repair facilities, a seaplane base, tank farm, a naval supply depot, a naval hospital, an ammunition depot, fleet recreation areas, and general harbor developments. During October, the 39th, 17th, 101st, and 117th Battalions and the 31st Special Battalion arrived at Saipan to construct the naval base. In December, the 51st Battalion reported to augment the construction forces. CBMU's 595 and 614 were also assigned to Saipan in the fall of 1944.

On October 11, the 39th Battalion, assisted by CBMU 595, began work on the seaplane base at Tanapag. They found the site littered with wrecked Japanese planes, wrecked masonry buildings, the twisted steel framework of Japanese hangars, a damaged concrete seaplane ramp, and a demolished concrete apron. The badly damaged buildings were destroyed and the area cleared of wreckage. Work was pushed to make major repairs to the Japanese ramp and parking area, to secure adequate drainage, and to increase the operating area.

Housing was provided for 1,750 men in quonset

DOUBLE-DECKER QUONSET AT SAIPAN
This chapel, photographed February 28, 1945, was built by the 117th Seabees

huts. and a 100-bed dispensary was erected. Quonset huts and steel arch-rib buildings were built for shops, and two portable seaplane hangars were provided. By the end of January, all work under the original plan for the base had been completed. During April and May, facilities were expanded to include an aviation supply annex, an aviation repair unit, and additional housing for 2,500 men. Expansion of the base also required drainage of a swamp.

Construction of a tank farm to supply fuel, diesel oil. and aviation gasoline for the Fleet as well as aviation gasoline for the seaplane base was started by the 39th Battalion on October 16, 1944. The tank farm was to consist of eighteen 1,000-barrel tanks for aviation gasoline, seven 10,000-barrel tanks for diesel fuel, and fifteen 10,000-barrel tanks for fuel oil, together with connecting pipe lines, pump housing. and 1.200 feet of submarine line for each type of fuel. The work was greatly delayed by the lack of material. By the end of November, however, the tanks and lines for aviation gasoline had been completed. By V-J day. seven of the fifteen 10,000-barrel oil tanks were in operation and the balance ready for tests; three of the original diesel tanks were in operation and the

other four under construction. All lines from tanker moorings to the tank farms were completed in March.

In October 1944, the 17th Battalion began construction of a naval supply depot, which was to support the Fleet and shore-based personnel in the area. Two 100-by-300-foot transit sheds were rushed to completion to provide for 2,500 tons of supplies due early in November. The supply depot. completed in February 1945, consisted of 64 steel arch-rib warehouses, 11 refrigerator sheds. and 8 quonset huts for administration.

Another task of the Seabees was the erection of their own permanent camps and naval base housing for 3,200 men. The latter construction, the project of the 117th Battalion, included two 1,500-man galleys and mess halls. Ten double-deck barracks and an office were constructed adjacent to the housing development for use as a receiving barracks.

Before development of the naval base, waterfront facilities at Tanapag Harbor consisted of three berths for Liberty ships at an existing masonry pier and two at a 12-by-72-pontoon pier. The concrete ramp at the seaplane base was used for the discharge of LST's, LCT's, and LCM's. Harbor

GARAPAN WATERFRONT DEVELOPMENT, SAIPAN
Creosote pile driver, photographed July 25, 1945, on south side of pier, widening pier approach and adding
berthing facilities

development was the major task of the 117th Battalion, with the assistance of a detachment of the 301st Battalion, which had as its special mission the dredging of an entrance channel and the clearing of isolated coral heads to develop Tanapag inner harbor.

The naval base plan called for the establishment of a mobile repair facility sufficient to maintain and repair hulls and engines of craft assigned to small-boat repair units and a small-boat pool.

The mobile amphibious base repair unit consisted of five, steel, arch-rib buildings, one 3-by-7-pontoon barge, one 4-by-7-pontoon barge with a 12-ton crane, one 6-by-18-pontoon drydock with a 4-by-7-pontoon tender barge, three 2-by-24 pontoon piers, and two 30-ton ramps. Fuel storage for this unit was provided in four 10,000-barrel diesel-oil tanks and two 1,000-barrel aviation-gasoline tanks, erected by the 39th Battalion as part of the major tank farm.

The small-boat repair unit included one, steel, arch-rib building, two 2-by-12-pontoon barges, and one 4-by-6-pontoon wharf, and a 4-by-15-pontoon drydock, two quonset huts, and mobile machine shops.

A small-boat pool and LVT-repair facilities were constructed on the site of an existing Japanese boat-basin. The Garapan pier, which had been partially repaired during the assault phase of operations, was further improved by putting in additional piling and coral-fill to provide 1,900 lineal-feet of marginal pier. During the spring of 1945, the 101st Battalion erected two 75-ton cranes on 6-by-18-pontoon barges and constructed an ammunition pier at Garapan, together with a 900-by-22-foot earth and coral causeway.

An industrial area, established in the spring of 1945 consisted of eight quonset huts and nine, steel, arch-rib buildings, with access roads and utilities. Three, steel, arch-rib buildings and two quonset huts provided shops for the repair of base equipment.

An ammunition area, a project assigned to the 101st Battalion, involved the construction of 112 steel magazines, 20 by 50 feet, each; four torpedo magazines; shops and a motor-maintenance shed; coral-surfaced bunkers and parking areas: and more than 6 miles of access roads.

Naval medical facilities at Saipan were provided by small dispensaries at individual naval activities and one 400-bed hospital constructed early in 1945 by the 17th Battalion. The hospital unit contained 40 quonset huts for wards, laboratories, mess halls, galleys, quarters, and administration buildings. Two, steel, arch-rib buildings with concrete decks and a refrigerator were constructed for general medical-storage. The hospital was used for casualties from the Iwo Jima and Okinawa campaigns.

The major medical installations on Saipan were for the Army, and the Seabees assisted in the construction of several Army hospitals. In March 1945, the 101st Battalion was ordered to construct Convalescent Hospital No. 5, a 3,000-bed unit of tents with wooden decks. Work was started on March 25, and 1,000 beds with necessary facilities were ready eight days later. The hospital was completed on April 28.

On March 14, 1945, the 39th Battalion was assigned the completion of the 2,000-bed General Hospital 148, which had been under construction by the Army for seven months. The work remaining to be accomplished was the erection of 45 quonset huts, 20 prefabricated huts, all utilities, and improvements to galleys and mess halls. About half of the battalion worked on this project, with aid from 180 men of an Army engineer battalion, and completed the work by the end of April.

For Army General Hospital 39 and Army Station Hospital 176, each of 600-bed capacity, the 17th Battalion erected quonset and wood-frame buildings.

Construction of the huge Kobler and Isely air fields for B-29's on Saipan was essentially an Army engineering job, but Seabees assisted in the erection of housing and the installation of utilities. Two small fields were established by the Seabees, one at Marpi Point and one at Kagman Point.

The 51st Battalion began the construction of Marpi Field in January 1945 and had nearly completed the facilities by the end of April, when the balance of assigned construction was turned over to the Air Corps. The field had a 4,500-foot runway, 15,000 feet of taxiways and parking areas, 45 buildings, and several portable hangars. CBMU 616 assisted in the further construction of the field. The 101st Battalion operated the coral pit and hauled coral to the field. By the end of July, the field had been increased to include a second strip, 3,500 feet long, and a 1,400-foot addition to the original runway.

In April, the 51st Battalion was assigned to the partial construction and revision of Kagman Field. The existing coral-surfaced strip, 5,000 by 150 feet, was repaved, and additional facilities were built, including two portable hangars, a 1,000-man mess hall, and 58 quonset huts for quarters, shops, and utilities.

Another major project was the construction of an ammunition-storage area (500 acres) by the 101st Battalion. Many of the bunkers were located in hard coral, which had to be blasted, a process which slowed production and resulted in excessive break-down of equipment. The original plan called for 248 bunkers and 22 steel magazines. Plans were changed on January 15, 1945, to 109 bunkers and 197 steel magazines. Work progressed as rapidly as the arrival of equipment permitted.

On V-J day the 39th, 51st, 117th, and 121st Battalions, the 31st Special Battalion, and five maintenance units were at Saipan, the 121st Battalion having returned from Tinian in June.

Guam

Guam, the second step in the occupation of the Marianas, was destined to become the nerve center of the final thrust against Japan. Within air-striking distance of the Japanese homeland and athwart the lines of Japanese air and sea communications in the western Pacific, Guam was developed as an air base to support offensive operations, became the Pacific Fleet headquarters, and was used as a huge storehouse of supply.

The island of Guam, at the extreme southern end of the Marianas archipelago, the largest and most populated island of the group, is about 32 miles long and varies in width from 4 miles near the center portion to about 8 miles across both northern and southern sectors. The entire island is surrounded by an extensive reef system.

The northern portion of the island is a high limestone plateau with an average elevation of 400 feet, broken only by two higher points, Mt. Santa Rosa and Mt. Barrigada. In general, the plateau is gently rolling and well adapted for the construction of airfields and related facilities. The southern part of the island has a rugged terrain and red volcanic clay soil which becomes very unstable under heavy rains.

The only important anchorage is Apra Harbor, on the western side of the island, formed by Cabras Island and Orote Peninsula. In spite of these protective arms, however, the harbor was open to

HANGARS AT HARMON FIELD, GUAM

heavy ocean swells and required considerable development before it could be considered a first-class anchorage.

Island climate is healthful and pleasant. However, a 100-inch annual rainfall and a flash run-off which follows sudden downpours created considerable drainage problems.

Prior to the outbreak of hostilities in Europe, Guam had been under United States control since the close of the Spanish-American War and was the site of a small navy yard at Piti and a Marine barracks at Sumay. Early in 1941, a CPFF contract was negotiated for the construction of a naval station at Guam. Although the Hepburn Board in 1938 had recommended the development of Guam as a heavily fortified naval base and later, as a major air and submarine base, only minimum development was authorized under this contract because of the strained relations between the United States and Japan. Construction work was limited to tank farms for fuel oil, diesel oil, and motor gasoline; a breakwater and other harbor improvements; additional seaplane facilities; together with housing, power, water, and roads.

Contract construction started on May 24, 1941, with the erection of five steel tanks for oil storage, and the next project was road construction.

Construction of the breakwater on Luminao Reef, to afford greater protection against typhoons than was given by Cabras Island, was not started

until August 1941. Huge limestone blocks, quarried on Cabras Island, were skidded along the reef to an improvised derrick which deposited them at desired points to form the breakwater.

A crew of experienced steel workers from the mainland was employed in the erection of the steel tanks. Other projects were carried out for the most part by native labor. Two other construction organizations worked in conjunction with the contractor's organization. One was the Guam naval station public works force, consisting of about 1,500 military and native personnel, who worked on the breakwater and oil pier, and on the development and extension of power, water, communications, and sewage-disposal systems. The other organization, operated under the Island Department of Industries, had a personnel of about 800 natives, chiefly concerned with road building and maintenance. Practically all construction equipment, plants, and utilities used by the contractors were facilities of the naval station, the Marine Corps post, or the Island Government maintenance department.

Work on the construction projects was scarcely well underway when Guam was taken by the Japanese on December 10, 1941. A road had been graded around the island, and other roads had been extended and improved. One mile of breakwater, 36 feet wide and 5 feet above sea-level, had been completed. An oiling dock had been constructed and piped, and some work had been accomplished on pump houses, barracks, and mess halls.

The contractor's organization had also done engineering and experimental work in connection with a proposed Orote Peninsula airfield. In a letter of August 6, 1941, the naval commandant reported surveys indicating that a 4500-by-400-foot landplane runway could be constructed.

No action was taken by the United States on this proposal, but the Japanese, during their occupation, recognized the suitability of the location and constructed a 4500-foot coral-surfaced airstrip on the peninsula. In addition, the Japanese brought a similar strip northeast of Agana to near-completion and partially cleared a third strip still farther north. Otherwise, the Japanese did very little to improve or extend the island facilities.

The United States assault to recapture Guam began on July 21, 1944, when landing forces struck at two points, one about 2 miles north and the other about 2 miles south of Apra Harbor. In the north, the assault was spearheaded by the Third Marine Division (Reinforced), which stormed and broke

the defenses on a beachhead extending along the west shore of the island, from Piti to Asan. In the south, the First Provisional Marine Brigade and the 77th Army Division struck on the beaches of Agat, forcing a beachhead along the west shore, from Orote Peninsula southward to a point beyond the village of Agat. By the evening of D-Day, assault forces had secured firm footholds ashore and were driving inland against considerable infantry, automatic-weapon, and mortar-fire opposition, to force a north-south junction and so cut off Apra Harbor and the surrounding hill-country.

The 25th Construction Battalion, one of several Seabee units active in the assault, landed with the Third Marine Division on the northern beaches near Asan. Acting as a shore party for the Third Combat Team, this unit had charge of Red Beaches One and Two, where landings were effected rapidly in the face of enemy fire. Personnel of this shore party were subjected to considerable fire throughout the first three days of assault operations. The 25th manned beach defenses in this area until increased security of the beachhead made it possible

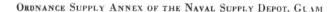

ORDNANCE SUPPLY ANNEX OF THE NAVAL SUPPLY DEPOT, GUAM

BLACK OIL TANK FARM, GUAM
This Seabee-built tank farm was part of the naval supply depot

to reduce these forces, and also provide rear guards in the combat lines.

On the fifth day of the assault, four 25th-Battalion road-repair units were brought ashore, and the road leading from Piti to the principal city of Agana was repaired for the advance. The remainder of the personnel of this unit was assigned as ship's platoons and acted as stevedores in unloading essential cargo for the assault troops.

Company B of the 2nd Special Battalion also took part in the Asan landings. This unit, consisting of six officers and 201 men, was assigned to working the supply dumps by day and occupying ridge defenses by night.

After July 28, the men and equipment of the 2nd Special were transferred to the southern beachhead, where the major part of unloading operations was in progress. On September 9, the remainder of the battalion arrived. The entire battalion then moved to a new camp location and swung into its regular routine of handling cargo from ships unloading in Apra Harbor.

CBMU 515 was attached to the 22nd Regiment of the First Provisional Marine Brigade and hit the southern landing beaches near Agat with the first assault waves. Casualties were numerous. Two sections of this unit were engaged in actual fighting for the first two or three hours after landing. The mission was to handle all equipment for the battalions and staffs of the 22nd Marines and to unload supplies for the inland assault. Cargo-handling across the reef was accomplished under continuous sniper fire. Late in the afternoon of D-Day, a bulldozer and a welding machine were landed and work was immediately started on the repairing of damaged LVT's.

CBMU 515 was assigned to night rear-guard duty for nearly a week. As equipment came ashore, road-building and supply of front-line Marine troops were carried on. As the fighting progressed northward, two Marine hospitals were erected.

A special group of the 53rd Battalion, composed of one officer and 18 men, landed just four minutes after H-Hour. Theirs was the difficult mission of anchoring landing-craft, LCT's and LCM's, at the reef edge, using waterproofed tractors, while the craft discharged their cargoes of armored field tanks. After securing the landing boats, the men marked out a lane, through waist-deep water, across several hundred yards of reef to the beach, and led the incoming tanks safely ashore. This work was carried on for more than nine hours under constant enemy fire, during which time some 50 LCM's and five LCT's were unloaded.

On July 22, the entire forward echelon of the 53rd Battalion, 18 officers and 520 men, went ashore to further assist in landing operations. In addition, the men hauled supplies, built combat roads, repaired bridges, established water points,

and set up command-posts. The second echelon came ashore on July 27. During the early phases of the assault, the battalion cleared the areas of some 23 tons of explosives.

Another Seabee outfit which had a hand in the assault phase was the 13th Special Battalion. Men from this unit landed with the southern forces on July 28. One man was wounded when enemy troops on Orote Peninsula opened up with mortars on the unloading LST's. On July 30, Orote Peninsula was secured, and the next morning the first vessels entered Apra Harbor. Before noon of that same day, the 13th Special had five stevedore crews aboard these ships. Unloading, without benefit of piers or established points, began at once,

APRA HARBOR AND BREAKWATER

with small landing-craft and self-propelled barges serving as lighters.

Meanwhile, the Japanese airstrip on Orote Peninsula had been cleared of enemy resistance on July 28 and was placed in operation the next day by the 2nd Marine Engineer Battalion.

On July 23, both the Island Commander, United States Marine Corps, and the Officer-in-Charge of the Fifth Construction Brigade came ashore with the assault forces at Agat. Operational control of all construction forces during the initial assault phase was administered by the Marine general commanding the assault forces. As enemy forces were eliminated from portions of the island, permitting occupation and base development by our forces, construction forces, such as the 2nd Marine Engineer Battalion and the 25th and 53rd Construction Battalions, were placed under the control of the Fifth Brigade Commander.

Organized resistance on Guam was officially ended on August 10, 1944, but enemy resistance from caves, jungles, and hillsides continued for many weeks. The Seabees had at least a small part of the subsequent mopping-up. Additional Seabee units came ashore shortly after the initial resistance had been overcome, and on August 15, 1944, the 5th Brigade assumed control of the island construction work.

The large-scale assault operations carried out by our attacking forces, together with minor demolitions set off by the Japanese, had destroyed a major part of the installations on Guam. Agana, the principal city and capital of the island, with a pre-war population in excess of 12,000, was utterly destroyed in the bombing and shelling of the assault. Two other towns of importance, Piti and Sumay, located on Apra Harbor, were also leveled by pre-invasion bombardments. With the exception of the Piti boat channel and quay-wall and the breakwater and oil dock at Cabras, all naval installations on Guam were damaged in the assault beyond any possible use except as a source of salvaged materials. Of the extensive water system, a large part of the overland pipe line was destroyed during the assault, but the reservoirs remained practically intact. The pre-war road system was also badly damaged by the bombardment and the greatly increased traffic. The only construction

WARDS OF FLEET HOSPITAL No. 115, GUAM

WARDS OF FLEET HOSPITAL NO. 103, GUAM
Example of quonset-hut adaptation for use in the tropics

work by the Japanese which could be used by our forces were the three airstrips.

Development of waterfront facilities in Apra Harbor was a task of highest priority. The tremendous importance of the harbor to base development had been recognized in the choice of an assault site. As the natural barrier reef precluded any considerable use of LCT's and the existing pier installations were negligible, the Seabees began the installation of pontoon piers to break a prospective bottle-neck of supply.

It was decided that the logical spot for installing the first pier was the site of an old Navy fuel station on Cabras Island. Blasting was first necessary to obtain a 35-foot depth of water along the outboard face of the pier. Construction was initiated on August 5, 1944, and the pier was completed by August 22.

All the actual pontoon-assembly work was done in deep water by a crew of Seabees quartered aboard an LST in the harbor. At the same time, another crew built a coral-fill causeway out to the pontoon string. Soon, pontoon piers were being completed on the average of one every twelve days,

in spite of bad weather, rough water, and the scarcity of material.

By the first of October 1944, six piers, 42-by-350-feet, were in full operation, and a seventh was under way. In the meantime, five concrete barges had been sunk for a temporary breakwater extension along Calalan Bank. Then disaster struck. A full-scale typhoon passed near Guam between October 3 and 9. Continued strong winds built up such heavy waves in Apra Harbor that they destroyed or severely damaged all the pontoon piers, carried away portions of the Cabras Island breakwater, and seriously damaged the sunken barges placed to form the breakwater extension. When the weather finally cleared and the heavy seas subsided, the supply problem was more critical than ever.

One pier at Sumay and one at Cabras were repaired as quickly as possible to permit time to redesign the construction of the others. One month after the typhoon, seven piers were again in full operation and in a more secure condition. A new elastic bridge connection was designed to absorb the shock of the tide rather than attempt to resist it. The "Hensen" connection is made from a steel

I-beam, welded to the pontoon bridge and clamped to the anchor string by a coil spring and a pendulum-type rod which allows the I-beam to slide back and forth on the anchor.

Two other phases of waterfront construction involved the breakwater along Calalan Bank and the development of the inner harbor. Limestone, quarried on Cabras Island, was used to construct the breakwater, 3260 feet long and 32 feet wide. The

of five airfields to support the offensive operation of heavy, long-range bombers against the islands of Japan. The three Japanese strips, which had been captured in varying stages of completion, formed the nucleus of the first three fields to be established. In addition, two huge fields of two strips each were constructed on the northern tip of the island for B-29 bases.

Orote Field, which had been completed by the

BASE HOSPITAL No. 18, GUAM
Large and small quonsets grouped to form units

entire protective arm, which was built along the north of Apra Harbor, from the main island through Cabras Island to the outer tip of the breakwater on Calalan Bank, measured 17,000 lineal feet.

Development of the inner harbor included 7,500,-000 cubic feet of dredging and the construction of 26,000 lineal feet of quay-wall. The quay-walls were built with steel sheet-piling, back-filled with coral. A small-boat pool and a submarine base with a finger pier were provided in this part of the harbor. Existing installations at Piti for small-boat repair were rehabilitated and augmented.

By July 1945, the piers in Apra Harbor numbered 14 quay-wall berths, nine pontoon piers, two wooden piers for fueling, ten LST berths, and one submarine pier.

As the waterfront facilities were developed to accommodate the heavy flow of supplies and equipment, other construction on Guam proceeded apace. Of prime importance was the establishment

Japanese to 4,500 feet and was the only existing strip to be rehabilitated during the assault, was completely rebuilt and lengthened to 5,500 feet by the Marine Engineers. Seabees assisted in the development of the field, constructing hardstands, shops, and warehouses. Orote Field was in constant use after the early part of August 1944, first for fighter operations and later for conditioning 1,800 planes per month for the Fleet and the Marines. Planes were tested, repaired, and cleaned of the preserving compounds with which they had been shipped overseas. An aviation supply depot and an aircraft repair and overhaul unit were established at the field.

The second step in airfield construction was on the 5,000-foot strip which the Japanese had almost completed near Agana. The initial runway was extended to 7,000 feet and paved with asphalt, and a second asphalt-surfaced strip, 150 by 6,000 feet, was constructed. The field was rotated several degrees in order to reduce flight interference from

ADVANCE BASE CONSTRUCTION DEPOT, GUAM

DISPENSARY AT MARIANAS HEADQUARTERS, GUAM

Mt. Barrigada. The first planes landed on the former Japanese strip on August 29, 1944, and the field was commissioned on October 22. Agana Field was used principally by Naval Air Transport Service and for Army passenger and freight traffic.

The Japanese had completed clearing a third strip, to the north of Agana Field. This site was chosen for the establishment of Depot (later, Harmon) Field, and again the orientation was shifted slightly. Two inches of asphaltic concrete were applied to the 7,000-by-150-foot strip; 12,000 feet of taxiway and 42 hardstands were constructed.

Eight superstructure hangars, 130 by 160 feet each, and ten 160-by-190-foot repair hangars were erected for the field. Cooperation between the Army Engineers and the Seabees produced the largest air repair base in the Pacific for the repair of B-29's in the Marianas. The first B-29's landed on November 24, 1944.

Early in 1945, attention was concentrated on the carving of the two B-29 fields, North and Northwest Fields, out of the dense jungle on the northern end of Guam. Each field comprised two asphalt-surfaced runways, 8500 by 200 feet, capable of sending off 160 planes per flight.

North Field was constructed entirely by Army Engineers. The first strip was commissioned on February 3, 1945, and three weeks later, the first B-29 Tokyo raid from Guam was launched from this strip. By the end of April, the second strip was in operation.

During April and May 1945, the combined efforts of the Army Engineers and the Seabees were centered on the construction of Northwest Field. In the construction, 26-foot cuts and fills were made through hard limestone. The south runway, completed two days ahead of schedule, was opened to service on June 1, 1945. Work was rushed on the taxiways, hardstands, and operational facilities for the south strip and also on the second strip and its appurtenances to accommodate the rapidly arriving B-29's. The north strip was in operation by July 1.

Another vital construction project on Guam involved the development of a road network. Road construction was undertaken during the rainy season, while the invasion battle was at full tempo. It was a road job different from, and more difficult than, any previously attempted in the Pacific. The terrain presented considerable difficulties, because

CHAPEL AT FLEET HOSPITAL No. 111, GUAM

THIRD MARINES' CHAPEL, GUAM

the rugged outcroppings of rock and sharp shore-line required heavy earth moves. Moreover, the roads were to be permanent.

Specifications were as rigid as those for super-highways in the United States. Main arteries were to be widened to 56 feet and made to carry four 11-foot traffic lanes. Curves on the main roads were not to exceed six degrees, and grades were to be held to a six-percent maximum. Primary roads were surfaced with two and a half inches of as-phalt; secondary roads were surfaced with coral and then oiled. Secondary roads would carry either three or two lanes, but this reduction in width did not relax any of the other rigid criteria.

The first major road job undertaken was the construction of a super-highway between Sumay and Agana. Three weeks after D-Day, the road was under construction. Constant two-way traffic made construction progress almost impossible; torren-tial rains reduced every new cut to an ever-deepen-ing gumbo and made the problem of fill acute; breakdowns in equipment came rapidly; and road

workers had to take precautions against Japanese snipers. A high expenditure of coral was necessary where the road was built across gullies, swamps, and former rice paddies; these sections took be-tween 10 and 18 feet of fill. At the end of 60 days, a four-lane highway, 12 miles long, had been con-structed, with nine bridges built to standard H-15 highway loading. Traffic on this main highway reached a proportion equal to the traffic in down-town sections of large cities in the United States.

Attention was then turned to regrading and straightening other existing roads and to building new roads for access to airfields, ammunition dumps, camps, and other facilities. The road net-work on Guam finally totalled more than 103 miles.

Due to the position of Guam in the forward area, it was essential that a large store of supplies, spare parts, equipment, fuels, and refrigerated foods be on hand at all times for the Fleet and for military forces on the island and in forward movements.

By March 1945, an extensive tank-farm system was complete. Storage had been provided for 328,-

PORT DIRECTOR'S HEADQUARTERS, GUAM

000 barrels of aviation gasoline, 130,000 barrels of diesel oil, 40,000 barrels of motor gasoline. and 448,000 barrels of fuel oil.

Several major supply depots were established. The naval supply depot comprised 464 steel, arch-rib warehouses, a large personnel camp, open-storage areas. a drum-filling plant, and 68,000 cubic feet of refrigerator storage.

The advance base construction depot covered 250 acres and had 369 buildings for general ware-

houses, spare-parts storage, equipment-overhaul and tire-repair, and a 2600-man camp. The function of the depot was to procure, store, and issue supplies and equipment, primarily for the Seabees. but equipment was issued to other military activities when available and if priorities warranted the issue.

The Marines had cognizance of the issue of all the staple foods on the island. which necessitated large warehouses. Five 96-by-540-foot buildings

NOSE HANGARS AT AGANA NAVAL AIR STATION. GUAM

were erected at Agana, and two at Agat, one 745 by 118 feet and the other 349 by 118 feet, for this purpose.

The medical supply depot was composed of 18 buildings. Total warehouses for all airfields consisted of more than a million square feet of space. The Marine depot for supplies was made up of 190 buildings. Army garrison forces had about 600,000 square feet of storage space.

The naval ammunition depot consisted of two

Shallow wells along the coastal areas, deep wells in the interior, a basal ground-water tunnel, dams, and springs were used until the total completed water system had a capacity of 12,000,000 gallons per day from 67 main sources.

The Almagosa system was the largest, supplying two million gallons per day for Orote Peninsula and for the Fleet. It consisted of a 12-inch pipe-line from Talofofo River, paralleling the main 10-inch line from Almagosa Springs to tanks at Orote, for

BACHELOR OFFICERS' QUARTERS, GUAM
These double-deck quonset huts served the headquarters for the Marianas command.

sections, one for the Fleet and one for ground forces. The Fleet unit comprised 44 quonsets for personnel and administration buildings, 202 pre-fabricated-steel magazines, 100 hardstands, and 20 fuse magazines. The ground unit had 26 quonsets, 550 shelters, 61 hardstands, and 50 magazines.

The water system on Guam at the time of the invasion was insufficient, because of bombardment damage and initial inadequacy, to meet the needs of the tremendous increase in population and the demands of the Fleet. Various methods were used in the development of an adequate water system.

facilities and docks at Orote; a 6-inch pipe-line loop for Orote facilities; and 10-inch pipe-lines from tanks to docks.

The Agana system supplied one and a half million gallons per day to the towns of Agana and Sinajana and units in the vicinity. The Ylig treatment plant, producing 300,000 gallons per day, consisted of plant pumps and pipe-lines to various activities in that area. The Pago River treatment plant, with rapid sand-filters, provided 500,000 gallons per day to mobile combat units in that vicinity. A 400-foot underground tunnel, with pumping stations, sup-

BARRIGADA RADIO STATION (ABOVE) AND MARINE CORPS FIELD DEPOT (BELOW), GUAM

plied one million gallons of water per day for Agana Field, the ABCD, and the Fleet hospitals. Deep and shallow wells and the dams produced water for all the other activities.

Hospital construction on Guam was initiated in September 1944. By March 1945, the hospitals, brought to usable completion by Seabees and Army Engineers, provided a total of about 9,000 beds and were pressed into service to handle casualties from

with a total capacity of about 150 beds. Screened food-preparation centers were provided, and food was distributed from the preparation center. Water and sanitary systems were set up. The camps were crowded and accommodations in many instances were primitive, but the civilians were returned to their own ranches, farms, and houses as soon as practicable.

Development of the major advance base at Guam

THIRD MARINES' RECREATION CENTER, GUAM

the Iwo Jima operation. Included were Naval Base Hospital 18 (1,000 beds); Fleet Hospitals 103 and 115 (1,000 and 2,000 beds, respectively); the 373rd Army Station Hospital (750 beds); and the 204th Army General Hospital (1,000 beds).

Devastation of civilian housing on Guam, as a result of bombing and naval bombardment, was extensive. There were few habitable buildings in the towns of Agana, Asan, Agat, and Sumay. Approximately 15,000 natives had to be housed, and three camps were set up at Agana, Agat, and near the Ylig River. Each camp had its own hospital

was accomplished by the cooperative efforts of the Seabees, the Army Engineers, and the Second Marine Engineer Battalion. Free interchange of equipment and materials was made possible by the operational control of the Fifth Brigade over all construction forces. The Seabees were responsible for approximately 75 per cent of the total construction.

Very little native labor was employed in construction, primarily because most of the natives were needed on the reconstruction of their own homes and on Federal Economic Administration farming projects aimed at producing fresh foods for natives and for garrison forces.

In all, some 37,000 construction troops were employed in the construction of Advance Base Guam.

Tinian

Tinian, the third of the three largest islands of the Marianas, lies just southwest of Saipan and is separated from it by a strait only 3 miles wide.

center of the island. Japanese construction on the northern plateau formed the nucleus of the great airfields the Seabees built on Tinian during the succeeding months.

In view of the magnitude of the development planned for Tinian, the Sixth Construction Brigade was formed and was assigned responsibility for all construction work on the island. It comprised, originally, the 29th and 30th Construction Regi-

ROUTE 6, GUAM
This photograph shows conditions in November 1945

The island is about 12 miles long, from north to south, and about 6 miles wide, with a generally flat and terraced terrain. The Japanese had developed extensive sugar plantations; the island's industry was confined to sugar-refining.

The northern part of Tinian contains an extensive plateau ideally suited for a large airdrome, a circumstance that had not been overlooked by the Japanese. During the months just prior to our Marianas offensive, they had done considerable work there on two airstrips, one a coffin-shaped field, 4,700 feet long, and another of more orthodox shape, 3,900 feet long. In addition, they had completed a 5,000-foot strip about midway of the west coast, and had begun a small runway near the

ments; later, while base development was in progress, the 49th Regiment was formed and became part of the Brigade. Two of the battalions, the 18th and the 121st, participated in the assault on Saipan and were again given an assault assignment in the Tinian invasion. As was customary, during the assault period these battalions were under Marine Corps control and did not formally become part of the construction brigade until the island was secured.

The invasion of Tinian was principally a shore-to-shore operation from Saipan by landing craft. On July 24, 1944, the Fourth Marine Division landed on two narrow beaches on the northwest coast of the island. They were accompanied by the

CAMP OF THE 94TH SEABEES, GUAM
Photograph taken October 1945

forward echelons of the 18th and 121st Construction Battalions. The remaining personnel of these battalions went ashore on Tinian on July 27.

The 18th and 121st had a different organization than was customary for construction forces assigned to Marine divisions. The men had been especially trained, prior to the occupation, to perform certain tasks that could be activated according to operational requirements in the field. Twelve assault units were set up, as follows: LVT-ramp maintenance, beach access, road reconnaissance, road construction, road maintenance, traffic circulation, railroad demolition, railroad construction. airfield rehabilitation, civil-affairs construction, water supply, and reserve.

One of the more significant tasks of the Seabees in the Tinian assault was the maintenance of LVT ramps — especially developed devices to allow LVT's to climb the steep banks that flanked the narrow landing beaches.

The ramp consisted of two side-rails, made of 10-inch I-beams, which supported an articulated mat of 6-by-12-inch timbers, and was carried to the landing point by the vehicle itself. The side rails were suspended from the sides of the LVT, with enough upward slope to permit their forward ends to clear the top of the bank. The timber mat was supported for its first 10 feet by the rails and for the remainder of its length by slides built over the vehicle's cargo well. At the point of landing, the forward ends of the rails were released so that

they came to rest on the top of the bank; the LVT then backed away a few feet, allowing the after ends of the rails to rest on the bottom. Further backing permitted the timber mat to come to rest upon the rails for its entire length, and the vehicle could then go ashore over the ramp thus formed.

The first echelon of the 18th Battalion installed and maintained these ramps, the work lasting three days. Harbor facilities were non-existent and everything had to come across the barrier reef, to be unloaded and transported inland.

Upon arrival of the remainder of the battalion, road-repair and construction details were assigned, emphasizing the construction of special roads for cleated vehicles. The terrain was level, and access roads were easily built from the beaches to the existing Japanese roads.

On July 27, the 121st Battalion began the repair of the 4.700-foot Japanese strip in the north, filling bomb and shell craters with swept-up shrapnel fragments. By evening, a strip, 150 by 2,500 feet, had been repaired. The next day the first plane landed. At the end of two days the field had been repaired for its full length, and on the third day, the Seabees widened it to 200 feet. Air transports immediately began operating from the field. bringing in supplies and evacuating wounded.

A few days after the initial assault, the surviving defenders fled to a network of caves in the hills and cliffs of the island; on August 1, the assault phase on Tinian was over. The Seabees were thereupon released from the operational control of the Marine commander and were assigned to the Sixth Construction Brigade, which began its full functioning on August 3.

Plans for the development of Tinian as a major air base had been carefully laid at Pearl Harbor during the months preceding the invasion, by a nucleus staff of the Sixth Brigade in cooperation with the 64th Army Engineers of the Army and the joint staff agencies of the area command. According to the plan adopted, two strips built by the Japanese, the 4,700-foot strip at the north end of the island and the 5,000-foot runway on the west coast, were to be extended to 6,000 feet each so that medium and heavy bombers could operate from them. After that extension had been made,

the northern runway was to be lengthened to 8,500 feet and the neighboring Japanese-started strip was to be completed to the same length, to support the opening operations of B-29's. The next scheduled step was to be the building of two more 8,500-foot strips on a new site in the vicinity of the west-coast strip. In addition, a field, having a 6,000-foot runway, for Navy use, to be designated East Field, was to be built at a location to be determined on the scene.

Immediately following the securing of the island the air base development was begun, but the plan was modified. The rehabilitated northern strip was extended by 1,000 feet at its west end and 650 feet at the east end and was widened to 300 feet. This strip formed the first element of what later was to

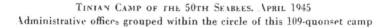

TINIAN CAMP OF THE 50TH SEABEES. APRIL 1945
Administrative offices grouped within the circle of this 109-quonset camp

NORTH FIELD, TINIAN
Across the water. in the background, is the island of Saipan

become the great North Field. The second task, undertaken in September, was the completion to a 6,000-foot length of the neighboring Japanese-started strip; thereupon, designated North Field, Strip No. 3. The existing Japanese field on the west coast of the island, which had been severely damaged during the assault period, was then reconditioned to serve as a 4,000-foot fighter strip.

During this early period, Navy patrol planes operated from the North Field runways. When the time arrived for enlarging those strips to permit their use by Superfortresses. it was necessary first to provide a new field for the Navy's use. A site, a mile east of the west-coast fighter strip. was chosen, adjoining the area selected for the proposed third and fourth B-29 strips; construction of a new 6.000-foot runway, designated West Field, Strip No. 3, was put under way. The East Field site. originally planned for the Navy field, was rejected as unsuitable for proper development. To expedite the construction of the Navy strip, on October 1 practically all construction at North Field was brought to a halt and all the heavy-duty earth-moving equipment on Tinian was moved to West Field. By November 15 the strip was complete, and the entire Navy air force moved to its new base. Accessories to this strip included 16,000 feet of taxiway. 70 hardstands, 345 quonset huts, 33 buildings for repair and maintenance facilities, 7 magazines. and a 75-foot-high control tower.

After the completion of the Navy air facilities at West Field, attention was directed again to North Field and to the extension and strengthening of the two 6,000-foot bomber strips to fit them for Superfortress use. At the same time the scope of the plan for North Field was enlarged, calling for four B-29 strips instead of two.

The North Field project was assigned to the 30th Regiment, which, in turn, divided it into several phases and assigned principal responsibility for each phase to a battalion.

The first phase was the development of Strip No. 1, to its required length of 8,500 feet and width of 300 feet, and the construction of taxiways, hardstands, and aprons necessary to serve it. The 121st Battalion. which had rehabilitated the old Japanese strip in this location during the assault period, was named as "lead battalion" for this phase. The other battalions of the 30th Regiment assisted it, acting as sub-contractors. Strip No. 1 was completed nine days ahead of the date set. The first B-29 landed on December 22.

The second phase included the extension of the No. 3 strip to 8,500 feet, with the 67th as the lead battalion.

The 13th Battalion drew the responsibility for the next phase, which was the construction of a strip, designated as North Field No. 2. between the two earlier strips, including taxiways, hardstands, and a service apron for a projected fourth strip. Strip No. 2 was completed and received its first long-range bomber on February 27.

Instead of proceeding immediately with construction of Strip No. 4, all construction effort was then directed to the development of the long-range-bomber strips planned for West Field.

Construction of West Field, Strip No. 1, the first B-29 strip at that location. north of the Navy's West Field strip (No. 3), had been begun on February 1 by the 49th Regiment. a newly formed unit; in March the battalions of the 30th Regiment were added to the project.

Construction of two 8,500-foot strips proceeded

Construction of the field would have been simpler if the runways had been only 7,000 feet long, the width of the Tinian plateau. The last 1,500 feet spilled over the edge of the plateau, and extensive fills had to be made on both the east and the west sides of the island. Moreover. after construction work had started the maximum permissible taxiway grade was reduced from two and one-half to one and one-half per cent, because of an opera-

NAVAL AIR BASE, TINIAN
General view of the apron and shops

simultaneously, and personnel and equipment from all battalions were freely exchanged in accordance with the needs of the job. Both strips, laid out parallel to each other, were 500 feet wide and included 53,000 feet of taxiway, 220 hardstands, 2 service aprons, sub-service aprons, and warm-up aprons. 251 buildings for administration, repair, and maintenance, and 4 personnel camps. On April 2. Strip No. 1 received its first B-29's. Strip No. 2 was completed on April 20.

After West Field was finished, the 30th Regiment again took up its unfinished work at North Field. Under the leadership of the 135th Battalion, the fourth 8,500-foot strip was constructed to a width of 500 feet. In addition. the other three strips were widened to 500 feet and additional hardstands were built. On May 5, 1945, North Field, Strip No. 4 was complete.

Total facilities at North Field, in addition to the four 8,500-foot runways, comprised 8 taxiways, aggregating nearly 11 miles, 265 hardstands. 2 service aprons, 173 quonset huts. and 92 steel arch-rib buildings. The four runways were parallel, 1,600 feet apart, with taxiways in the intervening spaces.

tional decision to taxi the planes under their own power to take-off line, instead of towing them by tractor as originally planned. This change increased the amount of earth to be moved at North Field by 500,000 cubic yards.

The construction of the Tinian fields represented a gigantic earth-moving operation. Deep cuts in hard coral and high fills characterized the work at both North Field and West Field. Cuts as deep as 15 feet and fills as high as 42 feet had to be made. North Field excavations totalled 2,109,800 cubic yards, and the amount of fill required was 4,789,400 cubic yards. At West Field the quantities of cut and fill were 1,718,050 cubic yards and 3,298,490 cubic yards, respectively. The great volume of excess fill necessitated development of huge borrow pits in the coral underlying the island.

Before the airfield program was put under way, test holes were dug to determine the extent of the over-burden and the characteristics of the underlying coral. They showed that the over-burden was usually from 8 to 12 inches deep, but that in certain areas there were soil pockets of considerable depth which characteristically occurred between hard coral heads that would be difficult to remove. Shortly after the beginning of these investigations, a soils expert was sent out from the office of the Director of the Pacific Division, Bureau of Yards and Docks, to study the many problems encountered and to assist in finding solutions that would assure runways able to support the heavy loads imposed by Superfortresses. This work was later carried on by a soils engineer on the brigade staff.

The design adopted for the fields required that the rolled-coral base course be not less than 6 inches thick where the sub-base was of pure coral, free of soil pockets. Where the pockets were deep, or where there were fills of relatively stable overburden, a base-course thickness of not less than 21 inches was specified. After construction was under way the 21-inch requirement was relaxed to 18 inches, after tests of the shear value of compacted coral had demonstrated that the thinner-base course would suffice to distribute the weight of prospective wheel loads.

Soil tests were continued throughout the entire construction period by six field parties. All test data were studied at a soils laboratory, set up at a battalion engineering office. Among the facts learned about Tinian coral, was the discovery that it had a 45-percent compaction factor.

The method of construction had to be studied individually for each runway. For example, the de-termining factor for procedure on West Field No. 3 was the availability of only twelve wagon drills, an insufficient number to permit making enough cuts to balance the volume of fill. Under the circumstances, rooting and panning were practiced as long as practicable, but upon encountering large coral heads of crystalline limestone it was necessary to abandon this procedure in favor of mass hauling from borrow pits. About 400,000 cubic yards were hauled a distance of 3 miles; during the 45-day construction period a total of more than 1,000,000 yards had to be moved.

Similarly, on North Field, the shortage of wagon drills did not permit cutting through a heavy bank of coral at the east end of the field, and made it necessary to use two heavy tractors with each pan. This was hard on equipment, but the permitted construction period was short.

In the early phases of the extensive dynamiting operation, material was blasted to a depth of a foot below sub-grade. It was soon discovered, however, that considerable follow-up was necessary to remove the coral heads that were left protruding above-grade. The depth of the drilling below-grade was subsequently increased from 2 to 3 feet to reduce the clean-up grading.

Coral on Tinian was considerably harder and more irregular in structure than that on Saipan and Guam, and, in view of the tremendous quanti-

B-29'S AND TAXIWAY, NORTH FIELD, TINIAN

NORTH FIELD, TINIAN
Photograph, taken in November 1945, shows taxiways, planes, and repair shops

ties that had to be handled, it was highly desirable to find borrow pits that could be dug with a shovel without extensive dynamiting. The coral pits developed on Tinian fell into three catagories:

(a) "Push Pits," in which coral could be pushed by a bulldozer working down a slope to a point where it could be shoveled into trucks.

(b) "Bailing Pits," in which the coral could be dug by power shovels, without preliminary blasting.

(c) "Blasting Pits." in which blasting was necessary.

Though it was desirable that borrow pits be located as near the airfields as possible, to minimize hauling time, it was found that a good "bailing pit" was advantageous even when the haul was relatively great.

It was also found that on deep fills the pocketing of water during heavy rains caused unstable sections if the relatively flat transverse grades were maintained. To avoid this, all fills were started on the center line, and the lifts were brought up with

not less than 5-percent cross-grade, to permit rapid runoff. until the top-level was reached. Then. working with coral alone, the transverse grade was gradually brought up to meet the flat grade specified. The rapid placement of fills almost 50 feet deep may be credited to the adoption of this procedure.

Earlier Seabee experience in other Pacific locations had shown salt water to be the best stabilizing agent for coral. The speed with which the fills had to be made on Tinian and the limited number of trucks available. however. made it impracticable to haul salt water in sufficient quantities. Moreover, compaction tests of the completed surface, especially where the fill had been placed in small lifts which had been extensively rolled with a sheepsfoot roller, indicated that the densities were practically as great with fill placed in the dry as with fill placed in the wet. In later phases of construction, the use of salt water was eliminated except for the final finishing.

In the finishing of the surface, a honing process, using patrol graders. brought the fines to the surface. At this stage, it was essential that adequate salt water be applied, to improve the cementing action of the coral particles, and to eliminate dust during the early field operations. These surfaces ultimately were to be topped with asphalt, but during the immediate operational stages it was imperative that frequent salt-watering be practiced as a dust palliative.

As a final step in the airfield-development program, runways and taxiways were paved with asphaltic concrete, 200 feet wide. The asphalt was placed to a thickness of two and one-half inches and rolled to slightly more than two inches.

During the early part of base development, all fuel consumed on the island was obtained from drums. Later, facilities were installed in Tinian Harbor for obtaining bulk aviation-gasoline from a steel barge, known as YOGL. Although this method necessitated trucking gasoline for 10 miles, over narrow, congested roads, the YOGL was an improvement over the dangerous and arduous system of drum-dumping.

Tank-farm construction was started in early September 1944. On November 3, after the construction of 25,000-barrel storage capacity, all future tank-farm construction was turned over to the 29th Regiment, which, in turn, assigned the 18th Battalion as "lead" battalion on the project. By November 27, 1944, a submarine pipeline and 56,000-barrel storage space were ready for use by the first tanker. The entire project was completed by March 8, 1945.

The island fuel system, as completed, consisted of a single 14,000-barrel storage farm for diesel oil, one 20,000-barrel farm for motor gasoline, and a series of six farms, with capacity of 165,000 barrels, for storage of aviation gasoline. All fuel was brought ashore through a submarine pipe-line, from a single tanker mooring just north of Tinian Harbor. Numerous pumping stations and 86,000 feet of main pipe-line distributed fuel over the island. The diesel-oil and motor-gasoline farms were located close enough to the tanker mooring to be filled from the tanker's pumps. Each was fed by a 6-inch line which permitted a filling rate of 700 to 800 barrels per hour. The aviation-gasoline storage was divided into two main farms and four secondary farms located near the two airfields. The system had six dispensing points for North Field and two for West Field.

Seabee ingenuity was called upon when the un-

foreseen expansion of airfield facilities necessitated the moving of an already completed aviation-gasoline tank farm of twelve 1,000-barrel, bolted-steel tanks to a new location about a mile distant. A method was worked out by the 18th Battalion to move the tanks intact, thus saving considerable time and material. The job was completed in five days.

In the selection of Tinian as a B-29 bomber base, because of its potentialities for development as a large airfield, consideration had to be given to the absence of any natural harbor. The only site on the island that was conceivable for a harbor was at Tinian Town, where the southwest side of the island formed a slight bay in which it was possible to anchor five or six ships at one time.

Waterfront construction was divided into two phases. The first phase lasted from D-Day until the middle of November, when all effort was directed to building and maintaining temporary facilities. When the island was secured, our forces found themselves in possession of two small beaches capable of accommodating landing-craft, a pontoon pier constructed by the assault forces, and two badly damaged Japanese masonry piers.

In August, two temporary marine railways for use in repairs to LCM's and LCVP's were built. A section base was started about a mile south of Tinian Town, but was abandoned because the location was too unprotected. A severe storm in early October destroyed the two railways, the existing work at the section base, the pontoon pier, and one of the masonry piers. To alleviate the critical situation resulting from this damage, a pontoon pier was constructed of three sections of 4-by-30-strings, connected by flexible bridges which enabled the pier to withstand the shock of rough water.

The second phase covered the period subsequent to the middle of November and involved the construction of permanent harbor facilities. The major project for this period was the provision for berthing eight Liberty ships.

The 50th Battalion, which arrived in November 1944, was designated to accomplish the permanent waterfront work at Tinian. Before the arrival of the 50th, the 92nd Battalion had driven about 120 lineal feet of sheet-piling along what was to become the south bulkhead. The 107th Battalion had done some grading along the waterfront and had built a ramp extending from the shoreline to a

TINIAN BREAKWATER
The sheet-piling circular cells are 30 feet in diameter

point on the coral reef, about 1,150 feet distant. This ramp later formed a portion of the breakwater.

The project for the berthing of eight Liberty ships consisted of three component parts. The south bulkhead, that portion of quay-wall paralleling the pontoon pier, was 600 feet long. The cargoship bulkhead formed that part of the quay-wall which turned from the south bulkhead, at an inside angle of 75 degrees, and extended northward for 2,000 feet. The cargo-ship piers consisted of two sheet-pile piers, 80 by 500 feet each, running parallel to the cargo-ship bulkhead and connected to it by a causeway, 88 feet wide. The project was started in late November 1944 and was completed on March 6, 1945.

The breakwater at Tinian Harbor, built on an existing coral reef that fringed the small harbor, was of circular cell design. The 120 circular cells, built of sheet piling, were 30 feet in diameter, plus-15-grade above mean low water, and were filled with coral.

Considerable dredging was necessary for the development of the harbor. A detachment of the 301st Construction Battalion, part of Service Squadron 12, began dredging on September 20, 1944, to pro-

vide a 32-foot channel and 28-foot berthing space. The dredging was completed by January 20, 1945.

An urgent need for pontoon equipment arose in connection with the waterfront development. To meet the demand for a floating pile-driving barge, a 6-by-12-pontoon barge was built and fitted with fair leads and anchor guide lines, 3 two-drum power winches, and a 12-inch-by-12-inch timber matting, to serve as a base on which to work a 20-ton crane. The next project was construction of a 6-by-18-pontoon barge with two propulsion units and a 75-ton fixed-boom crane to lift heavy cargo from ships and to raise small boats and landing craft out of the water. A T-shaped pontoon pier was built as a small-boat landing, and a 2-by-14-pontoon string was sunk for LCT landings.

Stevedoring operations were begun at Tinian Harbor on August 2, 1944, by CBD 1036, a detachment of half-battalion strength. The Seabees performed all transfer of cargo from vessels in the open stream to LCT's, and work parties of the Army and Marines unloaded the LCT's at the beach.

On November 19, 1944, the 27th Special Battalion, at that time only half of regular battalion strength, arrived at Tinian to handle the cargo in the stream, while CBD 1036 took over beach operations. On January 20, 1945, CBD 1036 was absorbed by the 27th Special Battalion.

From D-Day until the completion of docking facilities in March 1945, all cargo was moved to the beach by lighters, most of them LCT's and LCM's. Cargo-handling operations were under the supervision of an Army port superintendent. An Army port battalion of five companies shared stevedoring assignments with the Seabees.

When United States troops took Tinian, the construction forces inherited a network of roads that became the fabric of the island's road system. The general layout of the existing roads and the similarity in shape of Tinian to Manhattan Island resulted in the naming of the roads after the streets of New York.

The Japanese-built roads were too narrow for our heavy traffic, were poorly drained, and had no shoulders. Heavy trucks slid into the ditches and tracked a slippery coating of mud upon the road surface in climbing back.

The first problem was the maintenance of the 35 miles of existing roads, with the limited equipment which could be spared from high-priority airfield construction. The Japanese roads were resurfaced with 8 inches of pit-run coral, and the necessary shoulders and drainage were provided. Rainy seasons and dry seasons produced conflicting road-maintenance problems. In dry weather, the roads became dusty and rough, and a continuous wetting-down with salt water was necessary. It was found advantageous to mix clay with the coral surface during this season. During the rainy season, the roads had to be bladed to the center after each rain in order to be kept passable.

As equipment became available, new road construction was pushed to the utmost. Tinian consists of several plateaus of different heights, and road construction required a great deal of blasting in order to keep the grades down for heavy-truck traffic. The roads were built 22 feet wide, with 3-foot shoulders and ditches to carry off heavy rainfall. Major roads were surfaced to 30 feet

TINIAN HARBOR

in width to support heavy traffic. About 34 miles of new roads were constructed on the island. To solve the problem of rapidly increasing traffic on the two main north-south roads, a second 22-foot lane was constructed parallel to each road to provide dual highways.

Necessity for camp construction was considered to be of secondary importance to the completion of military installations on Tinian, once a unit had standard minimum facilities. Camps were divided into two main classes: temporary camps, of framed tents with wooden decks and screened sides, and semi-permanent camps with quonset huts for Navy and aviation personnel and prefabricated wooden barracks for Army personnel. Both types of semi-permanent buildings were allocated on the basis of 20 enlisted men or eight officers per building.

One difficulty in camp constructions was the clearing of cane fields, but removal of the valuable thin top-soil, with the roots, allowed erosion from heavy rains and winds. Bulldozers had piled both cane and top soil in huge pits that had to be removed by clamshell and truck. The Seabees, therefore, started using a sheepsfoot roller for clearing, removing the cane later, by hand. This method left enough roots in the ground to prevent extensive erosion.

Another problem was the building of mess halls and similar facilities for large units, with only 20-by-56-foot quonsets supplied. It was found that by using concrete floors, 20-foot-wide quonset floor-beams could be used for roof trusses and the quonsets stretched to both 34-foot and 39-foot widths where large buildings were necessary.

The development of housing on Tinian involved camps for more than 12,000 Seabees, 13,000 other naval personnel, and 21,500 Army personnel.

The first medical facility on Tinian, a 100-bed tent-hospital, was completed in September 1944. This served as the only hospital on the island for military personnel until the completion of the 600-bed Navy Base Hospital 19, in early December. Quonset huts, modified where required to suit operational needs, were used. Rearrangement of floor space increased the capacity to 1,000 beds. A 600-bed hospital of similar design was completed for the Army in March 1945. A 1,000-bed hospital was made available in June, with the reconversion of the camp area vacated by the 135th Battalion, which moved to Okinawa. On V-J day, construction

was nearing completion on a 1,000-bed hospital on the South Plateau.

General supply facilities for Tinian were of three types: those for the garrison forces; those for general Navy supply activities; and those for the Sixth Brigade, which handled construction supplies.

In early August 1944, the 92nd Battalion was assigned the layout and construction of the Seventh Field Depot for the Marines. The project, which included camp facilities for a Marine quartermaster battalion and the improvement of 300,000 square feet of open-storage space, was completed early in November. In December, the 18th Battalion began the reconstruction and expansion of the depot, then designated as the quartermaster depot of the Army garrison forces. The completed depot consisted of three camps, 386,000 square feet of warehouse storage, two million square feet of surfaced open-storage, and about 63,000 cubic feet of refrigerated storage.

For the naval supply depot, the Seabees erected seven, steel, arch-rib buildings and provided 16,000 square feet of storage space in frame warehouses.

A spare parts depot and an ABCD-Annex were constructed for the 6th Brigade. The spare parts depot, consisting of six, steel, arch-rib buildings and one quonset hut, was completed in January, 1945. By early May, seven, steel, arch-rib buildings, two quonsets, and a surfaced storage yard with 575,000 square feet of space had been constructed for the ABCD-Annex.

In September 1944, the first ammunition-storage dump of 11 revetments was constructed. Access roads were developed on the basis of existing roads. Expansion of this facility to include 254 coral-surfaced revetments, 25 by 75 feet, and almost 14 miles of main and secondary roads, undertaken in November 1944, was completed in February 1945.

On January 28, 1945, work was started on an additional bomb dump of 20,000-ton capacity, in an area near West Field. Work progressed slowly because of limited equipment; the 468 revetments were not finished until early summer of 1945.

In February 1945, the Seabees met a three-week deadline in the construction of an aerial-mine assembly and storage depot. The project involved the construction of two 40-by-200-foot quonset huts with concrete decks, surrounded by a 12-foot earth revetment on three sides; two 20-by-50-foot quonset magazines with concrete decks and an earth cover;

twelve 30-by-40-foot ready-storage revetments; and about one mile of 20-foot, coral roadway.

Tinian, though it contains not a single stream and has only one small fresh-water lake, is an island rich in water. The average yearly rainfall is in excess of 100 inches, and the porous coraline structure of the island permits the rain water to filter into the ground with very little runoff. The Japanese had developed a well-and-reservoir system, with the necessary pipe-lines to serve the Tinian Town area.

After the island was secured, the Seabees assumed the development and control of the water supply. Purification units were set up at four, small, shallow wells in the Marpo region, where the water was filtered and chlorinated. These wells, in addition to Hagoi Lake, provided sufficient water, with rationing.

The Seabees rehabilitated and extended the existing Japanese pipe-line from the reservoir. Well-drilling was undertaken, and the water system was eventually composed of 17 deep wells, Marpo well, Tinian Town well, and Hagoi Lake, providing 20 gallons of water, per man, daily. With the increased development of water sources during August, it was no longer necessary to ration water.

The water supply eventually included a skimming trench in Marpo Valley, designed to produce 1,800.000 gallons per day. The service-group camps and shops at North Field were supplied from two wells in that vicinity. The island system was designed for 30 gallons per man per day.

To provide drinking water, food, clothing, and shelter for the civilians held in custody at Camp Churo, reliance was placed on what facilities the Japanese had left.

Using Japanese four-by-four timber taken from damaged farm and village buildings, the Seabees supervised the native laborers in the construction of tarpaulin shelters for initial housing. As more materials were brought in by salvage crews, the tarpaulin shelters were replaced by wood-frame and corrugated-iron-roofed sheds.

A 100-bed civilian hospital, constructed largely of salvaged material, was completed in September 1944. A 100-bed quonset-hut hospital replaced this initial hospital in April 1945.

Captured Japanese civilians, who knew the location of food supplies, were assigned to food-salvage details. The existing food supply was supplemented by American food and by extensive agricultural development. When firewood supplies on the is-

MEN AND EQUIPMENT OF THE 62ND BATTALION WORKING ON THE SECOND AIRSTRIP, IWO JIMA
Photograph, taken March 22, 1945, shows steam rising from hot ground and Mount Suribachi in the background

766450—47—25

land showed signs of exhaustion, the Seabees improvised a diesel-oil stove for cooking, using cement and salvaged fire-brick, with burners made of salvaged scrap pipe and tubing.

Iwo Jima

The capture of Iwo Jima, halfway between Saipan and Tokyo, not only eliminated a base from which the Japanese could attack United States installations in the Marianas, but, more significantly, provided a site for the development of airfields to support the operations of fighters escorting Superfortresses in their missions over Japan and to afford emergency landing fields for crippled B-29's returning from the raids.

Iwo Jima, the largest island of the Volcano

90TH SEABEES EXCAVATING FOR TANK-FARM PIPELINE, IWO JIMA

group, is about five miles long and two and one-half miles wide at its broadest point. The most prominent feature is Mt. Suribachi, a volcanic cone rising to nearly 550 feet at the southern end of the island. The northern half of the island forms a broad dome, with maximum elevations of 340 to 387 feet. Iwo has enough flat land in its 8 square miles for the construction of airstrips. The entire shore is rugged and precipitous, with few good landing-beaches. The Japanese took advantage of

the terrain and developed Iwo Jima into an air base, two fields being operational and a third under construction at the time of the American assault. The southernmost field had two strips, 5,025 and 3,965 feet long, respectively. Two runways, forming an X, had been built to 5,225 and 4,425 feet in length, near the center of the island. A third strip, 3,800 feet long, had been started far-

IWO JIMA HANGAR ERECTED BY THE 8TH SEABEES
This hangar, which was completed April 7, 1945, measures 130 by 170 feet

ther north. These three fields, the main objective of the assault, became the nucleus for the development of an advance air base for United States aircraft.

The assault on Iwo Jima was initiated on February 19, 1945, by the Fifth Amphibious Corps and the Third, Fourth, and Fifth Marine Divisions. Three Seabee units, the 31st, 62nd, and 133rd Battalions, were assigned to the Marines during the assault, to act as shore parties and to start work on the airstrips at the earliest possible moment.

The Marines went ashore on the southeastern beaches of Iwo Jima, meeting relatively little resistance. However, the enemy, taking advantage of the hilly terrain, soon concentrated extremely heavy artillery and mortar fire against the Marine positions. By the evening of D-day, the Marines had cut across the narrow isthmus to the west shore of the island, isolating the southern airfield, which was captured the following day. By February

SEVENTH FLEET COMMAND HEADQUARTERS, IWO JIMA
Photograph taken in August 1945

26, the northeast-southwest Japanese runway had been made operational by the Seabees and was in use by observation planes.

The Marines continued their painful advance toward the northern tip of the island and by March 3 had captured all three airfields. On that date, transports began operating from South Field to bring in much-needed supplies and to evacuate the wounded. Effort was concentrated on the rehabilitation of the northeast-southwest 5,225-foot strip which had been constructed by the Japanese at Central Field. By the time Iwo Jima was secured on March 16, both South and Central Fields had one operational strip, and 50 Superfortresses had made emergency landings on their return from great incendiary raids over Japan.

With the close of the assault phase of operations, attention was turned to the execution of plans for the development of Iwo Jima as an important air base. The Ninth Construction Brigade was organized for this purpose. The Eighth Regiment, consisting of the 8th, 90th, 95th (Section Two), and the 23rd Special Battalions, and the 41st Regiment, composed of the assault battalions, made up the brigade.

Initial plans called for the development of three airfields, to be known as South, Central, and North Fields, on the sites of the existing Japanese strips. The 5,025-foot strip at South Field was to become a 200-by-6,000-foot fighter strip. The longer runway at Central Field was to be extended to 8,500

feet for B-29 operations, and a similar strip was to be constructed parallel to it. In addition, the second strip at Central Field was to be extended to 6,000 feet. North Field, where the Japanese had only started construction, was to have one 200-by-5,000-foot strip for fighter operations.

At South Field, the temporary strip was rebuilt and additional taxiways, shops, and service areas were constructed while the field was in constant operation. On April 7, 1945, fighters took off from South Field to form the first land-based fighter escort for B-29's on a strike against the Japanese homeland. By July, the runway had been extended

133RD SEABEES BUILD A CULVERT, IWO JIMA
This culvert, under taxiway No. 2, connects Central and North airfields

to 6,000 feet and had been surfaced with emulsified asphalt. Also constructed were 7,940 feet of taxiways and 258 hardstands.

By July 7, 1945, the first B-29 strip at Central Field had been paved to 8,500 feet and placed in operation. During the day, 102 B-29's, returning from a raid on Japan, landed on the field. Several subgrade failures occurred in the construction because of ground water and soft spots in the subgrade. In some places the paving sealed off steam which had been generated below the surface. When the steam condensed, the subgrade became saturated. At one time, poor subsoil under the paving made it necessary to remove about 1,500 feet of crushed stone and subgrade. By July 12, the B-29 strip had been completed and paved for a length of 9,800 feet. The east-west runway was developed into a fueling strip, 6,000 by 570 feet, with 60 fueling outlets. The second B-29 strip had been graded to 9,400 feet by V-J day, and was left unpaved.

Virtually the entire job at North Field was new construction in rough terrain which consisted principally of consolidated volcanic ash. The initial portion of the work in preparing the subgrade for the strip entailed the moving of about 200,000 cubic yards of rock and volcanic ash. Seabee construction was stopped on April 27, and the project was turned over to an Army Engineer battalion for completion. By V-J day a strip, 6,000 feet long, had been graded and was paved to 5,500 feet; 10,000 feet of taxiways had been graded; and 129 fighter hardstands had been provided.

All facilities on Iwo Jima were constructed to support the air base. Main projects were tank

CASU 52 CAMP AND ADMINISTRATION AREA, IWO JIMA
Constructed by the 90th Seabees

farms, water-distribution system, roads, hospitals, storage areas, and waterfront facilities.

A temporary tank farm, consisting of four 1,000-barrel tanks—two for aviation gasoline, one for motor gasoline, and one for diesel oil—was ready for operation on March 16, 1945. Dismantling of this farm began when the permanent farms were placed in operation. The permanent tank-farm system consisted of two central farms, called East and West Farms, and small farms at each of the three airfields. Small installations provided 1,000 barrels of aviation gasoline for South Field; 6,000 barrels

for Central Field; and 6,000 barrels for North Field. The East Tank Farm, for aviation gasoline only, had a capacity of 80,000 barrels. West Farm facilities consisted of 160,000 barrels for aviation gasoline, 50,000 barrels for motor gasoline, and 20,000 barrels for diesel oil.

All unloading of cargo at Iwo Jima was across the beaches. Berthing was later developed at both eastern and western beaches, the latter proving much more satisfactory. Stevedoring was extremely

MESSHALL AND GALLEY AT CASU 52 CAMP, IWO JIMA

difficult because of the heavy surf, bad weather, and sand conditions on the beaches. During the assault, marston mat was extensively used to make possible the landing of wheeled vehicles.

Harbor development consisted of a breakwater of blockships on the east side of the island and a small boat pool on the west side. A storm wrecked the blockship breakwater, and no further attempt was made to provide seaward protection for ships.

A project of high priority was the provision of a water-supply system. There are no perennial streams on Iwo and the water table lies at a considerable depth near the center of the island. A fresh-water lens, extending about 9 feet above sea-level, had formed, and wells were drilled to secure water from this lens. The Japanese had dug 14 wells, eight of which were used in the development of the water system. In addition, the Japanese had paved catchment-areas which were drained into cisterns excavated in the soft rock. The runoff from the two completed airfields had been stored in masonry and concrete reservoirs, which were repaired by the Seabees and became the basis of the water system. By V-J day, the system was only

90TH SEABEES MOVE A QUONSET HUT, IWO JIMA

half finished, with 58 small stills and eight drilled wells.

Establishment of storage areas for the ordnance, quartermaster, medical, engineering and chemical warfare departments involved the construction of quonset huts, frame buildings, and open-storage areas, as well as 27,000 cubic feet of refrigerated storage space.

Housing and messing facilities for 37,000 officers and men were set up, in addition to the individual battalion camps. Tents were used for living quarters, and quonset huts were provided for headquarters and mess halls. Medical facilities were provided at the 38th Field Hospital, the 41st Sta-

tion Hospital, and the 232nd General Hospital, with a total capacity of 1,250 beds. There were also 105 beds in Navy dispensaries.

The first Seabee road construction involved the hacking of a road up Mt. Suribachi to install radar equipment. The Japanese had made no attempt at this construction. After a demolition team had cleared the terrain of mines and booby traps, a bulldozer blazed a trail to the top, and within twelve days, graders, scrapers, and dump trucks had completed the road.

To link the various activities on Iwo Jima, 20 miles of primary and 40 miles of secondary roads were constructed.

PHILIPPINE SEA FRONTIER HEADQUARTERS, LEYTE
Members of the 61st Seabees erect a quonset village at Tolosa. Photograph taken January 1945

CHAPTER 29

BASES IN THE PHILIPPINES

Landings, on September 15, 1944, on Morotai Island by Southwest Pacific forces and in the Palau group by Pacific Ocean forces were the last preparatory land offensives for the reoccupation of the Philippine Islands. The Morotai action was designed to isolate Japanese forces on Halmahera, which would otherwise have been in a position to flank any movement into the southern Philippines. The occupation of Peleliu and Angaur in the Palau group accomplished the same objective for the eastern flank of the Philippine campaign.

After providing support for the Palau landings, the Third Fleet carrier task force returned to the attack on the Philippines. From waters to the east, they conducted the first carrier attack of the war on Manila and Luzon, September 21 and 22, inflicting severe damage on the enemy and suffering only light losses.

Initial plans for re-entry into the Philippines called for the securing of Morotai as a stepping stone to landings by the Seventh Amphibious Force on Mindanao some time in November. The decision to accelerate the advance by making the initial landings on Leyte in the central Philippines was reached when the Third Fleet air strikes of September disclosed the relative weakness of enemy air opposition. It was decided to seize Leyte Island and the contiguous waters on October 20 and thus secure airfield sites and extensive harbor and naval base facilities.

The east coast of Leyte offered certain obvious advantages for amphibious landings. It had a free and undefended approach from the east, sufficient anchorage area; it provided good access to the remainder of the central islands in that it commanded the approaches to Surigao Strait. Moreover, the position by-passed and isolated large Japanese forces on Mindanao. The accelerated timing of the operation and the choice of the east coast for the landing required, however, the acceptance of one serious disadvantage — the rainy season. Most of the islands in the Philippines are mountainous, and during the northeast monsoon, from October to March, land areas on the eastern sides of the mountains have torrential rains.

On October 19, two assault forces, the Third and Seventh Fleets, approached the east coast of Leyte with the Sixth Army aboard. The 10th and 24th Corps went ashore on schedule on October 20, after the Navy had paved the way with drum-fire bombardment. Assisting in the landing was a detachment of the 302nd Construction Battalion, which handled the pontoon barges and causeways. On October 24, elements of the 12th Construction Regiment were put ashore at Tacloban to start construction of naval facilities in the Leyte Gulf area.

Three days after the initial landing, General MacArthur directed the ground forces to secure their beach areas and await the outcome of the naval battle which was then impending between Admiral Halsey's task force and the Japanese Singapore fleet. The Japanese made the decision to commit their fleet, which comprised 60 per cent of Japan's major naval units, in the battle to prevent America's return to the Philippines. By October 26, it was apparent that the Third and Seventh Fleets had virtually eliminated Japan as a sea power.

In the six days of the great naval action the Japanese position in the Philippines had become extremely critical. General MacArthur's land wedge on Leyte was firmly implanted in the vulnerable flank of the enemy. The enemy no longer had an effective fleet to cover his forces in the Philippines or his communications to the empire of Malaysia, so easily conquered two and a half years before. If General MacArthur succeeded in establishing himself, nothing could prevent him from overrunning the Philippines.

The American advance continued. After winning the high ground overlooking Leyte Gulf, the 24th Army Corps penetrated inland to secure Dagami and Burauen. The 10th Corps swept across

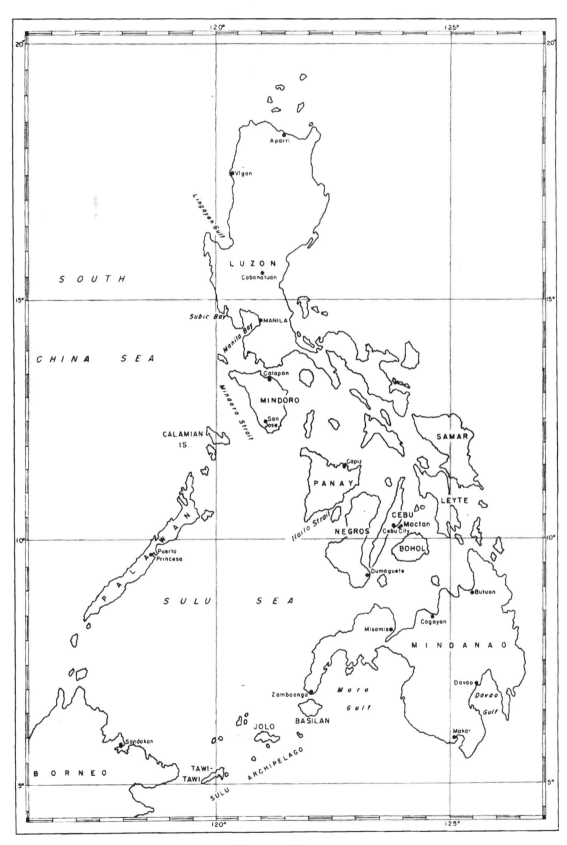

PHILIPPINE ISLANDS

San Juanico Strait to seize the south coast of Samar; they also landed troops in a short amphibious operation on the north coast of Leyte.

By November 5, American forces had reached Limon at the northern end of the valley road leading to Ormoc, on the western side of Leyte, the principal Japanese installation on the island. Bitter fighting for Leyte was now in progress, rendered all the more difficult by typhoons which inaugurated the rainy season.

While the Army was battling to free the island of the enemy, construction forces were struggling to construct airfields and facilities to support further operations. Monsoon rains and continuous heavy traffic churned the deep, clayey topsoil of Leyte into a sea of mud. Terrain features added to construction difficulties. Lack of space and unsatisfactory soil conditions forced the Navy to abandon the Tacloban area and move construction forces to the southern tip of Samar for the development of a naval base.

During the month of November, the 12th Regiment had been augmented by the arrival of two more battalions, bringing the total to five. In the succeeding months, battalions which had been engaged in the construction of naval facilities in the Hawaiian area were loaned to the Seventh Fleet service organization for work in the Leyte Gulf area. These battalions, plus several from rear areas in the Southwest Pacific, brought the number of battalions engaged in the construction of Leyte Gulf to 25. All naval construction forces, including several special battalions, detachments, and maintenance units, were organized into two brigades and placed under the Commander, Construction Troops, Leyte Gulf. This organization developed the area into a vast operating and repair base, capable of supporting the enormous sea forces that were soon to aid in the complete liberation of the Philippines and the ensuing invasion of Okinawa.

In the Ormoc Valley, the Japanese fought fiercely and delayed, but could not stop, the Sixth Army advance. By the end of November, American troops were closing on Limon and another column threatened Ormoc from the south. Violent rains and deep mud harassed the supply lines. Forward units were dependent on hand-carry methods. Casualties were evacuated by native bearers.

By December 1, seven divisions were well established ashore, five airfields were in operation, and the waters of the Visayas were under firm naval control.

The 77th Division landed south of Ormoc on December 7 and captured the town four days later. Toward the end of December, organized resistance on the island ceased.

While mopping-up continued on Leyte, a landing force of two regiments and a detachment of the 113th Construction Battalion was sent into southern Mindoro. Within 24 hours, American planes and PT boats were operating off the southern coast of Luzon.

In the first week of January a new American assault force gathered east of Leyte, slipped through Surigao Strait, over the sunken wrecks of Japanese warships, and passed into the Mindanao and Sulu Seas.

After several feints, designed to confuse the enemy, the Sixth Army, now composed of the 1st and 14th Corps, hit the beaches in Lingayen Gulf on January 9. By nightfall, 68,000 troops were ashore and in control of a 15-mile beachhead. The Army immediately launched its advance toward Manila, troops meeting with little resistance until they approached Clark Field.

On January 29, troops of the 11th Corps landed on the west coast of Luzon near Subic Bay. They drove eastward to cut off the Bataan peninsula.

The 11th Airborne Division on January 31 made an unopposed amphibious landing at Nasugbu in Batangas Province, south of Manila. Three days later the division's parachute regiment jumped to Tagaytay ridge dominating the Cavite area. That night, troops of the First Cavalry Division raced through Novaliches and reached Grace Park in the northeastern portion of the city of Manila. On February 6 the airborne troops reached Nichols Field. As the troops of the Sixth Army closed on Manila from the north, northwest, and south, the situation of Japanese forces in the city was rendered hopeless, but they fought bitterly from house to house. Organized resistance ceased on February 23.

On the morning of February 16, paratroopers were dropped on Corregidor. Simultaneously, troops hit the shore in assault boats at San Jose South Dock. Fighting on the island continued for two weeks before the Japanese destroyed the extensive tunnel systems and themselves with explosives. Manila Bay was open in early March. In less

SEABEES BUILD AN AIRSTRIP THROUGH A PHILIPPINE SWAMP

than two months, the Americans had accomplished what the Japanese had taken six months to do.

In late February, elements of the Eighth Army effected an unopposed landing at Puerto Princesa, Palawan Island. The force captured the town with its two airstrips and completely occupied Puerto Princesa peninsula. The airfields gave control of a wide area of the China Sea, greatly facilitating the severance of Japanese communication with Malaysia and Burma.

On March 10, troops landed on the western tip of Mindanao, second largest island in the Philippine group. Initial resistance was light and the city of Zamboanga fell the next day, but heavy fighting in the foothills continued for weeks.

Landings were made during March on Panay, Cebu, and Negros. Reconnaissance parties went ashore on Jolo, Tawitawi, and other islands in the Sulu archipelago, extending our holdings to within 40 miles of Borneo. In each instance, the landings were effected with a minimum of resistance. Stubborn and prolonged fighting, however, usually followed in the hills.

The objective of the Philippine campaign had been accomplished: The islands were liberated. As fast as an island was invaded, construction forces, both Army Engineers and Naval Construction Battalions, started building landing fields and facilities for the support of the fleet. A large portion of the 1,800 ships that engaged in the invasion of the Ryukyus were staged in the Philippines.

Leyte Island

On October 20, 1944, United States amphibious forces landed on the eastern shore of Leyte Island; the liberation of the Philippines had been begun.

Leyte, the eighth largest of the Philippine group of islands, is easily accessible from the Pacific Ocean, on the east, through the deep Leyte Gulf. Together with Samar Island, from which it is separated by San Juanico Strait, Leyte controls the Leyte Gulf and the eastern entrance to the Surigao Strait.

Because the area was beyond the range of fighter planes from any advance bases then held by the Allies, and because of the large number of enemy planes—on D-day the Japanese had 52 operational strips within a radius of 350 miles of Tacloban,

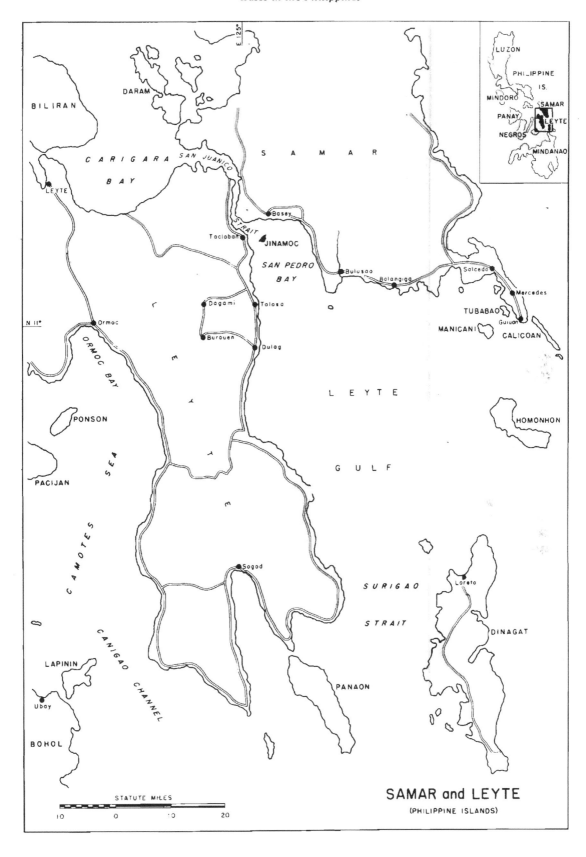

SAMAR and LEYTE

(PHILIPPINE ISLANDS)

STATUTE MILES

RECEIVING STATION, TUBABAO ISLAND, SAMAR

which had been picked by the planners as the naval base area—the first objective of the construction forces was to provide landing facilities for our fighting planes.

Locations selected for naval installations during the planning stage were on the east coast of Leyte, between Tacloban and Anibong Point. Headquarters for the Seventh Fleet was to be at Tolosa, 10 miles south of Tacloban.

A detachment of the 302nd Construction Battalion assisted the Army's landing on D-day, handling pontoon causeways and barges on the beaches of Leyte. As beaching conditions were favorable, however, the need for the causeways was soon over, and the Seabees then reassembled the cells for use as barges and pontoon piers.

Units of the 12th Construction Regiment, detachments from the 75th and 105th Battalions and CBD 1024 then operating under the Third Naval Construction Brigade, disembarked from LST's at Tacloban, on October 24. Camp erection was started within the city boundaries; work was begun on the renovation of several warehouses for Navy use; and heavy-equipment crews commenced maintenance of roads.

The 61st Battalion went ashore near Dulag, 20 miles south of Tacloban. They were assigned the task of completing a fighter strip for the Army Air Corps.

The regiment was joined on October 30 by a detachment from the 88th, and on November 12 by the 93rd Battalion. Second echelons of these units arrived on November 12, and other battalions arrived at Leyte, and later at Samar, throughout most of the ensuing months. A total of 25 battalions, in addition to stevedore battalions, maintenance units, and detachments, saw service at Leyte Gulf. A maximum Seabee population of about 32,500 in the Leyte Gulf area was reached, including all of the Second and Seventh and about half of the Third Brigades.

In the advance planning for the Philippine campaign, it had been decided to develop the Leyte Gulf area as a naval operating base to support further operations. Facilities to be provided including a PT base, landplane and seaplane landing areas, supply depots, a hospital, and a ship-repair base.

Study of available maps showed that although much of the island was mountainous, a broad valley facing Leyte Gulf for 35 miles and extending around the northern coast of the island, gave access to the inland waters of the archipelago. The beaches generally were sandy, though some stretches of mangrove swamps and marshlands existed, principally at the mouths of the many streams which drain the valley. Low hills intruded into the coastal plain at several points, in some places close to the shore. It seemed an excellent place for a naval base.

Military development of Leyte, however, was limited, by the elements. It was found that during the northeast monsoon (October to January) severe storms lash the east coast of Leyte, making ground operations practically impossible; the south and west coast of the island are almost as hard hit during the southwest monsoon (June to September). During the monsoons, torrential rains and high winds wash out bridges and hold up shipping, frequently for weeks at a time.

The usefulness of airfields would, accordingly, be limited. The port of Tacloban could accommodate 12 to 15 vessels of 20-foot draft, but had to be kept dredged alongside the wharf to permit larger vessels to dock. There were no other major port facilities on Leyte Island, although numerous indentations along the west coast afforded anchorage except during the southwest monsoon. Ormoc Bay, on the west coast, had unlimited anchorage for a large number of vessels but was also open to the southwest monsoons.

Construction was started in these areas but, except at Tolosa, the nature of the ground proved impractical for construction. Low-lying rice-paddies and swamp land were impossible to work and no rock, coral, or other surfacing material was available. Enemy action combined with the terrain and weather difficulties to make construction progress practically impossible.

The Army was having the same difficulties with its installations, particularly the airstrips under construction at Dulag and near Tacloban. Scarcity of usable area on the east Leyte coast led the Army to conclude that it would have to use the area that had been assigned to the Navy near Anibong Point.

To alleviate these conditions, an area was selected for the Navy base on the island of Samar, near the barrio of Basey, across San Juanico strait from Tacloban. Construction forces were moved to the area, but only a few days' work was necessary to show that this site also would not be practical. After a complete reconnaissance of Leyte Gulf area,

WHARF AREA OF THE NAVAL SUPPLY DEPOT, CALICOAN
Leyte Gulf in the background

the southeastern tip of Samar was selected as best suited to the Navy's needs. The location, near the town of Guiuan, 45 miles from Tacloban, was not ideal. The nearest water for a fleet anchorage was 20 miles away, but it was an area that could be developed rapidly, with room for an airfield for the tactical support of the Luzon push, and there was an adequate amount of coral available for surfacing roads, camp areas, and storage areas. Accordingly, most of the naval construction forces in the Tacloban area were moved to Samar in December.

Tacloban. The naval station at Tacloban was reduced to include only the headquarters for the commandant of the operating base, a communication center. a fleet post office, living quarters and a dispensary for the operating personnel, and receiving barracks. Although some facilities were housed in renovated buildings, most of the activities were provided with quonset huts for offices and living quarters.

Tolosa. At Tolosa, the original plans were carried to completion. Quonset huts were provided for the quarters. offices. and communication facilities for the Seventh Fleet and the Philippine Sea Frontier headquarters.

Jinamoc Island. A seaplane base was built on the small island of Jinamoc, 5 miles east of Tacloban, in San Pedro Bay. Work was started in December on the grading for a ramp. When the subgrade was finished, a pontoon barge was floated into position and submerged. The ramp was first used on January 14, 1945, when a scout plane was hauled from the water. When it was decided that the base was to be the permanent one for operations in that area, it was thought that the pontoon ramp would be inadequate, and in May construction was started on a steel and pre-cast concrete ramp. The final installation was 220 feet long.

The water surrounding the island was deep enough to be used for runways without the neces-

JUNGLE ROAD ON CALICOAN ISLAND

sity of dredging. Taxiways and hardstands were graded and surfaced.

Living facilities for both base and transient personnel were provided in 75 quonset huts. Construction included a mile and a half of access roads, a 200-bed dispensary, water supply, and utilities.

Samar Island

The principal naval development was at the southeastern tip of Samar. The naval base was located on a peninsula, 3 miles wide and 11 miles long, and on Calicoan Island, which is more than a mile wide and 7 miles long, and is separated from Samar by 800 feet of shallow water. Guiuan, site of the headquarters for this area, was in the middle of the peninsula on the eastern shore of Leyte Gulf.

There are no high mountains or ranges on Samar, but the terrain in general is rugged. Rainfall averages 12 to 15 inches per month, but the local geological structure makes rainfall relatively harmless. The underlying formation of the southeast peninsula and of Calicoan Island is porous coral; the higher ground carries an overburden of reddish clay mixed with coral and varying in depth from 2 to 40 feet. Leaching has produced many chimneys, underground caverns, and sinks. Porosity of the coral causes the static water table to rise only slightly above sea level, and inland wells tend to become brackish under sustained pumping.

Because rain and mud had stopped the 61st Battalion from repairing the Japanese strip at Dulag for the Army, it was necessary to build a field. As the Navy was to build two strips at Guiuan, it was agreed that the first strip was to be finished as soon as possible for the use primarily of Army's heavy bombers.

Guiuan.—A survey party of 4 officers and 100 men arrived at Guiuan on November 30 to lay out the site for the bomber field. Detachments of the 61st and 93rd Battalions landed the next day, and earth moving was started a week later. All work was maintained on a 24-hour basis: 780 operators and gradesmen were assigned to the strip and 184 to equipment maintenance. The first landings by heavy planes were made on December 22, just 14 days after the start of construction. The men produced 7,000 feet of 100-foot strip with 50-foot shoulders, five alert areas, 5000 feet of taxiways, and 50 hardstands, requiring the movement of more than 344,000 yards of muck and coral.

On December 31, the first fighter squadron was ordered to the field. Surfacing of the strip with yellow coral was finished on January 15, 1945, and on the next day the first bomber squadron arrived. After its completion, the strip was used principally by Liberators of the 5th and 13th Air Forces.

Facilities were provided for overhaul and repair; gasoline storage (15,000-barrels) and administration buildings were included. Constructed for the aviation-supply depot and auxiliary repair and overhaul facilities were housing and messing facilities for 2000 men. Construction on the air strip was carried on in the face of heavy rain and frequent night air alerts that delayed progress considerably.

Work on the second 7000-foot strip was suspended after 2000 feet had been completed, but was resumed in May. Excessive coral formations made excavation difficult and required a great deal of blasting. Equipment on this job required an abnormal amount of maintenance and repair. The major accomplishment on the project was excavation through a coral hill for 200 feet which required a maximum cut of approximately 26 feet. Practically every yard of the hill was solid coral, and shovels could remove only that which was blasted loose. Extensive hardstands, taxiways, and parking aprons completed the field installations.

Headquarters for the naval station was located within the boundaries of Guiuan. Office space was provided by renovating a schoolhouse and various other buildings and by erection of quonset huts and tents. The same type of structures provided quarters and messing facilities for 5,500 men.

Tubabao Island, a triangular-shaped island in Leyte Gulf, lying west of Guiuan and separated from Samar by a narrow strait, was selected as the site for a receiving station.

A quonset city, including messhalls, recreation facilities, and utilities for 10,000 men, was erected. Tubabao was connected to Samar by a timber bridge, 515 feet long and 22 feet wide, with a 58-foot clear span in the center of the channel.

A major destroyer-repair base and a ship-repair unit were built on Manicani Island, 8 miles west of Guiuan. This project included wharves, berths for several large floating drydocks, administration buildings, shops, water and steam lines, power system, and fire-protection system.

Construction of a pier to accommodate vessels of 45-foot draft required 100 lineal feet of coral fill

ADMINISTRATION BUILDING AT THE SAMAR NAVAL AIR BASE

and a timber approach, 40 feet wide. A 1500-by-80-foot pier was built, using one floating and two skid rigs for driving 3400 piles, up to 100 feet in length. Many of the piles were spliced.

Despite a delay of approximately six weeks due to lack of long piles, the project was completed in four and a half months. A pontoon pier and a jetty for LST's were constructed in the northwest cove.

Ship-repair facilities were housed in 80 quonset huts and 150,000 square feet of large timber trussed structures. When completed, the repair unit had facilities for the repair and maintenance of any ships of the fleet, from battleships to LCM's. Coincident with this work, 25,000 feet of lines were installed for a salt-water fire-protection system, sanitation, fresh water, and steam systems. Numerous power stations, each consisting of approximately two dozen 75-kw generators and all necessary distribution systems, were provided for the entire area. At least six floating drydocks, including the giant sectional ABSD's, were brought to Manicani Island.

Water for this activity was obtained from a watershed half a mile wide and three-fourths of a mile long. The water was pumped from the collection point to a water-treatment plant having a capacity of 840,000 gallons per day.

Personnel housing and messing facilities for 10,000 men were constructed with tents and frame huts. Approximately 150 acres of swamp land were converted to hard ground to accommodate the construction, 150,000 cubic yards of the coral being excavated from the bay. Harbor improvement at this activity included the moving of approximately 5,000,000 yards of material by blasting and dredging.

One of the Navy's largest motor-torpedo-boat bases was located on the northern end of the peninsula, near the barrio of Salcedo. A small bay on Leyte Gulf provided a harbor for PT's and auxiliary craft. This base had all the necessary facilities for the overhaul and repair of 25 boats, in addition to administration and operations buildings.

Drydocking for the PT boats was provided by three floating pontoon drydocks, moored to a pontoon pier. Other waterfront development consisted of a loading pier of two 4-by-18-pontoon strings, a pier for handling torpedoes, and one catwalk pier capable of mooring 30 boats.

Large quonset-type buildings were used to house the torpedo-overhaul department, ordnance department, and an engine-repair unit. Water for this activity was obtained by damming a stream and storing the water in fifteen 5.000-gallon wood-stave tanks.

Housing was at first provided in tents, but quonset huts were erected to house 3,000 men. The camp contained supply, dispensary, dental, and recreational facilities.

A 3,000-bed fleet hospital was constructed about 5 miles north of Guiuan. Wards, built in an H-shape, consisted of 311 prefabricated buildings and 14 quonsets, with a floor area of 320.000 square feet. The main mess hall, of frame construction, had a capacity of 3000 men. Construction began in April, and 1500 beds were ready for occupancy by July 2, 1945. By July 8, another 500 beds were available. and the entire unit was completed by September 15.

Northwest of the hospital a small ammunition depot was built. Personnel facilities and a barge pier were included in the work, also about 20 miles of roads leading to, and within, the site.

A tank farm was erected near Bulusao, on the southern coast of Samar, 35 miles northwest of Guiuan. Initial plans called for the erection of 55 one-thousand-barrel oil tanks, but change reduced the number to 31. The 105th Battalion started construction, which included earth-moving, piping, erection of a fueling pier, and driving of dolphins, on May 12, 1945. By August, all earth work was finished, piping was 30 per cent complete, and 19 tanks had been erected. Rain and lack of heavy equipment caused considerable delay in the early work.

A ship-watering facility was built on the Bulusao River, near the tank farm. Installations consisted of a pumphouse, a mile of 6-inch supply pipe lines, a 1,000-barrel storage tank, mooring dolphins and catwalk, a personnel camp, and a signal tower and shelter. This activity was placed in operation on February 10. Water could be supplied by two LST's and two LCI's daily.

One of the most necessary activities from a construction standpoint was the sawmill at Balangiga, east of Bulusao on the south coast of Samar. This mill, operated by 3 officers and 132 enlisted men, of the 12th Regiment, aided by 145 civilians, supplied lumber used in the construction of the naval facilities at Leyte Gulf. Lack of heavy equipment and sufficient water transportation handicapped the operations. The first mill was opened in February, and the second in March. The amount of lumber cut increased from 126,000 board feet of rough lumber sawed in March to 325,000 board feet of lumber in May.

Calicoan.—Wharves for cargo vessels were constructed on the Leyte Gulf side of Calicoan Island, rather than in the vicinity of Guiuan, where there

GENERAL VIEW OF THE SUPPLY DEPOT, SAMAR

were reefs and shallow water. Supply facilities on Calicoan Island were built as near the wharves as possible.

The naval supply depot on Calicoan Island was established to provide for storage and issue of general provisions. It was also to act as a spare-parts distribution center for the fleet and the surrounding shore-based activities. Facilities for storage of ship's stores, dry provision, oxygen, acetylene, carbon dioxide, perishable goods, and cement were provided.

Quonset warehouses were built in groups of twelve, the ribs of adjacent buildings overlapping about one foot to make a warehouse 120 feet wide and 300 feet long. Because of the shortage of cement it was necessary to finish all except five of the warehouses with coral floors, using concrete for foundations only. Three frame buildings were constructed for sorting and transit sheds, and twenty-four 6,800-cubic-foot refrigerators were set up.

Work on a 3600-man camp, which included offices, a 14-bed sick bay, post office, and theater, was started on April 18. By June the entire site was cleared of all temporary quarters, and 90 per cent of all grading was complete. By August all the huts were completed. Two 126,000-gallon steel tanks, a pumping station, and gathering lines were constructed to collect rainwater.

To handle the cargo shipped into the supply depot, three 500-foot timber piers and one 500-foot pontoon pier for seven cargo ships, and one jetty for five LCT's were constructed.

The total area for the advance base construction depot on Calicoan Island covered 80 acres. Seventy acres of this area consisted of hard coral with very little top soil and with coral heads projecting 3 to 8 feet higher than general level. The entire plot was covered with thick brush and large trees. Work was started on this project March 5, 1945. The brush and smaller trees could be cleared with bulldozers, but the large trees had to be cut and the stumps dynamited. In order to dynamite the coral heads and to level them with bulldozers, it was necessary to maintain five drilling and shooting crews seven days a week. By the end of April, 30 acres had been cleared; the project was completed in June.

Sorting and transit sheds, warehouses, and administration buildings were erected. The warehouses consisted of approximately 40 quonset buildings; the sheds for sorting and transit were

of frame construction. These buildings were erected on platform raised to truck height. A retaining wall was erected to enclose a 4,000-yard fill on which the concrete floor was laid. The work also included construction of water-supply facilities, fuel storage and distribution facilities, quarters, roads, waterfront developments, floodlighting, and 4,500 feet of underground power distribution.

Other facilities constructed on Calicoan Island were an automotive and construction equipment parts depot which supplied parts to the entire Philippine area, a pontoon assembly depot, a radio sound pool, and medical and ordnance depots.

Construction of a water-supply system had high priority throughout the work. The Samar water distribution and pumping system was completed in 90 days. All right-of-way clearing for the 12,000 feet of 12-inch water-main, running from the hospital area to the filter plant north of Guiuan, was completed in June. Approximately 8,000 feet of pipe were installed during this period. The entire line was placed in operation in July.

In addition, 20,000 feet of 12-inch line were laid north of the hospital area to Salcedo. Two feeder lines (one 6 inches; the other 8 inches) were laid in the Mercedes area with the 8-inch line connected to the PT-boat well and placed in operation. Access roads for the Salcedo pumping station and the Salcedo River pumping station were well underway by July. By August the 12-inch main from Salcedo to Mercedes had been completed and tied into the water system which supplied the naval station and north Calicoan.

At the Tubabao receiving station, 15,000 feet of 12-inch welded-joint pipe were laid for the Guiuan filtration plant. Of this, 12,000 feet of pipe were welded together on the Samar shore and floated across the bay, to be eventually sunk and anchored to the bottom of the bay.

Water supply to the Samar boat pool was completed during September, sources being either deep wells or surface water. Erosion at one time so muddied the surface sources that filter facilities were heavily loaded.

Many primary and secondary highways and roads were necessary. Among the primary roads was the Mercedes highway, running north from Guiuan for 20 miles. Another main road was the Guiuan-Calicoan highway, which stretched from Guiuan, eastward past the airstrip, south across a

MULTIPLE-QUONSET WAREHOUSES AT THE SUPPLY DEPOT, CALICOAN ISLAND

causeway between Samar and Calicoan, and across Calicoan for 2½ miles to the south end of the island.

This continuation of the Calicoan highway involved a considerable amount of blasting, as at least 75 per cent of it had to be blasted through solid coral. Sand excavated in the supply depot area was used by the 5th Battalion for rough grading; well-compacted rolled coral was used for surfacing. Huge holes in the coral formations, some of them big enough to swallow a large tractor, hampered operations, damaged equipment, and made efficient dynamiting difficult. By August 31, when the project was completed, the 5th Battalion had used a total of 150 tons of dynamite for grading and quarry work.

Access roads for all activities were constructed. All roads were surfaced with coral which made an excellent all-weather road.

Mindoro

Mindoro Island, nearly 300 miles northwest of Leyte, was invaded by United States forces on December 15, 1944. The area along the southwestern coast, where the landings were made, was low, sandy, and covered with scrub growth. Beyond the beaches, a cultivated plain extended inland for 5 miles, rising gradually to the mountains of the interior. There was little jungle. High mountains form an impassable barrier between east and west coasts and have a direct effect on the rainfall, so that from October to May the southwest coast is virtually without rainfall. The island was invaded to secure a site where landing fields could be developed, free from the rain and mud of Leyte and Samar.

On D-day, Detachment A of the 113th Battalion landed with Army forces at Caminawit Point. The detachment, consisting of 53 men and one officer, started work immediately on an advance PT base which they completed in February 1944. Tents were used for the housing and messing of 1800 men; tents and native huts for offices; two quonset huts for a post office and radio communications; several large tents and a quonset warehouse for storage; a 70-by-100-foot frame building for repair shops, a dispensary and sick bay. A 230-foot timber pier was also built.

On December 15, 1944, Detachment B of the 113th, consisting of 100 men and three officers, were enroute to Mindoro aboard an LST, which was badly damaged when an enemy plane, carrying bombs, crashed into it. Two men were killed, three missing, and seven wounded.

On January 14, Detachment C, with 150 officers and men, disembarked at Caminawit Point with orders to build an advance naval base in the area. They were followed on February 7 by Detachment D, consisting of the remainder of the 113th Battal-

Gulf to Manila Bay is 100 miles long and varies from 30 to 50 miles in width. It contains the capital city of Manila, the major concentration of the population and wealth, numerous airfields, and a network of roads and railroads.

Naval installations on Luzon were, as soon as was possible, placed under the command of naval headquarters at Manila. The facilities consisted, in addition to the naval base at Manila, of a sec-

STREET SCENE AT THE CALICOAN SUPPLY DEPOT
Photograph, taken in November 1945, shows the general view on the ocean side

ion, which went ashore at San Jose. Detachment A left the island early in March to install other advance PT bases. The remainder of the battalions worked at Mindoro until the Japanese surrendered.

During their stay at Mindoro, the 113th constructed headquarters for a section base, a port director's office in a quonset hut, three quonsets for communications offices and transmitters, a post office, a 40-by-60-foot frame building, three acres for open storage, four quonsets for a dispensary, a service apron at the Army airfield for Naval Air Transport Service planes, a tent camp for base personnel, and a 266-foot timber pier for small craft.

Luzon

Luzon, the largest of the Philippine Islands, with about the same area as the state of Virginia, is generally mountainous, but is cut by two large valleys. The central plain, extending from Lingayen

tion base at San Fernando on Lingayen Gulf, a naval base at Subic Bay, an airfield at Sangley Point, receiving barracks and hospital at Cavite, and a port director's office at Batangas.

San Fernando.—A section base was established on the east side of Lingayen Gulf, to coordinate with the Army in the routing and convoying of ships, to provide service to forces afloat, to coordinate naval activities in the Lingayen area, and to furnish local defense of the area, including harbor entrance control.

Included in the facilities at San Fernando were radio and visual stations, a dispensary, a boat pool, a fleet post office, and 93 anchorages.

Quonset construction, used for all personnel structures and shops, was erected mainly by local labor under the supervision of a detachment of the 102nd Construction Battalion.

Subic Bay.—Naval facilities were installed to provide a repair base for destroyers, submarines, and small craft; major overhaul of PT engines; service and supply to fleet units, a hospital, an amphibious training center, and a receiving barracks.

Subic Bay, on the west coast of Luzon, about 30 miles north of Corregidor Island and 50 miles northwest of Manila, was used during the war to accommodate deep-draft vessels.

Olongapo, on the east side of the bay, was the site of pre-war naval installations and of the native settlement of Olongapo. The other large native settlement, Subic City, was at the extreme northern end of the Bay.

The semi-tropical climate with high temperature and humidity and rainfall of about 125 inches yearly, the heaviest being in July, August, and September, characterized the area.

Water, which had to be treated, was available in an unlimited amount from streams and wells. The soil was a rather fertile clay mixture. Several sources of clean well-graded gravel and of good rock for road building and concrete aggregate were available. Native timber could be utilized for construction purposes.

Before the Japanese invasion of 1941, Olongapo was the site of a small United States naval base. In Subic Bay, near Olongapo, the floating drydock "Dewey" was moored. The old coaling station had been placed in an inoperative status, but a freshwater supply was available through a 12-inch line. At the naval station were offices, shops, a naval radio station, and Marine barracks.

The 115th was the first construction battalion to debark at Subic Bay, arriving on February 8, 1945, from Lingayen Gulf.

It was immediately assigned to construction work in the area adjoining Olongapo. The first task was the construction of facilities, which included camps for port director, communications, ship repair and base dispensary units as well as a base camp for housing 1200 men in 32 two-story barracks.

The base water supply was put back in operation. A 10-inch line from the Ealaklan River to Olongapo was rehabilitated, and work was begun on repairs to the 12-inch line from Binictigan River to the ship watering point at the old coal pier. This work later was taken over by the 102nd Battalion. When completed, the line was capable of delivering half a million gallons daily. A filtration plant capable of treating 810,000 gallons per day was installed in the 10-inch line to Olongapo.

The 102nd Battalion arrived in Subic Bay on February 28, 1945, with the 24th Regiment and set up camp at the site of the submarine base. The regiment, after a brief stay at the old ammunition depot at Maritan Point, settled in the administration area at Olongapo.

On March 7, 1945, the 24th Special Battalion reached Subic Bay. The first week was spent in discharging battalion cargo and setting up a temporary camp on the beach. On March 12, 1945, the battalion was divided into two sections. The first section remained at Subic Bay, and the second went to Manila. Stevedoring operations were begun on March 18, and continued until V-J Day.

On June 23 and 29, 1945, the 21st Special Battalion arrived to reinforce the 24th.

For the combined activities of a fleet post office, a chart depot, a port director, and a dental laboratory, a total of 29 quonsets were erected.

The establishment of a small-boat pool required, for housing, the construction of a 1000-man frame building, six 2-story frame buildings, and five quonsets. Waterfront facilities for small-boat operation included five quonset warehouses to house the various shops and three regular quonsets for offices. Two 1000-gallon storage tanks were installed, one for gasoline and the other for diesel oil. Two small, T-shaped pontoon boat piers were constructed.

The naval base dispensary was of the advance base, quonset-hut type. A total of 26 quonsets were erected for wards, storerooms, messhalls, galley, laundry, and offices.

Clearing and grading the site for an amphibious training center was started by the 102nd Battalion in April 1945. Quarters were provided by 24 quonsets, complete with latrines and other services such as water and electric power. A sick bay was set up in three quonset huts, with connecting covered walkways and facilities. Other buildings erected were a quonset warehouse for an enlisted men's mess hall, a frame galley building, and a laundry with all necessary equipment.

Water was obtained from four 20-inch wells, and three 15,000-gallon wood-stave tanks provided storage. A water-treatment plant, using four 5000-gallon wood-stave tanks for filters and two pontoons for back-washing, was built and placed in operation during May 1945.

A site was cleared for warehouses, and on the nearby beach a concrete apron, 80 feet by 400 feet, was poured. A 400-foot marine railway, using pontoons to support its rails, was about 15-percent complete on May 9, 1945, when the 115th Battalion assumed supervision of the amphibious training center project.

Construction as carried on by the 115th included erection of 68 quonset huts for living quarters, 11 for classrooms, 7 large quonsets for lecture halls, shop buildings, and galleys.

The amphibious training center was finished by the 11th Battalion, which arrived June 27 and erected the last fifteen quonsets, a recreation building, and a 500-man latrine. The 11th also finished work on the 400-foot marine railway, complete with landing winch and platforms.

Meantime, the 102nd Battalion was assigned to the construction of a 500-man beach-party camp. A 500-man wood-frame messhall was erected first; then a 30-by-56-foot wood-frame galley, with a concrete deck and all necessary services, was placed at right angles to the mess hall.

Living quarters were provided in 40 wood-frame tents, with screens and wood decks. The administration building and warehouses were of frame construction. On May 10, 1945, the 115th Battalion took over completion and maintenance at the camp. Work was completed by June 1, 1945, including installation of services and roadways.

Construction of a submarine base was the next assignment of the 102nd Battalion. Offices were set up in a 20-by-168-foot multiple-quonset hut, and quarters and mess facilities were also established in quonsets. Access roads throughout the area were gravel-surfaced, and sidewalks were built throughout the camp.

Radio facilities for the base were provided in two standard quonsets, placed end-to-end, with a third quonset connected to form a T-shaped building. The structure had a concrete deck. A wood-frame building with a concrete deck was erected to house the generating equipment.

Submarine repair facilities also were constructed by the 102nd, with the help of base personnel. Enlisted men were quartered in eight 24-by-176-foot double-deck wood-frame barracks. A wood-frame mess hall and galley to accommodate 2000 men was provided. Laundry and ship's store activities were located in two large quonset huts. A general-stores warehouse, 100 by 135 feet, was of multiple-quonset construction, and a wood-frame structure was installed to protect six 650-cubic-foot refrigerators. Medical facilities for the base were provided in five quonset huts.

Multiple-quonset construction was used to make a torpedo workshop, 123 by 200 feet, and a ship-fitter shop, 100 by 120 feet. The torpedo workshop was later equipped with an overhead crane, and a 20-by-100-foot frame addition was made to the shipfitter shop for use as a compressor shed. Two electrical shops, a photography shop, and a radio and radar shop were installed in quonset huts. A pontoon pier, complete with dolphins, was installed for cargo vessels. This was later supplemented by the construction of a timber pier.

Five miles of gravel-surfaced roadway and four timber highway bridges were constructed to provide access to the base.

To permit construction of the submarine supply center, a native village was relocated. Ten quonsets were built for quarters. A carpenter's shop, a packing building, and two 226-by-300-foot multiple quonsets were constructed as warehouses.

The base water-supply system was at first cared for in wood-stave water tanks erected by the Seabees. Later, three Japanese 160,000-gallon steel storage tanks, captured at the base, were erected for a permanent base water supply.

Work at the supply depot was done by several battalions. The bulk of the initial construction, including temporary and permanent camps for officers and men, six, 160-by-200-foot steel warehouses, and four standard quonsets for administration buildings, was performed by the 115th Battalion.

At the naval supply depot one steel warehouse, for which the deck had been poured and frame erected, was completed by the 11th. A block of twelve 1800-cubic-foot refrigerators with shelters, a power system, and a water-supply system were constructed. At Rifle Range Beach the 11th Battalion constructed a 1200-foot timber pier to serve the supply depot.

The 80th Battalion, which arrived at Subic Bay on June 18, 1945, assisted the battalions already at the base on the several jobs then in progress.

The 102nd Battalion constructed a degaussing station on Agustin Point. Piles were driven to support a small finger pier at the station. The 80th Battalion provided a 4000-man receiving barracks and mess hall with framed tents.

Access roads over rice paddies, including a 120-foot timber highway bridge over the Matain River, and 12 acres of open storage areas were built by the 11th Battalion.

A few miles northeast of Olongapo, the 115th

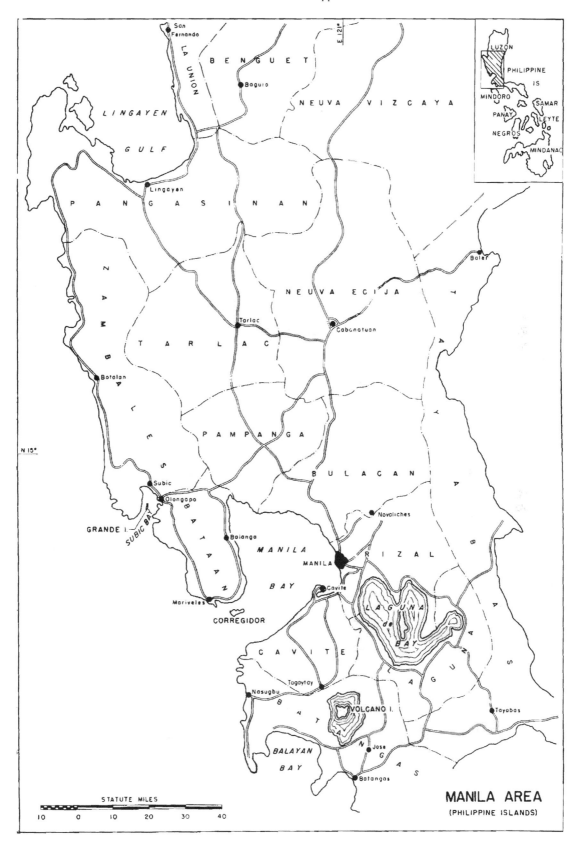

STATUTE MILES

MANILA AREA
(PHILIPPINE ISLANDS)

Battalion put into operation a Japanese sawmill, which they had transported from Botolan. However, the output of this mill was not sufficient to supply the area. Later, the 102nd Battalion set up another sawmill near the radio station at Agustin Point, and logging roads were built into the surrounding jungle.

In May 1945, CBMU 543 arrived at Subic Bay. During June they built a camp and began taking over some of the maintenance work in the area. By July 1, the unit was settled and fully occupied with its maintenance job.

When the Japanese surrendered, all Subic Bay facilities were operating at capacity. The 11th, 80th, 102nd and 115th Construction Battalions, plus the 21st Special Battalion and half of the 24th Battalion, as well as the CBMU 543 and CBD 1082, were still operating at this base.

Manila. In 1938, naval facilities at Manila were centered in the navy yard at Cavite. Several outlying activities in the vicinity, although set apart geographically from the yard, were loosely spoken of as divisions. Among them was the fuel depot at Sangley Point, a small peninsula extending into Manila Bay.

Other activities in the area were the naval hospital at Canacao, a radio station at Sangley Point, and a supply department in the city of Manila. Two small boat piers on the Manila waterfront were used for the landing of liberty parties from the many ships that anchored in the deep and extensive harbor at Manila.

Early in 1941, the United States government began planning a seaplane base for patrol activities in the Manila area. Sangley Point was selected as the location, and plans for the proposed station were approved by the Bureau of Yards and Docks, on April 10, 1941.

Field work started in May 1941 under a supplemental agreement to the contract providing Pacific air bases. Plans called for clearing of the site, dredging, bulkheading, filling, and grading; construction of a seaplane ramp and extension of the existing seaplane runways; erection of a seaplane hangar, a utility shop, an assembly and repair shop, an engine-test shop; construction of a power plant and distribution system, fuel storage facilities, magazines, barracks, messhalls, recreation facilities, roads, walks, and a fire-protection system.

Under the same contract and agreement, the contractors also were ordered to develop an ammunition depot at Mariveles on the tip of Bataan

Peninsula. This project called for 47 structures, including storage for mine and cartridge cases, ammunition overhaul shops, a general garage, a generating plant, distribution systems for electricity and water, telephone and fire-alarm service, quarters for military personnel and civilian workers, as well as walks, roads, and necessary drainage.

The contractors continued work on these projects until Christmas Eve of 1941, when Manila was declared undefended. Emergency defense work was continued by the civilian workers until April 8, when Bataan was surrendered to the Japanese.

In March 1945, shortly after the recovery of the Manila area from the Japanese, the 77th and 119th Seabees arrived at Manila to begin new construction and rehabilitate the existing facilities.

Several projects were immediately undertaken,

FILTRATION PLANT WITH 810,000-GALLONS-PER-DAY CAPACITY. SUBIC BAY

including construction of a communications system, the clearing for a receiving barracks at Cavite naval base, and the installation of facilities for a ship salvage unit at Manila.

On April 8, the 63rd Construction Battalion arrived at Manila to begin work on the Seventh Fleet headquarters, on a 40-acre site on the Manila waterfront formerly occupied by the Manila Polo Club. Quarters for personnel were quickly available in 33 quonset huts and 14 two-story frame units. Eleven prefabricated steel units were erected as office buildings. Eight 75-kw generators were set in a 40-by-128-foot prefabricated steel hut, which included a laundry and drying unit. In addition, electrical, water, and sewerage facilities, a 10-quonset hospital, an open-air theater, and a chapel were constructed. The project also included all walks, roads, and necessary drainage.

The communications center consisted of three units- a transmitting station, a receiving station,

NAVAL SUPPLY DEPOT AREA, SUBIC BAY
Shows units 1, 2, and 3, completed by the 115th Seabees

and a traffic center. At the transmitting station, 12 quonset huts, for living quarters, galley, messhalls, and sick bay, were erected. and 3 quonsets over concrete decks served the power plant. One quonset housed the transmitter. Poles, transmission lines, walks, roads, water and sewerage facilities were installed. The receiving center consisted of 40 quonsets for quarters, offices, and utilities buildings; the traffic center had seven large quonset huts and two frame buildings. By June 22, 1945, the 119th Battalion had completed the work on these centers, including all facilities.

Sangley Point. The 77th Construction Battalion accomplished the major portion of the work at Sangley Point. A 5000-foot runway was constructed, complete with taxiways and parking areas, all of them surfaced with pierced plank. A terminal building and appurtenant structures and facilities for Naval Air Transport Service were constructed adjacent to the strip. Two 1,000-barrel tanks and one 10,000-barrel tank, complete with a distribution and pumping system, were erected. Existing seaplane facilities were expanded to include a concrete ramp, temporary shops, and a

pontoon slip to facilitate loading and unloading operations.

Cavite.—Construction consisted chiefly of erecting 12 quonset huts to serve as a receiving barracks. A base hospital was started, but was still uncompleted on V-J Day. Local labor was used extensively, under supervision of the 77th Battalion.

The 119th Battalion erected three large quonset huts over concrete floors, to be used as shops for the ship salvage unit. Two small personnel camps and a dispensary were also in process of construction when the Japanese surrendered.

Palawan

A naval base at Palawan was set up to care for a fleet air wing, including three carrier aircraft service units and three patrol-bomber squadrons, plus base facilities for two seaplane squadrons.

Palawan Island, fifth largest of the Philippine group, is 265 miles long and varies from 5 to 25 miles in width. Puerto Princesa Bay, where the Seabees began operations, is near the mid-point on the east coast. The area around the bay, which was listed as a typhoon anchorage, is largely mountainous, except for coastal plain lying along the east shore. The mountains consist of two ranges, extending northeast-southwest, each a confused system of rugged peaks, some as high as 5,000 feet. Several good airfield sites. however, were found on the coastal plain.

Twelve days after the Army had overcome enemy resistance, March 12, 1945, the 84th Seabees landed at Puerto Princesa. All Japanese facilities had been rendered useless by the attacking bombardment, but one runway was deemed suitable for enlargement and a large looping taxiway was found to be repairable. The assignment was handled by Army Engineers, the 84th loaning heavy equipment and trucks.

Initial projects assigned to the 84th were the construction of facilities for landplanes and seaplanes, together with headquarters for a naval unit and for the port director.

Construction of a small landplane base was begun March 15, 1945. Facilities included 12 hardstands with connecting taxiways, personnel housing and messing for 2,500 men, nose hangars. and 6 miles of roads. The Seabees also were assigned the task of building a strip that would connect taxiways. The first hardstands were in use on March 28, and the remaining ones were completed and placed in use on May 31. The connecting strip was completed at approximately the same time. A temporary camp for 2,100 men was set up in April; permanent structures were usable on May 15. For unloading tankers carrying aviation gas, a fuel jetty, consisting of 175 feet of catwalk and pipe supports, was constructed. After May, only maintenance work was done on the landplane base.

Construction of the naval headquarters unit and facilities for the port director was started on March 16. The two projects included administration buildings, housing, messing, sanitation, dispensary, and operational buildings. The two units were in operation on April 1, and facilities were completed on April 15.

Although work was started on the ramp and hardstands for the seaplane base on March 15, it was not until May 15 that the first plane came up the ramp. By July 10, temporary seaplane facilities were in operation. Construction of permanent facilities was started on August 1, the completion date was September 7. These included a 500-man camp, administration buildings, and operational facilities.

The base was enlarged beyond its original plan to include a ship-watering-supply point and concrete paving on the ramps and hardstands. Water for ships was obtained from two wells and stored in a 126,000-gallon tank. Paving work on 120,000 square feet of ramps and hardstands was started on August 9; by September 1, it was practically complete.

In addition to this construction, Seabees were charged with maintenance of the station and steve-

SAMAR CAMP OF THE 100TH SEABEES, NOVEMBER 1945

Naval Aviation Repair and Overhaul Unit, Samar

doring on 22 ships as well as with the naval security of the island, which included handling the shore patrol and a stockade.

Mindanao

Zamboanga, on the southern tip of the Zamboango Peninsula in Mindanao, was the site of a naval section base. Ten miles across Basilan Strait, a major PT operating base was built on Basilan Island.

The 118th Construction Battalion arrived at Basilan Island on March 29, 1945 to erect facilities for repair, maintenance, and upkeep of 24 PT boats. These included a 1450-man camp complete with mess and recreation facilities, one 370-foot pier for small craft, two 400-foot piers for mooring the large speed boats, a marine railway capable of handling three boats at a time, seven 1,000-barrel and one 2,000-barrel, steel, fuel tanks, with facilities for fueling which included a 90-foot fuel pier.

While this construction was under way a 120-man detachment from the 118th was sent to Zamboanga to construct buildings and other facilities for the headquarters of the naval section base.

These included communications, supply, and a 10-bed dispensary.

Cebu

Cebu, a long finger-like island west of Leyte, lies also within the perimeter of Negros and Bohol. The naval section base was established at Cebu City on the central east coast of the island, overlooking the small island of Mactan. It provided facilities for a small port director unit, a visual station, a radio station, a small boat pool, a small motor pool, a fleet post office, a dispensary, and a tent camp for 250 men.

The harbor afforded good anchorage, but the excellent deepwater piers at Cebu City had been badly damaged by military operations.

The 54th Construction Battalion developed the section base, which required grading and preparing the sites for tent erection and, later, replacement with quonset huts.

Mactan

Mactan Island, a small island with an area of about 25 square miles, lies a mile across the channel from Cebu, opposite Cebu City. It is flat, except for a 100-foot hill at the northern end, and is surrounded by coral reefs except for a 4-mile stretch facing Cebu, which accommodates one cargo ship.

The island was selected for a dual mission, to support both landplanes and seaplanes. Four airstrips were begun but the Japanese surrendered before their completion.

Facilities were temporarily erected to provide overhaul, repairs, and maintenance service for all types of planes. Many of the personnel and shops were housed in tents, which were being replaced by quonset huts as fast as time and materials permitted, when the end of hostilities caused the work at the base to be stopped.

All work was accomplished by a detachment of the 54th Construction Battalion and Air Corps personnel.

Panay

Early in the summer of 1945, facilities for a port director and for communications were established at the port of Iloilo on the southeast coast of the island of Panay and fronting on Iloilo Strait, which could give protected anchorage to a large number of ships. Facilities, constructed by a detachment of the 5th Battalion, included administration offices (in Army buildings), a visual signal tower, a motor pool, and a boat pool. Facilities for the maintenance, upkeep, and refueling of one PT-boat

squadron that patrolled throughout the southern Philippine area were also constructed.

Borneo

Seabees accompanied the Australians in the invasion of Borneo. At the initial landings, in May 1945 at Tarakan, 7 officers and 140 men of the 111th Battalion participated as pontoon-causeway operating crews. On June 10, the same number of officers and men performed the same function at the Brunei Bay landings. Two officers and 35 men from CBMU 605 also participated in the D-Day operations at Brunei Bay, landing on Labuan Island, where they constructed port director facilities.

Less than a month later, July 1, 1945, men from three battalions participated in the landings at Balikpapan. The 111th furnished 14 officers and 280 men to operate three pontoon causeways established at Balikpapan, over which both supplies and personnel were landed. By nightfall of D-Day, the Tokyo radio admitted that more than 7,000 troops had been set ashore and had established a beachhead. The 111th also operated five strings of pontoons at the landing beach near the Sepinggang airfield, 5 miles from Balikpapan, and set up a ship-repair unit which serviced 16 LCT's in the first 11 days.

Facilities for servicing motor torpedo boats were installed by 55 men from the 113th Construction Battalion. A detachment from the 5th Battalion also participated. All the Borneo landings were made under fire.

CHAPTER 30

OKINAWA

By the summer of 1944, joint United States Army and Navy forces had pushed westward in the Pacific to the Marianas, and plans for the next major actions in the war against Japan were taking form. The Tenth Army had been formed for the purpose of seizing the island of Formosa and a section of the China coast near Amoy; however, the decision to invade the Philippines at an early date, as well as the discovery that landing beaches on Formosa were unsuitable, led to a reconsideration of the targets. Staff planners, thereupon, directed their attention to Okinawa and the Nansei Shoto, or Ryukyu Islands.

Strategically, Okinawa offered many advantages. Its occupation would place United States forces within 350 miles of the Japanese home islands. From bases established there, our forces could attack the home islands of Japan and their sea approaches with naval and air forces; could support further operations in the regions bordering on the East China Sea; could sever Japanese sea and air communications between the homeland and the mainland of Asia, Formosa, Malaya, and the Netherlands East Indies; could establish secure sea and air communications through the East China Sea to the coast of China and the Yangtze Valley; and could maintain unremitting military pressure against Japan. In view of these considerations, the Joint Chiefs of Staff directed the Commander in Chief, Pacific Ocean Area, to "occupy one or more positions in the Nansei Shoto." The target date was set for March 1, 1945, but was subsequently adjusted to April 1, 1945.

Okinawa Shima, with other islands of the Nansei Shoto, forms the boundary between the East China Sea and the Pacific Ocean. These islands resemble the floats of an enormous fish net, strung between Kyushu and Formosa, with Okinawa as the central, and largest, float. The island is 67 miles long and varies in width from 2 to 15 miles. The coastline is irregular, deeply indented with bays and inlets. Wide fringing coral reefs almost completely surround the island and limit access from the sea. North of a narrow isthmus at Ishikawa, the land is rugged, with peaks rising to elevations higher than 1500 feet; south of the isthmus the hills do not exceed 700 feet. Although broken by steep limestone scarps and terraces, there are extensive areas of gently sloping land in the southern portion of the island. Land too steep or unproductive to till is covered with a moderate growth of small pines and coarse grass. In the northern hills, vegetation is heavier and approaches the jungle type. The climate is subtropical, and although variations in temperature are not great, the extreme humidity makes even these small variations noticeable. Rains are frequent and often torrential, and typhoons of great intensity frequently sweep across the island.

The invasion of Okinawa began on April 1, 1945. Divisions of the Third Marine Amphibious Corps and the 24th Army Corps made simultaneous landings on the west coast, north and south of the Bisha Gawa and less than 20 miles north of the port of Naha. Meeting only light opposition, our forces rapidly advanced inland to capture Yontan and Kadena airfields and to extend the beach head to a depth of two and a half miles by nightfall. The advance was rapid for the next few days as the Marines cleared Bolo Point and the Army drove across the width of the island to the Awase peninsula. On April 7, Marine reserves landed near the town of Nago, at the base of the Motobu Hanto, augmenting forces advancing overland, and one week later, reached the northern tip of the island.

The 24th Corps found resistance considerably stiffer in the southern part of the island. Fighting from prepared positions, the enemy was able to defend a line extending eastward across the island from Machinato. This line held until April 19, when our ground forces, supported by the fleet, succeeded in breaking through. By the end of

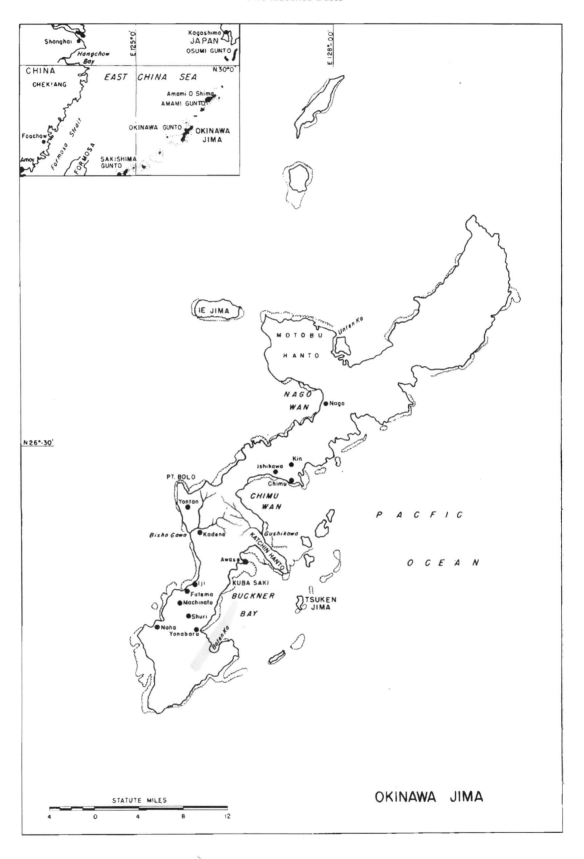

April, our troops had captured Machinato airfield, but were halted north of Shuri and the Yonabaru airfield.

Progress during May was slow and costly, and at the end of the month, the enemy still occupied the central Shuri salient. Early in June, our forces chased the enemy to his prepared position in the southernmost part of the island, where it was necessary to dig in and blast each enemy position, before organized enemy resistance ceased on June 21, 1945. Isolated pockets of Japanese were left for mopping-up operations; however, all sites required for construction purposes became available in the next few days.

Enemy installations of engineering importance on Okinawa consisted of limited port and harbor improvements, an extensive but narrow road system, four airports previously operational according to Japanese standards, two airfields on which construction had started, two water-supply systems, and miles of stone-masonry seawall. Of no use to our forces were two narrow-gauge railroads, the water-supply systems, and the caves and tunnels.

Enemy airstrips were too short and their construction too light to meet the requirements for operation of our heavier aircraft. Hardstands were small and some were surrounded by diamond-shaped revetments, open at the point. Taxiways and hardstands were elaborately camouflaged—mock villages with potted trees were used to hide aircraft in dispersal areas at Yontan.

The road network, although extensive, was constructed to standards completely inadequate to meet our minimum requirements. Cuts and embankments were narrow, and curves sharp. Native villages, with stone walls and deep gutters pressing the roadway on both sides, gave limited clearance. The best surface consisted of a thin layer of hand-placed coral stones, which failed under our heavy traffic and could not be maintained with our power equipment. Bombardment by our air and surface craft had destroyed many of the bridges and drainage structures of the road network, and the enemy, as he withdrew, wrecked with demolition charges those that were left.

The task of base development was delegated to the Island Commander, Okinawa, under whose control were the Army and Navy construction troops available for execution of the base development plan. The Island Commander, in turn, placed all construction troops in Task Unit 99.3.5, and assigned to Commander, Construction Troops, the mission of executing the base development plan and of all engineering construction on Okinawa. Construction troops under Commander, Construction Troops, consisted of three naval construction brigades, the 8th, 10th, and 11th, and one Army Engineer construction group, the 1181st. This construction group later was designated a provisional construction brigade.

Units of the command were staged for the target from bases as close as the Marianas and as distant as Seattle and New Caledonia. Some units went ashore as combat engineers with the assault troops, and others sailed in follow-up shipping echelons, but all construction units were brought forward as soon as the shipping priorities, based on limited beach capacity at the target, would permit.

The 44th Naval Construction Regiment, with the 58th, 71st, 130th, and 145th Construction Battalions assigned, was staged and shipped to the target with Marine units to which the battalions were attached. The 58th, 71st, and 145th Battalions were landed on D-Day with the assault troops; the 44th Regiment, on April 5; the 130th Battalion was held in Tenth Army reserve with the Sixth Marine Division until April 12. In addition to these regular battalions, the 130th pontoon and the 11th Special Battalions went in with the assault.

During the combat period, construction troop units landed with the assault troops, served as combat engineers in support of ground troops—rehabilitating and improving native roads and bridges and clearing enemy mines and demolitions. They located, developed, and operated water-supply points for all units; they cleared, repaired, and extended abandoned enemy airfields for early use by our fighter-planes; they installed communication facilities; they provided engineer supply for combat and garrison troops; and they began the development of the permanent facilities of the base for the support of future operations against the enemy. These activities were carried on night and day until the island was declared secured, and in spite of enemy sniper activity, artillery fire, and air attacks. Perimeter defenses of the command post of the commander of construction troops—established soon after D-Day—and, later, of the sector of the island containing the headquarters command post were manned by construction troops.

UNLOADING ACROSS A PONTOON CAUSEWAY, OKINAWA
Temporary causeway established by the 128th Seabees during the assault phase

In addition, construction units were assigned sectors and special tasks under the various area defense commanders.

Engineering reconnaissance was begun on April 2, the day after the initial landings, and continued throughout the campaign. This reconnaissance was often carried on in, and immediately behind, the front lines, in areas recently taken from the enemy and exposed to enemy bombing, sniper shelling, and mortar fire. The knowledge to be gained was considered so important to the accomplishment of the mission that the risks were accepted. Two civilian geologists, attached to the headquarters during the combat period, made extensive explorations and assisted in the location and development of quarries and water-supply installations.

The 43rd Naval Construction Regiment was the first American force to land on the east coast of Okinawa. Between the 27th and the 30th of April, the 36th, 40th, and 87th Battalions landed with the 7th, 14th, and 21st Battalions of the Eighth

Construction Brigade and the 79th Battalion of the 11th Brigade. It was realized early in the planning stage that shipping limitations would prevent the landing of Seabees early enough to accomplish their mission and at the same time avoid interference with the support of combat troops. Accordingly, these eight battalions were streamlined and staged at Saipan on LST's returned from the assault echelon. They were landed on the east coast of Okinawa and developed their own beaches. Construction troops landed in this manner were able to begin work on Chimu and Awase airfields at a date much earlier than would have been possible under the regular shipping schedules.

The first operation undertaken by construction troops was the rehabilitation of beach exit roads and main supply routes. Road work was carried on day and night and without interruption of the heavy flow of military traffic from the beaches to the combat fronts. Native roads were unable to handle the heavy traffic imposed upon them by combat operations, and deteriorated rapidly under the heavy loads and continuous rains which fell during the latter part of May. The situation became so serious that on the 25th of May, the island commander issued an order restricting all traffic to the minimum essential to the provision of water, rations, and ammunition. On the 26th of May, as heavy rains continued, the commanding general of the Tenth Army placed first priority on the maintenance of main supply roads serving the combat troops. Work on other construction projects, including airfields, was temporarily suspended, and all construction troops available concentrated on road maintenance. This condition prevailed until the return of good weather in mid-June when roads again became passable.

Initial road projects were begun in the first few days of the operation by units still attached to the assault forces. Between the 2nd and the 14th of April, when the first battalions, which had landed with the Marines, reverted to control of the commander of naval construction troops, work consisted largely of providing maintenance and keeping all roads passable. Improvements were made later, as equipment and personnel became available. Enemy demolition of bridges had been widespread; however, many of the damaged structures were quickly made usable by cribbing, filling, and shoring, and those demolished beyond repair were bypassed.

Great emphasis was placed on establishing airfield facilities for our forces at the earliest possible moment. Both Yontan and Kadena airfields had been damaged by the pre-invasion bombardment and were further obstructed with mines and booby traps. Construction troops occupied these fields on

ROAD-SURFACING OPERATIONS BY THE 71ST SEABEES ON OKINAWA
Photograph taken July 16, 1945

766450—47—27

YONABARU PIER IN OPERATION, JULY 23, 1945
This was a project of the 21st Seabees

April 3 and immediately began rehabilitation of the existing strips. The initial work at Kadena was accomplished by the 1901st Aviation Engineer Battalion and CBMU 624 on April 4. At Yontan, the 58th Battalion, CBMU 617, and the 802nd Army Aviation Engineer Battalion were at work on the strip by April 3. Initial efforts were concentrated on clearing runways, repairing bomb craters, and disposing of unexploded bombs and ammunition. One strip at Yontan was ready for fighter operation on April 4.

During the latter part of April, construction troops resurfaced the existing runways and constructed taxiways, hardstands, warm-up aprons, pilot housing, and gasoline storage facilities. Damage-control parties from the battalions on several occasions filled bomb craters on one end of the runway while enemy planes were strafing the other end. In spite of enemy interference, the runways were thus kept serviceable almost without a break. At the end of April, construction was started on a new bomber strip at Yontan.

Reconnaissance and surveys which began immediately after the initial landings on Okinawa revealed possibilities for an expansion of the airfield program. In addition to the sites at Yontan, Kadena, and Awase and the sites in possession of the enemy, possible sites were at Bolo Point, Nago, Majiya, Motobu Peninsula, Chimu, and Tsuken Shima. As a result of these and other considerations, it was decided to defer indefinitely the occupation of the island of Amami, north of Okinawa.

All construction forces and all aircraft units originally scheduled for the Amami operation were diverted to Okinawa. This addition brought the number of Army and Navy construction troops on Okinawa to 95,000 and called for construction of airfield facilities to accommodate 4,000 aircraft. At the close of the combat period, the first new bomber strip had been completed at Yontan, the airfields at Kadena, Chimu, and Awase were well under way, and construction was in the first stage at Bolo and Yonabaru airfields.

Reconnaissance parties had discovered that the site originally selected for the Awase airfield was unsuitable because of poor drainage and the absence of conveniently located construction material. A new site for the field was selected a mile south of the original site and on better terrain.

The 36th Battalion began work on a 5,000-foot fighter strip at Awase on April 23.

None of the five remaining airfield sites was available for construction in April because unexpectedly strong enemy resistance had halted the advance of our troops north of Shuri. New airfield sites to the north were surveyed; one on Bolo Point and one on the north shore of Chimu Wan harbor, near Kin, were found to be suitable. The 40th Battalion began work on Chimu airfield on May 6.

On June 14, the Seventh Battalion began construction of a seaplane base on Katchin Hanto. One of the ramps was available for operations by the first of July.

Pontoon structures were used more extensively at Okinawa than in any other previous Pacific operation. The 70th Seabees manned 96 barges of 3-by-

KATCHIN HANTO PENINSULA, OKINAWA
View looking westward, with the advance base construction depot in the foreground

EXTENSION TO PIER AT BATEN KO, OKINAWA
Both pier and extension were built by the 21st Seabees

12-pontoons, and the 128th Battalion managed 28 sets of 2-by-30-pontoon causeways allotted for the operation. The two Seabee units were placed under the commander of the amphibious forces, United States Pacific Fleet, for this operation. The men for this job were trained and embarked at Pearl Harbor. Practice-landings were made at Leyte Gulf and in the Russell Islands. A severe storm was encountered en route to Okinawa, with the result that eight causeways and 13 barges were either lost at sea or so badly damaged that they could not be launched for the invasion. Launchings started on the day of the assault, and by April 8 all available barges and causeways had been launched and were in operation.

The pontoon causeways were used at Okinawa in a slightly different manner than in the Philippines, as the character of the beach differed widely. The attack took place over a wide coral reef. LST's could come up to the edge of the reef, and at low tide it was possible to drive many vehicles ashore over the reef itself. However, pontoon causeways and finger piers were constructed to make the dry-shod landing of men and vehicles possible at high tide.

Actually, 92 pontoon barges were in operation at Okinawa. These were used as lighters, as crane transfer barges, to evacuate casualties, and as "bowser" barges to refuel small boats. A number of barges were also designated as pontoon warping tugs, and were found extremely useful for pulling stranded landing craft off the reef, and for placing moorings for causeways and landing craft. Each of these tugs had a 3,000-pound anchor and a heavy winch. During the first month of operations, the Seabee-manned lighter barges hauled more than 25,000 tons of miscellaneous cargo; the crane barges transferred 40,000 tons of cargo.

The waterfront construction program began on May 5 with preparations for placing an LST pontoon-barge pier near the town of Kin on Chimu Wan. Additional pontoon piers, constructed at Katchin Hanto, Awase, and Kuba Saki, were also placed in operation during the month, although

PONTOON PIER AT KATCHIN HANTO, OKINAWA, MAY 12, 1945

considerable work, such as clearing channels, dredging reefs, and improving access roads, was continued for some time. At Kuba, facilities were established for the storage and issue of pontoons and piling. Pontoon piers at Machinato and Yonabaru were rushed to completion for use in the support of combat troops. During the latter part of June, when the need for moving civilian refugees became great, a pontoon pier was constructed at Ora Wan.

Construction of some permanent facilities was begun during the combat period. On May 8, work was started on a pontoon pier at the section base at Chimu Wan. This installation facilitated the repair of harbor craft, minecraft, and minecraft equipment. Later, in June, construction of a minecraft storm refuge was begun at Unten Ko on Motobu Hanto. The project consisted of the installation of timber-pile mooring dolphins, concrete anchors for mooring buoys, and a small-boat pier.

Nearly two million tons of munitions and supplies were landed during the three-months campaign at Okinawa. All of this freight had to be handled from ships to lighters and from lighters to trucks on the beaches.

To support their operations, the Third Amphib-ious Corps had assigned to them the 11th Special Construction Battalion and two logistics support companies (the 26th and the 32nd). Initial cargo-handling plans evolved around these units. The 11th Special and the two support companies were organized into 90 ship's gangs. Men of all ratings and qualifications were used; all embarked with the assault forces.

As far as landing of supplies was concerned, the first thirty days of the campaign passed without incident, except for enemy aircraft attacks. The total cargo handled for 373 ships during that period was 778,992 measurement tons. In May, beaches were opened on the east coast, and shore-party personnel began to be replaced by organized Seabee Special Battalions and Army port personnel. During the month of May a total of 625,140 measurement tons of supplies were handled over the beaches in lighters and small boats.

On June 1, 1945, all shore-party personnel were relieved and the unloading operations became the responsibility of the commandant of the naval operating base, and was, in turn, delegated to Commander, Joint Freight Handling Facilities, in operational charge of Army and Navy cargo-handling troops.

The tactical situation in June made unprecedented demands for supplies and support on a scale far beyond any previous demands.

Although ample supplies had been behind the lines on June 1, the combat troops had advanced, and the heavy rain which fell all during the month made the roads to the rear impassable. A new and complete supply system had to be quickly devised. As overland transportation was impossible, the burden of supplying troops at the south end of the island had to be shifted to the lighterage used in normal unloading operations. To meet the emer-

AUTOMOTIVE CONSTRUCTION EQUIPMENT OVERHAUL AND REPAIR DEPOT, OKINAWA
Open storage area prepared by the 146th Seabees

KADENA TRAFFIC CIRCLE, OKINAWA
This was a project of the 130th Seabees

gency, cargo ships were spotted at dispersed anchorages and selectively discharged. Supplies were unloaded at every possible landing beach near the troops. Lighterage, after being unloaded on the beach, was used to evacuate casualties and natives caught in the path of advancing troops. Despite the huge burden of extra supply, 613,200 tons of supplies were unloaded during the month of June.

On July 1, the demands of the tactical forces diminished. Selective discharge of ships was no longer necessary. By July 17, the unloading rate had been increased to 35,000 tons per day. This was an increase of 15,000 tons a day over June. During July, 1,015,374 tons of freight were discharged and 206,000 tons loaded out. All of this freight was handled twice, from ships to lighters and from lighters to trucks on the beaches. In contrast, the original base development plan called

for the handling of 550,000 tons per month over completed ship piers and permanent installations.

Seabee units comprising Joint Freight Handling Facilities consisted of the 3rd, 4th, 11th, 12th, 23rd, 27th, and 36th Special Battalions, the 81st, 28th, and 148th (Pontoon) Battalions, and the 137th and 139th (Trucking) Battalions. On July 31, both Army and Navy resumed responsibility for its own unloading, and Joint Freight Handling Facilities ceased to exist as of that date. Naval personnel were reorganized to form the 12th Naval Construction Brigade.

The first major shipment of construction materials—15,900 measurement tons—arrived on Okinawa on May 21. Until the arrival of these materials, construction projects were limited to those which could be accomplished through the use of native materials or of the small supplies of general construction material brought to Okinawa as a part of battalion allowances.

Major construction projects completed by the Seabees during the combat period included three airstrips at Yontan field, the Third Amphibious Corps evacuation hospital at Yontan, Special Augmented Hospital 6, a traffic circle near Kadena Field, and pontoon piers at Kuba Saki, Machinato, Awase, and Bisha Gawa. Major construction projects begun by Seabees during that same period included airstrips at Bolo, Awase, and Chimu, a seaplane base at Katchin Hanto, six highways, Special Augmented Hospitals 7 and 8, a fuel pier and a pontoon pier at Katchin Hanto, a breakwater at Tengan, an ammunition depot at Chimu Wan, a section base at Katchin Hanto, a minecraft storm refuge at Unten Ko, a receiving station at Kuba Saki, boat pool facilities at Bisha Gawa, a degaussing station at Tsuken Shima. and a joint communication center.

Although the initial landings on Okinawa were accomplished without great difficulty, the enemy

BUILDING A RUNWAY AT YONTAN AIRFIELD, OKINAWA
Men of the 87th Battalion grading on May 13, 1945

thereafter did his utmost to harass our forces and to hinder the occupation of the island and the development of the base. The enemy's stubborn defense of the south quarter of the island prevented our occupation of airfield and naval base sites and made necessary the continued diversion of construction forces in support of ground troops, while transportation of construction material was delayed to accommodate the combat operations.

Air attacks against our installations, particularly the airfields, began during the first week of the occupation and continued until the Japanese surrender. The enemy made 261 air raids in the period from April 1 to June 30. Enemy night bombing raids were frequent, and, although the resulting damage was small, the interruptions to work and necessary rest were considerable. Kamikaze attacks against shipping in the harbor damaged some construction equipment and material. In fact, the first ship to arrive with a cargo of

unassembled pontoons and pontoon gear, the SS *Carina*, was struck by a suicide torpedo boat on the second night in the harbor of Nakagusuku, later called Buckner Bay. The most serious menace to construction personnel during enemy air attacks was found to be falling fragments from friendly anti-aircraft shell bursts and mis-directed automatic-weapons fire from ships in the harbor.

On land, the enemy employed mines and booby traps of all descriptions to destroy our equipment and delay our progress. Airfield sites at Yontan, Kadena, Machinato, Yonabaru, Futema, Ie Shima. and Tsuken Shima were heavily mined. Bomb-disposal squads of the 21st Construction Battalion removed tons of explosives from Tsugen Shima before construction could begin.

Bridges had been systematically destroyed by our own air forces in the pre-invasion attacks, and nearly all of those that were left were destroyed by the enemy before his withdrawal. In one case, an enemy patrol infiltrated our lines on May 18, demolished a bridge near the village of Iji, and ambushed the bridge repair party from the 14th Con-

OVERLOADED TRUCK TOWED THROUGH OKINAWA MUD

struction Battalion, when they set out to repair the damage. One repairman was killed and two were seriously wounded.

Direct attacks by enemy ground troops against Seabee bivouacks were neither frequent nor effective. Sniper fire was a constant annoyance, however, and resulted in the establishment of a rule that vehicles must not travel after nightfall except in convoy. Construction troops at work near the combat lines were interrupted by enemy artillery and mortar fire, and, before the capture of Machinato, the airfields at Kadena and Yontan were often subjected to the fire of enemy long-range artillery. During May, the 14th, 20th, and 40th Battalion camps near Chimu were attacked with light mortar and small-arms fire, and attempts were made to sabotage equipment and supplies with explosive charges, but the damage was small. The most frequent enemy contacts were made by reconnaissance survey parties and by battalion outpost guards intercepting small enemy patrols and armed stragglers. Some 168 enemy troops were reported killed and 25 captured.

Upon the cessation of organized enemy resistance on Okinawa at the end of June, construction troops were able to concentrate their efforts on base development, and during the following two months, important progress was made toward the accomplishment of that mission. Much sniper action continued during July and until the final surrender. Additional construction troops arrived during July and August, and, with the completion of additional cargo-handling facilities and the reduction of combat requirements, the availability of construction materials was improved.

Several important organizational and administrative changes in the task unit were accomplished during the period, without interruption of the work. Early in July, the plan for division of base development areas and the reassignment of battalions among naval construction brigades was placed in effect. Each naval construction brigade was made responsible for a type of work—waterfront, airfield, or general construction—in a particular area. As construction troop units were landed or were released from temporary duty with

WATER POINT, OKINAWA

combat forces, they were assigned on this basis. Battalions arriving during July were assigned according to the work load and the needs of the brigades under the new plan.

Construction troops reached a maximum strength during August, when 80,000 officers and men were attached to or under operational control of the Commander, Construction Troops. The figure does not include the 7,000 engineer and naval construction troops under Island Commander, Ie Shima, over whom the Commander, Construction Troops, as engineer for Island Commander, Okinawa, exercised only general supervision. The strength of construction troops, made up of equal numbers of Army and Navy construction personnel, included the following basic units: 36 naval construction battalions, 21 Army engineer aviation battalions, 14 Army combat engineer battalions, and 7 Army engineer construction battalions.

On August 15, joint Army-Navy command in the Ryukyus was dissolved; however, Commander, Construction Troops, maintained joint Army-Navy control of construction forces and construction work until September 1. During the interim, Commander, Construction Troops, was responsible to the Commanding General of the First Army Service Command for Army construction and to the Commandant of Naval Operating Base, Okinawa, for Navy construction. This arrangement was made to allow the expeditious completion of urgently needed Army facilities, including airfields and command posts upon which naval construction units were employed.

With the close of the combat phase, shipping arrivals at Okinawa increased daily, and unloading operations soon became a major problem. Although construction troops were assisting at the piers with additional cranes and loading crews, the piers could not be cleared with the trucks available from receiving units and those assigned to Joint Freight Handling Facilities. In order to alleviate this critical condition, the First Construction Battalion Provisional Truck Company, made up of officers, men, and equipment attached from each of the three naval construction brigades, was activated on July 2. This provisional company, under the administrative control of the 11th Brigade, was given the mission of keeping the east coast piers cleared by handling all classes of supply, from piers to dumps, until Joint Freight Handling Facilities could take over. The company began operations on July 5 and continued until August

31, when Navy Cargo Operations, reinforced by the arrival of regular trucking units, was able to relieve them.

One of the major engineering accomplishments of the Okinawa operation was the rapid construction of Awase airfield. The field was located in a rice-paddy area on the east coast of the island, where drainage was poor and the sub-base was a blue clay which became unstable when wet. The nearest sources of coral for fill and surfacing were located at Gushikawa and Myazato, 3 and 5 miles distant, respectively, although a limited supply of finger coral and coral sand was available on the Awase Peninsula. The field was urgently needed as a base for fighter aircraft conducting the air defense of the island, and the desired operational date was set at July 1.

The scheme of the Commander Construction Troops, for landing naval construction units on the east coast of Okinawa became a proven success when the 36th Battalion debarked at Gushikawa and was able to begin construction of Awase on the 23rd of April. Rice paddies were drained; large drainage canals were dug; and tide gates, installed in the sea wall. A bypass for the main supply road was constructed next, and traffic diverted around the field. These preliminary steps had been nearly completed and work was under way on the fills when the torrential rains of late May and early June caused the Commanding General of the Tenth Army to divert all heavy earth-moving equipment to the maintenance of main supply roads.

Upon the return of dry weather in mid-June and the return of normal priority to airfields, construction troops redoubled their efforts on Awase. The 36th Naval Construction Battalion was reinforced with all available equipment and operators. Six battalions cooperated in moving coral to the field from the quarries at Gushikawa and Myazato. The Island Command provost marshal assisted in the traffic control, and a continuous line of trucks and other earth carriers moved from the quarries to the field and back again.

Work continued night and day, except when enemy aircraft interrupted. The fill material was spread, compacted, shaped, and rolled as it was placed; the strip, taxiways, and hardstands rapidly took shape. Control towers and operational buildings were constructed concurrently.

On June 30, the strip was pronounced ready for initial operation; the desired operational date had been met. The obstacles and difficulties of drainage, material, weather, and interference by the enemy had been overcome. The first planes of Marine Air Group 33 landed on the strip that same day.

During the period from July 1 to August 31, construction troops were able to continue and complete many of the base-development projects begun during the combat period and to initiate the construction of all base-development projects which had been delayed because the enemy prevented occupation of the selected sites.

During the base development period, Seabees completed the airstrips at Bolo, Chimu, Awase, and Yontan, Special Augmented Hospitals 3 and 6, Mine Assembly Depot 8, a degaussing range at Tsuken Shima, a minecraft storm refuge at Unten Ko, and a pontoon-barge and LST pier at Baten Ko. As of August 15, the Yonabaru airfield became operational, with the completion of 6500 feet of runway.

During this period they also continued to work on the construction of communication facilities,

58TH SEABEES PLACE MAT FOR SEAPLANE RAMP, KATCHIN HANTO SEAPLANE BASE

including the erection of a joint communications center, the receiving station at Kuba Saki, naval facilities at Bisha Gawa, the repair base at Baten Ko, the fuel pier at Katchin Hanto, and the breakwater at Tengan.

An advance base construction depot was started during this period. It included a spare parts

depot and an automotive construction equipment overhaul and repair depot. New construction of port facilities included an ammunition pier at Chimu Wan, a pontoon barge pier at Tsuken Shima, a general cargo pier at Katchin Hanto, and two piers for the naval supply depot at Tengan. Large base facilities were started at the supply depot, the naval bases at Buckner Bay and Chimu Wan, and the section base at Katchin Hanto. Other new projects included a naval ammunition depot. Special Augmented Hospital 4, a fleet petroleum-storage facility, a tank farm, permanent water

TIDE-CONTROL GATES FOR DRAINAGE OF YONABARU AIRFIELD
This was a project of the 74th Seabees

systems at Tengan and Baten Ko, a ship repair base at Baten Ko, and docking facilities for aviation repair ships at Awase.

When the Japanese government formally surrendered on September 2, the mission of developing Okinawa as an advance base for the support of fleet, air, and ground forces engaged in prosecuting further attacks against the Japanese Empire had been completed in the degree necessary to that end. Pending a definition of the post-war mission of the base, naval construction troops were directed to proceed with projects underway.

Major projects developed by Seabees after the surrender of Japan included the naval operating base at Baten Ko, the Kuba Saki receiving station and staging area (for demobilization of troops), ammunition depot, Fleet Hospital 116, the Katchin Hanto section base, the aviation supply depot, Baten Ko fleet landing, and a fleet recreation area at Tsuken Shima, as well as additions to the naval supply depot at Tengan on Chimu Wan. The sep-

feet of wharves, 712,000 square feet of general covered storage, 11,778,000 square feet of open storage, 193,000 cubic feet of cold storage, as well as storage for 8,820,000 gallons of aviation gasoline, 30,000 barrels of diesel oil, 50,000 barrels of fuel

BUILDING THE OPERATIONAL UNIT FOR THE 301ST FIGHTER GROUP, IE SHIMA

DOCKING FACILITIES AT IE SHIMA
Photograph, taken June 1, 1945, shows a project of the 106th Seabees in operation

aration of joint Army and Navy commands in the Ryukyus became effective for construction troops on September 1, 1945. Commander, Construction Troops, was detached from duty under the Army Service Command and reported for duty to the Commandant, Naval Operating Base, Okinawa. Upon reporting, he was designated as Commander Naval Construction Troops, with the mission of constructing all base facilities designed primarily for naval use. Thus came to an end the largest joint force of Army and Navy construction troops ever assembled under one engineer commander.

Extensive damage to installations was caused by a severe typhoon, the center of which passed over the southern portion of the island on October 9, 1945. It necessitated the concentration of construction troops for the reconstruction of the fleet postoffice at Baten Ko, Special Augmented Hospital No. 4, and other facilities required for demobilization.

By the close of 1945, naval facilities on Okinawa covered 20,000 acres, and included 4,180 lineal

oil, 13,000 square feet for ammunition. Aviation repair shops covered 324,100 square feet and general repairs shops, 91,000 square feet. Hospital space amounted to 338,000 square feet, and quarters 4,755,000 square feet.

Ie, which was developed in conjunction with Okinawa, became a naval advance base. Its four airstrips were under Army control, but were used by Naval Air Transport Service. The naval base included 16,700 square feet of general storage space, 7,475 cubic feet of cold storage space, and 4,500 square feet of open storage. In addition to 700 lineal feet of wharfage, there were repair shops covering 5,500 square feet; hospitals, 2,400 square feet; and quarters, 67,692 square feet.

CHIMU AIRFIELD, OKINAWA
Photograph shows this project of the 40th Seabees as it looked on July 16th, 1945

CHAPTER 31

AFTER V-J DAY

When organized enemy resistance ceased on Okinawa, on June 22, 1945, the entire focus of attention was turned to the home islands of Japan. With the capture and development of the airfields on Okinawa, land-based planes were brought within easy range of the Japanese-occupied China coast and Korea, as well as the home islands of Kyushu, Shikoku, and even Honshu. Bombings from bases in the Marianas were intensified, and the fleet, with far-ranging air attacks and direct bombardment of the Japanese shores, completed the isolation of the islands.

These operations, together with the atomic bombing of Hiroshima and Nagasaki and the almost simultaneous entry of Russia into the Pacific war, with the resulting attack on Japanese forces in Manchuria and Korea, left Japan with the choice of surrender or annihilation.

On August 14, Japan announced her acceptance of the Potsdam Proclamation, the terms of which were complete disarmament and surrender of all military forces and equipment. The "cease-firing" order took effect the next day.

The instrument of surrender, which was presented to Japanese representatives on August 19, by General MacArthur, at Manila, provided that the Commander in Chief, Army Forces, Pacific, should receive the surrender of the Imperial General Headquarters, its senior commanders, and all ground, sea, air, and auxiliary forces in the main islands of Japan, minor islands adjacent thereto, Korea south of 38 degrees North Latitude, and the Philippines. The Commander in Chief, United States Pacific Fleet, was designated to receive the surrender of the senior Japanese commanders and of all ground, sea, air, and auxiliary forces in the Japanese-mandated islands, the Ryukyus, the Bonins, and other Pacific islands.

On August 27, an advance unit of the Third Fleet, guided by a group of Japanese naval officers, harbor pilots, and interpreters, and provided with maps and charts, moved into Sagami Bay, just southwest of Tokyo Bay. The next day, a small detachment of Army Air Forces parachuted onto Atsugi airfield, 14 miles southwest of Tokyo, to prepare the way for the large-scale air-borne landings on August 30, when General MacArthur arrived at the field and set up general headquarters at Yokohama.

Meantime, on August 29, Fleet Admiral Nimitz had arrived from Guam, to break his flag in the battleship *South Dakota*, and with Admiral Halsey, Commander, Third Fleet, aboard the *Missouri*, entered Tokyo Bay and anchored off Yokosuka naval base. The next day about 10,000 Marines and naval personnel landed and took possession of the base and neighboring fortress islands. On September 1, the Marines moved across the bay to occupy the Japanese naval base of Tateyama.

The formal surrender of the Japanese Imperial Government, the Japanese Imperial General Headquarters, and all Japanese and Japanese-controlled armed forces wherever located, was signed on board the battleship *Missouri* in Tokyo Bay on September 2, 1945. General of the Army MacArthur signed as Supreme Commander for the Allied Powers in the Pacific; Fleet Admiral Nimitz signed as representative of the United States.

Five days after the formal surrender, MacArthur entered Tokyo, and his troops raised the Stars and Stripes over the United States Embassy. This was the same flag which had flown in Washington on December 7, 1941, had been hoisted over Rome and Berlin, and been raised on the *Missouri* while the Japanese signed the surrender documents.

Seabees in Japan

On V-J Day, 13 construction battalions and 3 special battalions were awaiting assignment to Japan, where they were to aid naval forces at Hiroshima, Kabayana, Yokosuka, Omura, Nagasaki, Sasebo, and Kure. That very day, 16 officers and 541 men of the 136th Construction Battalion embarked in 12 LSM's at Guam; reported at Iwo Jima on August

21; and arrived at Yokosuka naval base on August
30, on which day they established their camp at the
site of the navigation school within the naval base.
After constructing galley and mess halls, the 136th
was assigned various projects furthering facilities
for the naval forces. They repaired housing, electric and telephone systems and roads at the naval
base; graded fields and remodeled buildings for
the fleet recreation area; repaired housing and
surfaced an airstrip at Kisarazu airfield.

Also, on August 30, the 602nd CBMU arrived at
Yokosuka from Guam to maintain runways and
roads at the Marine Corps air base. They also constructed a 2000-man galley, restored barracks and
facilities for personnel, constructed a chapel and
recreation facilities, completed a sawmill, public
works shops, a cold-storage plant, and a chlorination plant for water treatment, and installed hot-
water showers in all barracks.

During the month of September, the 41st Regiment, consisting of the 9th, 28, and 62nd Construction Battalions, together with the 90th and the
28th Special Battalion, joined the 136th at Yoku-
suka. Among the major projects assigned to the
90th Seabees in addition to work at the naval base
was the repair and maintenance of the Kisarazu
naval air station, which included overhauling the
gasoline system and providing housing facilities
for air station personnel and repairing and maintaining the airstrip. They also repaired buildings
and erected quonset huts for housing and messing
facilities for port director activities at both Yokosuka and Tokyo, and loaded gravel from the Atsugi River for use in repairing roads and runways.

In October, the regiment was reformed to include the 38th, the 127th, and the third section of
the 31st Special. The 31st had been divided into
four sections on Saipan. Section 1 embarked September 29; arrived at Kure, Japan, on October 8;
lay at anchorage five days; and then was ordered
to return to Guam. The second section embarked
from Saipan on September 28; reached Sasebo,
Japan, on October 22; was inactivated on November 5, its personnel being transferred to the First
Special Battalion. The third section had sailed
from Saipan September 20; reached Yokosuka on
October 4; and remained to work at the naval base.
The fourth section was given orders to embark for
Ominato, Japan, but these were cancelled.

The Seabees were withdrawn from Yokosuka in
the spring of 1946.

Sasebo on the island of Kyushu, not far from
Nagasaki, was the other big center of Seabee activity in Japan. For some time, the 7th Regiment,
consisting of the 43rd, the 98th, and the 116th Construction Battalions, and the 72nd, and the 31st
the First Special Battalions, were working simultaneously at Sasebo, but by the end of the year the
regiment had been withdrawn. It was followed by
the 72nd and the special battalion, leaving the
31st, which remained until the end of June 1946.

The 98th did considerable work in clearing the
dock area in the Sasebo navy yard, providing space
for roadways and facilitating the unloading of
ships. Clearing the dock area necessitated removal
of large quantities of scrap metal, heavy marine
equipment, and other debris. A Japanese floating
crane and Japanese barges, together with some
Japanese laborers, were used on the task.

The 116th Battalion had left Hilo on August 23.
The movement had been planned as a combat
operation and loaded as such. As a result, only
equipment for shore-party work was brought forward, plus an outfit for a bridgebuilding unit. As
soon as the shore-party phase of the operation was
concluded, the battalion was assigned the duty of
renovating a barracks to accommodate the main
elements of the 5th Marine Division. Lack of all
classes of tools and difficulty in adapting Japanese
installations to American living habits made progress slow. Operations were also hampered by bad
weather, which included a typhoon.

In addition to repairing and maintaining the Marine camp at Ainoura, the 116th Seabees rehabilitated and constructed 5 miles of road from Ainoura
to Sasebo, together with an alternate 5-mile stretch,
operated a quarry as an adjunct to the road work,
using Japanese labor, and eventually opened a second quarry. They also constructed a quonset-hut
camp to house 400 Seabees at the aircraft factory
at Sasebo.

The 72nd Seabees, which left Guam on October
16, reached Sasebo a week later. Their mission
was to construct a 2000-man camp, two 200-bed
hospitals, and recreational facilities. The Sasebo
area was found to be almost completely lacking
in acceptable material as source of concrete aggregate or road surfacing, but a sand-gravel deposit
was finally found in a tidal basin about 20 miles
away and was developed.

Upon its arrival in Japan, the 31st Battalion had
been sent to Omura, about 28 miles from Sasebo.
As there were no adequate railroads or suitable

roads for transportation of large numbers of troops between the two activities, it was necessary to unload all personnel into LCT's for transport to Omura. Sasebo Harbor and Omura Wan are connected by a narrow channel, with strong currents which necessitated ship operations being confined to daylight hours. with passage through the channel only at slack water, a condition which delayed unloading operations.

TEMPORARY QUARTERS OF THE 72ND SEABEES AT SASEBO, JAPAN

At Omura the battalion was given a former Japanese hangar for temporary barracks, messing, and work space, and assigned a former Japanese garrison force compound for permanent barracks and work space. The latter was satisfactory except for general cleanliness and sanitation. The area presented every evidence of deliberate attempt to inconvenience occupation troops; all the latrines were in disreputable condition, lighting fixtures had been torn out, and the general litter and debris throughout the approximately 1,440,000 square feet of area was so extensive that a 40-man cleaning crew worked for more than a fortnight removing debris and trash.

Seabees in China

After the surrender of Japan, the Third Marine Amphibious Corps was detailed to assist the Chinese government in the repatriation of Japanese troops. To assist the Marines, four construction battalions and two special battalions were sent to China.

The Marine unit set up headquarters at Tientsin, and in November 1945, part of the 33rd Seabee Regiment, consisting of the 83rd, the 96th, and the 122nd battalions and the 32nd Special Battalion, landed at Tsingtao and Tangku. Part of the 42nd Battalion and a detachment from the 33rd Special Battalion landed at Shanghai with Naval Advance Base Unit No. 13.

The 96th Seabees, after building quarters for themselves and repairing the 10 miles of road from the city of Tsingtao to a captured Japanese-built airfield, were assigned in early January the task of rebuilding and expanding the airfield for use by the Marines, Navy, and Chinese air forces. The two 3800-foot strips were repaired and extended to 5000 and 6000 feet, respectively, with 900-foot approach strips.

The project included the construction of a complete drainage system for the field. Extension of the runways required the removal of rock hills and the resulting excavation of 350,000 cubic yards of weathered granite.

Section B of the 122nd Battalion assisted the 96th in the trucking operations at Tsingtao, and Section B of the 32nd Special Battalion handled the stevedoring activities. Section A of the 122nd was assigned to Peiping, and Section A of the 32nd to Tangku, where the 83rd Seabees had been sent to construct harbor facilities.

By the end of January 1946, all personnel not eligible for release from the service had been transferred to the 96th and Section B of the 32nd Special Battalion, which remained in China. The other units were inactivated. The 32nd (Section B) was inactivated May 1, 1946, and the 96th was scheduled to be inactivated on July 1, 1946, when a Seabee detachment was to assume maintenance of the Tsingtao airfield.

Seabees in the Surrendered Islands

Mille Atoll in the Marshall Islands was the first of the many Japanese island possessions to capitulate. On August 22, just one week after the cease-firing order had been given, the Japanese island commander surrendered aboard the destroyer escort *Levy*. Nine days later, on the last day of August 1945, Rear Admiral Whiting, aboard the destroyer *Bagley*, received the surrender of Marcus Island.

In November, 93 men of the 117th Construction

Battalion and 36 men from the 616 CBMU were sent from Saipan to Marcus, to repair and construct facilities for the Navy.

The surrender which affected the largest number of islands was that which took place at Truk, when the commander of the 31st Imperial Japanese Army surrendered not only that closely guarded bastion, but also Wake, Rota, the Palaus, Maleolap, Enderby, Ponape, Wotje, Kusaie, Jaluit, Mortlock, Moreyon, and Pagan. At the same time the commander of the Imperial Japanese 4th Fleet surrendered the Japanese Navy-controlled bases of Namorik, Nauru, and Ocean. It was estimated that a total of 130,000 Japanese military personnel, in addition to a large number of civilians, were involved in the Truk surrender—on Truk itself, a total of 49,000 military and 9,000 civilians; on Babelthaup, 27,000 military and 12,000 civilians; on Ponape, 8,900. Additional large groups were surrendered on Rota and Yap.

At Truk Atoll, the 29th Construction Battalion took over construction details at the end of November, having left Guiuan in Samar on November 21 and arrived at Moen eight days later. At Moen, they built an airstrip, ramps for LST's, and all the buildings and roads necessary to maintain such activities. Part of the battalion moved to the island of Truk to carry on construction and repair work. Late in the spring of 1946, the 29th was relieved by CBD 1158.

One company of the 48th Construction Battalion was sent to Rota after the surrender of that island.

The 85th Seabees moved from Espiritu Santo to Wake in a convoy of four ships, the first arriving September 29; the last, October 12. After they had unloaded all their equipment and hauled it to stowage points, the 85th handled cargo for five other ships. They cleared and graded camp sites, erected camps and messing facilities, repaired a fuel-oil pier, built roads, maintained air strips, installed water-distillation units, and constructed buildings for both Army and Navy. By June 1, 1946, the 85th had left Wake, and CBD 1154 was operating there.

Early in 1946 one other island began to appear on lists of Seabee stations. That was Bikini, where the 53rd Construction Battalion was sent to help in preparations for the atomic bomb tests.

Work at all these areas was particularly difficult during this period because of the rapid demobilization. Not only were the battalions losing men; they were also losing their experienced workers at a disproportionate rate. In the nine-months period from August 1, 1945, to May 1, 1946, the number of construction battalions overseas dropped from 122 to 15; special battalions, from 32 to zero; CBMU's, from 106 to 12; CBD's, from 64 to 14. In the same period, the total number of officers overseas dropped from 6033 to 431; enlisted men, from 194,334 to 13,032.

By May 1946, the Seabees had entirely withdrawn from the South Pacific and the Southwest Pacific except Manus and Milne Bay. There were still regiments at Okinawa, Samar, the Marianas, and in the Hawaiian islands, and single groups, for the most part detachments or maintenance units, in various places in the Philippines, at Iwo, Eniwetok, Kwajalein, Peleliu, and Alaska in the Pacific. Maintenance units were still on duty in Iceland, Argentia, Trinidad, Bermuda, St. Thomas, and Panama in the Atlantic area, and a single detachment still remained at Exeter.

APPENDIX

Seabee Record

NAVAL CONSTRUCTION BRIGADES

No.	Date Comm.	Date Inact.	Places Served Overseas
1	8 May 43	May 44	Adak, Dutch Harbor
2	Sept. 43	19 Nov. 45	Samar, Pearl Harbor
3	Jan. 44	7 Dec. 45	Manila, Brisbane, Hollandia, Leyte
4	April 44	17 Feb. 45	Noumea, Manus
5	May 44	active	Guam
6	June 44	25 Oct. 45	Tinian
7	1 Aug. 44	Sept. 46	Hawaii, Samar, Manila
8	11 Aug. 44	15 Dec. 45	Okinawa, Hawaii
9	24 Oct. 44	5 Nov. 45	Iwo Jima
10	19 Dec. 44	27 Dec. 45	Okinawa, Noumea
11	19 Dec. 44	Jan. 46	Okinawa, Noumea
12	May 45	30 Nov. 45	Okinawa

NAVAL CONSTRUCTION REGIMENTS

No.	Date Comm.	Date Inact.	Places Served Overseas
1	28 Oct. 42	1 Sept. 43	Dutch Harbor
2	Jan. 43	1 Mar. 45	Noumea, Manus, Los Negros
3	Feb. 43	20 Dec. 45	Manila, Pearl Harbor, Samar
4	15 Jan. 43	15 Sept. 43	Kodiak
5	Jan. 43	Feb. 45	Noumea, Espiritu Santo, Manus
6	15 Feb. 43	5 Nov. 44	Adak
7	May 43	5 Dec. 45	Sasebo, Pearl Harbor, Maui
8	May 43	10 Sept. 45	Iwo Jima, Pearl Harbor
9	1 July 43	29 Oct. 44	Attu
10	July 43	3 Jan. 44	Argentia
11	11 Sept. 43	1 June 44	Trinidad
12	Nov. 43	18 Oct. 45	Samar, Brisbane, Milne Bay, Leyte
13	Oct. 43	8 Nov. 44	Devon, England
14	Oct. 43	7 Dec. 43	ComNavEu
15	Oct. 43	June 44	New Georgia
16	Nov. 43	13 June 44	Torokina, Bougainville
17	Nov. 43	26 Nov. 45	Okinawa, Noumea, Manus, Los Negros
18	20 Dec. 43	Feb. 45	Noumea, Guadalcanal, Emirau
19	20 Dec. 43	20 Nov. 45	Tacloban, Brisbane, Mios Woendi, Milne Bay
20	Feb. 44	9 Aug. 46	Oahu
21	15 Jan. 44	13 June 44	Treasury
22	15 Jan. 44	13 June 44	Green Island, Guadalcanal
23	Feb. 44	1 Feb. 45	Russells
24	Feb. 44	7 Dec. 45	Subic Bay, Hollandia
25	Mar. 44	Dec. 45	Le Havre, Plymouth, Cherbourg
26	30 May 44	20 Sept. 45	Guam
27	May 44	15 Sept. 45	Guam
28	May 44	15 Nov. 45	Guam
29	May 44	1 Oct. 45	Tinian
30	June 44	1 Oct. 45	Tinian
31	1 Aug. 44	17 Oct. 45	Samar, Pearl Harbor

CONSTRUCTION REGIMENTS *Continued*

No.	Date Comm.	Date Inact.	Places Served Overseas
32	1 Aug. 44	2 Dec. 45	Samar, Pearl Harbor
33	1 Aug. 44	1 May 45	Pearl Harbor, Samar, Tsingtao
34	1 Aug. 44	May 46	Maui, Samar
35	1 Aug. 44	10 May 46	Guam, Pearl Harbor, Okinawa
36	1 Aug. 44	24 Oct. 45	Guam, Pearl Harbor
37	1 Aug. 44	10 Dec. 45	Okinawa, Pearl Harbor
38	12 Aug. 44	1 Feb. 45	Peleliu, Ulithi
39	7 Sept. 44	10 Dec. 45	Okinawa, Saipan
40	7 Sept. 44	15 Nov. 45	Guam
41	24 Oct. 44	31 Jan. 46	Honshu, Iwo Jima
42	19 Dec. 44	10 Sept. 45	Okinawa, Saipan
43	19 Dec. 44	Dec. 45	Okinawa, Noumea
44	19 Dec. 44	26 Nov. 45	Okinawa, Guadalcana
45	19 Dec. 44	23 Nov. 45	Okinawa
46	19 Dec. 44	29 Nov. 45	Okinawa
47	19 Dec. 44	8 Jan. 46	Okinawa, Russells
48	19 Dec. 44	31 May 46	Okinawa
49	Mar. 45	1 Oct. 45	Tinian
50	8 July 45	27 Dec. 45	Samar, Mactan
51	6 July 45	20 Dec. 45	Cebu
52	6 Sept. 45	15 Dec. 45	Guam
53	Sept. 45	23 Nov. 45	Okinawa
54	Sept. 45	30 Nov. 45	Okinawa

NAVAL CONSTRUCTION BATTALIONS

Bobcats	Jan. 42	April 45	Borabora, Tutuila, Maui, Kwajalein, Eneiwetok
1	Mar. 42	June 44	Tongatabu, Efate
2	April 42	April 44	Upolu, Funafuti, Tutuila, Wallis Island
3	May 42	July 44	Noumea, Fijis, Borabora, Funafuti
4	May 42	Dec. 45	Dutch Harbor, Adak, Amchitka, Pearl Harbor, Guam, Okinawa, Eider Point, Unalaska
5	May 42	Dec. 45	Pearl Harbor, Midway, Palmyra, Johnston Island, French Frigate Shoals, Canton Island, Samar, Balikpapan, Kauai, Calicoan
6	June 42	Nov. 45	Espiritu Santo, Guadalcanal, Tulagi, Auckland, Noumea, Okinawa
7	June 42	Sept. 45	Espiritu Santo, Pearl Harbor, Saipan, Okinawa
8	May 42	Jan. 46	Dutch Harbor, Cold Bay, Adak, Pearl Harbor, Iwo Jima, Hiroshima
9	June 42	Dec. 45	Iceland, Pearl Harbor, Tinian
10	Nov. 45	July 46	Pearl Habor, Guam, Leyte-Samar, Oahu, Johnston, Canton
11	July 42	Dec. 45	Tutuila, Noumea, Ile Nou, Auckland, Banika, Los Negros, Subic Bay
12	Aug. 42	July 44	Kodiak, Dutch Harbor, Attu, Adak
13	July 42	Dec. 45	Dutch Harbor, Akutan, Pearl Harbor, Okinawa, Tinian
14	July 42	April 46	Noumea, Guadalcanal, Espiritu Santo, Pearl Harbor, Saipan, Okinawa
15	July 42	Nov. 45	Espiritu Santo, Auckland, Green Island, Banika, Pavuvu Island, Okinawa
16	Aug. 42	May 45	Pearl Harbor, Funafuti, Nukefetau, Nanomea, Tarawa, Apamama, Makin
17	Aug. 42	Nov. 45	Argentia, Saipan, Okinawa
18	July 42	June 45	Noumea, Guadalcanal, Wellington, Tarawa, Hilo, Saipan, Tinian
19	Sept. 42	Dec. 45	Noumea, Australia, Cape Gloucester, Goodenough, Oro Bay, Russells, Okinawa
20	Aug. 42	Nov. 45	Noumea, Woodlark Island, Olena, Viru Harbor, Kiriwina, Russells, Saipan, Okinawa
21	Aug. 42	Nov. 45	Dutch Harbor, Atka, Adak, Ogliuga, Pearl Harbor, Saipan, Ryukyus
22	Sept. 42	June 44	Sitka, Attu
23	Sept. 42	May 46	Kodiak, Cold Bay, Dutch Harbor, Atka, Adak, Attu, Pearl Harbor, Guam
24	Sept. 42	Nov. 45	Noumea, Guadalcanal, New Hebrides, Rendova, Kokurana, Baribuna, Munda, Auckland, Banika, Okinawa
25	Sept. 42	Nov. 45	Auckland, Pago Pago, Tutuila, Guadalcanal, Bougainville, Guam
26	Sept. 42	July 45	Noumea, Guadalcanal, Tulagi, Kodiak, Dutch Harbor
27	Oct. 42	Dec. 45	Tulagi, Guadalcanal, Auckland, Emirau, Okinawa
28	Oct. 42	April 46	Iceland, Hvalfjordur, Scotland, Netley, Fowey, Plymouth, Falmouth, Teignmouth, Cherbourg, Le Havre, Calais, Paris, Okinawa
29	Oct. 42	May 46	Rosneath, Londonderry, Exeter, Plymouth, Falmouth, Teignmouth, Cherbourg, Le Havre, Calais, Paris, Salcombe, Dartmouth, Heathfield, St. Mawes, Penarth, Subic Bay, Okinawa
30	Oct. 42	Dec. 45	Trinidad, Dutch Guiana, Curacao, British Guiana, St. Lucia, Pearl Harbor, Samar
31	Oct. 42	June 46	Bermuda, Hilo, Iwo Jima, Sasebo
32	Dec. 42	May 44	Dutch Harbor, Adak
33	Dec. 42	May 45	Noumea, Guadalcanal, Banika, Auckland, Green Island, Peleliu
34	Oct. 42	Dec. 45	Espiritu Santo, Halavo, Guadalcanal, Russells, Tulagi, Okinawa
35	Oct. 42	Apr. 46	Noumea, Espiritu Santo, Russells, Auckland, Lorengau, Manila, Manus
36	Nov. 42	Feb. 46	Espiritu Santo, Banika, Bougainville, Noumea, Saipan, Okinawa

NAVAL CONSTRUCTION BATTALIONS *Continued*

No.	Date Comm.	Date Inact.	Places Served Overseas
37	Oct. 42	Dec. 45	Noumea, Guadalcanal, Ondonga, Green Island, Okinawa
38	Nov. 42	Feb. 46	Kodiak, Kiska, Adak, Pearl Harbor, Tinian
39	Nov. 42	Sept. 45	Maui, Saipan
40	Nov. 42	Nov. 45	Espiritu Santo, Finschhafen, Los Negros, Noumea, Saipan, Okinawa
41	Nov. 42	Sept. 45	Kodiak, Guam
42	Oct. 42	Feb. 46	Dutch Harbor, Adak, Amchitka, Pearl Harbor, Leyte Gulf, Samar
43	Nov. 42	Dec. 45	Kodiak, Sand Point, Oahu, Maui, Saipan, Nagasaki, Japan
44	Dec. 42	April 45	Espiritu Santo, Manus, Noumea, Okinawa
45	Dec. 42	June 44	Kodiak, Sitka, Adak, Tanaga
46	Nov. 42	Mar. 45	Guadalcanal, Finschhafen, Los Negros, Milne Bay
47	Dec. 42	June 45	Russells, Noumea, Guadalcanal, Segi, Enogai, Munda, Ondonga, Espiritu Santo
48	Nov. 42	Oct. 45	Pearl Harbor, Maui, Oahu, Guam, Rota
49	Dec. 42	July 45	Bermuda, Guam
50	Nov. 42	Oct. 43	Pearl Harbor, Midway, Oahu, Angaur, Palau, Tinian
51	Dec. 42	Dec. 45	Dutch Harbor, Ulithi, Saipan
52	Dec. 42	Sept. 45	Dutch Harbor, Sand Bay, Adak, Pearl Harbor, Guam
53	Dec. 42	Aug. 46	Noumea, Guadalcanal, Vella Lavella, Bougainville, Guam, Bikini
54	Dec. 42	May 46	Algeria, Arzew, Oran, Mostaganem, Cherchel, Port-aux-Poules, Tenes, Beni-Saf, Nemours, Bizerte, Ferryville, Tunis, Karouba, LaGoulette, LaPerchie, Guiuan, Tubabao, Mactan Island
55	Dec. 42	April 45	Merauke, Kanakopa, Port Moresby, Palm Island, Brisbane, Hollandia, Mios Woendi
56	Dec. 42	April 46	Pearl Harbor, Guam, Oahu
57	Dec. 42	May 45	Espiritu Santo, Manus
58	April 43	May 46	Vunda Point, Guadalcanal, Vella Lavella, Auckland, Banika, Los Negros, Okinawa
59	Dec. 42	Sept. 45	Hilo, Kamuela, Pearl Harbor, Guam
60	Dec. 42	April 45	Brisbane, Townsville, Woodlark, Finschhafen, Owi, Neomfoer, Amsterdam Is., Leyte
61	Jan. 43	July 46	Espiritu Santo, Guadalcanal, Auckland, Emirau, Russells, Philippines, Leyte, Guiuan
62	Dec. 42	Sept. 45	Oahu, Maui, Iwo Jima
63	Jan. 43	July 45	Guadalcanal, Auckland, Emirau, Manus, Manila
64	Jan. 43	Mar. 46	Argentia, Pearl Harbor, Guiuan, Samar
65	Mar. 43	Dec. 43	Freetown, Sierra Leone
66	Jan. 43	Sept. 45	Adak, Sand Bay, Attu, Okinawa
67	May 43	Jan. 46	Pearl Harbor, Tinian, Eniwetok
68	Jan. 43	Nov. 45	Adak, Attu, Okinawa
69	Feb. 43	Sept. 45	Argentia, Plymouth, Falmouth, Dunkeswell, Omaha Beach, Southampton, Exeter, Rosneath, Belgium, Germany (Bremen. Frankfurt-am-Main)
70	Jan. 43	Oct. 45	Oran, Arzew, Bizerte, Nemours, Beni-Saf, Ainel-Turck, Mostaganem, Tenes, Port-aux-Poules, Salerno, Pearl Harbor, Guam, Oahu, Iwo Jima, Okinawa, Ie Shima
71	April 43	Dec. 45	Guadalcanal, Bougainville, Manus, Pityilu, Los Negros, Okinawa
72	Jan. 43	Dec. 45	Pearl Harbor, Barbers Pt., Iroquois Pt., Ewa, Guam, Sasebo, Kyushu, Japan
73	Mar. 43	July 45	Noumea, Guadalcanal, Roviana, Saseville, Munda, Banika, Pavuvu, Peleliu
74	April 43	Dec. 45	Pearl Harbor, Tarawa, Kwajalein, Okinawa
75	Mar. 43	Feb. 46	Noumea, Guadalcanal, Bougainville, Banika, Milne Bay, Leyte, Samar, Calicoan Island
76	Jan. 43	Nov. 45	Pearl Harbor, Palmyra, Oahu, Guam
77	Dec. 42	Oct. 45	Guadalcanal, Vella Lavella, Bougainville, Emirau, Brisbane, Manila
78	Feb. 43	Dec. 45	Noumea, Milne Bay, Finschhafen, Los Negros, Manus, Okinawa
79	Feb. 43	Nov. 45	Kodiak, Cold Bay, Amchitka, Adak, Saipan, Okinawa
80	Jan. 43	Sept. 45	Trinidad, Subic Bay
81	Feb. 43	Oct. 45	Rosneath, Milford Haven, Fowey, Penarth, Bicester, Falmouth, Salcombe, St. Mawes, Dartmouth, Newton Abbott, Plymouth, London, Utah Beach, Paris, Teignmouth, Pearl Harbor, Eniwetok, Ulithi, Okinawa, Hagushi, Kuba Saki, Nakagusuku, Ie Shima
82	Jan. 43	Nov. 45	Guadalcanal, Vella Lavella, Munda, Ondonga, Sterling, Nepoui, Russells, Eniwetok, Ulithi, Okinawa
83	Feb. 43	Dec. 45	Trinidad, Pearl Harbor, Leyte-Samar, Tangku
84	Feb. 43	Sept. 45	Brisbane, Milne Bay, Darwin, Thursday Island, Sydney, Townsville, Biak, Morotai, Puerto Princesa
85	Jan. 43	May 45	Dutch Harbor, Attu, Espiritu Santo
86	Feb. 43	Feb. 46	Adak, Great Sitkin, Amchitka, Tanaga, Andrews Lagoon, Okinawa
87	Feb. 43	Dec. 45	Banika, Treasury Islands, Noumea, Saipan, Okinawa
88	Feb. 43	Nov. 45	Mt. Dore, Guadalcanal, Treasury, Emirau, Ulithi, Leyte-Samar, Jinamoc, Guiuan
89	Feb. 43	July 44	Camp Parks, Calif.
90	July 43	April 46	Pearl Harbor, Angaur, Peleliu, Iwo Jima
91	Feb. 43	Dec. 45	Milne Bay, Ladava, Hilimoi, Swinger Bay, Gilli Gilli, Madang, Palm Island, Finschhafen, Brisbane, Manicani Island
92	May 43	Oct. 45	Kauai, Oahu, Saipan, Tinian
93	May 43	May 46	Russells, Green Island, Leyte, San Antonio, Samar
94	May 43	Nov. 45	Pearl Harbor, Guam, Marianas, Oahu
95	July 43	Sept. 45	Pearl Harbor, Apamama, Roi-Namur, Iwo Jima

NAVAL CONSTRUCTION BATTALIONS *Continued*

No.	Date Comm.	Date Inact.	Places Served Overseas
96	June 43	May 46	Terceira, Azores, Manicani Island, Samar
97	June 43	Sept. 45	London, Dunkeswell, Exeter, Heathfield, Lough Neagh, Devon, Southampton, Portland-Weymouth, Fowey, Falmouth, Milford-Haven, Rosneath.
98	June 43	Dec. 45	Oahu, Waiawa Gulch, Tarawa, Cora, Helen Islands, Pearl Harbor, Iroquois Pt., Maui, Oahu, Sasebo, Japan
99	June 43	Dec. 45	Oahu, Waiawa Gulch, Kauai, Johnston, French Frigate Shoals, Canton Island, Angaur, Aiea, Moanalua, Samar
100	July 43	Dec. 45	Pearl Harbor, Majuro Atoll, Angaur, Samar
101	July 43	Nov. 45	Pearl Harbor, Point Mugu, Moanalua Ridge, Saipan, Okinawa
102	July 43	Dec. 45	Finschhafen, Hollandia, Subic Bay, Luzon, San Fernando
103	Oct. 43	active	Pearl Harbor, Guam
104	Aug. 43	Dec. 45	Milne Bay, Los Negros, Australia, Sual Port, Leyte-Samar, Manus, Tacloban
105	Aug. 43	Nov. 45	Milne Bay, Hilimoi, Gamadodo, Swinger Bay, Leyte-Samar, Talosa, Guiuan, Balingiga, Osmena, Tacloban
106	Oct. 43	Sept. 45	Pearl Harbor, Eniwetok, Ulithi, Iwo Jima, Ie Shima.
107	July 43	Oct. 45	Kwajalein, Ebeye, Bigej, Tinian.
108	Aug. 43	Dec. 44	Rosneath, Plymouth, Netley, Normandy, Selsy, Richborough, London, Southampton, Tilbury
109	July 43	active	Oahu, Kwajalein, Roi-Namur, Guam.
110	July 43	Oct. 45	Pearl Harbor, Oahu, Eniwetok, Tinian
111	Sept. 43	Nov. 45	Plymouth, Falmouth, Dartmouth, Swansea, Samar-Leyte, Mindanao
112	Sept. 43	Nov. 45	Pearl Harbor, Tinian, Okinawa
113	July 43	Dec. 45	Hollandia, Mios Woendi, Amsterdam Island, Soemsoem Island, Samar-Leyte, Mindoro, Finschhafen
114	Aug. 43	June 45	Rosneath, Cherbourg, Nantes, Pontivy, Attu
115	Sept. 43	Dec. 45	Milne Bay, Brisbane, Luzon, Subic Bay
116	Sept. 43	Dec. 45	Pearl Harbor, Oahu, Tarawa, Japan
117	Sept. 43	Nov. 45	Oahu, Saipan
118	Aug. 43	Dec. 45	Gamadodo, Milne Bay, Mindanao, Zamboanga, Subic Bay
119	Aug. 43	Dec. 45	Milne Bay, Hollandia, Aitape, Wotje, Manila
120	Feb. 43	Aug. 44	Casablanca, Oran, Arzew, Pt. Lyautey, Algiers, Palermo, Sicily, Termini, Salerno, Naples, Ajaccio, Corsica
121	May 43	Sept. 47	Roi-Namur, Maui, Saipan, Tinian, Kwajalein
122	Oct. 43	Dec. 45	Milne Bay, Gamododo, Hollandia, Samar
123	Aug. 43	Oct. 45	Pearl Harbor, Midway, Samar-Leyte
124	Oct. 44	active	Adak
125	Aug. 43	May 45	Hawaii, Okinawa, Nakagusuku Bay
126	Sept. 43	Dec. 45	Eniwetok, Japan, Parry, Hawthorne Islands, Pearl Harbor, Okinawa
127	Oct. 43	Nov. 45	Pearl Harbor, Maui, Leyte-Samar
128	Sept. 43	Nov. 45	Pearl Harbor, Guam, Japan, China, Korea
129	Oct. 43	May 46	Oahu, Leyte-Samar
130	Sept. 43	Dec. 45	Pearl Harbor, Saipan, Okinawa
131	Sept. 43	Jan. 44	Camp Parks, Calif.
132	Oct. 43	Oct. 43	Camp Peary, Va.
133	Sept. 43	Dec. 45	Pearl Harbor, Iwo Jima
134	June 45	April 46	Guam
135	Oct. 43	Dec. 45	Pearl Harbor, Tinian, Okinawa
136	Sept. 43	Nov. 45	Pearl Harbor, Guam, Yokosuka, Japan
137	Mar. 45	Nov. 45	Okinawa
138	Feb. 44	June 45	Attu, Adak
139	Feb. 44	Dec. 45	Okinawa
140	Nov. 43	May 46	Manus, Ponam Island, Pityilu Island
141	Oct. 43	Jan. 46	Pearl Harbor, Kwajalein
142	June 44	Nov. 45	Pearl Harbor, Leyte
143	Dec. 44	June 46	Samar
144	Jan. 45	Jan. 46	Guam
145	Nov. 44	Nov. 45	Russells, Okinawa
146	Feb. 44	Mar. 46	Iceland, Plymouth, Omaha Beach, Utah Beach, Cherbourg, Okinawa
147	April 45	Dec. 45	Okinawa
148	May 45	Nov. 45	Okinawa
301	April 44	April 46	Pearl Harbor, Midway, Roi-Namur, Guam, Kwajalein, Saipan, Peleliu, Tinian, Iwo Jima, Okinawa
302	Aug. 44	Dec. 45	Pearl Harbor, Russells, Peleliu, Angaur, Leyte, Luzon, Oahu, Majuro, Kwajalein, Guam, Okinawa

NAVAL CONSTRUCTION BATTALION MAINTENANCE UNITS

No.	Date Comm.	Date Inact.	Places Served Overseas
501	Mar. 43	July 45	Auckland, Russells
502	Mar. 43	Nov. 45	Wellington, Vella Lavella, Manus, Guam, Emirau
503	Mar. 43	May 46	Fiji Islands, Russells, Peleliu
504	Mar. 43	Sept. 45	Wallis Island, Upolu, Tutuila, Noumea, Guam, Emirau
505	April 43	Nov. 45	Upolu, Tulagi, Saipan
506	Mar. 43	Dec. 45	Tutuila, Funafuti, Tongatabu, Samoa, Noumea, Guam
507	April 43	Aug. 46	St. Thomas, Roosevelt Roads.
508	April 43	Nov. 43	Dutch Harbor
509	May 43	Dec. 45	Amchitka, Adak, Tonaga, Kiska, Okinawa, Ie Shima (June 45)
510	May 43	Dec. 45	Atka, Cold Bay, Dutch Harbor, Otter Point, Adak. Sand Bay, Andrew Lagoon, Saipan
511	May 43	April 46	Efate, Tongatabu, Guam
512	June 43	Sept. 45	Sitka, Leyte, Samar, Guiuan
513	July 43	Nov. 45	Oran, Okinawa
514	July 43	active	Iceland
515		Sept. 45	Guadalcanal, Kwajalein, Eniwetok, Guam
516		May 44	San Juan, Roosevelt Roads.
517	Aug. 43	Oct. 45	Funafuti, Leyte-Samar, Ulithi. Nanomea
518	Sept. 43	Aug. 45	Guadalcanal
519		Jan. 45	Borabora, Noumea
520	Sept. 43	Aug. 45	Guadalcanal
521	Aug. 43	Jan. 46	Tulagi, Okinawa
522	Sept. 43	Oct. 45	Oahu
523	Sept. 43	Jan. 46	Oahu, Pearl Harbor, Iroquois Point
524	Sept. 43	Nov. 44	Midway
525	Oct. 43	June 46	Argentia
526	Nov. 43	active	Argentia
527	Oct. 43	Nov. 45	Palmyra
528	Sept. 43	Feb. 46	Milne Bay
529	Sept. 43	Feb. 46	Milne Bay
530	Sept. 43	Nov. 45	Oahu, Ewa, Midway
531	Sept. 43	July 45	Midway, Oahu
532	Sept. 43	Sept. 45	Guadalcanal, Russells, Angaur, Guam
533	Dec. 43	Feb. 46	Guadalcanal
534	Sept. 43	Jan. 46	Espiritu Santo, Noumea, Manus, Treasury, Okinawa
535	Oct. 43	July 45	Espiritu Santo
536	Sept. 43	Sept. 45	Noumea
537	Sept. 43	Sept. 45	Noumea
538	Sept. 43	Sept. 45	Noumea, Espiritu Santo
539	Sept. 43	Feb. 46	Espiritu Santo, Efate, Okinawa
540		Apr. 47	Bermuda
541	Oct. 43	Mar. 46	Espiritu Santo, Okinawa
542	Oct. 43	Jan. 46	Espiritu Santo, Okinawa
543	Oct. 43	Oct. 45	Finschhafen, Subic Bay
544	Oct. 43	Nov. 45	Brisbane, Leyte-Samar
545	Nov. 43	Oct. 45	Finschhafen, Milne Bay, Hollandia, Saipan
546	Nov. 43	Aug. 46	Cairns, Port Moresby, Milne Bay, Hollandia, Palawan, Samar Island, Subic Bay, Puerto Princesa.
547		Feb. 44	Attu
548		Oct. 45	Milne Bay, Gamadodo, Hollandia, Manila
549	Sept. 43	Oct. 45	Tarawa, Kwajalein
550	Nov. 43	Sept. 45	Efate, Noumea, Banika, Russells
551	Oct. 43	Dec. 43	Bermuda
552	Oct. 43	Feb. 46	Nukufetau, Green Island, Hollandia. Manus
553	Oct. 43	Sept. 45	Nanomea, Leyte-Samar
554		Nov. 45	Johnston Island
555	Nov. 43	July 46	Salinas, Balboa, Corinto, Taboga, Barranquilla
556		Dec. 44	Attu
557	Nov. 43	Nov. 45	Apamama, Guam
558	Nov. 43	Feb. 46	Finschhafen, Hollandia
559		Apr. 47	Trinidad, Curacao
560		Nov. 45	Trinidad
561	Nov. 43	Oct. 45	Munda, Ondonga, Manus, Hilo
562	Nov. 43	Oct. 45	Hilo
563	Nov. 43	Nov. 45	Kahului, Maui
564	Nov. 43	Nov. 45	Pearl Harbor, Kauai, Honolulu, Keehi Lagoon
565	Nov. 43	Feb. 46	Milne Bay, Morotai Island, Tarakan
566		Nov. 45	Casablanca, Agadir, Pt. Lyautey
567		Aug. 45	Palermo, Sicily, Salerno, Naples, Oran
568		Sept. 45	Munda, Samar
569		Sept. 45	Treasury Island, Samar

NAVAL CONSTRUCTION BATTALION MAINTENANCE UNITS *Continued*

No.	Date Comm.	Date Inact.	Places Served Overseas
570 ●	Nov. 43	Sept. 45	Ft. Pierce, Fla.
571	Nov. 43	Feb. 46	Russells, Peleliu
572	Dec. 43	Nov. 45	Russells
573	Dec. 43	Jan. 46	Russells
574	Nov. 43	Aug. 45	Pearl Harbor, Johnston Island
575	Dec. 43	Dec. 45	Puunene, Maui
576	Dec. 43	Dec. 44	Attu
577	Dec. 43	Jan. 46	Tarawa, Eniwetok, Engebi
578	Nov. 43	April 46	Okinawa
579	Nov. 43	April 46	Nettuno, Anzio, Arzew, Bizerte, Okinawa
580	Nov. 43	Oct. 45	Munda, Russells, Okinawa
581	Jan. 44	Nov. 45	Oahu
582	Jan. 44	Sept. 45	Torokina, Samar
583	Dec. 44	Jan. 44	Iceland, England
584	Jan. 44	Aug. 45	Dunkeswell
585	Feb. 44	Dec. 45	Milne Bay, Manus, Los Negros, Luzon
586	April 44	Sept. 45	Torokina, Tacloban, Samar
587	Jan. 44	Nov. 45	Treasury, Manus, Pityilu, Ponam
588	Feb. 44	July 45	Canton Island
589	Feb. 44	Feb. 44	Davisville, R.I.
590	Feb. 44	Dec. 45	Roi
591	May 44	Dec. 45	Majuro
592	Mar. 44	June 46	Eniwetok
593	Mar. 44	April 46	Pearl Harbor, Tinian, Guam
594	Feb. 44	Nov. 45	Engebi, Guam, Eniwetok
595	Mar. 44	Dec. 45	Pearl Harbor, Saipan
596	April 44	Dec. 45	Oahu, French Frigate Shoals, Kaneohe
597	Mar. 44	April 46	Tinian
598	Feb. 44	Nov. 45	San Pedro Bay, Tacloban, Leyte-Samar
599	April 44	Nov. 45	Pearl Harbor
600	April 44	Nov. 45	Pearl Harbor, Oahu
601	Mar. 44	Dec. 45	Ebeye Island
602	April 44	Jan. 46	Guam, Yokosuka, Japan
603	May 44	Dec. 45	Ulithi
604	June 44	July 44	Camp Parks, Calif.
605	June 44	Nov. 45	Biak, Borneo
606	June 44	Dec. 45	Milne Bay, Luzon, Lingayen
607	June 44	May 46	Tarawa, Kwajalein
608	June 44	Dec. 45	Eniwetok
609	Oct. 44	Nov. 45	Manus, Mindoro
610	Oct. 44	Nov. 45	Manus, Manila
611	June 44	June 45	Arzew, Marseilles, Toulon, Oran
612	June 44	Dec. 45	Manus
613		Feb. 46	Azores
614	Aug. 44	Jan. 46	Saipan
615	Oct. 44	Jan. 46	Okinawa
616	Oct. 44	May 46	Marpi Pt., Saipan, Marcus
617	Aug. 44	Feb. 46	Okinawa
618	Sept. 44	April 46	Okinawa
619	Sept. 44	Mar. 46	Guam
620	Sept. 44	July 46	Iwo Jima
621	Sept. 44	Nov. 45	Manus
622	Nov. 44	Nov. 45	Leyte, Guiuan, Samar, Tacloban
623	Sept. 44	Sept. 45	Leyte-Samar, Guiuan
624	Sept. 44	Dec. 45	Pearl Harbor, Okinawa
625	Oct. 44	Mar. 46	Okinawa
626	Nov. 44	June 45	Bizerte, Arzew, Oran
627	Nov. 44	July 45	Cherbourg
628	Nov. 44	Apr. 46	Le Havre
629	Nov. 44	July 45	Le Havre, Paris
630		May 47	Okinawa
631	Mar. 45	Dec. 45	Okinawa
632	April 45	Nov. 45	Okinawa
633	June 45	Jan. 46	Okinawa
634	July 45	May 46	Kodiak
635	July 45	June 46	Dutch Harbor
636	July 45	Dec. 45	Bremerhaven, Germany, Bremen

NAVAL CONSTRUCTION BATTALIONS
(Special Battalions)

No.	Date Comm.	Date Inact.	Places Served Overseas
1	Jan. 43	April 46	Guadalcanal, Auckland, Noumea, Espiritu Santo, Lingayen, (Sasebo, Kyushu, Japan
2	Jan. 43	July 45	Noumea, Guadalcanal, Guam
3	Jan. 43	May 46	Espiritu Santo, Okinawa
4	Jan. 43	Jan. 46	Noumea, Guadalcanal, Okinawa
5	Jan. 43	Dec. 45	Dutch Harbor, Adak, Sand Bay, Point Barrow, Tacloban, Leyte-Samar
6	April 43	July 45	Nandi, Guadalcanal, Bougainville, Treasury, Ulithi, Oahu, Vella Lavella, Russells
7	May 43	Aug. 45	Dutch Harbor, Adak
8	June 43	Oct. 45	Kodiak, Dutch Harbor
9	April 43	Oct. 45	Samoa, Guadalcanal, Russells, Tulagi, Sasavele, Bougainville, Green Island
10	July 43	Aug. 45	Pearl Harbor, Midway, Oahu
11	July 43	Oct. 45	Noumea, Russells, Guadalcanal, Okinawa
12	Aug. 43	Nov. 45	Russells, Okinawa
13	Aug. 43	Oct. 45	Pearl Harbor, Iroquois, Oahu, Guam
14	Sept. 43	Sept. 45	Pearl Harbor, Funafuti, Oahu, Tarawa, Marshalls, Gilberts, Kwajalein, Eniwetok, Majuro
15	Aug. 43	Dec. 45	Gamadodo, Hollandia, Kwajalein, Roi
16	Oct. 43	Nov. 45	Pearl Harbor, Eniwetok, Guam
17	Sept. 43	Dec. 45	Banika, Emirau, Palau, Peleliu, Ulithi, Guam, Leyte
18	Dec. 43	Dec. 45	Oahu, Pearl Harbor, Ulithi, Tacloban, Peliliu
19	Dec. 43	Dec. 45	Finschalfen, Biak, Hollandia
20	Dec. 43	Dec. 45	Manus
21	Dec. 44	Dec. 45	Manus, Subic Bay
22	Jan. 44	Dec. 45	Manus, Los Negros
23	Feb. 44	Dec. 45	Iwo Jima, Okinawa, Pearl Harbor
24	Feb. 44	Dec. 45	Milne Bay, Subic Bay, Manila
25	Feb. 44	Nov. 45	Milne Bay, Noumea, Gamadodo
26	Mar. 44	Nov. 45	Pearl Harbor, Oahu
27	April 44	Nov. 45	Pearl Harbor, Tinian, Okinawa
28	Mar. 44	Nov. 45	Pearl Harbor, Leyte-Samar, (Honshu, Japan
29	May 44	Nov. 45	Guam
30	July 44	Oct. 45	Rosneath, Plymouth, Leyte-Samar
31	May 44	Feb. 46	Saipan, (Yokosuka, Kuri, Sasebo, Japan
32	June 44	May 45	Samar, Leyte, (Tangku, China)
33	July 44	April 45	Milne Bay, Leyte-Samar
34	Sept. 44	Nov. 45	Pearl Harbor, Guam
35	Oct. 44	Feb. 46	Pearl Harbor
36	Jan. 45	Dec. 45	Okinawa
37	April 45	Jan. 46	Pearl Harbor
38	May 45	Aug. 45	Davisville, Port Hueneme
41	Nov. 44	Oct. 45	Hollandia

NAVAL CONSTRUCTION BATTALION DETACHMENTS

No.	Date Comm.	Date Inact.	Places Served Overseas
1001	Nov. 42	Dec. 43	Scotland, Freetown
1002	Nov. 43	Dec. 43	Scotland, Freetown
1003	Dec. 42	Jan. 43	Noumea
1004	Dec. 42	May 43	Argentia
1005	Mar. 43	Jan. 45	Bizerte, Maddelena, Sardinia, Oran
1006	April 43	Sept. 44	Algeria, Bizerte, Exeter, Plymouth, Falmouth, Dartmouth, Southampton, Normandy, Sicily
1007	May 43	Sept. 45	Espiritu Santo
1008	May 43	June 45	Florida Island, Tulagi
1009	June 43	June 45	Russells
1010	July 43	Dec. 45	Guam, Tulagi
1011	July 43	Feb. 46	Fort Pierce, Fla.
1012	July 42	April 44	Balboa, Nicaragua, Honduras
1013	July 43	Mar. 44	Espiritu Santo
1014	July 43	Mar. 44	Noumea, Espiritu Santo
1015	July 43	April 44	Espiritu Santo
1016	July 43	April 44	Guadalcanal, Noumea
1017	July 43	Feb. 46	Oran, Kodiak, Cold Bay, Attu, Dutch Harbor
1018	Sept. 43	Dec. 44	Attu
1019	Aug. 43	Feb. 45	Noumea, Espiritu Santo, Tulagi
1020	Aug. 43	Oct. 43	Davisville, R. I.
1021		Sept. 43	Port Hueneme Calif.
1022	Aug. 43	Oct. 45	Adak, Samar
1023	Aug. 43	Dec. 44	Milne Bay
1024	Aug. 43	July 45	Milne Bay, Samar-Leyte

NAVAL CONSTRUCTION BATTALION DETACHMENTS *Continued*

No.	Date Comm.	Date Inact.	Places Served Overseas
1025	Sept. 43	May 44	Gulfport, Miss.
1026	Sept. 43	Oct. 43	cancelled
1027	Aug. 43	Nov. 45	Davisville, R. I.
1028	Aug. 43	April 46	Quoddy Village
1029	Oct. 43	Sept. 45	Espiritu Santo
1030	Oct. 43	Feb. 46	Joliet, Ill.
1031	Nov. 43	Feb. 45	Davisville, R. I.
1032	Nov. 43	Feb. 45	Davisville, R. I.
1033	Feb. 44	June 44	Trinidad, Pearl Harbor
1034	Dec. 43	June 46	Majuro, Japtan Island, Eniwetok
1035	Dec. 43	Aug. 44	Pearl Harbor, Saipan, Tinian
1036	Feb. 44	Jan. 45	Pearl Harbor, Tinian
1037	Dec. 43	June 45	USS BOWDITCH
1038	Dec. 43	Aug. 44	Pearl Harbor
1039	Dec. 43	Aug. 44	Pearl Harbor, Marshalls
1040	Jan. 45	July 45	Bizerte, Salerno, Naples, Marseilles, Anzio
1041	Feb. 44	July 44	Pearl Harbor
1042	Mar. 44	Mar. 45	Pearl Harbor
1043	Dec. 43	Aug. 44	Pearl Harbor
1044	Jan. 44	Sept. 45	Majuro, Kwajelein, Eniwetok, Guam, Russells, Manus, Ulithi, Nakagusuku, Okinawa
1045	Jan. 44	Mar. 45	Toulon, Marseilles, Calvi, Ajaccio
1046	Feb. 44	Oct. 45	Espiritu Santo, Guam
1047	Feb. 44	Feb. 45	Davisville, R. I.
1048	Feb. 44	April 44	England
1049	Mar. 44	active	England
1050	Mar. 44	April 45	Manus
1051	Jan. 44	April 45	Manus
1052	Mar. 44	Mar. 46	Adak
1053	June 44	Nov. 45	Los Negros, Samar, Manicani Island, Guam
1054	July 44	Aug. 44	Pearl Harbor, Russells
1055	June 44	Feb. 45	Espiritu Santo, Manus, Guam
1056	June 44	Mar. 46	Guadalcanal, Espiritu Santo, Noumea
1057	Aug. 44	Oct. 44	Davisville, R. I.
1058	June 44	Mar. 46	Point Barrow
1059	April 44	Nov. 45	Guam
1060	July 44	Sept. 45	USS CARINA
1061	July 44	Sept. 45	USS ALLEGAN
1062	July 44	Sept. 45	USS APPONOOSE
1063	Aug. 44	Oct. 45	Manus, Manila, Noumea
1064	Aug. 44	Aug. 45	Guam, Manus
1065	Aug. 44	Oct. 45	Manus, Tinian
1066	Aug. 44	Nov. 45	Manus, Leyte, Samar
1067	Nov. 44	Dec. 45	Samar, Manus
1068	Sept. 44	Aug. 45	Guadalcanal, Kwajalein
1069	Sept. 44	Aug. 45	Saipan
1070	Oct. 44	Aug. 45	Guam
1071	Feb. 45	Aug. 45	Guam
1072	Oct. 44	Aug. 45	Guam
1073	Feb. 45	Aug. 45	Guam
1074		Aug. 45	Oahu
1075	Oct. 44	Sept. 45	Camp Parks, Calif.
1076	Jan. 45	Jan. 46	Dutch Harbor
1077	Jan. 45	Jan. 46	Attu
1078	Dec. 44	Sept. 45	Iwo Jima
1079	Nov. 44	Sept. 45	Oahu, Okinawa
1080	Jan. 45	Jan. 46	Tinian
1081	Jan. 45	Nov. 45	Okinawa
1082	Feb. 45	Dec. 45	Hollandia, Subic Bay
1083	Feb. 45	Mar. 45	Camp Parks
1084	Oct. 44	Nov. 45	Guam
1085	April 45	May 46	Hollandia, Samar
1086	May 45	Jan. 46	Peleliu
1087	July 45	Mar. 46	Okinawa
1088	July 45	Nov. 45	Okinawa, Oahu
1089	July 45	Oct. 45	Tinian
1090	May 45	Aug. 45	Guam
1091	July 45	Jan. 46	Okinawa
1092	July 45	Dec. 45	Milne Bay, Manus, Subic Bay
1093	June 45	Jan. 46	Saipan
1094	July 45	Sept. 45	Camp Parks, Calif.
1095	July 45	Sept. 45	Camp Parks, Calif.

NAVAL CONSTRUCTION BATTALION DETACHMENTS *Continued*

No.	Date Comm.	Date Inact.	Places Served Overseas
1101	July 45	Dec. 45	Manus, Hollandia, Bougainville Bay, Dutch New Guinea, Luzon
1102		Dec. 46	Okinawa
1103		Dec. 46	Okinawa
1104		Dec. 46	Milne Bay
1105		Dec. 46	Milne Bay
1106		Dec. 46	Manus
1107		Dec. 46	Manus
1108		Dec. 46	Oahu
1109		Dec. 46	Oahu
1151		active	Yonabaru
1152		Jan. 47	Subic Bay
1153		June 47	Manus
1154		Jan. 47	Wake
1155		July 46	Midway
1156		May 47	Eniwetok
1157		Jan. 47	Kwajalein
1158		May 47	Truk
1159		Dec. 46	Peleliu
1160		Jan. 47	Johnston Island
1161		active	Attu
1162		Jan. 47	Dutch Harbor
1163		Feb. 47	Tsingtao
3001	Nov. 43	Jan. 44	Camp Perry

NAVAL PONTOON ASSEMBLY DETACHMENTS

No.	Date Comm.	Date Inact.	Places Served Overseas
1	Dec. 42	Oct. 45	Noumea, Manus, Samar
2	Dec. 43	Nov. 45	Russell Islands, Guam
3	Jan. 44	Aug. 45	Milne Bay, Leyte-Samar
4	Oct. 44	Sept. 45	Hollandia, Leyte-Samar
5	Dec. 44	Jan. 46	Guam

INDEX

INDEX

    photographs, 185, 187
Attu Sector, development, 184–187
Auckland, New Zealand, 195, 221
    base development, 236 240
    Harbor Board, 238, 239
    map, (facing) 194
    roll-up, 240
Australia, 201, 236, 241, 277
    Allied Works Council, 280, 283
    base development, 280 286
    Board to determine base-development requirements, 277
    Government, 221, 283, 284
    maps, (facing) 194, 242
    Royal Australian Air Forces, 222, 284, 296
    Royal Australian Navy, 311, 312
    supply line, iii, 161, 191–195, 196
Australians
    augment U. S. facilities, 279
    Borneo, 396
    Efate, 202
    New Caledonia, 195, 221, 227
    road surfacing, 281
automotive construction equipment overhaul and repair depots, *see* storage, depots
automotive and construction equipment parts depots, *see* storage, depots
Avianca, *see* Aerovias Nationales de Colombia
aviation facilities
    air bases
        Admiralty Islands, 279, 295
        Antigua, 3, 22, 34–35
        Apamama, 317, 318
        Argentia, 22
        Australia, 277
        Azores, 91
        Bahamas, 3
        Bermuda, 22
        Bougainville, 268 272
        Brazil, 43, 44, 45, 46
        British Guiana, 3, 22, 35
        Colombia, 42
        definition, 22
        Dutch Harbor, 163
        Efate, 192, 193
        Eniwetok, 325
        Espiritu Santo, 196
        Funafuti, 232, 234
        Great Exuma, 22
        Greenslade Board recommendations, 3
        Guadalcanal, 241, 242, 243, 244, 246, 247
        Guam, 343
        Iceland, 56
        Iwo Jima, 370
        Jamaica, 3, 22
        Kiriwina, 279, 291
        Kodiak, 163
        Kwajalein, 313, 321
        Leyte, 380, 381
        Mactan, 396
        Midway, 154 155, 155–157
        Morotai, 311

        New Georgia, 241, 262, 264, 265
        Pacific, iii, iv
        Palau, 326
        Palawan, 393
        Pityilu, 301 302
        Ponam, 301
        Puerto Rico, 5
        Russell Islands, 257
        St. Lucia, 3, 22
        St. Thomas, 3, 10
        Samar, (photograph) 384
        Sitka, 163
        Tinian, 360, 361
        Tongatabu, 193
        Treasury Islands, 242
        Trinidad, 22
        Ulithi, 332
        Upolu, 194, 212
        Vella Lavella, 242, 266
        Wallis, 194
        Woodlark, 279, 291
    air bases, bomber
        Adak, 179
        Angaur, 314
        Attu, 184
        Bougainville, 242, 268, 270–272
        Efate, 195
        Emirau, 304
        Eniwetok, 313
        Espiritu Santo, 196, 228
        Green Island, 242, 274
        Guadalcanal, 246, 247–248
        Guam, 337, 350
        Iwo Jima, 339, 370, 371
        Johnston Island, 160
        Majuro, 313, 320
        Merauke, 286
        New Georgia, 265
        Palawan, 393
        Palm Island, 283
        Saipan, 337, 343
        Tarawa, 313, 317
        Tinian, 337, 339, 360, 361, 362–365
        Treasury, 267 268
    air bases, fighter
        Bougainville, 268 270
        Espiritu Santo, 228
        Green Island, 242, 274
        Guadalcanal, 244, 247
        Guam, 350
        Iwo Jima, 339, 370, 371
        Majuro, 320
        Merauke, 286
        New Georgia, 241, 265 266
        Okinawa, 399, 409
        Ponam, 301
        Tarawa, 313, 317
        Tinian, 361
        Treasury, 242
    air bases, fleet
        Fiji, 220
        Iceland, 56, 58, 59

☆ U. S. GOVERNMENT PRINTING OFFICE: 1947—

Made in the USA
Middletown, DE
02 November 2016